ALSO BY DAVID FROMKIN

*The Question of Government*

*The Independence of Nations*

*A Peace to End All Peace*

# In the Time of the Americans

# IN THE TIME OF THE AMERICANS

FDR, Truman, Eisenhower, Marshall,
MacArthur—The Generation That Changed
America's Role in the World

## DAVID FROMKIN

ALFRED A. KNOPF   NEW YORK   1995

THIS IS A BORZOI BOOK
PUBLISHED BY ALFRED A. KNOPF, INC.

Copyright © 1995 by David Fromkin

All rights reserved under International and Pan-American
Copyright Conventions. Published in the United States by
Alfred A. Knopf, Inc., New York, and simultaneously in Canada
by Random House of Canada Limited, Toronto.
Distributed by Random House, Inc., New York.

Grateful acknowledgment is made to the following for permission to
reprint previously published and unpublished material:
*Houghton Mifflin Company:* Excerpts from *Public Philosopher: Selected Letters of
Walter Lippmann,* edited by John Morton Blum, copyright © 1985 by John
Morton Blum; excerpts from *Turbulent Era: A Diplomatic Record of Forty Years,
1904–1945,* by Joseph C. Grew, edited by Walter Johnson, copyright © 1952
by Joseph C. Grew, copyright renewed 1980 by Elizabeth Lyon, Anita J.
English, and Lilla Levitt. Reprinted by permission of Houghton Mifflin
Company. All rights reserved.
*Yale University Library:* Diary entries for Sept. 29, 1917, Oct. 13, 1917,
Dec. 18, 1917, Dec. 30, 1917, Jan. 3, 1918. Edward M. House Papers,
Manuscripts and Archives, Yale University Library.

Library of Congress Cataloging-in-Publication Data
Fromkin, David.
In the time of the Americans : FDR, Truman, Eisenhower,
Marshall, MacArthur—
the generation that changed America's role in the world /
by David Fromkin.
p.    cm.
Includes bibliographical references and index.
ISBN 0-394-58901-7
1. United States—Foreign relations—20th century.
I. Title.
E744.F865    1995
327.73—dc20          94-30100
CIP

Manufactured in the United States of America

First edition

*To John and Martha Watts—*

who make it all worthwhile

# CONTENTS

# A NOTE TO THE READER

THIS IS THE STORY of the American leaders who defined America's role in the international politics of the twentieth century: Franklin Roosevelt, Truman, Eisenhower, Marshall, MacArthur, and their contemporaries. I see them as forming a coherent generation, shaped by shared experiences that brought them to see events from a common point of view. Historians often say that it is unscientific to think in terms of generations; but I think that in this case it helps to do so.

Born in the 1880s, FDR and his peers were old enough to fight in the First World War and to command in the Second. They changed their political enthusiasms and allegiances often as they rode the roller coaster that was at the same time the history of the twentieth century and their education.

They were offered a rare opportunity. Only a few times before in the history of the human race had a people been privileged to hold sway over much of the surrounding world. The handful of others mostly pursued traditional goals of gold and glory; but the Americans made use of the chance that came their way to try to change the political ways of the world. We will look into the upbringing that made them conceive that to be their mission, and we will ask what made them think that it was something that could be done.

This is not a full-scale history of the period. Nor is it a rounded generational history, describing in detail what FDR and his contemporaries wore and ate and drank and read and thought. It is focused uniquely—and in that sense narrowly—on their changing views about what America's role in the world ought to be.

The book is written for the general reader. It is not, for the most part, based on primary sources. It is a work of storytelling and of interpretation. I have undertaken original research only in the few instances, such as the drafting history of Wilson's Fourteen Points, where I could not make sense of the existing accounts.

I have studied a respectable amount of the secondary literature, but nowhere near all or even most of it: it is too vast. I have had to be selective.

Whenever forced to make choices, I have gone to the most recent sources based on the latest scholarship.

In trying to keep to a narrative path through the luxuriant overgrowth of information about America's twentieth century, I have followed and kept in sight several torchbearers to light up the way: characters who appear at times in the pages that follow, mostly to show where their generation was going. William Bullitt, in particular, has much more space devoted to him than his intrinsic historical importance would justify. He is here so often because when important things were happening, he so often was there.

Then, too, Bullitt was emblematic. His twists and turns were typical of liberal Americans in his generation, or at least of those who took a keen interest in world affairs. He was pro-Wilson and then anti-Wilson; he ran the gamut of opinions about communist Russia; and he was a stubborn isolationist and a passionate interventionist.

I wanted this to be a shorter book, but couldn't manage it: there was too much ground to cover. Americans of FDR's generation witnessed much of the world history of the twentieth century—wars, revolutions, market crashes, the collapse of empires—and took part in most of it. They had far more than their share of being where the action was.

Events were on an epic scale. So were men. Their life span in politics was unusually long because they began when they were so young. Douglas MacArthur already was an American general in the First World War. Franklin Roosevelt entered politics the same year that Woodrow Wilson did. William Bullitt was a key presidential foreign policy adviser only three years out of college.

Arriving early, they stayed late. Only death kept FDR from serving out his presidency through its sixteenth year; only the Constitution kept Eisenhower from being elected to a third term at the age of seventy—and perhaps a fourth one when he was seventy-four. Theirs was a long day in the sun.

A consistent theme in their politics, coming out of their July Fourth heritage, was their opposition to colonialism. Five centuries earlier, the countries of Europe had begun one of history's greatest adventures: the conquest or settlement of all the rest of the world. A previous book, *A Peace to End All Peace*, ended with the final achievement of European imperialism: the occupation by Britain, France, and the Soviet Union of the Middle East, the last place left. That was its high point, and what is about to come is its low. What follows is the story of how FDR's generation of Americans opposed all of Europe's imperialisms—and played a role in destroying them all.

The history that follows is done for the interest and pleasure of it, but is not without contemporary relevance. For example, the Europe-first agenda upon which the members of Roosevelt's generation finally agreed was in

sharp contrast to that espoused by their successors, junior officers in the Second World War who held the presidency in a line that began with John F. Kennedy and ended with George Bush, and who placed their emphasis on the politics of the Third World and found themselves mired in them. It might well be asked today whether that was—or is—the wisest course to pursue.

Then, too, the ethnic feuds and nationalist rivalries in the Balkans and central and eastern Europe that formed so conspicuous a feature of the political landscape of the world before the First World War, by resurfacing in the 1990s have made some of the concerns of young FDR's contemporaries into our headline news. It will be seen once again that the past is not dead when we turn in the next few pages to what Thomas Mann, in his foreword to *The Magic Mountain*, called "the old days, the days of the world before the Great War, in the beginning of which so much began that has scarcely yet left off beginning."

New York City
August 27, 1994

# In the Time
## of the
# Americans

# PROLOGUE

WASHINGTON, D.C., FRIDAY, JANUARY 20, 1961. At 6:15 a.m. Dwight David Eisenhower awakened in the White House for the last time. He was to remain in office only until noon; thereafter nobody born in the nineteenth century would ever again be President of the United States.

Change was in the air that day. Its winds swirled through the streets of the capital. At dawn the freak snowfall finally stopped, and the sun rose in a sky that was to become deceptively cloudless; but the thermometer stood at a cutting twenty-two degrees and the bitterness of the winds matched the bleakness of the President's mood.

He had dreaded the coming of this day. Earlier in the week, watching the reviewing stands being constructed outside for the inaugural, he had remarked to a visitor that "it's like being in the death cell and watching them put up the scaffold."

Even though his last term of office had been less than successful— there had been the U-2 incident and the rise of Castro and the humbling of America by Russia's launching of *Sputnik*—Eisenhower was loath to let go. It was not that he disliked the Democrat who had won the 1960 election or especially liked the Republican who had lost it. But, as his personal secretary noted the day after the election, "The President kept saying this was a 'repudiation' of everything he had done for eight years." If he himself had been allowed to fight the election—if the Constitution had not barred him from seeking a third term—he might well have won it.

Now, instead, there were the ceremonies of departure to be gone through. There was the White House staff to be seen to; like leftovers from yesterday that had been stored in the refrigerator, some thirty of its members emerged from underground that morning into the light of day. Trapped by the snowstorm, they had been obliged to spend the night in the White House bomb shelter, where they had thrown an impromptu party that ushered out an era. Later in the morning they lined up to say their good-byes to the President and his family.

The Eisenhowers' personal possessions already had been packed and shipped. The night before, Lieutenant Colonel John S. D. Eisenhower, the

President's son and aide, had emptied the last eight safes of all remaining documents. At 7:15 a.m. the President went to his office in the West Wing to dictate and sign a few papers. Suddenly there was nothing left to do. To John Eisenhower, it seemed that "the atmosphere in the West Wing of the White House was eerie. With no papers to sign or examine, we simply idled away the time." The President spent most of the morning leaning on an empty safe and reminiscing.

At 11:04 a.m. the long, black, bubble-top presidential limousine that had been dispatched to call for the President-elect and his party arrived at the White House—early, at Eisenhower's suggestion, so that his successors would have time to come in for a cup of hot coffee to brace themselves against the cold. While the Eisenhowers entertained the John F. Kennedys and their companions, painters moved in to start work redoing the Oval Office and the staff offices for their new occupants.

At about 11:30 a.m., Eisenhower and Kennedy emerged together from the White House and went out to their waiting car in the silk top hats Kennedy had prescribed for the inaugural—though Kennedy, not used to wearing a hat, quickly took his off. Eisenhower, still President, occupied the seat of honor at the right of the limousine.

Three thousand men using 700 plows and trucks had worked through the night to clear the principal Washington streets of their 7.7 inches of snow; so the presidential limousine moved smoothly along the mile-and-a-half route from the White House to the Capitol, where the inaugural platform had been erected.

At precisely twelve noon the presidency passed automatically, by the terms of the Constitution, from Eisenhower to Kennedy. But it was not until 12:20 that Kennedy appeared on the inaugural platform, and not until 12:51 that he rose to take the oath of office with a gesture that was to forever fix the image of that moment in the world's memory: he threw off his coat. Standing coatless and hatless on the windswept platform, he appeared even younger than usual—in contrast to Eisenhower, bundled up in coat and muffler and looking especially old.

Not merely the photo but the same picture in words was there the following morning on page one of *The New York Times:* "At 43 years of age, the youngest man ever elected to the Presidency, Mr. Kennedy took over the power vested for eight years in Dwight D. Eisenhower, who, at 70, was the oldest White House occupant." The youngest took over from the oldest; it was to be the refrain for decades to come whenever memories returned to that moment.

But in his inaugural address, delivered as American flags whipped in that day's now-storied stiff winds, the new President underscored the more important truth: he proclaimed that "the torch has been passed to a new generation of Americans—born in this century. . . ." Power had been taken away from those old enough to serve in the First World War; had passed over those (such as Adlai Stevenson, Estes Kefauver, and Stuart Symington) too young to fight in the first war but too old to fight in the second; and had passed directly into the hands of those who had been young officers in the Second World War, men like John F. Kennedy himself and those who were to become his successors, Lyndon Johnson and Richard Nixon.

With its promise of youthful renewal, the new President's brief address brought the inauguration to a successful climax; but parades, ceremonies, and revelries were still to come. And for the Kennedys, the day in the public eye had only just begun.

For the Eisenhowers, however, it had ended; and as soon as the inaugural ceremony was concluded, they sneaked off the platform by a side exit and slipped away to a private luncheon with friends and members of the outgoing cabinet at the 1925 F Street Club. There, out of the limelight, they relaxed as cocktails and champagne flowed; and after lunch, they drove away to their retirement farm in Pennsylvania.

NEVER BEFORE IN AMERICAN HISTORY had an incoming administration dismissed a generation as such from the corridors of power. For a century Democrats had been replacing Republicans, and Republicans, Democrats; for two centuries liberals had been replacing conservatives, and conservatives, liberals; and the young had been replacing the old since the beginning of time. But in January 1961, for the first time, one *generation* deliberately excluded another, arguing that the life experience of Eisenhower's contemporaries was such as to inculcate beliefs that were outmoded.

President Kennedy's articulate speechwriter and intellectual alter ego, Theodore C. Sorensen, later wrote of the inaugural that "grouped behind Kennedy as he removed his overcoat to speak were the young men of his new administration . . . men who were, with few exceptions, unschooled in the old pre–World War I dogmas and pre-depression doctrines. . . ." In other words, they had been educated during or after the 1930s—not before.

In making appointments to the most important positions, the new President did not ask of candidates who otherwise were qualified whether those under consideration had voted for him or not, so long as, like himself, they belonged to the combat generation of the Second World War. Of course, there were exceptions—Robert Lovett (who declined) was offered high office—but they were rare. As national security assistant—his chief White House adviser on foreign policy—the new President chose McGeorge Bundy, a Republican, but a man almost exactly his own age, a junior officer in the army in the Second World War who had landed on a Normandy beach the day after D day. To help him formulate world strategy, the President chose another Republican, Robert McNamara, who had emerged from the Second World War an air force lieutenant colonel. McNamara was only a year older than Kennedy.

Searching for a secretary of state who would execute rather than formulate policy, Kennedy was willing to consider somebody a bit older, but not very much so. At one point at the end, the leading candidate was David Bruce, a Democrat who was one of the country's most experienced and distinguished diplomats; but he was rejected by Kennedy and his team because (in the words of one adviser) "he was sixty-two years old" and, like so many of the older men, "his orientation was European." Another Kennedy adviser commented that Bruce "seemed to be very much of the old school, with Europe the touchstone of his thinking."

Kennedy and his advisers were right to see that they were different from the men of Eisenhower's and Truman's and Roosevelt's generation— and not in tastes and style alone. It was not just that the outgoing President relaxed by reading cowboy novels of the Old West while the incoming President read Ian Fleming's James Bond fantasies: tales of fast living, sports cars, recreational sex, and space-age weapons. There were differences of substance as well.

The generation of Eisenhower, Truman, and Roosevelt, born in a century when all the world outside our hemisphere was dominated by Europe, brought with it a sense of Europe's central importance in world affairs. It had lived throughout the great war of the twentieth century from its very beginnings in 1914 until the cease-fire in 1945—a war that directly or indirectly took between 50 and 150 million lives—and had accepted an unsatisfying temporary partition of Europe at the end of it for the indefinite future rather than go to war with the Soviet Union to impose a final peace settlement.

Eisenhower, the last of his generation to win the presidency, was expected by some to change this "containment" policy of merely holding the line and waiting through the decades or centuries for the Soviet empire to collapse from within. But he did not do so, and was criticized for not doing so. James Reston, of *The New York Times*, writing at the end of the Eisenhower years, admitted that "nothing vital to the free world has been lost," but summed up the failures of the outgoing administration by complaining that "nothing has been settled."

This was not good enough for the young men who flocked to the banner of President Kennedy. They pictured the Third World, not Europe, as the theater of combat; and many of them were eager to engage the communists in the field to defeat them militarily. Elite counterinsurgency forces—paratroops and rangers—were their chosen agents, supported by electronic gadgetry and helicopter-gunships. Cuba and Indochina, trouble spots inherited from the outgoing administration, were the battlefields they selected.

These were genuine departures from the outlook and world strategy of the Roosevelt-Truman-Eisenhower generation, and the young men of the Kennedy administration were right to see them as such. Indeed, by defining themselves and their approach to world politics so clearly, Kennedy and his associates helped to throw into relief the essential unity of the earlier generation. Roosevelt, Truman, Eisenhower, MacArthur, Marshall, Acheson, Dulles, Taft, and Vandenberg were different from one another, and some of them were adversaries, but they had a political life-experience in common; and it was a bond between them. Many generations of Americans had questioned what role the United States should play in world affairs, but theirs was the generation forced to give the answer.

Kennedy's young men took it for granted that the United States was a superpower with global interests and responsibilities, but Eisenhower's generation had not started from any such assumption; they had been obliged to question and search for themselves, often changing their minds, sometimes learning by trial and error as they groped for a definition of the world role their country should play, pursuing the exceptional mission that they believed history had ordained for the United States, while pursued by doubts that they had got it right.

Growing to manhood, they had been challenged by Theodore Roosevelt to make their country a great power. With President Wilson, they had agonized over whether they should allow America to be drawn into Europe's global wars. For them, this was personal experience: they had lived it, not learned it from books. Eisenhower's secretary of state, Christian Herter, had served on the staff of the U.S. embassy in Germany during Woodrow Wilson's first administration; had seen the unfolding European war from that vantage point; had watched as Germany and America drifted into conflict; and was one of the last Americans to leave German-held territory in the spring of 1917, when the United States entered the First World War.

Herter and Eisenhower, like Harry Truman, who was in Washington the day Eisenhower left office, and Dean Acheson, who still was in Washington every day, and Douglas MacArthur, who was fading away in the seclusion of New York's Waldorf Towers, were among the survivors of the long march through America's twentieth century. As Eisenhower retired to his Pennsylvania farm, the youngest and last of his generation to have held the highest office, he brought to a close the story of a remarkable quest: his generation's search for an answer to the questions of what the United States ought to be and ought to do.

The story began in an earlier, less experienced America, fresh from the conquest of the western frontier and seeking new worlds, if not to conquer, then at least to explore. And for most of Eisenhower's and Truman's and MacArthur's contemporaries, the highlight of their story was not the time of public acclaim and great achievement at the climax of their professional lives, but those earlier days especially in and around the First World War, when they were just beginning their education in life and all seemed possible; so that what marked them even more than what they did was what they might have done but did not.

It was in that earlier war, and in the peace that followed it, that they had invested their youthful hopes and dreams. It was that experience that formed the core of their lifelong schooling in politics. Those who encountered them only in the middle decades of the century, when they had become masters of half the world, missed knowing how they had become who they were. To understand them fully, one had to have known them when they were young.

# PART ONE

---

# GROWING UP

# I

# THE MIDDLE OF THE JOURNEY

AT THE BEGINNING OF SEPTEMBER 1901, as young people all over America prepared to start a new school year, an educational and entertaining world's fair opened its gates in the city of Buffalo, a port of entry to the United States in northwestern New York State. Located on grounds about a mile long and a half-mile wide, the fair occupied roughly 350 acres and its total cost came to more than $10 million. Tens of thousands thronged to see it, and 116,000 paid admission on a single day. It was called the Pan-American Exposition, and its theme was the achievements of the Western Hemisphere during the nineteenth century.

A guidebook to Buffalo and the world's fair, written by a team that included Mark Twain, explained that in order to focus on its theme, the Exposition limited its pavilions to countries located in the Western Hemisphere or in the outlying dependencies of the United States in the Pacific: the Sandwich Islands (later known as Hawaii), Samoa, Guam, and the Philippines, taken by America from Spain in the war of 1898. Mark Twain and his fellow authors emphasized how the fair's architecture was in keeping with the cultures of the Pacific and of the Latin south: "The buildings are low, with red-tiled roofs; are brilliant with color; are rich with ornament, with domes and towers and turrets, with balconies and loggias, and, above all, with pergolas, or arbors, covered with thickly-growing vines."

To the public swarming through its gates, attending the Buffalo fair, with its wonderful water and electrical displays, offered an opportunity to contemplate the thrilling achievements that might be expected of the new century. For, as recently reelected President William McKinley remarked to his secretary earlier that summer, "Expositions are the timekeepers of progress." The President had accepted an invitation to speak at the Buffalo fair on September 5, and a theme of his address was to be the new, expanded role the United States should expect to play in world affairs.

The exposition summed up and celebrated the achievements of the nineteenth century; it therefore was an appropriate venue—and 1901 the appropriate year—in which to consider the challenges of the dawning twentieth. It focused on the Western Hemisphere only years after the war of 1898 had raised the question of whether the United States should involve itself in the politics of the world outside the hemisphere. So the Pan-American Exposition was the right place and 1901 was the right time to deliver a speech of the sort that McKinley had in mind; but the President perhaps was not the *very* best person to deliver it. The very best would have been the newly elected Vice President and former governor of New York State, Theodore Roosevelt, the disturbing public figure most responsible for raising the issue of expanding America's power overseas.


AS THE CENTURY TURNED, the restlessly energetic Roosevelt challenged Americans to play a major role on the world stage. His views were changeable and not always consistent, but at times he seemed to want the United States to acquire an empire and become a great power like Britain or Germany. To play that role meant risking war, but he was prepared to pay that price.

He knew that his was a minority view. Americans were both isolationist and pacifist. They were opposed to fighting wars—at any rate, against European powers. They claimed to be against imperialism. In inspiring the 1898 war against Spain, which was followed by the annexation of the Philippines, the sensationalist press mogul William Randolph Hearst and his rival Joseph Pulitzer showed that American public opinion could be turned around on these issues for a time. But not for long. The fever of imperialism had died down after the Spanish war almost as quickly as it had come.

It was, in a sense, too soon for America to choose a new role in world affairs. The country was not ready for it. Like teenagers, Americans still were too much absorbed in the question of who they were going to be to address the question of what they were going to do. The United States was fully occupied in trying to deal with its own growth, and with the qualitative as well as quantitative changes that growth was bringing with it.

In the final decades of the last century, when George Marshall (1880), Douglas MacArthur (1880), Franklin Delano Roosevelt (1882), Harry S Truman (1884), Dwight D. Eisenhower (1890), and others who would lead the United States in the Second World War were born, and in the first dozen or so years of the twentieth century, when they became adults, America was in the middle of a journey. The United States was not what it had been when it began life in the eighteenth century as an independent republic: a rural, mostly agricultural society of a few million largely British-born colonists along the Atlantic seaboard. Nor was it still the pioneering, frontier society of hunters, farmers, and cattlemen toward which the Louisiana Purchase (1803) had pointed in the early nineteenth century. But it had gone only part of the way toward becoming something else.

The Civil War (1861–65) had visibly transformed the country, as had the completion of the first transcontinental railroad in 1869, opening up the West for settlement; but the movement away from the antebellum world, instead of exhausting itself in these efforts, seemed to pick up speed. Henry Adams, a chronicler of American history and also a witness to it, was inspired to believe that the wave of change was a manifestation of a universal law of acceleration: that history was speeding up.

Of course, Americans had always been on the move, multiplying their territory and population in every generation since the birth of the Republic; and as the nineteenth century moved toward, and then into, the twentieth, they went on doing so. But these movements and multiplications had become involved with other changes that were something else again, and that were altering the country's fundamental character.

America was caught up in powerful movements that were transforming her. There was the continuing push westward, propelling Americans ever farther from their European origins. There were the industrial, technological, and urban revolutions, moving Americans ever further from their origins in less literal but more important ways, by changing the nature of their work and of where and how they lived. The landscape of the continent was undergoing metamorphosis: the frontier was closed officially in 1890, forests and wilderness were fast disappearing, industrial cities were springing up, and farmers were moving into towns and becoming factory workers.

At the turn of the century it was possible to glimpse the outlines of the urban mass industrial society that might emerge when these movements were completed; but Americans were only en route toward that kind of society, not already there. So when the twentieth century dawned, which, it was widely predicted, would become the American century, the United States was adolescent rather than adult: it was not yet fully formed. It even looked incomplete: its country roads and city thoroughfares were unpaved, and western towns like Tulsa, in the Oklahoma Territory, consisted of only one street, as though the builders had started by throwing up a saloon and a few general stores, had gone off, and would be back to work later.

The old continued to function alongside the new: a look typical of an era of transition. The country, especially in the West, was dotted with one-story frame houses, while in the cities of the new age—New York and Chicago—builders were throwing up skyscrapers. In the streets of American cities, horse-drawn carriages still plied their trade alongside trolley cars and elevated railways; and gaslights still glowed at night, on the verge of being replaced by electricity.

The making of America was still in process, as was the making of Americans. The Statue of Liberty, with its Emma Lazarus sonnet ("Give me your tired, your poor / Your huddled masses, yearning to breathe free . . ."), was only about fifteen years old at the turn of the century, and never had the United States provided refuge for more foreigners. In 1900 almost *40 percent* of the country's white population was born in Europe or of a European parent; and another 8 million immigrants—more than 10 percent of the population of the United States—landed on American shores in the first ten years of the twentieth century alone.

Franklin Roosevelt's ancestors arrived in America in 1650, and were therefore among the original settlers of the country; but in terms of numbers of immigrants, the real settlement of the United States took place not in the seventeenth century but largely in Franklin Roosevelt's own lifetime.

Unlike the original settlers, many of these more recent immigrants were not from Great Britain. English was not their native language, and to forge an American nationality from the tens of millions of Europeans who flooded into the country was a challenge that the country had not yet finished meeting.

Henry James, the master of the American novel, who returned to the United States in 1904 for the first time in more than twenty years, visited Ellis Island and watched the immigrants being processed ("marshalled, herded, divided, subdivided, sorted, sifted, searched, fumigated"). He pictured this "visible act of ingurgitation" by American society as a sort of milling machine in which Europeans were fed in at one end and would emerge, a generation later, as Americans.

Meanwhile they lived in the slums of the big cities, where swarms of them huddled for the moment in tenements whose metal fire-escape stairs, deplored by Henry James for their lack of architecture, made the streets look like a "spaciously organized cage for the nimbler class of animals in some great zoological garden." But for them it was no cage; Europe was the cage, and they had been let out of it.

TO ACHIEVE NATIONHOOD—and the United States was moving close to that, but was not yet there—America had not only to convert the European immigrants into Americans, but also to persuade Americans that they were not, in the first instance, westerners, southerners, middle westerners, or easterners. Regionalism had nearly destroyed the United States in the nineteenth century, and had to be overcome.

The Union victory in the Civil War was only a step in the direction of bringing the country together. The revolutionary changes in American life after the Civil War were further steps in the same direction. None was of more importance than that announced in the first guidebook to the United States, published in 1893 by the German firm of Baedeker: "The United States now contain about 170,000 M. of railway, or nearly as much as all the rest of the world put together."

This immense and pervasive network held the country in its tight embrace, binding it together. The new transportation system linked all parts of the United States, and the new communications media—the telegraph and the infant telephone—did, too. So did national publications such as *McCall's* magazine, profiting from the new phenomenon of mass literacy.

Yet the differences in political life in the United States still fell largely along sectional lines, and in that sense the United States fell short of achieving nationhood; here, too, turn-of-the-century America was a country in transition. The South, the East, the Middle West (beginning at the Allegheny Mountains, and therefore including western Pennsylvania), and the lands west of the Mississippi were in some ways almost as different from one another as four countries.

The South lay in ruin from the Civil War, its agriculture in decay and its mansions crumbling into dust. Henry James, visiting in 1905, remarked on the enormity of it: "The collapse of the old order, the humiliation of defeat, the bereavement and bankruptcy involved, represented, with its obscure miseries and tragedies, the social revolution the most unrecorded and undepicted, in proportion to its magnitude, that ever was. . . ." Asking how, in a great and complex society, "can *everything* so have gone?" and "Had the *only* focus of life then been Slavery?" he found himself driven toward the conclusion that it had been: that the antebellum South, with the single-mindedness of the mad, had indeed bet everything on that one losing card.

Bitterly, the South at the turn of the century continued to look backward, taking ever stronger measures, legal and illegal, against its black population. In presidential elections it regularly voted for the Democrats, who normally lost. It offered no national leadership because its vision and its aspirations were irrelevant to those of the rest of the country. It had a basis for common action only with the West; both regions were rural and poor, and their white populations largely were of native Anglo-Saxon Protestant stock.

In terms of square miles, most of the United States lay west of the Mississippi River. But the West was sparsely populated, so it did not play a role proportioned to its size in electing congressmen or presidents. Besides, in 1900 Arizona, New Mexico, and Oklahoma had not yet been admitted to statehood, and accordingly sent no congressmen or senators to Washington. Then, too, the West was poor. It had its financial centers, but essentially it was peopled by ranchers, farmers, prospectors, miners, traders, and shopkeepers: borrowers, not lenders.

William Jennings Bryan, the populist, Bible-quoting orator from the prairies, brought the West and the South together in his three losing campaigns as Democratic candidate for the presidency (1896, 1900, and 1908). He appealed both to the economic interests the two regions had in common by championing small-town and farm debtors against the eastern banks, and to the social, ethnic, and religious background they shared as rural, white native Anglo-Saxon Protestants; so that he drew support, though for different reasons, at the start of his career from liberals and at the end of it, in the 1920s, from the Ku Klux Klan. Although celebrated as a public speaker, he appealed to the voters most strongly on ethnic, religious, and sectional issues that were unarticulated. Thus his advocacy of Prohibition, then one of the important issues in American politics, united rural, native-born Anglo-Saxon Protestants against such new immigrants as the wine-drinking Italian Catholics who swarmed into the slums of the big industrial cities.

While Bryan's choice of issues was divisive, his campaigning had the unifying effect of transforming the whole country into one forum: he ushered in modern politics by going out to all parts of the United States to meet the people. His 1896 campaign was the first time that a presidential candidate had traveled extensively and orated to the crowds from trains. He traveled 18,000 miles, spoke an average of 60,000 to 100,000 words every day, and addressed more than 5 million people.

THE EAST AND THE MIDDLE WEST, the one-sixth of the country that held nearly half its population, the heartland of the Union in the Civil War and the center of American wealth, minerals, manufacturing, and finance, were linked by politics but divided by geography and economics—and also by outlook, for east of the Allegheny mountain range, Americans looked across the ocean to Europe, while Americans west of the mountains did not.

America's largest industry, wholesale slaughtering and meat packing, was centered in the middle western metropolis of Chicago. The mineral wealth of the country and the steel and other industries upon which it was based were also to be found in the Middle West. At the turn of the century, Pennsylvania, the leading state in minerals (principally iron and coal), by itself accounted for about a third of all American minerals production; while Ohio, the original site of John D. Rockefeller's headquarters and the center of his empire, produced about 40 percent of America's oil.

Finance, however, was centered along the Atlantic coast, in Boston, Philadelphia, and New York City. Throughout the nineteenth century, the growth of the United States had been financed by British and continental European investors, who placed their moneys with and through the banks of the cities of the East, establishing a money power that the other sections of the country, even the wealthy Middle West, resented.

But the East and the Middle West had in common new social and political issues that growing urbanization and industrialization brought with them, and that the South, in particular, had therefore not yet encountered: such matters as the rights of labor unions, the regulation of working conditions, the prevention of industrial violence, the growth of slums, and the widening differences in wealth: on average a farm laborer in the 1900s earned $247 a year while the banker John Pierpont Morgan earned $5 million a year—and was regarded by someone really wealthy, Andrew Carnegie, as "not a rich man."

The flood of immigrants into the industrial cities created a political challenge the South and West had not yet experienced: for example, once popular election of senators was instituted, Roosevelt's political partner, Senator Henry Cabot Lodge of Massachusetts, a Protestant, a man of wealth, descended from Englishmen who had settled in America centuries before, had to appeal to Boston voters who were Irish, Catholic, poor, and newly arrived.

Republicans retained control of the two regions—and, except for the two Grover Cleveland victories, won every presidential election from 1860 to 1908—in an alliance that expressed itself as a balanced Middle West/East ticket. Typically the presidential nominee was from Ohio and the vice-presidential nominee was from New York. Thus, Ohio-born President Ulysses S. Grant and Vice President Schuyler Colfax (New York); President Rutherford B. Hayes (Ohio) and Vice President William A. Wheeler (New York); President James A. Garfield (Ohio) and Vice President Chester A. Arthur (New York); President Benjamin Harrison (Ohio) and Vice President Levi P. Morton (New York); and President William McKinley (Ohio) and Vice President Theodore Roosevelt (New York).

Of course, it was not an even balance: in American politics the presidency is everything, the vice presidency nothing—unless the President dies in office. Garfield's death brought the New Yorker Arthur the presidency in 1881; and in 1900, when the Republican party gave its vice-presidential nomination to New York's governor, Theodore Roosevelt, a personality so colorful that he was widely regarded as a lunatic, Ohio political boss Mark Hanna reputedly asked fellow Republicans: "Don't any of you realize that there's only one life between this madman and the White House?"


MCKINLEY, A MAJOR IN THE UNION ARMY, was the last Civil War veteran to serve as President. His Vice President, young Roosevelt, had taken no part in it, for he had been a mere two years old when the war between the states began; with his accession to high national office, the country moved another big step away from the Civil War and from the sectionalism that had given rise to it.

The Civil War had been about the preservation of the Union. If the United States had split into rival countries, like those of Europe, they could have been expected to behave like European states: they would have fallen, in the words of Henry Adams, a historian of the early American Republic, into the "local jealousies, wars, and corruption which had made a slaughter-house of Europe."

But the very purpose served by the United States was to be not like Europe. The immigration that had peopled America over the course of three centuries and that had risen to flood-tide levels by 1900 was a mass escape from Europe, while the American experiment in republican government based on a continentwide federal union was an escape from Europe's politics. The United States was the alternative to Europe: it was in order to fulfill that role that the United States had come into being.

IN THE 1880s, when Franklin Roosevelt and Douglas MacArthur and George Marshall were born, American history was not yet widely taught to schoolchildren. American history textbooks were not to be found in most classrooms, and the few that were available were of little value. A historian of these matters tells us that the early nineteenth-century textbooks supplied little information about "government . . . politics, or even . . . the shape of the country" and that their authors, for want of information, "tended to make things up." It was only in the 1890s, when Dwight Eisenhower and other younger members of the generation entered elementary school, that systematic American history texts came into general use in the classroom.

The United States that approached the turn of the century was a country on the edge, about to become conscious of its past only as it verged on moving away from it.

# 2

## EUROPE AND US

TO AMERICANS, wrote Henry James, "elsewhere" means Europe. In political terms, this was close to the literal truth at the time; for about a third of the human race lived in Europe and, outside the American sphere, all the rest of the earth was then dominated by Europeans. But Americans meant more than that. They meant that Europe represented what they had fled or had rebelled against. For they were starting afresh. As Henry Adams wrote, "The American stood in the world as a new order of man."

Characteristic of Europe's monarchical system, as seen from this side of the Atlantic, were intrigues at court, secret treaties, and the sort of balance-of-power politics that made warfare endemic. Americans condemned these characteristics, and the system that gave them rise.

Having settled a vast new continent that seemed boundless, Americans saw that opportunities were boundless—if human beings did not set up boundaries. With no internal frontiers or bars to trade, they prospered, and saw in this a lesson for the rest of the world. They argued that they themselves should be free to trade without hindrance anywhere in the world.

Contrasting the accumulation of wealth arising from their productivity with the wastefulness caused by Europe's wars and politics, Americans pictured economic activity as the alternative—the winning alternative—to war and politics; from which they later concluded that economic sanctions alone could bring an enemy to its knees.

As Henry Adams wrote of his countrymen, "Believing that in the long run interest, not violence, would rule the world . . . they were tempted to look upon war and preparations for war as the worst of blunders; for they were sure that every dollar capitalized in industry was a means of overthrowing their enemies more effective than a thousand dollars spent on frigates and standing armies. The success of the American system was, from this point of view, a matter of economy. If they could relieve themselves from debts, taxes, armies, and government interference with industry, they must succeed in outstripping Europe. . . ."

Americans did not recognize how British they were. They were like children who think themselves completely unlike their parents, though any outsider can see the family resemblance at a glance. There was, in the American view, an ocean of difference between the former colonies and their mother country; but to continental Europeans, what was striking was that Americans and Britons, in many senses, spoke the same language.

It is true that the colonies of the New World rebelled against England and fought for and won the right to go their own way. But even in revolting against British rule, American leaders were inspired by political principles and theories embodied in a British literature that stretched from the Magna Carta to the writings of John Locke; and having achieved their independence, they wrote a constitution for themselves heavily influenced by Montesquieu's theory of how Britain was governed. And they chose to continue being governed by British common law.

In seeking independence, their only enemy had been Great Britain. Thereafter, all they sought was freedom to trade around the globe; and wherever they found themselves shut out, it seemed to be the British who closed the door. They were so much alike that they always competed. Americans almost invariably discovered that their rival in manufacturing, in shipping, and in trading was Britain.

Yet it was the British upon whom Americans, especially New Englanders such as the Adams set, modeled themselves. Adams's pupil Henry Cabot Lodge went further: he admired England so much that he envied her and wished to take her place in the world. He believed British "stock" to be the world's superior race, but the American branch of it to be superior to the native variety. He was the same coin of which Anglophile and Anglophobe were the two sides.

So America continued to define herself in world affairs in terms of her political birth: her Declaration of Independence in 1776. More than a century later her foreign policy still was that of the Fourth of July. She had one basic political principle: that governments in Europe should not rule territories across the water. She had one basic economic principle: that all waters and lands around the globe should be open to her merchants. And in both her political and economic principles, she was brought back to having as her prime enemy Great Britain.

In the days when Henry Adams's grandfather John Quincy Adams had been secretary of state, the most astute American leaders saw that, nonetheless, Britain actually protected the United States. Her navies, which controlled the Atlantic and the Pacific, kept the other European powers, who were England's rivals, away from the shores of the Americas. John Quincy Adams, observing that it was not from love of the United States, but because her own interests required her to protect the Americas, that Britain performed this service, decided that America owed her nothing in return—not even an alliance to help England carry her policy into effect. This nineteenth-century New England policy of pursuing a rivalry with England while consciously relying on her protection was an intellectual inheritance, handed down to Henry Adams, Adams's pupil Cabot Lodge, and Lodge's young colleague Theodore Roosevelt. Most other Americans gave no thought to the question of how it happened that the United States was so secure against attack; those who did put it down to their country's moral superiority.

Should America venture forth to fight for democracy abroad? or for other colonies seeking to throw off the yoke of their mother countries? Despite the generous inclinations of some in the Revolutionary generation, the answer of many in their time and thereafter was negative. In the words of John Quincy Adams, America "is the well-wisher to the freedom and independence of all. She is the champion and vindicator only of her own."

Americans could show themselves to be "true friends of mankind," advised President Washington, not by taking part in world politics but "by making their country not only the asylum for the oppressed of every nation, but a desirable residence for the virtuous and industrious of every country." The United States, in other words, should not participate in European politics, should not try to challenge or change Europe, but should instead provide an *alternative* to Europe.

So well did the United States succeed that by the 1880s and 1890s and 1900s, millions and millions more Europeans were streaming across the Atlantic each year to become Americans. But as the United States increased in size, population, and wealth at the turn of the century, Americans like young Theodore Roosevelt and his friends longed to have their country play a great role in world affairs. They questioned the deeply held feeling in America, especially west of the Alleghenies, that becoming entangled in Europe's politics, or the world politics that Europe controlled, was dangerous.

THE AMERICAN FEAR of being corrupted by involvement in Europe's affairs was most memorably expressed not in a speech or in a state paper, but in a novelette; and though it came from the pen of Henry James, the master of the American novel, it was a slight work, by no means one of his substantial creations.

*Daisy Miller* was inspired by a story James had heard of a young American girl traveling in Italy with her mother in the winter of 1876–77, who in all innocence had picked up acquaintance with a good-looking young Italian man without understanding either the need for a proper introduction or the rules that required her to associate only with persons of suitable background. The point of the anecdote was its ending: when the girl later was introduced into Roman society, she was, predictably, snubbed—and was surprised.

In James's telling, of course, the tale took on new dimensions. The

Daisy Miller he created was intended to typify Americans in virtues as well as faults. Superficial, uninformed, and always on the move, Daisy was oblivious of the impression she created on the Europeans she met in her travels. In turn the Europeans, to whom her naturalness and openness were incomprehensible, misinterpreted her character and actions. In Rome, not realizing how such behavior would be viewed by Italian society, she visited the Colosseum after dark, unchaperoned and alone with a male companion. She contracted a fever in the night air—a malaria from off the marshes—and died of it.

That it was unhealthy for Americans to breathe the corrupt air of Europe was at least one reading of the story; and perhaps the oddest thing about it was that it was written by Henry James, whose subtle tales of the mutual misunderstandings of Americans and Europeans were informed by a sense that these misunderstandings were within the family. The peer of Flaubert and Turgenev, James, who lived in England and was at home in France and Italy, symbolized an essential unity of European and American culture of which turn-of-the-century America was becoming ever more aware.

James, the great American author, resided in the English countryside. In 1907 his friend Edith Wharton, the novelist of old New York, established herself and her salon in Paris in the aristocratic Faubourg Saint-Germain. Boston-bred Bernard Berenson, the art critic, lived in the hills above Florence. Henry Adams spent months of each year traveling in Europe.

In the steamship era travel had become easy; and eastern America was being drawn into ever closer intimacy with western Europe. Even in other parts of the United States, feelings about Europe were starting to turn around—a movement more easily discerned in retrospect than at the time. About Great Britain in particular, a turnabout in sentiment was under way. There was relief in both countries when they did not go to war against one another in the Venezuela crisis of 1895, and with the relief came a consciousness—at least on the part of some—of the madness it would have been for kindred peoples to fight. Americans were put in an especially good mood by Britain's decision to make the principal concession: she bowed to the American demand that the whole of the Venezuela matter be submitted to arbitration.

Britain's willingness to give in to American demands was due in part to her recognition that, challenged by the rising power of the newly united German empire, she might one day want or need the support of the United States. Though Washington in the nineties was still a sleepy, provincial town not much larger than Lima or Bogotá, the United States was becoming a power, and was being recognized as such: in 1892 the major European countries raised their legations in Washington to the status of embassies.

When America went to war against Spain in 1898, Great Britain gave further proofs of friendship by holding the line for the United States in Europe, restraining great power adversaries of the Americans from throwing their weight on the Spanish side. Without explicitly asking for anything in return, Great Britain acted the part of an ally.

On a personal level, as the growing number of society marriages between Britons and Americans attested, relations between the two countries were becoming closer. Transatlantic romance was in the air, as was transatlantic friendship. Cecil Spring-Rice, the British diplomat who became his country's ambassador to the United States, was best man at Theodore Roosevelt's wedding in London; and while the political importance of personal relationships can be overstated (Henry Cabot Lodge, Roosevelt's political ally, though immensely fond of Spring-Rice, "hated his country"), it seems not unlikely that "Springy's" informed and lucid analyses of European politics may have exerted some influence on the thinking of his American friends. In Washington, Spring-Rice occupied a privileged position unique for a foreigner, as one of the happy few admitted to the circle of Henry Adams (there were only six for breakfast and four for dinner at 1603 H Street, the Adams residence): a circle that seemed to be central to American policy making at the beginning of the twentieth century, for it included the majority party's foreign policy theorist in the Senate, the secretary of state, and Theodore Roosevelt.

ON SEPTEMBER 5, 1901, President McKinley, in his scheduled speech touching on America's new role in the world, told an audience of perhaps 50,000 at the Buffalo fair that the days of isolationism were over. America's wealth, he said, so great as to be "almost appalling," should inspire the country to bring wealth to countries less fortunate. New communications and transportation technologies had made the world one: "The same important news is read, though in different languages, in all Christendom"; and the speed of modern ocean liners was so great that distance had been abolished. The Atlantic no longer separated North America from Europe. "God and man have linked the nations together," he said, and "No nation can longer be indifferent to any other." The conclusion, according to the President, was inescapable: "Isolation is no longer possible or desirable."

ON FRIDAY, SEPTEMBER 6, the day after delivering his address, the President returned to the Exposition to enjoy himself. At four o'clock that afternoon, in the Temple of Music, he attended a scheduled reception: he shook hands with the crowds of visitors as they filed in to meet him, a chore to some politicians but not to McKinley, who took pleasure in it.

A little before 4:10, a man approached the President and shot him twice with a pistol. The man held no grudge against McKinley, but was an anarchist who believed all government to be wrong. He stood where he was, making no move to escape. McKinley said: "Don't let them hurt him."

After a week in which hopes rose and fell, McKinley died in the early hours of Saturday, September 14.

Unpredictable Theodore Roosevelt, at forty-two the youngest chief executive in the nation's history, became the twenty-sixth President of the United States.

# 3

## THE ENERGIES OF TR

THEODORE ROOSEVELT, a restless bundle of energy, came to power at the start of a new century that was expected to be an electric age. Typically, the handbook to the Buffalo exposition proclaimed that "the electrical features are said to exceed in variety, in novelty, and in quantity, those of all other expositions." One of the best-remembered theories of Henry Adams, fascinated by the dynamos he inspected at the Chicago and Paris world fairs, was that the dynamo was making history obsolete: that experience gained when humans had only the strength of animals, winds, and waves to augment their own had become largely irrelevant. The rising availability of mechanical power was the new thing: in 1898 the world generated 10,000 times more of it than in 1820, and more was being generated all the time. The genies were out of the bottle, and with their help all was possible: humans could descend to the floors of the oceans, explore the far side of the moon, fly among the stars. In intuiting that the twentieth century would be an era of energy, Henry Adams saw truly. Young people who visited the Buffalo exposition one day would read in their newspapers that Americans, by releasing atomic energy, had brought down fire from the sun.

The relative invention rate had reached the highest point in history by the turn of the century; Thomas Edison had invented professional inventing; and nowhere did inventions—the elevator, the bicycle, the typewriter, the camera, the auto—enter into everyday use more rapidly than in the United States. It seemed right that kinetic Theodore Roosevelt, who was always in motion, should become President in an era of change in which, for the first time, humans could travel speedily.

To countrymen and foreigners alike, Theodore Roosevelt—TR, as he came to be called—was characteristically American to the point of caricature. The improbable stories of his life were as well known as the tales they most resembled: the boys' adventure stories that were so popular in that bygone era of dime novels. The weakling who turned the tables on his tormentors by learning to box. The sickly lad who went west and became a man among men. The eastern dude with the Harvard drawl who learned to be a cowpuncher in the Badlands of the Dakota Territory, lived clean, did not swear or drink or smoke, but won the admiration of even the toughest gunslingers. The deputy sheriff who tracked down horse thieves with a Winchester rifle in his arms and a copy of *Anna Karenina* in his saddlebags. The weak-eyed historian who, in the field, transformed himself into the mighty hunter of birds and beasts. The aristocratic New York City police commissioner, attired in silk cummerbund, who smashed crime and corruption with a gloved but iron fist, and who, while others slept, roamed the streets by night to see that the laws were enforced. The young civil commissioner who, in the words of the then President of the United States, Benjamin Harrison, "wanted to put an end to all the evil in the world between sunrise and sunset." Having urged the United States into the 1898 war against Spain and sent the American fleet to take the Philippines, TR resigned his desk job as assistant secretary of the navy to fight in the field, emerging as the hero of the war by leading his Rough Riders in the charge up San Juan Hill.

TR had two marriages and six children, spoke or read seven foreign languages, and wrote fourteen books in his spare time. As President, he was the first American to win the Nobel Peace Prize; he made Panama a country; and he left his mark on the face of the planet by building the Panama Canal. TR's energies have astounded posterity almost as much as they dazzled his contemporaries; and it is not surprising that, to many in the generation of his young kinsman Franklin D. Roosevelt, TR seemed to be the greatest man in the world.


THE UNITED STATES, which had plunged into financial disaster in the early 1890s, was beginning a prolonged upswing in the McKinley/TR administrations. In 1900 the country produced a third of the world's steel, pig iron, silver, gold, and coal, and more than half the world's cotton, corn, copper, and oil. From then to 1910 the gross national product (GNP) grew 50 percent, the manufacturing component of GNP 100 percent, and steel production nearly 200 percent. Telephones rose 600 percent; the number of motor vehicles registered jumped from 8,000 to 458,000—and to 8 million a decade later.

But in this explosion of production and distribution, forces had been let loose with which TR felt obliged to do battle. The enormous new wealth was concentrating power on a scale hitherto unimaginable, and concentrating it in the hands of private interests that dwarfed the government. Between 1897 and 1903, some 40 percent of the country's industrial output was merged into giant corporate trusts. The banker J. P. Morgan exercised control over so many companies that Morgan-reorganized railroad corporations alone had half as much annual revenue as the government of the

United States did. In the panics of 1893 and 1907, Morgan was able to save the country from financial collapse.

What shocked some was that private interests were so powerful. What shocked TR was that the government, which alone represents the public interest, was so weak. Where others wanted to break up, and therefore weaken, private concentrations of wealth through antitrust laws, TR was more inclined to push for a bigger government that would regulate, not destroy, industrial combines, and that would be strong enough on the positive side to achieve national goals and pursue national greatness.

He told Congress that his program was "the enlargement of the scope of the functions of the National Government required by our development as a nation." It was a call for a break with the country's small-government past, and as such it was of a piece with the un-American program that the supposedly most typical of Americans urged upon the United States in foreign affairs.


TO BEGIN WITH the most heretical of his views, TR, unlike his countrymen, and even more unlike his countrywomen, was in favor of warfare: he thought it health-giving. He despised the peace-lovingness of the moneyed classes of his day, and feared that Americans might grow soft with easy living. He believed in the survival of the fittest, considered the manliest to be the fittest, and felt that manliness, which was the result of a strenuous life, was best earned and proved on the field of battle.

This ran so contrary to the sentiment as well as the traditions of the country that TR was obliged to emphasize that the military and especially naval preparedness programs he advocated would, by deterring potential enemies, help to keep the peace. But it was not easy to convince Americans of this, for they were inclined to believe just the reverse. They had always thought that large standing armies were the creatures of monarchical Europe, that they are ruinous to a civil society, and that arms races bring war while disarmament brings peace.

Of course, these traditional American opinions were not entirely consistent with American actions. Territorial expansion often had involved the United States in fighting, whether against Indians or others, and Americans had always aimed at expansion—within the Western Hemisphere. To that extent TR's countrymen, though they did not recognize it, were as bellicose as he was. TR was in the mainstream American tradition of John Quincy Adams when he wrote that "ultimately every European power should be driven out of America, and every foot of American soil, including the nearest islands in both the Pacific and the Atlantic, should be in the hands of independent American states, and so far as possible in the possession of the

United States or under its protection. . . ." But TR left the mainstream far behind whenever he inclined toward establishing an empire overseas—the very thing the United States had denounced in asserting its own right to independence from Great Britain.

At times, then, TR spoke the language of an imperialism that mainstream Americans had always disavowed. Also unlike his countrymen, TR had an instinctive feel and sympathy for the balance-of-power politics that Europe practiced and other Americans deplored. In his more lucid moments, he saw—and was one of the few who saw—that the growing power of Germany would one day threaten the United States, and that it would be in America's interest to back Great Britain against Germany.

But TR was realistic about how little support there was for many of his views on both foreign and domestic policy in the Republican party or in the country at large, whose leader, in both cases, he had become only by accident.

Indeed, TR was not only a more realistic but also a more complex thinker than his public personality suggested, or than his former patrons divined: he was underestimated not only by businessmen and politicians, but also by most of those in the Henry Adams circle who supposedly knew him best. Henry James privately considered TR "a dangerous and ominous jingo" and "the mere monstrous embodiment of unprecedented and resounding noise." Henry Adams, who remarked that TR "acts by the instinct of a school-boy at a second-rate boarding school" and that "mind, in a technical sense, he has not," claimed that TR misunderstood why his friends were so fascinated by his presidency: "Theodore is blind-drunk with self-esteem. He has not a suspicion that we are all watching him as we would watch a monkey up a tree. . . ." Secretary of State John Hay and others in the Adams social set found it hard to come to terms with the fact that TR, about whose adolescent self-dramatization they had made so many amusing comments, had become their chief; Hay told TR that other than in doing official business, he would refer to him not as "Mr. President," but as "Theodore."

The nation's youth, however, responded to TR with enthusiasm, and never more conspicuously than in 1912, in the aftermath of his presidency, when their elders stood against him.


TR EMBARKED ON a well-publicized career of adventure when he handed over the presidency to his handpicked successor, William Howard Taft, in 1909. He hunted big game. He rode in one of the first airplanes. He traveled the world.

It should have been predictable, however, that he would come back to politics. Like an opera star whose latest farewell tour is never the last, he craved the limelight. Even if his successor had carried on the good fight, he might have been tempted to return; as it was, the temptation proved irresistible. Taft, amiable but indolent, was not a man, let alone a President, in TR's mold. Taft was the last President of the United States to ride to his inaugural in a horse and buggy; TR was the first current or former President to fly.

Taft, as TR saw it, had been weak. Ignoring how little trust-busting his own administration had undertaken, TR charged that Taft had allowed the owners and representatives of concentrated wealth to take back control of the Republican party and of the government. TR, who had given Taft the presidential nomination in 1908, was determined to wrest it from him in 1912. To deny an incumbent President his own party's renomination is no small undertaking, but like his political emblem, the bull moose, an animal that can weigh 1,000 pounds and stand seven feet tall, TR was an outsize figure.

In his quest to regain the presidency, TR, like a Hindu deity, became at once destroyer and creator. In the past he had broken with traditional American ideas. Now he also smashed *things*—the existing structures of American politics—and opened the way for new ones to be built in their place. For Roosevelt was far and away the most popular man in the country, and his collision with the parties changed the face of American politics.

When the masters of the Republican party, disregarding public support for TR, renominated Taft, Roosevelt became the presidential nominee of the newly formed Progressive party—a nomination that otherwise had seemed to be destined for Robert La Follette. In doing so, TR shattered both the Republican and Progressive camps. For half a century the Republicans had been the majority party, but TR reduced them temporarily to third-party status: Taft, with only 3.5 million votes, came in third out of three in the 1912 elections. The Progressives, once the progressive wing of the Republican party, had put together an imaginative and constructive program responsive to the needs of twentieth-century America under the leadership of middle western and western reformers who were brimming over with ideas, and hoped to establish a lasting presence on the national scene; but when TR converted the party into a personal vehicle for the 1912 race, he ruined its chances (despite a second-place finish with 4.25 million votes) of becoming anything else.

The Democrats, a minority party since before the Civil War, nominated their candidate knowing that Taft and TR would split the Republican vote, guaranteeing a freak Democratic victory. At the party's national convention in Baltimore in June 1912, William Jennings Bryan, who had lost three uphill races for the presidency, unexpectedly blocked the seemingly inevitable nomination of his follower Champ Clark by throwing his support to a minority candidate—a newcomer to national politics, New Jersey's first-term governor, Thomas Woodrow Wilson. As Bryan must have known, he was giving Wilson enough votes to stop Clark but not enough votes to win.

Bryan thereby deadlocked the convention, making it possible for the delegates to turn to *him*. But the delegates knew it was a year when they could win the presidency at last—unless they threw it away. Nominating three-time loser Bryan *would* risk throwing it away. Since Bryan kept them from nominating Champ Clark, and they were not going to nominate Bryan himself, weary delegates on the forty-sixth ballot nominated the candidate Bryan seemed to prefer: Wilson of New Jersey.

The Baltimore convention of 1912 proved to be one of those seminal occasions when new actors make their debuts on the stage, and when people who are going to know each other all their working lives meet for the first time. Franklin and Eleanor Roosevelt agreed, sight unseen, to share the rental of a house in Baltimore during the convention with two other couples. One of the other couples turned out to be Mr. and Mrs. James F. Byrnes. The first-term New York state senator and the first-term South Carolina congressman formed a lasting political association.

Franklin Roosevelt, a leader of the Wilson faction of the New York delegation, also met Bryan's ally Josephus Daniels and made a powerful impression on him. Daniels was to play a major role at the convention and in the eventual nomination of Wilson.

Wilson himself was a new face. Like younger men such as Byrnes and Roosevelt, he had been in politics for only two years. He made a much more attractive candidate than Bryan, in the sense of being more fresh; though when the votes were counted, it was possible to argue that Bryan might have drawn greater support. Wilson had gone on to win the elections, but with only 6.3 million votes—fewer than Bryan had carried in *losing* the 1896, 1900, and 1908 elections—as against a combined total of 7.7 million for TR and Taft.

TR was the moving force in the 1912 elections; without him, Taft might not have sought renomination, Wilson might not have been nominated, and Wilson would probably not have won the election. Moreover TR, by helping the Progressives to break down the two-party system, had introduced a new fluidity into American politics. Young people coming into their own in the TR years were shown new possibilities and offered new choices; it was nearly two decades after the 1912 elections before the new alignments in American politics solidified. For many Americans it was not until the 1932 elections, when a kinsman of TR's ran for the presidency, that political loyalties once again became fixed.

TR spoke to and for a rising generation of Americans—even, in many cases, those who voted for his opponents. Whether or not they endorsed his program or shared his views, they were drawn to his personal belief that life should be lived at a high level of achievement: that a human being always should try to reach beyond what seems possible. To some extent, TR may have been expressing a current of feeling that was already in the air, but certainly he expounded it, exemplified it, and won converts to it.

He challenged, but also flattered, young Americans by setting high goals for them to achieve. It was the right time for TR to throw down his challenge; this was a generation that, for reasons of its own, wanted to meet challenges. Many measured themselves against fathers who had fought in the Civil War, and wanted in their turn to prove themselves. Others were excited by the seemingly limitless possibilities that transition from the nineteenth- to the twentieth-century world would open up for them. It was a generation of young Americans who were looking for a mission in life, and who therefore responded with especial enthusiasm to TR's call to greatness.

One day in January 1902 a visiting thirty-four-year-old New York lawyer, Henry L. Stimson, was on horseback in a park in Washington when he was sighted by his former employer, Secretary of War Elihu Root, and the President himself, grouped with others on the far side of a rain-swollen creek. Jesting, TR and Root ordered Stimson to jump the creek and join them—and felt sudden guilt when Stimson took them at their word, attempted the jump, fell into the swift-flowing water, disappeared underwater, and was swept downstream. Eventually Stimson and his mount were able to come ashore and join TR, who protested that he had never thought Stimson would attempt the jump, that he had assumed Stimson would understand that the order was given in jest because he could see for himself it was impossible.

"Mr. President," said Stimson proudly, "when a soldier hears an order like that, it isn't his business to see that it is impossible."

The episode became one of Stimson's treasured memories, and it typified the attitude of the younger men who were inspired by TR. They wanted to be called upon to do high deeds. They felt that they and their country had matured to the point where they were ready to play a great role in the world. They awaited the call.

# 4

# AMERICAN LIVES

FRANKLIN DELANO ROOSEVELT WAS NOT, as he longed to be, close to TR. TR in fact was his kinsman, but a distant one from a more illustrious branch of the family. When he was fourteen years old, Franklin bought a pince-nez in imitation of TR. At twenty-one he engaged to marry TR's favorite niece, Eleanor; and after their marriage he received invitations as the husband of TR's niece that he would not have received on his own. At the end of his honeymoon trip to Europe in the summer of 1905, he heard his wife applauded when it was pointed out that "Mrs. Roosevelt"— she, and not he—"had a connection with the President"; and he wrote from London to his mother that "everyone is talking about Cousin Theodore," and that they were saying that TR "is the most prominent figure of present day history." As for himself, he admired his famous fifth cousin more than anyone else on earth. He also found his relationship to TR useful. For the first decade or more of his political career, he lived off the capital of his cousin's name; indeed, he would never have been launched in politics without it.

But his doting mother, the former Sara Delano, claimed him for her own: he was "a Delano, not a Roosevelt at all," she said. Her family—they were French Huguenots, and the name originally had been de la Noye— was an even older one in the New World than was that of the Dutchman Claes Van Rosenvelt. Sara's father had gone out to Canton (1833–46) and made a fortune in the China trade, which essentially was the opium business; when he later lost his money in the stock market crash of 1857, he went back into the narcotics trade, this time in Hong Kong, and made a second fortune. His family came out to live with him both in Canton and in Hong Kong; so that while Sara did not discuss or acknowledge the source of her father's wealth, a connection with China loomed large in the background of her family, as of many American families.

Sara was only about half the age of James Roosevelt, the wealthy widower she married. The difference in age may have been one reason that she was so much closer than he was to their son. Franklin was born January 30, 1882, at his family's country estate a few miles north of Poughkeepsie, New York, in the tree-lined Hudson River valley. It was a long and overdue childbirth, and mother and son nearly died in it. Historians later were to see in it the psychic roots of the intense relationship, overshadowing all others, between Sara and her only child. In response to her stifling posses-siveness, he fabricated an inner mask for himself. What later was to chill his wife and his close associates, and to baffle politicians and biographers alike, was that he never took off the mask: he was unwilling or unable to open himself up to intimacy. Decades later one of his White House aides—Rexford Tugwell—was to remark that "Franklin himself did not possess the key to his own unconscious reticences. . . ."

When he was young, his contemporaries believed that there was noth-ing behind the mask. His cousins thought that Roosevelt was "superficial." They described him as "terribly self-conscious" and "without convictions."

Roosevelt was brought up in the society of adults, not children, and was off-puttingly polite from an early age. Seeking to make himself agree-able, he told people what they wanted to hear: conduct that he must have regarded as mannerly but others regarded as deceitful. Like a nephew hoping to inherit, he was too eager to please, and gave the impression of spending an unnatural amount of his time in the company of old ladies. Though he grew to be a handsome, slender, long-muscled six feet one, he did not entirely lose his air of tea party prissiness. TR's family called him "Miss Nancy" when he tried his hand at tennis, and one of TR's nieces said that she and her friends had called him "the feather duster." TR's daughter Alice said he was "a good little mother's boy whose friends were dull, who be-longed to the minor clubs and who was never at the really gay parties." She and her friends took no interest in him. She later said: "The joke was on us."

Roosevelt, biding his time, tamely allowed his mother to supervise his life until he was of age, and then—immediately—made a dash for freedom by seeking out someone with whom he could engage to marry. Roosevelts frequently married their cousins, and his eventual selection was artful; TR's favorite niece, despite shortcomings, could not be put down as unsuitable. Of course, Roosevelt's mother was right in saying that at twenty-one he was much too young to marry, but that position, no matter how well defended, was intrinsically temporary, allowing her to do no more than fight a delay-ing action.

Roosevelt obtained his mother's reluctant consent—for she thought politics to be degrading—and TR's approval before making his next move toward independence: he ran for the State Senate in 1910 on the Democratic ticket* and won, with the Roosevelt name and the votes of his normally

---

* Roosevelt's father had been a Democrat. It made political sense for him to join that party, too. True, his hero TR was a Republican; but TR had sons of his own who might want to enter politics in their father's party, and it would be awkward to appear to be their rival.

Republican family, friends, and neighbors. He did not become an outstanding state senator; but because of his name, his words and deeds were publicized by reporters in search of a story, while his sense of his importance as a Roosevelt led him to fight loose of party bosses, earning him a popular reputation for independence.

His mother would have preferred him to live in gentlemanly ease, devoting himself to a fine existence. But the next stop on Franklin's personal timetable was to be Washington, to follow in the path that TR had pioneered.


IN COLONIAL DAYS, when there were no great accumulations of wealth in the United States, an upbringing like Roosevelt's would have been inconceivable; and even in his own time, it was far removed from the experience of ordinary people. From infancy until adolescence, he had spent much if not most of his time in Europe, for his parents normally spent much of the year in England, France, or Germany. He spoke several foreign languages. He had been schooled by a succession of private tutors, many of them foreign, and was as familiar with the Luxembourg Gardens and the Eiffel Tower as with the trees and flowers of the Hudson Valley. He had little daily contact with the common run of Americans. Within the United States his family traveled in his father's private railroad car, the *Monon*. They were as little inclined to dine in restaurants—that is to say, in public eating places—as to employ public transport.

It was an upbringing like that of the landed British aristocracy; and it was something new in Roosevelt's United States, and that of his father, that Americans could live like that. His serious education, too—his boarding school years at Groton (for he took little interest in the schooling that followed at Harvard College,* or at Columbia Law School, from which he did not graduate)—was of a sort that was unavailable in America before his time, and it, too, was modeled on what was done in England.

Groton was the creation of the Reverend Endicott Peabody, son of a London-based Morgan partner, who had been so inspired by his own British education and by the Church of England that he gave up his family's Unitarian faith to become an Anglican clergyman and to found the equivalent of a British public school—an Eton or Harrow or Rugby—in the United States. Such was Groton School, in a tiny Massachusetts town west of Boston, in which Roosevelt was enrolled even before its physical foundations had been dug.

---

* Nonetheless he enjoyed the college experience, became editor of the student newspaper, the *Crimson*, and was elected chairman of the 1904 class committee.

Peabody aimed at imbuing his students—the sons of the wealthiest and most prominent in the land—with a sense of obligation. He urged them to enter the public service of their country and to bring ideals into politics. He formed their character and guided their faith into channels explicitly Episcopalian, implicitly Anglophile, and consciously patriotic.

Roosevelt was of the first generation of Americans to receive such an education. So, a decade or so later, were W. Averell Harriman and Dean Acheson. They learned to live in six-by-nine cubicles and to awaken at 5:45 a.m. to cold showers.

As a child of E. H. Harriman, the railroad tycoon, William Averell Harriman (born November 15, 1891) grew to manhood in the shadow of what was reputed to be one of the world's great fortunes. His childhood playmates were the children of domestics employed at his father's palatial estates, and he grew accustomed to assume that those around him were his servants. He was destined, he knew, to play a role in commanding a vast business empire, and he felt the need to prove himself worthy. Slow but persistent, he thought it important to win all games, taking them seriously and recalling that his father "could not imagine doing anything just for fun." Robert Lovett, four years younger, son of E. H. Harriman's general counsel, found that Averell was not only better at games but tried harder.

On his family's private lake a tutor had taught Harriman to row, so that when, at Groton, he offered rowing advice to Dean Acheson, a younger boy, he was able to be more coach than colleague. Later, after Harriman had studied crew technique in England, he was to coach Acheson on his college team. Acheson (born April 11, 1893) needed the help, not merely because he was two years younger, but because at school he found himself beaten at everything: he was a poor student and bad at sports, and was, besides, rebellious. The son of an Episcopal clergyman, he was kept on at Groton only because of the clerical connection; and in the end he graduated at the very bottom of his class, twenty-fourth out of twenty-four. But the school had its effect on him; a classmate later recalled that at Groton "the idea of service, so strong with Dean, was first instilled."

Reverend Peabody wrote that "if . . . Groton boys do not enter political life and do something for our land, it won't be because they have not been urged." The teachings of Peabody were much like those of his friend TR, whom he had once asked to teach at Groton and who proved to be a popular speaker at the Groton chapel. Peabody's school had begun to impart to the country's privileged youth at the end of the nineteenth century a sense of mission such as that which TR attempted to instill in Americans as a whole.

It was a proud day in the Groton career of Franklin Roosevelt when cousin TR came to school to regale the boys with tales of his crime-busting experiences in New York's police department. The boys were enthralled. It was not Roosevelt alone who took TR for a model; so did his entire generation.

THE OUTWARD CIRCUMSTANCES of his early life were so different from those of Franklin Roosevelt, his sixth cousin once removed, that Douglas MacArthur might as well have grown up in another time or a different country.

MacArthur was born on January 26, 1880, at an army camp in Arkansas, the son of a professional soldier. A half-year later the family moved to a new posting, at Fort Wingate in the wilds of the New Mexico Territory, which was an enormous but sparsely populated land of mountain ranges, canyons, and high plateaus. Built in the shadow of mountain peaks that reached to 11,000 feet, the fort was tiny. Quarters were cramped in the fort's primitive adobe structures; living facilities were crude; and it was a long way to Albuquerque, the nearest real town, about a hundred miles to the east. This was outlaw country, and the handful of soldiers were expected to help bring some sort of law and order to it. Shortly after the MacArthurs arrived, the most famous of the desperadoes, William Bonney ("Billy the Kid"), was in fact captured in their vicinity.

MacArthur's father had known some of the famous figures of the frontier, among them James ("Wild Bill") Hickok, the scout and lawman who had pacified some of the toughest towns in the West, and William F. Cody, "Buffalo Bill," the hunter and Indian fighter. So stories as well as scenes of the Wild West surrounded MacArthur in the first years of his life.

The 900-mile Santa Fe Trail, the oldest of the great wagon trails westward still in use, and the one that had seen the most Indian fighting, remained in service until the year the MacArthurs arrived in New Mexico. The era of wagon trains and stagecoaches was coming to an end, and one of the army's assignments was to protect the crews building the railroads that were replacing ox-drawn and horse-drawn transport.

The Indian wars were then in their last phase; and in northern New Mexico, where Fort Wingate was located, another of the army's tasks was to keep the Navajo on their reservation and to keep hostile Apaches off it.

When MacArthur was four years old, he was brought along on the monthlong march southward from Fort Wingate to his father's new post at Fort Selden on the Rio Grande, a distance of 300 miles. Historians doubt that he "trudged," as he later claimed, "at the head of the column" of his father's troopers for any sustained period of time, but there is no doubt that he was exposed to hardships and hazards. Lurking nearby were Geronimo's Apaches, then on the warpath, who terrorized the region until their surrender two years later.

MacArthur learned to ride and shoot before he could read or write. He and his older brother, barefoot and naked to the waist, mounted on spotted Navajo ponies, would ride off into open country to shoot rabbits. He became an expert horseman and a crack shot.

The sounds as well as the scenes of his life in isolated frontier forts were different from those with which boys his age growing up on the farms of the Middle West or the cities of the East were familiar. The hours of MacArthur's waking day were punctuated by hoofbeats, gunfire, and the barking of drill sergeants, while sleep at night was sometimes disturbed by the drumbeat of tom-toms. The commands that accompany such military ceremonies, as the inspection of uniforms and equipment, or the furling and unfurling of banners, became a part of his basic vocabulary. Bugle calls— taps and reveille, retreat and advance—signaled orders and ordered time.

Young though he was, MacArthur was where some of the great dramas of America's West were being played out. Before the MacArthurs, who had moved from Fort Selden to Fort Leavenworth, Kansas, left Leavenworth in 1889, soldiers of their unit were involved in one of the rites of passage in the growth of the United States. They stood guard to preserve order while, at a prearranged signal of gunshots, 100,000 Americans rushed to stake claims to nearly 2 million acres of formerly Indian lands in Oklahoma, leading the federal census superintendent to report the following year that the frontier was now closed: the era of land rushes had come to an end.

As his family left Leavenworth in 1889, Douglas's father, Arthur MacArthur—who bore a striking physical resemblance to TR—began to come into his own professionally. In 1890 he finally was awarded the Congressional Medal of Honor for one of the great acts of courage in the Civil War: twenty-seven years earlier, as an eighteen-year-old at the battle of Missionary Ridge, he had seized the standard of his home state of Wisconsin and led what seemed a suicidal charge uphill against 45,000 Confederate troops entrenched on the heights above him, driving them from the ridge.

Now, decades later, he finally was achieving recognition and also moving upward, first in the peacetime army, and then in wartime. When the United States fought Spain in 1898, he had the luck to be sent to the Philippines. By 1900 he was the general in overall command of American forces in the Philippines and was governor of the islands as well—until he clashed with William Howard Taft, who had been made civilian administrator of the islands by President McKinley, in a showdown that foreshadowed that of another General MacArthur and a civilian chief executive a half-century later. Arthur MacArthur was relieved of his Philippine command but promoted to lieutenant general, the highest-ranking officer in the U.S. Army—and remained the adored lifetime idol of his son, Douglas, as much as TR was of his young cousin Franklin.

EXTERNALLY, THE CIRCUMSTANCES of Douglas MacArthur's childhood were unlike those of Franklin Roosevelt's, but the inner lives of the two flowed in similar channels. Roosevelt modeled himself on his famous cousin; MacArthur, on his famous father. Both young men were dominated and shaped by mothers who burned with ambition for them, though the ambitions differed: Mary MacArthur's aim was for her son to win life's battles, while Sara Roosevelt's was for her son to rise above them.

Like Roosevelt, MacArthur attended a new school for boys founded by an Episcopal clergyman—the West Texas Military Academy (later named the Texas Military Institute)—which was operated by the church. MacArthur was required to supply not only his uniform, napkins, and napkin ring, but also his own Bible, prayer book, and hymnal. Much the same values and faith were instilled in MacArthur at West Texas as were imparted at Groton. But unlike Roosevelt, Harriman, and Acheson, mediocre students all, MacArthur was not only an all-around success at athletics but an outstanding scholar, winning awards, citations, and medals, and described by a teacher as "the most promising student that I have ever had."

On graduation Douglas moved with his mother to the MacArthur hometown, Milwaukee, Wisconsin, where they lived in the Plankinton House Hotel in the city's center while he attended courses at West Division High School, was specially tutored, and studied for competitive examinations to enter the U.S. Military Academy. Nauseous with nervousness, as he always was to be in the tense moments in life, but exhorted by his mother to "believe in yourself," he succeeded brilliantly. "HE WILL GO TO WEST POINT," headlined the Milwaukee *Journal*, June 7, 1898, over a story that reported, "Young MacArthur is a remarkably bright, clever and determined boy. His standing was 93⅓ percent against the next man's 77.9 percent."

Accompanied by his mother, MacArthur attended the military academy, graduating first in his class in 1903 with a 98.14 academic record, the highest since Robert E. Lee (98.33) in the class of 1829. A year after graduating, he found himself assigned to the Philippine Islands, where his father had won fame and glory as a general several years before.

As an army officer in 1905, he was appointed aide-de-camp to his father, and with his father and mother toured Asia: Japan, China, Hong Kong, Siam, Indochina, India, Burma, Ceylon, and Singapore. As Roosevelt, much of whose childhood and youth were spent on the Continent, felt about Europe, MacArthur came to feel about Asia. Much later he was to write that his Asian tour "was without doubt the most important factor of preparation in my entire life. . . . It was crystal clear to me that the future and, indeed, the very existence of America, were irrevocably entwined with Asia and its island outposts." He had now, therefore, acquired a view of America's mission that complemented his view of his own: he and his country had a rendezvous with greatness in the East.

AMIABLE, IF SOMEWHAT LETHARGIC, William Howard Taft, who weighed more than 300 pounds, was not cut out to be a hero. His firmness in facing down MacArthur's father in the Philippines was out of character. Usually he dealt with troubles by eating more: in times of crisis, his weight could go up to 320. And when TR broke with him, he retired to his Pullman car and cried.

To his firstborn son, however, he *was* a hero. Robert Alphonso Taft modeled his career and opinions on his father's as much as Douglas Mac-Arthur did on his. Taft came from a well-to-do family of lawyers, judges, and politicians, and he set his sights on following his father to the top. His goal in life was to become chief justice of the United States. His views on the sanctity of laws, contracts, and customary rules derived consciously from his father's.

He was born September 8, 1889, in sooty Cincinnati, then the principal manufacturing town in Ohio. It was a largely German-American city of 300,000 that had become a magnet for immigrants: nearly two-thirds of the population was of foreign parentage. In the beer taverns of the slums, customers breathed the air of the old country; but the Tafts lived in East End, the fashionable district where native-born Americans resided.

Both parents emphasized the values of hard work and discipline; and Taft, instructed at times by private tutors, was scholarly by nature. The American occupation of the Philippines affected his life, as it did that of others of his generation; as a ten-year-old in 1900, he followed his father to the East. For years he traveled in Asia and Europe before returning in 1903 to enroll in the Taft School in Watertown, Connecticut, founded and run by his uncle, and designed, like Groton and West Texas, to teach the virtues of service.

Taft excelled at studies—he was to graduate at the top of his class from Yale in 1910 and Harvard Law School in 1913—but not at sports. He shied away from the limelight. (When his father was President, a girl asked, "What does your father do?" and Taft replied, "He has a government job.") On graduating from law school, he was offered a clerkship by Supreme Court Justice Oliver Wendell Holmes—the most prestigious and exciting job a young attorney could be offered—and turned it down in favor of returning to Cincinnati to set up in practice.

Six feet tall and unbending, he was also unsmiling and undemonstrative. He did not give himself to intimacy or camaraderie; he was notoriously unwilling to let himself go. Dry and passionless, he nonetheless found himself involved in a romantic triangle as he returned to Cincinnati: he wanted to marry a woman his best friend also wanted to marry. She was Martha Bowers, the daughter of one of his father's oldest friends and colleagues; a pretty, witty, talkative young woman who demonstrated considerable diplomatic skills in dealing with her rival suitors. She resolved matters with a minimum of awkwardness, marrying Taft in October 1914 in a ceremony in which his best friend was the best man.

Marriage had also been proposed to Martha Bowers by John Foster Dulles, the young international lawyer who, in his law school days, had frequented the Taft household in Washington. It was a glamorous life that Dulles had been able to offer her, and far from the prosaic law practice of a Cincinnati attorney. He was embarking upon an international career not open to American attorneys until the end of the nineteenth century, and invented in part by his grandfather.

John Watson Foster, Dulles's maternal grandfather, who had served as U.S. minister to various foreign countries, did not want to return home to the Middle West at the end of his term as secretary of state (1892–93). Instead he stayed on in Washington to represent private interests involved in international transactions: a highly political law practice pioneered by him in Washington and by William Nelson Cromwell of the firm of Sullivan and Cromwell in New York.

It was at Foster's home on I Street in Washington that Dulles was born February 25 during the terrible blizzard of 1888 in which 400 people died. His father was a Presbyterian minister in Watertown, in northern New York, just east of Lake Erie. His family was steeped in the Presbyterian ministry, and had destined him for it; but from the first, like his younger brother Allen, who joined the diplomatic service, he was his grandfather Foster's child. He took time off from Princeton (he was the youngest in his college class) in 1907 to serve as a secretary-clerk at the Second Hague Peace Conference, to which Foster, serving as China's representative, brought him. In order to live with Foster, he attended law school at George Washington University in Washington, graduating in two years instead of three and achieving the highest grades in the university's history. Because he had not attended one of the "right" law schools—Harvard or Columbia—he had difficulty finding a job at a New York City law firm, but Foster took a hand in the matter, was in touch with Cromwell, and obtained a position for him with Sullivan and Cromwell.

Cromwell was a buccaneer thrown up by America's dynamic plunge into worldwide politically related business at the end of the nineteenth century and the beginning of the twentieth. Retained by French interests who had tried and failed to build a Panama canal, Cromwell helped divert the new U.S.-inspired canal project from Nicaragua to the isthmus, contributing $60,000 to the Republican party in the process, and reaped high rewards for himself and his clients. Dulles, who started work at Sullivan and Cromwell in 1911 at $12.50 a week, was soon roaming the world on behalf of clients.

Dulles came to the law firm as a person formed by his grandfather—and by another mentor as well. As an undergraduate at Princeton, he had fallen under the influence of the university's president, Woodrow Wilson. Wilson, like Dulles, was the child of generations of Presbyterian clergymen, and, too, had seemed destined for the ministry. After becoming president of Princeton, Wilson, who had been a professor of political science, continued giving lectures. Dulles, who attended them, was impressed. He later recalled that "the major benefit I got from Princeton was participating in Woodrow Wilson's courses, where I gained my interest in public affairs."

GEORGE CATLETT MARSHALL, JR., in his father's clear-eyed view, was so unlikely to pass a competitive exam to enter West Point that there was no point in trying. So, as members of his family had done for generations, he attended the Virginia Military Institute. His family traced its ancestry to John Marshall, secretary of state, chief justice of the United States, and one of the main architects of American constitutional government.

A child of the industrializing age, George Marshall was born December 31, 1880, the same year as MacArthur, to a prosperous owner of coalfields and coke ovens in Uniontown, Pennsylvania. The town had been a stagecoach stop on the National Road, but by 1880, though its trolleys were still horse-drawn, its streets had been paved and it could boast of gasworks and an electric company. Marshall's father sold his business and lost the proceeds in a land speculation when the good times of the 1880s gave way to the financial collapses of the 1890s. The lanky boy, fearing rejection and suffering from a sense of his own inadequacies, was now troubled by his unaffectionate, quick-tempered father's failure as well. He had to learn self-discipline to overcome shyness and launch himself in life.

After graduating from VMI, he obtained an interview with the President of the United States (for the country was still small enough so that matters were handled in this way) to ask to be allowed to take an examination leading to an army commission. President McKinley said yes, and young George Marshall, passing the exam adequately though not brilliantly, became a second lieutenant, and in 1902 found himself—as so many Americans of his generation did—in the Philippine Islands. The following year he was posted to Fort Reno in the Oklahoma Territory, a relic of the army's Indian wars, bringing him a taste of the life and surroundings in which Douglas MacArthur had grown up.

In 1906 Marshall succeeded in winning a posting to the Infantry and Cavalry School at Fort Leavenworth, Kansas. First Lieutenant Douglas Mac-Arthur was on Leavenworth's permanent staff at the time; although the two men met, they did not become friends. For Marshall, Leavenworth was a first step on the road to the Army War College and high rank. In full command of himself now, Marshall worked hard, and in his first year won promotion to first lieutenant and came in number one in his class. He was on his way.

THE ECONOMIC DOWNTURN of the 1890s, which affected the fortunes of George Marshall's family, ruined those of young Arthur Hendrick Vandenberg (born March 22, 1884) of Grand Rapids, Michigan. His well-off parents were wiped out in the panic of '93, and he took all sorts of jobs: carting shoes, operating flower and lemonade stands, selling vegetables, running a stamp-trading business, selling seasickness pills, ushering at a theater, and selling newspapers. Hoping to earn enough money to send himself through college, he took a position as a billing clerk at the Sears Biscuit Company—but lost the job in his passionate admiration for the hero of his generation. "I was an ardent Teddy fan," as he later recalled; and when TR, campaigning for Vice President in October 1900, stopped in Grand Rapids, Vandenberg, though allowed only twenty minutes for lunch, stayed two hours to see and hear him. Losing his job, he looked for another—and found work at the Grand Rapids *Herald*. It was the work he was cut out to do. Giving up thoughts of college, he stayed on as a newspaperman, became managing editor of the newspaper, and won himself a name—and a position in Republican politics—with his furious rhetoric.

OF DWIGHT DAVID EISENHOWER, an outstanding biographer has written that "his heritage was ordinary, his parents were humble folk, his childhood was typical of thousands of other youngsters growing up around the turn of the century . . ." and "everything about him appeared to be average."

On both sides his family's distant ancestors were Mennonites of the German Rhineland. In more recent times they had followed their Mennonite sect, the River Brethren, west from the Pennsylvania "Dutch" settlements in Pennsylvania to Abilene, Kansas, where they had found the abundance of farmland that they sought.

Dwight ("Ike") was born October 14, 1890, the year that the frontier closed. At the time his family lived in a shack beside the railroad tracks in Denison, Texas. His father, trying to escape from life as a farmer, had opened a store in Abilene and had lost everything in the worst of the agricultural depressions that, like earthquakes or hurricanes, unexpectedly struck the country from time to time. He had come to Texas in search of a new start, but could not find one.

The year after Ike's birth, his family trudged back to Abilene, where relatives rallied round. His father, who arrived with net assets of $24, was given a job as mechanic of the Belle Springs Creamery, owned by the River Brethren and managed by his brother-in-law, at a salary of $50 a month. The family lived in a rented shack, again by the railroad and on the wrong side of the tracks: the south side. Ike and his brothers took turns getting up at 5 a.m. to build a fire in the cookstove.

In 1898 the family moved to a more spacious home—much needed, for there were a half-dozen brothers—on three acres of land. The house had no running water and no indoor lavatory; four boys had to sleep in one room; and electricity was not installed until seven years later. On the other hand, there was a horse for plow and buggy, two cows for milking, and chickens, ducks, pigs, and rabbits. On the grounds grew fruits—cherries, apples, pears, and grapes—and vegetables. "I have found out in later years," said Ike in 1952, "that we were very poor, but the glory of America is that we didn't know it then."

Abilene once had been the terminus of the Chisholm Trail, a town of cattlemen, prostitutes, and card sharks; and Wild Bill Hickok, whom MacArthur's father had known, served at one time as town marshal. But its days of sin and glory were over; the long cattle drives that had ended at Abilene were in decline, and other railheads were taking away its business.

Now it was a dreary and dusty but hardworking and law-abiding town of about 4,000 people who took life and religion seriously. But Ike, apart from an uncontrollable temper, seems to have been as lighthearted as most children. He distinguished himself in the things that mattered most to schoolboys: fistfighting and athletics. From a middle-aged friend—an illiterate trapper whom Dwight would visit at his camp—he acquired skills in activities he would pursue all his life: hunting, fishing, and playing cards.

Sports were his passion. He set his heart on going to college so that he could play football and baseball. Though not a gifted student, he worked hard to get the necessary good grades in high school; and he took all sorts of jobs to help pay for a brother's college expenses and to save for his own. He worked as an iceman, loaded galvanized sheet metal, and became night manager at the creamery. Saving up enough money was a goal that proved elusive, in part because of his losses at card games.

A friend put him on to the idea of trying for a place at the U.S. Naval Academy in Annapolis, where an education would be free. It was not easy obtaining an appointment to the academy, but Ike persevered. Eventually he sat for a competitive examination, agreed in advance that West Point would do as well as Annapolis, and won a place at the former when the slot for the latter was taken. So Eisenhower went on to the army's academy, where he graduated with middling grades.

Eisenhower's Kansas ran next to Missouri, where Harry S Truman was born May 8, 1884; but though the states were neighbors, the central line of division in American life and history ran along the border between them. Kansas, after a mini–civil war of its own, had entered the Union in 1861 as a free state; but Missouri had been a slave state from the start. It was for that reason, and because of the stories they had heard of its rich soil, that Harry's pioneering maternal grandparents, the Youngs, had left Kentucky to settle in the state.

Independence, Missouri, was perhaps the first of the boomtowns on the trails west. It was the point of departure for trade and travel along the Santa Fe Trail. Grandfather Young prospered by leading wagon trains from Missouri to New Mexico, Utah, Oregon, and California.

When Harry was ten years old, his family left the Young farm, which was outside town, and moved into Independence so that he could go to school. It was a town like Eisenhower's Abilene, in that its population was almost entirely native-born American; but there the similarities ended. Abilene was of German stock, Republican, and of the Mennonite sect, while Independence was largely Scots-Irish in ancestry, Baptist, and Democratic. Abilene was North and Independence was South in the great regional division of American politics; the one had backed the Union, the other the Confederacy. Abilene was white, while Independence was split between the whites of the town and the blacks of its slums.

Harry was a child troubled at first by his poor eyesight, and then by having to wear the spectacles that corrected it. He avoided sports and fights, taking care not to break his glasses. He laughed and smiled a lot, enjoyed school, was fond of his teachers, got good grades, but tended not to mix with the other children. Reading was his passion; he especially enjoyed learning about history's heroes.

Unlike most other boys in town, Harry went on from elementary school to high school. But—unless one counts some courses he later began at Spalding's Commercial College in Kansas City—he never went beyond graduating from Independence High School. His father, a never very successful farmer who traded in livestock and real estate, had tried his hand at speculating in wheat futures—and lost everything about a year after Harry graduated. West Point turned Harry down because of his eyesight, and he could not afford to attend a college that was not free.

After taking jobs as a newspaper wrapper, a timekeeper for a railroad construction crew, and a bank clerk, Truman became a farmer like his father, and was proud of plowing straight furrows. He dabbled in other businesses, too, but his real taste was for politics. He began by serving as postmaster, road supervisor, and member of a district school board. In 1905 he became a charter member of the Missouri National Guard, and in 1909 he joined the Freemasons.

James Francis Byrnes, like Truman a born politician, avoided discussing his ancestry or early life. Catholic and Irish—the paternal grandfather he never knew came over from Ireland—and having some relatives in New York City, his family must have come from or at least through the immigrant slums of the big-city industrial Northeast; but Byrnes made himself over into the voice of the rural and Protestant Old South. He was born May 2, 1879—or, more likely, 1881—on King Street, the north–south thoroughfare in historic Charleston, the windswept South Carolina seaport shaded by palm trees, whose commerce was about to revive. Byrnes, along with his sister, cousin, aunt, and invalid grandmother, was supported by his widowed mother, who worked as a seamstress. Learning shorthand at his mother's suggestion gave him his start: he left school at fourteen to work in a law office. At twenty-one he became a court stenographer, which led him to become a lawyer four years later.

The young woman Byrnes courted sang in the choir of St. Thaddeus Episcopal Church in Aiken, South Carolina, where he began to practice law. Byrnes joined the chorus and later the church, marrying in 1906 and converting to the Episcopal faith. Becoming Protestant opened up a political career for him in the antipapist South: in 1908 he was elected public prosecutor, and in 1910 won a seat in Congress.

For red-haired, hot-tempered Joseph Patrick Kennedy, born September 6, 1888, a child of teeming big-city America, it was an advantage to be Catholic. With a genius for politics, the Irish immigrants who overflowed into the urban metropolises of the United States had organized themselves and almost everywhere had taken hold of City Hall. Their political machines provided the basic services to their communities that governments set out to provide only later.

A prosperous saloon keeper who was the political boss of his ward and later became a state senator, Joe Kennedy's father was almost as big a man in his world as were Douglas MacArthur's, Robert Taft's, or Averell Harriman's fathers in theirs—and was every bit as much his son's idol. One of Joseph Kennedy's earliest memories was the night of the presidential elections of 1892; he was four years old and remembered his father's campaign workers coming in to report: "Pat, we voted 128 times today."

Young Joe was a hustler. He sold newspapers, repaired clocks, ran errands, raised pigeons, sold candy, and invariably greeted the gang of children he led with: "How can we make some money?"

He was a fierce competitor who played only to win—and made sure that he did. Though a mediocre scholar, he graduated from the best schools; though not the choice of his father-in-law, he married the daughter of the mayor of Boston; though an outsider in the Brahmin world of State Street finance, he went on to make a fortune in business before going into politics.

James Vincent Forrestal's mother—a person of powerful character— was determined that he should become a priest. His father, an Irish immigrant who had become a successful building contractor, hoped that he would enter the family business. The senior Forrestal was also a figure in Democratic party politics who supported his young friend Franklin D. Roosevelt in his race for the State Senate in 1910. "Vince," born February 15, 1892, in the Hudson River town of Matteawan, south of Poughkeepsie, was a troubled person who fought free of his parents. At Dartmouth, which he attended for a year, and at Princeton, which he left at the end of his senior year without graduating, he was financially pressed because he could not bring himself to take money from the parents against whom he rebelled. He refused to become a priest; he declined to enter the family business; he broke with his Catholic faith; and to the extent that he concerned himself with politics, he became a Republican, not a Democrat. After leaving Princeton he quit three jobs in a row before finally finding the career for which he was suited: he became a bond salesman at the Wall Street house of Dillon, Read.

ON HIS FATHER'S SIDE William Christian Bullitt was related to Pocahontas as well as to George Washington's father, Patrick Henry's sister, and more to the point, Fletcher Christian, who led the mutiny on the *Bounty*. Bill Bullitt was a born mutineer.

The day he was to leave for Groton, he suddenly refused to go. "Every Groton fellow I know is a snob," he said. Yet he himself was proud of his family's position in Philadelphia society and of the fact that his father's forefathers were among the original settlers of the United States. An ancestor, a French Huguenot named Joseph Boulet, had arrived on American shores in 1634.

The malicious always would whisper that Bullitt was Jewish. Though the family of his mother, Louisa Gross Horwitz, had long since converted to Christianity, they descended from Haym Salomon, the Jewish immigrant from Poland who founded Philadelphia's first synagogue and who played so great a role in helping finance the American Revolution and the early Republic.

Born January 25, 1891, Bullitt claimed early on that "I'm going to be a lawyer and Governor and Secretary of State and President," and proved to be wrong on all counts. Yet he had all the talents. He was a superb athlete and was voted most brilliant man in his class at Yale. He was outstanding in college theatricals, and with his friend Cole Porter founded a club for satire.

The Cole Porter set, of which he was an intimate, was the social center of the college. Archibald MacLeish, future poet and adviser to Franklin Roosevelt, and Dean Acheson were among the younger men drawn to it. Acheson, much changed from his Groton self, had become dashing, and a wit. But at crew he was still the protégé of the commanding Averell Harriman, as he had been at Groton.

Harriman, who graduated with Bullitt in the class of '13—but without Bullitt's athletic and academic sparkle—was in a unique position and held in special awe. He had entered college just after his father's death. His mother, who inherited everything, and Judge Lovett, who had been his father's general counsel, took charge of the Harriman empire and clearly were grooming Averell to assume large responsibilities. His grades at school were not outstanding, but he was held in esteem by his classmates. Harriman was the first man in his class at Yale tapped for the grandest of the college clubs, Skull and Bones; and in the yearbook he was listed as the "Most Admired," "Most Thorough Gentleman," "Handsomest," and "Most Likely to Succeed."

In the event, the Yale man most likely to succeed did so only because, on a day nearly three decades later, he was thrown a career lifeline by one of his most unlikely-to-succeed contemporaries. Harry Hopkins, born August 17, 1890, in Sioux City, Iowa, was a poor boy from the Middle West. His father was a charming drifter who had been a prospector for gold and a traveling salesman, and who supported himself and his family by betting on himself in bowling matches. Eventually a personal injury lawsuit (he was run down by a horse-driven truck) gave him $5,000 with which he settled as a storekeeper in Grinnell, Iowa. Harry's mother had a very different character; deeply religious, she was active in the Methodist Missionary Society.

Harry was a skinny, gangling boy with an open face who was not very good either at sports or at schoolwork. He was an enthusiastic sports fan, a practical joker, and somewhat of a success in student politics. He graduated from Grinnell College with the class of '12 without any sense of what he would like to do in life.

He jumped at a chance to visit New York City. A summer job was on offer, as counselor at a camp for slum children outside the city. He took it, went to New York—and stayed, having found his vocation as a social worker. It was as though he had stopped being like his father, a lightweight charmer and aimless, and had started to become, like his mother, a missionary.

While Hopkins, having graduated, was walking in his mother's footsteps, and Harriman, entering the family business, was trying to walk in his father's footsteps, Harriman's companions at Yale were making their own dispositions.

In their respective classes Bullitt and Cole Porter, Acheson and Mac-Leish followed the traditional path: they entered the Harvard Law School. Acheson was to prove a serious student of the law, in large part because he was to fall under the influence of young Professor Felix Frankfurter. Archibald MacLeish, his lifelong friend, was to graduate from law school but would abandon the practice of the law for poetry. Cole Porter quit law school for music, but continued to be Acheson's roommate in Boston. Bullitt, who had entered law school only to please his father, dropped out in 1914 when his father died.

With his mother, Bullitt embarked for Europe. His career plan was less odd than it sounds now. He observed that the United States had no foreign intelligence service—and decided that he would gather firsthand knowledge of conditions in Europe and later trade it out for a job in the government of the newly elected President, Woodrow Wilson.

But his real hero in politics was TR. As a child, he had tacked pictures of TR to his wall. Like Franklin Roosevelt, he was a TR admirer drawn to Europe rather than to Asia.

A Harvard man for whom nobody would have predicted a career in public service was towering Christian Herter, nearly six and a half feet tall, who loved to play tennis, took no interest in politics, and could never make up his mind what he wanted to do in life. He became engaged to May Carrie Pratt, a great heiress, who at Yale socials had danced with Archibald MacLeish and Dean Acheson—but he was unable to tell her or her family what his plans were, for he had none. It was to be a classmate named Lithgow Osborne who later pulled him into the foreign service, and later still, a Harvard friend, Leverett Saltonstall, future Massachusetts governor and senator, who acted as a mentor in politics.

Herter's generation of public figures may indeed have been the first in American history for whom college ties became immensely important in later careers. Dean Acheson, Archibald MacLeish, and their young teacher Felix Frankfurter, for example, were intimates who helped and advised one another throughout life. It may have been no coincidence that after a run of Presidents from Lincoln to McKinley, none of whom had attended one of the elite eastern universities, from the opening of the twentieth century by TR through the end of the First World War, Herter's generation grew to manhood under the administrations, successively, of a Harvard man, a Yale man, and a Princeton man. The career importance of having attended such universities was growing at the same time.

Christian Herter was typical, too, of his generation in the eastern part of the country in the closeness of his ties to Europe. His grandfather, a German immigrant, made a fortune as the leading society interior decorator of the post–Civil War United States, and then returned to Europe to live in Paris. Christian's father and mother, artists both, also chose to live in Paris, where Christian was born and received his elementary education.

For Herter, as for others of wealth in his generation such as Roosevelt, Harriman, and Bullitt, a major educational experience was the encounter with Europe.

THOUGH FAR LESS COMMON, an encounter with Asia made its mark on the passage to manhood of a number of those who grew up in the age of TR: MacArthur, of course, and to some extent Taft and Marshall, but especially Willard Dickerman Straight, who was born only a few days after MacArthur.

Straight's ancestors were among the early English settlers of the New World. His parents were schoolteachers, were poor, and died when he was a child.

Feeling that America's horizons had been extended in his time to the far side of the Pacific, Straight, after graduating in architecture from Cornell, obtained a position with the British-led Imperial Maritime Customs Service in China. In its schools Straight learned Chinese, rose to the top of his class, and became personal aide to the chief and founder of the Service. Idealistic to the core, he was outraged by the behavior of white men in China. He told his diary (September 30, 1902) that "my heart shrivelled within me as I heard tale after tale of the roguery of American officials in the East, of the bribery, of a consul and a group of missionaries, such things of Americans, of the great, the proud home of the Eagle, such rotten corruption by the representatives of one's own native land, was enough to make me wish for an absolute despotism that the stable might be cleaned."

Like the Christian missionaries sent out from the United States—Episcopalians had been in the field in China since 1835, and others had followed—Straight felt that China's independence and territorial integrity should be assured, and that the great powers should be prevented from carving out spheres of influence or control for themselves within the country. But Straight felt that America's views carried no weight because her words were not backed up by deeds.

After a stint as a reporter in the Russo-Japanese War of 1904, which he covered from Japan, Manchuria, and Korea, he left journalism to become vice consul and secretary to the American minister to Korea. The victorious Japanese had promised to respect the independence of Korea, and the United States had pledged to uphold that independence with moral support; but Straight saw the Japanese crush Korea, its emperor, and his court, and drew his own conclusions about the value both of Japan's promises and of America's moral support.

Tall, slender, with reddish-brown hair and open features, Straight had a winning manner that charmed visitors to the U.S. consulate in Seoul. So when Japan's snuffing out of Korean independence led to the closing of the consulate, Straight was offered other positions by some of the important people he had met: TR's family and that of E. H. Harriman.

For a time he served as TR's U.S. consul general in Mukden, Manchuria, charged with the task of opening up northern China to American business enterprise. As the U.S. government's man north of the Great Wall, in the cockpit of Asia where the territorial interests of Japan, Russia, and China collided, he was located, he said, where "the biggest game in the East, save Peking itself, is being played."

In the Manchurian temple that he converted into his consulate, Straight sat in on that game, hoping to protect the independence of China against Japanese imperialism. He soon discovered that he was playing a lone hand. His own country would not support China in any tangible way; Britain, France, and Germany, caught up in dangerous rivalries in Europe to which they necessarily gave priority, were unwilling to risk alienating Japan; while Russia, after some initial wavering, deemed it more prudent to cut a deal with the Japanese than to take a chance on being defeated by them once again. It was true that Russia and Japan had solemnly pledged to uphold the Open Door in China; but the Russian minister with whom Straight dealt described this treaty language as nothing but "drool" inserted to please the Americans. In 1909 Straight decided to leave government service to work with E. H. Harriman and a financial group headed by the Morgan bank.

That year the orphaned Dorothy Whitney, one of America's great heiresses, met Straight when she visited Peking. He became her guide. Theirs were kindred, romantic natures. After taking her to the Great Wall one day, he realized that he had fallen in love. For two years thereafter he courted and pursued her, following her to Europe and then to the United States. She was president of the New York Junior League and a leading Long Island socialite, while Straight was, in society's view, nobody. But his new association with the House of Morgan helped, and TR, a great figure in Long Island society as well as in the world's affairs, interceded on Straight's behalf. Willard and Dorothy Straight were married in Geneva on September 7, 1911.

Straight's work with a Morgan-led China banking consortium continued until Woodrow Wilson became President in 1913, and Wilson, who held views of his own about China policy that the bankers did not share, blocked the consortium from going forward. Straight then took up a new project—the one for which he is still remembered. He decided to found a magazine to champion the sort of ideas that TR espoused. Though he recruited the social theorist Herbert Croly to edit it, decisions were to be made on a collegial basis by a group of founders, each (even the Straights, who financed it) having only one vote. It was to be called *The New Republic.*

One of the founders of *The New Republic* was tiny, birdlike Felix Frankfurter, a brilliant War Department lawyer about to leave the government to teach at the Harvard Law School. The unbelieving son of a poor Austrian Jewish businessman descended from six generations of rabbis, Frankfurter, born November 15, 1882, in Vienna, was brought to America through Ellis Island in 1894. His family's move from Vienna to New York was part of the great and continuing wave of immigration that, in the three decades beginning in 1890, brought a third of the world's Jews to the United States—a country that otherwise was entirely Christian.

Growing up in the teeming slums of Manhattan's Lower East Side, he escaped from some of its hazards: he was so short that the tough Irish teenagers who roamed the streets would not stoop to beating him. In the years that followed, his amazing mind took him out of the world of the immigrants, brought him through the New York school system and the Harvard Law School with distinction, and afterward brought him to the attention of Henry Stimson, a follower of TR's who was to become Frankfurter's patron.

On February 1, 1906, Stimson was appointed by TR to be U.S. attorney from the Southern District of New York; and in the best Rooseveltian tradition, Stimson selected assistants on the basis of merit alone—among them Frankfurter, who as a Jew could not have obtained a job at a major Wall Street firm. Frankfurter excelled, and made himself invaluable. When Stimson ran for the office of governor of New York in 1910, Frankfurter came along as his brain-trust and speechwriter. Defeated in the elections, Stimson (with what he believed to be TR's blessing) accepted appointment by President Taft as secretary of war, and brought Frankfurter to Washington as law officer of the War Department's Bureau of Insular Affairs. The doors of Washington society were of course closed to Frankfurter, but he was always welcome at the Stimsons' home. He also formed close ties with Supreme Court Justice Oliver Wendell Holmes.

In the War Department Frankfurter dealt with Cuba, the Philippines, Puerto Rico, Panama and the Canal, Haiti, and what is now the Dominican Republic—the unavowed American empire over which, in his words, "we had a kind of receivership." He was persuaded by Stimson and a newer patron and adviser, the Boston lawyer Louis D. Brandeis, not to follow his natural inclination to resign in 1912 to enlist in TR's presidential campaign. Indeed, he stayed on through the first year of the Wilson administration, but then threw himself with enthusiasm into the launching of *The New Republic* as an organ of Rooseveltian opinion.

In his available time Frankfurter wrote pieces for the new magazine, but its emerging star was young Walter Lippmann, one of its editors. Lippmann was of a Jewish family that had come two generations before from Germany but, unlike Frankfurter, he was born (in New York City on September 23, 1889) to wealth and privilege, earned by his immigrant maternal grandfather. In the words of his biographer, "Walter Lippmann was brought up to be a gentleman." Though he grew up surrounded by other descendants of wealthy German Jews, the values that he was taught and the style of life that he lived were much like—and ran parallel to—those of Groton boys like Roosevelt. Even the religion in which he was raised (and which he rejected) was much like theirs; Reform Judaism, created to bring the Jewish religion into the mainstream of the nineteenth-century Christian world, was shorn of many traditional Jewish beliefs, laws, and rituals, and emphasized instead the timeless ethical principles that Judaism shared with Christianity.

In 1906 Lippmann entered Harvard College, in perhaps its most illustrious class ('10) ever. Mentors included William James; teachers included George Santayana; classmates included the poet T. S. Eliot and John Reed, adventurer, journalist, revolutionist, and exemplar of the romantic life. Upon graduating, Lippmann threw himself into journalism and the writing of political philosophy. But it was his career at *The New Republic* that brought him into the limelight: it made him the most famous and influential political commentator in the United States, a position he was to hold almost all the rest of his life.

TR—"the image of a great leader and the prototype of Presidents," in Lippmann's words—was his lifelong hero. He wrote that TR "was the first President who knew that the United States had come of age . . . that they had become a world power. . . . He was the first to realize what that means. . . . The first President who realized clearly that . . . social justice had to be sought deliberately. . . . Theodore Roosevelt began the work of turning the American mind in the direction in which it had to go in the Twentieth Century." TR, he wrote, was "the first President who shared a new social vision."

In turn TR wrote, when Lippmann was twenty-five, that he was the "most brilliant young man of his age in all the United States."


THE COMING GENERATION in turn-of-the-century America knew the United States was growing much bigger, the world was growing much smaller, and their country might well be drawn into the affairs of hitherto-distant parts of the globe. Whether across the Atlantic or across the Pacific, the United States bumped up against the ambitions of European powers, but some of the young men who one day were going to become American leaders felt that a choice might have to be made as to whether their country's next frontier lay on the far side of the one ocean or of the other.

Like Americans before them, they received an education steeped in religion; indeed, many of them were schooled by churchmen. But new institutions like Groton and Taft were called into being by the felt need to teach children and grandchildren of the Gilded Age that the unprecedented creation of wealth in the United States to which they would become heir brought with it a responsibility to serve society. The message preached by the Endicott Peabodys was that of noblesse oblige.

TR, who believed that nobility was a quality earned rather than inherited, preached a parallel but different sermon: he exhorted young Americans to choose a life of exertion and danger. American pioneers and Civil War Americans had been given no option but to live such lives; what was new and extraordinary in American life at the end of the nineteenth century was that young people had other choices. TR urged young Americans to rise to the level of their forefathers by voluntarily undergoing the hardships and courting the risks that earlier generations had faced.

The young were proud that they could believe TR, an American, was the greatest public figure in the world, and that Europeans thought so, too. But many of them did not understand his thinking, others disagreed with it, and a great many others, who believed they wanted to follow his example, lacked the courage to do so when the occasion arrived.

In TR's vision the United States was becoming a great power like the others. His young admirers tended to continue believing instead that America was a unique country, that Americans were the bearers of a political message for mankind, and that in foreign policy the United States pursued principles while other countries pursued interests.

What the young seem to have found so appealing in TR was that he called on them to distinguish themselves. Like outstanding young people in all generations, many of those who were to become America's leaders felt a sense of personal mission; but they also felt—as earlier generations did not—that in their lifetime their country would be called on to play a new and larger role in world affairs. Their belief that their privileged birth as Americans brought with it responsibilities carried over at some point into the belief that America's newly earned great wealth and growing power required the United States to provide not merely a moral example, but also moral leadership, for the rest of the world.

Born in a candlelit, horse-drawn world, they were to be called upon one day to design the nuclear age. Many of them had started political life as TR's children. They were about to take their first steps away from him in 1913, as eloquent, enigmatic, reform-minded Woodrow Wilson became the first President to ride to his inauguration in an automobile, ushering in a new and modern era.

# PART TWO

## THE SUMMONS TO GREATNESS

# 5

# FRANKLIN ROOSEVELT
# COMES TO TOWN

IN MARCH 1913, in the first days of the Woodrow Wilson administration, young New York state senator Franklin D. Roosevelt came to the nation's capital to take his first Washington job. He had been appointed assistant secretary of the navy. Josephus Daniels, the rumpled, small-town North Carolina politician and newspaperman who had become navy secretary, believed the appointment was his idea; he remembered running across Roosevelt in the lobby of the Willard Hotel on Inauguration Day and asking the charming New Yorker, "How would you like to come to Washington as Assistant Secretary of the Navy?" But even before Wilson chose Daniels to be secretary, he turned down someone who wanted to be assistant secretary, saying that the position would be offered instead to Roosevelt. Roosevelt himself had angled for the job. And the Democratic political boss of New York, anxious to rid himself of the independent-minded state senator, is said to have engineered the appointment. "Go, Frank, go," cried the overjoyed New York Senate president pro tem when he heard the news; "I'm sure you'll be a big success down there."

It was as though the appointment had been foreordained. Roosevelt himself seems to have believed that it was meant to be. An avid sailor, he had always loved the sea, and as a child had hoped to join the navy. But the significance of the appointment was that he was pursuing the destiny he hoped and believed was his: he was following in the footsteps of TR. Henry Cabot Lodge had managed to secure TR's appointment as assistant secretary of the navy with the conscious purpose of setting him on the road to the presidency—and it had worked. It was no secret that Roosevelt planned to follow the same path.

TR wrote a congratulatory note, saying, "It is interesting that you are in another place which I myself once held." Josephus Daniels remarked in his diary, "His distinguished cousin TR went from that place to the Presidency. May history repeat itself"; and Daniels's newspaper ran a photo of Roosevelt captioned "He's following in Teddy's footsteps." The editor of the liberal New York *Evening Post* wrote, "I am truly glad of your appointment. . . . May it lead straight onward for you as it did for T.R.—but *not* by means of that barbarism known as war."

But, as Roosevelt was fully conscious, it *was* by means of war that TR had done it. Two months before the Spanish-American War began, TR had ordered the fleet to Manila with orders to be ready to attack. When Daniels briefly left town two days after taking office, the new assistant secretary reminded reporters, "There's a Roosevelt on the job today. . . . You remember what happened the last time a Roosevelt occupied a similar position?" Speculating soon afterward on what he would do should war come, he said, "I suppose that I . . . must follow in the steps of T.R. and form a regiment of rough riders."

Assistant secretary of the navy in 1897, TR had left to lead the Rough Riders in 1898, took office as governor of New York in 1899, was elected Vice President of the United States in 1900, and became President in 1901. From his appointment as assistant secretary of the navy, it was only fifty-three months until TR's swearing-in as President. It would have been a tight schedule for Roosevelt to follow—especially as there was no war on the horizon. Indeed, in world affairs the United States peacefully sailed "on a summer sea."

APPROPRIATELY, ROOSEVELT'S OFFICES in the massive State, War and Navy Departments Building* were next to the Executive Mansion—"the White House," as TR called it, and as it has been called ever since. The machinery of American foreign and military policy was small-scale enough at the time so that the State, War and Navy Departments Building's ten acres of floor space could house all three departments. The baroque granite building was under the superintendence of the War Department. Captain Douglas MacArthur, whom the army briefly placed in charge in 1913 just after Roosevelt's arrival, left his mark outside it by adding concrete planters to brighten the facade.

The outgoing assistant secretary briefed Roosevelt on his new duties, many of which were routine. An enormous number of papers required his signature, which his mother, critical of his handwriting, admonished him to improve: "not . . . too small, as it gets a cramped look. . . ." Writing to her on his first day in office, he claimed to have signed whatever was put in front of him; the new assistant secretary of the navy joked that he was "somewhat at sea!"

Although he found time for frequent rounds of golf, his official duties kept him busy. With the help of Louis M. Howe, his faithful aide from Albany days whom he had brought with him to Washington, he helped

---

* Later known as the Executive Office Building and now as the Old Executive Office Building.

prepare the departmental budget and supervised supply, procurement, and the navy's shipyard and dock facilities, with their thousands of civilian employees and problems of labor relations.

President Wilson at times called Roosevelt to his offices to deliver specific instructions. Occasionally, the former political science professor in the White House lectured him as well; Roosevelt later recalled that Wilson told him, "It is only once in a generation that people can be lifted above material things. That is why conservative government is in the saddle two-thirds of the time."

Though somewhat in awe of the President, Roosevelt (as his many biographers have pointed out at length) failed to appreciate the strengths of his immediate superior, Secretary Daniels. Typically, soon after taking office Roosevelt wrote to his wife that he had been obliged personally to take over from the secretary some matters about which Daniels's opinions were "half-baked"—adding grandly that he was sure the older man, too, eventually would have arrived at the right conclusions had he only given himself "the time to learn." Roosevelt was not disposed to be anybody's subordinate, let alone that of a small-town, small-time bumpkin such as Daniels pretended to be. (On first meeting Daniels, Roosevelt thought him "the funniest looking hillbilly I had ever seen.") Roosevelt was too young to perceive the shrewdness (shown in avoiding pitfalls and in dealing with congressmen) and masterfulness (shown in putting power-seeking naval officers in their proper place) that lay hidden behind Daniels's seemingly artless, simple-country-boy manner. Roosevelt's frequent acts of disloyalty were always overlooked, and his failings and indiscretions, always forgiven, by a chief who acted more like the best of fathers.

One of the many differences between them was that Roosevelt lived an animated social life in Washington, while Daniels and his close friend and ally, Secretary of State William Jennings Bryan, teetotalers and church-goers both, were essentially family people, disinclined to frivolity. They in any event would have been out of place—wrong clothes, wrong manners, wrong political party—in the homes into which Roosevelt was invited; for Washington society was Republican, and welcomed the assistant secretary not as a Democrat, but as a Roosevelt.

TR's inner circle took him in as one of their own. He and Eleanor were entertained by the capital city's leading hostess, dazzling Alice Roosevelt Longworth, and by the witty British ambassador Sir Cecil Spring-Rice. They were allowed to call upon Henry Adams—which in Washington was the supreme social distinction. They were sought out by TR's early political partner, proud and powerful Senator Henry Cabot Lodge, who thereafter disregarded the secretary of the navy when he wanted a favor— he had a nephew in the navy for whom he wanted a promotion—and communicated directly with the assistant secretary, who was happy to oblige.

One of the others who asked his help was Joseph C. Grew, a Groton boy two years ahead of him and a fellow club member of Fly at Harvard, who had joined the foreign service and been posted to the U.S. embassy in Berlin. Grew was afraid that he would lose his job to a Democrat; for President Wilson, intensely partisan, tended to reward his own. Roosevelt corresponded with Grew, but at that time Germany seemed a world away from his concerns as an ambitious young politician in his first year of office in Washington.

JOSEPHUS DANIELS was not only a teetotaler but a pacifist. His appointment realized the worst fears of the professional navy and its civilian supporters as to what might happen if Democratic populists were to come into power. Roosevelt was conveniently out of town and unavailable for comment when the secretary brought Prohibition to the fleet, decreeing that naval officers henceforth were to be deprived of their alcohol ration. Nonetheless, he served as a shield protecting the secretary on the military preparedness issue.

The name Roosevelt stood for the proposition (among others) that if America were militarily strong, she would be left in peace—an opinion shared by young Americans otherwise as different from one another as Averell Harriman and Douglas MacArthur. The assistant secretary, much influenced by the theories of TR's friend Admiral Alfred Thayer Mahan, brought to his job a fervor for a strong navy that was reassuring to such opposition leaders as Senator Lodge.

The navy's especial sphere, and that of the marines, was the mini-empire in Central America, the Gulf of Mexico, and the Caribbean that the United States administered with scant regard for the nominal independence of the countries in the area. U.S. forces were permanently stationed in Panama, while by the terms of the so-called Platt Amendment (1901), Cuba had become a U.S. protectorate. Haiti was to undergo U.S. military occupation from 1915 to 1934. Santo Domingo was to be controlled by an American military governor from 1916 to 1924; and Nicaragua was subject to almost continuous U.S. armed intervention from 1912 to 1925.

When Roosevelt came to Washington, these tropical lands were where the action was to be found. Felix Frankfurter, still in the State, War and Navy Departments Building in 1913, was busily tidying up the legalities of it all in what he supposed would be his last year in the War Department. John Foster Dulles of Sullivan and Cromwell was traveling the West Indies, scouting out chances for his clients to compete against British trade in the English colonies; and a disease contracted in the tropics left him with an eye tic for the rest of his life. In pursuance of American interests, Roosevelt found himself repeatedly ordering warships and marines to Caribbean lands.

In Roosevelt's second year in office, war with Mexico threatened to erupt, and his spirits soared. For a time it seemed that his moment might have come, and he spoke excitedly of annexing the whole of America's southern neighbor. But despite the temporary occupation of the Mexican port of Vera Cruz by the United States Navy, the war failed to ignite; and glory in the field was won only by Roosevelt's contemporary Douglas MacArthur.

In April 1914 Captain MacArthur was sent out from Washington to Vera Cruz, arriving on May 1 with orders "to obtain . . . all possible information which would be of value" to an American expeditionary force advancing on Mexico City if war should come. MacArthur was acting under the direct command of the War Department, and independently of the American command in Vera Cruz, whose orders were to stay put and to avoid hostilities against the Mexican forces surrounding the city. MacArthur was not bound by such orders; on his own initiative, but in pursuance of his mission, he set out on a one-man reconnaissance patrol behind Mexican army lines. Having spied out the position, he was able to return to his own lines only after a series of fast-action gunfights. Fired on by five armed men at Salinas, he shot two of them with his short-barreled pocket pistol. Three bullets whizzed through his clothes at Piedra as fifteen horsemen attacked; he got four of them. He dropped one out of three near Laguna, as bullets again ripped through his uniform.

After returning safely to his own lines, MacArthur wrote a brief report. It did not dwell on his own exploits. A few months later he was brought back to the General Staff in Washington.

When the general to whom MacArthur had reported in Washington became aware of the details of the young officer's adventures, he recommended that he be awarded the highest of military decorations, the Medal of Honor. But then others were heard from. The American commander in Vera Cruz, bypassed in an operation in which MacArthur had taken orders directly from Washington, wrote stiffly that "as the reconnaissance was made on the theory that Captain MacArthur was not a member of my command at the time, and as I had no knowledge of it until many months later, I am at a loss to know how I can properly make official recommendation on the subject." He questioned "the advisability of this enterprise having been undertaken without the knowledge of the commanding general on the ground," and claimed that the success of the mission with which he had been entrusted by the secretary of war had been jeopardized by MacArthur's actions.

A special board convened by the army chief of staff to consider the MacArthur case took the same view. Overlooking the fact that it was Washington (in the person of former chief of staff General Leonard Wood) that had chosen to send MacArthur out on a mission independent of the local army commander, the board recommended against awarding the Medal of Honor, saying that though he had risked his life to accomplish his mission, "to bestow the award recommended might encourage any other staff officer . . . to ignore the local commander, possibly interfering with the latter's plans with reference to the enemy."

For many decades his father had been unjustly denied the Medal of Honor and the recognition that had been his due, and now MacArthur felt the pattern recurring. The board's decision fueled what was to prove his lifelong suspicion that "they" were conspiring against him; and in his intemperate expression of his disappointment, he confirmed the enemies that he was making in their view that he was arrogant and unbalanced. He was bitter, but he had won glory and, in 1915, promotion to major.

For lack of adventures like MacArthur's, Franklin Roosevelt felt frustrated. Not even the outbreak of what was to become the First World War in Europe seemed to lead to any excitement. Roosevelt's instant reaction was that it would be "the greatest war in human history," but he remarked that "to my astonishment on reaching the Dept. nobody seemed the least bit excited about the European crisis. . . ."

# 6

## THE OUTBREAK OF
## THE GREAT WAR

IT BEGAN IN THE OLD COUNTRY, from whose hatreds, quarrels, and entanglements Americans believed they had escaped. Its first stirrings were on a peninsula crisscrossed by mountains and rivers—the Balkans—where the crumbling empire of the Ottoman sultans retreated before the only slightly less shaky empire of the Hapsburg emperors. Inhabited by peasants and traders whose customs and beliefs were rooted in the dim past, it remained a land of fierce clans and undying feuds. The remains of a Neolithic settlement, found and excavated nearby, went back perhaps 7,000 years. Close by, too, a spa, still functioning, dated to the days of the Roman Caesars. More than a millennium before, the Slavs had come, and had remained. Once Bogomilian Christians, many of the Slavs had become Muslims during the centuries of occupation by the Ottoman Turks. The Hapsburg Empire (Austria-Hungary) had taken possession of the province—Bosnia and Herzegovina—from the Turks in 1878, unilaterally annexing it in 1908, which provoked the Slavs to plot attacks against Hapsburg officials. Millions of Slavs lived uneasily under Hapsburg rule, many of them dreaming of a free southern Slav confederacy; but the Hapsburg regime believed that the unrest was fomented from the outside, by Serbia, an independent, neighboring Slav state that was a client of Russia's.

The town where it happened—Bosnia's capital, Sarajevo, an assemblage of wooden buildings at the bottom of Mount Trebevic—stretched along a narrow river valley through which flowed a turbulent stream that (so claimed a later observer) ran red. It was a mining town that had become a trading center; indeed, in 1914 many of its streets still were named for crafts and trades, and the Turkish market in the town center continued to flourish. Clashing with the east European facial features of most of its inhabitants, and with the central European cut of the uniforms worn by the soldiery of its new Austrian and Hungarian rulers, the town had an Oriental aspect. A third of its population was Muslim; minarets shot up from its skyline; and five times a day muezzins, from the heights of their mosques, called the faithful to prayer. It was evident at a glance that, like so many towns in eternally warring Europe, it had changed hands often.


TO AMERICANS, almost every aspect of the tragedy at Sarajevo in the summer of 1914 was foreign—not least of them, Francis Ferdinand's title of archduke, and his position as heir to the Hapsburg throne of Austria-Hungary, in line to inherit not just properties but provinces, peoples, and countries. It was odd and European that one born so powerful could *not* do what even the humblest American could do—marry for love. Yet it was true, for his beloved Sophie, as a mere countess, was too lowly to be married to an archduke. In espousing her, he therefore was allowed to contract only a "morganatic" marriage, so that the children of their marriage were disinherited. More to the immediate point, it pained him constantly that she was not allowed to take her place by his side on formal occasions. So it is not inconceivable, as an English historian suggested decades ago, that Francis Ferdinand may have scheduled the Hapsburg army's annual maneuvers in Bosnia—and on that fateful day—because under the arcane rules of Hapsburg court etiquette, the frontier province was the only place in the empire where he was permitted, even on June 28, the fourteenth anniversary of his wedding, to have his consort seated by his side in public.

Foreign though they were, and far away, the events that occurred in Sarajevo on Sunday, June 28, soon were burned into memory in the New World as in the Old: the procession of four open cars, bringing Francis Ferdinand and Sophie and their party, moving into Sarajevo along the quay that followed the river; the half-dozen Slav nationalist students, nineteen-year-old Gavrilo Princip among them, waiting by the side of the road to attack, and then bungling the attempt; the flight of the failed conspirators, and Princip's retirement in despair to a café; the decision by Francis Ferdinand's party to cut short their visit; the failure of Hapsburg officials to tell the archduke's chauffeurs of the change in plans—that they now were to stay on the main thoroughfare and drive straight ahead, to the hospital and then out of town; the driver, not having gotten the word, turning, as in the original plan, into the narrow side street that led to the market; the angry shouts, "What are you doing? We're going the wrong way!"; the driver stopping, by a terrible coincidence, at the very café in which Princip gloomily was sipping a glass of water to wash down his morning coffee; Princip looking up, astonished to see the archduke seated in a stopped car only two yards away; and Princip leaping up, jumping on the running board of the car, shooting at point-blank range, and killing Francis Ferdinand and Sophie.

The archduke's last words were: "It is nothing." Nobody was ever more wrong. For the rest of the century, the images of his final hours were to be recalled, peered at through magnifying glasses, and scanned in enlargements for hidden meanings. For from the apparently meaningless acts of violence in the far-off Balkan peninsula that day came the greatest disaster in modern history, the outbreak of the Great War, with far-reaching consequences— some evil, some extremely good—within the lifetime of Franklin Roosevelt's and Harry Truman's and Dwight Eisenhower's generation: the practical disappearance of traditional rural societies; the destruction, after at least 5,000 years, of the monarchical system of government; the legal emancipation of women; the collapse of colonial empires; the coming to an end, after five centuries, of Europe's hegemony over the rest of the world; the eruption of fascism, Nazism, and communism; the discovery of how to release nuclear power; the end of America's isolation; and the rise of the United States to global hegemony.

WHAT WAS NOT CLEAR AT THE TIME, especially to Americans, was why the murder of these two people had to lead to the killing of tens of millions of others. Yet evidently there was some eerie, apparently inescapable—and foreign—logic to it. As absurd and blurred as a nightmare, the events that unfolded after Francis Ferdinand and Sophie died moved from the apparently accidental to the seemingly inevitable.

After consulting with Germany's leaders on July 5, the government of Austria-Hungary presented Serbia with an ultimatum on July 23, in effect demanding that Serbia surrender her independence; rejected Serbia's abject and nearly total acceptance of the ultimatum on July 25; and on July 28 declared war. On July 30 Russia, as Serbia's protector, started to mobilize. In response, Germany delivered ultimatums to Russia and to Russia's ally France, and on August 1 declared war on them. Germany commenced hostilities by attacking France through neutral Belgium and Luxembourg in violation of treaty obligations. The treaties entitled Britain to go to war to defend Luxembourg, but obliged her to do so to defend Belgium. After receiving no reply to her demand that Germany stop the invasion, Britain came into the war at midnight (German time) August 4.

HISTORIANS EVER SINCE have disagreed about why the war really started and are likely to go on doing so. But the works of those who wrote in the first half-century after the event were rendered obsolete in important respects by the publication, beginning in the 1960s, of revealing German documents dating from the first decades of the century. As a result, we know that the conclusions that the Roosevelt, Truman, and Eisenhower generation drew from their formative political experience in the First World War were based on faulty information about Germany's role in the origins of the conflict.

The question that Americans focused on during the first years of the war—and that, for example, William Bullitt pursued as a journalist seeking a "scoop" in wartime Europe—was whether Germany had known and approved of the Austrian ultimatum of July 23 before it was sent to Serbia. It was an important question (to which the answer was "yes"), but did not go to the heart of the matter.

Perhaps more attention should have been given to what Colonel Edward House, President Wilson's confidant, had observed in Germany *before* the assassination. On June 17, 1914, House, in London on his way back from Berlin, told the British foreign secretary, Sir Edward Grey, "of the militant war spirit in Germany and of the high tension of the people, and I feared some spark might be fanned into a blaze. I thought Germany would strike quickly when she moved: that there would be no parley or discussion; that when she felt that a difficulty could not be overcome by peaceful negotiation, she would take no chances but would strike. I thought . . . the army was militaristic and aggressive and ready for war at any time." The British foreign secretary, however, and Prime Minister Herbert Asquith treated such reports as alarmist and no cause for concern. They were taken up with other matters, Ireland in particular, and it was not until nearly four weeks after the assassinations in Sarajevo that foreign affairs were even discussed by the British cabinet.

It was difficult for Britons—or Americans—to imagine, when they read of Francis Ferdinand's death in the distant Balkans, that it could affect their own lives. The British prime minister did not see it coming, any more than did the man or woman on the street in Europe or the United States. Even later, during and after the war, it seemed so unlikely a chain of events that led from Sarajevo to the trenches of the western front, that Americans throughout the twentieth century have tended to believe that the war came about through mischance or miscalculation, or through flaws in Europe's political, social, economic, or international relations systems that made it possible for accidents and mistakes to cause a war that nobody wanted.

This assumed that nobody wanted the war—which we now know to be untrue, for the powerful chief of the German General Staff certainly desired it. In picturing the outbreak of war as accidental, what always has carried conviction is the observation that on June 28, 1914, nobody could have foreseen that an unlikely and unexpected shooting in the Balkans would bring about a war that would draw in all of Europe. We now know that to be untrue, too; a handful of men in Berlin had foreseen it—and in large part had planned it—long before.

IN THE UPPER REACHES of German business, political, and military life before 1914, as historians now have shown, there was a widespread desire for Germany to be supreme on the continent of Europe. This was not an unusual sort of goal for a nation's leaders to harbor at that time; TR and Henry Cabot Lodge, for example, were ambitious for the United States to dominate the two continents of North and South America as well as much of the Pacific.

Germany's leaders were aware that if their country expanded beyond a certain point, Russia or Britain would step in to stop her, and that to achieve her goals, Germany would have to fight a war. That thought did not deter them. They were determined to expand no matter who tried to stand in their way. That is what they meant when they told one another that a European war was inevitable; they meant that their own actions were going to make it inevitable.

Germany's military leaders carried their logic further. They argued that rather than wait the extra couple of years until the enemy was ready to fight (for Russia was making alarming progress in strengthening her army), it would be only prudent for Germany to launch a preemptive strike immediately against Russia and her ally France.

Such, or something like it, was the thinking of the chief of the German General Staff, tall, heavy, balding, gloomy Field Marshal Count Helmuth von Moltke. He had focused his attention on central and eastern Europe as the direction both of Germany's expansionist goals and of her vulnerability. He saw in the ferment in that area a fated, ages-old conflict between Teutons and Slavs. In 1909 Moltke, in correspondence with the Hapsburg chief of staff, Franz Conrad von Hotzendorff, committed Germany to side with Austria-Hungary if Russia intervened in a war between the Hapsburg Empire and Serbia. Moltke, who made the point that it would be better to wait until Serbia committed an act of aggression that provoked the Hapsburg Empire into making war, kept the kaiser and the German chancellor aware of this correspondence.

The kaiser ("caesar," or emperor) was Wilhelm II. When war broke out in 1914, he was fifty-five years old and had reigned for twenty-six years. He ruled a German federation of states that had kings and princes of their own, but in it he and his state—Prussia—were supreme. Germany had a parliament, the Reichstag, but especially in foreign policy and national security matters, it tended to defer to the kaiser. The chancellor was the civilian head of government; he was appointed by the kaiser, and an important part of his job was to win support in the Reichstag for the government's policies and especially for the raising of the money—the appropriations—that the government required.

Military matters were the special province of the kaiser. The army and navy chiefs were appointed by him, and reported to him, rather than to or through the chancellor. Wilhelm II enjoyed having this power, for he loved playing soldier. He identified himself with the Homeric hero Achilles, though the resemblance between the two was clearer to him than to others.

Germany was Europe's growing power in almost every sphere. Another emperor might have seen in this a reason to keep the peace and wait until the industrial greatness of his country brought with it the effective domination of the Continent—as it was bound to do eventually. Wilhelm II was inclined to follow a different path. His impatient desire was to force the issue: to intimidate the other countries of Europe into conceding immediately the German supremacy to which her might entitled her. But Britain, an empire he admired but envied, seemed always to thwart him.

It was to discuss Britain's attitude that Moltke was summoned by the kaiser to a conference Sunday morning, December 8, 1912, along with three high naval officers. Kaiser Wilhelm was enraged that a British cabinet minister had said that Britain would *never* allow Europe to come under complete German domination. The kaiser and Moltke decided to go to war. Moltke wanted "to launch an immediate attack," saying that "war was unavoidable, and the sooner the better." The navy, however, claimed that it was not ready and would need a year or a year and a half to accomplish certain preparations. The kaiser (and the gloomy Moltke) agreed to the postponement only reluctantly.

Moltke was well acquainted with the character of the vain, strutting, boastful, insecure kaiser, whose withered arm gave him an asymmetrical look in keeping with his unbalanced personality. He was someone who let people down. Caught up in enthusiasm or bragging, he would announce bold decisions that he would weakly retract the morning after.

So Moltke may not have counted overly much on the "decision" of December 1912 to go to war, even though the civilian chancellor was made privy to it within a week. Yet all along Moltke looked forward to an inevitable war, sparked, as he had indicated in 1909, by a Balkan incident that could be portrayed as a Serbian attack on Austria-Hungary; and the 1912 decision provided him with a rough timetable.

Only a month or so before the actual outbreak of war in 1914, the German foreign secretary noted that Moltke told him that in two or three years the "military superiority of our enemies would . . . be so great that he did not know how he could overcome them. Today we would still be a match for them. In his opinion there was no alternative to making preventive war in order to defeat the enemy while there was still a chance of victory. The Chief of the General Staff therefore proposed that I should conduct a policy with the aim of provoking a war in the near future."

Though some historians still dissent, modern scholarship seems to indicate that the German government did just that. It was not (as used to be believed) that a local crisis in the Balkans somehow spun out of control; it was rather that the kaiser's government had been waiting for something like the Sarajevo incident to happen. When it did occur, Germany deliberately seized on it as a pretext to provoke a war.

"Provoke" was indeed the word, for the German government was not willing to bet that its citizens or its parliament would support an act of aggression. The German people, like the peoples of the powerful neutral countries, would have to be persuaded that Germany was defending herself against an attack by others.

In May 1914, a month before Sarajevo, Moltke took the baths at Carlsbad in company with the Austrian army chief Conrad. Conrad, whose position in the Hapsburg government was far less powerful than Moltke's in the German regime, had long advocated an Austro-Hungarian attack on Serbia. At Carlsbad the two generals refined war plans they had adopted five years before. Moltke assured Conrad that on the thirty-ninth or fortieth day after mobilization, Germany would have defeated France and would turn against Russia.

By June 1914 the German navy had completed its preparations. So the time to go to war had arrived. Moltke had told his colleagues that if Germany was to have a chance of winning it, the sooner the better. All of them were acquainted, and had been at least since 1909, with the scenario: a Serbian attack on the Hapsburg Empire in the Balkans would trigger the sought-for war. Everybody knew that Bismarck had predicted that "some damned foolish thing in the Balkans" would be the cause of the next big war. Indeed, they counted on it, knowing that provocative acts happened in the Balkans all the time; the kaiser and his ministers had only to wait.

And then came the shootings in Sarajevo. Austria-Hungary consulted Germany, and both the kaiser and Chancellor Theobald von Bethmann-Hollweg not merely gave the Hapsburg Empire a blank check to take action against Serbia—with Germany guaranteeing to fend off Russian interference—but left the Hapsburg government with the feeling that Germany was urging the strongest possible action and indeed might abandon Austria-Hungary if she were feeble and failed to act. Some evidence uncovered relatively recently suggests that the more offensive language in the ultimatum sent by Vienna to Belgrade might even have been the kaiser's.

Wilhelm went yachting with the armaments tycoon Krupp von Bohlen and told him that "no one would ever again be able to reproach him"—the kaiser—"with indecision." Another source quotes him as saying (in a curiously modern idiom that must be the result of free translation): "This time I haven't chickened out."

BUT HE SPOKE TOO SOON. When Serbia accepted almost all of the terms of the Hapsburg ultimatum, he tried to back down: "But that eliminates any reason for war," he exclaimed, forgetting that he wanted one. Believing that France might stay neutral, he asked Moltke not to invade her—only to be told that what he asked was no longer possible: armies were on the move and it was too late to stop them. "How did all this happen?" Kaiser Wilhelm asked his chancellor.

Of the motives of the chancellor, Bethmann-Hollweg, more than much has been written. On all sides it is recognized that he knew what giving the blank check to the Hapsburgs and urging them to act strongly meant: that it almost certainly would lead to a general European war. He knew that the generals regarded such a war as inevitable, and thought that Germany could win only if it were fought now rather than later ("The military keep on urging for a war now while Russia is not yet ready," as a Saxon official reported). He knew that Moltke wanted war and had been waiting for a Balkan incident to ignite one. And he knew that he was doing what Moltke wanted done to bring about a war.

That said, some believe that Bethmann-Hollweg hoped against hope for a peaceful resolution of the crisis nonetheless—which is to say, that Serbia would surrender without a fight. As late as July 25, the German foreign minister candidly admitted that "neither London, nor Paris, nor St. Petersburg want war." But London, Paris, and St. Petersburg might have no choice in the matter if Austria-Hungary attacked Serbia, as Germany encouraged her to do; the number two official at the German Foreign Office conceded that such an attack would lead "with a probability of 90 percent to a European war." Perhaps, as some claim, Bethmann-Hollweg tried to keep at least Britain out of it; but it is not unfair to say that it was with eyes open that he allowed the war to occur.

To his own people, but to them alone, Bethmann-Hollweg successfully painted Russia as the aggressor. The decisive moment was when Russia started to mobilize. "I run to the War Ministry," a Bavarian official wrote. "Beaming faces everywhere. Everyone is shaking hands in the corridors: people congratulate one another for being over the hurdle." On August 1, 1914, the head of the kaiser's navy cabinet wrote that "the mood is brilliant" because "the government has succeeded very well in making us appear as the attacked."

AT THE TIME, however, there was no conclusive evidence that Austria-Hungary had consulted Germany before initiating the crisis: it was possible to believe that Germany had been dragged into the conflict by the terms of her alliance with the Hapsburg Empire, forced to defend an Austrian move of which she herself had not known in advance and did not approve. Alternatively, Germany's leaders, even if they had known what Austria-Hungary was going to do, might not have foreseen where the Austrian move might lead. The war could have come about, in other words, through error rather than design: through miscalculation, misinformation, and mis-understanding.

To Americans, it was natural to believe, too, that the causes of the war were mired in the complexities of Europe's intricate power politics: the arms races, the secret treaties, and above all, the rival alliance systems. Yet it transpires that such was not the case. It was not the Austrian alliance that sucked Germany into the conflict; Germany acted of her own volition. Nor did alliances bring Russia and France into the war; it was Germany's declaration of war on them that brought them into it. Great Britain entered the war not because of a treaty of alliance, but because Germany invaded a country whose neutrality Britain had guaranteed.

But Americans were not necessarily wrong to believe that the coming of war showed the political system of Europe to be deeply vicious. Although Germany deliberately tossed a match into it, Europe already was a powder keg. Social, cultural, class, and ethnic tensions were widespread, as was industrial strife, creating a climate in which politicians found it expedient to pursue a bellicose foreign policy. There was a sense in the air that Europe suffered from some malady that required bloodletting for its cure, or that called for a cycle of death and rebirth. On the announcement of the outbreak of war, foreign observers noted with surprise that crowds in the belligerent countries were seized by a frenzied enthusiasm: a wild happiness, a sort of mass delirium.

# 7

# "... I WAS GOING TO STOP THE WAR"

IT WAS JULY'S END, 1914. A year out of Yale, dapper twenty-three-year-old William Bullitt, a handsome young man of medium height with wavy brown hair, had reached the capital city of tsarist Russia in the course of his European travels with his mother, Louisa. The Bullitts moved into the National Hotel in St. Petersburg, but at night could not sleep: through their windows came the sounds of impending war. There was shouting in the streets. The city was awake. Crowds were singing the national anthem. The Bullitts heard strains—or so they believed—of Tchaikovsky's *1812* Overture.

It had all come about as suddenly and without warning as the eruption of a sleeping volcano. After Austria-Hungary had declared war on Russia's ally Serbia, on July 30 it had ordered a general mobilization to warn off Russia from coming to Serbia's defense. Now Tsar Nicholas II was responding by marshaling a general mobilization in Russia. Throughout the territories of his empire—one-sixth of the land surface of the globe—the tsar was calling what ultimately would be 5 million civilians into military service to meet at assembly points according to plan for transport to their assigned units.

Bullitt later wrote that "I was young and . . . I hated war, and I'll confess . . . that I was naive enough to make up my mind that I was going to stop the war. . . ." He and his mother caught the last train out of St. Petersburg to Berlin. There they registered at the Adlon Hotel, and promptly contacted James Gerard, a family friend who served as U.S. ambassador to Germany. Gerard, who as late as July 27 had advised Washington that there would be no war, now warned the Bullitts to leave at once.

The Berlin correspondent of *The New York Times* wrote that the city was "raging mad for war." The streets were filled with "shrieking, singing" mobs. " 'War! War!' they shouted." From the window of their railroad train compartment as they left for London, the Bullitts watched German troops marching off to fight.

Like the Bullitts, other Americans heard singing everywhere in Europe. The New York *Evening Post* reported that in Munich students were chanting war ballads and mobs were singing "Watch on the Rhine." In Vienna, according to the New York *World*, "half the population of the city seemed to be on the streets . . . singing national hymns and cheering." In Paris, wrote a correspondent of the Philadelphia *Public Ledger*, "a howling mob" had marched to a statue of Joan of Arc and was singing the "Marseillaise."

ON AUGUST 4, 1914, thirty-one-year-old Felix Frankfurter, who had just accepted appointment as a professor at the Harvard Law School, was a guest at Sagamore Hill, TR's three-story mansion in Oyster Bay on Long Island's north shore. Sagamore Hill had served as the summer White House (1901–09), and from it the former President kept a watchful eye on fast-moving events in Europe. German troops had invaded Luxembourg August 2 and neutral Belgium the night of August 3–4. The question these invasions posed to the House of Commons was whether Britain should honor her treaty commitment to Belgium.

Another guest at Sagamore Hill August 4 was an Englishman, Charles Booth, head of the great shipping line Cunard. Frankfurter described the ex-President as doing "a tomahawk war dance" around Booth, while crying "You've got to go in! You've got to go in!" At 6 p.m. New York time, 11 p.m. London time, and midnight Berlin time, Britain did so.

A keen and realistic student of international politics, TR understood both why Germany may have had to violate Belgium's neutrality and why, in response, Britain had to declare war on Germany. As the war went on, he was also among the first to see how America's interests might be affected by its outcome. In August 1914, however, not even he foresaw an American involvement in the drama being played out in Europe. But his young distant cousin in the Navy Department did.

FRANKLIN ROOSEVELT BELIEVED that "the greatest war in human history" was about to begin, and seems to have been the only person in the government who thought the United States might be drawn into it. Secretary of the Navy Daniels, wrote Roosevelt, was "feeling chiefly very sad that his faith in human nature and civilization, and similar idealistic nonsense, was receiving such a rude shock." He claimed that "I started in alone to get things ready and prepare plans for what ought to be done by the Navy."

Daniels and Secretary of State Bryan, in Roosevelt's view, had no "conception of what a general European war means." Receiving the news in early August that Germany had invaded France, Roosevelt told his wife that "a complete smash up is inevitable." Daniels, he said, "is bewildered by it all."

Over the course of the next few months, Roosevelt was to wage an undercover campaign for increased military preparedness, secretly under-mining Daniels and the President. In the autumn of 1914, TR waged a public campaign for military preparedness, which President Wilson op-posed, saying that increased defense spending would mean that "we had been thrown off our balance by a war with which we have nothing to do, whose causes cannot touch us. . . ."

Having proclaimed America's neutrality in the European conflict, and having asked all Americans to be neutral in thought as well as action, Wilson designated Sunday, October 4, 1914, as a day of "prayer and sup-plication," and urged his fellow citizens "to repair . . . to their places of worship" on that day to petition God to bring peace. Prayers were recited and speeches declaimed in churches, synagogues, and meeting halls through-out the country on Peace Sunday, and in addressing one such meeting, the governor of Illinois pointedly remarked that "if this Republic can live in peace, others ought to be able to do the same."

IN AUGUST 1914, as the war broke out in Europe, ceremonies were held to mark the opening of TR's great monument, the Panama Canal. An editorial in *The New York Times* noted the coincidence of the two events: "The European ideal bears its full fruit of ruin and savagery just at the moment when the American ideal lays before the world a great work of peace, goodwill and fair play."

Robert A. Taft, not long out of the Harvard Law School and just beginning his practice in Cincinnati, observed: "Aren't the nations of Eu-rope a queer lot, to go to war for nothing." Taft's sympathies were with the Allies, but even so, the war illustrated for him, as for other Americans who gave it any thought, how different Europe was from America and how right it was for the United States to have stayed away from Europe's politics. A small-town newspaper, the Wabash, Indiana, *Plain Dealer,* remarked of the war in Europe that "we never appreciated so keenly as now the foresight exercised by our forefathers in emigrating from Europe."

Though the war reinforced Americans in their view that they were superior to Europeans, it also aroused their sympathy for the suffering that Europeans were undergoing. Herbert Hoover, a successful engineer-businessman living in London, gave practical expression to that sentiment: he created and managed a volunteer organization—the Commission for Re-lief of Belgium—that fed and clothed the entire population of German-occupied Belgium. It was the only sort of foreign involvement with which Americans felt comfortable: a humanitarian, not a political, endeavor.

A parallel activity, in part inspired by the multimillionaire former steel manufacturer Andrew Carnegie, was launched by a Baltimore publicist named Theodore Marburg at the Century Association in New York City on

January 15, 1915. It was an organization dedicated to creating a league of nations: the League to Enforce Peace. Intended to prevent the outbreak of another 1914 war, its idea was for the powers—the United States and the countries of Europe—to agree to act together to force countries involved in disputes to submit them to arbitration. Former President William Howard Taft became president of the organization.

Bryan attacked Taft's group because its program would pledge the use of force to compel nations to arbitrate. This would require the United States to send troops into combat abroad to settle disputes between Europeans— the very thing that Bryan, in the mainstream of the American political tradition, wished to avoid. TR attacked from the other side: he claimed Taft would sign a piece of paper establishing a league but then would fail to build the armed forces to back it up. TR had proposed a league of nations of his own back in 1905, which would have been a cartel of the great powers. The cartel would have policed the rest of the world.

Leagues of nations were very much the stuff of political discourse east of the Mississippi in the first months of the war, as Americans observed with dismay what Europeans were doing to one another. West of the Mississippi, Americans felt too remote from the foreign conflict to give it much attention.

WILLIAM BULLITT, employed in 1915 as a journalist by the *Public Ledger* back home in Philadelphia, had his chance to return to Europe when yet another American businessman decided to do something about the European war. Henry Ford, the billionaire auto magnate, had been persuaded by a Hungarian pacifist, Rosika Schwimmer, that the warring countries of Europe wanted to stop fighting, and would do so if only a disinterested party would intervene to offer mediation. Ford thereupon chartered the *Oscar II,* a steamer of the Scandinavian Line, to transport himself and a delegation of fellow peacemakers to Europe to offer to mediate. It was November 1915, and Ford set a tight deadline by pledging that "we'll get the boys out of the trenches by Christmas." Bullitt was assigned to cover the story, and syndicated his reports.

The *Oscar II* sailed December 4, 1915, with 149 peace delegates aboard. Bryan came to see it off, and compared it favorably to Noah's Ark. Bullitt reported that "10,000 howling men and women" were at the dock to watch them leave, and that as the ship shoved off, one man "plunged into the river . . . saying he would swim behind the ship to ward off torpedoes."

Ford's "peace ship," a subject of jokes and laughter, docked in Norway, where Ford disembarked and—perhaps conscious of how ridiculous he had been made to appear—fled back to America. The delegates toured Europe throughout 1916; but the press and public lost interest in them.

The experience of the Ford peace delegation proved to be a foretaste of things to come. As Americans traveled through the twentieth century, they often were to find themselves voyaging in foreign waters seeking in all sincerity and with the best of intentions to do good—and yet somehow appearing foolish, or worse.

# 8

## AMERICA QUARRELS WITH BOTH SIDES

SOON AFTER BRITAIN WAS DRAWN into the German war in Europe, TR wrote to his close friend Ambassador Sir Cecil Spring-Rice that "it is a singular thing to reflect that seventy years ago, when there was practically no Irish or German vote in this country, we would have been unquestionably anti-English. . . . Now there is a very large German and Irish vote, and yet that does not make the slightest difference in the trend of national feeling being favourable to England."

A poll of 400 newspaper editors by the magazine *Literary Digest* in the autumn of 1914 suggested that, with wide regional variations, arguably based on ethnic origin, most Americans did not take sides in the war, but that the minority who did were largely pro-Allies. At least in the South and East, and certainly in Washington, D.C., there was considerable sympathy for the Allied cause, but no disposition to give practical expression to it. No significant body of opinion anywhere in the United States favored entering the war, or even considered doing so.

In the summer of 1914 Americans were preoccupied with problems of their own. The economy had been in a slump, as had Wall Street; so the domestic outlook already was bleak when, like a tornado that strikes without warning, the news arrived that Europe's armies were mobilizing for war. For a long time the growth of America's industry and trade had been financed by European investors; were they—all at the same time—to try to cash in their holdings in order to pay for the war, it would be in the nature of a run on the bank, and the United States would face ruin.

Hence Wall Street's violent reaction to the news that in far-off central and eastern Europe, Austria-Hungary and Russia were mobilizing their armies. Thursday, July 30, saw the biggest one-day fall in prices on the New York Stock Exchange since the panic of 1907. Worse threatened to come. The major bourses of the Continent had shut down by the thirtieth; all of them had gone out of business indefinitely as of the three p.m. close in New York that day. At ten o'clock the following morning, the world's principal financial center, the London Stock Exchange, closed its doors. Winston Churchill, then Britain's youthful First Lord of the Admiralty, wrote from London to his wife that the city's financial district "has simply broken into chaos. The world's credit system is virtually suspended. You cannot sell stocks & shares. You cannot borrow. Quite soon it will not perhaps be possible to cash a cheque. Prices of goods are rising to panic levels."

At dawn on Friday, July 31, the New York Stock Exchange, which was scheduled to open its doors as usual at 9:30 a.m. and to commence trading at 10 a.m., was the only major bourse in the world still in business: for practical purposes the only place remaining on the planet where stocks and bonds still could be exchanged for cash. Early that morning Wall Street stockbrokers arrived at their offices to find so many accumulated sell orders—an avalanche that had arrived overnight for execution at Friday's opening—as to threaten utter collapse. Heeding a summons from the leading firm in the financial district, Wall Streeters rushed to the headquarters of J. P. Morgan and Company, where Henry Davison, the Morgan partner for whom Willard Straight had worked in supporting the government of China, took command.

Even as the leaders of Wall Street met at Davison's call, the doors of the Corinthian-pillared seven-storied temple of commerce that was the New York Stock Exchange were opened for business, and those who worked there streamed inside to take up their positions. A few minutes before 10 a.m., the man who was to ring the gong signaling the start of trading was about to do so when the president of the Stock Exchange, who had rushed over to Morgan headquarters to ask what to do, called by telephone to order the Exchange to close.

The financial situation was terrifying ("THE CREDIT OF ALL EUROPE HAS BROKEN DOWN ABSOLUTELY . . . ," Davison cabled to his partner Thomas Lamont, who was in Montana fishing for trout), but Davison presciently sensed that great opportunities accompanied the grave dangers; "WE WILL SOON GET TO RIGHTING THINGS," he concluded.


AS HOSTILITIES BEGAN, Britain's Royal Navy took control of the Atlantic Ocean, and soon effectively blocked all commerce by sea with Germany and her neighbors. This was in flagrant violation of the tenets of international law as understood by the United States and most other countries. Americans believed it their right as neutrals to continue trading with both sides in wars, and had regarded their freedom of trade as central to their world policy ever since the first days of their Republic. They had protested in vain when Britain blocked their trade with the Continent during the Napoleonic wars a century before; and, in part on that issue, had fought the War of 1812.

A few weeks after the European war started, President Wilson expressed himself strongly against the developing British policy in a conversation with his adviser Edward House. According to House, Wilson "read a page from his history of the American people telling how during Madison's administration the War of 1812 was started in exactly the same way as this controversy is opening up. . . . The President said: 'Madison and I are the only two Princeton men that have become President. The circumstances of the War of 1812 now run parallel. I sincerely hope they will go no further.' "

Although House warned the British government of the President's mood and of stiff American protests to come, the British carried their blockade strategy into effect, cutting off the Central Powers, Germany and Austria-Hungary, from overseas sources of supply. British officials treated the official American position as all talk and no action, and were vindicated in doing so when the Wilson administration failed to back up its words with deeds.

In 1914 Americans had a sense that they were becoming a power in world politics, and yet their neutral rights were being disregarded by the Royal Navy as high-handedly as ever before. For most of America's existence, Great Britain had been the country's chief foreign enemy, and now again it was Britain who denied Americans their due. So it signified a great change in American attitudes toward Britain that Wilson did not pursue the quarrel with any great warmth.

Of course, Washington sent letters of protest to London, but they were of no avail. Diplomacy proved useless, while the alternative, the application of force, appeared impractical: the American fleet, of which Secretary Daniels and Assistant Secretary Roosevelt were so proud, was efficient and modern, and was the third-largest navy in the world, but it was no match for the Royal Navy, the largest and most powerful fleet of all.

There seemed to be nothing the United States could do to break Britain's illegal blockade. Yet as time went on, a question arose as to whether the Wilson administration was trying as hard as it might. As 1914 drifted into 1915 and 1916, it transpired that while Britain might be trampling on America's neutral rights, the United States had a powerful motive for looking the other way: it paid to do so.


WILLARD STRAIGHT, the thirty-four-year-old founder of *The New Republic* who worked at the House of Morgan, claimed to have suggested to Henry Davison in the autumn of 1914 that all British purchases in the United States be coordinated through a single agent. It was a sensible suggestion, because the British had stepped up their buying in the United States when war began and had been bidding up prices on themselves. Davison and Straight boarded ship for Great Britain in November 1914, and in London negotiated an agreement that established Morgan as Britain's agent.

With so much purchasing power at its disposal, Morgan was able to drive a hard bargain with U.S. suppliers to keep prices under control. To head Morgan's newly created export department, Davison's partner Thomas Lamont chose Edward R. Stettinius, Sr., a former commodities speculator, who assembled a hardworking staff that eventually numbered 175 people.

So immense was the scale of British wartime buying that, as a historian of the House of Morgan has written, "Stettinius became the single most important consumer on earth. . . . He bought, shipped, and insured supplies on an unprecedented scale. . . . Each month, Stettinius presided over purchases equivalent to the *world's* gross national product a generation before" (emphasis added). Morgan encouraged American companies to expand and create mass production facilities in order to meet Britain's increasing orders, and loaned them the money to do so.

The war was dramatically changing the terms of world trade. For the United States between 1914 and 1916, the positive balance of trade (the dollar amount that tells how much more Americans sell to foreigners than they buy from foreigners) rose 600 percent.* In a short time the United States had become the arsenal of the Allies, expanding its industrial capacity and converting to war industries with a speed that German and other foreign observers found stupefying. Henry Adams, the doyen of Anglophile Washington society, wrote that "apparently we are working day and night for the Allies, but also for money."

Britain, although still the world's banker in 1914, needed credit to pay for these sudden and enormous purchases from the New World. At first Wilson agreed with Bryan that it would be unneutral to allow American banks to make war loans to the Allies, but within weeks he changed his mind; these loans were financing the sales to the Allies that were making America prosperous. As Britain's banker in the United States, Morgan arranged the largest foreign loans in Wall Street's history. In August 1915 Wilson again thought of cutting off these financings, but was dissuaded by his cabinet; without further loans to the Allies, warned one cabinet member, there "would be . . . industrial depression, idle capital and idle labor, numerous failures, financial demoralization, and general unrest and suffering among the laboring classes."

During the period of America's neutrality in the European war, U.S. investors bought $2 billion of Allied bonds and only $20 million of German bonds, a ratio of a hundred to one. As trade with Germany and Austria had been cut off by the Royal Navy while billions in U.S. exports went to the Allies, German-American organizations lobbied Congress for an embargo on

* Excluding gold, which really was a payment, not an "import."

all arms sales to either side—effectively putting an end to sales to the Allies, since none were being made to Germany. Despite the blow this would have struck at the country's new prosperity, there was substantial support for such an embargo throughout the country (outside the Northeast), and in the Senate it secured thirty-six votes out of ninety-six. Particularly in the heavily German-American Middle West, the hated Morgan bank and the East Coast financial interests it symbolized were seen to be attaching America to the Allied cause out of greed. Charles Lindbergh, a congressman from Minnesota, was typical of those in Middle America who denounced the "money interests" for pushing the country into the Allied camp in order to rake in inordinate profits.

Indeed, what was taking place was perhaps the largest transfer of wealth in a short time that the world had known. On the sidewalks of New York's financial district, activity perked up; what began with "four boys and a dog" became a hundred stock brokerage firms buying and selling stocks and bonds out of doors, until in the spring of 1915 the New York Stock Exchange opened its doors for business once again. By then, no danger was posed by foreigners who wanted to sell; Americans now had the money to buy.

Years later, when the war in Europe was over, it could be seen that the United States, which had been one of the world's principal debtor nations in 1914, owing about $3.7 billion, had become the world's creditor, owed about $3.8 billion. A net effect of the war was that much of Europe's wealth was transferred to America in payment for arms and other supplies, causing the United States to replace Great Britain as the leading financial power on the planet.

BRITAIN'S BLOCKADE of Germany was contrary to international law, and so was Germany's response to it. Unable to challenge the Royal Navy on the surface of the Atlantic, imperial Germany launched a submarine campaign, sinking, without warning, Allied shipping and also ships bringing supplies to the Allies.

In March 1915 a German U-boat torpedoed a British steamship called the *Falaba* off the coast of Africa. One hundred eleven lives were lost, one of them an American passenger. On several counts this violated prewar rules on international law. Under those rules, the U-boat should have surfaced and warned the *Falaba* before opening fire. In any event, the German commander should have taken steps to ensure that the American, as a neutral, would not be harmed in the fighting.

Within the American government, responses to the *Falaba* incident were various. Bryan argued that in wartime Americans who choose to travel on the ships of one side or another must do so at their own risk—for it is only to be expected that the ships of a nation at war will be attacked. State Department Counselor Robert Lansing claimed that a time for decision had arrived: the United States should either confront Germany on the legality of submarine warfare or back down and do nothing. Wilson was uncertain what to do.

On May 1, 1915, advertisements placed by the German embassy appeared in newspapers along the eastern seaboard of the United States warning Americans not to travel on the British liner *Lusitania*, a Cunard steamship about to cross from New York to Europe. Only one *Lusitania* passenger heeded the warning and shifted to another ship.

Anger against Great Britain was gathering in the country. Three miles outside New York harbor, British warships waited to stop and board vessels, and to detain those bound for neutral ports. On the other side of the ocean, the Royal Navy prevented American ships from docking in neutral Norway, Sweden, or Denmark; and British authorities had intercepted and detained nearly a half-billion dollars of meat products that Americans had exported to European destinations. In Boston, anti-British demonstrators demanded the creation of an enlarged merchant fleet to break through the blockade.

But sentiment in the United States shifted violently on the morning of May 7, 1915, when a German U-boat torpedoed and sank the *Lusitania* as it steamed past the coast of Ireland. The lives of more than 1,000 passengers were lost, including more than 100 Americans. The ship went down in less than fifteen minutes.

Americans were shocked but also confused. They denounced Germany angrily, but few of them (only 6 percent in a poll of newspaper editors) believed that the United States should punish Germany by declaring war. Even those swept away by anger sometimes reconsidered later. A journalist who happened on Walter Lippmann on the street the day after the sinking reported that Lippmann was all for going to war to avenge the *Lusitania*. A month later Lippmann wrote to *The New Republic* correspondent in Paris that "we here . . . want to avoid getting into the struggle, if it is at all possible. We have everything to lose and nothing to gain by taking part in it. It would only mean that the last great power was engulfed in the unreasonableness of it all and that American lives far from being safer would be a great deal more in danger."

Wilson's predecessor, William Howard Taft, wrote him to say that Congress would back him if he chose to ask for a declaration of war. Others advised the President otherwise. He was navigating in uncharted waters, and the tides of opinion were treacherous. He was preoccupied with personal matters (he was courting the lady who later became his second wife) and always found it difficult to concentrate on more than one matter at a time.

When Wilson decided to protest against Germany's behavior without also protesting against that of the Allies, Secretary Bryan resigned. "You people are not neutral," Bryan told the cabinet. "You are taking sides." In resigning, Bryan also complained that the President's adviser Edward House had been the real secretary of state.

On the other hand, supporters of TR found Wilson's stance against Germany too weak. TR's longtime political partner, Henry Cabot Lodge, the Republican foreign policy leader in the Senate, later claimed that this was the moment of no return in his decision to oppose Woodrow Wilson. Later, too, Germany's ambassador wrote in his memoirs that Wilson's conduct in the *Lusitania* matter left him "firmly convinced" that the President "would never initiate a war with Germany." The kaiser's government may also have been confident of this because, in a moment of indiscretion before resigning, Bryan had told the Austro-Hungarian ambassador that the United States had no intention of going to war.

Americans who were out of sympathy with the pacifist inclinations of the administration made their views known. On the initiative of General Leonard Wood, an associate of TR's and now commander of the army's Department of the East, a military training camp for civilian volunteers was established at Plattsburg,* New York, in the summer of 1915. It provided a rallying point for TR's young supporters who favored his policy of preparedness and were opposed to the do-nothing attitude they ascribed to Wilson. Drawn especially from Wall Street and the other financial centers of the Atlantic seaboard, 1,600 ambitious young professionals took time off from their careers to be trained in the basics of soldiering by regular army officers.

Word of the summer camp for adults spread, and by the summer of 1916 the program had become a movement: 16,000 men enrolled in a number of "Plattsburgs," preparing themselves to form the nucleus of an officer corps in a citizens' army should the need arise. Among trainees at the camps were future Secretary of War Robert Patterson, future Assistant Secretary John McCloy, and, though he was over the normal age, former Secretary of War Stimson. Taking over from Wood as the head of the movement was a young New York attorney named Grenville Clark, who had started in the law practice with Franklin Roosevelt. Whether or not they consciously intended to do so, the Plattsburg volunteers—mostly Republicans of the Theodore Roosevelt persuasion—were sending a political message not only to Berlin but to Washington.

Caught between TR and Bryan, the President walked a political tightrope. In the aftermath of the *Lusitania* sinking, facing opposition from the pacific and the belligerent alike, Wilson set out to outline his view of America's proper role in a speech that proved to be an utter disaster. Explaining to an audience of 15,000 that America was so right that there was

---

* Now spelled Plattsburgh.

no need to use force to prove it, he hit upon the unfortunate phrase that "there is such a thing as a man being too proud to fight." In TR's country there also was such a thing as a man being too much of a sissy to fight, and the popular revulsion against Wilson's apparent weakness was instantaneous.

For the administration, it clearly was a time to alter course.

# 9

## AMERICA PREPARES—
## BUT FOR WHAT?

FRANKLIN ROOSEVELT, like TR, had been in favor of American military preparedness even before the outbreak of war in Europe. His enthusiasm for a bigger navy had brought him support from outside the constituencies normally served by the Democratic administration in which he served. While his faithful assistant Louis Howe dealt skillfully with administrative details of wages and working conditions in such a way as to win a following for Roosevelt in organized labor, the assistant secretary of the navy developed a cordial relationship with the Navy League of the United States, which brought him the friendship of big business as well as retired and serving naval officers.

The Navy League, incorporated in New York December 29, 1902, with the stated aim of teaching the public the need for a strong navy, had languished for lack of finances and membership throughout most of the first decade of its existence. But as war broke out in Europe, it came into its own. In campaigns in 1915–16, League officials addressed 120,000 people and distributed 500,000 pamphlets.

A feud between the League's officials and Secretary of the Navy Daniels that seems to have begun sometime in 1914 widened with time. But the assistant secretary was on close personal as well as political terms with the League's president, Robert M. Thompson, chairman of the International Nickel Corporation, and the League's vice president, New York attorney Herbert Satterlee, son-in-law of J. P. Morgan. Only a month after taking office in 1913, Roosevelt had addressed the League in full support of its program. In the years that followed, he had become the League's friend at court. The League spoke for the industrialists and bankers of the East, the very groups that Josephus Daniels and William Jennings Bryan and the rural America they represented regarded as their enemies; so, as the League's advocate in the Wilson government, Roosevelt staked out a position that distinguished him from his fellow Democrats.

In December 1914, at a public meeting in the Hotel Astor in New York, Roosevelt called for universal military training just days before President Wilson, in his annual message to Congress, denounced proposals for compulsory military training. The day after the President delivered his message, Daniels, in an appearance before the House Naval Affairs Committee, presented evidence to show that the U.S. Navy, "ship for ship," was the equal of any in the world and could be fully manned and ready for action in a few days with a few thousand more men; whereupon Roosevelt testified before the committee that the U.S. Navy was only third or fourth best, and would need months and tens of thousands of men to be fully manned and ready. In the spring of 1915, when Daniels, in a speech to the Navy League, praised the Congress for enacting Wilson's domestic reforms, Roosevelt, who spoke before him, suggested that, insofar as strengthening the navy was concerned, the Congress had not done enough: ". . . trust to the judgment of the real experts, the naval officers. Let us insist that the Congress shall carry out their recommendations."

WITH THE SINKING of the *Lusitania* and the adverse reaction to his "too proud to fight" speech, Wilson changed course and in the summer of 1915 ordered the armed services departments to embark on programs of military preparedness. On November 4 he announced his new military expansion proposals in New York City ("We have it in mind to be prepared for defense, to protect our security," he told his dinner audience), and in top hat jauntily led a Preparedness Day parade down Fifth Avenue. As 1916 began, the aloof and unapproachable President uncharacteristically brought his case to the people on a tour that took him to the West.

The heart of the Democratic party in Congress and the country still belonged to William Jennings Bryan, a pacifist. Therefore, to win the support in the House and the Senate that he needed to carry through his new program, Wilson had to persuade his fellow Democrats that preparedness would not lead to war. Military strength, he claimed vaguely, would enable him to uphold America's "honor" while keeping the country neutral.

Not even TR advocated intervening in the war. His followers avoided the issue by claiming that if TR had been President in 1915, Germany would not have dared to sink the *Lusitania*. They did not specify what should have been done once the vessel had been sunk. TR faulted Wilson for being slow to formulate a preparedness program and for then proposing a program that was inadequate: for being too late with too little. TR's supporters continued to maintain that they were not warmongers, but that, in the words of young Grand Rapids (Michigan) newspaperman Arthur Vandenberg, "preparedness does not cause war, if anything it helps to preserve the peace."

Franklin Roosevelt, who agreed that the administration's program was inadequate, urged upon the President the creation of a Council of National

Defense to coordinate and mobilize America's resources; but Wilson would not pursue the matter. On his own initiative, in September 1915 Roosevelt then created a 50,000-man Naval Reserve force.

THE TRUTH about the reclusive President's real views and objectives always will be a subject of controversy. At times he said one thing; at other times, another. But there is strong cause to believe that for many reasons, some political and some principled, he did not want to bring the United States into the war. However pro-Ally he may have felt privately in 1914 —and he had reservations even then, for despotic Russia was among the Allies—by 1916 he had come to distrust and disapprove of the Allies as much as, or perhaps even more than, the German-led coalition.

The news of the war in Europe was not such as to encourage a desire to participate in it. Trench warfare—a type of fighting that the world had not known before—had commenced in the autumn of 1914. Nobody knew how to win it, and it was not evident that those involved would survive. Each of the two rival coalitions had dug trenches across the Continent from the Atlantic Ocean to the Alps. The two lines of trenches ran parallel to one another and blocked each other's way. The lines of trenches were heavily fortified with barbed wire, sandbags, and land mines. Each long line was more or less impregnable, yet the two sides continuously bombarded and charged one another as though a sustained breakthrough were possible. The charges were suicide attacks.

The armies of the western front lived underground in growing hope-lessness in the perhaps 35,000 miles of trenches that they eventually dug for themselves, amid mud, rats, excrement, and squalor. The deadlock, by the end of 1916, had lasted for two years, and there were those who believed that it would last forever. What was occurring on the battlefields of the war was less a military campaign than the mass execution of the young male population of Europe.

Erich von Falkenhayn, the German war minister who had replaced Moltke as chief of the General Staff, believed that 1916 was the decisive year: that Germany could not hold out much beyond that. Though Germany seemed to be coming out ahead on the western front by pursuing a defensive strategy behind powerful fortifications, he feared that Allied superiority in population and supplies eventually would tell. He lacked the manpower to launch a knockout blow, but argued that he could accomplish the same thing by attacking a fortress town so important to the French that they would "throw in every last man they have. If they do so the forces of France will bleed to death. . . ." The town in France that he had in mind was Verdun, a gray citadel on the river Meuse that had been a fortress of the

Gauls even before the coming of the ancient Romans, and that was a spear-head of the French defensive system.

Attacking Verdun on February 21, 1916, Falkenhayn began the longest and arguably most terrible battle in history. It raged for ten months. Per square foot of ground (the battlefield was three and a half square miles) there were greater losses than in any other battle before or since. Total casualties ranged somewhere between three-quarters of a million and a million and a quarter. In the end neither side gained: no ground of any significance was won or lost.

Americans who read accounts of the nightmarish new kind of warfare, symbolized by Verdun, that was being waged in the mudfields of northern France and Flanders were bound to be thankful that they were not involved in it.

BETWEEN LATE 1915 and late 1916, realistic hopes for a British or German victory shifted mostly to attrition and economic warfare, and therefore largely from land to sea. The British naval blockade and the German U-boat campaign each aimed at strangling the other side by cutting off all supplies. No matter how much it upset the United States, neither of the warring camps engaged in this life-or-death struggle could afford (or so their military chiefs believed) to let go.

Yet Woodrow Wilson found himself in 1916 in a position in which he needed the various political forces with which he had to contend to show some willingness to give. It was a presidential election year, and his prospects for reelection were uncertain. Wilson had squeaked into office in 1912 with less than 42 percent of the vote only because the majority party had split in two. Now the Republicans mostly were reunited, and on a straight party vote, on past form, would beat him by better than seven to six.

Wilson had made himself personally unpopular by remarrying in late 1915, too soon (the country felt) after the death of his first wife in August 1914. Politically, he had gone downhill since the 1914 midterm elections. In foreign policy he was attacked by TR's followers as weak in defense of American interests at sea against both British and Germans. Yet short of going to war against Britain or Germany or both, which Americans did not want to do, the only way to safeguard Americans and their merchandise from being attacked when crossing the Atlantic would have been an embargo prohibiting Americans from shipping supplies to either of the warring sides or from traveling on ships belonging to the Allies or the Germans. In turn, an embargo on trade would have destroyed America's prosperity and doomed whatever chance Wilson might have had to be reelected. So the President found himself blocked in 1916 in every direction in which he looked to extricate himself from his foreign difficulties.

In an effort to stave off the German challenge in the Atlantic, the President sent a series of stiff notes to Berlin following the *Lusitania* incident. Only months later, in the summer of 1915, a British liner (the *Arabic*) was torpedoed by Germans, taking two American lives; and though Germany then promised Wilson to curb the U-boat campaign, she sank more Allied ships without warning the following winter, with further American casualties. After the last of these sinkings, the French channel steamer *Sussex* on March 24, 1916, Wilson threatened to break off diplomatic relations with Germany.

The President had failed to think of a response more imaginative than ceasing relations, complained Walter Lippmann; "That's why we are so utterly discouraged about Wilson." In the pages of *The New Republic*, which had been studiously impartial in the European war, Lippmann now proposed a "differential neutrality" in which the U.S. would use a military force to protect against U-boats. Though Lippmann and *The New Republic* still did not want the United States to enter the war, this proposal, which was bound to upset the conservative Middle West, also aroused the anger of the Left —and Lippmann was particularly wounded by an attack in that respect from a member of his graduating class in college.

John Reed ("Jack" to his friends) was a curly-haired young man from Oregon, an outsider with no friends in the East, who had spent his Harvard years looking for a team or club that would let him join. In those days the idol of the Socialist Club on campus had been high-minded Walter Lippmann ("Who builds a world, and leaves out all the fun," teased Reed in a lighthearted verse). Reed showed enthusiasm for socialism, but also for sexual freedom, atheism, votes for women, anarchism, modern art, and other advanced causes. On graduation both Reed and Lippmann had been given jobs by Lincoln Steffens, the famous muckraking journalist, who had introduced both young men to Greenwich Village bohemian society and to the salon at Fifth Avenue and Ninth Street of Mabel Dodge that was its social center. Reed went on to ride with Pancho Villa in the Mexican revolutionary war in 1914, winning fame as a journalist for his vivid accounts of his experiences. Though he broke off his turbulent love affair with Mabel Dodge (and entered into an even more turbulent affair with the wife of a Portland dentist, Louise Bryant, who came east to live with him), his outlook remained that of the romantic Greenwich Village bohemian prorevolutionaries of the Dodge set. The war in Europe, he (and they) thought, was "a clash of traders," a struggle for markets and monopolies, in which sympathies should lie with Germany as the newcomer and underdog. England, he wrote, "grips the Red Sea, sucks the blood from India, menaces a half billion human beings from Hong Kong, owns all Australia, half North America, and half of Africa . . . the great intriguer, sitting like a spider in the web of nations. . . . It was England's will that Germany should be destroyed."

Of the Allies, perversely, he was attracted by tsarist Russia: "Russian ideals are the most exhilarating, Russian thought the freest, Russian art the most exuberant, Russian food and drink are to me the best, and Russians themselves are, perhaps, the most interesting human beings that exist. . . ."

In 1916 Reed urged socialists to support Wilson (even though Wilson was against socialism) in order to keep the United States out of the war. He charged that Lippmann's idea of taking a stand against the German U-boat campaign was a betrayal of the Left, a selling out to the Wall Street of *The New Republic*'s owner. Lippmann replied bitterly. "I do not suppose that I was entitled to expect any kind of patient fairness from you," he wrote, "even though I have tried to be pretty patient and fair with you for a good many years. I continued to believe in you even though many times I have felt that you had acted like a fool or a cad. . . . I cannot help saying that you are hardly the person to set yourself up as a judge of other people's radicalism. You may be able to create a reputation for yourself along that line with some people, but I have known you too long and I know too much about you. I watched you at college . . . trying to climb into clubs . . . and to tell you the truth I have never taken your radicalism the least bit seriously. . . . I got into this fight long before you even knew it existed and you will find that I am in it long after you quit."

Lippmann believed that Reed knew nothing about the Wall Street he so often attacked. Reed certainly was wrong if he believed that Willard Straight, publisher of *The New Republic,* was typical of it or representative of its views. In the Lippmann-Reed-Straight generation, a representative Wall Street figure instead would have been someone like John Foster Dulles, the young international lawyer at Sullivan and Cromwell.

In 1915–16 Dulles was busily exploiting every wartime opportunity for the benefit of his clients. The war had led to an outburst of American global commercial and financial activity, and he was part of it, especially after his uncle Robert Lansing became secretary of state in May 1915. When in Washington, Dulles stayed at his international lawyer grandfather's house on I Street: the house where he was born, where his grandfather Foster still lived, and where Lansing and his wife lived, too. Dulles continued to ask Lansing for favors for clients in Europe, Latin America, and China. As counsel for Merck and Company, he had obtained the Department of State's help with European shipments. In April 1915 State wrote letters of introduction for him in Europe as he made his first business trip to deal with interests in France, Holland, and Britain, and to obtain war-risk insurance for his clients. He maintained his connection with the Caribbean, a region that had marked him forever with his disconcerting tic. In New York City he arranged dinner parties at which he introduced current and prospective clients—bankers and businessmen—to the secretary of state. Like so many in the East in 1915 and 1916, the Dulles family of the house on I Street prospered from the war.

CIVILIAN ELEMENTS within the kaiser's government were worried from 1915 onward that their country's unrestricted submarine warfare might bring the United States into the war. After the sinking of the *Lusitania* and the *Arabic* in 1915, Chancellor Bethmann-Hollweg prevailed upon the kaiser to pledge that Germany would stop sinking passenger liners and unarmed merchant vessels without warning. When the German authorities broke their word and resumed sinking such vessels as the *Sussex* in March 1916, leading Wilson to threaten to break off diplomatic relations, the chancellor again was able to prevail upon the kaiser to pledge a halt to the unrestricted U-boat campaign. Bethmann-Hollweg warned Wilson, however, that the new pledge might be withdrawn if the President could not force the Allies, too, to respect the rules of international maritime law.

Wilson's apparent diplomatic victory allowed him to be portrayed by his supporters at the Democratic convention and in the autumn presidential campaign as the candidate who "kept us out of war." Wilson also began speaking of a league of nations to prevent future wars. "I have come around completely to Wilson," wrote Walter Lippmann, "chiefly because I think he has the imagination and the will to make a radical move in the organization of peace." Although the candidate of the reunited Republicans, the colorless Charles Evans Hughes, also was not in favor of going to war, Wilson's record enabled him to bid for the support of Progressives in the West who did not share the enthusiasm of their onetime leader, TR, for flexing America's muscles in dealing with Germany. (TR accused the West of being "yellow." Kansas newspaperman William Allen White replied: "Man! You are clean, plumb crazy.")

THROUGHOUT 1916 President Wilson was conscious of the precariousness of America's neutrality. He was uncomfortable with the "he kept us out of war" slogan that emerged at the Democratic convention and that was to be used by his supporters in the autumn elections, because he was not sure it was going to prove true: if the U-boat truce in the Atlantic did not hold, he might well have to bring the United States into the war.

Increasingly Wilson's hopes and ambitions came to center on mediating an end to the European war, as TR had settled the war between Russia and Japan in 1905, winning a Nobel Peace Prize. Wilson's friend Edward House, whose special interest was foreign policy, long had thought in terms of making peace between Britain and Germany, and from 1914 onward was encouraged by the President to take the matter in hand. In international dealings as in face-to-face politics at home, House listened and spoke for Wilson, acting as a surrogate and alter ego for the reclusive chief executive. Without any formal authorization, House was (or at least seemed) the President's plenipotentiary.

A small, urbane man who moved through the world of affairs with catlike agility, House seemed never to put a foot wrong. He had earned a reputation for discretion and had a way with him that led his interlocutors to believe that he fully understood not merely what they said, but also what they left unsaid.

Nonetheless House seemed in his initial meetings with the Europeans not to grasp the essentials of their outlook. Indeed, he appeared to be naive about international politics in general when, for example, he told the Allied ambassadors to Washington in January 1915 that if they agreed to make peace, he would keep Germany from starting more wars by obtaining the German chancellor's promise to give up militarism. The ambassadors refrained from asking House what such a promise would be worth.

In their bones, Wilson and House did not seem to understand why Europe was at war. So the plans they proposed to end the conflict never came to grips with the concerns of the powers involved, and were viewed in London, Paris, and Berlin as irritatingly simpleminded. Of course the various foreign offices and their ambassadors in Washington were diplomatic in feigning serious interest in whatever the Americans suggested, with the result that House felt encouraged to voyage to Europe in the winter of 1915, where he learned firsthand that at that time there was no serious interest on either side in a negotiated peace. Germany was unwilling to quit while ahead. Britain and France did not want to quit while behind. Suffering losses that became ever more catastrophic as time went on, the Allies wanted to continue the war until they could inflict even more catastrophic losses on the Germans to match their own. Unless Germany was beaten decisively, any peace (in the Allied view) would be a mere cease-fire allowing Germany to rebuild strength before launching another war.

House journeyed to Europe on another peace mission a year later, in the winter of 1915–16. This time his proposal was that the Allies, at a moment they judged opportune, should ask the United States to convene a conference of belligerents for the purpose of ending the war. At the conference President Wilson would recommend moderate but pro-Ally territorial peace terms and also would propose to establish a league of nations to guarantee the security of the powers thereafter. British Foreign Secretary Sir Edward Grey, certain that Germany would reject the proposal, agreed to it on condition that the United States would pledge without qualification to go to war against Germany if the German government said no. House was clients—bankers and businessmen—to the secretary of state. Like so many in the East in 1915 and 1916, the Dulles family of the house on I Street prospered from the war.

CIVILIAN ELEMENTS within the kaiser's government were worried from 1915 onward that their country's unrestricted submarine warfare might bring the United States into the war. After the sinking of the *Lusitania* and the *Arabic* in 1915, Chancellor Bethmann-Hollweg prevailed upon the kaiser to pledge that Germany would stop sinking passenger liners and unarmed merchant vessels without warning. When the German authorities broke their word and resumed sinking such vessels as the *Sussex* in March 1916, leading Wilson to threaten to break off diplomatic relations, the chancellor again was able to prevail upon the kaiser to pledge a halt to the unrestricted U-boat campaign. Bethmann-Hollweg warned Wilson, however, that the new pledge might be withdrawn if the President could not force the Allies, too, to respect the rules of international maritime law.

Wilson's apparent diplomatic victory allowed him to be portrayed by his supporters at the Democratic convention and in the autumn presidential campaign as the candidate who "kept us out of war." Wilson also began speaking of a league of nations to prevent future wars. "I have come around completely to Wilson," wrote Walter Lippmann, "chiefly because I think he has the imagination and the will to make a radical move in the organization of peace." Although the candidate of the reunited Republicans, the colorless Charles Evans Hughes, also was not in favor of going to war, Wilson's record enabled him to bid for the support of Progressives in the West who did not share the enthusiasm of their onetime leader, TR, for flexing America's muscles in dealing with Germany. (TR accused the West of being "yellow." Kansas newspaperman William Allen White replied: "Man! You are clean, plumb crazy.")

THROUGHOUT 1916 President Wilson was conscious of the precariousness of America's neutrality. He was uncomfortable with the "he kept us out of war" slogan that emerged at the Democratic convention and that was to be used by his supporters in the autumn elections, because he was not sure it was going to prove true: if the U-boat truce in the Atlantic did not hold, he might well have to bring the United States into the war.

Increasingly Wilson's hopes and ambitions came to center on mediating an end to the European war, as TR had settled the war between Russia and Japan in 1905, winning a Nobel Peace Prize. Wilson's friend Edward House, whose special interest was foreign policy, long had thought in terms of making peace between Britain and Germany, and from 1914 onward was encouraged by the President to take the matter in hand. In international dealings as in face-to-face politics at home, House listened and spoke for Wilson, acting as a surrogate and alter ego for the reclusive chief executive. Without any formal authorization, House was (or at least seemed) the President's plenipotentiary.

A small, urbane man who moved through the world of affairs with catlike agility, House seemed never to put a foot wrong. He had earned a reputation for discretion and had a way with him that led his interlocutors to believe that he fully understood not merely what they said, but also what they left unsaid.

Nonetheless House seemed in his initial meetings with the Europeans not to grasp the essentials of their outlook. Indeed, he appeared to be naive about international politics in general when, for example, he told the Allied ambassadors to Washington in January 1915 that if they agreed to make peace, he would keep Germany from starting more wars by obtaining the German chancellor's promise to give up militarism. The ambassadors refrained from asking House what such a promise would be worth.

In their bones, Wilson and House did not seem to understand why Europe was at war. So the plans they proposed to end the conflict never came to grips with the concerns of the powers involved, and were viewed in London, Paris, and Berlin as irritatingly simpleminded. Of course the various foreign offices and their ambassadors in Washington were diplomatic in feigning serious interest in whatever the Americans suggested, with the result that House felt encouraged to voyage to Europe in the winter of 1915, where he learned firsthand that at that time there was no serious interest on either side in a negotiated peace. Germany was unwilling to quit while ahead. Britain and France did not want to quit while behind. Suffering losses that became ever more catastrophic as time went on, the Allies wanted to continue the war until they could inflict even more catastrophic losses on the Germans to match their own. Unless Germany was beaten decisively, any peace (in the Allied view) would be a mere cease-fire allowing Germany to rebuild strength before launching another war.

House journeyed to Europe on another peace mission a year later, in the winter of 1915–16. This time his proposal was that the Allies, at a moment they judged opportune, should ask the United States to convene a conference of belligerents for the purpose of ending the war. At the conference President Wilson would recommend moderate but pro-Ally territorial peace terms and also would propose to establish a league of nations to guarantee the security of the powers thereafter. British Foreign Secretary Sir Edward Grey, certain that Germany would reject the proposal, agreed to it on condition that the United States would pledge without qualification to go to war against Germany if the German government said no. House was willing to give the pledge. At that point he may even have come to share Britain's real goal of using what appeared to be a peace proposal as a means of bringing America into the war.

But the American President was willing to say only that the United States "probably" would enter the war if Germany said no. That was not good enough for Great Britain, though there was no need for Grey or his ambassador to offend Wilson by saying so; the House-Grey formula called for the President to try to make peace only when the Allies told him that the time was right, so the Allies never told him that the time was right.

In fact, from an Allied point of view, the time suddenly was *not* right. The Allies had counted on things going better, but instead they were getting worse. The bloodletting at Verdun in the spring of 1916 was such that General Joseph-Jacques-Césaire Joffre, France's commander in chief, warned that by midsummer the French army might cease to exist. The British hoped to save their Allies and turn the tide of battle against Germany by mounting a summer offensive in northern France. But in the event, when the British attacked that summer, opening the battle of the Somme River valley, the army they destroyed was not Germany's but their own.

The British lost 25 percent of their attacking forces in the first half hour of fighting, and 50 percent in the first day as a whole. "God, God, where's the rest of the boys?" asked a Scottish lieutenant looking back for the battalion with whom he had gone over the top, and finding only two survivors. When the Battle of the Somme ended four and a half months later, the British army, despite suffering losses of close to a half-million men, far from winning the war had failed to achieve even its first day's territorial objectives.

Wilson did not accept, or perhaps did not understand, the reasoning behind the Allies' contention that they had to drag Germany down to their level of weakness before they could talk peace; that after being bloodied by Germany for two years, they could not afford to let the fighting be stopped before they had a chance, in turn, of bloodying Germany.

Waiting for the call that never came—the call from the Allies to step in to try to stop the war—Wilson doubted that the Allies, if they had been dealing with him in good faith, would choose to go on absorbing such horrendous losses when he had given them a chance to stop it all and, on the basis of House's proposals, get the essentials of what they claimed to want. The obvious explanation was that they were lying to him and to the public about what they actually desired. Britain and France claimed to have gone to war to repel aggression and to rescue Belgium, but Wilson was driven to suspect that had been a mere pretext, and that the Allies really were waging a war of conquest.

The truth was at once more simple and more complex than Wilson seemed to suppose. What was simple to understand was why the Western democracies had gone to war in the first instance. France had not had a choice; without having given any provocation, she had been invaded by Germany, and had no alternative but to fight back. Britain then had come into the war on France's side for reasons of both head and heart: a minority seriously concerned with foreign policy thought it mortally dangerous to allow any one power—in this case, Germany—to achieve total mastery in Europe, while the majority felt that Britain, having pledged by treaty to uphold Belgium's neutrality and the inviolability of her frontiers, was morally bound to rescue Belgium from Germany's invasion.

Once the fighting started, ideas about war goals began to change; but that outlooks were shifting in all the belligerent countries was one of the many aspects of wartime reality that Wilson seemed not to grasp. Germany's successes in the first two years of the war showed its military machine to be far more effective, as compared with the forces of the Allies, than Allied leaders had recognized before 1914. It was only natural that London and Paris would be more conscious than they had been in antebellum days of the danger that would continue to be posed by Germany in the future and that a level of German power that might have seemed acceptable to the Allies a few years earlier might now seem ominously high. The circumstances of Britain and France no longer were what they had been, and they sought to crush Germany's military machine in the fighting to come—not only (as Wilson seemed to assume) in order to obtain the peace terms they desired, but also because, with their own armies devastated, the Allies would be inferior to Germany in the postwar world if peace were negotiated before the German army, too, could be destroyed.

So as the war raged, both the Allies and the Central Powers adopted new war goals, responding to changes in circumstances and in the fluctuating fortunes of war, but also to shifts in their own governments and politics. Thus Prime Minister Asquith, who had been opposed to England's taking any territorial gains in the war, was replaced in 1916 by David Lloyd George, a political figure of a very different sort. Once a radical and an enemy of imperialism, Lloyd George now was neither. British strength and prosperity were being destroyed in the war, and Lloyd George, in addressing himself to the task of turning that situation around, came to believe that only by acquiring new territories, with the wealth and strategic advantages that they would bring, could Great Britain be made whole. Moreover, Britain (even in the opinion of Asquith and Grey) could hardly stand aside and take nothing if her Allies advanced large claims in the postwar world. And the number of Allies, and therefore of claims, kept expanding, for there were new recruits, drawn not to the cause, but to its rewards: the Allies were obliged to promise territorial bribes to countries like Italy to come into the war on their side.

Wrongly suspecting that the imperialist ambitions harbored by the

Allies in 1916 might explain the origins of the European war, Wilson (and Marxist observers as well) misperceived the process that was occurring. Wilson guessed that he was seeing imperialism beget war when he really was seeing war beget imperialism.

To the extent that he became aware of the rewards that Britain and France were promising to themselves and their allies, President Wilson became disillusioned with the Allied cause in 1916 and confirmed in his fears that the true animating force of Allied policy must be the lust for conquest. In spurning Wilson's offer to mediate, in choosing instead to fight on and endure numbingly horrible losses, the Allies, in Wilson's view, were showing their true colors as imperialists.

In the spring of 1916 the President learned that the Allies—Britain, France, Russia, and Italy—had met secretly in Paris to concert a program for beating off the American economic dominance they feared might otherwise arise in the postwar world. They discussed such matters as the creation of trade barriers to keep American products out of their markets. It was news that could not help but color Wilson's perception of what the Allies sought to achieve.

In the United States and abroad, politicians and journalists who spoke with Edward House at one point or another in 1916—believing, as everyone did, that speaking with House was the same as speaking with Wilson—imagined that the President was pro-Ally and might even be seeking some basis on which he could bring the United States into the war if he could do so without dangerously dividing the country on that issue.

House, it is true, remained pro-Ally, but the President did not, and increasingly thought not of Germany, but of Great Britain, America's traditional enemy, as the adversary. Military preparedness, the program Wilson had taken over from TR after the *Lusitania* affair, could be of more than one sort. An army would be of use in fighting Germany. But as against Britain, it was a navy that would be needed—and it was into naval preparedness that Wilson threw himself. Incensed by Britain's restrictions on America's trade with Germany, Wilson told House in September 1916: "Let us build a navy bigger" than Britain's "and do what we please."

FROM THE BRITISH POINT OF VIEW, it seemed evident that Wilson wanted to be asked to mediate the war in 1916 because it would help him win the presidential elections. Tory statesman Arthur Balfour, a former prime minister, told the cabinet on the first day of spring 1916 that the House proposal "was not worth five minutes' thought" but that "no doubt, if carried out, it would get the President of the United States out of political difficulties." Spring-Rice, the British ambassador in Washington, who never had gotten on well with Wilson, warned London for the future "against the danger of entrusting the United States with any large measure of influence over the affairs of other nations . . ." and reported that in the United States "there is nothing so sacred . . . no consideration of right and wrong . . . that . . . is not subordinated, without a semblance of shame or hesitation, to the party calculations of an election year."

IT IS AXIOMATIC that in good times people tend to vote for the incumbent, so the prosperity of the United States in 1916 to some extent offset Wilson's disadvantage as the candidate of the minority party and gave him a fighting chance of being reelected. His breakthrough came in winning normally Republican Ohio, with its big bloc of electoral votes, a result that may have reflected the growing strength in that state of trade unions, which in the years ahead were to become a mainstay of the Democratic party.

In the end, though, as in 1912, Wilson's victory was a fluke made possible by a split in Republican ranks. The last and deciding vote in the 1916 presidential campaign was cast by California, which was believed to be safely Republican. But the state's powerful Progressive Republican governor, Hiram Johnson, was bitterly offended when a factional opponent was treated by Charles Evans Hughes as the leader of the party in the state. With Johnson and his supporters walking out on the Republican campaign, Wilson squeaked by to carry the state by a plurality of less than 4,000 out of a million votes cast. California's thirteen electoral votes put Wilson over the top.

With less than 50 percent of the popular vote, Wilson carried the solid South, the border states, and almost the entire West, winning thirty states (with 277 electoral votes) to Hughes's eighteen (with 254). Wilson won the antiwar West but lost the antiwar Middle West, including states such as Wisconsin with heavily German-American populations. So it is not clear what role the war issue played in the election.

Even if it played no material role in the minds of the voters, it was an issue that haunted the campaign—and haunted Wilson. For the President recognized that the fate and direction of his foreign policy now were in Germany's hands. He could emerge as the peacemaker who ended the war—but only if Germany helped him do it, for the Allies would not. Or he could become the first President to embroil the United States in a war on the continent of Europe—if Germany drove him to it by ending the U-boat truce, as from a military point of view she might have to do sooner or later in order to defeat the Allies. For the United States the issue of war or peace would be decided not in Washington, but in Berlin.

# 10

## BERLIN DECIDES

THE UNITED STATES, having loaned Britain and France so much
money, was bound to come into the war on the Allied side: such was the
opinion of William Bullitt, the twenty-five-year-old star reporter of the
Philadelphia *Public Ledger*, who had returned to America in February 1916
from reporting the adventures of Henry Ford and his peace mission to Europe. Bullitt reasoned that the countries he should get to know while there
still was time were America's enemies-to-be, Germany and Austria-
Hungary; for he continued to pursue his plan of acquiring firsthand information about Europe that the government lacked so that one day President
Wilson would appoint him to high office.

The dashing young man-about-Philadelphia was about to marry. His
bride, Aimee Ernesta Drinker (whom Felix Frankfurter, too, had courted),
had qualities that Bullitt especially prized: her family was older than Philadelphia itself, and she was of a startling beauty that led passing strangers
to stop and stare. She wished to be a writer, and the young couple chose to
spend their honeymoon in Germany and Austria-Hungary so that they both
could pursue their ambitions.

"We were broad-minded before we touched Germany," wrote Ernesta.
"We—particularly Billy—were ready to understand Germany. Billy said
he could see their point of view perfectly." But in fact he and she could
not. On entering Germany they were shocked at the first thing said to them:
a young German who boarded their train explained "how much he hated
America, because the United States was selling munitions to the Allies."

On arriving in Berlin May 29, 1916, the Bullitts were invited to a
luncheon at the American embassy by the U.S. ambassador, James Gerard,
the family friend who had advised Bullitt and his mother to leave Germany
in 1914. At the embassy the young couple met the staff, whom Gerard's
deputy, Joseph Grew, had made a point of recruiting from Harvard, his
alma mater. "The Embassy is filled with Harvard secretaries," wrote Ernesta,
quoting a diplomat she had met, "whose lips . . . are still wet with the
milk of Groton."

In exploring life in Berlin, the Bullitts found food shortages ("there's
scarcely any butter") as a result of the war, but no real hardship. "We have

given up the romantic idea of starving," wrote Ernesta, and "Billy says he's not going to be the first to complain of the high price of caviar and *pate de foie gras.*" What struck Ernesta was the efficiency and discipline with which Germany carried out the rationing of food; no other people, she remarked, had it "in" them to do it.

As guests of the German government, the young Bullitts traveled to Belgium in midsummer 1916. There they moved about freely enough so that Ernesta could report, of the Belgian people, that "their confidence that the English will soon be back to rescue them never dies. . . . They think the English are gods and tell you stories of their bravery." Americans were much loved, too, for the wonders accomplished by Herbert Hoover and his American Committee for Relief in Belgium in feeding the population. "Mr. Hoover," Ernesta discovered, "is considered by Belgium . . . the greatest American alive today, and they fully expect him to go home and move to the White House when the war is over."

"I wish I knew how this war started," mused Ernesta. "If one knew whether Germany knew beforehand of the Austrian note to Serbia one would know better just how deliberately Germany went into this." That, indeed, was a question that Americans wanted to have answered, and born journalist that he was, Bullitt contrived to find the answer. The Bullitts traveled to Austria and Hungary, meeting government leaders there, and when they returned to Berlin September 17, Bullitt, in an interview with German foreign minister Gottlieb von Jagow, pretended to have uncovered a good deal more than he had. When Bullitt asked what were Jagow's intentions in writing the Austro-Hungarian ultimatum to Serbia, Jagow, protesting innocence, said, "I did not have a hand in preparing that note. I saw the note for the first time at eight o'clock the night before it was presented in Belgrade." So the German foreign minister *had* seen it beforehand.

Bullitt discussed a question even more important to Americans with Walter Rathenau, the brilliant industrialist and socialist who became the director of the German economy during the war. The question was whether Germany would resume unrestricted U-boat warfare—whether, in other words, the United States would be brought into the war. Rathenau, who personally was opposed to the war ("the most absurd, mad thing that has ever happened") and to resuming the U-boat war ("It would make us the most hated people on earth and would prolong the war indefinitely"), told Bullitt that nonetheless there was "an even chance" that those who favored submarine warfare would win out in the Reichstag in the spring of 1917. He reasoned that after a winter of intense hardship for the German people, politicians would find it difficult to resist the military chiefs when they argued that it would be foolhardy for Germany to refrain from using the one weapon that could win the war for her.

ON RETURNING TO BERLIN, the Bullitts had found an agreeable new arrival at the American embassy. He was lanky, twenty-one-year-old Christian Herter, who still had not decided what to do in life but had come over as a volunteer clerk to help out the overworked foreign service. Harvard but not Groton, Herter had been sent by a college friend to be interviewed by Grew, who had agreed to take him on.

Making excuses to his fiancée for leaving her—indeed, in his letters protesting so much that one gets the impression he did not expect her to believe him—Herter had crossed over in late July on a Dutch liner. His job was to help the embassy staff in the work of representing Allied interests in the enemy country—which meant visiting prisoner-of-war camps to see whether inmates were being treated correctly. The whole business of the war appalled him; "I can only pray to heaven we won't ever get mixed up in it," he wrote his fiancée.

Herter enjoyed the company of the American newspapermen in Berlin, Herbert Bayard Swope of the New York *World* and Raymond Gram Swing of the Chicago *Daily News*. Above all, he was entertained by the dazzling Bullitts. Bullitt, a born storyteller, had wonderful stories to tell of his travels. It is not clear whether young Herter's outlook on German affairs had an influence on Bullitt.

All through the autumn—and the Bullitts departed halfway through it—Herter was in the process of becoming privy to secret information about German politics. His contact was Kurt Hahn, a German Jewish employee of the German government's press office. Hahn belonged to a small group of liberals who looked for guidance to the great military historian Professor Hans Delbruck. Hahn may have misunderstood Delbruck, or Herter may have misunderstood Hahn; in any event, Herter came to believe that, through Delbruck, it might be possible for him to work for a negotiated compromise peace between England and Germany. Though he and his closest embassy friend held secret meetings with the Germans without informing their superiors, Herter found occasion in mid-October to compose a background memo for Grew in which he outlined the views, as he understood them, of the Delbruck group.

Though nothing came of them, the secret meetings were exciting. At twenty-one, Herter was being much like his friend Bill Bullitt in imagining that he could play a lone hand that would bring peace to the war-torn world.

BULLITT STORED UP the information he gathered from his interviews and travels, and in October 1916, when he and Ernesta returned from their honeymoon, his articles on the European crisis made the front pages of the *Public Ledger.* The Bullitts had returned to America on the same ocean liner as had Ambassador Gerard, traveling from Berlin to Washington amid a swirl of rumors that he brought with him a peace proposal from Kaiser Wilhelm; and Bullitt reported in the *Ledger* "with absolute certainty" that the ambassador brought with him no such message.

Bullitt gave his readers a firsthand account of what was happening: ". . . at the present moment Germany is thinking a great deal less about peace via the United States than about war with the United States." He told them of the political tension in Germany between Chancellor Bethmann-Hollweg and the military chiefs, and warned that it was "a struggle whose outcome will determine whether or not the United States is to be drawn into the war."

Bullitt elaborated on this theme for a wider audience later in the month. In the October 28, 1916, issue of *The New Republic,* Walter Lippmann published an article by Bullitt that addressed the question of whether there was any point in trying to distinguish between "worse or better Germany." In it Bullitt wrote that almost all Germans believed in Germany being supreme; believed, too, in maintaining strong armed forces to keep the peace; and did not believe in international organizations to keep peace (such as the league of nations that William Howard Taft had proposed and that Woodrow Wilson recently had espoused)—did not believe, that is, that Germany could disarm and safely entrust the defense of her frontiers to such an organization. Nonetheless, argued Bullitt, there was an important difference between the liberal Germany represented by the chancellor and the conservative Germany that followed wherever the military led. The United States had to "bother about distinctions between Germans," he wrote, because "we cannot continue to enjoy our . . . neutrality unless Bethmann remains Chancellor. The day conservative Germany overcomes liberal Germany, sinking without warning will be recommenced, and we shall be drawn into war."

Bullitt brought back information not meant for publication, including reports of statements made to him in confidence by foreign leaders, which he offered to Frank Polk, counselor and second in command at the Department of State. Transferred to the Washington desk of his newspaper in November, Bullitt became a valuable source of authentic information for State and later for the President's adviser Edward House. On the basis of his own observations, Bullitt was able to alert the government to such significant developments as the growing disintegration of the Russian army.

Bullitt tended to discuss events in terms of personalities, which makes for lively journalism but not always for accurate analysis. In focusing his readers' hopes on Bethmann-Hollweg's survival in office, he gave insufficient weight to what Walter Rathenau had told him: that if the war continued, political pressures would mount on the German government—any German government—to employ the only weapon that seemingly could bring victory. In the autumn of 1916, Bullitt was reporting that it was still an open question whether or not to resume U-boat warfare. Meanwhile, Joseph Grew, who headed the Berlin embassy while Gerard was on home leave, wrote to Edward House warning that the pressures on the chancellor were overwhelming and that "our Government should therefore be fully prepared for an eventual resumption of the indiscriminate submarine warfare against commerce in violation of the rights of neutrals on the high seas."


BY AUTUMN 1916 German Chancellor Theobald von Bethmann-Hollweg no longer believed that Germany's armed forces could win the war. Falkenhayn's battle of Verdun had been the last army action that Bethmann-Hollweg, and even Falkenhayn, had been able to see as offering a breakthrough to victory, yet like earlier campaigns, it had ended in stalemate—though at a staggering cost in lives lost. Falkenhayn's excuse was that the navy had not done its job and that the decision to discontinue submarine warfare—a decision with which he had gone along at the time—was what had robbed him of victory at Verdun. Bethmann-Hollweg did not believe this, and feared that resuming submarine warfare would bring the United States into the war and cause Germany's defeat. In August 1916 he allowed Washington to understand that he would welcome President Wilson's efforts to mediate an end to the war. He believed that it was time for Germany to quit while she could; but he also may have figured that if Germany fell in with Wilson's peace views while the Allies did not, the President might be moved to stand aside and not enter the war should Germany later decide to resume submarine warfare.

Winning approval from Kaiser Wilhelm for a peace bid at last had become possible. When Romania joined the Allies in August 1916, Germany's mercurial monarch, breaking into tears, suddenly decided that the war was lost and that his country had no option but to sue for peace. But Bethmann-Hollweg believed that to protect themselves politically in seeking a compromise peace, he and the kaiser would need the support of the chief of the General Staff. Falkenhayn would have to be replaced. Bethmann-Hollweg looked around for an army leader of sufficient weight to be nominated for the job and on whose political support he could depend.

In the east, great victories won by General Erich Ludendorff had been credited to Ludendorff's superior, Field Marshal Paul von Hindenburg, who had become a popular hero. Duped into believing that Hindenburg was in favor of negotiating peace, Bethmann-Hollweg persuaded the reluctant kaiser to bring back Hindenburg to replace Falkenhayn and to take command of the armies. The kaiser seems to have sensed that this was a step on the road to abdication, and that Hindenburg, as the nation's hero, along with the inevitable Ludendorff would take command not only of the army but of the government.

It was in August 1916 that the kaiser installed Hindenburg in office, and from then until the end of the year, as the power of decision slipped away from the monarch and his civilian prime minister into the hands of the new military chiefs, Bethmann-Hollweg's foreign policy was more and more a race against time. In one area after another, Hindenburg and Ludendorff trespassed on civilian territory, even in foreign policy, with apparent support from the Reichstag. In October the German parliament directed the chancellor—even though the constitutional authority to decide was his—to follow the guidance of the military chiefs on whether to resume submarine warfare. By December, a mere five months after the chancellor discussed installing a new chief of the General Staff, the chief was holding discussions on the installing of a new chancellor.

No longer able to keep on waiting for Wilson to step forward as mediator, Bethmann-Hollweg dispatched a note to the United States on December 12, 1916, proposing to talk peace but not specifically offering any concessions—for he dared not reveal how stiff were the peace terms on which Hindenburg would insist.


AS BETHMANN-HOLLWEG RACED against time in Berlin, so did Woodrow Wilson in Washington. Sometime during the last half of 1916, he became fixed in his idea that if the war continued, the United States was going to be dragged into it. He concluded that America, in her own national interest, ought to step in to bring the war to an end—whether the belligerents wanted her to do so or not.

House told the President that the Allies would consider it an unfriendly act for America to come forward to stop the war just as they were starting to win it, and advised him to continue waiting until the Allies were ready. But Wilson rejected the advice. Soon after being reelected, the President sat down at his typewriter to tap out a note to the belligerent powers.

Though perhaps not fully aware of how financially vulnerable Great Britain had become, the President was conscious of the Allied dependency on the United States. In fact, England was running out of money, and John Maynard Keynes, speaking for the British Treasury, of which he had become an important official, told the cabinet in London in 1916 that by the end of that year, "the American executive and the American public will be in a position to dictate to this country." In December 1916 Wilson interfered with a J. P. Morgan financing for Britain, underlining his point that the

Allies must bend toward the American viewpoint in the matter of making peace.

Wilson had decided on a strategy of asking the belligerents to state their minimum peace terms, in hopes of then narrowing the distance between them. He had almost finished drafting his proposal when Bethmann-Hollweg's note arrived, stealing Wilson's thunder and causing complications. If Wilson dispatched his own note at once, it might look to the Allies like collusion; but if he waited, they might already have rejected Bethmann-Hollweg's note as uncompromising, thus aborting the peace process. So Wilson sent his own note without delay.

Germany could not reply responsively to Wilson's questions about war aims without revealing how unyielding her position had now become, and accordingly, in answer, stated only that she was prepared to talk. The Allies—to some extent hoping that what House and Robert Lansing said reflected Wilson's hidden thoughts, and therefore that the American note really called upon them to propose attractive goals that would convince the United States to rally to their cause—articulated some new and popular objectives. These included the freeing of the Christian and other peoples of the Middle East from the tyranny of the Ottoman Empire, which of course had nothing to do with why the war had started in Europe or why it still was being waged.

The Allies did not know how far away from House's thinking the President had moved. House was thinking of war, Wilson of peace. By the end of 1916 Wilson was more determined than ever to keep the United States out of war, more pacifist in his mood, less sympathetic to the Allies, and more convinced that the European powers were motivated by nationalist or imperialist objectives he deprecated. On the other hand, House, who thought in terms of American intervention, worried in his diary (December 14, 1916) "that my worst fears as to our unpreparedness were confirmed. . . . I am convinced that the President's place in history is dependent to a large degree upon luck. If we should get into a serious war and it should turn out disastrously, he would be one of the most discredited Presidents we have had. . . . We have no large guns. If we had them, we have no trained men who would understand how to handle them. We have no air service, nor men to exploit it; and so it is down the list." On January 2, 1917, House quoted a remark that the President's frame of mind was disturbing in that he was "for peace almost at any price."

Seeing, from the response to his note, that the belligerents were unwilling to envisage realistic peace terms, Wilson decided to advocate his own. House credited himself with the suggestion that he should do so. Wilson's note asking the belligerents to define peace terms had been the first step on the road to imposing America's vision on the European world; this was the second.

The President spent the first weeks in January 1917 drafting his statement: his last chance of persuading Germany and the Allies to make peace before they forced America to make war. He then, unexpectedly, sent a letter asking the Senate for permission to appear before it at once to make a statement. Other than Edward House and Secretary of State Lansing, William Stone, chairman of the Senate Foreign Relations Committee, was the only political figure to be given the document to read in advance. After reading it, the senator had looked "stunned," Wilson told House.

WHILE WILSON WAS TYPING DRAFTS of his address, Germany's vice chancellor was at work drafting for the chancellor a document exposing fallacies in the argument for resuming unrestricted U-boat warfare, for that argument once again was being made. On January 8 Bethmann-Hollweg received a telegram from Hindenburg asking him to attend a meeting to discuss the U-boat issue at the military's Supreme Headquarters at the distant castle of Pless.

It should instead have been the chancellor who summoned the military chiefs; he must have been apprehensive as he traveled to the frontier at their call. Pless,* a historic Silesian river town on a tributary of the Vistula, was some 300 miles from Berlin. It was situated at the southeastern edge of the kaiser's European domains, where the borders of the German empire marched with those of the Russian empire and of the Austro-Hungarian empire: the meeting place of the Hohenzollerns, Romanovs, and Hapsburgs—three dynasties, centuries old, whose continued existence had come to be staked on the outcome of the European war.

In the castle of Pless on January 9, Hindenburg, Ludendorff, and the naval chief, Admiral Henning von Holtzendorff, discussed who should become chancellor if Bethmann-Hollweg should fail to accede to their wishes when he arrived the following day. They discussed, too, the obtuseness of the kaiser (Holtzendorff: "His Majesty doesn't understand the situation." Ludendorff: "Absolutely not"). For them the conference on the submarine issue was no more than a formality, and Hindenburg seemed to have forgotten why they were going to the trouble of convening it. Reminded that the chancellor was due to arrive on the morrow, the field marshal asked: "What's troubling him now?" Though nobody had told Bethmann-Hollweg or the other politicians, the decision to launch unrestricted submarine warfare already had been reached. The key advocates, Admirals Reinhard Scheer, commander in chief of the German High Seas Fleet, and Adolf von Trotha, chief of Naval Staff, having concluded that the army now made all decisions, had bypassed their own naval chief and also the kaiser (who "had vision but

---

* Now, as it was before 1742, the Polish city of Pszczyna.

lacked nerve," said von Trotha). At year's end the two had taken their case directly to Ludendorff at Pless, who had decided in their favor.

When Bethmann-Hollweg traversed the long avenue to the entrance of the 300-room castle of Pless on the morning of January 10, was ushered inside by liveried servants, climbed the marble staircase to the conference room, saluted Kaiser Wilhelm, who had arrived to preside over the conference, settled himself and listened to the navy's chief, Holtzendorff, explain why unrestricted submarine warfare provided Germany's last and only chance to win the war, and then launched into his own hourlong rebuttal, he evidently believed that the U-boat question was still an open one. He also seemed to think that the 200-page memorandum supplied by the navy in support of its position, with its detailed charts and statistics, was an advocate's brief that the memorandum his vice chancellor had prepared for him could counter. He was mistaken. The kaiser yawned and fidgeted throughout most of the chancellor's presentation. Bethmann-Hollweg must have sensed that he had lost his audience, for he began to retreat. Finally he said: "But if the military authorities consider the U-boat war essential I am in no position to contradict them."

They did consider it essential, and indeed essential to sign the necessary orders that very day. In exactly three weeks—on February 1—the submarine campaign then could begin. In no more than six months thereafter, the military chiefs promised, Germany would win victory. The United States might declare war, but there would be no time for Americans to gear up to fight before the Allies surrendered. "I guarantee on my word as a naval officer that no American will set foot on the Continent!" pledged Admiral von Holtzendorff that morning. Hindenburg said: "We can take care of America."

The kaiser, bored with all the talk and impatient to conclude matters, signed his name to an authorization already prepared ("I order that unrestricted submarine warfare be launched with the utmost vigor . . .") and went in to lunch. Bethmann-Hollweg, in what seemed to be a state of collapse, told intimates that the decision just taken meant that Germany was finished, an opinion immediately recorded in a diary for posterity; but he trimmed his sails to a different wind in speaking to his colleagues. "If success beckons," he told the military leaders who predicted that the submarines would bring a quick victory, "we must follow." Advised to resign as chancellor by those who shared his fears of what retribution submarine warfare might bring, Bethmann-Hollweg instead was of the view, not uncommon among politicians, that he owed it to his country to stay in office; and he remained chancellor until pushed out six months later.

In the three weeks between the conference of January 10 and the launching of Germany's unrestricted submarine warfare on February 1, the utmost secrecy was to be preserved. Nobody was to know that the decision to unleash the U-boats had been taken. Peace proposals advanced by the United States were to be treated as though they were being seriously considered. Germany's military leaders had convinced themselves and the kaiser that the war would be over by harvest time.

WHEN THE SENATE of the United States assembled at noon on Monday, January 22, Vice President Thomas R. Marshall, its presiding officer, read aloud a letter he unexpectedly had received the night before from Wilson, in which the President asked permission to address the Senate. Within hours Wilson, fresh from a morning on the golf links in Virginia, was on the speaker's podium delivering his statement.

What the President read aloud to the Senate was a message to the warring powers, but his thought processes were so thoroughly American, so utterly alien to Europe, that his message could not have been appreciated in Berlin, Vienna, St. Petersburg, Paris, or possibly even London. Wilson addressed Europeans in a language more foreign to them, even, than American English: "The question upon which the whole future peace and policy of the world depends is this," Wilson declared. "Is the present war a struggle for a just and secure peace, or only for a new balance of power?" This question, as posed, could only have been mystifying to the great powers, for Europe's experience had been that a stable peace and a just one, in the sense of protecting the rights of the weaker countries, could be achieved *only* by a balance of power.

Europeans on both sides of the terrible conflict believed deeply that it was justice and security for which they fought, but Wilson dismissed the beliefs of both camps, urged them to abandon the gains they already had won and the war goals they had set for themselves, and advised them instead to settle for "a peace without victory."

Wilson linked his peace proposals to his espousal eight months earlier of a league of nations. The United States, though historically unwilling to participate in world politics, now (said Wilson) would agree to do so, through participation in an international peacekeeping league—but only on condition that the warring coalitions in Europe make peace on America's terms. It was only right, he argued, that Europe should make peace on the basis that the United States urged; for America, by joining a league to keep the peace, would be making a long-lasting commitment to guarantee those terms. He could not ask the American people to uphold a settlement in which they did not believe.

Among the basic terms of the peace agreement, Wilson said, should be those that the United States long had advocated, such as freedom of the seas. This meant that Great Britain, with which America had been quarreling and sometimes even warring on this vital issue for more than a century, would surrender to the claims of the United States, giving up the strategy on which her position in the world was based and abandoning the control of the world's oceans in wartime that both ensured Britain's survival and maintained her supremacy.

It was not unnatural that Europe's leaders should resent rather than welcome these proposals. For two and a half years their countries had been engaged in fighting one of the bloodiest wars in history, enduring suffering and losses of every kind on an unprecedented scale, only to be told that it was not to be their terms but America's on which the war was to be ended. To some, the lofty tone in which the President spoke was irritating in itself, as the American leader depreciated the war goals of Europeans as selfish while portraying policies that would benefit the United States, such as freedom of the seas, as noble. Wilson, commented the noted British historian George Otto Trevelyan, "is surely the quintessence of a prig." To Anatole France, urbane and ironic grand old man of letters, the peace terms suggested by the American President, coming as they did after all that the Allies had suffered, were "fetid, ignominious, obscene. . . ."

Though Wilson's plea for peace and his idealism compelled admiration, his specific proposals met with less success, even in the United States. With the exception of Progressive senator Robert La Follette, who was enthusiastic, Wilson's approach was not supported by America's political leaders. Wilson's eloquent address, regarded by contemporaries and by posterity alike as among his most important statements, was like a flash of lightning suddenly illuminating a scene that had been dark: it lit up the foreign policy differences among America's politicians with stark clarity. Those who opposed Wilson's package of a league of nations tied to "without victory" peace terms (i.e., no gains by either side in the war) were of three minds: some were for the league but against the terms, others were for the terms but not the league, and still others were against both.

1. William Jennings Bryan praised Wilson's proposals as a "brave and timely appeal to the war-mad rulers of Europe"; but true to America's isolationist traditions, he opposed American membership in a league of nations because time after time it would require the United States, in order to keep the peace, to use its armed forces overseas. Farm-state Republican senator William Borah, expressing views widely held everywhere from the Allegheny mountain range west to the Pacific coast, launched a battle for isolationism that he was to wage until his death in 1940.

2. Theodore Roosevelt had been the first (in 1905) to propose creation of a league of nations. But his had been a much different conception. His league was to be an alliance of the few but powerful: a club of like-thinking great powers who would act together to police the globe and keep the peace. Edward House, in the years just before the outbreak of the European war, had proposed a similar scheme: an alliance of Germany, Great Britain, and

the United States, perhaps along with France and/or Japan, to direct the affairs of the world.

TR regarded Wilson's notion of a league to which all countries would belong as impractical. More important, he and Senator Henry Cabot Lodge thought the American public did not fully understand, and eventually would fail to honor, the commitments that Wilson's sort of league entailed. Like Bryan, they saw that membership in Wilson's league meant that America was pledged time after time to fight wars abroad to stop aggression; but unlike Bryan, they feared that when the point came, Americans would back down and refuse to send armies abroad. This, believed Lodge and TR, would be dishonorable. It was a long-standing theme in the thought of both men that Americans never should sign a treaty—never should make promises—they were unlikely to keep.

3. Former President William Howard Taft, who for the past two years had headed an organization to promote a league of nations, gave his public support to the President's proposals, which, insofar as establishing a league was concerned, were inspired by proposals of his own. Privately, however, Taft complained of the way Wilson had framed the issue, for Taft was opposed (as were TR and Lodge) to linking the league issue to the peace-without-victory terms that Wilson advocated. Taft (like his Republican rival TR, and like Senator Lodge) wanted the Allies to win the war and to impose their own peace terms.

I FEEL CONFIDENT,'' President Wilson told the Senate in his January 22 address, "that I have said what the people of the United States would wish me to say." He added: "I would fain believe that I am speaking for the silent mass of mankind everywhere." Of his proposals, he affirmed that "these are American principles, American policies. . . ."

As he was to do two years later, the President, despite opposition from politicians in both parties, claimed to speak for the people of the United States. As he was to do then, he linked acceptance of his attractive plan to establish a league for peace with the acceptance of peace terms that many found objectionable. He identified America's principles with those of the world, believing in all good faith that to pursue America's interests was for the general good, while for other countries to pursue their interests was selfish. As he was to do in 1919, he said that he, and not their national governments, spoke for the people of Europe. As in 1919, he misconstrued the motives of foreign leaders and failed to understand the rationale of the policies they pursued. And as they were to do at Versailles after the war, the leaders of Europe failed to appreciate at their true value the wisdom of Wilson's counsel and the clairvoyance of his prophecy, which seemed to be so strangely intermixed with naiveté.

Duped by the charming German ambassador, Count Johann von Bernstorff, who did not know the full truth himself, America's President believed that his message was receiving careful consideration in Berlin. He did not know that the issue had been decided weeks before, that he was wasting his words on deaf ears, that the kaiser had already signed the order sending the U-boats out from their home ports into the depths of the Atlantic in search of victims. So while Wilson, on his podium in Washington, spoke of peace, beneath the surface of the oceans the submarine fleet unleashed by the German High Command scanned the horizon through periscopes in search of American merchant vessels to blow out of the water.

# 11

# America Finds
## a Foreign Policy

Washington, D.C., Wednesday, January 31, 1917. The German ambassador, Count von Bernstorff, paid a formal call on Secretary of State Robert Lansing to deliver a message to the surprised secretary. Bernstorff stated that he had been instructed by Berlin to announce that, weeks before, the kaiser's government had decided to resume unrestricted submarine warfare. "I know that it is very serious, very," said Bernstorff, adding, "I deeply regret it. Good afternoon." Later the ambassador told reporters that "I am finished with politics for the rest of my life."

President Wilson went into shock. He had believed that the Germans, unlike the Allies, were giving his views serious consideration; but now it was clear they had been stringing him along. He told House that he "could not get his balance" and that he felt as though the sun suddenly had reversed itself and "had begun to go from west to east." He spent hours in seclusion trying to think things through.

At his home in New York that day, January 31, Edward House also received a communication from Bernstorff. Apparently replying to Wilson's December note—though not in terms that would move the peace process forward—the German government notified House, too, of the submarine blockade. Promptly after dinner, House went to the railroad station and caught the midnight train to Washington. He arrived in the capital the following morning and went to the White House after breakfast to confer with Wilson. Later Secretary of State Lansing joined them.

Lansing, who had come by the White House the night before to urge Wilson to break off diplomatic relations with Germany, wanted the United States to intervene in the war. So did House, who believed that a break in relations was bound to be followed by entry into the war. But Wilson, in discussing the matter that Thursday morning, February 1, still hesitated; he neither wanted to enter the war nor believed it inevitable that the country should do so. He told Lansing that " 'white civilization' and its domination of the planet rested largely on our ability to keep this country intact."

At the regular cabinet meeting the following afternoon, Wilson argued that the United States had to stay out of the war in order "to keep the white race strong against the yellow—Japan, for instance. . . ." Then, too, he did not really believe in the Allied cause: "Probably greater justice would be done," he told the Cabinet in assessing the situation in Europe, "if the conflict ended in a draw."

Reluctantly, on February 3 he asked Congress to approve breaking with Germany. But he clung to the hope that matters would stop there. He told Congress that he refused to believe that the Germans, when it came to the point of moving from words to deeds, really would sink American and other neutral ships, and that only "actual overt acts on their part" could make him believe they would do so. "We are the sincere friends of the German people," he declared, and "we shall not believe they are hostile to us unless and until we are obliged to believe it."

This was too meek for such warriors as Theodore Roosevelt, who commented that Wilson was "a very timid man when it comes to physical danger. . . . As for shame, he has none, and if anyone kicks him, he brushes his clothes, and utters some lofty sentiment." Others, even those less hostile than TR to the President, were uncertain in what direction Wilson proposed to go.

Walter Lippmann, however, believed that *he* understood where Wilson was leading the country. The young editor, whose phrase "peace without victory" had been used by the President in his January 22 speech, enjoyed the heady sensation of being at the center of things. In close and frequent communication with Edward House, Lippmann fell into the common error of assuming that House's thoughts and sentiments reflected the President's. Lippmann had come to believe by the end of 1916, as House did, that the United States should join the Allies. It would be "something to boast of," he wrote in *The New Republic,* "that we have lived in a time when the world called us into partnership."

As against the U-boat danger, he wrote, "The safety of the Atlantic highway is something for which America should fight." His new concept was of an "Atlantic community" in which the United States and Great Britain were partners. Britain, as he now saw it, had used her dominion of the oceans to shield the Western Hemisphere from attack by the great powers of the Continent. In now building its own naval strength, the United States should seek to play a role as England's partner in shouldering the burden, hitherto borne by the United Kingdom alone, of policing the "vital highways of our world" to keep them open to Americans while denying their use to those who would endanger the Americas.

Lippmann wrote to Felix Frankfurter February 19 to explain what he imagined was Wilson's hidden design. After breaking with Germany February 3, Lippmann claimed, "the administration absolutely expected a sensational outrage within a few days"—a German U-boat sinking of some unarmed vessel—"and had set its mind in preparation for war on the strength of it. They miscalculated the facts." For in the days and weeks after February 3, nothing had happened, and pacifist and isolationist feelings in the country had reasserted themselves. So Wilson, Lippmann explained, was obliged to hold off. "If he acts now the aggression will seem to come from Washington," he wrote; "if he acts aggressively and seems to desire war he will lose the very public opinion which he most needs."

Wilson lived through a very different winter of 1917 than Lippmann believed. In retrospect it seems that the President waited to see if there would be a German attack at sea—not in hope, as the young journalist thought, but in fear. He deliberately avoided provoking or offending the Germans, knowing that his record in this respect would help unify the country behind him if he were obliged to ask for a declaration of war. But that was not the reason he was doing it; it now looks very much as though he was doing it in sincerity to try to avoid the coming of war.

THE SAME MONTH in which Walter Lippmann wrote to Felix Frankfurter outlining what he believed to be Wilson's political strategy for bringing the United States into the European war, Kansas newspaperman William Allen White wrote to a British acquaintance that "the war is not a first page story in the West. A score of things interest the West more. . . ." The farther away from the Atlantic seaboard that Americans lived, the more remote and irrelevant events in Europe seemed to them to be. Middle and western America were not even considering getting involved in the faraway fighting.

Retrospection distorts. Looking back, the events of the twenty-three months following the torpedoing of the *Lusitania* led to the American decision to fight Germany. But that is not how people saw those months as they were living through them—and not just because of the remoteness of the war or because of America's lifelong isolationism. For those in their twenties and thirties, it also was because their generation—that of Roosevelt, Truman, and Eisenhower—was at an age in which the normal focus of immediate concern is personal: marriage, family, and the first steps in a career.

On a sunny Sunday south Texas afternoon in October 1915, Dwight Eisenhower was on guard duty at Camp Wilson on the edge of Fort Sam Houston when the wife of a superior officer called him over to meet Mary Geneva Doud. On Valentine's Day 1916 he proposed; in July 1916 they married; during the Christmas season, they conceived a son.

Some $12,500 in debt, Kansas farmer Harry Truman lost $7,500 more in a lead and zinc mining company, contrary to his hopes of earning enough money to marry Bess Wallace. He told Bess, "You would do better perhaps if you pitch me into the ash heap and pick someone with more sense and ability. . . ." Then a promoter persuaded him to go into an oil speculation—Truman borrowed $5,000 from his mother, who raised the money by mortgaging her farm—and that venture collapsed, too.

In New York, Averell Harriman, one of the world's richest men, was settling with his bride, Kitty, into the life of Manhattan high society. In his second year at the Harvard Law School, 1916–17, dashing Dean Acheson, who had become a school athlete under Harriman's tutelage, was flowering intellectually under the inspiration of his new mentor, Felix Frankfurter.

William Bullitt, once the carefree star of the college social set to which Acheson had belonged, wrote on March 23, 1917, to his friend Walter Lippmann that his wife, Ernesta, "bore a son day before yesterday, and I buried him today." Bullitt had married only twelve months before, but it was the beginning of the end of their marriage; Ernesta could not have another child, and Bullitt wanted a child above all else.

In March 1917 Franklin and Eleanor Roosevelt had been married twelve years. Their fifth surviving child had been delivered the year before, but there was an emptiness in the marriage, and neither husband nor wife felt fulfilled in it. Franklin, indeed, now looked elsewhere for companionship and romance.

Arthur Vandenberg, editing the Grand Rapids *Herald* in Michigan, was struggling to bring up his three children on his own after the death of his wife in 1916. In Cincinnati, a comfortably married Robert Taft in his mid-twenties was fully occupied with his growing law practice, his family, his work for the Legal Aid Society and the Boy Scouts, his fund-raising for charities, his position as secretary of the Cincinnati Yale Club, and his gardening and golfing.

Despite a record of continuous success, George Marshall was not satisfied by his career in the army. He had remained a lieutenant for fourteen years before being promoted to captain in mid-1916, and had considered resigning to seek out a business career while he was still young enough to make a fresh start. In 1916 and early 1917 he was for the most part in San Francisco, training civilian volunteers who came to learn drilling and other military skills as part of the national enthusiasm for the "preparedness" cause that President Wilson had taken up. Marshall was disappointed by the assignment. He had wanted to see combat in the war.

One of the many reasons Americans were not paying attention to the conflict with Germany, even when it was only months or weeks away, was that to them at the time, *the* war—the war that made headlines in the press, the war that Marshall meant—was not the one in Europe; it was the undeclared war that the United States was waging in Mexico.

HENRY ADAMS WAS PROVEN RIGHT in his belief (c. 1913) that Woodrow Wilson ("loathed in advance by everyone within my circuit, Democrat or Republican") would not stop the American military involvements south of the border that had been so conspicuous a feature of the Roosevelt and Taft administrations. Far from it; Wilson proved to be the most interventionist of America's Presidents. Even young Vandenberg, an American imperialist and an admirer of TR, denounced Wilson for establishing a "protectorate against the will and best wishes of the central Americans themselves" that was "bound to damn us now and forever."

Mexico was the principal theater of U.S. Army operations. The initial goal of the Wilson administration in 1913–14 was to overthrow the Mexican dictator, Victoriano Huerta; to accomplish this, Wilson ordered such actions as the occupation of Vera Cruz, the episode in 1914 in which Douglas MacArthur so distinguished himself.* Huerta resigned and fled the country in 1914. Huerta's opponents then quarreled among themselves, and Wilson provided assistance to the forces of Venustiano Carranza, supported by Álvaro Obregón, against those of Pancho Villa, supported by Emiliano Zapata. In retaliation, Villa raided across the frontier in the United States, deliberately provoking Wilson to order U.S. Army troops into Mexico. Villa's calculation apparently was that the invasion by the United States would be perceived as an intervention in support of President Carranza, which would so compromise the Mexican president as to unite all forces in the country against him.

Having obtained the consent of the Carranza government, Wilson ordered American troops under the command of Brigadier General John J. Pershing to cross into Mexico in pursuit of Villa. On the morning of March 15, 1916, 5,000 of Pershing's troops crossed the frontier, later to be followed by 10,000 more. Eventually four-fifths of the American regular army was occupied in the campaign on one side or the other of the border, and Wilson felt obliged to call up the National Guard. Forbidden the use of Mexico's railroads by a government that did not want to appear to be a puppet of foreigners, the Americans had to bring along their supplies in horse-drawn covered wagons and in their few trucks. All eight of the U.S. Army airplanes intended for reconnaissance broke down in the first few weeks of the campaign. Pershing's troops penetrated hundreds of miles into Mexico, through desert and rugged hill country, enduring temperatures as high as 122 degrees, riding and marching from one suspected haunt of the elusive Villa to another and never finding him.

As the American troops crossed and crisscrossed Chihuahua province,

* See pages 61–2.

Carranza turned against the gringo invaders and ordered the Mexican army to block their advance. The two armies clashed repeatedly but inconclusively. It was only to be expected that Mexico would turn for support to Japan or Germany.

The American government knew that Mexican and Japanese officials had been in communication with one another, and knew, too, that German agents had been interested in embroiling the United States in a conflict with Mexico that would distract American attention from events in Europe. Urged to do so by Lansing, Wilson on January 25, 1917, ordered Pershing to withdraw from Mexico in order to strengthen the American position in dealing with warring Europe.

Earlier that month Arthur Zimmermann, who had been promoted to foreign minister of Germany under pressure from the military, had traveled to Pless and obtained permission from the High Command to try to incite Mexico and Japan to attack the United States. In pursuance of his strategy, Zimmermann sent coded telegrams instructing the German imperial minister in Mexico to offer President Carranza an alliance: "MAKE WAR TOGETHER, GENEROUS FINANCIAL SUPPORT, AND AN UNDERSTANDING ON OUR PART THAT MEXICO IS TO RECONQUER . . . TEXAS, NEW MEXICO, AND ARIZONA."

Intercepted and decoded by British intelligence, the Zimmermann telegram was turned over to the United States government. On Wilson's instructions, Lansing secretly released news of the cable to the Associated Press. The story provided banner headlines in the newspapers March 1. On March 3 Zimmermann, at a press conference in Berlin, admitted that the telegram was authentic.

Predictably, publication of the Zimmermann telegram strengthened those who advocated intervening in the European war. But in his second inaugural address, delivered March 4, the President would take the country no further along the road to war, even while warning that events in Europe had "made us citizens of the world" and that "there can be no turning back."

In pursuit of preparedness, the President ordered the arming of merchant vessels. But though he finally had brought the army back from Mexico, he still refused to bring the fleet back from the Caribbean.


ON JANUARY 21, as German U-boat commanders readied their coming campaign against American shipping, Assistant Secretary of the Navy Franklin Roosevelt left Washington to inspect American-occupied countries in the Caribbean. Roosevelt traveled with a party of friends in what was really a pleasure jaunt; he enjoyed the tropical sunshine, the sporting life, the daiquiris, the dancing, and the outdoor dining.

Roosevelt had planned an itinerary for himself and his friends that consisted in touring Cuba and the two sides of Hispaniola, Haiti and Santo Domingo. The countries of Hispaniola were marine-occupied and navy-ruled, in theory to restore order but in practice to further American business interests. Roosevelt fell in with the official view that the American occupation was bringing civilization to savage lands.

The trip was cut short by the break in relations with Germany; Secretary Daniels sent for Roosevelt in early February. Expecting war, Roosevelt was disappointed on returning to Washington to find that Wilson still was waiting on events.

On a day when Daniels was out of town, Roosevelt, briefly acting as secretary, went to see the President to ask permission to order the fleet, then anchored in Cuba, to steam north to be fitted out in preparation for whatever hostilities might arise. Wilson refused. As Roosevelt later recalled, the President said that "I want history to show not only that we have tried every diplomatic means to keep out of the war; to show that war has been forced upon us deliberately by Germany; but also that we have come into the court of history with clean hands."

The reply did not satisfy Roosevelt, who on the war issue was on a collision course with the administration in which he served. Briefly he indulged in thoughts of resigning, which led Thomas Lamont, the Morgan banker then living in Roosevelt's Manhattan house as his tenant, to express the hope that Daniels would retire "so that we could have the satisfaction of seeing you Secretary of the Navy!" The Navy League's leader was ready to urge that Daniels be replaced by Roosevelt—though Roosevelt asked him not to do so—and others went forward to do so without asking his permission. Louis Howe, Roosevelt's devoted assistant, surreptitiously organized a campaign along these lines.

On Sunday morning, March 11, Roosevelt visited Edward House in New York and privately complained of Daniels being too slow in getting the fleet ready for war. More dangerously Roosevelt met that night with TR and several of his most powerful colleagues. Around the table at the eight o'clock dinner in a private room at the Metropolitan Club on Fifth Avenue, Roosevelt and the Republican President, who was his idol and the leading figure in his family, concerted strategy to push the Democratic President, who was his political chief, into line with their interventionist thinking.

Roosevelt was so committed to the interventionist cause that he took to intriguing even with the most rabid of Republican anti-Wilson, anti-liberal anti-Democrats: Robert McCormick, a fellow Groton student and now publisher of the reactionary Chicago *Tribune*, to whom Roosevelt secretly supplied news stories. Such disloyalty to President Wilson and Secretary Daniels—his leaders in the Democratic party and in the government, to whom he owed his glamorous and highly visible job—has been put down by biographers to youthful selfishness, arrogance, and indiscretion. Similarly his enthusiasm for intervening on the Allied side, expressed immediately on the outbreak of war in 1914 and unwaveringly thereafter, has been interpreted as the unthinking desire of a shallow young man to be involved in an adventure in which he might earn glory.

There appears to be some truth in that portrait of the youthful Roosevelt. Yet somehow it misses something. For later in life, too, Roosevelt, though lacking in depth and intellect, was to see what the United States had to do before others did. In both of the world wars of the twentieth century, Franklin Roosevelt and Walter Lippmann understood that America's interests obliged the United States to intervene; but in both cases Roosevelt, a person of great charm but supposedly without much of a mind, understood this before the brilliant and highly educated Lippmann did.

Comparing Henry Cabot Lodge with his political protégé, TR, Henry Adams had written that "Lodge was a creature of teaching," while "Roosevelts are born and never can be taught." Franklin shared with his cousin Theodore a feel for how the world works, and an instinctive sense of the national interests of the United States. He had no need to learn about these things in books.

It was the intellectually lightweight Roosevelt rather than Wilson, America's only Ph.D. President, who had the truer appreciation of Europe's thinking and motives during the winter of 1916–17, as the President watched and waited and worried, refusing to anticipate that which he dreaded and half-expected to happen.


THEN, AT LAST, the long-threatened attack occurred. On March 18 the German U-boats struck, torpedoing and sinking three unarmed American merchant vessels: the *City of Memphis*, the *Illinois*, and the *Vigilancia*. Wilson met with his cabinet March 20 to solicit counsel from its members as to whether to call the Congress into extraordinary session. If he did convene such a session, what (Wilson asked cabinet members) should he ask Congress to do? The President then listened to what each member of the cabinet in turn had to say. Every one of them advised calling Congress into session, and each—even pacifist Secretary Daniels, though with tears in his eyes—advised the President to ask for a declaration of war. "I think there is no doubt as to what your advice is," Wilson told the cabinet members.

Wilson gave no indication of his own views; but he did remark on the "apparent apathy of the Middle West." This touched not only on his domestic political problem but on the more profound dilemma Wilson faced as the leader of a country of immigrants: Was it reasonable to expect the tens of millions of Americans born in Europe or of a European parent to sever blood ties to their native lands? Would it be fair to draft those born in Germany or of a German parent—about 10 percent of the population—and order them to kill Germans? Had their adopted country the right to ask that of them?

It could be argued that until the melting pot process was completed, the United States was by its nature disabled from taking sides in a war in Europe. Wilson, as the British ambassador had reported to London some time before, feared that if America were drawn into the conflict between Britain and Germany, the United States might dissolve into ethnic tribes whose mutual antagonisms could well erupt into civil war.

One thing was clear: even Americans who might be willing to fight against Germany would not be willing to do so merely to help Britain or France. Joseph Patrick Tumulty, the President's faithful and longtime private secretary, wrote to him on March 24 that editorial opinion in newspapers all over the country was overwhelming; if the United States went to war against the Germans, "it should be on an issue directly between us and them."

Of course, choosing to fight Germany—even on an issue in contention just between Americans and Germans—inescapably meant fighting alongside the Allies. But that no longer was an unpalatable option: in mid-March the tsar's regime collapsed in the first of the Russian revolutions of 1917. Tsarist government, loathed by Americans as tyrannical and reactionary, had tainted the Allied cause. A Russia seemingly moving toward democracy, on the other hand, was a fitting comrade in arms.

After asking the Congress to reconvene in extraordinary session on April 2, the President, on the morning after his cabinet meeting, gave himself a sabbatical week. He played pool, went on outings, and spent time with his wife. Not until the week had ended did he start (on March 28) to flesh out an outline of the topics to be covered when he addressed Congress.

Leaving word that he "did not wish to be disturbed by anyone," Wilson then secluded himself in his library beginning March 30. He worked there by himself for days. His was the most agonizing decision for a President to make since April 1861, when Abraham Lincoln was called upon to respond to the Confederate attack on Fort Sumter. What Wilson was about to do would mean a change in America's relations with the outside world greater than any since July 4, 1776, when the Continental Congress voted in favor of a Declaration of Independence from Great Britain. Nobody had to remind Woodrow Wilson, once a professor of history, that his was the most fateful decision that an American leader had been called upon to make in the twentieth century.

On April 2 the tensed, high-strung American leader was ready to do what had to be done, but the Congress was not; it took that deliberative body all day to get organized, while Wilson, under strain, waited at the White House. He showed his speech in advance only to Edward House, who had come down from New York to be with him. Afternoon came and went. At 6:30 p.m. the President, a few family members, and House sat down to dinner. After dinner, the time finally came; the President left the White House to go up the Hill.

WASHINGTON, D.C., Monday evening, April 2. Bathed in flood-lights, the shining white Capitol stood out against the darkness of the night sky as President Wilson drove toward it through the rain to ask Congress for a declaration of war against the German empire. Wilson's career had been based on his eloquence as a public speaker, but this was to be more than eloquent: it was to be the speech of his life.

Once arrived in an antechamber of the Capitol, he paused to prepare. Chin shaking, skin flushed, features distraught, he stared steadily at himself in a large mirror for a time as, by an effort of will, he made his face calm. Then, shortly after 8:30 p.m., he entered the chambers of the House of Representatives, where both houses of Congress had assembled. Squeezed just as Roosevelt and Daniels were into seats on the floor or in the visitors galleries were justices of the Supreme Court, members of the cabinet, foreign diplomats, and other dignitaries; but the President, as everyone present must have known, spoke that night to an audience far beyond the bounds of the Capitol building.

Germany, the President said, had attacked the United States by sinking three American vessels; and the only honorable course of action for America was to strike back.* The Germans had gone "beyond the pale of law" and should be treated as "pirates." It was, said Wilson, with a "profound sense of the . . . tragical character of the step I am taking" that he asked the Congress to declare war.

The war that he asked Congress to declare was not to be in support of the Allies' objectives, but of America's, which were unlike theirs. "We have no selfish ends to serve," he said, echoing the sentiments of his "peace without victory" proposal made ten weeks earlier. He distinguished the goals of the United States from those of England and France, who sought reparations for their losses and suffering, saying that Americans "seek no indemnities for ourselves, no material compensation for the sacrifices we shall freely make."

The United States was responding to the attacks on its ships in March

---

* In 1917 "honor" still was taken seriously. It was thought normal to go to war to uphold it—and shameful not to do so.

1917. It still was not choosing sides in the conflict between rival coalitions about the rights and wrongs of the Sarajevo crisis of July 1914 and its immediate aftermath. So in his address that night, the President did not ask for declarations of war against Austria-Hungary, Bulgaria, and the Ottoman Empire—Germany's allies though they were in the 1914 war—for they had not joined in the 1917 attack against America. And as Wilson later was to make explicit, in fighting alongside England, France, Russia, and the others against Germany, the United States would be not an ally, but an associated power.

The United States would wage war against the German government but not against the German people. America was going to fight "for the ultimate peace of the world, and for the liberation of its peoples, the German peoples included." The distinction that Wilson drew between the Germans and their government could be viewed as playing politics, for it enabled him to soften the impact of the blow he was striking at German-American voters. But even had no ethnic issue been involved, it would have been usual for an American leader to draw such a distinction—a distinction that was deeply rooted in the political thought of the United States. From the earliest days of the Republic, Americans had maintained that wars were caused only by the functioning of monarchies, and that there were no fundamental quarrels between peoples; if all countries were to become democracies, there would be no more wars.

These views always had sprung easily to the lips of an American politician, but in the First World War they were to have real consequences. For the difference between Wilson's view of the challenge posed by the kaiser's Germany and the views of Britain and France on that point were more than merely theoretical: they lay at the heart of the argument that Wilson had started with the Allies about the causes of the war and the terms of an eventual peace. The Allies believed that the fighting had its origins in Germany's bid for mastery in Europe, and that the war was about *power*: Germany was too powerful relative to her neighbors, and she had to be radically weakened. Wilson, who already had indicated that he saw no point in blaming one side more than another, was arguing that the war was about *political systems*: Germany was militaristic in government and political culture, and she had to be radically changed—had, in fact, to be changed into a democracy.

But implicit in Wilson's analysis was the proposition that it was not Germany alone that had to be changed; the rest of Europe had to be changed, too, as did the world that Europe had shaped in its own image in Africa and Asia. In a phrase that was to become famous, the President in his war message the night of April 2 invited Americans to join with him to "make the world safe for democracy." There may have been some significance in the fact that the senator who first applauded that stirring phrase was deaf.* It is certainly doubtful whether the multitudes who acclaimed the President's message that evening heard the overtones in his words—understood, that is, that he was summoning them to a crusade that could fairly be regarded, both in the noble sense and in the slighting one, as quixotic.

The theme upon which Wilson expanded was traditional: since George Washington's day, the United States had refused to involve itself in Europe's quarrels on the grounds that it would be dangerous and corrupting to do so. Wilson's variation on the theme was to propose its converse: if the United States were forced nonetheless to become involved in the affairs of Europe's world, America would be obliged to change that world so as not to be contaminated by it.

This was a natural extension of the thinking behind Wilson's "peace without victory" speech ten weeks before, in which America now offered to emerge from isolation to play a continuing role in world affairs—but only on condition that the European powers forswear their own ambitions and make peace on America's terms.

Now the United States, forced to take up arms, was going to fight not just to defeat and then remake the other side in the war, but to remake *both* sides: that is what Wilson was edging toward saying, without explaining how he was going to get victorious Britain, France, Russia, Italy, and the other Allies to change themselves and their ways once, with America's help, they had won the war.

It was not until long afterward that such explanations were asked for and that Wilson's seductive language was exposed to the cold glare of critical scrutiny. On the evening of April 2, all was given over to euphoria. The President concluded his address to cheers. As he left the Capitol, the crowds outside flocked around to shout their support. Within days the Senate and the House approved the war resolution that the President had proposed. He signed it on Good Friday, April 6, 1917, bringing the United States into the Great War. Wilson's move, on a day normally reserved for commemoration of the Crucifixion, was inauspicious for those who feared that the war might be mankind's road to Calvary.

At last America had found her new role in world affairs: she was to remake the world.

---

* Senator John Sharp Williams of Mississippi.

PART THREE

A CALLING HIGHER
THAN SOLDIERING

# A MISSED RENDEZVOUS

TO HEAR WOODROW WILSON'S war speech in person, the Michigan newspaper editor Arthur Vandenberg made the long trip to Washington. In the past he had accused Wilson of violating the spirit of American neutrality by not taking a strong stand against the British blockade. Now he thought the President was doing the right thing in making a stand against Germany. Often inconsistent and given to bursts of enthusiasm, Vandenberg was overwhelmed by the April 2 speech. Once he had idolized TR, but now he had found a new idol; he later wrote that "from that date Wilson was my President just as completely as though I had personally named him."

In this he did not speak for the Middle West as a whole. The region's popular Progressive Republican leaders, Senator Robert La Follette of Wisconsin and Senator George Norris of Nebraska, denounced the war as serving only the purposes of European imperialism. So did the Socialist leaders, presidential candidate Eugene V. Debs and former Milwaukee Congressman Victor Berger. Though ethnic passions ran high ("I do like the Kaiser. I am a German and will fight for Germany" was a statement not untypical of those made by Wisconsin defendants who were prosecuted during the war for unpatriotic speech or conduct), it was not only the German-American electorate to whom La Follette and the others appealed. These men also attracted strands of idealist opinion that President Wilson thought of as his own, and Wilson resented them much as lovers resent rivals.

Walter Lippmann's particular value to Wilson and House was that he was seemingly able to bring over to their side the Progressive and Socialist idealists who might otherwise have followed La Follette, Norris, Debs, and Berger—or even the former Progressive presidential candidate Theodore Roosevelt, who attacked the President from the other political flank. Lippmann, whose first political love, like Vandenberg's, had been TR, wrote to President Wilson April 3 that "I have tried to say a little of what I feel about your address in the following words, which are to appear in *The New Republic* this week." In the paragraph that followed, and that appeared in the magazine a few days later, Lippmann wrote: "For having seen . . . that this is a war between democracy and autocracy . . . our debt and the world's debt to Woodrow Wilson is immeasurable. . . . Only a statesman who will be called great could have made America's intervention mean so much to the generous forces of the world, could have lifted the inevitable horror of war into a deed so full of meaning."

It was Lippmann's special gift to be able to articulate what others felt but could not put into words. Among the outstanding men in their twenties and early thirties who had grown up worshiping TR and now transferred their allegiance to Woodrow Wilson, there seems to have been a sense that the President was supplying something that they had needed but until then had lacked: a moral framework for the sense of mission that TR initially had inspired in them. Theodore Roosevelt, who thought war glorious, had urged them to do battle in order to prove that they were tough enough to meet the best that other countries could field; while Wilson, who thought war terrible, called on them to fight only in order to make the world better—to make it a world in which there would be no more wars. Wilson appealed to their belief that they and their country were exceptional: that their goal was not (as TR's was) to prove that America now was the equal of Europe, but rather to make Europe, now morally inferior, as good as America. Unlike TR, Wilson did not ask them to undergo hardship or horrors for their own sake; he asked them to do so in pursuit of a moral ideal. To that which they were about to experience in the trenches of the western front, Wilson thereby had given, in Lippmann's word, a *meaning*.

THE WILSON ADMINISTRATION, facing the question of how America could best contribute to the war effort, at first thought in terms of fulfilling a support function: of supplying loans, financial credits, food, war matériel, and transport to the Allies and their armies. When British and French statesmen arrived in Washington in April 1917 to coordinate war plans, they made it evident that this was not enough: they needed soldiers, too.

The American army of which President Wilson was commander in chief in April 1917 was smaller than that which had fought under General Washington's command in the eighteenth century; and it had been designed for Indian fighting. Without committing himself on the issue of what role U.S. ground forces would play in the warfare on the continent of Europe once America's armies were raised and ready, Wilson, in response to Allied pleas, ordered a buildup of the U.S. Army.

The President was determined to plan the war effort in a rational and systematic way. His administration instituted a draft, after opposition had been overcome through a public relations campaign led for the War Department by Major Douglas MacArthur. Wilson's conscription program—selective service, as it was called—was designed to call able-bodied young men to the colors without disrupting the flow of industrial and agricultural production that the President expected would provide the United States with the key to victory. Emphasis was placed on exempting from military or combat service those who could make a greater contribution in some other capacity.

Those who were rejected for military service as physically unfit, or who obtained exemption from service, were of course in various frames of mind as to how to think about it. Some took it for granted that if they could accomplish more for their country in some civilian or staff position, it would be wrong for them to serve in combat. Others were persuaded that they were shirking their duty—or at any rate would be thought by others to be cowards—if they were not engaged in battle. As happens in wartime, the country was swept by patriotic ardor and challenged by such examples of bravery as that of Alan Seeger.

Seeger, born in New York City and a college classmate of Walter Lippmann's and John Reed's, was a poet little known before the war, whose works sometimes were published in *The New Republic.* When the European war began in the summer of 1914, he embraced the Allied cause and enlisted in the French Foreign Legion. He served almost continuously in combat for the next two years. Attacking a German-held village in northern France in 1916, he was mortally wounded by machine-gun fire on July 4, and died the next day.

Of all the poems out of the United States about the war, Seeger's "I Have a Rendezvous with Death" became the most famous: "I have a rendezvous with Death/ At some disputed barricade," he wrote, and "I shall not fail that rendezvous." Others of the elite of his generation—Groton boys, and Yale and Harvard men—were bound to be affected by their sense of whether their appointed place, too, had been at some disputed barricade.

ROBERT A. TAFT WAS NOTHING if not honest. The prosaic young Ohio lawyer admitted that he did not want to be a soldier; but he had a strong sense of duty that led him to try to enlist in the armed forces. He was rejected as physically unfit (his eyes were weak).

Determined nonetheless to perform national service in wartime, Taft went to work for Herbert Hoover's Food Administration in Washington, D.C. He served as one of the four attorneys designated as assistant counsel. As such, he dealt with such regulatory matters as the pricing and grading of food products. It was congenial work for a young lawyer who enjoyed paying attention to detail, and he was good at it. He probably would have made an indifferent soldier; he served his country far more effectively as the capable attorney he was. Yet as he rightly observed, "My failure to enter the army requires and always will require explanation, and I shall always feel that those who have suffered in the war . . . are regarding me as one who failed to do his real duty."

Arthur Vandenberg seemed to be troubled by no such feelings. Though an ardent supporter of TR and an enthusiast for the American side of the world war ("the greatest revival the world has known since Christ came upon the earth"), the young newspaperman, a widower with three young children, felt that family responsibilities precluded him from enlisting or serving in the armed forces.

The outbreak of war found international lawyer John Foster Dulles in Central America on a secret mission for his uncle, Secretary of State Lansing. Dulles, who was experienced in doing business in that part of the hemisphere on behalf of corporate clients, had been instructed by Lansing to make sure that whenever the United States declared war on Germany, Panama—site of the canal vital to the U.S. Navy—declared war, too. His mission accomplished, Dulles returned to the United States to be appointed by Lansing as state's special counsel for Central American affairs. Dulles applied for entrance into Officer Training School in the summer of 1917, but like Taft, he was rejected because of poor eyesight. Dulles succeeded, however, in obtaining a direct commission as a captain in the Signal Corps, assigned to intelligence duties, and became head of the economic section of the Military Intelligence General Staff. It was a position for which he was well qualified, and he had become even more of an enthusiast for Woodrow Wilson, whose teaching had meant so much to him in college. Dulles was enthralled by Wilson's vision of making the Allied war effort into something higher: into "an idealistic crusade" for a world based on international cooperation.

James Forrestal, if he had to serve, wanted to do so as an officer, too. The Wall Street bond salesman, facing a call by the Naval Reserve, applied instead for a commission in the Marine Corps, but was turned away by a recruiting sergeant who said (as Forrestal later recalled), "I see that you're another one of those goddamn leaders. Well, we've got enough of them, and we don't need any more." Called to service in the navy, Forrestal trained as an aviator and spent his war at staff headquarters in the United States.

Joseph P. Kennedy pulled political strings to get a job that would exempt him from the draft. He became accountant and assistant general manager of the Bethlehem Steel Corporation's Fore River Shipyard at Quincy, Massachusetts. Though lacking in physical courage, he was tough as a businessman, and made money out of avoiding military service: he was earning a base salary of $20,000 a year (then a large sum of money), plus a bonus, and profited in addition by owning the cafeteria at which many of the 22,000 workers ate. Though most of the credit belonged to others, Kennedy's shipyards broke production records. But according to Ralph Lowell, a Boston patrician, the Harvard class of '12 to which they both belonged "didn't appreciate a man not going into the war, as, for instance, in the case of Joe"; and one of Kennedy's biographers writes that later, "Kennedy confessed to a twinge of regret at having remained a civilian."

Averell Harriman also went into shipbuilding. With money borrowed from his mother, he bought an interest in a shipyard in February 1917, after the United States broke relations with Germany, and acquired the rest in April after the declaration of war. He then acquired a second shipyard and financially consolidated the two companies. He and his associates put $9 million in the venture and obtained favorable contracts from the government—initially, as he wrote to his brother, to build eighty-seven ships. The government put in $92 million and guaranteed him profits on the vessels he was to construct. Harriman undertook also to create a new town, a new plant, and new shipbuilding facilities; but under his management, the record was dismal. He was able to launch only one vessel during the war. When the director-general of the United States Shipping Board wrote to him on August 23, 1918, to ask where the ships were and to remark, "This seems to me to be an awfully bad record," Harriman wrote (but did not send) a reply blaming conditions inherited from previous management.

In a magazine interview in 1920, Harriman remarked of his wartime shipbuilding that "I felt that in no other way could I contribute half as much to the urgent needs of the nation in the supreme emergency that had arisen." But in a book published more than a half-century later, he was paraphrased as saying that "he had long regretted the family and business circumstances that had kept him out of action in the world war." He went on to say that "I felt very strongly there should be a draft. Intellectually, I could reason that I had done the right thing, because I thought that shipping was the real bottleneck of World War I. But emotionally, I never felt entirely comfortable." He went on to suggest that this emotional discomfort may have been responsible for the missions he later was to undertake in the Second World War: "That tended to square the balance."

Of the stars of Yale's graduating class of 1913—Cole Porter, Averell Harriman, and William Bullitt—Porter was the most shameless in avoiding military service. Apparently disregarding the law that required him to register for selective service, he boarded an ocean liner to France and spent the war living in Paris, where he dressed in Foreign Legion and other French military uniforms, leading everyone to assume that he was serving as an army officer. He kept up the charade in front of his friend and college classmate, the future actor Second Lieutenant Monty Woolley, and in front of Archibald MacLeish, who was to fight in the second battle of the Marne. MacLeish, a close friend of Porter's Harvard roommate, Dean Acheson, had left Harvard to join the army, while Acheson stayed on to finish law school before enlisting (as it happened, just before the Armistice brought the war to an end).

MORE THAN ANY OTHER AMERICAN, Theodore Roosevelt stood for the proposition that one should risk one's life for one's country. And as always, he set the example. A few years earlier his body had been practically destroyed in an expedition in Brazil that searched for the source of the River of Doubt. Yet when war was declared, TR, though physically a wreck, nearly sixty, and half-blind, desperately sought permission to lead a volunteer unit to France to fight. President Wilson rejected his offer, in patronizing terms that foreshadowed the partisan spirit in which the chief executive would conduct the war and the peace.

Wilson hated TR and was jealous of him. TR despised Wilson. As he came out of his meeting with the President, the ex-President encountered Colonel House and complained of the reception he had just received. As Winston Churchill later told the story, Theodore Roosevelt said: " 'Wilson was very rough with me. After all, all I asked was to be allowed to die.' House (*in his silkiest tones*): 'Did you make that last point clear to the President?' "

As soon as war came, all four of TR's sons enlisted in the army. But cousin Franklin did not. TR told Roosevelt, "You *must* resign." He said, "You must get into uniform at once!" Not merely did he say it, he said it often. Eleanor Roosevelt remembered that TR "was *always* urging Franklin to resign."

Roosevelt did offer to resign, but dropped the matter when Josephus Daniels told him that Wilson wanted him to remain in his position. His old daydream of being another TR—of winning glory on the battlefield—seems to have flamed up only fitfully and then to have fizzled out. He seems, too, to have been torn between a feeling that it looked wrong for him not to enlist and a strong desire to stay where he was. Despite his athletic appearance, he was not robust; he suffered from frequent colds. He could well take the view that he was making a greater contribution to the war effort as assistant secretary of the navy than he could make as a fighting man. He also had strong inducements to stay put: His political life in Washington was fulfilling. So was his personal life; he and twenty-six-year-old Lucy Mercer, once his wife's secretary, were in love. At last he had found a woman who suited him physically, temperamentally, and socially. Their clandestine affair was facilitated by her employment for a time at the Navy Department. But Washington was a small town, and though the lovers were discreet, there were those who noticed and who gossiped. Daniels seems to have learned of the affair, and in October 1917 terminated the employment of Yeoman Second Class Mercer. But Roosevelt did not break with her, despite Daniels's unspoken disapproval; the liaison, whatever may have been its nature, continued.

In this he was encouraged by his cousin Alice Roosevelt Longworth, TR's daughter and Washington's most brilliant hostess. Franklin and Lucy had taken an automobile drive in the country one day. Alice happened to see them and, looking at the expression on Franklin's face, guessed all.

"You didn't see me," she teased her cousin later. "Your hands were on the wheel but your eyes were on that perfectly lovely lady."

"Isn't she perfectly lovely?" he agreed.

Alice proceeded to be helpful. Whether out of sentiment or mischief, she provided a cover: when Eleanor was out of town, she would invite the lovers to dinner, giving them a place to meet and be together.

A lifetime later, when Alice was eighty-three but still known for her malicious wit, she was asked about the role she had played in the affair. She defended herself. Franklin, she said, "deserved a good time. He was married to Eleanor."

Despite cousin TR's often-voiced exhortations, the charming young assistant secretary of the navy lingered in Washington, far from the sea battles of the North Atlantic.

# 13

# FOCUSING ON THE PEACE

WILLIAM BULLITT, who was often a step ahead, had grasped the importance of focusing on foreign policy in 1914, years before even such brilliant contemporaries as Walter Lippmann had seen that events in Europe might involve the United States. By 1917 he had made himself into an outstanding Washington journalist and foreign correspondent. His longtime plan had been to trade his firsthand information about European affairs into a high position in the Wilson administration. America's entry into the war enabled him to do it.

The President's adviser Colonel House had come to value Bullitt's views. On July 15 Bullitt wrote to House that "the unhappy results of an appendicitis operation make it impossible for me to do active military service" and that he wished to serve on the White House staff. By the end of the year, House managed to obtain for Bullitt—who was only four years out of college—an appointment as assistant secretary of state. The State Department then requested that he not be inducted into military service.

At State, Bullitt continued to communicate directly with Colonel House, although in theory he was to report to and through Joseph Grew, the State Department's chief of the Division of Western European Affairs. Grew, who had served as number two at the U.S. embassy in Berlin until war came, had gone on to a brief stint at the embassy in Vienna before being brought back to the United States. He was not physically eligible for the armed forces because he was partially deaf—able to make out what was said to him face-to-face, but not what was said if he turned away.

Bullitt had known Grew at the Berlin embassy, and Christian Herter, too, who finally had dealt with his fiancée's objections to his leaving her for public service by marrying her. Rejected by the army as underweight for his enormous height, Herter had become a State Department officer. Among the other draft-age officials of the department was austere, forbidding Sumner Welles, a Groton boy, Harvard '14, a page at Franklin Roosevelt's wedding, recommended by Roosevelt for the foreign service in 1915, who had been posted to the embassy in Tokyo.

THIRTY-FOUR-YEAR-OLD Felix Frankfurter, professor of law at Harvard, became an assistant to Secretary of War Newton D. Baker when the war began, and as such was exempt from the draft. Walter Lippmann, twenty-seven, wrote to Frankfurter and to Secretary Baker as well to ask if he, too, could obtain an exemption from military service. "What I want to do is to devote all my time to studying and speculating on the approaches to peace and the reaction from the peace," Lippmann wrote. "I am convinced that I can serve my bit much more effectively than as a private in the new armies."

Baker agreed, and appointed Lippmann one of his special assistants. For Lippmann, this meant leaving *The New Republic* and New York City. Frankfurter and a handful of other brilliant young bachelors already were in residence at the Washington house of a friend at 1727 Nineteenth Street, and Lippmann (and his wife, for he had just married) moved in, too.

The redbrick house was an intellectual center pulsating with the vitality of young men on the move. A frequent visitor, Supreme Court Justice Oliver Wendell Holmes, teasing them for their seriousness and sense of self-importance, dubbed their residence the "House of Truth." Holmes, who had served with gallantry in the Civil War, was a survivor of a more robust era in which young men were not always so high-minded.

At first Lippmann, like Frankfurter and Roosevelt (all of whom now had offices in the State, War and Navy Departments Building), was drawn into administrative work, notably dealing with labor questions (wages, working conditions, and the like) in docks and arsenals. In the course of these proceedings Lippmann, as army representative, met Franklin Roosevelt, the navy's man, who had been detailed to such committee work for years. But the two did not get to know each other or to form any particular bond.* For one thing, Roosevelt often was absent from committee meetings; his assistant, Louis Howe, frequently showed up in his place, for the assistant secretary tended to focus instead on public appearances. Lippmann, in turn, did not remain in his War Department job long.

For Lippmann's star was rising. When on August 1, 1917, Pope Benedict XV called upon the warring countries to stop the war and to make peace on the basis of disarmament, arbitration of disputes, no annexations or indemnities, and a return by all parties to wherever they started from in the summer of 1914, President Wilson turned to Lippmann to supply an

---

* Roosevelt had become acquainted with Lippmann's friend Frankfurter long before, however, and the two began to know each other better during the war years. As young lawyers in 1906, they had been introduced to each other at a lunch arranged by a common friend. They also had dealings together at State, War and Navy in 1913, in Roosevelt's first year at Navy and Frankfurter's last year (during that stint of government service) at War.

explanation of why the United States was rejecting the appeal. The pope was proposing the "peace without victory" that Wilson himself, only months before, had asked all belligerents to accept. But now that the United States was in the war, the President wanted to remake the world of 1914, not return to it. Lippmann responded with a draft reply to the pope that said that in order to prevent a recurrence of the war, Germany had to be changed. Just going back to July 1914 would solve nothing, for it would mean that someday, August 1914 would come again.

Lippmann's memorandum (for his chief, the secretary of war) in August 1917 was a somewhat muddled attempt to think through the President's policy toward Germany. "We are conducting the war," Lippmann began, "on the assumption that there is a distinction between the German government and German people. The question is: Why had the German people supported this government in the past and why do they continue to?" Lippmann's answer was that Prussian militarism had won for Germany things that matter—national security, prosperity, respect from others—and that the Germans had been led to believe that only the kind of government they had could get these things for them.

It followed, Lippmann argued, that "if the German people are to be weaned from their governing class they must be made to believe that they can be safe, prosperous, and respected without dependence upon the government as it exists." Lippmann did not say how this could be done. Nor did he mention the obvious corollary of his proposition: that the United States should fight on until the power of Germany's military ruling class was broken. If Germany were beaten badly enough, her people might be persuaded that Prussian militarism did *not* provide safety, prosperity, or respect—and therefore might be induced to opt for a different kind of regime.

Lippmann urged Wilson to say that Germany was not a fit partner with which to establish a peaceful world. He explained that "by a fit partner we understand a Germany in which control of foreign policy and of the military machine has passed to the representatives of the people. We go on the assumption that it is possible to deal in good faith with a democracy."

But that contradicted what he had said about the German people having been deluded into believing that only Prussian militarism could secure the country's legitimate objectives. If they went on believing that, the German people would be no more fit than Germany's government to work with America in designing a peaceful and disarmed world.

Nonetheless Wilson was impressed by Lippmann's memorandum. "Lippmann is not only thoughtful," the President said to the secretary of war, "but just and suggestive." Wilson went on to reply to Pope Benedict along lines Lippmann had suggested, emphasizing the distinction between the German people and their government.

THE NEED TO REPLY TO THE POPE focused attention on the question of American war goals. Even before the United States entered the war, House had suggested to Wilson that a body of experts should be convened to supply American delegates to the future peace conference with the information they would need. Then, shortly after the pope's appeal in August 1917, Felix Frankfurter, visiting Paris, reported to Lansing that the French had assembled several committees to plan ahead for the peace. Frankfurter suggested to Lansing that the United States should do likewise. Frankfurter's report was forwarded to Wilson, who wrote to Lansing that he had read it "with a great deal of interest."

House, who had heard from Frankfurter directly, was worried that little or nothing was being done to follow through. In fact, Lansing, in September 1917, had made a start, though not a particularly ambitious one. He asked Joseph Grew and two others to draft secret memorandums that would help in thinking about peace terms, and to begin by describing and analyzing the development during the war of "the aims and desires of the present belligerents." A William Bullitt or a Walter Lippmann would have jumped at this chance to design a new world, but with a bureaucrat's weariness, Grew wrote that "my share of this seemingly colossal task includes Germany, Austria-Hungary, England, France, Belgium, and Portugal." After searching in vain for somebody to draft the memo for him, Grew decided that he could do it himself if State would give him a week's leave of absence.

But the President took the inquiry into war goals away from the Department of State. At the time, professional foreign and consular services were only just being established by the United States—indeed, Grew was to become (in the words of the Council on Foreign Relations) "the first American to manage a complete foreign service career"—and it could well be argued that the department lacked the expertise, experience, and manpower to plan a global peace conference. In any event Wilson's was a personal style of government. On the occasions when foreign policy issues drew his attention, he decided them himself; the rest of the time—which was most of the time—he wanted his alter ego, Edward House, to deal with them. So it was in character for him, when the issue of peace terms arose, to instruct House to secretly assemble a group of experts—bypassing the State Department—to help formulate America's plans for the postwar world. The group was to be located in New York in order to preserve secrecy, which proved to be a convenience for House, who resided there.

Wilson suggested that members of the team should be recruited mainly from the academic world and that names might be solicited from the president of Harvard and from the editor of *The New Republic*. The group, anonymous for the moment, later was to be code-named "the Inquiry." To ensure his continuing personal control of it, House appointed as its director his wife's brother-in-law, Sidney Mezes, president of the College of the City of New York.

At the end of September 1917, House visited Washington and came by the War Department. He invited Walter Lippmann, for some months special assistant to Secretary of War Baker, to a stroll with him and a talk, in the course of which he revealed the secret project and asked Lippmann to be part of it. It was exactly what Lippmann wanted. It validated his decision to stay out of combat and save himself to make more important contributions to his country's cause—contributions that he uniquely was capable of making.

As soon as House returned to New York, Lippmann wrote to him that "the work outlined is exactly that which I have dreamed of since the very beginning of the war, but dreamed of as something beyond reach. I'd literally rather be connected with you in this work in no matter what capacity than do anything else there is to do in the world."

So it was that a mere five months after arriving in Washington to work in the War Department, Lippmann, who had just turned twenty-eight years old, returned to New York to focus his extraordinary intelligence on the problems not of war, but of peace. He rented an apartment at 21 East Fifty-seventh Street for himself and for fun-loving Faye Albertson, whom he had married in the late spring, and immersed himself in questions of high politics—which bored his wife, but gave meaning to his life.

There were five of them in the inner group: Mezes, the head; Lippmann, who became general secretary; James Shotwell, a historian from Columbia University; attorney David Hunter Miller, a law partner of House's son-in-law; and Isaiah Bowman, director of the AGS (the American Geographical Society). At first the Inquiry made its headquarters at the New York Public Library on Fifth Avenue at Forty-second Street. Later Lippmann and his colleagues moved to the premises of the AGS at Broadway and 155th Street.

The AGS provided professionally drawn maps that were outstanding. Nonetheless, the Inquiry's other productions tended to be amateurish. There was a comic side to the notion of assembling a group of academics, many of them unworldly or impractical, a number of them narrow specialists in obscure and irrelevant fields, some of them historians of long-dead peoples and remote times, and asking them to resolve all the questions facing the twentieth century.

Yet for a moment it seemed to be the best club in the world. Felix Frankfurter longed to join, but Lippmann, on House's instructions, wrote: "The job goes well, but it has not reached a point where you can be drafted into it with any fairness to the work you are now doing." One of the great American jurists, Judge Learned Hand, suggested that he might join the

Inquiry, and the educator John Dewey wanted in, too, but House and his lieutenants fended off the volunteers.

It was heady stuff: Lippmann was one of the mere handful of people in their twenties who had the luck to be engaged in the remaking of the world. TR's children who had become Woodrow Wilson's offspring, they had been shown the way by a President who was priest and prophet. TR had summoned them to make war, but Wilson, whom they now followed, summoned them to make peace. This, they had come to believe, was their destined mission as young Americans growing up with the twentieth century. Only a handful of them could represent their generation in fulfilling its historic task. It was their privilege to be among that handful.

Tears running down his cheeks after a speech at the end of 1917, Woodrow Wilson exclaimed: "I hate this war! I hate all war, and the only thing I care about on earth is the peace I am going to make at the end of it." Clearly that was what Lippmann felt, too. The vocation of others might be to make war; his was to make peace.

While those contemporaries for whom his classmate Alan Seeger spoke kept their rendezvous with death on the battlefields of France and Flanders, Lippmann in New York, like Bullitt and Roosevelt in Washington, kept an individual appointment with destiny—and they had every reason to believe that history would remember it as the one that mattered.

# PART FOUR

## A Separate War

# 14

# A WAR OF OUR OWN

DAYS BEFORE AMERICA'S ENTRY into the war, the Navy Department sent Admiral William S. Sims to London to coordinate with the British admiralty. His instructions from William S. Benson, the chief of naval operations—the uniformed head of the navy—were: "Don't let the British pull the wool over your eyes. It is none of our business pulling their chestnuts out of the fire. We would as soon fight the British as the Germans."

Benson was known to be anti-British, but what he said was in line with views expressed by the President, who in 1914 had been privately pro-Ally but had become increasingly skeptical about Allied motives as time went on. At the end of 1917, when the American ambassador to Britain suggested that former President William Howard Taft and other prominent figures should visit England as part of a program to foster mutual understanding, Wilson objected, telling Taft that "he questioned the desirability of drawing the two countries too closely together. He said that there were divergences of purpose and that the United States must not be put in the position of seeming, in any way, involved in British policy. . . . He intimated that the motives of the United States were unselfish while those of the British Empire . . . seemed of a less worthy character."

Even though the United States after April 6, 1917, was committed to fight, at least in some fashion, alongside the Allies, the President stressed his resolve to retain diplomatic independence. He made that clear to Arthur Balfour, the British foreign secretary, when British and French missions arrived in the United States at the end of April 1917 to discuss coordination of war efforts. Wilson told Balfour that the United States reserved the right to make a separate peace, and Balfour recognized that if he were in Wilson's place, he would insist on the same freedom of action.

The question to be resolved was how the United States would contribute to the war against the common enemy. Marshal Joseph Joffre, who headed the French mission, asked that one division of American troops be sent to France to show the flag. President Wilson agreed to his request, though it meant creating a division: the United States did not have one formed at the time. It remained an open question whether American participation in the war should include dispatching any additional soldiers to Europe. To recruit and train armies would take time; the war might well be over before it could be done.

An aide to Newton Baker, testifying at about that time before the Senate Finance Committee in support of the War Department's request for appropriations, was asked by the chairman of the committee, Senator Thomas S. Martin of Virginia, what the money was going to be spent for. The department's spokesman began: "Clothing, cots, camps, food, pay. . . . And we may have to have an army in France."

"Good Lord!" said Martin, "You're not going to send soldiers over there, are you?"

The administration knew it was going to ship a division of soldiers "over there," but knew little more than that. When Baker appointed General John J. Pershing to command the division and whatever additional forces would be sent to France, he left it to the general to advise what additional level of forces, if any, should be sent. Pershing was to go on ahead to Europe immediately.

Wilson and Baker ordered Pershing overseas as commander of the American Expeditionary Force—the AEF—with broad powers. The President appeared to believe that he should leave military matters to the military. As Baker remembered them, Wilson's parting words to Pershing were "I will give you only two orders, one to go to France and the other to come home. . . . If you make good, the people will forgive almost any mistake. If you do not make good, they will probably hang us both from the first lamppost they can find."

Baker told Pershing that "the underlying idea must be kept in view that the forces of the United States are a separate and distinct component . . . the identity of which must be preserved." Pershing believed that in telling him that, Baker in effect had answered his own question about force levels. Pershing had been ordered to preserve the American identity of his forces, and in his view, the United States could fight its own war in Europe only with an army of at least a million men. He therefore began to plan immediately for a force of at least that size.

THERE WAS AN EXCEPTION to the rule that American troops were to fight as a separate unit—and the exception showed the blind side of American democracy. Pershing provided France with four black infantry regiments, and alone among American troops, they fought the entire war under French command. Three of the four regiments were awarded the Croix de Guerre; and in one of them, the "Harlem Hell Fighters" of the New York National Guard, a number of officers and enlisted men individually won either the Croix de Guerre or the Legion of Honor.

In the South and elsewhere, there was widespread fear of inducting blacks into the armed forces and training them as soldiers. Neither the Wilson administration nor the U.S. armed forces were willing to confront the color issue. Both attempted to dodge it, hence the handing over of some of the black units to France. Secretary Baker, caught between his own brand of liberal politics and the prejudices of his countrymen, decided that it was not his official responsibility to deal with the matter. He stated that "there is no intention on the part of the War Department to undertake at this time to settle the so-called race question."

IN A HEAVY RAINSTORM Captain George C. Marshall escorted General Pershing and his staff to the docks at Governors Island in New York Harbor on May 28, where they boarded the ferry that would convey them to their appointed rendezvous with an ocean liner headed for England and crossing to France.

Marshall had hoped to go with them, but the army could not spare him from Department of the East headquarters at Governors Island. The department's commanding general was in the hospital, and Marshall, who had arrived from California only weeks before, found himself in effective command. Conditions were chaotic; it was a price the country was paying for its lack of military preparedness. There had been no adequate planning for war, for recruitment, or for the creation of a citizens' army—not even of the single division that had been promised to Joffre and that was supposed to be following Pershing over to France.

Marshall coped as best he could. He also pulled strings, and within weeks had secured an appointment on the staff of the commander of the about-to-be-formed First Division. With other officers and men who formed the nucleus of the First Division, he boarded a converted fruit ship in June for the long, dangerous Atlantic crossing through submarine-infested waters; he overheard sailors rigging a gun on the foredeck, complaining that they had no ammunition. "My God, even the naval part isn't organized . . . ," he exclaimed.

At the end of June, Marshall and his companions landed at the French shipbuilding port of Saint-Nazaire, at the southeastern tip of the Brittany peninsula where the Loire estuary meets the ocean. A small crowd had gathered to greet the Americans; almost all were women, and of these, most were dressed in black to mourn their dead.

During the summer, as more troops arrived and Marshall took up his duties as chief of operations of the First Division, Pershing prepared and sent his reports to Washington. Commanding generals naturally want to increase the size and independence of their commands, but Pershing in addition had solid military reasons for desiring to do so. He asked for enough troops to wage a war of his own in Europe in part because he worried that the British and French generals had sunk into the mire of trench warfare. Like other Americans who had learned from Philip Sheridan and Stonewall Jackson, he believed instead in waging a war of movement. He was afraid, too, that if Europeans were in command, his troops might be sent "here and there" and employed for reasons of imperial policy in theaters other than the all-important western front.

Then there was the political aspect of it. As Pershing wrote to Secretary Baker, "When the war ends, our position will be stronger if our army acting as such shall have played a distinct and definite part." So his initial request from Paris was for an AEF of a million men. Then he talked at length with the Allied generals—and learned that he had better double or triple or quadruple that number.

FROM CONTACTS WITH THE FRENCH in the summer of 1917, Pershing came to the conclusion that the Allies were on the verge of losing the war. The British commander, General Douglas Haig, was not of that view. But from the new French commander, Philippe Pétain, Pershing received a gloomy account of troop morale in the wake of mutinies in a French army that seemed no longer willing to fight. Felix Frankfurter, who was on a fact-finding mission of his own in Paris that summer, reported that the French were so demoralized that they no longer cared about their own war goals—liberating Alsace and Lorraine—let alone Wilson's vision of designing a better world.

In the months that followed, the Allies staggered from one military crisis to another as German generalship proved superior, and as Russia went out of the war, allowing Germany to bring back her armies of the east to reinforce those on the western front.

Though Pershing had asked Washington to send several million more troops, this gratified the Allies less than it might have done, because the general continued to insist that the additional soldiers be dispatched to his independent command. By 1918 Britain and France recognized that they had exhausted their manpower, and both nations sought fresh troops to throw into their trenches. Pershing's refusal to let them expend American lives moved them to seek his dismissal; but the general had his government's full support.

AN IMMEDIATE QUESTION for decision was the choice of an area in France to be used as a training center. Pershing accepted a French suggestion that the Americans establish themselves in Lorraine in the east, in a relatively quiet area behind the lines. He set up headquarters in Chaumont in the Haute-Marne, not far distant; while in Lorraine, Marshall and other staff officers busied themselves in dealing with billets for the troops and other details.

In the summer of 1917 troop training was conducted by French officers, but by September Pershing had become critical of the emphasis they placed on trench warfare. Marshall insisted on first training the new troops in elementary drill, and Pershing ordered that training in marksmanship be emphasized.

Marshall, promoted to major, found his first six months in France so depressing that they amounted to a Valley Forge. There was the mud, the fog, and the constant effort to make do in the face of scarcity. By winter only about a quarter of a million American troops had arrived, and they were far from ready for combat.

Spring began with a German offensive that threatened to knock France out of the war before the Americans were ready. In the emergency Pershing relented and offered the four divisions he had to the French general Pétain: "All that we have are yours," said Pershing.

Pétain started by moving the First Division to Picardy, opposite the German-held town of Cantigny. There the Americans dug in, as ordered, and defended themselves against German bombardment. It was not Pershing's idea of how to fight a war. He ordered the First to attack and take the town.

As operations officer, Major Marshall did much of the planning for the assault, working out what each soldier in the lead Twenty-eighth Regiment should do. On May 28 the Twenty-eighth Regiment of the American First Division went over the top, charged across no-man's-land, and stormed the town, holding it against seven German counterattacks. It was a victory not merely for Americans but for American military doctrine. Pershing cabled the War Department, "Our troops are the best in Europe and our staffs are the equal of any."

Pétain next took 45,000 soldiers and marines of the Second and Third American Divisions and threw them into Belleau Wood and Château-Thierry to make a last stand in front of Paris to stop Ludendorff's armies. The Americans bore the brunt of the fighting, bayonet to bayonet, and halted the Germans.

The crisis having been managed, the Americans returned to Lorraine to continue building their own army—and from the point of view of the Allies, taking much too much time to do it.

# 15

# THE AEF IS TOO LATE

IN 1918 the Germans launched climactic offensives on the western front that threatened to prove decisive. Though America had declared war in the spring of 1917, she would not have an AEF that could launch its own offensive until the spring of 1919. So Wilson's decision to wage a separate war meant that his armies did not arrive in time. France and Britain, backs to the wall, had to fight the final battles largely on their own.

Perhaps a different administration could have done it more quickly. After the United States declared war, the government wasted time in trial and error. For this, Wilson was blamed by his critics, but the task would have been a daunting one for anyone. Total war, in which whole populations and industrial economies clash, requires a big government, but the United States in 1917 had a small one. World wars require an ability to transport large armies across the globe, and America lacked that as well.

Creating a manpower registration and selective service system for a continentwide country of civilians was challenging enough; with the shipping bottleneck added to it, the task of getting a mass army to the other side of the ocean in time to shift the tide of battle proved to be overwhelming.

Alliance politics contributed to the problem. Only Britain had a large enough merchant navy to transport the millions of American conscripts overseas, but she wanted the Americans sent to Britain's sectors of the battlefield rather than France's. Then, too, there was the haggling over costs: in the end the United States paid Britain $81.75 a head to carry American soldiers to France, and somewhat more than half of the AEF was brought over to Europe in British ships.

A year after the United States entered the war—and a year in the life of a war is an immensely long time—the AEF still was not ready to take the field: only half of the million troops that Pershing needed to create an American army had arrived in France. In the next six months a million and a half more disembarked, but another 2 million army troops were still in America awaiting transport.

Even when soldiers arrived from the United States, their war matériel did not. As late as 1918 the American forces still had to buy most of what they needed from the Allies. Of the AEF's 3,500 artillery pieces, only 500 were made in the USA.

As a learning experience, Pershing planned to launch the first independent American action of the war as a carefully defined operation, with limited objectives, in a sector next to the one in which his troops were assembling and training. He decided to have his army attack a German-occupied wedge of territory in Lorraine called the Saint-Mihiel salient. But the army would not be ready to undertake the operation until the late summer or early autumn of 1918.

Meanwhile the Allied armies soldiered on in the killing fields of France and Flanders, with no more reserves of manpower to provide replacements for their depleted ranks, and with none forthcoming from their American cobelligerents.

WAGING A MODERN WAR posed a challenge that the Wilson administration was not ready to meet. It was not until 1918 that the President had his men and measures in place.

The amount of money needed to pay for such a war was staggering. The entire expense of governing the United States from its foundation in 1789 until the declaration of war against Germany on April 6, 1917, had been $24 billion, and that is less than what World War I was to cost: perhaps $22 billion in 1917 dollars, or more than a million dollars an hour through 1918 only, with more to come. In the 1970s one historian added in the later expenses of the war as well, including veterans' benefits, and came up with a total figure in 1970 dollars of $112 billion.

Taking charge of the economy and of railroad transport, solving labor disputes, building ships and airplanes, and administering prices proved to be formidable tasks. The key officials who emerged were Secretary of the Treasury William McAdoo, who oversaw finances and the railroads; Bernard Baruch, a financier from South Carolina who took effective charge of war industries in 1918; and Herbert Hoover, who administered the output, distribution, and price of food and all that concerned it, while Harry Garfield, president of Williams College, exercised similar powers with regard to fuel.

Their preference was to rely on voluntary means wherever possible, to keep dislocations of the economy to a minimum, and to take the easy way. As a general rule, organized interests were bought off while unorganized ones were disregarded; and costs were passed on to the consumer. As administered by the government, the railroads and other industries benefited from a suspension of the antitrust laws and began to function with the efficiency of monopolies. For socialists and Progressives such as Walter Lippmann, this realized a prewar ideal of a rational economy that eliminated the wasteful duplication inherent in competition, that realized the economies that come with scale, and that was regulated in the public interest. Still, there was always a danger that the administrators would serve private or special interests instead.

To those who believed in the benefits of competition, the growth of a monopolistic warfare state foreshadowed questions that were to arise repeatedly and in different guises throughout the century: whether, in order to crusade for American ideals of government abroad, the country paradoxically was being untrue to its political and economic ideals at home.

Another and immediate criticism leveled against the Wilson administration was that the American economy did not produce the ships and airplanes that were needed in 1917 and 1918; that not until 1919 did American production come into its own. Among the Allies, there were suspicions that this was intentional. It appeared that the American government really was gearing up its economy not to wage war, but to take over markets from others after the fighting was over, before the European countries had a chance to convert their war industries to peacetime uses.

The British newspaper magnate George Riddell, an intimate of David Lloyd George's, told the prime minister in December 1917, "I don't trust the Americans. Naturally they desire to make America the first nation in the world; they will have a huge mercantile fleet, which they have never had before; and they will have opened new markets all over the world, markets which they have been developing while we have been fighting."

Lord Riddell's suspicions were not entirely unfounded. On entering the war the United States embarked on an economic warfare program against Germany with a view not merely to winning the war, but to improving America's competitive position after the war. The American Alien Property Custodian took German ships into service, seized German ownership interests in U.S. industry, and transferred the ownership of German patents to Americans, particularly in the chemical industry, where Germany had been dominant before the war.

The U.S. War Trade Board, established in the autumn of 1917, focused on Latin America, where it succeeded in forcing the sale of German interests to Americans. But the Americans went ahead to supplant British as well as German interests. Britain's exports to Argentina, for example, declined 30 percent between 1914 and 1917, while those from the United States soared 300 percent and came to exceed Britain's.

The Latin American countries accounted for about 25 percent of Britain's investment abroad in 1918, and Britain relied on exploiting her position in the markets of those countries to bring about her economic recovery after the war. But as the British Chamber of Commerce in Argentina pointed out in guarded language in 1918, "The chief danger threatening our rapid and complete post-war recuperation is the extent to which American trade and general penetration may prove to have passed from the transient to the permanent stage."

The only limit to the U.S. export drive appeared to be the lack of American ships in which to carry goods. When America entered the war, the British merchant fleet was 800 percent larger than hers, but as the war ended, that was down to only 250 percent larger. What gave cause for suspicion in London was that the American shipbuilding program was only just getting under way as hostilities in the Great War seemed to be approaching their final phase.


THAT THE CLASH OF IDEALS and interests between the United States and Great Britain did not produce even more harmful consequences than they did was due to the fortuitous friendship of Edward House and Captain Sir William Wiseman, a British intelligence officer, who happened to meet in December 1916. An instant professional intimacy developed between the two men, and soon they were transacting political business together. A few months after the United States entered the war, Wiseman moved into an apartment in the building in which House lived, at 115 East Fifty-third Street in New York City, and the two men coordinated policy, Wiseman acting for the Lloyd George government and House for Wilson.

Wiseman's greatest virtue was his cards-on-the-table candor. He understood the thinking of both governments, and could spot areas of potential accommodation of one to the other. He was also frank in explaining that there were areas in which disagreements could not be resolved, although his policy was to get differences out into the open. He recognized that Wilson's aim was to instill democracy in Germany, while Britain's goal was to reestablish a balance of power in Europe; and he knew that neither could bring the other to a change of mind.

In the course of meetings in Europe in the autumn of 1917, House and Wiseman arranged American participation in a Supreme War Council on an observer basis—which was as far as Wilson was prepared to go at the time, as American differences with the Allies about war goals continued to fester. While waiting for his armies to fully materialize, the President turned his attention to the war of ideologies that in some senses paralleled the war of armed forces.

# 16

## THE BATTLE OF IDEAS

EVER SINCE THE SPRING OF 1917, Woodrow Wilson had held the moral high ground by the terms in which he defined America's quarrel with Kaiser Wilhelm's Germany. In denying that the United States was at war with the German people, and in asserting that the country's purpose was to make the world safe for democracy, the American President portrayed his government as one, unlike others, that pursued no selfish goals.

In doing so, Wilson expressed a worldview quite different from that of the Republican who planned to run for the presidency in the next election. TR argued in the autumn of 1917 that the United States "did not go to war to make democracy safe." According to the former President, ". . . first and foremost we are to make the world safe for ourselves. This is our war, America's war. If we do not win it we shall some day have to reckon with Germany single-handed. Therefore, for our own sake let us strike down Germany."

Whatever its other virtues, this was not the spiritually uplifting message that America wanted to hear in the first flush of enthusiasm for the crusade in Europe. Wilson had taken the measure of his domestic audience, and in 1917's battle of words, he emerged triumphant.

Now, in the winter of 1917–18, during the seemingly endless waiting period while the American armies were getting themselves set to launch their campaign and the United States was contributing, for the most part, only the financing that enabled the Allies to keep on fighting until the AEF was ready, Wilson continued to wage his and America's campaign on the battlefield he found most congenial: that of ideas.

The new and unexpected challenge to which he responded was the Bolsheviks' seizure of power in Russia. In ideological terms it foreshadowed a meeting of armies at the river Elbe nearly three decades later. Lenin called for a revolution in world politics and so did Wilson; in 1917 as in 1945, the question was whether the forces of the American revolution and of the Russian revolution encountered one another as allies or as rivals.

The communist coup was a central event in Wilson's presidency and tested his concept of America's new role in world affairs. Appeals to public opinion were his chosen weapons; and in trying to reach out to the Russian people, Wilson composed and delivered his most famous foreign policy statement: the Fourteen Points.

IN THE RUSSIAN CITY OF PETROGRAD—the former St. Petersburg—the Bolsheviks, an underground communist faction led by Vladimir Ilyich Ulyanov ("Lenin") and a handful of fellow conspirators, seized control of the Russian government on the night of November 7, 1917. One of the reasons they were able to do so was that they had received, and continued to receive, large sums of money from the German government.

Another reason that the Bolsheviks were able to take power—and perhaps the only reason that they had a chance to hold on to it—was that they were the only political party in Russia led by someone who proposed to end the war. War had reduced Russia to chaos; the weary peasant conscripts who were the Russian soldiery were in no mood to go on fighting, and Lenin's appeal was that he, and he alone, offered a way out.

On November 8 the revolutionary regime in Petrograd adopted a "decree on peace," calling on all parties in the European war to make peace without annexations or indemnities: the peace without victory that Wilson had pleaded with the belligerents to accept eleven months before. But in seeking a separate peace, the new leaders of the Russian government were breaching a pledge that their country had given the Allies.

Implicitly defending themselves by denouncing the alliance whose terms they were violating, the Bolsheviks published to the world in the newspaper *Izvestia* the hitherto secret treaties between tsarist Russia and her allies, Britain, France, Japan, and Italy, outlining the rewards they would divide among themselves if they won the war. Whole empires were to be shared between the Allies in Africa, the Middle East, Asia, and the Pacific.

This was the very opposite of the kind of peace settlement President Wilson had led Americans to suppose they were fighting to achieve. Leftist and isolationist critics seemed vindicated in their claim that Wilson had led the country into what was basically an imperialist venture. The President, who had known and worried about the secret treaties for many months, at first denied knowledge of them. He also tried to suppress publication of the treaties in the United States, but failed.

America was not a party to the treaties and therefore was not bound by them. Nonetheless, Wilson feared that he and his administration might be tainted by them. It transpired after they were published that he had no cause for alarm: in 1917–18 the revelations—for whatever reason—did not strike a responsive chord in the United States. Almost nobody in America seemed to care.

The real question, as Wilson and his associates came to see it, was whether the sordidness of the secret treaties would have an effect on public opinion in Europe, especially among liberals, labor unions, and socialists. On the Allied side, these were groups to whom Wilson looked for support in persuading their governments to moderate their war goals; and inside the Central Powers, Germany and Austria-Hungary, these were the groups that Wilson hoped might bring pressure on their governments to make peace. For in appealing to the peoples of the belligerent countries over the heads of their governments, the Bolsheviks were not being original; they were following a path pioneered by Woodrow Wilson.

Much more even than Wilsonians, the Bolsheviks had deluded themselves into believing that the European masses would rise at their call. Events would disappoint them. Nearly three weeks elapsed after they broadcast their call for peace, but the Bolsheviks received no response from the citizens, let alone the governments, of Europe or the Americas. There were no acceptances, no counterproposals, no uprisings, no revolutions. So, to the surprise of the Bolsheviks, the war continued.

This caused an intellectual crisis for the Soviet leaders. Communist ideology called on Lenin to continue pursuing a suicidal policy of focusing on a world revolution that showed no signs of occurring, while taking no part in the imperialist war in which Germany was about to seize his territory and crush his regime. But Lenin chose not to do that; instead he threw his ideological baggage overboard in order to keep the ship afloat. Doing what he had to do if he and his movement were to survive, he sued for an armistice with Germany on November 26. Germany agreed on the following day to armistice negotiations commencing December 2 in Brest Litovsk, an old Polish river town that had belonged to tsarist Russia for more than a century.* The Bolsheviks asked the Allies to attend the conference, too, but they refused; so the Russian delegates had to face the Germans (joined later by Germany's allies) alone. The delegations signed an armistice December 15, leaving the armies in place and providing for peace negotiations to begin a week later.

The Bolsheviks were of divided mind about the negotiations, with only Lenin and his faction prepared to accept peace at any price. To gain a majority on the Bolshevik Central Committee, Lenin had to enter into a temporary alliance with Lev Davidovich Bronstein ("Leon Trotsky"), newly appointed commissar for foreign affairs, who believed (in a sort of caricature of Wilsonianism) that the peace negotiations would be rather like a public trial: the Russians would cross-examine the Germans so effectively that the German case would collapse before the court of world opinion.

So the Brest Litovsk negotiations began. Meanwhile, to encourage the Russians to defy the Germans, as well as to meet the challenge posed by

* It is now in Belarus.

the Bolshevik appeals for peace, Colonel House decided (as did other Americans, independently) that Woodrow Wilson had to respond in public—for Americans, like the Bolsheviks at that time, held an unwavering faith in the power of words and ideas.

EDWARD HOUSE WAS IN EUROPE conferring with the Allies when the events described above occurred. His immediate reaction, seconded from afar by the President, was to seek a common public statement of war goals by the Allies that might strengthen the hand of those in Russia who favored fighting on.

It should be remembered that House and the other Allied leaders knew little of the Bolsheviks or of their situation, other than that it was precarious. Lenin and his associates, though they ruled Petrograd and Moscow, held only one section of what had been the tsarist empire; in the rest of it, rival governments took hold, some of which proposed to march on the capital to overthrow Bolshevism. It was a widely held opinion that communist rule, even in the corner of the former empire where it had been imposed, would prove brief.

There was a question, too—which would be debated for decades to come—of who the Bolsheviks really were. The revolutionary slogans that they chanted convinced some observers that the Bolsheviks were men of the Left: liberals, only more so. If that were the case, it might be possible to persuade them to moderate their views so as to meet those of the Wilson administration. On the other hand, there were those who believed the Bolsheviks were German agents, for they had been financed by Berlin in subverting the pro-Ally government of Russia; others thought they were terrorists who aimed at one extreme or the other, anarchism or dictatorship.

In trying to achieve consensus with the Allies on a statement of war goals that might appeal to Russians of the Left, House was allowing for the possibility that the Bolsheviks could be won over, and if not, that pro-Wilson Russians could be inspired to push Lenin and his colleagues aside. He also had in mind public opinion within the Allied countries themselves. He told their representatives in Europe in December 1917 that a statement was needed "because of the Bolshevik peace proposals and the increasing demand on the part of liberal and labor elements in Allied countries for an assurance that the war was not being continued for imperialistic ends." House agreed with Aristide Briand, a leading figure of the French Left, that such a statement could also help induce the peoples of the Central Powers to urge or even compel their governments to make peace.

Woodrow Wilson cabled his agreement from Washington, urging the Allies to offer terms on the basis that he himself had outlined to Congress on January 22, 1917, in his peace-without-victory speech. "Our people and

Congress will not fight for any selfish aims," he warned, adding that "it would be a fatal mistake to cool the ardor of America." But House could not bring the Allies to agree on the sort of terms that he and Wilson regarded as unselfish.

It seemed clear what House therefore had to propose to the President. Before the United States entered the war, Wilson had focused his foreign policy on obtaining public statements of war goals from the belligerents. In the eight months since America declared war, House from time to time had suggested that the President should issue a statement of liberal war goals of his own. Now in Paris in December 1917, confronted with the challenge thrown down by Russian communism but unable to reach agreement with the Allies on a common response, House fell back on the idea of issuing a statement of American war goals unilaterally; he cabled Wilson, asking him to hold off making any foreign policy pronouncements until the two of them could discuss the matter in person.

Wilson replied by cable: "Sorry impossible to omit foreign affairs from address to Congress."

House left Paris December 6, boarded the USS *Mount Vernon* December 7, and on December 14 cabled Wilson that he would debark the afternoon of December 15. He added that he would catch the 11:08 train from New York to Washington Monday morning, December 17, and would arrive in Washington at 4:40 that afternoon. House and the President conferred from five to seven o'clock. The Wilsons and House dined alone and then went to the theater.

In a diary entry for December 18, House wrote that "an important decision the President and I made was to formulate the war aims of the United States. I never knew a man who did things so casually. We did not discuss this matter more than ten or fifteen minutes. . . ." This was, in the view of the editor of House's papers, the "moral turning point of the war."

House noted that "the President asked me to have Mezes"—the head of the Inquiry team in New York—"give a memorandum of the different questions which a peace conference must necessarily take up for solution. I told him I already had this data in my head. He told me that he also had it, but he would like a more complete and definite statement such, for instance (as) a proper solution of the Balkan question."

House suggested cabling Sir William Wiseman to return from Europe at once; Wiseman could be of help by telling them "the way England would receive what we had to say." Wilson said: "No, we shouldn't consult with anybody or we have to consult everybody."

Returning to New York, House "intimated" to three members of the Inquiry—Sidney Mezes, Walter Lippmann, and attorney David Hunter Miller—that the President planned to make the major speech of his life. He did not tell them at that point what it was to be about, but he did ask them for a memorandum and must have told them that it should deal with international issues that had to be resolved.

Lippmann drafted such a memorandum for the three of them, dated December 22, entitled "The Present Situation, the War Aims, and Peace Terms It Suggests." Much of it would be of little help to the President in his endeavor. It began by analyzing the current military situation of the various countries at war, the challenges faced by them, and their strengths, weaknesses, and goals. It then discussed what America's objectives ought to be, and the assets and liabilities the country brought with it in pursuing them. It suggested themes that the United States might employ in propaganda campaigns. It urged Wilson to formulate a public program of liberal war goals. And, in a concluding section (Part III), it offered a brief list of war goals the President might proclaim.

House took the memorandum with him when he caught the noon train back to Washington December 23 to spend the Christmas holidays; later that day he handed it to the President, who did not read it at the time. Dining at the White House on December 27, the colonel was worried by Wilson's appearance: "I could see some signs of weariness in him and I begged him to take, as nearly as possible, a week's rest before we get at the war aims message. He promised to do the best he could." Wilson asked House to return in eight days, saying that he had to address Congress on the railroad question January 4 "and after that," House wrote in his diary, "we will prepare together his address on war aims which he hopes to deliver to Congress."

WILSON WAS BEING BOMBARDED during the Christmas–New Year holidays with advice about a statement of war goals—although, unknown to its authors, he did not read or heed it. Most of the suggestions he received were alike: William Boyce Thompson, a wealthy American businessman who had become leader of a Red Cross mission to Russia, returned from Petrograd on Christmas morning and (having been denied a personal interview with the President) submitted a memorandum urging him to make a statement of war goals to Congress. Such a statement, he said, would show the Russian people that there was common ground between the aims of the United States and some of those professed by the Bolshevik government.

At about the same time, the American ambassador to Russia dispatched two communications to Wilson asking him to make a public statement of war goals—along the lines of his earlier peace-without-victory address—intended to hearten the Russians and encourage them to hold out against German demands. Edgar Sisson, who represented the American government's Committee on Public Information in Petrograd, wired a similar request January 3: "Re-state anti-imperialistic war aims and democratic peace requisites of America . . ."

Back in New York, House asked the Inquiry to assemble the maps and atlases that would be needed, but the material proved to be so unwieldy that he took an Inquiry professor with him to Washington to carry it. He brought back also a new memorandum from the Lippmann team dated January 2, which deleted Parts I and II and was a revised version of Part III only—the war aims section—of the earlier one. Lippmann believed that it was the President who asked for the cuts and augmentations, unaware that Wilson had not yet read the document.

The new memo was entitled "A Suggested Statement of Peace Terms," which previously had been the heading of Part III. Instead of merely listing proposed peace goals, it discussed each proposed goal in some detail. As it later turned out, the President was not interested in such discussions; all he wanted was a list of the issues he would have to deal with.

In preparing a statement of war goals, one of Wilson's unavowed but evident purposes was to score a victory in his rivalry with Lenin on the one hand and Lloyd George on the other. He wanted to stake out a claim to be the worldwide leader of progressive opinion.

He could not have wanted the British prime minister to believe, however, that he was merely seeking the limelight; and he called in London's ambassador to disclaim any such desire. On January 3 the President met with Cecil Spring-Rice, whom he disliked and almost never saw. Concealing his hope of appealing to opinion abroad, Wilson said he was about to address a statement to the American public. On the face of it, there was no need for such a statement; Wilson conceded that domestic opinion was solid for war and that revelation of the Allied secret treaties had produced no visible effect. But what of the future? Might not continuing Bolshevik calls for unselfish peace terms be heeded eventually? It was to obviate that possibility, Wilson told Spring-Rice, that he must answer the Soviet propagandists by telling the American people what their government's war goals truly were.

The following day Spring-Rice cabled the foreign secretary in London that Wilson planned to outline war goals in a speech designed to quiet the doubts of the American public, and that he had this news on the highest authority. The prime minister may have had this in mind as he pondered what he himself would say in a hastily scheduled speech the next day to a labor union conference. His object was to obtain certain concessions from the workers in furtherance of the war effort; and a liberal statement of peace aims might counter communist influence in their ranks and whip up their enthusiasm for the war.

On January 4 House's train was delayed and he arrived three hours late at the White House, but dinner had been saved for him, and after he had eaten quickly, he went to work with the President until 11:30 p.m. They resumed their labors the next day.

But then there was bad news. Only a couple of days before, House had noted, "I wish to again call attention to the selfishness which seems to lurk in the minds of those in authority. The President is anxious to state his peace terms before Lloyd George and Clemenceau have an opportunity to forestall him." But on January 5, even as Wilson began to work on his speech, Lloyd George delivered his own. The worst of it was that it was a stirring expression of liberalism that offered views nearly identical to the President's. Addressing the labor unions, the British prime minister called for a postwar world in which the shackles of class and empire would be cast off, economic issues would be resolved by international cooperation, and all peoples would be accorded the right of self-determination. Wilson, plunged into gloom, decided to abandon the idea of articulating American war goals. But coaxed by House, he changed his mind. House argued, as did British Foreign Secretary Balfour, that it was desirable for both the prime minister and the President to issue statements so long as the statements were consistent with each other.

The two friends went to work, but we have only House's account of what each of them said, thought, or wrote. Much of what they composed must have come from Wilson's pen, for although he worked a good deal of the time with House, at other times he drafted alone.

Freedom of the seas, nondiscriminatory trade practices, disarmament, fairness in dealing with colonial issues, generosity in dealing with Russia, and open rather than secret diplomacy were goals that were basic to the Wilson-House political philosophy, although none of them were listed in the Inquiry memorandums. The two men decided that these goals should be placed at the beginning of their list of terms, and they devoted their Points 1 through 6 to them. House claimed to have thought of numbering the various war goals.

Disregarding the January 2 memorandum and instead writing in longhand in the margin of Part III of the Inquiry memorandum of December 22, then working on successive drafts that he typed himself, Wilson turned to Points 7 through 13, dealing with the claims and conflicts of other countries. These were not American war goals as such. They merely set forth impartial America's best judgment as to how the most divisive issues in world politics could be resolved in fairness to all. Wilson and House decided, therefore, that in framing *these* points, they would use the word "should" rather than "must."

Point 14—a "must"—provided the climax to Wilson's proposals. It advocated the establishment of a general association of nations after the war to guarantee the independence and territorial integrity of all countries. It remained a vague proposal, but provided a rallying cry for the millions who hoped to see a different and better world emerge from the ashes of the war.

The principal purpose of the Fourteen Points was to reassure the people of Russia that if they decided to fight on, they need not fear that they would be doing so for anybody's imperialist goals. Major subsidiary purposes were to win over the Left in the Central Powers, and to win it back in the Allied countries. Wilson and House must have hoped that if enough public support were forthcoming for their formulation of terms, the governments of the Allies might feel compelled to accept them as an agreed basis on which to offer peace to their enemies.

Sometimes by himself, sometimes with House, the President drafted and redrafted for four days. Then, on January 8, 1918, having asked permission that morning to address a joint session of the Senate and the House of Representatives, he delivered his speech to Congress. The Fourteen Points, though imperfectly understood, were an instant success with peoples abroad, many of whom read their own desires into Wilson's words.

The authors of various memorandums to Wilson took self-awarded pats on the back. At least four American officials in Petrograd flattered themselves that they had inspired the Fourteen Points, and the U.S. ambassador believed that Wilson had quoted his exact phrases. Walter Lippmann bragged that he had "put words into the mouth of the President."

In Lippmann's case, there was some truth to the claim, for his list of eight of the war goals had been used by Wilson as a first draft. But because he was not privy to the drafting process, he did not grasp the President's intentions, which he wrongly assumed to be the same as his own. Outraged by the Allied secret treaties, Lippmann read into the Fourteen Points a disavowal of them, and therefore an implicit pledge to keep the Allies from adding to their empires in Africa, the Middle East, Asia, and the Pacific. As a result, he was to feel betrayed—as did his friend Bullitt in a related connection—by Wilson's stance at the peace conference a year later.

At the time Lippmann merely misunderstood; later, he forgot. His reminiscences of how the Fourteen Points came to be formulated, provided in interviews that were taped decades later, were hopelessly wrong, with dates, places, and persons muddled.* As historians have tended to take his word for it, histories and biographies in use today often provide an inaccurate and often misleading account.

---

* In his taped interviews Lippmann says that publication of the Allied secret treaties "shook the morale of this country" and that House came back from Europe "not later than the middle of November and told Wilson the only way to right the situation was by a statement of American peace terms which would override those secret treaties. Wilson agreed . . ." and House met with Lippmann in midtown Manhattan to tell him that "our organization was assigned the business of drafting that statement."

Later, Lippmann quoted House as having told Wilson: "You're going to have to disentangle the Allied cause from these treaties, and you can only do it by the restatement of the terms of peace. . . ."

But far from returning in November, House was in Europe that month, heading an American mission to Britain and France to confer with Allied leaders (as his records and theirs show) and exchanging

The real intention of House and Wilson in drafting the President's statement was to persuade the peoples of Europe that, contrary to what the Bolsheviks charged, America was fighting the war in order to build a better world.

---

London-Washington and Paris-Washington cables with the White House into the first week in December. His ocean liner took the second week of that month to make the Atlantic crossing. House, who debarked December 15, went immediately to Washington, concluded his business at the White House December 18, and could not have seen Lippmann in New York until December 19.

From the House diaries and the Wilson papers, it is evident that making a public statement of war goals was House's idea and that his notion of what such a statement could accomplish had nothing to do with the secret treaties, which he seems never to have mentioned to the President.

Lippmann's "organization," the Inquiry, was *not* assigned to draft the statement. As a reading of the December memorandum shows, its authors did not know what information the President was asking for or whether his speech would touch on war goals. Its final section begins: "What follows is suggested as a statement of peace terms *in case a general statement of terms at this time is desired*" (emphasis added)—which indicates that Lippmann and his colleagues did not know whether such a statement was wanted or not. The bulk of the memo is a confidential discussion of war strategy, and could not possibly have been intended as the draft of a public speech.

"We spent three weeks on it . . . ," Lippmann recalled repeatedly, and finished it the week before Christmas; but at most, it could have been three days. Wilson decided December 18 to make the statement; the earliest House could have seen Lippmann in New York to ask for a memo was December 19; and the memo was submitted to House December 22.

Modestly, Lippmann said that he had not done it all: "Isaiah Bowman played a big part. . . ." But Bowman did not come into the Inquiry's work until later. (Lippmann's memory betrayed him on many of these things; later he described how he and Admiral Grayson were at Willard Straight's side in Paris when Straight died—at a time when Grayson, far from Paris, was attending Wilson in America.)

Lippmann claimed that "it was we"—he, Mezes, and Miller, the authors of the two memos—"who invented the form of doing it in points." This became central to his memory of the whole affair, because he claimed that they had summarized the provisions of the secret treaties point by point, and then had given America's answer to each in the same numerical order. So the fact that he had numbered the peace goals supported his claim that what he was doing was restating war goals of the Allies, as shown in the secret treaties, while cutting out their "poison." "It was all keyed upon the secret treaties," he claimed. "I've never seen an adequate discussion of the Fourteen Points, because the Fourteen Points are exactly fitted to the secret treaties."

But a look at the two Lippmann memos disposes of that claim: the goals are *not* numbered. And we have House's notes, written at the time, telling us that it was he and Wilson, working alone and without anyone else present, who hit on the idea of numbering the points.

In the Lippmann papers at Yale are two copies of the beginning of a memo, one in longhand, one typewritten. The fragment is undated, and has been misidentified as part of the January 2, 1918, memo, to which it bears no resemblance. As no copy of it has been found in the Wilson or House papers, it is unlikely that it was submitted to the President—the more so as neither Wilson nor House made any known reference to it. It is merely the start of what looks as though it would have been a lengthy document, and it is possible that Lippmann never got around to writing it.

The introductory paragraphs indicate that this will be a discussion of how the great powers will be forced by their peoples to openly disclose their war goals, and how, in the process of doing so, they will feel obliged to change those goals to bring them more in line with what the common people want —and would be prepared to continue fighting for. Lippmann begins his discussion of the goals of the powers with Great Britain. The document stops after the first paragraph. But it is suggestive that Lippmann has numbered Great Britain "1."

Could this be the memo, either written or projected, in which Lippmann summarized and numbered the terms of the Allied secret treaties—and which he confused with the one Wilson used?

# 17

# WILSON VERSUS LENIN

ONE OF THE YOUNG MEN whose suggested phrases did find their way into Wilson's rhetoric was Lippmann's friend William Bullitt, who from his office in the State Department communicated directly with House. Bullitt followed the press in the enemy countries with great care. His notion, which seems to have been accepted by House and Wilson, was that the President should criticize the German and Austro-Hungarian governments in the same words and on the same grounds as did their domestic labor, liberal, and socialist opponents. With Wilson, House, Lippmann, and Trotsky, Bullitt shared a belief in the power of public opinion; and like them, he underestimated the extent to which nationalism, and solidarity in the face of a wartime enemy, would keep even opposition groups within the Central Powers loyal to their governments.

To Bullitt, the weeks following the Fourteen Points address seemed ripe for an American peace offensive. In Germany the new chancellor, conservative and almost blind seventy-four-year-old Count Georg von Hertling, and his foreign secretary, Richard von Kuhlmann, looked to be making at least some attempt to fight free of military control. In Austria-Hungary, which was crippled by strikes and food shortages, the new emperor, Charles I, and his foreign minister, Count Ottokar Czernin, had come to believe that the Hapsburg empire could not survive another year of war. Only later would it be learned that Hertling and Kuhlmann differed from Germany's military leaders more about methods than about objectives. As for Charles and Czernin, though they wanted peace, they did not intend to make a separate peace: they would go on fighting as long as Germany did.

In public statements responding to Wilson's Fourteen Points speech, Hertling and Czernin seemed to accept some of Wilson's proposals, each man, though, in different measure. In memorandums January 29 and February 3, Bullitt supplied House with a detailed and careful analysis of their statements. Like the German generals, Hertling (as Bullitt saw it) wanted to gamble that another offensive would win the war. But the chancellor recognized that the German public was unwilling to do that. So Hertling (in Bullitt's view) was only pretending to enter into a public dialogue with Wilson, and he was pretending in order to buy time. He was going through the motions of talking peace in order to keep the German people quiet until the generals could launch their attack.

Bullitt urged the President to follow up the Fourteen Points address with another, couched in the terms used by German liberals and socialists, and plainly advocating a peace with no annexations or indemnities. In conclusion, Bullitt wrote grandly that "the common people of the world desire to build a new world of international order. Is it too much to hope that the President may now become the leader of the liberals of Germany and Austria-Hungary as he had become the leader of the liberals of France and England?"

In a memorandum dated January 31, Bullitt claimed that the liberals and socialists of the Central Powers would follow Wilson. "They trust him," wrote Bullitt. With a vision close to that of the Bolsheviks (who believed that international class war would replace war between countries), Bullitt sensed that ". . . the air of Berlin and Vienna is quick with the first stirrings of revolution" and that "the war has entered the era in which it is no longer a war of rival states, but a world-wide social and political revolution." He argued that "the President of Germany and Austria are not yet prepared to follow Trotzky [*sic*]. They are prepared to follow the President into a new world of international order and social justice."

Perhaps influenced by Bullitt, Wilson delivered a speech on February 11 appealing to the peoples of Europe over the heads of their governments and outlining four principles on the basis of which peace terms should be drawn. He apparently intended to exploit the political schisms that seemed to have opened up within the enemy countries, but ironically he aggravated instead those that separated the United States from the Allies. Wilson's principles were those of self-determination. He asserted the right of peoples to choose independence for themselves, and made no mention of the precedent established by Abraham Lincoln in denying such a right to the Confederate States of the American South. He pointedly attacked the goal pursued by Britain and France, of reestablishing a balance of power on the continent of Europe. On the other hand, and without intending it, Wilson was enunciating principles similar to those advanced by von Kuhlmann, who had been attempting to negotiate a treaty of peace with Bolshevik Russia at Brest Litovsk.

KUHLMANN'S POLICY, as it now appears, was to fashion a peace treaty with Russia that, in the name of self-determination, would break the country up into manageable pieces. He proposed to recognize the independence of units of the former tsarist empire. Many of the new countries, too weak or vulnerable to stand on their own, would be expected to fall within the German sphere of economic and political influence. Having made these gains in the east, Germany could afford to be generous. She could turn west to offer the type of terms that Wilson and the pope had long advocated: a peace without victory. Germany could withdraw from France and Belgium, return to the frontiers of 1914, and emerge from the war, on the basis of her winnings in the east, as the preponderant power in Europe. She would also have been successful in overthrowing the prewar balance of power, in which she had been "balanced" by the alliance of the Russian empire with France—for now there would be no more Russian empire.

But Kuhlmann was frustrated by Trotsky, whose delegation made speeches and played to the galleries of world public opinion instead of negotiating seriously. When no significant progress had been made after three weeks of peace talks, the German generals pushed Kuhlmann aside and presented their own harsh terms. The Bolsheviks did not respond, so Germany signed a separate peace with a Ukrainian delegation, making Ukraine an independent country. Trotsky refused either to make peace on Germany's new terms or to make war. Calling Trotsky's bluff, the Germans resumed fighting. The Bolsheviks hastily asked to resume peace talks. The Germans issued an ultimatum offering a five-day session in which to sign on Germany's terms.

Trotsky, seeing his mistake, came over to Lenin's view that Russia should accept whatever terms she could get. On March 3 the Bolshevik government agreed to what the Germans proposed, surrendering claim to Ukraine and a stretch of territory from Poland through the Baltic states to Finland, and the treaty was ratified March 15.

In Germany, the Treaty of Brest Litovsk (as Bullitt reported to House) won the enthusiastic support of all parties except the one on the extreme Left. Bullitt had overestimated the ability of civilian leaders like Kuhlmann to break away from the control of Ludendorff and the military; and he had underestimated the nationalism of the German masses. On March 6 Bullitt wrote a memorandum to Frank Polk (his superior at State) and to House (for the President) saying that "Germany to-day is more unified in support of the policy of the Government than at any time since the first months of the war." For Wilson to issue further appeals to the German people for a peace without annexations would only unite the people further behind their leaders, said Bullitt; annexations tend to be popular with those doing the annexing, as Bullitt now seemed to see. He advised his leaders that "for the present, therefore, we had better fight and say nothing."

Good advice, perhaps, but in March 1918 the AEF was still about a half-year away from being ready to launch its first campaign, the proposed drive on the Saint-Mihiel salient. Wilson had been waging a war of ideas in default of being able to wage a war of any other kind.

According to a recent biographer of the President, "Wilson was pro-

foundly and bitterly disappointed" by the Brest Litovsk terms, which he
saw as "condemning the Russians to total military and economic subordi-
nation." As had been the case with the U-boat campaign that brought
America into the war, Wilson had expected better of the Germans. Losing
his illusions about Germany, Wilson now allowed himself none about the
Allies; he recognized that given the chance, Britain and France would impose terms equally harsh on a defeated Germany. "From this time on,"
concludes Wilson's biographer, "Wilson knew that his chances were slim"
of bringing the war to a close on the basis of America's vision of a better
world.

The President was losing faith in his ability to carry out his mission,
and somehow was losing his touch. It was to be a cruel spring for him. In
the second quarter of 1918, his failures came home to the American public.
When the German armies, freed by Brest Litovsk and brought back from
the Russian front, overwhelmed the Allies in fresh offensives, they dramatized the failings of the United States a year after declaring war: the troops
who had not yet arrived in Europe, the ships and airplanes and guns that
had not yet been produced, the AEF not yet formed and therefore not yet
ready to launch its first attack at Saint-Mihiel.

To Wilson's young followers, men like Bullitt and Lippmann, it was
also painfully evident that in the ideological contests they and the President
regarded as so important, America needed to do better.


THE BOLSHEVIK COUP D'ÉTAT in Petrograd in November 1917,
followed by the peace of Brest Litovsk in March 1918, had put the Russian
government in the hands of men who were Woodrow Wilson's ideological
rivals, for they claimed that Wilson was a representative of the system that
brings about wars and that only *their* system, not his, could bring into being
a new world in which there would be no more wars. So in 1918 Wilson
found that his war of ideas had become a two-front war. As against the
nationalism and ambition of the European powers, he had to continue to
oppose his generous vision of a peaceful world in which there was justice
for all; and as against the competing generous vision in which the Bolsheviks
claimed to believe, he had to show that his was the real thing and theirs
was the fraud.

To the extent that he was helpful to Wilson in formulating the Fourteen Points, Walter Lippmann had been an effective clarifier of Wilson's
vision. By an odd coincidence, it was a college classmate of Lippmann's who
became one of the most effective propagandists for the competing vision.
John Reed, who always had opposed America's entrance into the war, had
gone to Russia with his wife, Louise Bryant, in the summer of 1917 to

observe and report; while there, he became a witness of the unlikely events that delivered a great country into the hands of what had been an underground fringe of the revolutionary Left.

Seen through Reed's romantic eyes, the rise of the Bolsheviks was a stirring drama that promised one day to bring history to a happy end. He was careless of facts, but claimed that as an artist, he aimed at the essential truth. When the illustrator of his works objected, "But it didn't happen that way!" Reed replied, "What the hell difference does it make?"—and went on to show that the illustrator's drawings were inaccurate, too, in the literal sense, even though designed to convey a truthful overall impression. Whether the impression it conveyed was truthful or not, Reed's eyewitness account, *Ten Days That Shook the World* (1919), was to give readers a sense of immediacy—of having been there and lived those days themselves. It was through this account, rather than any book written by Russian Bolsheviks themselves, that much of the world eventually came to learn of the events of November 1917.

To Walter Lippmann, who persuaded Colonel House and Secretary of War Baker of it, Reed seemed the right person to help convince the new Russian leaders that Wilson was sincere in seeking an unselfish peace, a peace with no gains for any of the belligerents, a peace such as the Bolsheviks claimed to espouse themselves. But Reed, when asked, would not undertake the mission; he looked beyond world war to world revolution.

Bringing the notes for his book with him, Reed returned to the United States a month after the signing of the Treaty of Brest Litovsk. Government agents searched his luggage when his boat docked and confiscated the notes as revolutionary propaganda. A friend suggested asking Lippmann to help get the notes back, but the classmates had quarreled years before about who was the more serious and dedicated radical,* and Reed said, "I wouldn't ask Walter L for anything for the whole world." For help, Reed turned instead to Bullitt, who tried but failed.

On May 20 Bullitt wrote to the President through House that Reed had been back for a few weeks, that he had "served for a time as Director of Revolutionary Propaganda for the Bolsheviki," and that he had written a memorandum for Bullitt, which was enclosed. Page 14 of the memo, Bullitt claimed, contained policy recommendations that, though coming from Reed, might as well have come from Lenin and Trotsky, who would have made the same proposals themselves. A copy of Bullitt's covering memo has been found in the Wilson papers, but the attached memorandum from Reed is missing.

---

* See pages 89–90.

FEW ASPECTS of Wilson's war leadership were more difficult for his admirers to explain than his attempts to stifle dissent, especially from the Left, and to manage domestic public opinion. When the United States entered the war, Wilson appointed a controversial journalist, George Creel, to head the Committee on Public Information. And from then on, to civil libertarians, it was downhill all the way.

Creel's mandate was to tell the truth about the war to the American public, an endeavor he described as "the world's greatest adventure in advertising." Creel went ahead with vigor to censor newspapers, magazines, and films; to ban books; and to disseminate the administration's message in all media.

Using executive orders or powers granted by such legislation as the Espionage Act, the Trading with the Enemy Act, and the Sedition Act, the Wilson administration drove publications of which it did not approve out of business, while prosecuting dissenters personally and sending them to jail. The postmaster general, the attorney general, and other officials of the administration would resort to such means as denying the right to use the post office. Socialist Eugene Debs, who had received almost a million votes in running for president in 1912, was sentenced to ten years in prison, while antiwar labor leader William Haywood was sentenced to twenty.

Wilson was fiercely loyal to those in his administration who suppressed dissent, and especially to Creel, who painted the President's war leadership in a glowing light. Less partisan observers were appalled. Allen Dulles, the knowledgeable young State Department official who kept watch on central European affairs from his office at the U.S. legation in Bern, Switzerland, wrote on April 29, 1918, that "we have fallen down in our year's war effort. Creel sends over daily long bombastic telegrams of the marvels which we are accomplishing, which are regularly consigned to the waste basket."

Walter Lippmann, who deplored the crudeness of Creel's efforts, was delighted in the spring of 1918 to be asked to join a small group that would run an independent propaganda effort abroad on behalf of the army. With his keen interest in public opinion, propaganda, and the war of ideas, Lippmann was sure that he could do right everything that Creel was doing wrong. Moreover, the job opportunity came at just the right time; rivalries within the directorate of the Inquiry had grown intense, personal relationships were strained, and Lippmann was on what seemed to be the losing side of a power play in which Isaiah Bowman eventually would take over de facto leadership from Sidney Mezes. It was time to leave, so Lippmann gratefully accepted the new assignment.

Lippmann received a commission as a captain in army intelligence, and embarked for Europe in July in that capacity as well as in the role of House's liaison with the British counterpart of the Inquiry. His mission was not a success. His cabled reports to Washington criticized Creel's propaganda and urged that Wilson's liberalism be emphasized in appealing to European opinion. Wilson took the criticism personally. "I am very jealous in the matter of propaganda," he told Lansing, and "want to keep the matter of publicity in my own hands." He associated Lippmann with *The New Republic*'s denunciation of the administration's attacks on civil liberties. "I am very much puzzled as to who sent Lippmann over to inquire into matters of propaganda," Wilson remarked to House. "I have found his judgment most unsound. . . . [H]e, in common with the men of *The New Republic*, has ideas about the war and its purposes which are highly unorthodox from my own point of view."

Wilson did not say how his own view of the war's purposes differed from Lippmann's. But he did order Lippmann and his unit to be put under Creel's command. Although Creel had demanded Lippmann's recall from Europe, he acquiesced in new dispositions: Lippmann was sent to France at summer's end, with offices at AEF headquarters in Chaumont, to write propaganda leaflets to be dropped behind enemy lines.

For the great news—more than a year after entering the war—was that the AEF at last was ready to mount its first campaign.

# 18

## How to Fight the War

EVEN BEFORE THE AEF finally took the field, it had become clear that General Pershing was right: the United States wanted to fight the war under its own officers—not only because America had her own goals, but also because Americans had their own ideas about how the war ought to be fought. In American eyes Allied military leadership was mired in defensive thinking. The United States believed instead in carrying the war to the enemy.

As soon as America entered the war, President Wilson learned the seriousness of the threat that German submarines might cut off the British Isles from all supplies. Using a convoy system to increase the defensive power of Allied ships was an innovative approach pushed by British prime minister David Lloyd George and approved by the Americans. The President's instinct was not to stop there, but to hunt the U-boats down and destroy them. Wilson's idea, which was carried into effect, was to build vessels with sound equipment to locate the U-boats, and to use those vessels to chase and kill subs.

Assistant Secretary of the Navy Franklin Roosevelt championed another valuable approach to ending the U-boat menace. He urged stringing a mine barrage across the mouth of the North Sea bay from which German submarines put out to sea—effectively fencing them in. There was some substance to his view that only bureaucratic foot-dragging kept the Roosevelt program from becoming effective before the war's end.

Robert Lovett, who had dropped out of Yale in his junior year to serve as an aviator, discovered another successful way to go after the U-boats. Lovett, who had trained with the air arm of the British navy, found that at any given time about 85 percent of Germany's submarine fleet was in dock. Rather than searching the oceans for them, therefore, Lovett urged attacking and destroying them at their bases. He developed the aerial tactics to carry out such bombing attacks, and led death-defying raids that won him promotions and the Navy Cross. Risks were run with eyes open; his friend Kenneth MacLeish, Archibald's younger brother, lost his life in one of the sorties after refusing a promotion that would have taken him out of combat.

Another American who became fascinated by aviation was William

Mitchell, a Signal Corps officer in his late thirties. Billy Mitchell, like his friend Douglas MacArthur, was from a politically prominent Wisconsin family; MacArthur's grandfather was a judge, Mitchell's father a U.S. senator. Mitchell had enlisted in the army at eighteen to serve in the Spanish-American War, and when he came back to Milwaukee a hero at the age of twenty, had invited MacArthur to his parties. Like MacArthur, Mitchell had been appointed to the small Army General Staff in Washington in 1913. In April 1917 he was sent to Paris in advance of Pershing, Marshall, MacArthur, Patton, and the others, and served as the senior U.S. officer in France until Pershing arrived. In Europe he became intrigued by military aviation—his only avenue, as a Signal Corps officer, to combat service. He took flying lessons from the Allies.

"The only interest and romance in this war," he decided, was "in the air." He studied and then created aerial tactics for fighters and bombers. He suggested dropping troops by parachute behind enemy lines: paratroops were his idea.

Mitchell found a great deal being done wrong (to his way of thinking) in the air war, and pioneered ways of doing things right. He complained of the wastefulness of maintaining separate army and navy air arms. He discovered that none of the American military aircraft were fit for combat. To prepare for the first AEF campaign, the long-planned assault on the Saint-Mihiel salient, Mitchell begged and borrowed military aircraft from Britain, France, and Italy to ensure the air superiority that he believed would be essential.

CAPTAIN GEORGE S. PATTON, JR., was another American career soldier who, in Europe during the First World War, found the weapon in which he came to believe. In a sense he went looking for it, for he was someone in quest of a cause. Though he was from a socially prominent, wealthy, cultured, and loving family, he was awkward in personal relations, and crude in expressing himself to or about women. Incapable of friendship, he made toughness his cult. Biographers have blamed it on the undiagnosed dyslexia that afflicted him—all the more frustrating and humiliating for being inexplicable.

America's entry into the war found Patton serving as acting aide to General Pershing. Escorted by George Marshall to the ferry at the pier on Governors Island, New York, he embarked with Pershing and the rest of the staff at the end of May 1917 on the voyage that would take him with Pershing to London, to Paris, and then to headquarters in Chaumont. Thirty-two years old, trim, and more than six feet tall, the fiercely ambitious cavalry officer who was the best swordsman in the U.S. Army would have been an ornament to any general's staff. But his ambitions were for combat ("a fire-eater . . . longs for the fray," noted Field Marshal Douglas Haig, the British commander, in his diary); and because Pershing was engaged to marry his sister, Patton naturally looked about for a situation independent of the general's headquarters. As commander of the increasingly large headquarters company at Chaumont, Patton could have counted on promotion, but he wrote that he was "darned sick of my job."

Thought was being given by the American army to the use of tanks: the newly developed Allied armored vehicles that were designed to cut a path across trenches or through barbed wire. Patton, though contemplating the offer of an infantry command, also put in an application to be considered for a tank command. The new vehicle had been imagined by Winston Churchill, then Britain's First Lord of the Admiralty, in September 1914. It also had been thought of by a British army officer, Colonel Ernest Swinton, whose design proved workable when that of Churchill's admiralty did not. But despite championship by Churchill as well as by Sir Maurice Hankey of the British cabinet's secretariat, little had been done to prove the worth of the new weapon, the heavy tank—or of the light tank that the French army had developed on its own.

To confuse German spies, the designs for the new weapon had indicated that it was a sort of tractor intended to carry large quantities of water to troops on the battlefield. Using a term suggested by Colonel Swinton, it was labeled as a water "tank."

The American army decided to take a chance on the new machine. On November 6, 1917, Patton wrote to his father that "I believe that with my usual luck I have again fallen on my feet. It is so apparently a thing of destiny that I thought I would discribe [sic] it." He had been promoted to major and asked to start and head a tank school, to be located in eastern France at Langres, a fortified town of the Middle Ages. "Here is the sporting side of it. There will be a hundred Majors of infantry but only one of Light T. The T are only used in attacks, so all the rest of the time you are comfortable. Of course there is about a fifty percent chance that they wont [sic] work at all but if they do they will work like hell."

To his wife, Patton wrote (November 9, 1917), "What do you think of me. I am detailed in charge of the School for Light Tanks. To begin with I will have to go to the French Tank school for two weeks then to the Factory for a week then start the school. . . . The proposition is this. I am doing no good here, that is to my self. . . . By starting the Tank School I am sure of getting command of the 1st Battalion of tanks. . . . The gamble is this. The light tank is a new invention and may not work at all. If it does not I . . . would only have lost my time. . . . I did not mention the tanks much before as I feared it might not come out but if it works I have pulled one of the biggest coups of my life so far."

Although officers of higher rank were placed over him, Patton became the first American expert on tanks: how to build them, how to drive them, how to use them on the battlefield. At the end of 1917 he wrote his wife that "the Tanks were I truly believe a great opportunity for me. I ought to be one of the high ranking men one of the two or three at the top. I am fitted for it as I have imagination and daring and exceptional mechanical knowledge. I believe Tanks will be much more important than aviation and the man on the ground floor will reap the benefit."

But no tanks were forthcoming; the attempt to produce them in the United States was proving to be a failure. At the beginning of 1918 he wrote to his wife that "I am feeling very low over the Tanks again to day. Every thing seems to be getting in the way and no one can tell when we will ever get any tanks. I am disgusted with the whole business." The next day he wrote again that "unless I get some Tanks soon I will go crazy. . . ."

Though promoted to lieutenant colonel, Patton worried that the war, even if it lasted a few years more, might be over before the tanks arrived. General Pershing made a start at solving the problem by borrowing twenty-five tanks from the French army for Patton. As months went by, arrangements were made to borrow more from the Allies.

On August 20, 1918, Patton was told of the attack on the Saint-Mihiel salient scheduled for September. It was to be the AEF's first campaign. Patton was to have a tank command, leading his own men and a tank battalion loaned by the French army. The equipment was French and some of the troops were French, but the leadership was American, and the belief that the new weapon could change the hopeless pattern of trench warfare was held firmly by Patton.

THE AMERICANS BROUGHT to the war an enthusiasm for new weapons and for new tactics. Woodrow Wilson, Franklin Roosevelt, Robert Lovett, Billy Mitchell, and George Patton could hardly have been more different from one another as human beings, but in this they all were typically American.

Another trait that Americans brought from their egalitarian democracy into their conduct of warfare was a belief in leading by example. Generals, in this view, should share the hardships and the dangers with their men. No officer demonstrated this style of leadership better than Douglas MacArthur.

MacArthur, who was to play so conspicuous a role in the first American campaign in Europe, had been involved in the AEF's affairs since its inception. As a major in the regular army serving as an aide to the secretary of war, it was he who had solved the politically treacherous question of which state's National Guard unit should be the first sent overseas. He proposed combining the excess of guard units from twenty-six states into one division "that will stretch over the whole country like a rainbow." Having inspired its creation and its name, he went on to serve with it gloriously. Promoted to colonel, MacArthur became chief of staff of the Forty-second Division— the Rainbow Division—and landed with it at the French port of Saint-Nazaire in November 1917.

The division encamped for training in the designated areas, where French instructors schooled it in the new and foreign techniques of trench warfare. "Though it is to be borne in mind that our methods are to be distinctly our own," MacArthur told his troops in advance of the arrival of the French instructors, "it would be manifestly unwise not to be guided by their long practical and recent experience in actual trench warfare."

In February 1918 the Forty-second was ordered to Lunéville, a lovely town in southern Lorraine where, a century and a half before, Voltaire had produced plays for the court of exiled King Stanislas of Poland. The division trained there behind the French army, which held the front line. The Americans were distributed along a sixteen-mile expanse of plain between the Moselle plateau and the Vosges Mountains, stretching from Lunéville, with its Versailles-like château, to Baccarat, famous for it crystal. With its peaceful landscape of crops and livestock, it was a countryside whose appearances, as well as its associations of courts and crystal, were eerily at odds with the mass slaughter of armies that was taking place only miles away.

At the end of February, MacArthur became one of the few U.S. officers allowed by the French to accompany them on raids. Not content to merely observe, he plunged into the combat (of which he said, "the fight was savage and merciless"). He returned with prisoners. He was decorated with the Croix de Guerre, the first soldier in the AEF to be so honored; the United States awarded him a Silver Star, and his commanding officer told correspondents that "Colonel MacArthur is one of the ablest officers in the United States Army and also one of the most popular."

Eventually the Americans were allowed to plan and execute raids on their own. MacArthur devised a brilliant costume for himself in which to lead such raids. It was a dandy's outfit: a bright turtleneck sweater, a scarf around the neck and tossed casually over the shoulder, a riding crop, shining leather leggings, and a cap reconstructed by him to look especially dashing. He was, to say the least, noticed.

It was a costume that went with the battlefield role that he created for himself, one that he was to play in one campaign after another. Apparently relaxed and indifferent to danger, he would stroll into enemy fire with nothing but a riding crop in hand. Such displays of reckless courage always caused him nausea; if after his return from the battlefield he fell prey to shaking and vomiting, there was no one to see it. To his men he seemed simply to be without fear. He ensured that his troops took precautions, but took none himself. He refused a helmet and a pistol in an assault on enemy lines March 9. He would not wear a gas mask March 11—and was gassed, receiving a Purple Heart. He made his subordinates do the division's paperwork so that he could be free to fight.

At the end of March, MacArthur's opportunities to fight were enlarged. Freed by Russia's submission to the Treaty of Brest Litovsk, Germany's army, reinforced by troops brought back from the east and now outnumbering the Allies, punched a hole through northern France that French troops from Baccarat were rushed off to fill. So the Rainbow Division found itself holding the Baccarat front on its own for three months, and stepped up its raids; there were ninety in the first two weeks of June alone.

According to one American officer, "Raids became almost as popular as going for the mail to a country post office. Everybody must have part in one. . . ." Father Duffy, the division's senior chaplain, said that "some older heads" thought MacArthur had no business going on these raids himself. Certainly MacArthur's style of leadership from the front was foreign to the European war. A popular historian was later to write that "in earlier wars, and in the Second World War, generals, even marshals, also ran risks and died in action. In the First World War they led comfortable lives. [Other than Lord Kitchener, who drowned, no] . . . outstanding military figure on either side . . . came to a violent end."

Admirers argued that boldness such as MacArthur's was an inspiration to the troops. Major William J. Donovan, a National Guard officer of the Rainbow Division, claimed that "it would be a blamed good thing for the army if some General got himself shot in the front line." Donovan, a New York lawyer who had been a classmate of Franklin Roosevelt's at Columbia Law School, was the only officer in the division to win more medals in the war than MacArthur, and was awarded the highest of all, the Congressional Medal of Honor.

In retrospect it seems especially odd that MacArthur's mother continued to pull strings on his behalf at this period in his career even though he was so noticeably winning life's prizes on his own. Her stream of cables, letters, and pleas for promotion of her boy to brigadier general appear to have been a particular trial to General Pershing. Pershing's staff was already irritated by MacArthur's self-promotion; after MacArthur escorted Secretary Baker on a battlefield tour, the secretary—presumably briefed by his guide—called MacArthur the AEF's "greatest fighting front-line" officer. At headquarters at Chaumont, where George Marshall served, MacArthur was known simply as "the show-off."

In turn MacArthur was convinced that those on the staff at Chaumont—the "Pershing faction"—were conspiring against him. If so, they were meeting with little success. At the end of June the American press reported that he had been promoted to brigadier general; and *The New York Times* reprinted a release from the secretary of war saying that Mac-

Arthur "is by many of his seniors considered the most brilliant young officer in the army."

That was the summer the Americans allowed themselves to be pulled away from their own front to help the French stave off Ludendorff's march on Paris: the summer of Belleau Wood and Château-Thierry. Near Châlons-sur-Marne, MacArthur earned another Silver Star and high praise from his commander: "MacArthur is the bloodiest fighting man in this army."

In a battle to storm German-held heights near Châlons, joined early July 28, MacArthur again distinguished himself. It was a seesaw struggle in which a town below the heights changed hands seven times July 28, and four more times July 29. MacArthur won his third Silver Star July 29, and was promoted to command of a brigade. The battle continued, and he went on to gain a Distinguished Service Medal. Later the brigade's staff were to give him a gold cigarette box inscribed "The bravest of the brave."

At 3:30 a.m. on August 2, MacArthur, accompanied by only one aide, set out through no-man's-land to scout out German forces remaining on the heights. He found only corpses—about 2,000 of them. Returning to his own lines, he reported that the Germans had withdrawn. Not having been to bed for ninety-six hours, he then fell asleep. He was awarded his fourth Silver Star.

As soon as MacArthur awakened on August 2, he led his forces forward four miles—an enormous advance in war in which territory had been changing hands by the inch. From the field, MacArthur reported to headquarters in his usual style: "Have personally assumed command of the line. Have broken the enemy's resistance on the right. Immediately threw forward my left and broke his front. Am advancing my whole line with utmost speed."

Having been in combat for nine days, MacArthur's brigade was then relieved. MacArthur received his second Croix de Guerre and was named to the Legion of Honor. On August 3 *The New York Times* reported that MacArthur had been ordered back to the United States to train troops—a plot by Pershing, MacArthur of course suspected, that was thwarted when the commanding officer of the Rainbow Division protested that MacArthur could not be spared. So MacArthur returned with the rest of the troops to the staging area in Lorraine from which the first American offensive of the war—the long-awaited assault on the Saint-Mihiel salient—was to be launched in early September.

# 19

# THE AEF MAKES ITS MOVE

FOR FOUR YEARS the Germans had held the Saint-Mihiel salient, a sort of dagger some sixteen miles in depth and 200 square miles in area that plunged into French territory below Verdun. Ever since Pershing's arrival in France, it had been understood that destroying the salient was to be the AEF's first undertaking. Pershing scheduled the attack for summer's end in 1918. Yet when the moment arrived, doubts arose.

The French High Command had come to believe that the salient no longer was of primary importance. The locus of combat had shifted farther north, and there was a possibility that the Germans would withdraw from the salient in any event to shorten their line.

Within American ranks there were doubts as well. It was not just that the Americans were still obliged to use Allied tanks, airplanes, artillery, and other military equipment rather than weapons of their own manufacture. It also was because the troops were not yet ready. In their emergency service alongside the French during the summer, the Americans had suffered heavy losses of trained soldiers, whose places had been filled with relatively raw recruits. The fearless and much-decorated "Wild Bill" Donovan was one of those who worried that the Rainbow Division was not yet prepared to mount the planned operation; in his battalion 65 percent of the men and 75 percent of the officers were untried, untrained new replacements.

Douglas MacArthur, who spent weeks trying to whip new recruits into shape, was appalled to discover how little they had been taught in the United States before being shipped over. At one point he saw about a hundred troops out of formation, gathered about a sergeant, and was about to issue a reprimand when the sergeant explained: "Sir, I am teaching them how to load rifles." MacArthur backed off quickly. "When an army is in the fix we are," he said to the sergeant, "the knowledge of how to load and fire a rifle is rather basic."

AT 1 A.M. THE NIGHT of September 11–12, the AEF artillery suddenly opened fire on the Saint-Mihiel salient. Its almost 3,000 guns fired more than a million shells during the next four hours. It was the most intense concentration of artillery fire in history, according to the War Department, but was not highly effective. The outnumbered German defenders promptly began a withdrawal they may have planned in advance.

At 5 a.m., almost 600,000 strong, the American First Army moved forward. This, at last, was its battlefield debut, yet it advanced uncertainly. "Get forward, then!" shouted Donovan at the New York Irish recruits of his battalion. "What the hell do you think this is, a wake?"

The American troops advanced under an umbrella such as had never been seen before. Overhead, under the command of Billy Mitchell, flew the largest air armada ever assembled: almost 1,500 airplanes. Mitchell took instant control of the skies from the outnumbered Germans who, within a short time, were down to 243 aircraft.

Leading his Eighty-fourth Infantry brigade in the assault on the German fortification, Douglas MacArthur was the first man over the top at 5 a.m. He and his troops quickly overran the positions as the Germans fled.

At 6:30 a.m., from a command post on a hill, George Patton sighted a couple of his tanks that had bogged down, and walked forward two miles to get them dug out. He continued onward, and at 7:30 reported that sixteen tanks were actively engaged. At 8:30 he learned that five tanks were out of action. At 9:15 a runner brought word that some of the French tanks were being held up by terrain, so Patton went forward under fire to consult with the French commander dealing with the problem. Going farther past infantrymen seeking cover in shell holes, and nonchalantly smoking a pipe despite the deadly fire, Patton saw MacArthur standing on a small hill. He went over to join him.

The two officers chatted together as the Germans fired upon them. It was a comedy of demonstrated courage, as each tried to appear the more oblivious of danger. A creeping barrage of enemy fire moved steadily toward them. "I think each one wanted to leave," Patton wrote, "but each hated to say so, so we let it come over us. We stood and talked but neither was much interested in what the other said as we could not get our minds off the shells." MacArthur told the story differently. He claimed that at one point Patton, at the sound of fire, involuntarily flinched, and then immediately looked annoyed at himself, whereupon he (MacArthur) had remarked, "Don't worry, Major, you never hear the one that gets you."

MacArthur won his fifth Silver Star in the Saint-Mihiel assault, but essentially it proved to be only a matter of moving forward as the Germans moved out. In forty-eight hours, the salient disappeared. One hundred seventy-four American and French tanks had been engaged, of which 135 emerged intact; but Patton reported with chagrin that the weak German resistance had deprived him of a chance to prove the effectiveness of tank warfare.

For a year and a half, Pershing and his colleagues had worked away at

creating the American First Army. For months they had counted on bringing it into action and demonstrating what it could do in the assault on
Saint-Mihiel. But when the assault was launched, it proved to be an
anticlimax. After all of that planning and training and worrying and hoping,
when the Americans pushed, it proved to be against an open door.

WITHIN DAYS OF THE SUCCESS at Saint-Mihiel, the American
First Army, on short notice, was shifted sixty miles northwest to fight alongside the Allied armies in a new offensive. The Americans were assigned a
zone between the Meuse and Aisne rivers in the Meuse-Argonne offensive,
which was launched September 26, 1918.

In this second operation conducted by the American First Army, AEF
artillery opened fire at 2:30 a.m. and continued the heavy barrage for three
hours. At 5:30 infantry and tanks attacked through a heavy mist. Soon
troops lost touch with their units—and tanks with the infantry they were
meant to support. Tanks got stuck in terrain that proved impassable. Patton
eventually located these tanks and, under fire, directed men with picks and
shovels in digging them out so that they could move. Then, sending the
tanks ahead, Patton rallied about a hundred men in a charge over the crest
of a hill, where machine-gun fire cut them down.

Waving a walking stick, Patton jumped up and charged, followed by
six men. Four were dropped by enemy fire. Only Patton kept going, with
his orderly, Private Joseph Angelo.

"Let's go!" cried Patton.

"We are alone," said Angelo.

"Come on anyway," Patton urged—and then was shot through the leg
and fell. Angelo pulled him into a shell hole and bandaged his wound, but
neither man could move without attracting fire.

They waited for a long time. When finally they sighted AEF tanks,
Patton sent Angelo to tell them where the German guns were, and the
tanks then went after them. Later one of Patton's sergeants found him, and
Patton ordered him back with a message turning over command to his
number two and telling the unit not to send anyone to rescue him because
they would be cut down by enemy fire. When all the German machine-gun
nests had been cleaned out, stretcher-bearers came and carried Patton back
to headquarters. From there he went to a hospital, where he remained for
nearly five weeks.

MacArthur, too, continued to perform heroic feats as the Meuse-
Argonne offensive rolled on. Twice, without wearing a mask as usual, he
was gassed; he received another Purple Heart. In mid-October, after all
attempts had failed to take German-held high ground at the Côte-de-
Châtillon, a position that dominated the open country below, MacArthur

assumed personal command. In rain and mist on an autumn day, he took it. He reported that "officers fell and sergeants leaped to the command. Companies dwindled to platoons and corporals took over. At the end, Major Ross had only 300 men and 6 officers left out of 1,450 men and 25 officers. That is the way the Côte-de-Châtillon fell."

MacArthur was nominated for the Congressional Medal of Honor and promotion to major general, but was awarded neither, which further fueled his feeling that the authorities were unjust. He did receive a second Distinguished Service Cross (with Oak Leaf Cluster), and for action on the Meuse heights, a seventh Silver Star.

For all of the bravery of soldiers like MacArthur and Patton, the AEF campaign was less than successful. The terrain was difficult; the fighting was intense; the progress, slow. By mid-October, two and a half weeks after they commenced their attack, the Americans found themselves only halfway to their immediate objectives.

Hundreds of thousands of Americans—maybe even a million, depending on whose numbers one accepts—took part in the Meuse-Argonne offensive, and most of them were seeing combat for the first time. They still had much to learn. Officers were constantly being replaced, so that those in charge were new to their jobs. Bickering was endemic between regular army and National Guard officers, resulting in high casualties, and in the distintegration under fire of such units as the Thirty-fifth Division, in which among others, Harry Truman served bravely.

# 20

## AN ARMY OF TOURISTS

IN HIS LATER YEARS Harry Truman used to claim that as a young man he had been "afraid of a gun and would rather run than fight." At the age of twenty-one, he had enlisted in the Missouri National Guard nonetheless, believing that a man had to have some experience of soldiering if he were ever to become great—and the young middle western farmer and sometime bank clerk was determined to become great. Twelve years later, in the spring of 1917, he helped organize the National Guard regiment in which he would serve. Essentially it was a regiment of hometown buddies.

"I went to war," he said later, because "all great men had." When the war came, he and his fiancée, Bess Wallace, had been "ready to get married, but since I had to go I didn't think it was right to get married and maybe come home a cripple and have the most beautiful and sweetest girl in the world tied down. I'll never forget how my love cried on my shoulder when I told her I was going. That was worth a lifetime on this earth."

In the summer Truman was elected a lieutenant by his fellow guardsmen, and was sent to a camp in Oklahoma for training. It was not until the spring of 1918—a year after America declared war—that he was ordered to the East Coast for shipment overseas. As it was to prove for so many who lived west of the Alleghenies, the trip east was in itself an adventure for the young Missourian; but at first sight the fabled and often reviled financial capital of the country did not please. New York, Truman wrote as he passed through the metropolis, was "a vast disappointment." The hotels back home were better than the New York ones, he claimed; "Wall Street is an alley"; and "Kansas City can produce more good looking girls than two New Yorks."

But France, where he was sent from New York, was something else. He found himself billeted in "a real Chateau with a park, a moat and a cute little picture book village out in front. There are marble stairs hand carved wood work and everything like you read about. . . ."

Truman was appointed a captain, and was placed in command of Battery B of the 129th Field Artillery Regiment of the Thirty-fifth Division: the combined Missouri and Kansas National Guards. Taking over his battery, Truman, peering through thick glasses like a schoolteacher, gave the sort of rousing speech to the troops that he imagined a commander ought to give, saying, "You boys stick with me, and I'll bring you all back." But as one of the men later remembered, Truman spoiled the effect of his exhortations: "His knees were knocking together" and "you could see that he was scared to death."

It was a difficult and rowdy outfit, and indeed there had been talk of breaking it up. But Truman sensibly delegated the job of disciplining the troops to the noncommissioned officers, asking no questions about methods. Soon enough, the fists of the sergeants and corporals knocked the men together into some semblance of a military unit.

For most of the summer of 1918, they trained, and then in mid-August they were moved east to the Vosges. There, at the end of the month, the unit for the first time came under fire—and broke under it. The troops turned and ran, abandoning two guns and twelve horses.

In September the Thirty-fifth Division was ordered into the Meuse-Argonne offensive on twelve hours' notice, to be supported by Patton's tanks. But as later army investigations would show, the division of citizen-soldiers had not been organized for battle. Both the commanding officer and his chief of staff left headquarters as battle was joined, and they failed to establish any main post where communications could be centralized.

The attack by the Thirty-fifth began at 4:20 a.m. in the darkness of September 26, with a barrage of American artillery fire. Truman told his artillery battery that "right tonight I'm where I want to be—in command of this battery. I'd rather be right here than be President of the United States. You boys are my kind. Now let's go in!"

Truman and his battery performed well, and only one of his men died of wounds in the war. But the division itself fell apart for lack of command structure. By the third day of the Thirty-fifth's offensive, the division effectively had ceased to exist as a unit. On October 2 it was pulled out of the fighting. After resting, Truman and his men were sent to Verdun, though the great battle was over long since; there they fired some barrages at enemy lines. Essentially, however, their battlefield days were over. They had been in combat for a week.

FOR ALL OF HIS SPECIAL QUALITIES, Truman in the First World War was in some respects an everyman. His experience of the war was similar to that of many other American civilian soldiers. He served in the army during the war for two years, yet saw only seven days of real combat. Even that was a lot. Of the 4 million men in the U.S. Army at the end of 1918, half—some 2 million—were still in the United States awaiting transport to Europe. Of the 2 million in Europe, somewhere between a third and a half had not seen combat; and of the million or more who had, most had participated only in one operation (the Meuse-Argonne offensive), and even in that operation, had fought for no more than a few days.

MacArthur and Patton were professional soldiers and exceptions; in general, the American experience of the First World War was either not very much, or not at all, an experience of fighting. It was instead an experience of waiting, of training, of serving in or dealing with staff bureaucracies—and of being bored by doing nothing. For the half of the army that had come to Europe, it was overwhelmingly one more thing: a tourist experience.

In that bygone era, before the advent of commercial aviation and mass tourism, travel overseas was only for the few who were rich. Had it not been for the First World War, the chances are that a Harry Truman would never have seen a foreign country until he was past middle age. In sending young Americans to France, and then in giving them free time to travel, the government provided them with an extraordinary and unexpected experience that affected them far more than the fighting (which few of them did, and of which none of them did very much).

A substantial number, Willard Straight and Walter Lippmann among them, were assigned to staff duties that were much like civilian occupations. Their schedules allowed them time to visit Paris, and their conferences often were conducted over elaborate meals at châteaux.

Even those who did see some frontline combat, as Truman did, had plenty of time to explore the French countryside, and were also given leaves and passes to travel farther afield. A couple of months after his service in the Meuse-Argonne offensive, Truman, on a leave of absence, was in Paris. He had the leisure time and the opportunity to sample the principal tourist attractions of the City of Light, though not all were to his taste: he found the show at the Folies-Bergères "disgusting." With friends, he made a tour of the Italian and French Rivieras, which he and his party did enjoy a great deal. He was thrilled to see the Princess of Monaco in a restaurant, but upset when she ordered beer: "It gave all of us common people a letdown," he wrote.

Among American servicemen, there was a certain similarity of outlook that expressed itself in their accounts of travel and army experiences. A leading historian of the period has written that "thousands of men who had never before recorded in writing their daily doings, and never would again, faithfully kept journals while they were in the Army. . . . [E]ven a modest sampling . . . reveals common responses to the shared enterprise." Much of what they wrote dealt with topics other than the war. Seeing old women in black as the only inhabitants of ruined towns in France, they came away with the impression that the French were "a tired people in a blighted land" who "pursued antiquated ways." Those of the troops who came from farm country (and there were a great many of them, for half of the American population was rural at the time) were shocked to find the French peasantry still harvesting with cradles and sickles.

To believe in the redemptive mission of the United States in Europe was far easier an ocean away than it was up close. One had to be a strong Wilsonian indeed to think that France could or would help the United States build a shining tomorrow after encountering the people of the French countryside, who seemed to be so set in their ways and to belong so much to the past.

On the whole, the men of the AEF appear to have had a good time, and certainly a stimulating and exciting one. For most of them, service overseas seems indeed to have been the big event of their lives. But although they enjoyed themselves and were glad they had been sent to France, they were convinced by their firsthand acquaintance with Europe—or at least many of them were—that it was no concern of theirs what happened on the Continent. They reverted to the original American view that the United States should not involve itself in the politics of Old Europe. But while Englishmen and Germans and Russians were embittered once they came to believe that it had been a mistake for their country to have entered the war, American soldiers were not. They did not object to having been given a trip to Europe, but now they wanted to go home.

Harry Truman kept up his travels until the very end of his tour of duty in the spring of 1919. In March he was in Paris and caught a glimpse of President Woodrow Wilson, who had come over to talk peace. Though a passionate and partisan Democrat, Truman wrote that "I am very anxious that Woodie cease his gallivantin' around and send us home and quickly. As far as we're concerned most of us don't give a whoop (to put it mildly) whether Russia has a Red Government or no Government and if the King of the Lollypops wants to slaughter his subjects or his Prime Minister it's all the same to us. The Hun is whipped . . . so why should we be kept over here to browbeat a Peace Conference that'll skin us anyway."

TWENTY-ONE-YEAR-OLD aspiring novelist F. Scott Fitzgerald wrote to his friend and mentor Edmund Wilson on September 26, 1917, to ask "what effect the war at close quarters has on a person of your temperament. I mean I'm curious to see how your point of view has changed or not changed—." But Wilson, serving in the Hospital Corps, had to reply that he had gotten no nearer to the front than the Detroit State Fairgrounds.

Fitzgerald himself took (and passed) exams to become an officer in the regular army in order to see combat more quickly. In the autumn of 1917 he reported to Fort Leavenworth, Kansas, for three months of training as an officer. The officer in charge of Fitzgerald's platoon was Captain Dwight

Eisenhower. For professional reasons both Lieutenant Fitzgerald and Captain Eisenhower desired intensely to serve in battle. Eisenhower was too good at his job to be replaced, but his lack of combat experience was to cast a shadow over his future career as a professional soldier.

Fitzgerald thirsted for war experience as material for his writing. He was sure that he was going to be sent overseas to fight. He was ordered to Camp Taylor, Kentucky; to Camp Gordon, Georgia; and to Camp Sheridan, Alabama. He was being trained for combat service in the AEF, and the units in which he served were being organized into what eventually became the Ninth Division. From Camp Gordon in May 1918 he wrote that "we're probably going inside of two months and, officers and men, we're wild to go."

At a country club dance in Alabama in July, Fitzgerald met beautiful seventeen-year-old Zelda Sayre. They fell in love—as they were to do everything—madly; yet he willingly bade farewell in order to do battle overseas. At Hoboken he boarded a troop transport to Europe, but then was ordered to disembark. The orders to reembark never were issued.

In *Tender Is the Night*, Fitzgerald pictures himself (in the guise of the protagonist, Dick Diver) as haunted by the Great War in which he did not fight. Dick, "his throat straining with sadness," guides two companions in visiting a battlefield in France. Filled with excitement, Dick tries to communicate his sense of the enormity of what had taken place on that spot to the other two. One of his companions had fought in the war and no longer thought about it; he had put it behind him. But Dick, who had not lived it, remained fascinated by it. " 'This land here cost twenty lives a foot that summer,' he said. . . . 'See that little stream—we could walk to it in two minutes. It took the British a month to walk to it—a whole empire walking very slowly, dying in front and pushing forward behind. And another empire walked very slowly backward a few inches a day, leaving the dead. . . .' "

But the experience that Dick Diver was describing and that so seized the imagination of Fitzgerald was not the American experience of the First World War: it was that of Old Europe. Oddly, writers who, unlike Fitzgerald, did reach the battlefield did the same thing: they described the ordeal of Europeans at war, not Americans at war. Malcolm Cowley, a chronicler of that literary generation, explained that it was due to the branch of service many of them had chosen. "It would be interesting," he wrote, "to list the authors who were ambulance or camion drivers in 1917." In addition to himself, he named "Dos Passos, Hemingway, Julian Green, William Seabrook, E. E. Cummings, Slater Brown, Harry Crosby, John Howard Lawson, Sidney Howard, Louis Bromfield, Robert Hillyer, Dashiell Hammett. . . . [O]ne might almost say that the ambulance corps and the French military transport were college-extension courses for a generation of writers."

Some of the lessons they learned might have been learned in any army or service. But according to Cowley, "ambulance service had a lesson of its own: it instilled into us what might be called a *spectatorial* attitude." The war became "a spectacle which it was our privilege to survey. . . ." Cowley believed that "this spectatorial attitude, this monumental indifference toward the cause" for which soldiers were risking their lives, eventually expressed itself in their literary works.

Other reasons suggest themselves, too. Those the Americans were watching were Frenchmen; it was not unnatural that they should feel more detached than if they were watching fellow countrymen fight and die. The Americans might sympathize with the French cause, but it was not, after all, their own. Nor were the goals France hoped to achieve if she won the war objectives about which Americans were likely to care deeply. And by the time Americans arrived on the battlefield, many Frenchmen had become discouraged and cynical about the causes of the war, and may well have communicated that feeling.

Then, too, a certain indifference to the Allied cause was implicit in the very project of coming to the war in order to use it for literary purposes. In a sense, the ambulance drivers/writers were on the field of battle as voyeurs rather than as participants. One of the characters in the Dos Passos novel *1919* is quoted by Cowley as saying, "This ain't a war . . . it's a goddam Cook's tour. . . ." To be there and take part in it in order to write home about it was to be, in a certain way, a tourist.

The spectatorial way—the tourist way—of seeing the fighting, the suffering, and the bloodshed and trying to grasp and feel the tragedy of it, while at the same time remaining indifferent to the causes and goals of the war, led to the conclusion that the war was pointless and wrong: that the Europeans had been wicked to start it and Wilson's Americans had been fools to join in it. This reinforced the impression brought back by the everyman soldiers, the Harry Trumans, that Americans should go home and not get involved in any more European conflicts.


THROUGH PARIS IN 1918 there passed yet another species of tourist from the United States. It was natural that politicians would want to visit the battlefield and to be able to say that they had seen war firsthand. Of the many in Washington eager to travel to Europe, none can have been more ambitious to make the trip than Assistant Secretary Franklin Roosevelt.

Roosevelt was determined to go overseas. Throughout 1917 and 1918 he kept urging Daniels to let him undertake a mission abroad, but the secretary continued to say no. By the summer of 1918, however, it seemed advisable for either the secretary or the assistant secretary to make an inspection trip to Europe; congressmen were scheduled to go on such trips of their own, and it seemed only prudent to anticipate whatever criticisms Republicans might direct against the Democratic civilian administration of the navy. It was out of the question for Daniels to leave Washington, for he was indispensable; so Roosevelt, whose role at the Navy Department was never vital, was allowed to be the one to go.

The trip began well. Putting out of mind how badly it ended, Roosevelt always was to regard it as a high point in his life. On July 9 he embarked for Europe on a new destroyer, the USS *Dyer*, making her maiden crossing. A gun drill, a false alarm, the fear of submarines, a brief disablement of the *Dyer* that called for minor repairs: out of such materials Roosevelt imagined a rich wartime experience for himself upon which he drew deeply in the years to come.

The *Dyer* landed in England at Portsmouth. Roosevelt was greeted in style and brought to a suite at the Ritz in London as a guest of the admiralty. He was taken to meetings with the civilian and uniformed heads of the Royal Navy, the foreign secretary (Arthur Balfour), the prime minister (David Lloyd George), and even the king. Indeed, so grandly was he received that his private audience at Buckingham Palace with King George V lasted forty-five minutes, Roosevelt noted, rather than the usual fifteen.

After ten days in the British Isles, Roosevelt crossed to France, landing at Dunkerque and proceeding the next day to Paris, where the French government installed him in the Hotel Crillon, once an eighteenth-century palace, on the Place de la Concorde. Again he was received by heads of state and government. He attended a luncheon in honor of Herbert Hoover at the presidential palace, where he met President Raymond Poincaré; he also visited Premier Georges Clemenceau.

At a little house near the Arc de Triomphe, Roosevelt took tea one afternoon with two of TR's sons, Theodore, Jr. ("Ted"), and Archibald. Both had outstanding war records and been severely wounded in battle; Roosevelt wrote that "Archie was . . . looking horribly badly."

Most tragic was the fate of the son who was not there. Quentin, TR's youngest, a lieutenant in the U.S. Army Flying Corps, had been shot down and killed on the western front two weeks earlier. The twenty-year-old had been the best-loved of TR's children. Nearsightedness should have kept him out of the service, but he fooled the examiners by memorizing the eye charts in advance. Nothing would keep him away from combat when his country was at war. "We boys," he said, "thought it was up to us to practice what Father preached."

"But Mrs. Roosevelt, how am I going to break it to her?" TR had said when told about Quentin. To an old friend, he wrote that ". . . if I had not myself gone to war in my day I don't think I could have borne to send my sons to face death now."

After tea with his cousins, Franklin Roosevelt returned to his hotel, where he dined, and then joined traveling members of the House Naval Affairs Committee, who also were staying at the Crillon, in a night on the town. They began at the Folies-Bergères, and then were guided elsewhere, returning raucously at 4 a.m. Roosevelt nightclubbed all the next night, too.

Although Roosevelt spent several days visiting the scenes of some of the fiercest battles and proved to be a tireless tourist who was determined to get as close as possible to the front, he occupied almost all the rest of August and early September in merrymaking. In the words of his companion Livingston Davis: "FD having joy ride." According to one biographer, in Scotland, where they went fishing, Roosevelt and Davis "drank like undergraduates," and Roosevelt awakened to find a fox in his bed.

Then there was more partying back in London before Roosevelt crossed to France to embark for home September 12. Through all the carousing, he had been talking about finally becoming a fighting man, as though all the madcap weeks of parties and nightclubs in Europe were one gigantic farewell party before at last he went to war. But in his cabin aboard ship, he collapsed. He had come down with double pneumonia. He was carried off the boat when it docked in New York September 19, and was taken to his mother's house.

Eleanor came to be with him, but in unpacking his clothes came across letters from Lucy Mercer, from which she learned of the love affair between her husband and her friend and former secretary. "The bottom dropped out of my . . . world," Eleanor said later. The crisis engulfed Franklin. Weak, with his health shattered (he no sooner recovered from the pneumonia than he was seized by influenza), he faced the loss of his wife and five children, the destruction of his political career, and his mother's threat to cut off his income and his inheritance if he disgraced the family by divorcing.

For once he could not make everyone happy by telling each what he or she wanted to hear. Indeed, he could not make *anyone* happy. To avoid ruin, he would have to break with Lucy, which would hurt her badly and make him miserable. He would deprive himself of the love, support, and companionship of the only woman who fulfilled his needs. He had shattered Eleanor, who would never really recover: "I can forgive," she said years later, "but I cannot forget." His marriage, the physical part of which was at an end, from now on would be something more in the nature of a political alliance; and neither Franklin nor Eleanor would be comforted by love or intimacy until the day they could negotiate an agreement to allow one another the freedom to form relationships with others.

Roosevelt's illness dragged on, and he was in no fit state to make decisions that suddenly had to be made nonetheless. Things had caught up with him. An hour before midnight October 31, he went to see President

Wilson to say that he could wait no longer and must join the fighting forces, only to be told that it was too late: he had lost his chance. An armistice seemed to be imminent. In a few weeks or even days, the fighting was likely to end.

For Wilson, too, and in affairs of far more general concern and greater consequence, midnight was about to sound. The war was coming to an end too soon for the AEF to play a major role in winning it. Yet the President's hopes for forcing his own kind of peace terms on the reluctant Allies rested on the ability of Pershing's armies to emerge as the dominating force on the European battlefield. For that to happen, the war would have to last for another year or two. Pershing's plan was to launch the first big American offensive in the spring and summer of 1919; given the chance to do so, he believed he could win the war on America's terms.

THROUGHOUT THE WAR, Dwight Eisenhower had bombarded his superiors with requests to be sent overseas for combat duty. He had been too valuable a training officer, and they had kept him in the United States.

But on his twenty-eighth birthday, October 14, 1918, his luck turned. He was promoted to the temporary rank of lieutenant colonel with orders to embark for France on November 18, 1918. He was directed to take command of an armored unit in Pershing's long-planned spring offensive of 1919. As such he would be in the forefront of battle as the United States finally made its debut on the European battlefield as an independent great military power.

Eisenhower was shaken when the news came that it was too late, that Pershing would never launch his offensive—and that the orders sending him to Europe were canceled.

"I suppose we'll spend the rest of our lives explaining why we didn't get into this war," he said despairingly to a fellow officer.

# 21

# DISILLUSION
# BEFORE VERSAILLES

DESPITE WHAT Wilson told Franklin Roosevelt the night of October 31, and despite the fact that what Wilson predicted at the time turned out to be true, nobody could have been certain that evening that peace was close at hand. Only months before, Britain's Imperial War Cabinet in London had been advised by the chief of the General Staff that victory in Europe could not be won before the middle of 1919 and was more likely to be over in the summer of 1920. Although in October 1918 serious armistice proposals were being circulated by Germany and her allies, the war continued, and it was entirely possible that the war would continue for some time.

Wilson was nowhere near as effective a war leader as Lloyd George had been in Great Britain or as TR might have been in the United States. Not until 1919 would he have a chance to show how he could perform in a role that he found congenial: that of peacemaker. But many—even among those who had been his supporters—had come to believe in advance that he was going to fail even at that. A majority of voters in the United States were about to repudiate his leadership without waiting to see whether he could prove more effective in making peace than he had in making war.

What is commonly supposed to have happened only after Wilson went to Europe to negotiate the peace in fact occurred several months earlier, before he had left American shores and while he was still directing the war. The story as handed down is that America's hopes—and mankind's—were shattered by the peace conference that assembled in Paris in 1919, and that disillusionment was a product of the Treaty of Versailles. But Americans began losing faith in Woodrow Wilson and his promises well before the peace conference assembled. Indeed, their disillusion played a role in undermining the President's position in the negotiations.

They were disappointed that in wartime Wilson acted as a party, rather than a national, leader. Historians claim that his last-minute appeal to the voters to elect a Democratic Congress in the autumn of 1918 was a damaging blunder, but perhaps they attach too much weight to the effect of that single plea. His partisanship in deeds, rather than words, proved far more harmful in the end.

When war came, he did not invite leading figures of the Republican party to join his government and provide it with a national character. He did not offer a wartime role to TR, although a leading role for the warrior-statesman would have raised morale at home and abroad; nor did he associate Republican leaders, however capable, with the conduct of the war. The result was that the humiliating shortcomings of the American economy, and the delays in getting the AEF ready to fight, were blamed entirely upon him and his party.

For use in the midterm elections of 1918, TR delivered an indictment of the administration that attacked Wilson for not having adequately prepared for war before April 1917 and for not having effectively mobilized to wage war thereafter. It rang true.

By the spring of 1918, when Ludendorff launched his deadly offensives with troops brought back from Russia—and nearly won the war—he gave Americans and the Allies the scare of their lives. Voters in the United States were shocked into a realization that the AEF was still not ready to fight or equipped to fight.

The United States was a giant of a manufacturing country. It was difficult to understand why it was unable to produce boats, tanks, guns, or airplanes effectively, and why the AEF had to fight with tanks, artillery pieces, and aircraft borrowed from the French. Wilson, by choosing to lead a party rather than a national government, had assumed sole responsibility and therefore blame for it all. And though he fired the administrators who failed, and though his new appointees were making a creditable start at war administration in 1918, he was not forgiven for having lost a year in trial and error.

Wilson's position in the congressional elections of 1918 would in any event have been a vulnerable one. His Senate supporters who were up for reelection that year were those who had won their seats in the freak election of 1912, the year that the split in the Republican party between TR and Taft had allowed Democrats to slip into office with less than a majority. Now such Democrats faced an uphill fight to retain seats they would not have won in the first place except for a lucky accident.

Indeed, in 1918 luck ran against them; it was a bad year for a northern or western politician to be a Democrat. Since the Civil War, the Democrats had been perceived as the party of the South. Their congressional leadership was disproportionately southern. Southern-born Woodrow Wilson's undoing in the midterm elections of 1918 was that he made decisions that could be misrepresented convincingly as benefiting the special interests of the South.

It had to do with administered prices. The war brought about an inflation that the government failed to control; consumer prices doubled in the second Wilson administration. Farmers, though they saw the value of their crops rise, saw the costs of farming soar even more. They sought and obtained price supports as protection. But after wheat farmers in 1918 asked that their guaranteed minimum price of $2.20 per bushel be raised to $2.40, the press attacked the proposed legislation. Great Britain protested that the rise would cost her, for current purchases alone, an extra $100 million. So Wilson, who also feared the effects of yet more inflation, rejected the rise in price supports for wheat.

Yet cotton *had* gotten its minimum price raised. Cotton, of course, was grown in the South, and wheat in the West; thus it looked (or could be made to look) as though Wilson were favoring the South at the expense of the West.

The West, which had given Wilson the presidency in the election of 1916, now turned against him and started him on the road to political ruin. It was in the West that the Republican party wrested control of the Senate and the House of Representatives in the midterm elections of November 1918. The President's party went down to a defeat made all the more dramatic by contrast with what happened when Great Britain went to the polls a few weeks later—and gave a landslide victory of historic proportions to supporters of Lloyd George.

That the President's party was defeated meant that Wilson could not really speak for his country at a future peace conference. The leaders of other nations were on notice that they might be wasting their time in dealing with the President: that the Senate might not ratify a treaty that he negotiated. And it was an opinion held widely that Wilson would be defeated if he stood for reelection to a third term in 1920, and that the Republican victor would be TR.


IN 1918 A NUMBER of Americans were unhappy that their country was not yet playing the great role in the war that would be worthy of her. At the same time some of the outstanding young Americans in noncombat positions began to feel that they, too, had not been performing their proper role in the war. On July 26 John Foster Dulles, an intelligence officer engaged in economic warfare, formally requested a line commission that would allow him to go into combat. Robert Taft wrote to Herbert Hoover, his chief at the Food Administration, on October 18, saying that physical standards for induction into the armed forces had been lowered; there was a chance that he might be accepted for duty despite his poor eyesight, and he strongly requested permission to enlist. It was two weeks later that Franklin Roosevelt went to the President with his own request to join the armed forces.

Willard Straight, former Morgan banker and founder of *The New Republic,* who had tried always to set an example, was another whose thoughts turned to combat service. He began to feel unease in staying with his army job dealing with war risk insurance when his contemporaries actually were exposing themselves to risk. In Straight's reflections, many of the growing doubts ran parallel: his doubts about himself, about Wilson, about the Allies, and about America's role in world affairs.

On October 13 he wrote to his wife that "what I'm afraid of now is that the British and French . . . may demand their pound of flesh. The jealousy in England of our increasing power is more manifest, I understand, all the time . . . ," and Britain might join France in blocking America's plan to offer "a fair deal with Germany." Woodrow Wilson "is not a leader—not for a minute. He's no more ready for peace than he was for war. The people have done everything, forced everything that has been done. He has merely made speeches. . . . He has anticipated nothing and prepared for nothing that I can see. What's more, he's refused to let others do it. We stand in a fair way of having fought the war, lost thousands of lives and millions of dollars, upset everything, and of not getting the peace we started for"—and all because Wilson did not bring the Allies to terms when they were down. "The trouble is that it should have been done when our Allies were much less cocky than they are now. They would have agreed to anything then. It will be difficult to line 'em up now."

Since the war, in his view, was coming to a swift end, Straight was despondent. He had not distinguished himself in the conflict, and there was no more time in which to do so. He had served throughout as a staff officer, not as a commander in battle, and he asked his wife, ". . . what do I take to you? A record of performance, something of which you can be proud? No—nothing."

He despaired for his country, too, and for the American ideals that alone, in his view, justified Wilson's decision to bring the United States into the war. Walter Lippmann, his friend and one of his original band of editors at *The New Republic*, now serving as an intelligence officer interrogating German prisoners taken by the AEF, was at army headquarters in France with Straight the last weeks of the war, and recalled that "I was closer to Willard than ever before. Up at the First Army we talked far into the night. . . ." Mixed with hope the two earnestly idealistic young leaders of liberal opinion felt "a fear that what we had meant, and what alone could justify it all, was *not* going to be in the minds of the decision-makers."


WILSON'S DRIFT INTO CONFLICT with Bolshevik Russia was what most disturbed William Bullitt, House's man at the European desk of the State Department. The enormous land mass that had been the tsar's empire had over the centuries swallowed up some of the greatest invading armies in history, and there was no reason to believe that American troops sent to occupy Russia would fare any better.

Wilson, who at first resisted French and British proposals to send an expedition to take possession of Russia's northern ports, argued as he always had that no forces should be diverted from the western front. He always had feared that the Allies would try to send American armies to far-off theaters of war to serve French and British national or imperial ambitions; indeed, one of the reasons that he had insisted that Americans serve in their own army under Pershing's command had been to prevent that from happening. And it could well be suspected in 1918 that the Allied proposal to intervene in Russia was animated at least as much by political as by purely military motives.

Nonetheless Wilson, fearing, he claimed, that he had opposed Allied proposals too often, finally gave his consent. British and French leaders saw their plan (or at any rate presented it) in the context of the war against Germany. Although Bolshevik Russia had made peace with Germany in March 1918, the war in a sense continued on what once had been tsarist soil. The Russian empire had disintegrated, and in the fluid, volatile, confusing situation that followed, dozens of leaders, parties, and nationalities aspired to rule some or all of it. Rival tsarist officers in various parts of the former empire, aiming at a future position on or behind the throne, led armies that regarded themselves as still at war against Germany, while German forces remained active in the Caucasus and Ukraine.

At stake were vast quantities of supplies in many parts of the former empire that might fall into the hands of the Germans. Even more important were various armed groups of former soldiers—some from prison camps that had broken down as a result of the Russian revolutions—who moved across the chaotic sixth of the earth's land surface that had been the Romanov domains in an attempt to rejoin the German or Allied armies.

What Wilson allowed himself to be persuaded to do was send an American expedition under British command to occupy the ports of Murmansk and Archangel in the far north of Russia. It was argued that supplies of military importance would thus be protected from seizure by German or pro-German forces operating from nearby Finland. Wilson claimed he was using the troops "to guard the military stores" and, puzzlingly, "to make it safe for Russian forces to come together in organized bodies in the north." He did not identify the forces he had in mind.

Britain and France also pressed America to organize, with Japan, an intervention in Siberia. Again, Wilson at first refused. Then the situation changed suddenly. A corps of pro-Ally Czech soldiers, stranded within Russia and blocked by Germany and Ukraine from moving west, seized control of the Trans-Siberian Railroad and traveled east on it to its terminus, the Pacific coast port city of Vladivostok, taking possession of the town.

Wilson, one of the many admirers of the Czech liberal leader Tomáš Masaryk, met at the White House with advisers on July 6, 1918, and decided to dispatch forces "on sentimental grounds" to help the Czechs. He decided that "in view of the inability of the United States to furnish any considerable force within a short time," he would request the government of Japan to provide 7,000 troops to match the 7,000 troops he *could* send.

At the White House meeting, observing Army Chief of Staff General Peyton C. March, Wilson asked, "Why are you shaking your head, General?" and then, answering himself, said, "You are opposed to this because you do not think Japan will limit herself to 7,000 men, and that this decision will further her schemes for territorial aggrandizement. . . . Well, we will have to take that chance."

Wilson's decision brought the United States into conflict with the Allies, with Japan, and with Russia—indeed, with everyone except the actual enemy, Germany.

The Allies were furious at not being consulted or even informed. Britain replied in kind by unilaterally ordering forces to Vladivostok from nearby Hong Kong, followed by a British military mission and then a British high commissioner. So with no coordination, British troops moved into town alongside units of the American and Japanese armies.

Japan pushed aside the limitations Wilson sought to impose upon her and pursued her own ambitions for expansion on the mainland by sending 72,000 troops instead of the proposed maximum of 7,000.

By not clarifying what the American forces were going to help the Czechs do, Wilson also brought the United States into collision with Lenin's regime: perhaps without meaning to, he allowed America to be sucked into aiding the opposition White armies in the first stages of the Russian Civil War. The President ignored the role the Czechs were playing in fighting against the Reds. By not transporting the Czechs back to Europe, but instead supporting them inside Russia in their battle against the Bolsheviks, the United States was entering that conflict, too—but not doing so effectively enough to defeat the communists.

In a statement made public in August in which he justified the military landings in Russia, the President claimed that his government had no intention of interfering with "the Russian people in their endeavor to regain control of their own affairs, their own territory, and their own destiny." He did not explain why he thought that occupying Russian territory in order to help one side against another in a Russian civil war was not a form of interference.

As always, the President purported to be acting in the service of high ideals. One might have imagined that his decision had been to send out to Russian lands not military or political missions, but charitable and educational ones. "It is the hope and purpose of the Government of the United States," Wilson wrote in outlining his policy, "to send to Siberia a commission of merchants, agricultural experts, labor advisers, Red Cross representatives, and agents of the Young Men's Christian Association. . . ."

These decisions distressed the President's liberal supporters. In June William Bullitt wrote to Edward House that he was "sick at heart because I feel we are about to make one of the most tragic blunders in the history of mankind" by intervening in Russia against Lenin's government. Bullitt still believed that the Bolsheviks might be won over to the Allied and American cause, and pleaded with House to change sides in policy toward Russia: "Let us join the Soviets," he wrote.

In September, after the American intervention, Bullitt feared that Wilson's policy might drive Soviet Russia into alliance with Germany. "One year ago today," he wrote House, "Russia was fighting by our side against Germany. . . . Today we are fighting Great Russia, and it is possible that before summer one million Russians will be acting as German depot and supply troops on the western front. This is the year's achievement of our Russian diplomacy. When the men charged with aircraft production failed, the President threw them out. . . ." Those in charge of America's policy toward Russia should be thrown out too, Bullitt argued.

WILSON'S OUTSTANDING ADVISER when he sought his first term as President had been Louis D. Brandeis, the intellectual and spiritual giant of the Progressive movement who had been appointed by Wilson to the Supreme Court, but retained his interest in the foreign and other policies of the administration. Several years after the events recounted here, Brandeis remarked that President Wilson "should be judged by what he was and did prior to August 4, 1918, the date of the paper justifying the attack on Russia. That was the first of his acts which was unlike him; and I am sure the beginning of the sad end."

# 22

# A STAB IN THE BACK

THE FINAL ACT in the drama of 1914–18 began in an unexpected corner of Europe and followed a script that had been submitted and rejected long before. On New Year's Day 1915 David Lloyd George, then chancellor of the exchequer, had circulated to the British cabinet a proposal to launch an attack from the Greek port of Salonika (Thessaloníki) through the Balkans and Austria-Hungary directed at Germany's vulnerable southern flank. Britain's generals vetoed the plan and year after year had argued against such "Eastern" projects. But in the summer of 1918 French general Louis-Félix-François Franchet d'Esperey, newly appointed Allied commander in Salonika, won permission to launch an offensive in the Balkans against Bulgaria, the smallest of the Central Powers. His plan of attack was based on one formulated earlier in the war by a general in the army of Serbia, the Balkan kingdom whose rivalry with Austria-Hungary had led to the outbreak of hostilities in 1914.

Franchet d'Esperey's forces attacked on the morning of September 15 and smashed through Bulgarian lines. Racing forward against an enemy who had lost all will to fight, the Serbian, Greek, French, and British troops of the Salonika command advanced at rates of twenty and twenty-five miles a day. They knocked Bulgaria out of the war in two weeks. On September 26 the Bulgarians asked for an armistice, and on September 28 they accepted unconditionally the terms of one dictated to them by Franchet d'Esperey; they signed it the next day.

Talaat, the grand vizier of the Ottoman Empire, was stopping for a few days in Bulgaria on his way back from a conference in Berlin when the Bulgarians sued for an armistice. Bulgaria was the land bridge between Germany and Turkey, and now that it was collapsing, the Turks would be cut off from all sources of supply and reinforcement from Germany. Talaat hastened back to Constantinople to tell the members of his cabinet that Ottoman Turkey must ask for peace. He informed them that Germany was going to do so, too. Talaat and his cabinet then resigned, on the theory that a new Ottoman government less guilty in the eyes of the Allies might be able to obtain from them more generous terms.

Ludendorff, on receiving the news of Bulgaria's capitulation, came to the same conclusions. He told Hindenburg, the kaiser, and Chancellor Hertling that Germany must sue for an armistice immediately; that an approach should be made to the United States, not the Allies; that Germany should sue for peace on the basis of the terms Wilson had outlined to Congress; and that like the Turks, the Germans should change their government to make it more acceptable to the other side and therefore more likely to be able to obtain generous terms. Adopting this program advocated by Ludendorff and also by Foreign Minister Admiral Paul von Hintze, the Germans swiftly carried out a revolution from above. In less than a week commencing the night of September 28–29, they introduced fundamental constitutional changes subordinating military to civilian authority, and installed a new chancellor, Prince Max of Baden, sustained in the parliament by the Socialist party. Prince Max on the night of October 4–5 dispatched a note to Wilson asking him to help in arranging an armistice and in initiating peace negotiations on the basis of the Fourteen Points and the other principles the President had articulated since then.

So in a matter of days, Germany had changed from a de facto military dictatorship supported by the parties of the Right and determined to fight on, into a civilian democracy supported by the Left, and in search of a liberal Wilsonian peace. And it all had been done on orders from Ludendorff.

The dark genius of the German army had lost his nerve on the western front in the face of British advances during the summer. But he had pulled back to a strong defensive position, and his professionalism kept him going. It was possible that he could have held out behind his fortified lines until the AEF was fully ready to mount an offensive. But against an attack from Bulgaria through Austria-Hungary, Germany was defenseless.

The coming into existence of the AEF had doomed Germany, but only in the sense that it had set some sort of time limit within which she had to bring the war to an end. On the other side, the creation of the AEF provided the Allies with a guarantee that if the war continued long enough, Germany would be defeated someday by somebody—even if not by them. But in the autumn of 1918 it turned out that the Allies would not need to call upon that guarantee. They had won the war on their own. They had won it in a campaign in which the Americans took no part; indeed, the United States never had declared war on Bulgaria.

For Germany, which otherwise might have had until the spring or summer of 1919 to negotiate a compromise peace—or until sometime thereafter to surrender to an AEF that would impose terms that were generous—the success of Franchet d'Esperey's thrust through the Balkans meant that time had run out unexpectedly soon. Hence, in Berlin, Ludendorff's stage-managed coup d'état against his own regime.

IN LIFE AS IN CHESS, the endgame usually is the treacherous one. The minor pieces that provide cover and slow down the action by standing in the way have been eliminated long since. The play is swift, and there are no more chances to recover from mistakes. No matter how far ahead a survivor appears to be, one false step can bring sudden death, resulting in a forfeit of all winnings and undoing all advantage gained since the very beginning.

It was because the end was approaching with all its dangers, and because their faith in the President had been so shaken, that Americans—not just the Allies—were disquieted when Wilson engaged in a public correspondence with the new German chancellor, Prince Max, on the subject of peace terms. In reply to the chancellor's note sent October 4–5, Wilson posed questions as to Germany's intentions, to which Prince Max in turn replied.

Joseph Grew, head of the State Department's European desk, recorded in his diary the effect produced by this public exchange of notes: "The country from coast to coast was afraid the President would take the German bait, that he would let himself be drawn into the quibble of words, a repetition of the *Lusitania* notes, that the war would end in an inconclusive peace and that all our sacrifices were in danger of going for nothing. The country was unable to fathom the President's purpose in asking the German Government questions when it felt that there was only one answer to give to the original peace offer—a perfectly straightforward 'complete surrender or nothing.' "

But according to Grew, this was because the American people failed to understand that the President was addressing the *German* public and attempting to persuade it to stop supporting a militarist regime. In Grew's view, America's doubts about the President's course of conduct— if not the doubts of the Allied leaders, who were unhappy about his not consulting them when corresponding with Germany—disappeared after October 14 when Wilson sent a second note to Berlin, this time taking a hard line.

After consultations and reflections, Wilson had concluded (as he informed Prince Max) that the constitutional changes in Germany did not go far enough. Moreover, the sinking of a British liner on October 12, killing about 600 people, focused the President's attention on the need to stop German atrocities. And a message from the Allied prime ministers had reminded him that the terms of any armistice would have to be such as to preserve the military supremacy of the Allies. America's terms for an armistice stiffened.

WITH MATTERS COMING to a head, Wilson sent House to Europe to meet with the various military and Allied leaders and coordinate a response to Germany's overtures. House brought along with him his son-in-law and secretary, Gordon Auchincloss, a young lawyer who had served for a year as assistant to the State Department's counselor, and Joseph Grew.

Aboard ship October 18 Grew wrote in his diary: "A great piece of good fortune has come my way, for Colonel House has asked me to accompany him to the Supreme War Council in Paris, and, if things work out as we now hope and expect, to the final Peace Conference of the war. I had hardly dared let myself hope for this, but now that it has come it is agreeable to think how trivial everything else in the world seems. . . . [G]reat events have come . . . yet through it all we have looked forward to the Peace Conference as the greatest event of all. It will indeed be the great event of this age or of any age, just as this war has been the greatest war in history, and so Dame Fortune is smiling kindly on those who are to be in at the death."

He wrote that the "army of officials who will attend the final Peace Conference have not yet . . . been chosen except in the minds of two men, the President and Colonel House, in whose hands their selection will lie." Contemplating himself and his few shipmates on October 18, Grew exulted that "this little group which now starts for France are the trail blazers, the pioneers who go forward . . . and their leader, Colonel House, is the confidential adviser and official representative of the man who now, above all others, is directing and will direct the destiny of the world."

GERMANY'S LEADERS WERE DIVIDED about how to respond to Wilson's new and harder line. The navy wanted to continue its unrestricted submarine warfare. The army was prepared to fight on; Ludendorff had regained his nerve. But Prince Max, with the support of his cabinet, won the backing of the kaiser for a note to Wilson on October 20 that went far toward meeting the President's terms. It promised to end submarine warfare, assured the United States that Germany now had a parliamentary government, and agreed that armistice terms would reflect "the actual standard of power on both sides of the field."

The President replied on October 23, pushing for more changes in the German political system and referring consideration of the terms of a future armistice to a newly created Supreme War Council of the United States and the Allies at Versailles.

Hindenburg and Ludendorff issued a public statement saying that Wilson's October 23 note was unacceptable and that the war must go on. Disobeying orders from the chancellor, they journeyed to Berlin to make their point. Prince Max forced a showdown in front of the kaiser, on whose orders Ludendorff resigned (October 26) and Hindenburg did not. It now was Hindenburg's job to ensure that the military obeyed Germany's civilian chancellor, who replied to Wilson October 27 in an effort to meet America's terms.

IN SOME WAYS what Wilson was doing in the year 1918–19 was rather like what a chess master does in playing a number of games at once. He found himself engaged on one playing board in a contest against domestic political opponents; on a second, against international rivals for the affection of the European Left, Lloyd George and Lenin; on a third, for the United States against the Allies on the issue of peace terms; on a fourth, for America and the Allies against Germany—and all at the same time.

General Pershing, whose advice on armistice terms Wilson had solicited, reported to the President that he had told the Supreme War Council the military prospects were favorable and that the United States and the Allies should demand an unconditional surrender from Germany. In demanding unconditional surrender a quarter century later, in the Second World War, Franklin Roosevelt may have remembered this advice; for in years to come, the virtues of Pershing's proposal would become more evident. Such a surrender, swiftly followed by an end of the Allied blockade, would have saved the German people much suffering in the months to come; while the unconditionality of it—frank and stark—would have kept them from believing that promises were made to them that later were broken.

From the point of view of Wilson's desire to remake world politics, a demand for unconditional surrender, followed by German refusal, followed by a continuation of the war into 1919 or 1920, would have been a scenario that—albeit at the cost of much additional bloodshed—might have brought success. The Allies and Germans both would have become too exhausted to fight on, and the fresh and ever-growing AEF, having just begun to fight, would have been in a position to impose its will on all sides. That was to be the situation in Western Europe in 1945, and for now it was the way in which Wilson's program could be realized of not only remaking the German, Austrian, Turkish, and Russian empires, but also reforming and purifying the politics of the Allies.

But far from appreciating the suitability of Pershing's strategy for achieving his objectives, Wilson saw the general's unauthorized proposal as the gesture of a political rival. The American people were hostile to Germany and feared that their President was weak and too accommodating to the enemy; so Pershing's initiative, were it to become known to the public, might set up a bid for the presidency. Wilson suspected that Pershing harbored such ambitions, and Mrs. Wilson was sure of it.

Wilson neglected to tell the Allies his own ideas about the military terms of an armistice, so they took what they could get, pushing the Germans down a slope—and the President saw his own position slipping away, too. "It is certain," he told House October 28, "that too much success . . . on the part of the Allies will make a genuine peace settlement exceedingly difficult, if not impossible." His strategy for getting what he wanted had been to play off the Germans and Allies against one another, but the disintegration of Germany undercut it; he no longer could threaten the Allies with a Germany that might fight on if they overreached. And if they overreached in setting peace terms, the peace settlement, as Wilson rightly saw, would not endure.

Wilson and House asked the Allies to tie an armistice with Germany to the Fourteen Points. They were loath to do so. Point 2, freedom of the seas, had never been accepted by the Allies, and Britain saw in it a threat to her world position. As to the rest: when it was asked at a meeting of the British War Cabinet on October 22, 1918, whether the Allies were committed to granting Germany an armistice on the basis of the Fourteen Points, "it was generally agreed that this was not the case."

House, whose brief it was in Europe to persuade the Allies otherwise, had the inspired notion of supplying an official interpretation of the Points that might narrow their meaning and applicability sufficiently to make them acceptable. At his request, Walter Lippmann provided the gloss, assisted by Frank Cobb, editor of the New York *World*, and Wilson approved it. On November 4 the Allies—with reservations—approved, too.

Lippmann imagined this to be a triumph of American diplomacy. "I must write you," he told House in a letter, "because I couldn't possibly tell you to your face how great a thing you have achieved. . . . I did not believe it was humanly possible under conditions as they seemed to be in Europe to win so glorious a victory. This is the climax of a course that has been as wise as it was brilliant, and as shrewd as it was prophetic. The President and you have more than justified the faith of those who insisted that your leadership was a turning point in modern history."

Lippmann at this point had been taken onto House's informal staff. So had his friend and sometime employer Major Willard Straight. They joined Grew and Auchincloss.

Now that the United States and the Allies had papered over their differences, they were prepared to negotiate an armistice. On November 7 the Allied command ordered a local cease-fire at Compiègne, a town some fifty miles northeast of Paris, so that a German envoy could pass through in order to discuss terms. A local correspondent of the United Press wire service mistakenly understood the order as calling for a cease-fire everywhere in Europe, and cabled the news at once. There was hysterical rejoicing at the news the war was over, until the story was retracted. It was, according to *The New York Times*, "the most colossal news fake ever perpetrated upon the American people."

The real Armistice was signed November 11, and it appeared to promise the generous peace that Wilson had outlined to the world. There were many who later would believe that the November 11 Armistice therefore was an even greater hoax than the one of November 7.

THE SIGNING OF THE ARMISTICE took place in a French railroad car near the town of Rethondes in the forest outside Compiègne. In great confusion the German delegates had been waiting there for some sort of authorization from whatever government functioned in Germany to affix their signatures.

In due course the authorization had arrived. Meanwhile the Allies had granted their one and only concession to objections raised by the waiting German delegates. The Allies had demanded that the German army surrender 30,000 machine guns upon signing the Armistice. The delegation spoke for the army in protesting that "there would not be enough left to fire on the German people, should this become necessary." Marshal Ferdinand Foch, the Allied generalissimo,* thereupon relented and allowed the Germans to keep 5,000 of the 30,000 machine guns—so that their army could indeed use them against their civilian population.

Only a year and a half before, the President of the United States had told the Congress that America was going to war not against the German people, but against their military regime. Times had changed. The President never had been in a position to speak for the Allies on the German question; but now they were in a position to speak for him.

Shortly after 5:30 a.m. on November 11, Willard Straight had phoned in the news that the Armistice had been signed, to take effect (as House's relative Sidney Mezes later put it) "on the stroke of the eleventh hour of the eleventh day of the eleventh month" of 1918.

Unnoticed in the excitement was a fact that should have been disturbing: the Germans and the Allies had not accepted the same armistice terms. The Germans had agreed on the basis of Wilson's publicly stated Fourteen Points, Four Principles, and Five Particulars. The Allies had accepted, with reservations, only on the basis of Walter Lippmann's secret gloss that nar-

---

* In March 1918, under pressure from Lloyd George, Wilson had agreed to the appointment of an overall military chief in Europe, while maintaining the integrity and independence of the American army. Looking forward to mid-1919, when most of the troops on the western front would finally be American, Pershing assumed that he would then replace Foch as generalissimo.

rowed and to some extent explained away the Fourteen Points—a gloss of which the Germans knew nothing. So trouble lay ahead.

Meanwhile November 11, according to Joseph Grew's later account, "was the greatest day I have seen or ever shall see." The streets of Paris overflowed with singing, cheering crowds, while women danced down the boulevards kissing every man in uniform. The celebrations went on, wrote Grew, for three days.

Straight came up to Paris, to the Hotel Crillon, the day the Armistice was signed. Grew now appointed him general executive officer of the secretariat. Grew and Straight drew up a detailed chart organizing the work of the American delegation, which they submitted to House. Although a chart earlier had been prepared by the Inquiry, House (according to Grew) said of the Grew-Straight plan that it was "the best and in fact the only practical one he had yet seen."

Grew, Straight, and Lippmann set out to put the plan into operation. On the night of November 17, they dined together. The next morning, all of them woke up with the chills, aches, pains, and headaches of the influenza that was then reaching epidemic proportions. Within a week Grew and Lippmann had recovered, but Straight never did; he passed away December 1. Willard Straight had embodied the idealism of his generation of Americans, and it was an ill omen that he should die at the start of the peace conference in which he and his fellows had invested all their hopes for remaking the world. He was buried on a small hill overlooking the Seine.


BETWEEN THE END OF OCTOBER 1918 and the middle of November, the Hapsburg Austro-Hungarian empire disintegrated and then disappeared. In its place were newly proclaimed independent states: Czechoslovakia, Hungary, and Yugoslavia. All that remained was German Austria, which awaited such terms as the Allies might impose. The last of the Hapsburg emperors, Charles, fled into exile.

In November Germany broke apart under the strain of the Armistice negotiations. In the port of Kiel, admirals who feared an ignominious surrender planned to order the fleet to steam out into the high seas to attack the British navy; but rumors of the plan led to a mutiny in which a sailors' council took charge. Then a similar council took power in Wilhelmshaven, Germany's largest naval base. Inspired by these successes, sailors, soldiers, and workers took control of cities throughout northern Germany in the first week of November.

In the south, Bavaria, threatened with invasion through Austria by Franchet d'Esperey and fearful that Prince Max might not surrender in time, seceded under Left Socialist leadership, proclaiming itself an independent republic.

This led Kaiser Wilhelm to abdicate on behalf of himself and his dynasty, and to flee the country. Prince Max resigned on November 9 in favor of the Socialist leader Friedrich Ebert as authority disintegrated. Spearheaded by the Spartacists—the communists—the Left blocked Ebert's formation of a government, and Ebert turned for support to the army's Supreme Command. But even the army was disintegrating. To prop up Ebert, the Supreme Command called on individual officers to recruit volunteer forces of their own. These "free corps" armies then waged and won a bloody civil war against Bavarian secessionists, and against communists and their allies, that was not concluded until June 1919.

So two of Woodrow Wilson's objectives in Germany, the overthrow of the kaiser's government and the defeat of the communist revolt, were achieved; but they were accomplished by the very military clique that Wilson believed made Germany a threat to the world's peace—and left that clique, albeit behind the scenes, in a position to exert power.

IN A SPEECH IN NEW YORK CITY in the autumn of 1918, Wilson had said that he would never come to terms with people as dishonorable as Germany's rulers. In a similar vein his young State Department adviser William Bullitt counseled (in a memorandum dated October 4, 1918) that no offer of armistice or peace, however reasonable, be entertained unless it were offered by a "government controlled by the German people." Wilson himself, in his notes to Prince Max in October 1918 leading to the Armistice, made it clear that he would not accept an armistice or peace proposal if the offer came from a government headed by Kaiser Wilhelm.

Unlike the leaders of Britain and France—who thought in traditional terms of national security, vital interests, and balance of power, and to whom "the German problem" was that Germany was much too powerful as compared with her neighbors—Wilson was a spokesman for a new and American doctrine of politics, according to which the German problem was that Germany had the wrong kind of government. In this view, Germany could be infinitely powerful and yet not disturb the peace if she became a democracy. History provided examples of democracies that were imperialist and war-loving, but Wilson ignored them. In his speech to Congress asking for a declaration of war, and in his reply (aided by Walter Lippmann) to the 1917 peace plea of the pope, the President had outlined his view that it was the militarism pervading German society and the German government that had caused the outbreak of the war.

The President's program therefore was to change Germany. To do that—to persuade the German people to alter their social and political system—he would have had to show them that their existing system, their militarist system, did *not* bring them what they wanted—happy, secure, prosperous lives—while democracy could and would. That meant being brutal to Germany when she was militarist, and kind to her when she was not. It meant offering her harsh peace terms so long as she continued to follow the kaiser and his generals, but easy and generous terms if she over-threw them.

Once Wilson had decided on stiff peace terms in any event, it should have been clear to him what road he had to follow. Instead of denying Kaiser Wilhelm and the Ludendorff military regime a chance to surrender, the President should have *insisted* that they do the surrendering—and in public. The German people should have been obliged to see their military leaders—not their civilian ones—humbled. Wilson then should have seen to it that a military regime stayed in place during Germany's months of collapse, disorder, and bitter hardship.

Only if and when he could persuade the Allies to treat Germany generously should Wilson have encouraged Germany to change to a democratic regime. That would have shown the German people that a civilian government, a democratic society, and a peaceful foreign policy bring rewards.

Instead Wilson allowed the kaiser to run away, Ludendorff to resign, and both of them to avoid the odium of defeat. It was kept secret from the public that the generals were the ones who had asked for an armistice. All responsibility for the disgrace of surrender and for the horrors that followed it were shifted onto the shoulders of democrats, socialists, and civilians.

It was Wilson's muddled approach to armistice-making, including his decision to end the war before the U.S. and Allied armies had a chance to invade Germany, that made it possible for German text writers, inspired by Ludendorff and the military, to teach their young that the German army had not been defeated in the war; that Germany's generals had wanted to continue the fight; that unpatriotic Leftists had allowed themselves to be fooled into signing an armistice by fraudulent Allied promises of generous terms; and that it was only a collapse on the home front engineered by socialists, Jews, and other civilians—"a stab in the back"—that had brought down the German army. It was on the basis of this false history that young Adolf Hitler and his colleagues were to start in 1919 along the path that would lead to power, world war, and mass murder.

The real stab in the back at the end of 1918 was the one administered to the hopes for German democracy. The knife was wielded by the German army's Supreme Command, and in particular by Ludendorff, who was to become the godfather of Hitler's Nazi party. But the deed was made possible only by Wilson's failure to grasp the basic principle of behavioral psychology: you reward conduct that you want to encourage and punish conduct that you want to discourage.

Wilson rewarded militarism by insisting that the kaiser and his generals not assume the responsibility for surrendering. When Germany adopted a democratic form of government, he then punished her by stiffening his peace terms—and continuing a blockade that brought hardship to the German people. He should have done it the other way around.

# PART FIVE

# A Separate Peace

## 23

# THE *GEORGE WASHINGTON* GOES TO EUROPE

EVEN BEFORE PRESIDENT WILSON and his men brought the United States into the war, they had been thinking about the peace. In a diary entry dated September 29, 1917, Colonel House noted that "in speaking of the peace conference, I told Howard [Roy Howard, head of the United Press] of my suggestion to the President of more than a year ago that he should go in person. Howard thought it an admirable suggestion."

It would be unprecedented. Theodore Roosevelt had traveled to Panama, but no President had ever gone overseas during his term of office. On the other hand, the peace conference was going to be the biggest event since the Congress of Vienna. Wilson aspired to change the world and bring about perpetual peace; if that could be accomplished at the conference, it would be the biggest moment in history. The President could play the leading role in it: thus, the temptation to go proved irresistible.

Even the postmaster general, House told Wilson in October 1917, "desired to be a peace commissioner, in fact, everybody I knew desired to be one. The President replied, 'Do you think the American people would sustain me in being the only representative from the United States at the conference?' I did not know. . . ." House recalled that he had suggested the idea two years earlier but that conditions had changed; now there would be committees at the peace conference, so at least three American representatives would be needed.

A year later, when the time for decision arrived, Wilson was determined to go to Paris himself, even though there were real questions as to whether his leaving the country was legal (a statute enacted in 1913 forbade it), let alone wise. Not merely would he go, but his notion was that in meeting overseas with the Allied prime ministers, "I assume also that I shall be selected to preside."

House, already in Europe as the President's plenipotentiary, became aware of some of the problems that might arise were Wilson to spend any considerable time at the peace conference, and cabled him November 14 in search of a compromise. Putting the blame for the unwelcome advice on others, House claimed that British and French leaders were worried that Wilson, as head of state, would outrank their prime ministers, who were merely heads of government; they therefore suggested that Wilson spend only a short time in Europe at a preliminary meeting that would set the main lines of the peace agreement, leaving it to others to work out the details in the lengthy peace conference that would follow.

Wilson was put out of humor by the cable, and replied that he would not allow his superior rank to become a problem. No point of dignity, cabled the President, "must prevent our obtaining the results we have set our hearts upon and must have." Turning a blind eye and a deaf ear to the considerable resistance to his proposed voyage, Wilson told House that "it is universally expected and generally desired here that I should attend the conference."

Wilson's son-in-law, Secretary of the Treasury William Gibbs McAdoo, proposed that he himself should go but that the President should not. Both of his suggestions were rejected, and he resigned from the cabinet.

The President's face turned grim when Secretary of State Lansing, too, advised him not to go. Wilson never forgave him. But it would have been awkward to have left the secretary of state behind, so Wilson appointed Lansing a peace commissioner, along with himself and House.

General Tasker Bliss, the U.S. military representative on the Supreme War Council, sent message after message to Wilson telling him that it was essential that the President personally come to Europe to push the American peace program. Wilson happily made Bliss a peace commissioner in place of (and at the suggestion of) Secretary of War Baker, who felt duty bound to remain in Washington.

For the fifth and final place on the American Peace Commission, Wilson sought a token Republican. But he wanted one whose support he could count on, which ruled out the obvious choices: ex-President Taft, former Secretary of State Elihu Root, and Senator Henry Cabot Lodge. Having rejected several nominees, he and Lansing chose a retired diplomat named Henry White, who carried no weight in the Republican party but whose views the President found congenial.

So long as he was the solitary commissioner in Europe, House had been happy to have Wilson stay at home. But he was glad the President was coming to Europe now that there were to be more commissioners. The other three might not have let House have his way were the President not there. As explained in a diary entry by Willard Straight, who was in House's confidence: "I think he [Wilson] wants to come. It's obvious the others don't want him to. They're afraid of him. House is afraid of the rest of the American mission."

Wilson planned to make decisions not only for the American mission, but for the peace conference as a whole. He told a Swiss scholar that he intended to "run it all" at Versailles, but would do so without hurting the feelings of the leaders of the Allies.

But the President was obliged to delay his departure until December 2, 1918, when he was scheduled to deliver the annual State of the Union speech on Capitol Hill. At midnight on December 2–3, only hours after addressing the Congress, Wilson boarded a train for Hoboken, New Jersey, where he was awaited by the *George Washington*, the liner that would bring him and America's message to the Old World.

The brother of Elly Axson (Wilson's deceased first wife) wrote the President that "you carry overseas with you the hearts and hopes and dreams and desires of your fellow Americans. Your vision of the new world that should spring from the ashes of the old is all that has made the war tolerable to many of us. . . . Nothing but a new world is worth the purchase price of the war. . . ."

Wilson himself claimed that his showdown in Paris with the leaders of Europe would prove to be "the greatest success or the supremest tragedy in all history."

WHEN HE BOARDED THE OCEAN LINER, the President, evidently exhausted, was suffering from a cold and a cough. His doctor and constant companion, Admiral Cary T. Grayson, was by his side. The ship's commander plotted a southerly route to give the President a more pleasant crossing. The Wilson suite was comfortable and the President's schedule was leisurely: he went to bed early, slept till noon, was served meals in his rooms, and took restorative walks on deck. After a couple of days at sea, he was back to normal.

The State Department, relegated by the President to the role of arranging the details of the American expedition to Paris, took full advantage of its position and assigned to itself the best staterooms aboard ship as well as a private dining room and bar, where Lansing, Bullitt, and other of its officials congregated to be served by a staff taken from a New York hotel. Meanwhile, members of the President's entourage, including the outside experts on the staff of the Inquiry, were herded into cabins on "D" deck that had been used for troop transport.

Bullitt, who maintained contact with the Inquiry people, became aware that for them this was the final blow. They had been allowed little or no contact with those who were to make the decisions, and they felt unappreciated. They invited Henry White to tea, and he brought Lansing along, but it was the President they really wanted to meet. Bullitt contrived to speak to Wilson and "explained that everybody on board was in a thoroughly skeptical and cynical mood" and suggested that he talk to them so they would not feel ignored.

Though surprised, the President adopted the suggestion and spoke informally to some of the assembled scholars for about an hour. He discussed the establishment of a new world order. He said that the traditional European balance, in which the peace was kept by countervailing power, with each alliance checked and balanced by a rival alliance of roughly equal power, was a system inherently flawed. An alternative that he also rejected was an alliance of the victorious powers to uphold the peace settlement, such as was done in 1815 after the Napoleonic wars and such as TR urged now; but, Wilson argued, such an arrangement brought repression rather than stability.

What he had in mind (he said) was a broad general agreement by the countries of the world to join together in a league that would guarantee to each its independence and its present frontiers. Of course, existing frontiers might be—or because of changing conditions, might become—unjust; if so, the league would change them. He was not prepared to say how this would be accomplished; indeed, his point was that the specific procedures and machinery of the league should not be detailed in advance but should, like the Common Law of England, grow through experience.

The United States was qualified to lead the countries of the world into a new system of international relations because it had proven itself in peace and in war. Claiming that "at Château Thierry we saved the world," the President said that he had it from Pershing that the marines thrown into combat in that battle had stopped a German thrust at Paris that otherwise would have lost the war for the Allies. America's historic diplomacy, as exemplified by the Open Door policy in China, showed the country to be— unlike other countries—disinterested, and concerned only to do what is fair. The other nations, he said, could bring their disputes to the league of nations and trust the United States to be an impartial umpire of their claims.

Wilson encouraged the scholars to come to him during the peace conference if there were something vital they felt he had to know. "Tell me what's right and I'll fight for it," he promised.

BULLITT HAD TRAVELED on the first American peace boat to Europe—Henry Ford's—and in his newspaper dispatches had ridiculed it. Ford's notion had been that the European powers could and would settle their disputes by allowing Americans to referee them. That was Wilson's theory, too.

On his second peace-boat voyage, Bullitt took such claims more seriously. Only later, when embittered, did he poke fun at the idea of the President sailing off with a boat full of professors to cure the world's ills. The voyage of the academics provided an easy target. It was something out of a medieval allegory: the voyage of a ship of fools. Not unnaturally, Bullitt did not see the humor of it until after he ceased serving as one of the President's learned doctors.

What did bother him, he claimed, was that the President was ill informed about the issues that would be raised at the peace conference. Wilson championed the right of national self-determination, which meant that each group—Serbs, Croats, Slovaks, Czechs, Poles, Germans, Magyars, or whatever—should be free to choose its own political destiny and identity. In, for example, merging Bohemia, Moravia, and Slovakia into Tomáš Masaryk's new "Czechoslovakia," it therefore behooved the President to learn which national groups lived in those three provinces in order (according to his own principles) to consult them as to their wishes. But according to Bullitt, the following conversation took place:

WILSON: "Bohemia will be a part of Czechoslovakia."
BULLITT: "But Mr. President, there are three million Germans in Bohemia."
WILSON (*puzzled*): "President Masaryk never told me that."


A FEW DAYS INTO THE VOYAGE, the ship's newspaper, the *Hatchet*, carried a misleading news item. The British election campaign was in full swing, and on November 26 Winston Churchill, the colorful cabinet minister and Liberal member of parliament, had delivered a typically eloquent speech to his constituents in seeking reelection to the House of Commons. It was this speech that was the subject of the news item.

Churchill had begun by arguing that the war had been won by Liberal ideals—justice, freedom, tolerance, and humanity—as much as by the force of arms. He urged his audience to continue supporting constitutional and parliamentary government as against the antidemocratic doctrines of the new radical revolutionary movements in Germany and elsewhere. He also urged moderation in Allied treatment of defeated Germany.

He went on to ask: "Why should war be the only cause large enough to call forth really great and fine sacrifices?" and "Why is war to have all the splendors, all the nobleness, all the courage and loyalty?" He asked, "Why cannot we have some of it for peace?" The British people had given their all to the war for the past five years; now he urged them to pledge themselves to bringing the same effort and courage and national unity over the next five years to accomplishing constructive rather than destructive goals. "Five years of concerted effort by all . . . would create an abundance and prosperity in this land, aye, throughout the world, such as has never yet been known or dreamt of.

"There is enough for all," he said. "The earth is a generous mother."

Pointing to the miracles made possible by modern science, he concluded with the lines: "Repair the waste. Rebuild the ruins. Heal the wounds. Crown the victors. Comfort the broken and brokenhearted. There is the battle we have now to fight. There is the victory we have now to win. Let us go forward together."

In the course of his speech, Churchill reminded his listeners that the world remained dangerous and unsettled, and that even though peace was at hand, it was only prudent to maintain the strength of the Royal Navy. It was this, reported in alarming fashion by the *George Washington*'s newspaper, to which President Wilson, taking it as a military threat, responded with tirades against England and the Allies in conversations with the three journalists who accompanied his party.

It was American ships and American troops that had won the war, he claimed. By proposing an ambitious new shipbuilding program for the American navy, Wilson indicated, he could challenge Britain to an arms race that the wealthy United States could afford and the impoverished British empire could not. He would use this threat to get his way at the peace conference on the adoption of his program.

He said the Allied leaders "are evidently planning to take what they can get frankly as a matter of spoils. . . ." He was not going to let them do it. He would insist on a peace with justice—a peace, therefore, without victory. He regarded colonial empires such as those of Britain and France as inherently vicious, and saw in the Allied approach to peace terms a greediness and disregard of ethical principles that were the product of a corrupting political system.

In the course of his conversations aboard ship, Wilson touched on a number of other points, too, that were part of his American program for remaking world politics. Implied or stated, these were some of his goals: (1) the seas no longer to be dominated by Great Britain, but rather to be free, with American vessels always at liberty to go anywhere; (2) the European powers no longer to have colonial empires; (3) defeated Germany not to be destroyed, but rather reformed and given another chance; (4) the European powers to work together in unity rather than to balance against one another in rival blocs; (5) all countries to join a league that would keep boundaries from being changed by force; (6) diplomacy, including negotiation and conclusion of agreements between countries, to take place in public; (7) disarmament by all; and (8) foreign policies to be aimed at seeking achievement of ethical principles rather than pursuing the national interest or safeguarding national security.

At no time in history would such a program have had a chance of being accepted, let alone actually adhered to, by an imperfect human race. It was the stuff of dreams; it was too good for this world. Of course, the world war had brought about profound changes. Wilson was right to believe that politics in the winter of 1918–19 were in important ways different from what they had been in the past. But had the world changed so much as that? Even in the altered political circumstances of 1918–19, it was difficult to conceive of any way in which the United States could persuade or force victorious Britain, France, and Italy to accept such a program. The Allies looked forward to gaining, rather than losing, by winning the war. They intended to expand their empires, not surrender them.

At one time or another, Wilson had believed he would have in hand several levers with which to budge the Allies. But by the time he was aboard the *George Washington*, it should have been clear to him that none of those levers was available:

- Had the war lasted until 1919 or 1920, in all likelihood the exhausted Allies would have fallen by the way, the AEF would have entered the war in full force and with its own equipment, and Pershing could have imposed America's will by force of arms on Allies and enemies alike. But that did not happen.
- Wilson often spoke of cutting off credits and loans to the Allies, but for reasons of domestic politics he could not carry out such threats, as these credits and loans went to purchase American goods and farm products.
- As he so often did, Wilson spoke of going over the heads of the Allied leaders to public opinion; but it would have done him no good, for public opinion was against him, too. On such issues as whether to punish Germany and whether to expand their empires, the peoples of the Allied countries were on the side of their leaders, not on Wilson's. Even in the United States, opinion favored harsh peace terms for Germany, not the benign ones that Wilson seemed to have in mind.

The brilliant young liberals who had left off idolizing TR in order to rally to Wilson had therefore begun to reproach the President for having articulated a political program without having thought through how it could be achieved. According to Willard Straight,* whose views were generally shared by Lippmann and Bullitt, Wilson should have gotten the Allies to agree to America's terms early in the war, at a time when they needed help desperately. But even earlier in the war, America had helped the Allies only as an incidental by-product of helping herself; so she could have brought pressure to bear on the Allies only by threatening to harm herself —hardly a convincing threat. Besides, even if the Allies, under duress, *had*

* For Straight's criticism of Wilson, see page 190.

agreed to America's terms, they could (and probably would) have walked away from their concurrence once the war was over.

A more convincing explanation of why Wilson in 1918–19 was not in a position to achieve his American program was that it was unachievable— at least at the time. Only decades later, in the aftermath of the Second World War, would Western Europe finally be so helpless and desperate as to be ready to accept some of the terms of his program.

In those later years mature men who had served Wilson in their youth would find his program there where he had put it down, waiting to be picked up and used, and would marvel at his foresight in understanding what their needs would be. So it would be said that Wilson was a prophet. But he was not: not, that is, in the sense of being clairvoyant. He did not foresee the events that led some of his program to become practical politics in 1945–60, any more than he understood why none of it was practical politics in 1918–19. He believed that with God's help he would see his program adopted at the peace conference in Paris in 1919. Repeatedly he spoke of the coming conference in apocalyptic terms, and was not hopeful of a second chance if the conference failed. For him it was a matter of now or never. He believed, and was not alone in believing, that the peace conference in Paris was going to be the big event in human history.

FRANKLIN ROOSEVELT was determined to be there. He had missed serving in the war, he had been blackballed from the Porcellian Club at Harvard, and he had made up his mind that he was not going to lose out a third time. As always of late, his health was in poor condition, as was his marriage, but his thoughts were focused not on them, but on getting himself to Paris; and his plausible theory was that he was needed in France to deal with naval demobilization overseas. But Josephus Daniels refused to give permission and remained adamant.

"We've lived in suspense from day to day," said Eleanor, "never knowing what would happen next" . . . in love or war. She said that because of his health, Franklin would "have to be careful this winter. Of course now"—after the Armistice—"he can't go over and join the Naval guns at the front as he had his heart set on doing. He is anxious to be sent back to see to Navy things over there, but so far the Secretary can't be brought to see that some civilian with authority must go over. In time, however, F. may convince him."

AS THE *GEORGE WASHINGTON* STEAMED at a leisurely pace across the Atlantic, peace commissioner Edward House, assisted by Roosevelt's friend from Groton and Harvard, Joseph Grew, was at work in Paris setting up a staff, arranging housing, and paving the way for the President's arrival.

Among those whom Grew rewarded with an appointment to the staff was Christian Herter, whom he had first met at the Berlin embassy before the war, who had worked for him in Washington, and who had been doing a first-rate job dealing with prisoner-of-war issues out of the American legation in Bern. After the Armistice—which provided that U.S. and Allied prisoners were to be immediately released and returned to their own lines —Herter had been dismayed, on inquiring how the repatriation was proceeding, to learn that neither the Red Cross nor the army seemed to know anything about it. Taking three Red Cross officers with him, the young American had driven across France and Germany without authorization, making sure that American captives were being well treated. "What do you think of your old husband being the first . . . of the Allies to cross the Rhine?" he wrote to his wife. "Speedy stuff—what?"

In Germany, Herter saw authority disintegrating and red flags flying. On returning to the U.S. legation in Switzerland, he heard warnings of the Bolshevik peril to central Europe. He passed on to Washington the advice he received from German and other sources: that the United States should distribute food to the starving masses of the former German and Austro-Hungarian empires in order to combat the menace of communism. He also arranged secret meetings between aides of Herbert Hoover and German and Austrian officials to try to work out something along these lines. The meetings were kept secret from the Allies, who according to Herter were "watching us closely—fearing that we are trying to put some hooks in their present scheme of completely ignoring the Americans generally & President Wilson in particular."

At Christmas he was elated to receive word that Grew had appointed him a member of the secretariat of the peace conference, and had attached him to the Republican commissioner Henry White. Though happy to watch what he called the "royal battle of minds & wills" at the approaching conference, Herter had seen enough to fear the "terrible danger" of the fruits of victory "being nullified by the restoration of a . . . Europe based on the foundations of the old orders," which would result in "the destruction of faith . . . among the great masses of the people"—thus "giving bolshevism its great moral hold. . . ."

Young though he was, Herter presciently wrote of the coming peace settlement that "it looks as though it would be rotten & that sooner or later America would retire from Europe the laughing stock of imperialist politicians or the greatest hypocrite . . . ever. . . ."

THE *GEORGE WASHINGTON* DROPPED ANCHOR a mile off the French port of Brest at a little after 1:30 p.m. Friday, December 13;

the President believed that 13 was his lucky number. Warships had been firing twenty-one-gun salutes in his honor ever since sighting his vessel offshore early that morning.

General Pershing and other dignitaries were there to greet the President and his party, who came ashore after lunch. Bands played, bouquets were presented, and soldiers stood at stiff attention all along the way as the Wilsons drove to the private train of the president of France, which had been sent to fetch them.

Cheering crowds lined the length of the railroad track from Brest to Paris. "WIL-son! WIL-son!" they cried. "*Vive* WIL-son!" Children waved American flags, and overhead were signs that read: "HAIL THE CHAMPION OF THE RIGHTS OF MAN. HONOR TO THE APOSTLE OF INTERNATIONAL JUSTICE. HONOR AND WELCOME TO THE FOUNDER OF THE SOCIETY OF NATIONS." As the President wryly remarked, such congratulations were a bit premature.

# 24

## DECIDING THE FATE OF THE WORLD

THE VISION THAT Woodrow Wilson offered to the world—perpetual peace, disarmament, freedom, and justice—was not original. Priests, prophets, and philosophers had spoken of such things ever since the first stirrings of human conscience evidenced themselves in Middle Eastern river valleys millennia ago. What surprised in 1918–19 was to find it the stuff not of a sermon, but of a political program. What was new was that the leader of the greatest power in the world pledged his country's best efforts to carry it through. To Europeans, it was novel, too, that the President should address the concerns not only of his own country, but of the human race. Above all, the Americans offered food and financing to revive a ravaged world; never before, in the thousands of years of warfare that constitute recorded history, had the conquerors on the morrow of victory stepped forward not to take, but to give.

The impact of Wilson's message on the world outside the Americas was unique. For a fragile moment, even men of the world who should have known better allowed themselves to believe. In the United States, voters and politicians alike had lost faith in him; but many of the young men who followed the President to Europe—even those who later were most disillusioned and embittered—remembered their time of service under him as the high point of their lives.

AS THE PRESIDENT of the United States headed toward Paris to remake the world, so did hundreds of others, in pursuit—unlike Wilson—of their own narrow interests. The central political fact of the winter of 1918–19 was that the old order had broken down throughout central and eastern Europe and western Asia and had to be replaced. The Hohenzollern, Hapsburg, Romanov, and Ottoman empires all had come apart, leaving their neighbors, as well as hundreds of indigenous ethnic, religious, and linguistic groups, to battle for their share of the inheritance. Some—for example, Jews who hoped to establish a state in Palestine—wanted a small country of their own; others, hoping to achieve a larger presence on the world scene by joining forces, proposed to establish such federations as Yugoslavia and Czechoslovakia; while still others, among whom the Italians were notable, wanted to annex adjacent lands that hitherto had belonged to different countries.

To France they all went, to submit their claims to the judgment of Paris. To the European mind it occurred that something similar had happened at least once before. It was remembered that after the fall of Napoleon, the allies who had overthrown him had met in Vienna in 1814–15 to draw up a new map for Europe.

But to President Wilson's mind, the Congress of Vienna was a different affair altogether; indeed, there was no precedent in history for what he had in mind to do. At Vienna, statesmen, having erased existing kingdoms, states, and frontiers from the map, had merely sketched in new ones in their place. That was what the Allied leaders planned to do in Paris in 1919; it was only in that sense that they planned to remake the world.

But Wilson saw the task ahead as a remaking of the world in a more profound sense, never before attempted. He wanted to change forever the way in which countries deal with one another. He proposed to do away with international power politics and with war. In their place would function a worldwide association of states. Other than with House, his coauthor, Wilson had not discussed how his proposed league would work; he had not even told the scholars on the *George Washington.* But one might have guessed at the broad outlines of the plan gestating in the President's mind, for its origins were in the recent traditions of American diplomacy.

The notion to which American presidents and secretaries of state had been drawn for decades past was that of arbitration. In disputes among states, instead of scheming or fighting against one another, each would argue its case before a neutral referee and would agree to be bound by his decision.

In the sophisticated version of this plan that was growing in President Wilson's mind, representatives of every country would assemble on a regular or continuous basis to bring to the surface and articulate all disputes of a potentially disruptive nature; and then the countries that were neutral as between the disputants—and in Wilson's view, this usually would be the United States—would decide the issue and everyone would agree to abide by that decision.

So in believing that the proper purpose of the Paris conference was to remake the world and determine the political destiny of the human race, Wilson took a much larger view of what "remaking" might mean than did the leaders of the Allies; and his first priority was to get them to agree to remake the world in his broad sense, not in their more limited one.

But the three leaders of the principal Allies did not share the President's vision, nor were they even thinking, as he was, in long-run terms.

The prime minister of Great Britain, David Lloyd George, a dapper, white-thatched, electrically energetic little man of fifty-five—charming, devious, a political wizard from the magical land of Wales—was a Liberal whose coalition government was in power thanks only to the votes of the Conservatives, who in 1918 had won a landslide victory at the polls and thereafter held a great majority of the seats in the House of Commons. Although he personally favored moderation in dealing with Germany and accommodation in treating with Soviet Russia, in public he felt obliged— at least for the moment, until passions subsided—to take the hard line advocated by Parliament and demanded by the mass-circulation press. He would do the right thing (as he believed it to be) only if he thought he could afford to do it; for above all, the nimble-witted prime minister was an opportunist whose principal goals were to stay in office as prime minister and to acquire as much new territory for the British empire as he could without having to pay a price for it.

Georges Clemenceau, the French premier, in his late seventies, partly deaf, and portly, was a dedicated patriot: he cared for his country but for nothing else. He was a survivor of the National Assembly that in 1871 had been forced to accept the punishing peace terms that Bismarck's victorious Germany had imposed upon a beaten France.* In his mind's eye, he still saw the images of 1870–71: of starving, frozen Paris under siege by Prussians whose cannons shelled the city night and day. He was of an acid skepticism about people and theories, but harbored a lifelong passion: hatred of Germany. His goal was to keep Germany from being able to harm France again.

Vittorio Emanuele Orlando, fifty-eight, prime minister of Italy, led a country that need not have joined the Allies—indeed, need not have entered the war at all—and had done so only in order to win new territories: the share in the spoils of victory that England and France had promised. Orlando's mandate from his parliament and his public was to take as much as possible for Italy. Orlando represented a worldly Mediterranean people with no interest in changing the old game of politics, only in increasing their share of the winnings.

It was toward a meeting with these unillusioned, ethically pagan statesmen, as well as with the envoys of a narrowly focused and unsentimental Japanese government, and with the representatives of other associated powers of expansionist inclination, that America's visionary preacher-president journeyed on the railroad tracks from Brest to Paris while, lining his path, tens of thousands cheered him on.

---

\* Clemenceau, who had protested against France's acceptance of an armistice in that war, also had voted against the peace terms of 1871.

# 25

# PARIS IN THE PLAGUE YEAR

*I am describing what was, in fact, not a Conference, but a very serious illness.*
—Harold Nicolson, a young member of the British delegation,
later writing of the Paris Peace Conference of 1919

FRANCE BLAMED THE FLU ON SPAIN, and Spain, on France. The United States suspected that it came from eastern Europe, while western Europe believed that it came from the United States. In the Middle East, Edmund Allenby's victorious Egyptian Expeditionary Force contracted it from the Turkish troops they defeated. But the epicenter of the plague seemed to be the wartime front line in Europe.

Somehow the virus was born in the abattoirs that the western battlefields of the Great War had become. It seems to have arisen from the intermixture of mass armies in the principal arena of combat: northern France. For four years most of the killing had been concentrated in that small region. Millions of corpses had been dumped into its earth and waters to rot and be digested. Within its narrow bounds the native French and neighboring German troops fought against or alongside millions more who had been brought from all corners of the world—Africa, Asia, the Americas, the Pacific—each group carrying within it germs and viruses from its native land to which it alone had developed immunity.

Influenza is, in any event, unstable, mutating easily into different types to get around human defenses; and the mass meeting of the living and the dead from all over the planet on the western front—Flanders, Artois, Picardy, Champagne, and Lorraine—gave it an unparalleled opportunity. It was from these provinces that the deadly new strain of the influenza virus emerged.

For the American leaders who had come to Paris, it was Henry James's *Daisy Miller* writ large; it was in the corrupt, diseased air of Old Europe, amid the subtleties and deceits of cultures centuries old, that they fell ill. In some cases, most notably that of the President, it was to be a sickness not of the body alone, but of the soul.

WOODROW WILSON'S ARRIVAL in Paris was one of the great scenes in the drama of humanity. "When President Wilson left Washington he enjoyed a prestige and a moral influence throughout the world unequalled in history . . . and [as] the man of destiny . . . coming from the West, was to . . . lay for us the foundations of the future." So wrote the young English economist John Maynard Keynes, who served as an official of the British Treasury at the Paris conference. If anything he understated the case. Wilson was welcomed with rapture by masses who hailed him as a savior from dangers past and as a messiah who would deliver them from dangers future.

In Gene Smith's gem of historical narrative, *When the Cheering Stopped*, we read that the day Wilson came to Paris, "there waited the largest throng in the history of France. . . . It seemed the whole of France stood in the streets . . . men and boys clung to the very tops of the chestnut trees. The housetops were covered with people. Lines . . . of thirty-six thousand French soldiers, the cream of the Army, stood fast to hold back the crowds. . . . [A] new sound, like the distant rumblings of thunder . . . grew louder. . . . '*Wil-son. Wil-son*' . . . the cheers coming like waves as he moved. '*Vive* Wil-son! *Vive* Wil-son! *Vive* Wil-son!' . . . The American Secret Service men were in a frenzy of fear for their charge, but it was impossible to do anything; the crowds were too enormous, the noise too loud, the press of bodies too great. People grew giddy; women wept as they screamed his name."

A hundred thousand people had crammed themselves into the Place de la Concorde alone, crying the President's name. Of the acclaim for Wilson that day, Prime Minister Georges Clemenceau said, "I do not think there has been anything like it in the history of the world."

William Bolitho Ryall, a British journalist who was to win fame with a book about great men, wrote that "no one ever had such cheers. I, who heard them in the streets of Paris, can never forget them in my life." He remembered that "I saw Foch pass, Clemenceau pass, Lloyd George, generals, returning troops, banners, but Wilson heard from his carriage something different, inhuman—or superhuman."

What Wilson heard was the peoples of the world crying for justice; what he may have failed to hear amid the clamor of "WIL-son! WIL-son!" was that they were calling for justice not as he, but as each of them, conceived it to be.


THE AMERICANS HAD ARRIVED for the peace conference too soon in every sense. The European powers were not yet ready for them;

indeed, they would not be ready for the message the Americans brought with them for another quarter of a century.

In the month of free time at his disposal while the Allied leaders tended to domestic politics, President Wilson traveled. At Christmas he journeyed to the British Isles; at New Year's, to Italy. The applause continued, and Wilson continued to misinterpret it. The French, British, and Italian peoples took to the streets to shout hurrah for the President because each thought he was on their side; but Wilson believed they were cheering because they were on his side.

The politicians did not share the popular enthusiasm for the President. In London, the Imperial War Cabinet found it incredible that Wilson should wish to deny overseas colonies to those who had won them from the enemy. William Hughes, the prime minister of Australia, demanded to know what contribution to the war entitled the United States to enact laws for the rest of the world, while Lord Curzon, of the inner War Cabinet, suggested that Britain and France go ahead to frame a peace settlement without bothering with the Americans.

In Paris, Clemenceau made clear to his appreciative parliament that Wilson's ideas—disarmament, ending the balance of power, establishing an international league—held little appeal for him. On the contrary, well-defended frontiers, adequate armaments, and the establishment of a solid balance of power were what would bring peace. If in 1914, he said, the United States, Britain, France, and Italy had agreed that an attack on one was an attack on all, there would have been no war: Germany would not have dared. Such an alliance, therefore, was what was needed to preserve national security in the future. The "old system" of politics remained good enough for him, he said; and in nuanced phrases, he suggested that Wilson was an innocent—someone a bit simple.


WILSON RETURNED FROM ITALY to gray, cold Paris early in January. It was rainy, and the swollen Seine had overflowed its banks. Late at night, the weather cleared; but the days were dark, chilly, and wet. Wilson was tired, and Dr. Grayson, his physician, ordered a couple of days of total rest.

# 26

# A WHO'S WHO
# OF AMERICANS IN PARIS

THE FRENCH GOVERNMENT had installed the President in the
Villa Murat, a three-story eighteenth-century palace near the Parc Monceau,
set back from the street, surrounded by trees, and guarded by sentries. It
belonged to the descendants of the Napoleonic cavalry general, marshal of
France, and king of Naples for whom it was named. In its luxurious interior,
attended by his wife and his physician, Wilson was able to live the secluded
life he preferred; while at the same time, there was a direct telephone line
between his bedroom and the quarters of Colonel House.

The French government requisitioned the entire Hotel Crillon on the
Place de la Concorde for the use of the American delegation, so that is
where the offices and apartments of the American Commission to Negotiate
Peace were located, not much more than a mile from the Villa Murat; but
Dr. Grayson forbade Wilson to work there with the others.

House had to bridge the gap between the President and the U.S. headquarters. He would relay news and views from the Crillon to Wilson, and
then Wilson would direct him to tell the American delegation what was to
be done. So not only the staff but also the other commissioners had to get
their orders from House.

At the Crillon, House occupied space, and headed a staff, larger than
those of all three other commissioners combined. The other three were in
the awkward position of not knowing what they were supposed to be doing.
Lansing asked; and in reply, Wilson sent a message telling him to feel free
to make any appointments or plans he chose, as he (the President) had
nothing particular in mind for him (the Secretary of State) to do. Commissioner White wondered why he himself was there.

House recognized that he had been placed in an invidious position,
and went out of his way to soothe the hurt feelings of the others. But it
was not enough.

Nor could House solve the basic organizational problem: that Wilson
was not acting as chief executive of the American delegation, so nobody
was. For nobody would presume to act in the President's place while the
President himself was there.

The nearest thing to an organizing head was Grew, who dealt with staffing and logistics. At the beginning, the army tried to take over from him, while the navy made a grab for control of communications, but he fought off both of them.

As Grew's assistant, House's protégé, and State's liaison with the Inquiry, William Bullitt was awarded the choice job of briefing the American commissioners each morning (including White, though he had his own aide, Christian Herter). This made him the conduit on substantive matters between the staff and the commissioners. Bullitt, Grew, and Herter, familiar since Berlin embassy days before the war, had been together at State ever since the war began; unlike some of the other Americans in Paris, they worked together easily.

The Inquiry was installed a few steps from the Crillon in the Hotel Coislin, where the rue Royale meets the Place de la Concorde. But it also was given space next door, above gaudy Maxim's, onetime playground of the demimonde, and scene of many frivolous and often scandalous episodes in the Naughty Nineties. The scholars were lodged upstairs, in the individual private rooms in which the restaurant had served clients who chose to do whatever they were doing behind closed doors. These quarters, associated in the popular mind with playboys and courtesans, may well have contributed to the general feeling among the Inquiry scholars that they were not being taken seriously.

Bullitt seems to have pressured House into giving the Inquiry something to do; for on December 31, House asked the experts to advise on all important territorial questions. At least one of the scholars suspected that this was no more than make-work. The professors had seen nothing of the President in the United States, and aboard the *George Washington* had seen him only because of Bullitt's intervention. In Paris at the end of January, the Inquiry scholars formally complained that during their first seven weeks in the French capital they had seen the President only once—for five minutes.

A long-simmering power struggle among the scholars had climaxed earlier when Isaiah Bowman shoved aside House's relative Sidney Mezes as leader of the group. Bowman then settled long-standing accounts with Walter Lippmann, who until then had not realized how much he had provoked the older man; as the litany of his misdeeds going back to New York days was recited to him, he finally understood. Seeing no role for himself in Paris, Lippmann, at the end of January, returned to New York and *The New Republic*.

Earlier in January, the Inquiry's head of economic studies, Professor Allyn Young, was surprised to learn that before leaving the United States, the President had appointed another body, the Central Bureau of Research and Statistics in Washington, to provide the economic data for the American delegation to the Paris conference. Young found that twenty-eight-year-old lawyer John Foster Dulles had arrived in Paris as representative of the Central Bureau, and apparently expected to take charge. Conflict was averted when Dulles settled for a compromise in which he and his staff would remain in Paris as the sole liaison between the Central Bureau in Washington and Young's Inquiry people in Paris. Dulles therefore was able to work in Paris alongside his uncle, Secretary Lansing, and his younger brother Allen, a colleague of Christian Herter's and an expert on Central European affairs, whom Grew and the State Department had brought up from the Bern legation.

An economic area of special concern (as the secretary of the treasury warned the President) was the treatment of America's loans to Europe; so at the President's request, the secretary early in January appointed and sent over to France an adviser to help deal with such matters. He was Thomas Lamont, the Morgan banker, a Republican, who was renting Franklin Roosevelt's house in New York City.

Earlier the President had summoned Bernard Baruch to Paris to help deal with economic issues. The South Carolina financier, a Democrat who made it his business to befriend the powerful, had made a success of heading the War Industries Board in 1918; "You have made yourself indispensable," the President had written to and of him. On arrival in January, Baruch took up residence in lavish style at the Ritz, assembled a personal staff, and began picking up the bill for some of President and Mrs. Wilson's extra expenses. A vain man, Baruch later implied that Colonel House felt threatened by him. As it happened, House fell ill with a kidney stone attack and was given up for dead not long after Baruch arrived, so the South Carolinian filled in for the colonel for a time. After House recovered, Baruch joined Mrs. Wilson in putting doubts into the President's mind about House.

S O M E   W E E K S   B E F O R E, on January 1, 1919, when Bernard Baruch boarded the *George Washington* to cross to France, he found Assistant Secretary of the Navy and Mrs. Franklin Roosevelt and their party, including Roosevelt's incorrigible partying companion Livingston Davis, among the mere handful of other passengers. It may have been Roosevelt's mother who finally succeeded in persuading Secretary Daniels to let him make the trip to Europe, charged with the mission of disposing of naval property overseas. It was evident Roosevelt wanted to go to Paris to be there when the fate of the world was being decided, but his mother was more likely to have been thinking in terms of repairing his shattered marriage to Eleanor.

It was a heavy sea. Eleanor—who had spent her autumn brooding over the statue in which Henry Adams, after his wife's suicide, had, through the medium of a chosen artist, personified grief—now spent her hours aboard ship reading the Christmas gift she had given Franklin: the autobiography in which Adams, with a deep sense of futility and failure, told of his search for an education. Published for the first time only months before (from the 1906 private printing, later corrected), *The Education of Henry Adams* told of a vanished fellowship, the five friends who called themselves Hearts, and of the others to whom they were attached: public figures, most of them, given over to probing the great issues of history and politics, religion and philosophy, while secretly engulfed (though one would not know it from the *Education*) in personal tragedies, private passions, and hopeless, illicit relations.

Henry Adams himself had been the last of the Hearts; he had passed away in his sleep the night of March 26–27, 1918. The youngest in their set, the protégé of Adams's student Henry Cabot Lodge, was TR, the most dynamic of the characters described in *Education.*

Reading about the young TR during the course of her stormy ocean passage, Eleanor must all the more have been shocked when the news, tapped out by wireless to the *George Washington* in the middle of the voyage, was announced to all on board: the former President—who was widely expected to be elected President again in 1920—had died of a pulmonary embolism in his sleep. In politics, all bets were off now; it would be a new game, played by new men—Franklin Roosevelt, among them.

THE YOUNG ROOSEVELTS spent thirty-five days in Europe. As Franklin's naval aide Commander John Hancock ably dealt with the complicated questions they had come to Europe to resolve, Franklin had a good deal of free time.

In Paris the Roosevelts stayed at the Ritz. The French capital, despite the flu epidemic, the cold, and the rain, was starting to come alive. After the wartime blackout, it was the City of Light once again; and Eleanor, at least at first, was enthralled. "I never saw anything like Paris," she wrote home. "It is full beyond belief and one sees many celebrities and all one's friends!" It was something that other young Americans discovered, too; Robert Taft arrived on Hoover's staff, and found Paris filled with college classmates from Yale. The Paris conference turned out to be a place of American school reunions.

The streets, restaurants, and hotels swarmed with delegations of every religion and color and nationality from every continent in the world. For most, hotel rooms were unfindable and restaurant meals unaffordable. Shopping was irresistible, and Eleanor admired the courage and self-control with which Franklin surveyed the bills for what she had bought.

Celebrities were everywhere. Sarah Bernhardt was sighted at luncheon, and young Harold Nicolson had the experience of dining with Marcel Proust at the Ritz. Robert Vansittart, another young British diplomat, later remembered that it was at the Paris conference that the Americans first introduced the British to that modern entertainment, the cocktail party, from which, Vansittart wrote, "women barely tore themselves away in time to undress for dinner."

But it was not a social scene to everyone's liking. For Eleanor Roosevelt, who in any event had fallen ill, the pleasures began to pall. She tried to broaden her tolerance; she condoned the drinking of wine with meals ("The cheer would certainly be too cold without it"). But "the scandals"—the way many of the American men behaved in Paris—"would make many a woman at home unhappy." When Franklin seemed too much drawn to another woman at a dinner party, she dragged him home early.

She understood that Franklin and his friend Livy Davis would want to go out on inspection and battlefield trips without her. But after one such trip, she became worried and annoyed. It was on February 8, and he was scheduled to return that afternoon; as he knew, she had planned a dinner at eight that evening, but he did not appear until after midnight.

The next night was the one too many. Franklin, Livy, and other members of Harvard's Fly Club held a reunion party from which her husband staggered back in the early hours of the morning.

Eleanor turned against Europe, as did so many Americans who had an experience of the peace conference. The women of Paris, she decided, were dangerous for her husband; they were brazen, and "you wonder if there are any ladies." She went further: "I've decided there is very little real beauty in France!"

When the Roosevelts returned to America, Franklin's companion in dissipation Livy Davis turned over a new leaf: he signed on with Herbert Hoover, whom many hailed as a new savior, to feed the hungry in Czechoslovakia.

# 27

# A CLASH BY NIGHT

THERE WERE MORE THAN 1,000 Americans at the peace conference—perhaps as many as 1,300—and a great many of them later published books describing their experiences in Paris. Indeed, many were preparing from the start to do so. "It is amusing, going about as I do, to discover . . . [everyone], more or less surreptitiously, keeping diaries . . . ," Ray Stannard Baker, the journalist who had become head of the American delegation's press bureau, noted—in his diary, of course.

Felix Frankfurter, who was there himself, later said that "the best book I know on the Paris Peace Conference is Harold Nicholson's [sic] *Peace Making* . . . and the reason why I say it's the 'best book' is that he gives you the sense of disorderliness, the hubbub, the hallabaloo. . . ." According to Nicolson, an essential element of the story of the peace conference was confusion; "my study, therefore," he wrote, "is a study of fog."

Nothing had been planned in advance, not even when the conference would begin or how long it would last or what matters it would deal with. Matters, when the time came, were not taken up in a predetermined order, or indeed in any order. Most important of all, it had not been decided whether this was to be a meeting of the Allies and their associates to decide what peace terms they should *ask*, in which case the terms would be pitched high, as "asking prices" normally are—or whether it was to be a peace conference, in which case the other side, the Germans and their associates, would be invited to attend, and the conference would decide on peace terms that would be *accepted* by all sides, therefore representing a series of compromises.

As nobody invited the Germans to attend, one might have assumed that the former was the case, that a preliminary conference was in session, and that what was being drafted was not an agreement, which would take full account of the needs and desires of the other side, but a negotiating position, which would not need to do so. But though nobody got around to thinking the matter through or discussing it, it transpired that such was not the case; for months later, when the drafting was concluded, the document was submitted to Germany not as a proposal to be responded to, but as a treaty to be signed.

Similarly, those who were about to meet failed to talk through and reach agreement on an agenda; and of the thousands who streamed into Paris for the conference, it seemed at times as though each had an agenda of his own. Wilson, who had decided on a set of priorities, found himself repeatedly elbowed out of the way before he had been given a chance to assert it.

Herbert Hoover did it first, albeit with the President's consent. Beginning the week before the Armistice, Hoover had agitated as a first priority for the creation of a program under his direction to distribute American food supplies in Europe. The U.S. government had accumulated large surpluses of food supplies during the war; by donating them to the starving peoples of central and eastern Europe, the government at the same time could protect farm prices at home and keep countries abroad from falling prey to communism. Wilson and House were in agreement with Hoover about this, and about his insistence that the program should be an American one, independent of the Allies: "Let it have our brand," said Hoover.

However, the British, who were needed to supply the ships to transport the food, opposed Hoover's plan: they insisted on maintaining a blockade of Germany, which shocked Americans, who saw no reason to starve German civilians now that a cease-fire was in place and the war was effectively over. The French and Italians, in turn, did not want the United States to win the power that would come with controlling the food supplies: they desired it for themselves, aspiring to monopolize food distribution in the neighboring areas they hoped to bring into their orbits.

Blunt Herbert Hoover talked tough. "This government," he proposed to tell the Allies, "will not agree to any programme that even looks like inter-Allied control of our economic resources after peace. After peace over one-half of the whole export food supplies of the world will come from the United States and for the buyers of these supplies to sit in majority in dictation to us as to prices and distribution is wholly inconceivable. The same applies to raw materials."

Coming over to Europe for the peace conference, Hoover decided to send an American mission to Germany to report on conditions there. The British government objected to such a mission unless they, too, participated in it. Hoover ordered his own men to go anyway, and advised House to tell the British he was doing so. "Do nothing else," Hoover said to House, telling him not to ask permission from the British; "simply inform them."

Lloyd George was afraid, first, that American aid would go to the defeated countries when it was still needed by the Allies, and second, that the Americans would use control of food distribution (as he himself would have done) to achieve political ends. As the British ambassador to the United States put it, the hand that fed Europe would control its destiny.

In Paris Hoover lobbied Wilson, who sent a note (drafted by Hoover) to the Allies, informing them that because the situation in Europe was desperate, the United States was going ahead on its own to set up a Food Administration for the Continent—and would notify them of what it did so that they could make plans of their own.

Hoover bullied Joseph Grew into giving his organization thirteen rooms at the Crillon, despite expressions of alarm from the peace commissioners in residence there; threatened to leave Paris if any of the thirteen were taken away; and demanded more rooms. For others of his staff, he found and took over fifty rooms in an apartment house, though some must have been housed elsewhere, for Robert Taft a few months later sublet a furnished apartment for himself at 33, avenue Montaigne. Hoover also went out and recruited some 1,500 American officers from the armed forces. Eventually he agreed to report to an Inter-Allied Council for Supply and Relief (which convened in January 1919) and then to a Supreme Economic Council (which replaced it in February), but he continued to act on his own responsibility as director general of his agency.

Hoover commandeered the railroad system of central Europe, sent battleships hither and yon, took control of coal mines, distributed food only through his own officers, dictated policy to municipal and other authorities, and actively intervened in all sorts of areas of life and politics in the chaos that once had been the German, Austrian, and Russian empires. At House's request, Hoover also used his operation as a cover for military intelligence officers, who wore civilian clothes and were provided by Hoover with titles in his organization. Lewis Strauss, one of Hoover's chief aides and a future head of the Atomic Energy Commission, reported to the American delegation in Paris at the end of 1918 that this had been done. Although time and again Hoover said that his provision of aid to the starving and needy of Europe was intended to save them from communism, he regarded the work he was doing as nonpolitical.

Earlier, House had asked Hoover about his politics. Hoover said he could support either the Democratic or Republican party: whichever had "a progressive program." He claimed that he had no wish to be President, but House thought Hoover was fooling himself. The colonel had been dealing with politicians all his life; he knew a man who wanted to be President when he saw one.


YOUNG WILLIAM BULLITT also had his own agenda, and was well placed to get a hearing for it, for he had the ear of the commissioners, of his State Department superiors, and through House, of the President. Bullitt's goal was to seize for Wilson and the United States the leadership of the noncommunist Left in Europe, so as to mobilize the masses against what he saw as the reactionary tendencies of their own governments, and also against the Bolsheviks, with their leaning toward dictatorship. He proposed to summon up British and French support against Lloyd George and Clemenceau and their old politics, and at the same time, socialist and working-class support against Lenin and his version of the new. Bullitt's vision, though, was a clouded one, and at times he imagined that Lenin could be won over to democracy, while at other times he recognized that the Bolshevik leader was not open to persuasion.

Bullitt pressed his case in January 1919, as the peace conference was beginning, because European socialist and labor leaders proposed to hold their own international conference in the same city at the same time to deal with the same agenda, publicly urging the governments to heed the promptings of those who claimed to represent the masses.

In the end, the leaders of the Left were persuaded to hold their conference elsewhere, so they met not in Paris, but in Bern, Switzerland. Bullitt wrote a memorandum to House and Wilson asking that Samuel Gompers, leader of the American Federation of Labor, be persuaded to attend. Gompers was in Paris as an adviser to the American delegation. Staunchly anti-socialist, Gompers refused to go to Bern.

Won over by Bullitt, the American peace commissioners on January 29 sent him to Bern as their representative. The International Labor and Socialist Conference convened on February 3, with representatives from twenty-six countries in attendance. The debates showed sharp differences along national lines—for example, between French and German delegates as to who should be blamed for having supported the war in 1914—but Bullitt, as Americans often did, tended to downplay the importance of the nationalist feelings that were expressed. He was fully satisfied by the program the conference finally adopted. It called for a league of nations open to all countries, in which parliaments (rather than the executive branch of government) would be represented; disarmament; an international court; free trade; no territorial annexations; carrying on the class struggle only through democratic means; freedom of speech, press, and assembly; parliamentary government; everybody to have the right to vote; and the establishment of a charter for labor outlining the rights of working people.

One of the socialist leaders remarked at the Bern conference that "the President of the bourgeois U.S. Republic . . . represented a higher stage of humanity than the bourgeois governments of Europe." Bullitt, when he returned to Paris, reported that "the entire conference showed an almost pathetic confidence in President Wilson."

Yet when the Paris Peace Conference convened, it was not the American but the British delegation that proposed giving priority to international labor legislation, and it was Wilson who was not prepared to deal with it. On the President's agenda, which he was about to try to persuade the others to adopt, the League of Nations question was to be taken up first; but he had been sidetracked, first by Hoover's issue of food distribution, and then by this, which led Lloyd George to propose the creation of an agency that came into existence three months later and still exists: the International Labor Organization (ILO).

WILSON HAD BEEN WAITING in Europe impatiently and uncomfortably for nearly a month before he was able to sit down with the Allied leaders in Paris January 12. The conference was somewhat informal, and it assembled in an overheated conference room at the quai d'Orsay. It took the form of an enlarged meeting of the Supreme War Council, but when the military leaders left the room, it became the Council of Ten: the heads of government and foreign ministers of the United States, Great Britain, France, and Italy, and two spokesmen for Japan.

Wilson was squeezed for time. He would have to go back to the United States in mid-February to sign legislation at the end of the congressional session, and while he would return to Paris thereafter, he hoped to have something in hand to bring back with him to Washington in February.

At the January 12 meeting a revised French plan of procedure for the peace conference was presented that put territorial and economic issues first and the creation of a league of nations last. To Wilson's mind, that was the wrong way round; and on January 13 he urged his colleagues to put the league first.

Nobody will ever know what Wilson really thought, but what he often said was that with a league of nations in place, any decisions made at the peace conference that turned out to be wrong could be put to rights later. It would provide an insurance policy against the possibility that the conference might fail to adopt the peace terms Wilson had advocated—which in fact turned out to be the case. And the President ignored the objection that once it was agreed that decisions of the league had to be unanimous, every country would have a veto. So whoever benefited from the existing state of affairs was bound to veto any change in it.

It may be, however, as he sometimes suggested, that the President attributed such importance to establishing a league because he believed that it would be a first step toward changing the nature of world politics, and that once a first step was taken, a second and a third were bound to follow.

The issue of where the league question should be placed on the agenda remained to be decided when the peace conference opened formally on January 18 in the airless nineteenth-century quarters of the French Ministry of Foreign Affairs on the quai d'Orsay. Seated at a giant horseshoe-shaped table covered in green, around which were arranged sixty-nine red chairs, the delegates were welcomed by Raymond Poincaré, president of the French

Republic, in terms that outlined concisely his country's conception of the task at hand. Reminding the delegates that this was the anniversary of the taking by the Germans of the provinces of Alsace and Lorraine from a prostrate France, he said: "On this day, forty-eight years ago, on the eighteenth of January, 1871, the German Empire was proclaimed by an army of invasion . . . at Versailles. . . . Born in injustice, it has ended in opprobrium. You are assembled in order to repair the evil that it has done and to prevent a recurrence of it."

Moving that Georges Clemenceau, the head of the French government and its premier, be elected chairman of the conference, Wilson tried to return to universal themes (the "fortunes of all peoples are involved . . ."), but in accepting the chairmanship Clemenceau announced: "The greater the . . . catastrophes which devastated and ruined . . . France, the more ample and splendid should be the reparation."

There in a nutshell, as France's leaders saw it, was what had to be done: compensate France for the evil that Germany had wrought, and protect France against German wickedness in the future. But Clemenceau, especially after conversations with the persuasive Colonel House, saw no reason why Wilson should not have what he wanted, too. So long as France's security could be assured, he had no objection to establishing a league, nor even to incorporating the agreement establishing the league in the peace treaty (which Wilson wanted, on the unsound theory that then the U.S. Senate would have to swallow its objections to the league in order to obtain an agreement ending the war).

So when Wilson argued that the question of a league of nations ought to be the first item on the agenda of the peace conference, it followed, in the powerful logic of the French premier, that even before discussing that first item, he had to be assured that France's security needs and reparations claims *were* satisfied. And as the future of Germany's colonies was related to reparations, the question of colonies and empires had to be discussed before the first item on the agenda, too.

DURING THE WAR Great Britain and her dominions had captured many of Germany's colonies in Africa and the Pacific. Japan also had taken German possessions in the Pacific and had assumed the German position in China. Britain in addition had liberated the Middle East from the Ottoman Empire on behalf of herself as well as France and Italy.

Not even Woodrow Wilson advocated returning these territories to Germany or to the Turkish sultan. He had told the Inquiry aboard the *George Washington* that his thought was to turn them over to the proposed League of Nations; such territories would be administered by small countries, with their resources to be exploited for the benefit of all mankind. It was odd of him, even if in the American tradition, to imagine that small nations were morally superior to large ones and would be altruistic in dealing with colonies: little Belgium, in the Congo, was the most rapacious of the European colonialists in Africa. In any event, Wilson found no support in Paris for his plan.

As an American, Wilson had inherited the belief that the European powers ought not to possess colonies overseas. Face-to-face with the leaders of the victorious Allies, he was realist enough, however, not to go through the useless motions of asking them to divest themselves of their empires. Moreover, he found himself unable to resist their insistence on keeping the territories they had taken from the Germans and the Turks.

One of the weaknesses in America's anti-imperialist program was that Americans agreed with Europeans that "natives" were not, at least as yet, capable of governing themselves. When the United States forced a European power to abandon one of its overseas colonies (as it did in the 1898 war, pushing Spain out of the Philippines), it knew of no alternative government to propose but its own (as it did in annexing the Philippines). This made Americans look like hypocrites who were as much disposed to imperialism as anybody else, and whose real objection to Europe's colonies was that America coveted them for herself.

Turning that weakness into a strength, George Louis Beer, forty-six, a successful tobacco merchant who had retired at thirty-one to begin a second career as a historian and who was now a member of the Inquiry, provided Wilson with a face-saving formula on the issue of occupied German and Turkish territories: he offered the concept of trusteeship, of League of Nations "mandates." Jan Christiaan Smuts, the much-admired South African statesman, proposed something similar. The idea was that the Allied powers should govern former German colonies and Turkish domains only temporarily, in order to educate and develop them with a view toward eventual self-government and independence.

On the face of it, this allowed the President to claim that he had achieved America's anti-imperialist goals in dealing with lands captured from the enemy. If it were granted that they were not ready to govern themselves, it followed that he had set them on the only available path headed in the right direction: one that would lead them to responsible independence at some point down the road.

Of course, much depended on the good faith in which the mandatory powers took up their responsibilities. France, for one, frankly imperialist, regarded the business of being awarded a mandate as no more than a charade; in sending in an army in 1920 to occupy Syria (for which France was to receive a mandate from the League of Nations), the then premier of France, making no reference to eventual independence, proclaimed Syria to be a possession—"the whole of it, and forever."

AT THE SECOND FULL SESSION of the peace conference, on January 25, Wilson proposed a resolution calling for the establishment of a league of nations. Speaking without notes but with eloquence, though still suffering from a cold, he argued that such a league had to be established if the human race was to survive. House was enthusiastic: "What you have said today will hearten the world as nothing that you have said before . . . ," he wrote in pencil on a note he passed to the President. The Europeans were less impressed, and the secretaries omitted to report Wilson's statement that the league would do a better job of keeping peace than Christianity had done. (Lloyd George later recalled Wilson as having said that Jesus Christ had failed to get the world to follow his teachings because he had not thought of a practical way for people to achieve ideals, and that "that is the reason why I am proposing a practical scheme to carry out His aims.")

Once the colonies issue was settled to their satisfaction, the Allies agreed to let the President head a committee that would draft the charter (the "Covenant," as Wilson would call it, reminding his colleagues of his Presbyterian background) of an international organization; and he did so in ten meetings at the beginning of February.

Meanwhile, Clemenceau explored the question of how such an international entity would help ensure French national security. One approach (which the United States and Britain opposed) was for the proposed League to have an army at its disposal. The army would be the French army, and in effect it would be deputized by the world community to act in the world's name, enforcing the decisions of the League. Under cover of a league of nations, a French military hegemony in Europe would be established.

A rival concept was proposed from America by Walter Lippmann, who published a proposal calling for U.S. and British seapower to be combined as "the nucleus of world organization." Picturing seapower as essentially nonaggressive, he saw in it the ideal weapon with which to keep the peace in a world in which Britain and America would be the main arbiters between the nations. As for the League, it should be in continuous session, he wrote; it should be perceived as a process, taking the place of war. Quoting Smuts, Lippmann offered a bold solution to the threat (stressed by Bullitt) of chaos in the former Central empires. "Europe is being liquidated," Smuts had written, "and the League of Nations must be the heir to this great estate. The peoples left behind by the decomposition of Russia, Austria, and Turkey are mostly untrained politically; many of them are either incapable or deficient in power of self-government. . . ." Lippmann, in quoting Smuts, seemed to be suggesting that the international organization Wilson was creating ought to govern much of Europe and the Middle East.

At a general session of the peace conference February 14, the day he was scheduled to return to the United States, Wilson, with his hand on the Bible, read aloud the proposed Covenant of the League of Nations that he, House, Britain's Lord Robert Cecil, and others had drafted over the past fortnight. He then spoke in its favor. A French representative pointed to flaws in the proposed League, and a Japanese envoy repeated a request, always denied, for a written commitment by the framers of the League to racial equality. But Wilson's draft now was before the conference with the general expectation that it would be approved.

Wilson then left for Brest to board the *George Washington*. Franklin and Eleanor Roosevelt went aboard, too, returning to Washington at the same time. On the boat train carrying them to Brest, they read the draft of the Covenant, which they obtained from a journalist. Aboard ship, they hoped to spend time with the President and discuss it with him, but as he so often did, Wilson kept to himself. In the end, though, he did invite the Roosevelts to lunch, and spoke of American entry into the League: "The United States must go in or it will break the heart of the world for she is the only nation that all feel is disinterested and all trust."

ON THE VOYAGE HOME, Roosevelt stood on the bridge of the ocean liner one afternoon and spoke of his disappointments to a cousin, Sheffield Cowles. There was the old matter of having been blackballed from the Porcellian at Harvard, and the new matter, of which he would not speak, of the fragility of his marriage. For him the death of TR cast a pall over everything, personal and political. Roosevelt said that he recognized now that he should have followed TR's advice and joined in the fighting during the war. Usually hopeful, the charmed and charming young politician looked his future in the face and found that it had turned bleak.

# 28

## WAR OR PEACE WITH COMMUNISM?

IN LEAVING PARIS for a few weeks, the President left affairs in the charge of Colonel House, nominally in tandem with Secretary Lansing. He told House what he wanted him to negotiate in his absence, but on the understanding that he would make no binding agreements until the President returned.

The day of his departure, Wilson told the Supreme Council of the Allies that he would like to open informal talks with the Soviets—not to recognize them, or even to reach agreement with them, but to get information. During Wilson's absence, House and Lansing decided to follow up on this, having earlier been told by their own advisers, too, that the United States lacked reliable current data about Soviet Russia.

House, who was sensitive to currents of liberal opinion, was aware that the publication of the Soviet Constitution in the *Nation* had aroused some sympathy for the communists. He knew, too, that Bullitt on January 19 had suggested that America and the Allies send missions to Russia "to examine conditions in Russia with a view to recommending definite action."

On February 16 Lansing told House that he was in favor of sending Bullitt on such a mission to Russia to "cure him of Bolshevism." House instructed Bullitt to go to Russia secretly "for the purpose of studying conditions . . . for the benefit of the American commissioners." House and Lansing took into their confidence Lloyd George's aide Philip Kerr, who supported the project strongly, phoned the prime minister about it, and— as historians are inclined to believe—obtained his approval. Kerr drafted for House an unofficial statement of the terms on which he believed a settlement with the communists could be achieved. House sent the statement to Wilson.

Bullitt was given a copy of the proposed settlement terms, but was warned that it was a personal statement by Kerr that had no official sanction; to protect the prime minister, Kerr thus ensured that, if necessary, Lloyd George could wash his hands of the matter. It seems not to have occurred to the young American envoy that should news of his mission become public, he, too, along with Kerr's statement, might be disowned.

Bullitt set out on a path strewn with hidden land mines. Many on the Allied side were violently opposed to entering into contact with the Bolsheviks, and would have aborted Bullitt's mission had they known of it. Certainly the French would have done so. Clemenceau, a Radical, had been imprisoned briefly by revolutionaries more leftist than he in the civil war of March 1871, and hated communists with the passion that so often animates rivals for the same political constituency.

Adding fuel to the fire of Clemenceau's hatred for them, the communists of Moscow and Petrograd had dealt France two powerful blows. They had repudiated Russia's government debt, bonds that largely were held by French investors. France's losses on the tsar's securities would be all the more painful if the Ottoman sultan, as seemed likely, were driven to default on the bonds of his empire, too, of which the French again were the principal holders. It could mean financial catastrophe for French investors.

Even more harmful was the world policy blow the Leninists had struck: by taking Russia out of her alliance with France, they had destroyed the geopolitical strategy that alone allowed the French Third Republic, a weaker country, to confront her powerful enemy Germany on equal terms.

It was true that on the Left of the French political spectrum, there were those who took a less dim view of what the Bolsheviks had done. At the time of the Bullitt mission, Marcel Cachin, a socialist editor, had a luncheon meeting with Adolf A. Berle, Jr.—the youngest man ever to graduate the Harvard Law School and now, at the age of twenty-four, the head of the Russian section of the American delegation in Paris—in which Cachin said the French Left would support a settlement with the Bolsheviks that included their pledges to stop their propaganda campaigns abroad and to withdraw from the Baltic states. But Berle, like Bullitt, may have overestimated the popular support on which Socialists like Cachin could count.

For in the Western world, communism was not regarded as a legitimate ideology. In speaking to the scholars of the Inquiry aboard the *George Washington*, Wilson, according to Bullitt's notes, had referred to Bolshevism as a "poison." In plague-stricken Paris, the metaphor changed: what Lenin was spreading was labeled a disease. Transcripts of meetings between the Allied leaders that later were turned over by Bullitt to the U.S. Senate have Italian prime minister Orlando saying in early 1919 to the other government heads that "to prevent a contagious epidemic from spreading, the sanitarians set up a *cordon Sanitaire.* If similar measures could be taken against Bolshevism . . ." In time they were, and they were almost always described in Orlando's terms, as a cordon sanitaire: the roping off of an area of contagion by a line of guards.

The metaphor of communism-as-disease proved infectious. It was repeated often, thinkingly at first, unthinkingly later. Soon the words were in many mouths and on many tongues. Reminding his listeners that the

German General Staff, in order to overthrow the Allied regime in Petrograd, had facilitated Lenin's return to Russia and had supplied him with enormous quantities of the gold that enabled him to launch his bid for power, Winston Churchill, minister of war and air, told the House of Commons toward the end of 1919 that "Lenin was sent into Russia by the Germans in the same way that you might send a phial containing a culture of typhoid or of cholera to be poured into the water supply of a great city. . . ."

SENSIBLE PEOPLE do not try to compromise with an epidemic, they eradicate it; they treat an illness, not treat with it. In the United States, Britain, and France, there were enough people of importance who would have thought Bullitt's mission dangerously wrongheaded so that it could not have gone forward openly. To be undertaken at all, it had to be undertaken in secret.

But it was evident that Bullitt was going somewhere: his job of briefing the peace commissioners each morning ("Chief of Division of Current Intelligence summaries") was taken over temporarily by Christian Herter. One could have guessed where Bullitt was going; Germany and Russia were his two areas of special responsibility, so it was likely to be one or the other. But throwing observers off the scent, Bullitt and his companions, Captain Walter W. Pettit of U.S. military intelligence and the muckraking journalist Lincoln Steffens, mentor of John Reed and Walter Lippmann, traveled west instead of east: they left Paris for London. From there they went north to Sweden. Leaving Stockholm for Petrograd, Bullitt began his confidential talks with the Bolshevik leaders Chicherin and Litvinov March 9, and then went on to Moscow March 11.

The Bolsheviks, holding on to the capital cities of Petrograd and Moscow and to a stretch of territory in Russia, yet surrounded by the armies of foreign and domestic enemies, were at one of the low points in their fortunes. They were being hurt badly by an Allied blockade; the population was starving. They tried to hide it by serving Bullitt whatever they had, so at first, as he savored quantities of caviar three times a day, he was given the impression that the stories current in the West of hard times in Russia were exaggerated. But Bullitt was quick to learn, and he soon understood why Bolshevik officials so often dropped by to talk business at mealtimes: they were hungry, and hoped he would invite them to share in what he was eating.

The starvation, in Bullitt's view, was due to the Allied blockade and should not be blamed on Lenin's regime. But he grew rapturous about what the Bolsheviks had been able to accomplish in other areas. The streets were safe, he reported by cable to Colonel House, and "prostitutes have disappeared from sight, the economic reasons for their career having ceased to exist." Again and again he told Steffens and others that "we have seen the future, and it works"—a sentence that Steffens later published, without attribution, as his own.

The afternoon of March 14, by appointment, Bullitt finally met alone with Lenin in the Kremlin. Lenin already had read the Kerr statement of Allied terms, and in the desperate circumstances in which his government found itself, was prepared to accept it with only slight modifications. He told Bullitt that by throwing his weight in the Central Executive Committee against Trotsky and the generals, he had been able to force a committee decision to listen to a proposal from the Western world. But the proposal had to come from the West, he said. The terms were tough, and Lenin may have wanted to be able to tell his own people that they had been forced on him by the other side.

Lenin informed Bullitt that if by April 10 the West asked his government to do so, his regime would agree to a peace settlement on what essentially were Kerr's (and Britain's) terms: an immediate cease-fire; an amnesty in and out of Russia; free movement in and out of all the countries of formerly tsarist Russia; all the governments on Russian soil, including those still ruled by the tsarist military, to be recognized within their existing frontiers; a resumption of trade and an end to the Allied blockade; the Soviet and other Russian governments to pay all of Russia's debts and financial obligations; the withdrawal of all foreign troops from Russia; and the convening of a conference in a neutral country to arrive at a formal settlement.

"The Allies, as subsequent events were to demonstrate, would have been well out of it on these terms. It is a pity they were not accepted." Such was the mature judgment of George Kennan, America's foremost student of U.S.-Soviet relations, some four decades later. Even if circumstances had strengthened Lenin's hand such that he could have repudiated the agreement later, the Allies would have been no worse off than they were with no agreement at all.

But Bullitt was mistaken in his estimate of Soviet intentions. He did not understand Lenin's agenda. During the month of Bullitt's stay in Russia, the Soviets formed the Communist International (the "Comintern") as a rival to the Socialist international conference that Bullitt had attended in Bern the month before. Communism was cutting itself off from socialism on the basic issue of democracy: Bern was for it, Moscow against it. Moreover, the Bolshevik regime did not regard any peace agreement with the West as other than a temporary expedient: in Lenin's words, "The existence of the Soviet Republic together with the imperialist states is in the long run unthinkable."

So while Bullitt returned to Paris with an opportunity for the West to grasp, it was not so great an opportunity, nor could its benefits be expected to endure for so long, as he supposed.

Bullitt was jubilant about his having secured Lenin's agreement to Britain's settlement terms. House, too, was delighted, seeing a chance to quickly restore order in Europe—all the more desirable because a communist revolution had taken place only days before in Hungary. So when Bullitt reported to him in Paris the night of March 25, House phoned and sought an immediate audience for Bullitt with the President, who had recently returned to Europe. But Wilson refused, saying he had a headache. He also said that he had a one-track mind and could not deal with Russia while concentrating on other issues; he told House to take the matter in hand.

House scheduled meetings for Bullitt the next day with the other American peace commissioners. The following day Bullitt met at breakfast with the British: Lloyd George, Kerr, Smuts, and Balfour. In principle they should have been pleased, for it was Kerr's terms that Lenin had accepted. In fact, Lloyd George did want to agree to those terms. But he would not step forward; he did not want to get out in front on such an explosive issue and be the one to draw fire. He said he would follow if Wilson would take the lead. According to Bullitt, the British prime minister waved a copy of the mass-circulation, scare-headline *Daily Mail* in front of him—a newspaper that denounced the proposed agreement—and asked, "As long as the British press is doing this kind of thing how can you expect me to be sensible about Russia?"

The editors of the *Daily Mail* had the story of the secret agreement Bullitt had brought back with him because Gordon Auchincloss, House's secretary and son-in-law, had leaked it to them. Auchincloss had done so to try to wreck the agreement, of which he strongly disapproved. American newspapers followed the *Daily Mail* in denouncing the agreement with Lenin, and Wilson's press secretary on April 2 cabled from Washington: "The proposed recognition of Lenin has caused consternation over here."

Wilson turned his back on Bullitt, who became House's exclusive responsibility and political liability. Even before Bullitt's breakfast with the British, the President quietly had made his move. Wilson, who had begun to lose confidence in House the week before (of which more will be said presently), asked Herbert Hoover to advise him what to do about Soviet Russia. Hoover's advice was to not get involved in any military operations against Bolshevik Russia but also to not recognize Lenin's regime ("We cannot even remotely recognize this murderous tyranny . . ."), to demand that communist Russia unilaterally cease fire and cease agitation beyond its frontiers, and to offer to feed the people of Soviet Russia as a humanitarian gesture.

House, sensing which way the wind was blowing, quickly abandoned the Bullitt proposal (though without telling Bullitt) and opted for fighting Bolshevism with food. Auchincloss and his law partner David Hunter Miller drafted a document for House along these lines; while Bullitt, bewildered, could not understand why a new approach was being adopted just when the one he had explored in Moscow was on the verge of succeeding.

In his pride at what he had accomplished in Moscow, Bullitt had not noticed the strength of the political currents running against his project. A letter signed by 200 members of Parliament appeared in the London *Times* opposing recognition of Soviet Russia. Winston Churchill wrote to the prime minister telling him that the House of Commons was practically unanimous on the point. Churchill urged that Wilson "not be allowed to weaken our policy . . . " and, referring to the Bullitt mission, claimed that the President's "negotiations have become widely known and are much resented."

Quickly leaving the scene of a political accident, Lloyd George, on a flying trip to London, told the House of Commons that "of course there are constantly men of all nationalities coming from and going to Russia, always back with their own tales. . . . But . . . nothing authentic. . . ." He denied that he or his government had made an approach to Lenin. He said: "There was some suggestion that a young American had come back from Russia with a communication. It is not for me to judge the value of this communication, but if the President of the United States had attached any value to it he would have brought it before the conference, and he certainly did not."

Not knowing what to do, but angry and tired, Bullitt left town: he went off on a brief vacation. Then he returned, to urge sending a reply before the deadline expired, but found that he could not get through to anybody in a position of authority.

He wrote a letter to the President in which he tried to explain, in the context of the dangerous disorder then prevailing in central and eastern Europe, the importance, as he saw it, of achieving an accommodation with Lenin's regime. The "peoples of Europe have been seeking a better way to live for the common good of all," he wrote, but they "have found no guidance in Paris"—which is to say, from the President and the Allies—and so "they are turning towards Moscow." He claimed that "to dismiss this groping of the peoples for better lives" as "Bolshevism" was to misunderstand everything. These were peoples, he wrote, whose first instinct had been to turn toward the United States and its President; they had turned away, toward Soviet Russia, only because Wilson had failed them. "Six months ago all the peoples of Europe expected you to fulfill their hopes. They believe now that you cannot. They turn, therefore, to Lenin. . . ."

It was a sort of revolution, Bullitt claimed, that was occurring all over Europe, and it had arrived at a crossroads. If the United States cooperated with the "constructive and kind" leaders of the revolution—and Bullitt must have included Lenin among them in order to arrive at the conclusion he reached—then the energies of the revolution could be diverted into "peaceful and constructive" channels. But to support military interventions against the revolutionaries instead, as the President and the Allies were doing, would drive them "in self defense, to terror and massacres," as had happened, Bullitt claimed, in "the French Revolution more than a century ago and the Russian Revolution last year."

One did not need to agree with this analysis in order to be convinced that the Lenin offer should have been accepted; there were quite different grounds for believing it. In his proposals to Bullitt, Lenin was accepting the loss of most of prewar Russia, and if confined to a relatively small territory and surrounded by enemy Russian as well as non-Russian states, Bolshevism might be neutralized, or might even wither and die. Indeed, in hindsight it looks as though backing the Bullitt-Lenin agreement offered a better chance of containing communism in Russia than did supporting the armies of the tsarist officers Admiral Kolchak and General Denikin in the wars they were waging against the Reds.

But Bullitt and his negotiations had become political liabilities, and nobody in power wanted to be weighed down by him or them. The expiration date of Lenin's offer, April 10, came and went; but the West made no move to follow up on the proposals that Bullitt had brought back with him.

NOW THAT THE WORLD has had a long experience of communist government and has developed an understanding of the goals of Lenin and Stalin, it can be said with some degree of confidence that there was no real chance of bringing the Soviet regime into a peaceful and friendly long-term relationship with the Western democracies; but in 1919 one could not have been sure.

So the repudiation of Bullitt by Wilson and Lloyd George left questions unanswered that would trouble the democracies for decades to come. Had the West thrown away—as many would come to believe—the last, best chance to win the trust of Russia's new rulers? Was the outlaw behavior of the Soviet government in subsequent years due to its having been treated as an outlaw from birth? To those of Bullitt's generation who in the 1930s, 1940s, and 1950s would be called upon to define America's policy toward the Soviet Union, his unfulfilled mission left behind a disturbing legacy of doubt. Many of them would operate under the disadvantage of having a conscience that was not entirely clear where Soviet Russia was concerned, for they worried that in 1919 the United States might have been at fault.

# 29

# WILSON COLLAPSES

*You Americans are broken reeds . . .*
—John Maynard Keynes, in a letter to
Norman Davis (June 5, 1919)

WHILE WILSON WAS GOING to and from the United States in February and March, and Bullitt was going to and from Russia, American peacemakers who stayed on in Paris became aware that somehow they had lost the affection in which they had once been held: they had become unpopular. In the words of Joseph Grew, "the honeymoon between America and France is over. . . ."

It finally had sunk in to the French mind that the Americans did not agree that the war had been about France—and that the peace consequently had to be, too. The war had begun in a German invasion of France. The war essentially had consisted in the battle for France. The battlefield of the war had been northern France. The French army had suffered 6 million casualties in the fighting, which was more than those absorbed by the armies of Britain, the British empire and commonwealths, the United States, Italy, and Japan combined. Now, Frenchmen believed, there were only two questions to resolve: how to compensate France for what Germany had done to her, and how to prevent Germany from doing it again. It all was so simple to a French mind; why could the Americans not see it? And why did not the American President, on his arrival, go out to see for himself the battlefields and cemeteries that would give him a firsthand sense of what the war had been and what it had meant?

Instead of intervening in the war to help France (which is what Frenchmen had supposed that the Americans, however tardily, had come to Europe to do), it now appeared that America had other objects in view. The President instead intended to protect Germany from mistreatment; he had come to Paris to *prevent* Clemenceau and Foch from doing what had to be done to safeguard France against future German invasions. In place of the concrete measures the French planned to take to defend themselves, Wilson asked them to entrust their safety to a League of Nations that had no force behind it—and therefore no reality to it. That was bad enough, but there was worse: it was known in Paris that Wilson might not have enough votes in the

Senate to ratify whatever treaties he signed in Paris. So the President, if he had his way, would force France to leave herself undefended in return for a mere piece of paper—the Covenant—which the United States then would not sign, and this would leave France, not America, to pay for Wilson's folly.

Writing home on February 10, 1919, Joseph Grew reported that "the French press is complaining that we came into the war at the last moment . . . and now want to boss the whole show and rob them of their fruits of victory by helping Germany. . . . Furthermore the papers say that our only interest is to establish a League of Nations, impose our ideas on the Allies and then go home, leaving them to bear the brunt and shoulder the responsibility if anything goes wrong."

And, wrote Grew, there was ill will between the French and American armies in the areas in Germany they now policed (and in which Douglas MacArthur and others were now stationed). "The Americans . . . have angered the French by their friendly attitude towards the Germans in the occupied territories. . . . The Americans compare the neatness of the German towns, their cleanliness, their love of music, their morality . . . to the disfavor of the French."

WHEN PRESIDENT WILSON RETURNED to Paris from Washington in mid-March for his second and final session at the peace conference, there was considerably less fanfare than there had been on his first coming ninety days earlier. The French government assigned him new and less imposing (though perhaps more comfortable) quarters: the private residence— the *hôtel*—of Prince Roland Bonaparte on the Place des États-Unis, halfway between the Trocadéro and the Étoile.

Clemenceau, having recovered from an assassination attempt, led the French government in a barrage of territorial and economic demands against Germany that Wilson fought against but found hard to resist. For, as the conference knew, Wilson had learned in Washington that it was politically essential for him to obtain certain amendments to the proposed Covenant of the League of Nations—amendments, moreover, that exposed to the mercilessly logical and mocking French the wide gulf that separated what America preached from what she practiced. According to the young British diplomat Harold Nicolson, this was a less humiliating experience for Wilson ("He and his conscience were on terms of such incessant intimacy that any little difference between them could easily be arranged") than it was for other members of the delegation, on whom "the suspicion that America was asking Europe to make sacrifices to righteousness that America would never make, and had never made, herself, produced a mood of . . . increasing despair."

Three principal amendments that the President was obliged to move were: that states should have the right to secede from the League (a right that the American Union had denied to South Carolina and the other confederated states of the South); that the League should have no right to probe into matters that are a state's internal affairs (so that race prejudice in the United States, especially anti-Japanese legislation, could not be questioned); and that the validity of the Monroe Doctrine should be affirmed (so that the United States could maintain its exclusive sphere of influence in the Western Hemisphere, while continuing to deny to other countries the right to have spheres of influence anywhere).

In the end the French government allowed the President to have his way on these matters—and on others too, for House reported on April 14 that the French had permitted Wilson, in all, thirteen changes. But in doing so, it allowed him also to dramatize the extent to which political morality was something that Americans demanded mostly of others, seemingly having given themselves a dispensation from it.

IN PARIS DURING THE SPRING OF 1919, the President, his relationship with Colonel House, and the American program for world peace and reconstruction all collapsed. It remains a subject for speculation whether—and if so, how—these collapses were interrelated. Young Americans whose hearts were broken by the tragedy of Versailles and who were passionately concerned to discover why it had happened were driven to inquire, too, whether these events occurred there and then, or whether they merely manifested or were the culmination of processes that had originated earlier and elsewhere.

Did Wilson start to break with House because, on returning to Paris in mid-March, he found that his adviser had made too many compromises in the President's absence? That is the story related in her memoirs by the second Mrs. Wilson: "Woodrow . . . seemed to have aged ten years,"* she wrote, and he had told her at the time that "House has given away everything I had won before we left Paris. He has compromised on every side. . . ." Or since Wilson, during his absence, had been kept informed by cable of what House was doing, and had approved, was the President unwilling to admit even to himself how extensive were the compromises he himself had made—and was he trying to shift the blame to House?

Did the issue of compromises in Paris merely bring to the surface earlier grudges: House's opposition to the President's remarriage, or House's

---

* Decades later, Bullitt recalled that Dr. Grayson, Wilson's physician, said at the time that after Wilson talked to House in mid-March on the Brest–Paris train to receive House's report, the President "was hysterical."

nepotism in giving jobs to his son-in-law and his wife's brother-in-law, or his friendship with newspaper editors who glorified him at the expense of the President? The last was a point picked up by Harry Truman, who could identify with Wilson, and who wrote decades later, after leaving the presidency, that ". . . when House got to the point where he thought he was greater than the president, where he thought he *was* the president, why, then Wilson had to pull out the rug from under him and let him go, just like every president has had to do with some of his confidants."

Yet the political friendship with House had been supremely valuable to the President—had been, in many ways, the making of him. In destroying the relationship, Wilson damaged himself. The aspects of the inflexible twenty-eighth President that were entirely his own—the stubborn and illiberal sides of his mind and temperament—were increasingly troubling to the young progressives and liberals who once had rallied to his banner; while the large-minded, forward-looking aspects of him that so attracted Lippmann, Bullitt, and other luminaries of their generation were represented by, shared by, and in some measure a creation of, House. Knowing the President only through the colonel, they were dismayed, disappointed, and surprised by the Wilson who emerged in Paris after his quick trip to Washington. In the spring of 1919, as they watched the steady distancing of the President from House, what they saw was Wilson turning against what they had supposed to be himself.

Was it the illness clouding his mind that drove the President to do it? On the afternoon of April 3, while meeting with Lloyd George, Clemenceau, and Orlando to hear Yugoslavia present its case against Italy, the President suddenly was stricken. He returned to his residence in the grip of intense pain in the stomach, back, and head, in paroxysms of coughing, and with a fever of 103 degrees. Medical authorities ever since have disagreed as to what it was: influenza, a stroke, acute respiratory disease, or something else.

Though he recovered in a few days, the effects of the attack lingered on. His massive stroke six months later in the United States, causing physical breakdown and partial paralysis, led to the question of whether his collapse in Paris might not have been a precursor. Evidence now available enables historians to trace the breakdown of the President's health even further back: to a supposed neuralgia attack in 1896, with loss of use (for a time) of his right arm; to a then undiagnosed stroke in 1906 that destroyed central vision in his left eye; to a series of small strokes suffered after that; and to continuing hypertension—high blood pressure and arteriosclerosis. Those inclined (as so many have been through the years) to blame Wilson's failings after a certain date on his physical impairment now have an embarrassment of dates from which to choose, for his entire political career had been lived under the shadow of strokes and physical collapses.

It may be the opposite that is more true; it may well have been political failure that led to the April 3 attack. Wilson had been in frail health all his life, easily tired, not able to work more than about five hours a day, and unable to cope with stress. In student days the strain of study had been too much for him; severe indigestion had forced him to drop out of college and out of law school, and headaches and nerves caused breakdowns in graduate school.

So in the dark days of March 1919, as his American program for remaking the world collapsed in the face of stubborn political realities in Paris, it is possible that it was the political breakdown, with the ravages it worked on Wilson's nerves and emotions, that led to, or at least contributed to, his physical breakdown.


AMONG THE PRESSURES to which the President was sensitive, and which he felt with increasing force in returning to Europe for his second and final session, was the clamor in the United States and elsewhere for finally bringing matters in Paris to a conclusion.

"Wilson very impatient with the slow progress of the deliberations," Ray Stannard Baker, his Paris press secretary, noted on March 27. "Says Clemenceau is the chief obstacle. . . ." Two days later Baker wrote that House "now begins to be worried; blames the 'Four' for not getting down to business. . . ." Baker was one of the many who worried that anarchy or Bolshevism would prevail in central and eastern Europe if decisions were not reached promptly at the peace conference; on March 31 he "talked with the President about the feeling everywhere of the danger of the situation. 'I know it,' he said."

There was a widespread feeling that what was holding matters up was the President's insistence on dealing with the League of Nations first, and in the same conversation of March 31, Baker told Wilson that he was being blamed on all sides for the delay. "I know that, too," Wilson said, according to Baker's diary.

On April 2, the day before the President was stricken, Baker recorded that "I found the President tonight again much discouraged. . . . I suggested that the time might come soon when he would have to speak out"; to which Wilson replied, "If I speak out . . . I should have to tell the truth and place the blame exactly where it belongs—upon the French."

The President supposed that if he revealed to the world what the French leaders were doing—digging in their heels and insisting on harsh terms for Germany—their government would be overthrown. But even Wilson, according to Baker's diary, knew that "a new premier would probably be no better than Clemenceau."

For the obstacle facing Wilson was not just the French government; it was the French people. France was hostile to Germany and afraid of Germany—and what is more, had reason to be. To overcome the arguments of Clemenceau, Wilson would have had to address the real concerns of France and would have had to show her people as well as her government that they were mistaken in believing that harsh peace terms would achieve France's objectives.

IN HIS APPARENT SURPRISE that it was France that proved to be the obstacle to his peacemaking, Wilson reflected a thoroughly American prejudice. The defining issue in foreign policy for the United States had been opposition to British imperialism, and ever since the Revolutionary War, England had seemed to be America's principal world enemy.* Even in bringing the United States into the war, Wilson had focused on America's objection to British naval supremacy as a chief stumbling block to American unity of purpose with the Allies. Americans therefore tended to sympathize with Britain's rivals; within the Allied side, that was France.

Yet as Harold Nicolson observed on first meeting the American Inquiry experts in Paris: "Nice people. . . . A feeling . . . that our general views are identical." But the usually similar and often shared outlook of Americans and Britons was something that Americans in their anti-imperialism did not always notice.

CENTRAL TO THE PRESIDENT'S CONCEPTION of a new world order was universal disarmament. That was to be the guarantee that there would be no more war. If nations had no weapons, they would be unable to wage war. In place of trial by combat, disputes between countries would be settled not by the arms that they no longer would have, but by the judgment of their assembled peers: representatives of the countries of the world seated together in one room as a planetary council called the League of Nations.

Lord Robert Cecil, at the Foreign Office, and others among the British delegates had arrived at a similar conception. But France refused to entertain that notion, which in French eyes looked not merely impractical and utopian but dangerous and hypocritical. The United States and Britain proposed to retain their navies, which were all they needed to protect an Atlantic frontier. Unlike them, France required land forces, for her frontier with Germany was on land, not water.

The French government insisted on maintaining a powerful army to

---

* TR had seen that this no longer was the case. But when it came to foreign policy, his views were not those of the majority of his countrymen.

provide national security. If France did, so would others: yet if countries continued to command armed forces capable of winning wars, the likelihood dropped to zero that all nations, in cases when the League ruled against them, would always forgo the opportunity of winning on the field of battle—the claims the League denied them, but to which they considered themselves entitled. So the League could not guarantee against war.

Without armies of its own, the League could not provide France with a guarantee of national security in case of such a war. Unable to dispute the point, Wilson bowed to the French view in the March–April negotiations to the extent of agreeing to the permanent demilitarization of Germany's Rhine frontier, limitations on Germany's armed forces, and a French occupation of the Rhineland for fifteen years. Wilson refused to let France separate the Rhineland from Germany permanently, but in return agreed to sign a treaty binding the United States (and Britain) to come to France's aid if she were attacked by Germany.*

Between January and April 1919 the terms to which Wilson agreed meant (whether he recognized it or not) that in the postwar world, as before, there were to be political alliances and therefore rival blocs; there would be combat-ready armed forces, and wars; and there would be empires and colonies. The only sign of a new world order was the flawed Covenant of the League, and during his second session in Paris, in order to obtain Japan's adherence to the League (the Japanese "will go home," said Wilson, "unless we give them what they should not have"), the President promised that Japan could take over the German concession in China's province of Shantung—a bargain that was regarded as odious not only by Wilson's enemies in Washington but also by his friends everywhere.

Forgotten was the promise of a peace without victory. The Allies took over Germany's overseas colonies and her merchant marine, occupied some of her territory and gave away parts to Poland and others, and seized ownership of her coal-, iron-, and steel-producing industrial heartland in the Saar basin.

The most outrageous of the Allied demands was so obviously unreasonable that historians such as Arthur Link, Wilson's chief champion in the academic world, believe that if the Americans had dug in and made a stand, the Europeans would have backed down. The Allied demand was that the reparations bill due from Germany should be computed and assessed without regard to whether Germany could pay it. The issue was joined the morning of April 5 at Wilson's residence in the Hôtel Bonaparte. The stricken President lay in bed. The Allied prime ministers were seated in

* This was the sort of alliance treaty that Wilson had always deplored and that in the past the United States had rejected. As it turned out, the votes were not there in the Senate to ratify it, so the American guarantee of France's frontier never came into effect.

the salon. Through a bookcase that doubled as a secret door, House went back and forth between the bedchamber and the salon repeating to each side what the other had said. Wilson and House were in despair when they discovered that not even Lloyd George would agree to limit Germany's liability to what she could afford. A soul-sick House advised the bedridden President to surrender—and Wilson did.

# 30

## BLOOD MONEY

THE WAR HAD RUINED Europe financially. The Allies had spent all their cash and borrowed the rest from the Americans, to whom they now were deeply in debt. The essence of the reparations issue was that driven by domestic public opinion, the politicians of France and Great Britain insisted that Germany should make their countries whole.

Wilson, House, and such economic advisers as Bernard Baruch saw that imposing reparations on so vast a scale would be self-defeating for the Allies. Baruch predicted "that if Germany were left economically prostrate, all Europe would suffer."

Not even Baruch could have foreseen the scorched-earth policy to which the desperate Germans would be driven. In the early 1920s they would run money off their printing presses in order to pay reparations in worthless paper currency: one German mark in July 1914 became one trillion marks on November 15, 1923. They would succeed in cheating the Allies, but only by completing their own ruin. The inflation would crush the middle class; the social fabric would be torn, and first steps would be taken on the road to Nazism.

While the Americans were alive to the danger of pushing Germany too far, they were less sensitive to the problems of the Allies in repaying what they had borrowed from the United States. Lloyd George proposed that the United States forgive some of that debt and work with the Allies to foster Germany's recovery, in return for which Britain and France would reduce their reparations demands. Wilson refused, explaining why Britain and France would have to waive reparations.

"You have suggested," Wilson wrote to Lloyd George, "that we all address ourselves to the problem of helping to put Germany on her feet, but how can your experts or ours be expected to work out a *new* plan to furnish working capital to Germany when we deliberately start out by taking away all Germany's *present* capital? How can anyone expect America to turn over to Germany in any considerable measure new working capital to take the place of that which the European nations have determined to take from her?"

Oddly, something rather like that was what was going to happen over

the course of the next dozen years. There would be negotiations and rene-
gotiations of the reparations due the Allies, which originally had been set
as high as $33 billion. When Germany finally defaulted on what remained
of her debt in 1931, she had, according to Baruch, "paid less than five
billion in reparation, and half of that had been borrowed in the United
States."

But at the Paris conference, the wrangling over reparations wrecked
the prospects of a recovery plan for the Continent as a whole. Wilson's
economic advisory staff in Paris, spearheaded by Thomas Lamont of Morgan
and Norman Davis of the Treasury, had prepared a far-reaching scheme
for the economic reconstruction of Europe, in which America's financial and
manufacturing companies were to join hands under the aegis of the American government in a sort of forerunner of the Marshall Plan. A precondition
was that the Allies drop their reparations demands, which they refused
to do.

The narrowness and selfishness of the European outlook made a lasting
impression upon the young Americans in Paris. According to Lamont, writing to his wife June 7, 1919, the British were telling the small nations that
whenever Herbert Hoover's food aid program came to an end—a program
of aid with no conditions attached—Great Britain would take care of them,
but only if they did all their business with England. Lamont was the British
government's New York banker, but he wrote in disgust that "Great Britain
has been on the make from start to finish."


TORN BY DISPUTES OVER MONEY, the proceedings in Paris
had reached a stage of ugliness in which bitterness was generated on all
sides. The reparations madness of the Allies, and the weakness of Wilson
in agreeing to them, evoked a protest that surfaced in America at the end
of the year, when Lippmann published in *The New Republic* a serialized
version of *The Economic Consequences of the Peace* by John Maynard Keynes,
who had quit the British Treasury in protest. It was a powerful and immensely persuasive indictment of the reparations arrangements, and of the
President who had accepted them.

For Congress and the American in the street, what was to lead to the
most lasting rift in relations with Europe was the failure of the Allies to
pay their war debts to the United States.

In Germany, what added insult to injury was the unintended result of
some thoughtless phrase-making by John Foster Dulles, the American attorney who served as legal adviser to the American reparations team. The
issue Dulles faced was that although the President had agreed to the full
Allied reparations bill, nobody knew how much it amounted to. It would
take time to calculate it. Dulles proposed referring the matter to a com-

mission. To define the full parameters of German legal liability broadly enough so that the commission would be free to arrive at almost any figure it chose, Dulles drafted what became Article 231 of the Treaty of Versailles, by the terms of which the German government was compelled to admit "the responsibility of Germany and her Allies for all the loss to which the Allied and Associated Governments and their nationals have been subjected as a consequence of the war imposed upon them by the aggression of Germany and her Allies."

This "war guilt" clause, which flatly contradicted what President Wilson had said when urging Congress to declare war—that the war was not against the German people—was exploited in the years that followed by Nazi demagogues of the street and the beerhall who sought to destroy the peace and the Allies who had imposed it.

# 31

## CLOSING UP SHOP AT THE PEACE TALKS

*We lived many lives in those whirling campaigns, never sparing ourselves: yet when we achieved and the new world dawned, the old men came out again and took our victory to re-make in the likeness of the former world they knew. Youth could win, but had not learned to keep: and was pitiably weak against age. We stammered that we had worked for a new heaven and a new earth, and they thanked us kindly and made their peace.*

*—T. E. Lawrence*

THE BRITISH PRESS LORD George Riddell, a confidant of the prime minister's, noted in his diary March 21, 1919, "Great dissatisfaction at slow progress of Peace Conference negotiations." On March 24 he wrote: "Later saw Philip Kerr"—Lloyd George's secretary—"and told him the feelings of dissatisfaction were growing and that a general attack by all sections of the Press might be expected"; and the same day, after seeing a news release about a minor matter that was taking up the time of the Allied leaders: "I thought it advisable to let the public know that drastic steps were being taken to conclude terms of peace."

On March 28 Riddell noted that the prime minister "is very angry with the Press for criticizing alleged delay of the Conference. . . ." Lloyd George told him that "you really must try to get the papers to be more reasonable. They must not lose their heads. They must remember that we are settling the peace of the world. It is a gigantic task." Indeed, the work of the conference was being carried on not just by the President and the prime ministers, but by fifty-eight committees that were engaged in deciding even the most technical and obscure of questions, including the delineation of the frontiers of far-off countries unknown to most Britons or Americans.

But there were perhaps 500 reporters in Paris in the spring of 1919 looking for the story of the German peace settlement; they had been there all winter, and still there was no story; their readers and editors were impatient; and they themselves were bored. Lloyd George felt pressure not merely from the press, but also from Parliament and the people; ever since the cease-fire, they had demanded the imposition of the harshest terms on Germany and, inconsistently, immediate demobilization of Britain's troops—whose continuing presence on the European battlefield would be needed if terms were so harsh as to arouse resistance. (Although Winston Churchill warned the House of Commons, "Do not disband your army until you have got your terms," the advice went unheeded. Military conscription terminated in March 1919, and Britain's armies melted away.)

Under all of these pressures to show that a settlement finally was about to be achieved, Lloyd George persuaded Wilson and the Allies to invite the German government to send a delegation to Paris to be given a proposed peace treaty—an invitation designed to convince the world that matters were being wound up. The invitation was sent toward the end of April. About 160 German delegates, not knowing what to expect, arrived on April 29 and were confined to the unheated old Hotel des Réservoirs in Versailles, surrounded by barbed wire.

The Allies and Americans were in disarray, for they had no treaty to show, and the disarray turned almost to panic a week later when the Germans, tired of waiting, announced they were going home. Frantic deal-making took place between the leaders of Britain, France, and the United States, and compromises were hammered out on some of the main issues. The Council of Four (the United States, Britain, France, and Italy) scheduled a formal ceremony in the suburbs of Paris, at the Trianon Palace in Versailles, for May 7, on which date they proposed to present a treaty to the German delegation.

The moment of truth was at hand, and a drafting committee of the wartime victors was charged with the task of summarizing what had been decided over the course of the previous four months at the Paris Peace Conference. One of the difficulties in doing so was suggested by a letter that Joseph Grew—who as chief of staff to the American Peace Commission should have been fully informed—wrote on April 13. It said that the "Commission itself knows very little as to just what is going on; all important questions are now discussed and decided by the Council of Four (President Wilson, Lloyd George, Clemenceau, and Orlando) and as no secretaries or stenographers are present at their meetings and no notes are taken we hear little of the results achieved. . . . Our right hand does not know what the left is doing. Colonel House never attends the daily meetings of the other Commissioners and his office frequently takes action unknown to them and often disapproved of by them when they finally learn of it. Our only link with the President"—and that was no longer House—"has . . . become more sphinx-like than the Sphinx." At a reception Robert Lansing went over to one of the State Department's most junior employees, Christian Herter, and asked if *he* knew what agreement the President had reached with the Allies about an Italian-Yugoslav dispute; Herter did not know, and the Secretary of State was overheard to say, "Snoop around a bit and see if you can find out."

Yet in a matter of days the drafting committee was called upon to set out in writing all that had been decided since January, mostly in secret sessions, by the Councils of Ten, Five, Four, and Three. To these the committee had to add the reports prepared (some as working drafts, some as "asking terms," some as proposed treaty language) by the committees and subcommittees of the conference: papers composed in ignorance of the broad decisions arrived at by Wilson and the prime ministers, that had not been coordinated with one another and that had not been reviewed by anyone— for the drafting committee had no time. The accumulation of documents, described as the "Conditions of Peace," was sent to the printers on May 5. It comprised some 200 pages—roughly 75,000 words—and was divided into 440 articles.

On the afternoon of May 6, Clemenceau convened a conference at which the Council of Four went through the motions of consulting the smaller Allies about peace terms. The treaty was not back from the printers, so it was summarized for them in French, a language many of them did not understand. Marshal Foch, the Allied generalissimo, took the floor to protest that Clemenceau had not safeguarded his country's security, for the French frontier had not been moved to the Rhineland; the French premier angrily dealt with his insubordinate officer by adjourning the meeting.

Foch telephoned the chief of the British Imperial General Staff, General Sir Henry Wilson, to tell him that everything had been mixed up in the treaty as it had gone out from the drafting committee. Decisions had been reversed, clauses had been misnumbered, names had been gotten wrong: it was a shambles.

At a meeting of leaders of the British empire's delegation, Lloyd George had to read a summary of treaty provisions to his colleagues because the document in its entirety was still at the printer's. Smuts, the imperial statesman from South Africa, and Andrew Bonar Law, leader of the Conservative party in the House of Commons, had not been able to get hold of a copy of the treaty itself; it was a "hopeless mess," they told Sir Henry Wilson, who remarked that "no one has ever seen it in its completed form, for it does not exist." Yet the Allies were about to confront the German delegates and present them with the document, imposing peace terms, as Sir Henry marveled, "without reading them ourselves first. I don't think in all history this can be matched."


COPIES OF THE TREATY, fresh off the press, were brought to various of the delegates during the night of May 6–7. Herbert Hoover was awakened at about four in the morning by the delivery of his copy. He read it through immediately, and was horrified. He could not go back to sleep. At daybreak he dressed and went out to pace the empty streets. Within blocks he encountered first Smuts, and then the young British economist John Maynard Keynes. "It all flashed into our minds," according to Hoover, "why each was walking about at that time of the morning."

Hoover, Smuts, and Keynes (who wrote to his mother: "I've never been so miserable. . . . [T]he Peace is outrageous and impossible and can bring nothing but misfortune . . .") were not so alone in their reactions as they may have believed when setting out on their solitary walks at dawn that morning. All of the American peace commissioners were dismayed by the treaty. One of them, Secretary of State Lansing, set down in writing his first impressions of the document he had just read; the words he used were ". . . disappointment . . . regret . . . depression."

Ray Stannard Baker, the press secretary of the American delegation and (since the rift with House) the only official who spent time with the President every day, called the proposed treaty "a terrible document . . . with scarcely a parallel in history." The President himself told Baker: "If I were a German, I think I should never sign it."


THE PROPOSED TREATY denied to Germany, for the moment, membership in the League of Nations. It forbade the unification of Germany with Austria. It presented to Germany for payment a bill for the entire cost of the war incurred by the Allies—without adding it up and without fixing a ceiling on the amount that might be due. At the same time that this potentially ruinous fine was levied, Germany was to be deprived of the assets she would need in order to raise the money to pay it. She was to be stripped not only of her colonies and her merchant fleet, but also of one-eighth of her metropolitan area holding 10 percent of her population, 10 percent of her industry, and 15 percent of her arable land for agriculture.

The younger members, in particular, of the American and British delegations saw in the transfer of so many Germans to Czech and Polish rule a violation of the principle of self-determination that Woodrow Wilson preached and in which they believed. Regardless of the merits of that principle, it was a fatal weakness in the proposed treaty that it ran counter to the strong beliefs of those who were proposing it. It meant that when the time came to stand up and fight to enforce the treaty, Americans and Britons would be loath to do so; they would be unwilling to defend a settlement in which they did not believe. In the 1930s, as Hitler went about undoing the Versailles treaty by occupying and militarizing the Rhineland, merging with Austria, and seizing the predominantly German-speaking areas of Czechoslovakia, the leaders and opinion makers of Britain were going to be paralyzed in their response—for, as a glance at the 1939 edition of E. H. Carr's *The Twenty Years' Crisis* will show, they believed that Germany was in the right: that the Treaty had been unfair to Germany.

In retrospect, what really was wrong with the proposed treaty was not that it was too hard on Germany, though it was, while in some ways it was also not hard enough. What was wrong was that it made no sense—from any point of view. Nobody had written, nobody had edited, and nobody had even read the treaty as a whole; and its terms contradicted and defeated one another.

A treaty that expressed the political philosophy professed by Woodrow Wilson would have been so generous to defeated Germany that she would not have been provoked to start a future war to try to change its terms. On the other hand, a treaty that accomplished the goals of Georges Clemenceau would have destroyed German power so completely and permanently that Germany would have been unable to wage war successfully ever again. But the treaty that the Allies were about to propose at Versailles fell between the two. It hurt Germany enough to provoke her to start another war, but not enough to keep her from winning it.

"When you strike a king," Mr. Justice Holmes is alleged to have said, "you must kill him." It was advice the victors en route to their encounter with the German delegates at Versailles ought to have heeded: they should have struck to kill—or else they should not have struck at all.

WEDNESDAY, MAY 7, the day set for imposing the "Conditions of Peace" on the Germans at Versailles, outside Paris, was (as Harold Nicolson wrote in his diary) "a lovely day: great chestnut trees drinking gulps of sunlight." There was not a cloud in nature's sky. In the midafternoon the newspaper magnate Lord Riddell was enjoying a leisurely drive from Paris through the woods toward Versailles when he heard insistent honking from behind, and found his car overtaken by Clemenceau—"the Tiger," as he was called—racing in a Rolls-Royce toward the scheduled confrontation with the Germans. There was "a smile on the face of the Tiger," Riddell observed.

The ceremony was scheduled for 3 p.m. in Versailles at the Trianon Palace. It was a large, white luxury hotel set in a private park, and had served as Allied headquarters throughout the war.* On the stroke of three the victors began to take their assigned places around a horseshoe of three tables in the formal conference room, looking like a judicial panel. The defeated Germans were led in later and were seated at a fourth table, facing their accusers.

---

* Bought recently by Japanese, the hotel has been refurbished and reopened.

Clemenceau rose to his feet and addressed the Germans briefly. He said, "You have asked us for peace. We are disposed to give it to you. The volume which the secretary general of the conference will shortly hand to you will tell you the conditions which we have fixed. . . ." He stated that the Germans would have fifteen days in which to respond in writing to the proposed terms.

During the weeks that followed in May and June, German officials bombarded their counterparts on the Allied and American side with objections to the various and numerous terms of the Conditions of Peace, while Wilson and his colleagues pushed to achieve agreement on an early signing date for a formal treaty.


ON MAY 6, the day before the Conditions of Peace were formally presented in Versailles, the precociously brilliant young head of the American delegation's Russian section, Adolf A. Berle, was writing to his father of his bitter disappointment in Woodrow Wilson: "I have come to the conclusion that no statement of ideals by anybody will ever get any reaction from me again." Like most of the world, Berle was still ignorant of the proposed peace terms; but he was disgusted by what was being done and not done about Russia.

"Yesterday Bullitt called me in," he wrote, "and asked that an offensive and defensive alliance be made; wanted to start a new drive on the Russian situation, and asked me to come in on it: and I will though Bullitt is in disgrace in a sense and though it is taking one's life in one's hands."


ON AN EVENING in the second week of May 1919, a group of the younger members of the staff of the American Peace Commission assembled in a private room at the Hotel Crillon to discuss the proposed peace treaty, the terms of which they now knew. Bullitt, Berle, Herter, and the young historian Samuel Eliot Morison were among them.

Most of those present agreed with Bullitt that the proposed peace terms were a betrayal of the beliefs for which the United States stood and for which President Wilson had claimed to stand. Like Bullitt, they had come to Paris only months before as enthusiasts for their idealistic President. When Bullitt, returning from Moscow in March, had said that if Wilson took up Lenin's offer, the President would become "the greatest man in history since Jesus Christ," he spoke for many and perhaps all of them. But Wilson instead had rejected the Soviet peace offer, and now had joined in proposing peace terms that violated all the principles that he had professed.

"This isn't a treaty of peace," Bullitt argued. "I can see at least 11 wars in it." It was full of "black inequities." Young men had won the victory, and now the old men were trying to take it away from them. It was time to take a stand, Bullitt urged. He proposed that all of them—all the brilliant young men who staffed the American delegation—should resign in protest. It was on that issue that Bullitt lost some of his audience, for while all seemed to agree that the treaty was shameful, many said it would do no good to give up their jobs.

After the meeting the young men went in to dinner at the hotel. The Crillon had decorated their tables with red roses and yellow jonquils. At the end of the meal, as some remembered it, Bullitt took up the flowers, awarded the red to those who would join him in resigning—and tossed the yellow at those who would not.

Over the course of the next few weeks, about thirty experts (as Bullitt later recalled it) told their superiors that they were thinking of resigning from the American delegation in protest. Most were talked out of doing so. About a dozen went ahead to resign, spelling out in some cases those provisions of the Conditions of Peace they found most offensive.

In letters to Joseph Grew for the secretariat, one of the experts, John Storck, wrote (May 14): "Protesting vigorously against the treaty . . ." which "will by wronging Germany make her eager for revenge." Another, Joseph V. Fuller, charged (May 15) that "we have bartered away our principles in a series of compromises with interests of imperialism and revenge. . . ." Yet another, George B. Noble, termed it "an exceedingly dangerous settlement—if it could be called a settlement . . . provocative of future wars. . . . I feel that the idealism of America has been very largely sacrificed on the altar of imperialism."

Asking to be relieved of his duties, Adolf Berle wrote to Grew on May 15 that the proposed treaty violated "both letter and spirit" of the principles to which the United States was pledged in declaring and waging war; some of its provisions, "notably the Japanese clauses," would "create a situation thoroughly dangerous to the interests of the United States." (His reference was to the privileged position Japan was being awarded on Chinese territory.)

Samuel Eliot Morison, who served with Berle in the Russian section, wrote at the same time describing the treaty as in flagrant contradiction "both to the interests of the United States and to the ideals and principles for the vindication of which the United States was supposed to be waging war. . . ." Though both young men were pressed to stay on, Morison resigned and Berle was released from duty a month later. Writing at that time, Morison protested in particular the Allied decision to back the tsarist Whites in the Russian civil war.

"SENSATION AT CONFERENCE—NINE AMERICAN PEACE DELEGATES RESIGN FROM MISSION TO PARIS—DISGUSTED WITH TREATY" was the headline of a London *Daily Herald* story May 22, 1919. The newspaper reported that "practically the whole of the membership of the American Commission at Paris are disgusted and disappointed with the Peace Treaty. You will not find a half dozen of them who approve it. They are convinced that so far from being a basis of lasting peace, the Treaty will be the direct and certain cause of further wars. . . . They find that they have assisted in the making of a peace based, not on the ideals for which America fought, but upon the greeds and ambitions of European Imperialists. The general feeling of the delegation is that they have been duped. . . ."

Bullitt's was the biggest name in the group of young rebels. Before taking his stand, he had discussed his course of action with the three "outside" American commissioners, Lansing, Bliss, and White—all of whom shared his dismay at the proposed peace terms. Henry White, foreign affairs veteran that he was, had lectured Bullitt on his responsibilities as an official, and counseled him against resigning; it was the duty of a diplomat to further his government's policies, said White, not his own. Nonetheless, Bullitt resigned on May 17. Typically, he broke the rules: first, by sending his letter of resignation not to Grew, but directly to the President, and second, by having the letter published in the press.

"I was one of the millions who trusted . . . in your leadership," he wrote, "and believed that you would take nothing less than 'a permanent peace' based upon 'unselfish and unbiased justice.' But our Government has consented now to deliver the suffering peoples of the world to new oppressions, subjections, and dismemberments—a new century of war." Listing some of these injustices that he claimed would lead to new conflicts, Bullitt made the point that when taken together with the Covenant of the League of Nations, they would drag the United States into one war after another, turning the League not into an instrument of peace, but into an engine of war.

"That you personally opposed most of the unjust settlements," Bullitt concluded, was not enough; "if you had made your fight in the open, instead of behind closed doors, you would have carried with you the public opinion of the world. . . ." This was a Wilsonian concept in which Bullitt still believed. "I am sorry that you did not fight our fight to the finish and that you had so little faith in the millions of men, like myself, in every nation who had faith in you."

Publication of the letter caused a sensation. Bullitt was only six years out of college, as his detractors were able to remind one another. "How about Bullitt?" Frank Polk of the State Department in Washington cabled to Gordon Auchincloss, who had helped to undermine the Bullitt-Lenin accord. "A spanking seems desirable."

Bullitt, in turn, wondered how he and his talented friends ever had come to admire Woodrow Wilson—and decided that it all was because of tiny, plausible Edward House. He and such friends as Lippmann (he wrote to Lippmann) had been "bamboozled" by "little Eddie."


AS LATE AS MAY 6, the day the proposed peace treaty was at the printers in Paris, Walter Lippmann, back in New York City in his old editorial position with *The New Republic*, supposed that although its terms would not be to his liking, he would be able to support it. To his friend the art historian Bernard Berenson, he wrote that "I expect a compromise all along the line. . . . We here shall grumble and accept the results for two reasons—no peace means Bolshevism everywhere in Europe, and we don't want that; and the League is enough to build on . . ." so that in future, if more enlightened governments were to come to power in England and France, it would be possible to revise the peace terms through decisions of the League.

But a week later, as the terms approved by Wilson became known, Lippmann was appalled ("For the life of me I can't see peace in this document . . . ," he wrote to Ray Stannard Baker in Paris) and was persuaded by *The New Republic*'s other editors that the magazine ought to oppose the treaty. "IS IT PEACE?" the magazine asked on its May 17 cover; "THIS IS NOT PEACE," it answered the following week.

To his former chief, Secretary of War Newton Baker, Lippmann wrote two long letters explaining in detail why he now felt compelled to oppose the administration that, until a short time before, he had supported and served. The denial of self-determination to persons of German nationality (and to others) was not merely contrary to the principles Wilson had proclaimed but, Lippmann argued, as had Bullitt, it would lead to many wars. Focusing, as had Bullitt, on the League of Nations pledge of existing frontiers as well as on the separate and special American guarantee of France's frontier with Germany, Lippmann concluded, as Bullitt had, that the United States would be dragged into endless wars. As for Wilson, whom he once had admired so much, Lippmann wrote, "I can find no excuses in the fact that he had a difficult task in Paris. No one supposed that he would have an easy one."

Seeing the Covenant of the League of Nations as a guarantee of the peace terms, Lippmann argued that it was in the interests of Britain and France to persuade the United States to adhere to it. They needed America's support, in his view, but Wilson had failed to understand this: that *they*, not America, needed the League. Instead of buying European support for the League by agreeing to imperialism, he should have done the reverse, and forced Europe to buy American support for the League by renouncing "the Imperial program."

Then there was the matter of American support for the White armies in Russia. To Baker in Washington and to House in Paris, Lippmann addressed the same reproach: "I can understand these things happening in a reactionary administration. I can't understand them happening where Woodrow Wilson is President. . . ."

Lippmann now inclined to the late Willard Straight's view that Wilson should have forced the Allies to agree to American terms before coming to their aid in the war. He did not offer to explain why he had not suggested it at the time. Nor did he come to grips with the real difficulties of such a position: that the Allies, even under pressure, might not have concurred; that even had they consented under duress, they would have disavowed the agreement later; and that the United States, while it could have threatened to withhold aid from the Allies, could not have carried out the threat without jeopardizing its own national interests—for America supported the Allies to help herself, not to help them.

It was an essential element of Woodrow Wilson's greatness that he lifted people's eyes to higher things. He made the otherwise unbearable sacrifices and tragedies of the war meaningful by asserting that they would lead to a world without war or injustice in which no one nation would dominate another. The dark side of his gift for arousing hopes was that in the end he was bound to dash them, for there was no way in which he could fulfill such promises. Walter Lippmann, who ought to have asked at the very beginning how Wilson could possibly achieve the war goals he proclaimed, now blamed the President but not himself. The trouble with Wilson, said Lippmann, was his "curious irresponsibility in the use of language which leads him to make promises without any clear idea as to how they are to be fulfilled."

The President remained in Paris in May and June, impatient to conclude matters by signing a treaty with Germany so that he could return home. In their written responses to the Allied Conditions of Peace, the Germans, however, called into question practically every proposal; so that an agreement with them on a treaty seemed maddeningly far away.

Isolated from others, as he always insisted on being, Wilson was startled to be told on May 22 that Smuts, the most respected figure on the British delegation, and American Peace Commissioners House, Lansing, and Bliss were thinking of not signing the treaty. The President found it impossible to believe, but an envoy he sent to sound out Lansing confirmed that the secretary of state described the proposed treaty as "unjust and unprincipled," and rejected Wilson's argument that it could be revised by the League, pointing out that the veto power wielded by each member of the League made that impossible.

The President also was surprised by the attitude of Great Britain. Spurred on by Smuts, Lloyd George began to worry about the treaty. Questions arose; with the British army largely demobilized, what if the Germans refused to sign? He himself had never been in favor of harsh terms; he had insisted on them only because the press, the Parliament, and the public had demanded them. But now the German reply to the Allied proposals, received on May 29 (an extension of time had been granted by the Allies), made some points that the prime minister and his political partner, Andrew Bonar Law, found persuasive.

To consider the German reply, Lloyd George invited to dinner all of the British cabinet then in Paris. Among the prime minister's guests were Bonar Law, Foreign Secretary Arthur Balfour, Lord Robert Cecil, Winston Churchill, and a number of their colleagues. One of them noted in his diary that "For 3 hours after dinner we discussed the peace Terms . . . and it was amazing what unanimity there was in criticizing *all* the Peace terms."

On June 2 Lloyd George informed the Council of Four that after two days of meetings the British empire delegation had decided unanimously that the terms of the proposed treaty had to be revised to meet the German objections, and that unless major concessions were made to Germany, Britain would not join the others if the war resumed.

But the revolt in American ranks took a different turn. In the wake of Bullitt's rebellion, Wilson's four fellow peace commissioners wrote to the President (May 27) suggesting that he call the first general conference of the staff of the U.S. delegation to let everyone have his say. It was actually Hoover's suggestion, House wrote to Wilson—"for your own protection." And of the staff experts, House wrote that "if you do not confer with them, I have a feeling that some of them will be disgruntled and perhaps make trouble."

With some thirty-nine persons attending, the American commissioners met with their staff of experts on June 3—in Lansing's study, not (as would previously have been the case) in House's quarters. Flaws in the treaty were pointed out by the experts, but in the end nobody was prepared to join the British in reopening issues that had been fought through and settled. For the exhausted President, it was out of the question; he was too tired even to think of it. "The time to consider all these questions was when we were writing the treaty," he said.

Later that day the President met with the Allies and told them that the United States was against making any major changes in the treaty proposals. As a result, the British initiative failed.

M Y   M O N T H S  at the Paris Peace Conference in 1919 were probably the saddest in my life," Felix Frankfurter later recalled.* "The progressive dis-

---

* Frankfurter's principal role in Paris, assigned to him by Louis Brandeis, had been to aid the cause of Zionism. William Bullitt, whom Brandeis and Frankfurter regarded as a friend, was one of the officials whose support Frankfurter was supposed to enlist. But by the spring of 1919, Bullitt was no longer in any political position to render assistance.

illusionment of the high hopes which Wilson's noble talk had engendered was not unlike the feelings that the death of near ones brings." These were feelings that the young Harvard Law School professor shared with his patron, Justice Brandeis, and with his protégé, Dean Acheson, who in June 1919 became Brandeis's clerk.

Frankfurter found the atmosphere of the peace conference at the end of spring much like that when a congressional session draws to a close. In the rush to wind up, legislative proposals previously thought to be of vital importance are put out of mind, while other matters are resolved arbitrarily with a quick stroke of the pen just to close them out. "Paris was like a session of Congress," Frankfurter reminisced. "You finally had to shut up shop." The delegates, he said, would do "any old thing to close up shop."

Domestic disturbances demanded their attention, and the world's leaders could not afford to spend any more time on the German settlement. In June there were mutinies in the French army and strikes in Paris. In America there were bomb outrages; across the street from Franklin Roosevelt's house, the home of the attorney general was blown up, and a nationwide Red scare ensued.

It was time to close up shop at the peace conference.


THE GERMAN CABINET resigned rather than accept the treaty that the Americans and the Allies sought to impose. It was what Lloyd George, among others, had dreaded; for if Germany refused to sign, the belligerents would have to go back to war—and what was left of the Allied armies was in no fit condition to do that. But the high command of what remained of the German army, more keenly aware of the weaknesses of its own forces than of those of the Allies, advised the politicians that the military could not defend against a renewed Allied attack. So a new cabinet was formed in Berlin to do its bitter duty—which was to take upon itself the onus of signing the hated treaty.


ON JUNE 28, 1919, five years to the day after the assassinations at Sarajevo that provided Germany and Austria with an excuse to launch the world war, the treaty of peace was ready to be signed. Places at the historic ceremony were eagerly sought. Lansing wrote that the American secretariat "has had a very unhappy time with the applications for tickets" and that the conference secretariat "must have been nearly wild with the pressure brought to bear to obtain admission." He added that "there were some heart-burnings I know but that was unavoidable"; there was not room enough for everyone.

Clemenceau opened the ceremonies promptly at 3 p.m. on June 28 in

the long (240 feet), narrow (35 feet) seventeenth-century Hall of Mirrors of
the Palace of Versailles, where in 1871 Kaiser Wilhelm I, in a ceremony
meant to humiliate a defeated France, had been crowned emperor of Germany. The French premier, with his strong sense of the historic moments
in the blood feud between France and Germany, had deliberately chosen
not only the day—the anniversary of Sarajevo—but also this setting. He
was bringing the Germans to the bar of justice at the very scene of their
decades-old crime against France.

Clemenceau was nearly seventy-eight, and for half a century he had
been waiting for the hour between three and four o'clock on the afternoon
of June 28, 1919. But spectators that day in the Hall of Mirrors were seated
too close to view the old warrior's triumph in its fullness. They would have
had to be seated nearly a quarter of a century away to see the irony of it:
to see French officers, in a mirror image of the scene at Versailles, endorsing
an armistice of surrender in 1940 in the same railroad car at Rethondes,
outside Compiègne, in which German delegates had been forced to sign
such an armistice in 1918.

In the Hall of Mirrors on June 28, representatives of more than two
dozen victor countries sat at a horseshoe-shaped table along the mirrored
side of the hall. Pale and trembling, Dr. Hermann Mueller and Dr. Johannes
Bell, the German representatives, were led past mutilated Allied soldiers to
sign the treaty—"as if . . . called upon to sign their own death warrants,"
noted Lansing. All the victors signed except the Chinese, who were absent
to protest the awards to Japan at their expense. In less than an hour, Clemenceau brought the proceedings to a close.

House later was sorry the United States had not held out for the sort
of settlement President Wilson originally had promised: "I wish we had
taken the other road . . . ," he wrote.

At the time, some of the other participants put it more pointedly. "To
bed, sick of life," wrote Harold Nicolson in his diary. "What a wretched
mess it is," American Peace Commissioner Tasker Bliss wrote to his wife.
The treaty, according to Lloyd George, was "all a great pity. We shall have
to do the same thing all over again"—that is, fight another world war—
"in twenty-five years at three times the cost."


THE LEADERS DEPARTED for home as soon as they could. The
ceremony at Versailles was adjourned just before four o'clock the afternoon
of June 28, and at 9:30 that evening Woodrow Wilson was driven to the
Paris railroad station, where a private train waited to carry him to the port
of Brest. On Sunday June 29 he boarded the *George Washington* to return to
the United States.

Robert Lansing followed Wilson two weeks later, and his deputy,

Frank Polk, who had been in charge in Washington during Lansing's absence, then crossed the Atlantic to France to take his place there. Grew remained in Paris, heading the secretariat, and two of the American peace commissioners, Bliss and White, also stayed. House left for England to work with Lord Robert Cecil on fleshing out plans for the League of Nations; he did not acknowledge that Wilson had broken with him, and did not know that his onetime most intimate friend would never see him again.

The peace conference continued after June 1919, and indeed in one venue or another went on with its deliberations until the signing of the Treaty of Sèvres, in another town outside Paris, in August 1920. For the Versailles accord was only the first; other treaties, including the one dealing with the Middle East, still remained to be negotiated and much still had to be done in connection with Versailles. Pursuant to Versailles, thirty-five committees or commissions were to be established. The Dulles brothers were charged with leading roles in dealing with these: Allen Dulles served as chairman of the steering committee of the peace conference. John Foster Dulles was responsible for organizing the reparations committee, and was to deal with all matters concerning finance. In addition, as U.S. representative on the commission whose task was to see that the treaty as a whole was executed, he was involved in the appointment of American representatives to each of the thirty-five committees.

But in the name of Woodrow Wilson, his former teacher at Princeton, John Foster Dulles soon received startling and frustrating instructions: there was to be no American participation in the work of the Versailles treaty committees until the Senate ratified the treaty. There was no response from Washington to pleas from Paris to permit at least temporary appointment of U.S. representatives to the thirty-five committees.

So while the Allies went ahead with the remaking of the world, the American team was sent to the sidelines. For the United States, political paralysis had set in.

# 32

## THE IDOLS FALL

ON RETURNING FROM EUROPE in July, the President began talking to individual senators about the Versailles treaty and about the Covenant of the League of Nations, which he had made an integral part of it. He found that the senators wanted certain changes made in the Covenant. These proposed alterations have been much debated ever since, but particularly in retrospect, it looks very much as though they would have been acceptable to the Allies, that they would have made no material difference in the way in which the League eventually went about its business, and that it would have been wise of Wilson to accept them.

Senator Henry Cabot Lodge, now chairman of the Senate Foreign Relations Committee, became the campaign manager for amendments to the Covenant. Whatever he hoped to accomplish (and it is by no means clear), he threw down his fourteen Reservations to the Covenant as though they were a gauntlet, and the President took them up in the same spirit—as though, regardless of their merits, the proposals had to be beaten because they challenged his authority.

Since the meetings with senators were not producing the desired results, the President decided, as he so often did (and of late, so wrongly), that he would take his case to the people over the heads of elected officials. He would rely on public opinion. The precedents should have discouraged him: In November 1918 he had appealed to the voters for a Democratic Congress, and they had elected a Republican one. In December 1918 he had appealed to the people of Britain to curb British imperialism, with no noticeable effect. In the spring of 1919, he had urged the people of Italy to disown their leaders and to give up claim to the spoils of victory—and the Italian crowds had shouted, "Down with Wilson!"

At summer's end Wilson set out on his courageous but ill-fated whistle-stop trip around the United States. Aboard a special seven-car train—in his own blue car, the *Mayflower*, which was the last in line of the seven—he set out on a trip of almost 10,000 miles. He traveled to Columbus; to Indianapolis; to St. Louis; to Omaha; to Sioux Falls, South Dakota; to Billings, Montana; to Spokane, Washington; to Portland, Oregon; to Los

Angeles. . . . On and on he went, from one side of the continent to the other, bone tired, often unable to sleep, racked by headaches, hands trembling, seeing double—but not letting on, trying not to let it show, speaking with eloquence of his vision, crusading for his plan to rid the world of war.

He was on the Pacific coast when he heard that Bullitt had given damaging testimony before the Senate, and despite its impact and his anger, he went on. It was not until the return swing of his trip, at Pueblo, Colorado, on September 25, that he stumbled in a speech, burst into tears when speaking of soldiers who had died in the war, and later collapsed. He could go on no longer.

The President and his party headed home without stopping for more speeches. After pulling into Union Station in Washington, D.C., they transferred to an automobile: an open touring car. It was a Sunday, and the streets down which they drove toward the White House were practically deserted. Yet as he passed, the President took off his hat and bowed to the empty sidewalks: to phantoms, to the throngs that in his imagination had turned out to greet him. From somewhere—perhaps from behind closed windows—he was observed; and the rumor spread quickly through town that he had gone mad.

On October 2 Wilson woke up to find his left arm useless. Helped into the bathroom, he fell unconscious. When Dr. Cary Grayson arrived, he found that the entire left side of Wilson's body was paralyzed. Though later described by historians as a thrombosis, it seems that what Wilson had suffered was an occlusion of the right middle cerebral artery: a massive stroke.

It was known that Wilson had fallen ill, but to preserve the President's authority, Edith Wilson and her stricken husband ordered Dr. Grayson, a serving admiral, to keep the nature and seriousness of it a secret. Lansing convened the cabinet to determine whether the chief executive had been incapacitated; and under questioning, Grayson described Wilson's illness as a combination of nervous breakdown and indigestion.

The weeks and months that followed were among the strangest in the annals of the presidency. Twenty days passed after the attack before the President was able, even guided by his wife's fingers, to sign his name. But both Wilsons refused to acknowledge that he was disabled and resolutely refused to allow decisions to be made without him. The result was that decisions were not made. Positions fell vacant, but were not filled; letters, memorandums, and state papers arrived, but were neither read nor answered; pardons were prayed for, but fell on deaf ears. A strike broke out in the coal mines; race riots erupted throughout the country—but the executive branch of the American government did nothing. It was paralyzed.

IN THE THIRD WEEK of October 1919, the Franklin Roosevelts had dinner in Washington with the Harold Butlers. Butler, formerly an official of the British government, now was secretary general of the International Labor Organization (ILO) that Lloyd George, Wilson, and the others had created in Paris at the beginning of the year. He fell under the spell of his dinner companion, and after dinner, unburdened himself to Roosevelt of all his troubles.

The President had invited the ILO to hold its organizing conference in Washington. Under his patronage, the conference was scheduled to convene October 29. But Wilson had made no preparations and obtained no appropriations, and now he was incommunicado and nobody could do anything. The secretary of labor had gone through the motions of asking Congress for $200,000 to pay for the conference, but did not believe the request would be granted. There was "no money, no offices, no typists, no messengers, no machinery . . . ," said Butler. With only a week to go before the conference was due to open, he had borrowed $50,000 from Britain, but did not know where else to turn.

Roosevelt laughed. "Well, we have to do something about this," he said. "I think I can find you some offices, at any rate. Look in at the Navy Building tomorrow morning."

The next day, as Butler later recalled, "the Assistant Secretary received me as if he had known me all his life, and with that characteristic snap of the jaw told me that a set of forty rooms had been put at my disposal. With a broad grin he added that he would have to eject a number of admirals and captains, who were using the most nautical language about him, but . . . next day everything would be ready."

AS IF SURROUNDED by a moat, the White House had become a fortress that had pulled up its drawbridges. Nobody from the outside world could communicate with the President. Mrs. Wilson, a woman with only two years of boarding school by way of formal education, gave instructions from time to time to cabinet and other officials that, she said, came from her husband, and occasionally, in her childish scrawl, she would write letters giving orders that she said came from him.

In November Wilson revived sufficiently to receive an occasional state visitor. His brain had suffered permanent injury, and Dr. Grayson despaired of full recovery; but he made progress, if slowly—and before long he could be seen outdoors in a wheelchair.

It was in this invalid state that he exercised command of his political troops in the battle for ratification of the Versailles treaty and of the clauses he had insisted on making inseparable from it for U.S. entry into a league of nations.

WALTER LIPPMANN SPOKE for many of the outstanding figures of his generation in opposing the Treaty of Versailles. But they were in the minority in the country as a whole. The United States was in the grip of frightening strikes (including a police action in Boston), of terrible fears of communism (fanned into flame by Attorney General Mitchell Palmer, who hoped that anticommunism would help elect him President), and of a continuing anti-German hysteria, which all came together: the Germans had aided the Bolsheviks and the Bolsheviks fomented radical labor unrest, so Germans, communists, and labor agitators were all of a piece. On his nationwide speaking tour President Wilson had warned that "there are apostles of Lenin in our own midst," and that the only antidote to "the poison of disorder, the poison of revolt" was the ratification by the Senate of the documents he had brought back from Paris, designed to establish a new world order.

Other than such isolated figures as Senator La Follette of heavily German-American Wisconsin, few were prepared to argue that the treaty was unjust to Germany. The treaty was popular, and almost all senators wanted to vote in favor of ratifying it. The President, foreseeing that, had incorporated the League of Nations provisions into the treaty, so that in order to vote for the treaty, the senators would have to vote for the League.

Most senators wanted to vote for the League anyway, either in the form Wilson proposed or with some modifications. Only between twelve and sixteen senators (out of ninety-six) were opposed to a league in any form. Their leaders were Progressive Republican senators Hiram Johnson of California and William Borah of Idaho. In the American tradition, they were opposed to contracting permanent alliances with foreign powers. They pictured the League as an instrument of British and French imperialism. They were nicknamed "the irreconcilables"; and it was to them that Lippmann turned in mounting a campaign against Wilson's foreign policy package. He was taking Wilson up on his double-or-nothing wager, for Johnson and Borah were obliged to defeat the treaty (which is what Lippmann principally wanted to do) in order to prevent U.S. entry into the League (which was the focus of Johnson's and Borah's concern).

On August 17, 1919, Lippmann sent a letter to Johnson outlining at length the specific questions he and the other senators should ask the President. The questions were based on inside information Lippmann had gathered while working for Wilson and House, and were designed to uncover and cast a spotlight on every skeleton in the closet.

Next, Lippmann arranged for the senators to call William Bullitt as their witness, to appear in a public hearing to supply a behind-the-scenes account of the proceedings of the American Peace Commission in Paris.

Bullitt appeared before the committee on September 12 in the Senate Office Building. He told at length of his mission to Moscow and of how badly he felt he had been treated. He also testified that at the end of his stay in Paris, he had discussed the Versailles treaty and the League of Nations with House, Lansing, Bliss, and White: in other words, with all the American commissioners except President Wilson. He had taken notes of these conversations. As these conversations were private, the senators did not press Bullitt to reveal what the commissioners had said.

Nonetheless, Bullitt did volunteer information about one of these conversations, repeating remarks that had been meant for his ears only. He said that Lansing privately had condemned the treaty as unjust, and quoted him as having said: "I consider that the league of nations at present is entirely useless. The great powers have simply gone ahead and arranged the world to suit themselves. England and France in particular have gotten out of the treaty everything that they wanted, and the league of nations can do nothing to alter any of the unjust clauses. . . ."

RATIFICATION OF THE TREATY required the consent of two-thirds of the Senate. Slightly more than a third followed Senator Henry Cabot Lodge; they were willing to vote in favor of the treaty only as amended—only, in other words, if the fourteen Reservations proposed by Lodge were adopted. That made Lodge master of the situation. Even without the dozen irreconcilables who were opposed to the League on any terms, he had the votes to block ratification if his terms were not met.

Lodge was careful to obscure his own motives and objectives, for as Republican majority leader, he felt it his duty to provide a tent under which all members of his party could meet. As the last of a dwindling band—Henry Adams, who had been his teacher, and TR, who had been his protégé, had both died within the past twelve months—Lodge felt an emotionally charged duty to do his best to create a Rooseveltian peace: an alliance of the victors in the war to guard against Germany's resurgence. But the votes were not there for such a program—not in the Senate, not in the country.

All his life he had wanted the United States to play a larger role on the world stage, but as a realist, he knew that his choice was between

Wilson's League (as he himself had amended it) or no League, between a flawed internationalism or no internationalism at all.

The game was played out on the Senate floor in November 1919, and then was replayed in March 1920. In November Lodge could muster only thirty-five votes for his Reservations (which therefore were defeated), but Wilson could not find enough senators for his unamended treaty either. Newspaper polls suggest that the American public overwhelmingly—by odds of perhaps four to one—wanted to enter some kind of league; and by March everybody except the President was moving toward some kind of accommodation. A broad range of political personalities that included Edward House, William Jennings Bryan, and Herbert Hoover were in favor of accepting the Reservations.

But when the matter again came up for a vote in the Senate in March 1920, and Lodge assembled forty-nine votes in favor of the League with Reservations (more than were needed, when added to the twenty-three votes controlled by Wilson), Wilson directed his die-hard supporters to vote *against* the League rather than accept the Lodge Reservations. And that decided it; the United States had rejected membership in the League of Nations.

The League had been the President's handiwork; yet it was he who led America to walk away from it at a time when about four out of five Americans and about four out of five senators were in favor of joining.


FOR THE PRESIDENT, the cause of the League had become a personal crusade. In going to Paris he had said (according to Felix Frankfurter), "If I didn't feel that I was the personal instrument of God, I couldn't carry on." On returning from Paris, he had told the Senate in the summer of 1919 that the League had come about "by no plan of our conceiving but by the hand of God who has led us into this way."

Now the stricken leader gathered himself up to do battle for the League. In February 1920 he demanded and obtained the resignation of Lansing, who, claimed Wilson, had convened cabinet meetings without authorization while the President lay ill. Statements streamed out of the White House designed to give the impression that the President now had fully recovered. It was announced that he was back at work at his desk every morning. One of Wilson's physicians, in an interview in the Baltimore *Sun* February 10, stated that "in many ways the President is in better shape than before the illness came."

The point of such statements soon became clear. Defeated in the Senate, Wilson had decided that he would win his campaign for American membership in the League of Nations by going to the people in a vast national referendum. The referendum would be the presidential elections of 1920. From his sickbed, the President had decided to run for an unprecedented third term.


FRANKLIN AND ELEANOR ROOSEVELT were on what a later generation would call the White House enemies list. Their offense was that they had invited Viscount Grey of Fallodon, among others, to their home for Christmas dinner in 1919. The almost blind retired British foreign secretary (1905–16) had been a friend of TR's, so Eleanor had asked him to join them along with TR's daughter Alice and other members of the family. But Grey had brought upon himself the wrath of the Wilsons by refusing to send back to England a staff aide who at a party a year before had repeated a slanderous joke about Mrs. Wilson: to the question of what she had done when Wilson proposed marriage, the joke's answer was that "she fell out of bed."

Grey had brought word from England that Lodge's Reservations mostly were acceptable to the British government. From the President's point of view, that made Grey doubly an enemy, and Roosevelt doubly a traitor for having entertained him.

In Washington the first half of 1920 was in any event a time of partings of the way. Long-standing alliances and allegiances were coming apart. Members of the cabinet were leaving, including the secretaries of state, treasury, interior, commerce, and agriculture.

Roosevelt found himself entangled in two potentially damaging matters in which naval officers charged that the Navy Department had been badly, and indeed scandalously, mismanaged during the war. One set of accusations was leveled against Assistant Secretary Roosevelt, the other against Secretary Daniels. Seeking a way out, Roosevelt apparently tried to buy himself immunity by going over to the side of the naval officers. At the Brooklyn Academy of Music on February 1, he made a public attack on his chief's record as secretary of the navy.

Daniels went to the White House intending to ask Wilson to fire Roosevelt. But as he became aware of how much the President hated the young politician, some of his old feeling for Roosevelt returned, and he relented.

If he felt free to sever his ties with Daniels, Roosevelt certainly felt free to cut those with Wilson. Along with others of his generation, he no longer looked to the failing President for leadership. TR, the first idol of Roosevelt's generation, had fallen; Wilson, the second, was now a fallen idol. To Roosevelt and others in his circle, the new hero who had emerged from the war and the peace as an outstanding American statesman was the food administrator, Herbert Hoover.

Louis Wehle, a Kentucky lawyer and a friend of Roosevelt's from Harvard days, came to see him on January 10 to propose a 1920 Democratic ticket of Hoover for President and Roosevelt for Vice President. Wehle told Roosevelt that the people with whom he had already discussed the ticket were enthusiastic about it. Roosevelt said: "You can go to it so far as I am concerned. Good luck!"

To a friend, Roosevelt wrote of Hoover that "he is certainly a wonder, and I wish we could make him President of the United States. There could not be a better one."

The day after talking to Roosevelt, Wehle went to see Colonel House. House said that running Hoover for President was "a wonderful idea and the only chance the Democrats have in November." But Hoover was not a party man—indeed, much of his appeal to Americans was his nonpolitical orientation—and nobody knew whether he would choose (if he had to) to be a Democrat or a Republican.

Wehle put the proposition to Hoover. He reported that Hoover remarked, "I don't believe that I want to get into a situation where I have to deal with a lot of political bosses." Wehle, as he remembered, replied: "Let me tell you if you expect ever to get into American political life, you'll have to take it as you find it. You can't make it over first from the outside."

Wehle's reply went to the heart not only of the problem of the Hoover candidacy, but also of the problem faced by the generation of young Americans who had gone to Paris in 1919 without being willing to deal with the existing system of world politics—and who had returned disillusioned.

Hoover promised Wehle that he would discuss matters with House. When he did so, he told House he was not a Democrat, but a Progressive Republican in the TR tradition. In March he announced publicly that he was a Republican—which was not astute of him, because it meant that the Republicans got him without having to offer him anything.

Lewis Strauss resigned as Hoover's secretary that month to join the banking firm of Kuhn Loeb, and Christian Herter left the State Department to replace him. Hoover was too taken up with his humanitarian activities to campaign for himself, so Herter joined Robert Taft and other young staff members in pushing Hoover forward for the Republican nomination for President. Herter turned to Massachusetts friends; at his urging, Archibald MacLeish, whose closest friends were Dean Acheson and Robert Lovett, became head of the Hoover League at Harvard.

*The New Republic* promoted the Hoover candidacy, but Walter Lippmann, though an enthusiast, soon detected the political amateurishness that would doom the cause. Lippmann wrote to Felix Frankfurter on April 7 that at Hoover's phoned request, he had gone to see him; he had found Hoover "in a bewildered state of mind at the political snarl in which he finds himself. He really wants to take only a liberal line, but he does not know how. . . ." According to Lippmann, Hoover knew how to draw up a long and detailed technical program, but not how to paint in broad strokes a picture of his political vision. Thus, he was unable to rally support. Lippmann reported some advice that House had given: if Hoover were to walk out of the Republican party in protest if and when the National convention nominated a reactionary as President, he then could have the Democratic nomination, for the Democratic convention met later.

But such political maneuvers were not for Hoover, who remained too proud to fight for the nomination, and whose candidacy therefore petered out.

# 33

## THE UNITED STATES
## SIGNS ITS SEPARATE PEACE

MEETING IN CHICAGO in mid-June, the Republican convention deadlocked on the choice of a presidential nominee. A compromise candidate, Senator Warren G. Harding of Ohio, was selected on the tenth ballot after middle-of-the-night discussions that were commonly supposed to have taken place in a "smoke-filled room." Governor Calvin Coolidge of Massachusetts, popular because of his handling of the Boston police strike, won the vice-presidential nomination on the first ballot. It was a traditionally balanced Ohio/East Coast ticket.

The Republican platform denounced certain unspecified provisions of the Covenant of the League of Nations as signed by the President in Paris, but pledged support for "agreements among the nations to preserve the peace of the world. . . ."

Wilson continued to imagine that he would run for reelection on the Democratic ticket. Both his wife and his physician knew that it was out of the question: that the exertion of standing for election almost certainly would bring on another stroke. But neither they nor anybody else told him the truth.

The Democrats convened two weeks later in San Francisco. As there was no sentiment at all in favor of nominating Wilson for a third term, nobody made a nomination speech for him—which disposed of that issue without embarrassment. But there the consensus stopped. The convention soon deadlocked. There were twenty-four candidates for the presidency, and though this soon narrowed to four, ballot after ballot proved inconclusive. On the evening of the third straight day of voting, Governor James M. Cox of Ohio was chosen on the forty-fourth ballot. Cox picked Franklin D. Roosevelt of New York as his vice-presidential running mate—another traditionally balanced ticket, Ohio/New York.

The Democratic platform pledged support for the League of Nations, but explicitly did not oppose the Reservations to the Covenant.

In the general elections in the autumn, Harding and Coolidge won with 60 percent of the popular vote and 75 percent of the vote in the electoral college, the greatest landslide victory in a century.

Roosevelt sportingly described his run at high office as "a darned fine sail." His smile had won hearts everywhere, but a friend reported, "I've been getting around in the crowds. They'll vote for you, but they won't vote for Cox and the League." The experience had been good for him, though. He had learned to become a popular speaker—too much so for some tastes; Joseph Grew, refusing to meet him after the elections, wrote to a friend that "Frank Roosevelt got right down in the gutter and trotted out all the usual catch phrases, mudslinging and campaign slogans that one associates with the lowest form of ward politics."

Cox and Roosevelt had campaigned openly for American entry into the League of Nations. Harding, moving away from his anti-League position, had done his best to straddle the issue so as not to alienate voters on either side. Once elected, however, he came out into the open. In his inaugural address March 4, 1921, he proclaimed that "America . . . can be party to no permanent military alliance. . . . [A] world supergovernment is contrary to everything we cherish."

Voicing a sentiment for which he would be remembered, he told the nation that "we must strive for normalcy to reach stability." "Normalcy" became the catchword of his administration.

NOTHING COULD HAVE BEEN less normal than the state of relations between the United States and its former enemy in the late war. Having failed to ratify the Treaty of Versailles, America had not ended its state of war with Germany. Congress attempted to address this situation by a joint resolution signed by President Harding July 2, 1921, declaring the state of war at an end (without prejudice to any rights accruing to the United States from various accords).

The resolution, however, was unilateral. In order to obtain Germany's agreement, it was arranged that Ellis Loring Dresel, who had served as the principal U.S. State Department expert on Germany at the Paris Peace Conference, should sign, and have Germany also sign, a treaty embodying the terms of the congressional resolution. Dresel's title was U.S. commissioner to Germany, and he was designated the plenipotentiary to execute the document on America's behalf. The ceremony of signing the agreement was scheduled for August 24 at the German Foreign Office in Berlin, but at the last minute it was postponed by Dresel to obtain clarification from Washington of what journalists were told was a minor technicality.

THE 53,513 BATTLE DEATHS suffered by the U.S. armed forces in the war were few in comparison with those of France or Germany, but were no less painful to the relatives of those killed. The living were at a loss for words to say over the graves of the American dead. Henry James, in a 1915 interview published in *The New York Times*, had said: "The war has used up words, . . . they have deteriorated . . . and we are now confronted with a depreciation of all our terms. . . ." To the same effect, Ernest Hemingway had his hero in *A Farewell to Arms* say: "I was always embarrassed by the words sacred, glorious, and sacrifice and the expression in vain. . . . There were many words that you could not stand to hear."

Not only was it trite to offer the consolation that the dead "had not died in vain"; in large part it was untrue. Open-faced earnest boys from the West who had barely heard of Europe and cared nothing for its quarrels had been brought over the ocean to a foreign battlefield in order, so their President had told them, to make the world different: to make it safe for democracy. From Idaho and Oklahoma and Kansas, they had come a long way to do that. Now it turned out that the world, including the democracies of Europe, did not want to be made different. To the extent that the Americans buried in the military cemeteries on French soil had believed that it was in that cause that they were laying down their lives, their sacrifice *was* in vain.

On the strong advice of General Pershing, the War Department decided not to move the American war dead from France. Pershing's view was that their bodies should remain in the fields they had died to defend. Public opinion in the United States, or at least a part of it, was of the contrary view:\* that even in death, the boys should be brought home.


DETAILS OF THE SIGNING of the Treaty of Berlin—the treaty ending the 1917 war between the United States and Germany—are little remembered today. They form one of the more obscure episodes in the history of American diplomacy.

At five minutes before 5 p.m. on Thursday, August 25, Commissioner Dresel and four officials of the American mission in Berlin emerged from the U.S. embassy building on the Wilhelmstrasse. In the street they posed for the lone American press photographer who was there. Then they entered a khaki-colored U.S. Army vehicle and were driven a hundred yards to the German Foreign Office at 75–76 Wilhelmstrasse, followed by a few American correspondents. There were no Germans in the street, no curious crowds, no staring children, no local journalists.

Entering the German Foreign Office, Dresel and his colleagues were led into a reception room on the second floor promptly on the stroke of the appointed hour of five. A few seconds later the German foreign minister,

---

\* According to an editorial reprinted by the *International Herald Tribune* August 1, 1994, p. 4, from its pages fifty years earlier.

Dr. Friedrich Rosen, entered the room, followed a bit later by his own official party. Because the Germans, not liking to be reminded of their humiliating surrender, had especially requested the United States to play down the importance of the occasion, Dresel and his companions were in loose-fitting business suits and had worn straw hats. The German diplomats, not having intended the Americans to depart quite so far from decorum, had dressed formally in black cutaways and gray-striped trousers. Even in trifles, the United States and Europe seemed bent on misunderstanding one another to the end.

Despite efforts by the Germans to sidetrack them, six journalists, five of them American and one English, managed to gain entrance to the ceremony ("through rough reportorial technique and luck," according to *New York Times* correspondent Cyril Brown). The English newspaperman was struck by the lack of pomp; he remarked that it was the first time in history that a treaty had been signed in lounge suits. (The next day *The New York Times*, though it put the story of the signing on its front page, stated that "it was a cut-and-dried formality of the utmost unpicturesque simplicity.")

While the others stood, Dresel sat down at a desk and signed both copies of the treaty on behalf of the United States; whereupon Rosen sat down at the opposite side of the desk and signed on behalf of "the German Empire." It was 5:10 p.m.

Rosen then said he hoped the treaty would lead to friendship between the peoples of their two countries, and Dresel said he hoped so, too. There was no speechmaking and no lingering. Dresel and his party left the Foreign Office building less than twenty minutes after entering it.

So the war was over. It had been wasteful of life but was brought to an end without wasting time; it was not yet 5:30, and there were hours to kill before cocktail time and dinner.

# 34

# THE EDUCATION OF THE ROOSEVELT GENERATION: FIRST LESSONS

IF ONLY FROM THE AUTOBIOGRAPHY of Henry Adams, which so many of them had read, the Franklin Roosevelts and others their age were familiar with the thought that life is an education. But in the 1920s they did not know how enormously valuable their recent experience in making war and peace would prove to be. Because they did not expect the United States to repeat the experiment of sending an army overseas, they could not fully appreciate the worth of the preparation they had undergone. Wilson's young men supposed that history would put them down as the only Americans to involve themselves in Europe's wars and politics; as it turned out, they were not the only ones, merely the first.

The cost of their learning experience had been low. Casualties had been few; most American troops had not been exposed to any danger or fighting, and many of those who had gone overseas had enjoyed it. Moreover, the war had paid off America's foreign debt and made the country rich. If indeed it had been a mistake for the United States to enter the war—and increasingly a consensus was developing that it had been—then at least it had not been a terrible one, and the country was lucky enough to have gotten off lightly.

Wilson himself remained unrepentant. He never wavered in his faith that he had led the nation and the world in the right direction, and that he had been betrayed and abandoned. But the crippled ex-President commanded little support. On ceremonial occasions he could count on the attendance of only such die-hard loyalists as Congressmen James F. Byrnes of South Carolina and Cordell Hull of Tennessee. Others who wrote and came by to see him did so only out of sympathy: he could not walk, his eyes were failing, he would forget the words of the speeches he had rehearsed, his voice would break down, and often he would burst into tears.

Felix Frankfurter later claimed that he had always known how the Wilsonians would excuse themselves in recounting the story of what happened at the Paris Peace Conference. They would tell it, he said, as a tale of American innocence, in which Wilson and his followers acted in good faith and were frustrated only because the Europeans did not. The appearance in 1923 of a detailed account by Ray Stannard Baker, incorporating documents made available by Wilson, fulfilled Frankfurter's prediction.

The contrast drawn by Baker between the virtue of the Wilsonians and the sordidness of the Europeans did indeed belong to the long tradition of American loss-of-innocence literature. Though written by an internationalist, it could however be read as an argument for the isolationists who had opposed Wilson on the war issue: if the Allies were so lacking in virtue, why had the United States fought on their side? Would it not have been wiser for America to remain uninvolved in Europe's debasing feuds and politics?

THEY WILL DISBAND THEIR ARMIES/ When this great strife is won/ And trust again to pacifists/ To guard for them their home . . . ," wrote George Patton, during the fighting, of his countrymen; he mocked his short-sighted fellow Americans and concluded happily, "THERE IS NO END TO WAR." The regular army colonel was one of the few Americans in the postwar years who regarded war as a normal form of international behavior. He studied hard and read omnivorously to prepare himself for his country's next major conflict.

Patton was assigned in 1919 to a command post at Camp Meade, Maryland, where a heavy tank battalion commanded by Lieutenant Colonel Dwight Eisenhower had moved from Pennsylvania. Patton got hold of an army tank handbook—seventy problems with approved solutions—that he and Eisenhower then studied together. The two officers decided to collaborate on writing articles about the future of tank warfare. They took a tank apart and put it back together again. They championed the work of a designer who aimed at building a vehicle that could speed over rough terrain.

Eisenhower's real military education was about to begin—in the 1920s, when most Americans assumed that there would be no more wars. After Camp Meade, Ike was assigned to Panama, where he came under the influence of a general named Fox Conner, who had been the operations officer of the AEF in France. Conner was a cerebral officer who introduced Eisenhower to the pleasures of military literature: first historical novels, then history, then works of military history and theory. Conner taught the younger officer that the Peace of Versailles was no more than an armed truce; that there would be another round in the world war; that in thirty years the Germans again would take the field against an alliance of western Europe and the United States; that the alliance would fight under a unified command; and that American officers should learn to master the art of commanding multinational coalitions. The officer to watch and to follow,

Conner told Ike, was George Marshall: a man who had the qualities needed to lead the allied armies in the war to come.

PERHAPS THE ONLY COMMON GROUND between Conner and the American public was that the negotiations in Paris had been a failure. In the years to come, those who wanted to learn from the experience set out to inquire what had gone wrong.

One answer, supplied by Harold Nicolson in 1933, was that it was France that had blocked the United States and Britain from realizing their vision of a durable peace, and that she had been driven to do so because her geographic position was different from that of the English and the Americans. The English-speaking powers were surrounded by water and could not be invaded by Germany. France had no such defenses, and therefore had to take steps to protect herself that Wilson and Lloyd George regarded as either unnecessary or unwise.

Nicolson had not yet discovered that a resurgent Germany could threaten Britain with invasion as well as France. Nor did he take full account of the progress of modern science, which had shrunk the crossing time and value of even America's ocean moats. Nicolson was not alone in failing to see how greatly technology had changed the fundamentals of military geography. In 1923, writing with the authoritativeness of one who had been assistant secretary of the navy, Franklin Roosevelt, in an article in *Asia* magazine, argued that it was technologically impossible for Japan to attack America's Pacific coast.

WALTER LIPPMANN SENSED that Wilson's failure to put his program across in Paris had been due to some cause other than the moral failings of European politicians or the exposed geographical position of France. The Wilsonians, as Lippmann well knew, had gone to Paris convinced that they held the power to remake foreign politics in the image of America's. They were aware in advance that Europe's old-line politicians would oppose them; but they had been confident of overcoming that opposition. Wilson had counted on public opinion to bring the heads of other governments around to his views. That did not happen, so Lippmann concentrated on the question of why public opinion did not perform as Wilson expected it to.

Lippmann's *Public Opinion* (1922) proved to be a troubling book. A firsthand knowledge of journalism and of wartime propaganda led him to conclude that the public forms opinions on the basis of faulty information. The media, he explained, are not set up in such a way as to either discover or reveal the true story. His unconvincing solution was to create and publicly fund intelligence agencies of experts who would provide unbiased knowledge to those who need it.

Lippmann missed seeing the more basic flaws in Wilson's theory—and his—that public opinion can be relied on to compel governments to behave decently. One was that public opinion carries little or no weight in countries that are not democratically self-ruled—which was most of the human race in 1919, and almost the entire globe outside of western Europe, Canada, and the United States. The second flaw was that, even in democracies, the mass of the people favor the interests of their own countries. The President's theory that even in their own cause people will judge fairly and impartially proved in practice to be every bit as naive as it sounds. A third flaw was that, considerably more than Wilson supposed, opinions differ as to what is right and wrong; alien cultures and foreign political philosophies may produce views that Americans regard as unacceptable. Finally—and most visibly—public opinion is of no avail against invasion by an enemy army.

As of 1922 Lippmann's education in these matters was just beginning. Even in his disillusionment he still failed to grasp the essential inadequacy of his and Wilson's approach to the remaking of world politics. They placed too little emphasis on irrational impulses, on national and religious fanaticism, on xenophobia, on the darker side of human nature, and on the realities of military and political power—and too much on the power of ideals and speeches and the value of promises.

On display in the 1920s were two outstanding examples of America's belief that laws and treaties can change people and peoples. One was the law prohibiting the consumption of alcoholic beverages. The other was the negotiation by the United States of a multilateral treaty, the Kellogg-Briand Pact, in which the countries of the world agreed to renounce war forever.

Yet nations continued to make war; Americans continued to drink alcohol; and the effect of the attempt to enforce Prohibition was to turn normally law-abiding citizens into criminals, and such cities as Chicago into communities ruled by gangsters.

# 35

# GOING ON THE BIGGEST SPREE
# IN HISTORY

IN RESIGNING HIS POSITION at the Paris Peace Conference, William Bullitt told his friends that he was so disgusted by Wilson's betrayal of liberalism that he was giving up on ideals and causes; he was going to the Riviera "to lie down on the sand and watch the world go to hell." As he so often did, he set the trend for his generation. They were going to give up on doing good. They would make a lot of money and have fun.

Harry Truman and a partner opened a haberdashery in Kansas City. Their plan was to stock merchandise of top quality to attract a wealthy clientele—good business contacts, they reckoned, for the future.

Averell Harriman, a failure in wartime shipbuilding, decided he would make a fortune in sea transport like the one his father had made in railroading. He raided a competitor, set up a business combination with a leading German shipping line, and in a short time had made himself "the Steamship King." But a bust in shipping followed the boom, and he was lucky to be able to sell out his interest to his German partners.

In downtown New York he opened offices as "W. A. Harriman & Co." in his own building. He gathered wealthy contemporaries around him. He was joined by David Bruce, scion of a famous Virginia family, who had distinguished himself in the war and who had married Ailsa Mellon, perhaps the richest woman in America. Another recruit was the son of the lawyer who had taken over the management of the Harriman empire from Averell's father: Robert Lovett, somehow unable to concentrate his mind on finishing law school after years of excitement as a naval aviator, threw in his lot with the new firm, too. Another partner was George Herbert Walker, whose grandson George Bush grew up to be elected President.

While Harriman continued to dabble in business, he devoted himself increasingly to playing polo. Tall, thin, rich, athletic, and good-looking, he became a playboy star of the international set. His romantic liaisons were a feature of the tabloid press, and eventually led his wife to divorce him. His idle and luxurious life was envied by many.

But it was noticeable that many of the fortunes on Wall Street were being made by new men who, unlike Harriman and Bruce, had neither inherited their money nor married it. Tough and unscrupulous, they were not always easy to distinguish from the bootleggers who supplied their whiskey. F. Scott Fitzgerald had it pegged: in his novel about Jay Gatsby, the mysterious, debonair millionaire turns out to be not the financier he appears to be, but a creature of the crooked gamblers notorious for fixing the World Series of 1919. Not until 1929 did the hordes of ordinary Americans who played the stock and bond markets discover that the game in which they were gambling their savings was as rigged as the baseball finals of ten years earlier.

Rough, redheaded Joseph Kennedy, leaving the shipbuilding business at war's end, speculated in stocks, bonds, and real estate, profiting from inside information. He alternately organized and foiled bear raids, took over companies and sold them, and went long the booms and shorted the busts. His escapades with movie stars and other glamorous ladies were another expression of his acquisitive lust, less noticed at the time than in the later glare of publicity focused on his famous sons.

Nobody in real life was more a figure out of nowhere—like Gatsby—than James Forrestal, who wiped out all memory not merely of his Catholicism, but of his family origins. He never spoke of his past.

His best friend since college, Frederick Eberstadt, joined him at Dillon Read, the bond house to which he returned after the war. Eberstadt also was running away from his past: in his case, a father who was Jewish. Their employer, Clarence Dillon, had erased his background, too; he did not wish to be known as the son of a Jewish clothing store owner named Samuel Lapowski.

They were a lean, driven, innovative team, specializing in syndications that allowed them to compete against better capitalized rivals. Forrestal and Eberstadt earned fortunes in their daring corporate rescues and reorganizations. Forrestal married a dazzling ex–chorus girl and society columnist; and though he and his wife went on living the promiscuous sex lives that the jazz age seemed to demand, and therefore ran with a fast set of friends, they were enabled to mix with the traditionally wealthy, too. The Robert Lovetts, to whom they became increasingly close—both husbands having been naval aviators during the war—opened the doors for them into established society.

Forrestal continued to remain silent about his origins, refusing to tell even his wife, and later his sons, who his parents were and where he had come from. But the America of the 1920s was a country in which people no longer cared. It was unlike prewar America: Not even the old families to whom Lovett introduced him asked Forrestal about his family origins. What mattered was that he had money.


EVEN THOUGH NOT EVERYONE lived the 1920s that way, many did: those years as Fitzgerald wrote about them—the gaudy years of the jazz age—were what impressed themselves on the national consciousness. The young novelist spoke the same language Bullitt and Berle did in Paris in saying that "we were tired of Great Causes." The postwar decade was "an age of miracles, it was an age of art, it was an age of excess. . . ." It was discovered that "we were the most powerful nation," and the proof of it was that British tailors were obliged to change the cut of their suits to accommodate "the American long-waisted figure."

The automobile, enabling couples to park in distant secluded spots, out of sight of others, had made it possible for unmarried young people to explore the pleasures of sex. Then their elders "had discovered that young liquor will take the place of young blood." The sequel, wrote Fitzgerald, was "like a children's party taken over" by the adults. It was "a whole race going hedonistic, deciding on pleasure."

"The people over thirty, the people all the way up to fifty . . ."—and for young Fitzgerald that seemed a terminal age—"had joined the dance." The generation that had fought overseas to change the world no longer cared about changing anything; "the Jazz Age now raced along under its own power, served by great filling stations full of money."

THE SOLDIERS HAD RETURNED under the guidance of a self-effacing staff officer of whom few were aware. Colonel George Marshall had become Pershing's aide in the aftermath of victory, and as such had organized the transport of 2 million American troops from Europe back to the United States. The financiers in whose circles Pershing moved grew to respect and admire the general's aide. The Morgan bank offered Marshall a position at $30,000 a year. He declined, but in 1921 entrusted Morgan with the management of his investment portfolio—for even he was in the market. It seemed that everybody in America was.

At the end of the war, the army chief of staff, General Peyton March, continued a long-standing feud with Pershing. Searching for a new superintendent for West Point to modernize the service academy, March was determined not to award the post to any of Pershing's favorites, especially not the staff officers such as Marshall who had served under Pershing at his French headquarters in Chaumont during the war. He hit upon the idea of appointing MacArthur, who regarded himself as the victim of intrigues organized by "the Chaumont clique."

MacArthur adored West Point. His mother joined him there, proud of his star and his position, and served as his official hostess. But one night at a party on the Hudson, MacArthur met a wealthy, divorced, sophisticated woman of the jazz age, and they decided to marry. "Of course the attraction is purely physical," snorted MacArthur's mother, who was shocked as well as brokenhearted. Pershing's was a parallel but different unhappiness: he had understood that the lady was to marry *him.* *

Douglas and Louise MacArthur were married Valentine's Day 1922. MacArthur's mother moved out of, and his wife moved into, the superintendent's mansion at West Point. But soon afterward Pershing posted MacArthur to the Philippines—and Louise complained to the press that she was being exiled as a punishment for jilting Pershing.

Louise was bored by the Philippines. She tried to persuade Douglas to quit the army and become a stockbroker; that was where the action was at the time. She induced Morgan to make him an offer, but he declined it.

Deciding that if he were promoted they could go home, she went to Washington and used her money and connections to obtain a second star. "I don't care what it costs," she told her political attorney. "Just go ahead and send the bill to me personally. . . ." MacArthur's mother campaigned, too, pleading with Pershing ("Dear Old Jack"), now chief of staff, to give her son a second star. Just before retiring, Pershing granted the promotion.

MacArthur was posted to Maryland, where Louise had a large estate. But the move did not reconcile her to her husband's profession. She went about with other men, enjoying the nightlife she had missed and the gaiety of society. She decided to divorce again, and her attorneys arranged it. The decree became final, as did many things, in 1929. So ended Douglas MacArthur's romance with the jazz age.


BILL BULLITT KEPT ON THE MOVE, with all the restlessness of his generation: a generation that either did not find what it was looking for or was not satisfied with it when it was found. For a time he edited film scripts for Paramount Pictures in New York. When his wife left and then divorced him, he married Louise Bryant, the widow of his romantic revolutionary friend John Reed. Some guessed that he wanted to *become* Reed. With Louise he went to France; then, for a while, to Turkey. There he rented a villa on the Bosporus, where he and Louise settled—for a short time—to write.

He wrote a novel about the Philadelphia society in which he had grown up, only thinly disguising the characters. Indiscretion had been his weakness; he made it into a career. The book when published was a sensation and a best-seller; Bullitt claimed that it sold 150,000 copies. The Bullitts returned to France.

He now lived the ideal Lost Generation life. In the Paris of the 1920s, of Gertrude Stein and Fitzgerald and Hemingway, where everyone wanted

* Earlier Pershing had cooled to the idea of marrying Patton's sister, as he had long intended to do.

to be a famous writer, he *was* a famous writer—and his novel sold more copies than other people's books did. Hemingway was jealous of him.

Moreover, he was tinged with the glamour of the revolutionary Left: John Reed's mantle was on his shoulders, John Reed's widow was on his arm. Yet he also enjoyed the luxury of an independent income.

And still he was not satisfied. He seems to have been unable to forget that in the war and in the peace negotiations, there had been something further that he had been looking for in life.

GEORGE KENNAN, who served as a young diplomat under Bullitt in Moscow in the early 1930s, once wrote: "I see Bill Bullitt, in retrospect, as a member of that remarkable group of young Americans, born just before the turn of the century [it included such people as Cole Porter, Ernest Hemingway, John Reed, and Jim Forrestal—many of them his friends] for whom the First World War was the great electrifying experience of life."

At first that seems puzzling, for on both a personal and a public level, the war was disappointing and profoundly unsatisfying to Americans who dreamed of doing high deeds. Of course, it was not a terrible experience, as it was for Britons and Frenchmen who suffered the tortures of years of trench warfare; and indeed, American authors who wanted to show the absurdity or the horrors of war had to write their stories from a European point of view. Ernest Hemingway, though he much preferred to write from personal experience, could make his antiwar point in *A Farewell to Arms* only by writing of the Italian defeat in 1917, which he had not witnessed, rather than the victory of 1918, which he had.

The Allies and the United States won a victory, but it was not, for America or Americans, a success. As a rough and generalized truth to which obviously there were many exceptions, the wartime experience of Americans was that they were too late. The economy was not mobilized in time to supply even the AEF with war matériel; the tanks and planes and ships were not ready to be sent out until 1919, when the war was over. Three-quarters of the American army had yet to see combat when the firing ceased. Even the quarter of the army who had been in the front lines had been there, for the most part, only for a few days; they had just arrived.

So the war was over before the Americans could really get to it. The typical experiences were those of Eisenhower, in waiting for a year and a half to get orders sending him overseas and then having the orders canceled, or of F. Scott Fitzgerald, whom Eisenhower had trained, actually boarding ship at an American port before being sent back ashore.

During their training at army camps in the United States, the young civilians who were becoming soldiers had acquired an aura of romance on which they traded at dance parties with the local girls. They had received romantic favors because they were going off to fight, perhaps to die. Posturing for family and friends, they had written letters (and the tone of letters and diaries from the period is indeed, or at least seems so now, stiff and self-conscious) filled with heroic sentiments. And then it had not happened after all!—so that in a sense, and through no fault of their own, they had been made into frauds.

Fitzgerald's regrets (he wrote later in *The Crack-Up*) "at not getting overseas during the war* . . . resolved themselves into childish waking dreams of imaginary heroism. . . ."

The regrets and the dreams were widespread; for the overwhelming majority of Americans who aspired to glory, it had not been a satisfying war. Nor had it been satisfying for the handful who had aimed at winning glory at the peace table rather than on the battlefield; indeed, for men like Lippmann and Bullitt, the First World War experience had been even more deeply disillusioning and embittering.

But—and it helps explain Kennan's observation about how electrifying the experience had been—it was a time when, for themselves, for their country, and for the world, Bullitt and the others had felt that everything was possible. In part it was because they were young, and in part it was because the war had destroyed so much of the old order in Europe as to make any new political scheme seem possible. Bullitt could believe he would usher in a world of justice and peace, John Reed could believe he would lead a world revolution, and F. Scott Fitzgerald could believe he was going to win fame as a war hero.

One could become anyone, one could invent oneself: hence the great Gatsby. The excitement, the (in Kennan's word) "electrifying" aspect of the experience, was that anything might happen. The special sensitivity to life's possibilities, ascribed by Fitzgerald to Gatsby, was shared at that time by the generation to which Gatsby would have belonged.

So two central experiences that shaped the emotional life of the generation were the excitement of having once lived through a magical time of limitless possibilities, and the bitter disappointment that so much that seemed possible had not in fact happened.


TO HIDE THE HURT and the disappointment, they became tough. They learned the racy idiom of the gangster language that later—in the late 1920s and the 1930s—was picked up out of the gutters of the big cities by Dashiell Hammett and Raymond Chandler. The attitudes and postures they assumed were portrayed in the years to come by actors who played

---

* Ernest Hemingway, who always was competing against Fitzgerald, could brag of having been wounded in the war. But he was wounded in the course of a tame activity: distributing chocolate candies.

the role of tough guys in motion picture films: George Raft, James Cagney, Humphrey Bogart.

The overwhelming majority of Americans, including such responsible souls as Walter Lippmann, were going to watch terrible things happen throughout Europe during the 1930s while strongly protesting that they were not going to intervene: they were not going to fight anybody else's battles.

It was only much later that their political attitude was embodied on the screen—by Humphrey Bogart playing Rick in *Casablanca* (1942). "I stick out my neck for nobody," he says. "I'm the only cause I'm interested in." That was what the speakeasy generation had to say throughout the 1920s and early 1930s. Victims of one catastrophe after another appealed for help, but Americans who had lost their faith either on the western front or in the plague year in Paris chose to stand aside: it was none of their concern. The personification of the generation was Rick, at the bar of a gin joint with only a shot of whiskey for company, closing his eyes to the wickedness closing in on civilization—or it was Bullitt, in the public rooms of the Crillon in Paris, bragging that he was going to do nothing but "watch the world go to hell."

# PART SIX

# AMERICA GOES IT ALONE

# 36

## THE AGE OF THE DICTATORS

THE WORLDWIDE BINGE of the 1920s had been America's party. Round after round of drinks had been served to everyone in the house; but as Europe had lost its money in the war, it always was the United States that picked up the bill.

Although America's agriculture was in trouble, few saw the danger that a rural recession might pose for the rest of the economy, which boomed. A historian of the era tells us that "during the second half of the twenties the United States, with about 3 percent of the world's population, accounted for 46 percent of its total industrial output. During the same period it produced 70 percent of the world's oil and 40 percent of its coal." It invested some of its profits abroad, largely in the form of short-term loans that kept Europe financially afloat. The Allies, impoverished by the war, had tried to recoup by forcing Germany to pay them a fortune in reparations; while the Germans, ruined by the peace settlement, borrowed from America the money to pay the Allies. So the countries of postwar Europe lived on America's riches, passing around the largesse from one to the other.

Then American investors and speculators lost their money in the Wall Street crash of 1929.* They no longer could afford to lend, so they did not renew Europe's IOUs as they became due. As Europeans had little money of their own, the liquidity to finance world trade evaporated. The Congress believed it could save the American economy by keeping out competition; it enacted the protectionist Hawley-Smoot Tariff Act, which ironically helped to make everyone poorer, including the United States. America was going it alone.


ON NOVEMBER 21, 1930, Douglas MacArthur—"a dashing, fascinating figure," according to *The New York Times*—was sworn in as chief of staff of the U.S. Army, the eighth person in history to fill that position.

---

* From the autumn of 1929 to the summer of 1932, stocks listed on the New York Stock Exchange lost an aggregate $74 billion in value. In 1993 dollars that would be $740 billion.

His mother glowed in admiration of the four stars that denoted his new rank: "If only your father could see you now! Douglas, you're everything he wanted to be."

The fifty-year-old general and his mother moved into the chief's red-brick mansion house, Quarters Number One, at Fort Myer in Virginia, across the Potomac from the capital city. He took luncheon with her there every day. His devotion to his mother was striking; *More Merry-Go-Round*, an anonymous book of political gossip, remarked that "he takes as good care of his mother as she once took of him." But on his own side of the Potomac, in an apartment and later in a Washington hotel suite only a few blocks from his office, he kept an exquisite Eurasian mistress from the Philippines to whom he was "Daddy."

The habits of personal life he had brought back from the Far East tended to arouse distrust. From ancient history he ought to have remembered that the foreign tastes Caesar and Antony acquired in Egypt were held against them back in Rome; it was feared that they had forgotten their virtuous republican principles. MacArthur therefore should have known that his un-American ways would excite comment. It became common knowledge that in his office he dressed in the flowing comfort of a ceremonial Japanese kimono. *More Merry-Go-Round* reported, too, that "he uses a small Japanese fan, and an assortment of long ivory cigarette holders are always on his desk. Either through nervousness or affectation he uses a fresh holder with each cigarette." Disquietingly, the authors added that "in recent years the office of Chief of Staff has come to be that of virtual dictator of the army." MacArthur, who had started referring to himself in the third person, was not unlike such pharaonic contemporaries as Benito Mussolini. He projected a monumental image of himself by placing behind his office desk a mirror fifteen feet high.

IN MAY 1931 an event occurred that shook the world: the failure of Austria's largest bank triggered a European panic. Financial collapse in Germany followed. Great Britain was driven off the gold standard. Climaxing several years of dislocating shocks to the world's trade and finances, and coming after the 1929 American stock market crash and the 1930 Hawley-Smoot tariff, the Austrian bank failure led within months to the worldwide depression of the 1930s. Economies collapsed; institutions went under, and the financial system disintegrated. Trade between countries ground to a halt. Tens of millions were thrown out of work, while governments tottered.

In September 1931 MacArthur, after attending army maneuvers in France and Yugoslavia as an official observer, was called home by a crisis of a different sort: Japan, having staged a provocative incident at Mukden as a pretext, had invaded the Chinese province of Manchuria; and the government of President Herbert Hoover was uncertain what to do about it. Protecting the independence and territorial integrity of China had long been America's doctrine. The doctrine originally had arisen out of a desire to keep the Chinese market open to the United States. It drew its moral strength from ties developed by generations of American missionaries, though it could have been aimed as well (had America's leaders thought in such terms) at preserving a balance of power in Asia. But it was preachment rather than policy; America was reluctant to take action to back it up.

MacArthur seems to have been inclined, as Secretary of State Henry Stimson may have been for a time, to impose economic sanctions on Japan. But the President would not hear of it; he felt that the public would not support an action that ran the risk of provoking a war.

It was a private citizen, Walter Lippmann, who inspired the American response to Japan's attack. Reading his new column in the New York *Herald Tribune* ("Today and Tomorrow," which was syndicated throughout the country) "was becoming a matutinal rite as inevitable as coffee and orange juice," writes a social historian of the period. In his column, the famous journalist—at the height of his profession and earning the then immense sum of $60,000 a year—proposed that the United States refuse to recognize the territorial changes brought about by Japanese aggression. After advancing his proposal in public print, Lippmann traveled to Washington to make his case in person to Hoover and Stimson. In the end they agreed and promulgated it; it became known as "the Stimson doctrine."

It would be wrong "even to consider the coercion of Japan," Lippmann wrote. It was curious that he should have thought so; for, driven by ideological and economic imperatives, the Japanese surely were not going to stop unless they *were* coerced. Of refusing legal recognition, Lippmann wrote, "I don't see how the policy can fail . . ."; but Willard Straight could have told him how. Straight had spent much of his young life in the Orient observing Japanese expansionism and warning that the United States would count for nothing in the shaping of Asia's future—because American words were not followed by deeds.*

Stimson, having expressed disapproval of Japan's actions, regarded the episode as closed; he later told New York governor Franklin Roosevelt that there was nothing further to be done. But the episode proved to be no more than a prelude; the forces that drove Japan into Manchuria were to drive her further. A decade later it could be seen that the invasion of Manchuria was the first step on a road that led to Pearl Harbor, and that in one sense, the Second World War began in 1932.†

---

* See pages 49–50.

† In April 1932 Mao Tse-tung's Chinese Soviet Republic in Kiangsi province declared war on Japan.

THE PATTERN OF POLITICS that MacArthur observed in Europe as he traveled to observe army maneuvers there in 1931 and again in 1932 was not unlike that in Japan—and was entirely different from that which had been envisioned by Woodrow Wilson when he brought the United States into the European war in 1917. The war had shattered states, governments, economies, and societies; but peace-loving, free-trading democracies had not arisen in their place. Instead the world was moving in the opposite direction. The United States and the Allies at great cost had won the Great War, but the world that had emerged from it was, by 1932, far more dangerous and terrible than the world they had set out to change.

In Italy the once-socialist adventurer Benito Mussolini, who had taken power in 1922, had become dictator in 1926, giving the postwar world a new word: *fascisti* (the plural of *fascio*, a "bundle," used to signify his bundles of supporters). The Russian revolutions, which had aroused so many false hopes, by 1922 had led to the primacy of Joseph Stalin in the Kremlin and, by the 1930s, to his totalitarian dictatorship. Stalin, even more than Mussolini, exerted a pull on loyalties outside the frontiers of his own country; and communism and fascism, despite or because of their similarities, were seen as rivals.

By 1932 eyes had turned to Germany, economically the hardest-hit country in Europe. Versailles had crippled German industrial capacity; by the late 1920s the country's prosperity was based on the American loans, which were withdrawn after the Wall Street collapse. So in 1932 6 million Germans were unemployed and, though other factors also were involved, were vulnerable to the demonic appeal of Adolf Hitler.

Among the lesser European powers, dictatorship had become commonplace. Miguel Primo de Rivera y Orbaneja had made himself dictator of Spain in 1923. Marshal Józef Piłsudski took power in Poland in 1926. A military revolt in Portugal in 1926 eventually had led to the dictatorship of Antonio de Oliveira Salazar. Alexander I proclaimed Yugoslavia a royal dictatorship in 1929. Admiral Miklós Horthy de Nagybánya ruled Hungary. Mustafa Kemal Atatürk, though he encouraged the forms of democracy, served as Turkey's dictator. The chancellor of Austria, Engelbert Dollfuss, was in the process of destroying the country's republican government and establishing his own authoritarian regime. Greece was only years away from the dictatorship of General Ioannis Metaxas.

Republics, parliaments, and politicians were discredited by their ineffectiveness. They were unable to deal with mass unemployment. They proved helpless in the face of the violence introduced into politics by extremists of Right and Left. Traditional society, with its restraints, had been destroyed by the war and the crash. Europe and Japan now lived in a dark age of coups and conspiracies in which ultranationalist killers assassinated the civilian leaders who might stand in their way, gunning down, among others, German foreign minister Walter Rathenau, Bulgarian prime minister Alexander Stamboliski, and Japanese prime minister Osachi Hamaguchi.

The worldwide communist organization that served as an agency of the Soviet regime fought the militarist-nationalist-fascist networks with their own weapons: deceit, violence, conspiracy, and mass organization. Caught in the crossfire of Right and Left, those in the middle of the road evacuated their position: in large numbers, liberals looked to the Communist party to lead the fight against fascism while conservatives turned to the various fascist movements to protect them against communism. Secret police, street gangs, hired killers, and paramilitary troops replaced the debating hall and the ballot box.

Europe's politics were overshadowed by fear. To the extent that the Continent's most dynamic leaders looked forward, it was to a final conflict that would cleanse Europe of her corruption, however defined. In observing army maneuvers overseas in 1931 and 1932, Douglas MacArthur heard from civilian and military leaders that if Germany went Nazi, there would be a war.

In Great Britain, even though pacifist sentiment was strong, there was a party of militarist inclinations that aimed at dictatorship. Sir Oswald Mosley, a charismatic leader and the most creative mind in the Labour government, founded the British Union of Fascists in 1932 in slavish imitation of Hitler and his Nazi party and program.

MacArthur understated the case in describing the Europe he visited in 1931 and 1932 as "troubled and confused."


MAJOR DWIGHT EISENHOWER —"Ike" to practically everyone— lived a life insulated from the world's troubles. Stationed since 1929 in Washington, D.C., he lived with his wife and son in a block of apartments on Connecticut Avenue near Rock Creek Park. His youngest brother, Milton, who ranked high in the civil service, was a near neighbor; Ike and Mamie often were with Milton and his wife, Helen. The Dwight Eisenhowers also spent a great deal of time with the George Pattons, who were stationed at Fort Myer; the two men, who had plotted tank commander tactics together in the early 1920s, now often played golf together.

Eisenhower worked under Major General George Van Horn Moseley in the office of the assistant secretary of war. Their job was to plan the mobilization of the American economy in the event of another war; but as nobody (other than a few fringe figures such as Patton) believed the United States would enter into another war, Eisenhower and Moseley lived in a world of their own, engaged in work almost universally regarded as irrelevant. MacArthur's predecessor had made a point of having no contact with the two officers or their project.

As chief of staff, MacArthur brought Moseley and Eisenhower back into the center of things. MacArthur was tremendously impressed by Eisenhower, and later was to appoint him as his only aide. It was a period when even MacArthur camouflaged himself by wearing civilian clothes to work, for the country was overwhelmingly antiwar.

Earning a decent salary in an assured job at a time when prices were low and falling, Ike Eisenhower had no personal experience of what other Americans were going through in 1931 and 1932. Yet even he wrote, after the 1932 elections, that "things are not going to take an upturn until more power is centered in one man's hands. . . . For two years I have been called 'Dictator Ike' because I believe that virtual dictatorship must be exercised by our President . . ."—and, he added, "I still believe it!"

THE UNITED STATES IN 1932 looked like a country that had just been struck by a hurricane or an earthquake, although it was the people rather than the trees or houses that had been uprooted and blown away. Factories, farms, and banks had collapsed. As in Germany, which was in the process of turning to Nazi dictatorship, a tenth of the population— between a quarter and a third of the entire workforce—had lost their jobs. Two million took to the road—"nomads of the Depression," as former War Secretary Newton Baker called them—and found that the next town was no better off than their own. In one year, and on one railroad line alone, guards reported throwing almost 700,000 stowaways off freight trains. Fifteen million Americans were out looking for jobs. In their ranks were not only farmers and factory hands but also professionals who had thought of themselves as insulated from economic distress. People who only a couple of years before had been lawyers or civil engineers or bankers or architects wandered in a daze, hopeless and defeated, wondering where to sleep or to get food.

As with an earthquake or a hurricane, too, it was something that people could not understand. They did not know why it had happened. It had struck without warning, seemingly out of nowhere, wreaking havoc indiscriminately across the continent. This was the United States, the land of abundance; and yet from California to New York, from Wisconsin to Texas, Americans were sleeping in ditches and starving.

President Hoover withdrew into the White House. He refused to visit soup kitchens. He would not meet with deputations of the unemployed; he could not bear to look victims of the Depression in the eye. He would not admit that the disaster was happening.

Many Americans remained prosperous or wealthy. Some of them began to experience, when looking out at the teeming jobless, a sense of disdain, and with it, fear; to them, onetime friends and colleagues who had lost their jobs or homes had become "them"—troublemakers, radicals, real or potential criminals. Others chose not to notice. Behind the high walls surrounding their estates, it was possible for the rich to live through the Depression without really being aware of it. In the early 1990s an elderly lady in a Washington mansion indignantly denied that as a girl she had been unaffected by the Great Depression: "I distinctly remember that my mother told me we should cut down on my dress allowance!"

THE STORY OF THE BONUS MARCH on Washington has been recounted often; it needs no retelling in any great detail. The bonus was a bit more than $1,000 per soldier; it had been awarded to veterans of the First World War by an act of Congress in 1924, and was to become payable in 1945. When the Depression struck, the veterans petitioned for immediate payment. Over President Hoover's veto, the Democratic Congress elected in 1930 voted to pay them half: more than $500 each.

In May 1932 an unemployed ex-sergeant named Walter W. Walters of Portland, Oregon, became leader of a group that asked immediate payment of the remaining half. Walters's followers marched across the country to Washington, D.C., to present their case. Walters imposed strict discipline: there was to be no begging, no drinking, no incorrect behavior. By June, helped by a friendly Washington police chief, the veterans were camping peacefully in shacks and tents across the river from the capital city while Congress debated their case—and in the end, voted against it. When he heard of the congressional vote, Walters said to his followers: "I have bad news," but "let us show them that we can take it on the chin. Let us show them that we are patriotic Americans. I call on you to sing 'America.'" So the twenty or twenty-five thousand impoverished veterans joined in patriotic song.

They did not know what to do next. About 5,000 of them left. Most stayed. It was a hot summer, with the kind of weather in which any spark can ignite a riot.

A few Communist party members camped separately, led by a man named John Pace. Walters had made a point of excluding them from his ranks, not wanting to give the Hoover administration a pretext for labeling the bonus marchers Reds. Pace was hoping for a chance to seize control of the bonus movement, or at any rate to claim credit for it.

While police patrolled the grounds of the executive mansion day and night, President Hoover ordered the White House gates chained shut, banned traffic for one block all around, and erected barricades. At Fort Myer, cavalry troops and horses practiced antiriot mob control maneuvers. Secretary of War Patrick Hurley complained that the bonus marchers were too law-abiding; if only they would provide him with an outrage, he could declare martial law and set the troops on them.

On July 21 the civic authorities ordered the police to evict veterans from vacant buildings on Pennsylvania Avenue in which some of them had been camping. The buildings were scheduled for demolition; the land on which they were situated was to be developed as a park. On July 28 the evictions began. That morning police ejected the occupants of the first of the buildings. The veterans cursed, but left peacefully. Then a group of Pace's communists came by to provoke a riot; they threw bricks at the police, but the police chief restored order.

Two hours later the police tried to enter a second building, but the steps into it were missing. Someone had put down two planks to take their place. A policeman slipped on the planks, panicked, drew his pistol, and began firing into the crowd of veterans. Taking their cue from him, other policemen drew and fired, too. One of the two veterans killed was an out-of-work Chicago butcher who had joined the bonus march on Washington because (he had told his brother at the time) "I might as well starve there as here."

The disturbances provided the Hoover administration with the excuse it had been seeking to use force. The President ordered Hurley to have MacArthur dispatch troops to help the police clear the Pennsylvania Avenue buildings. The chief of staff sent for infantry from Fort Washington and for cavalry from Fort Myer.

Though he did not take personal command of the operation, MacArthur decided to accompany the troops. He passed word to his mother, at their quarters in Myer, to send him his uniform. When it arrived, he changed from his white civilian suit into it. He brought Eisenhower along with him.

Patton was not in command of the Fort Myer cavalry that rushed to Washington to carry out MacArthur's orders. But like MacArthur, he chose to come along. He did so even though he knew that a public relations disaster awaited him: journalists were aware that among the bonus marchers was Joseph Angelo, the wartime orderly who had saved his life on the field of battle in northeastern France in the autumn of 1918.*

Bayonets and sabers at the ready, the troops threw tear gas into the crowd of veterans, driving them out of their buildings and then through the crowded streets of the capital. The veterans streamed back toward their main encampment across the Anacostia River. Hurley, on behalf of the

* See page 176.

President, sent orders to MacArthur to break off the engagement and pursue no further.

Foreshadowing what he would do in Korea two decades later, Mac-Arthur disregarded the President's orders. Apparently it was his view that once the civilian authorities had placed him in charge of a military operation, they had no business interfering with how he carried it out. MacArthur, according to Eisenhower's later account, refused to hear the orders from Hurley and Hoover; "he said he was too busy and did not want either himself or his staff bothered by people coming down and pretending to bring orders."

Forty-five minutes before midnight, MacArthur's troops crossed the river to attack the tents and shacks where the veterans and their families camped. "Shortly afterward," Eisenhower later remembered, "the whole encampment of shacks and huts just ahead began burning." He and his fellow officers claimed that their troops had not started the fire. But as the whole encampment went up in flames, they attacked, driving the already fleeing men, women, and children before them, and dispersing groups of veterans with gas. According to some accounts, Patton and the veteran who had saved his life confronted each other as Patton led troops in the attack on Angelo's hut.

MacArthur then returned to the War Department and met the press to discuss his victory. The general told the journalists, "That mob down there was a bad-looking mob. It was animated by the essence of revolution. . . . [T]hey were about to take over in some arbitrary way . . . control of the Government. . . ."

As Eisenhower wrote later, "I think this meeting led to the prevailing impression that General MacArthur himself had undertaken and directed the move against the veterans and that he was acting as something more than the agent of civilian authorities." With his authoritarian personality, his bombastic rhetoric, his riding boots and glamorous uniform, the chief of staff seemed the very type of the man on horseback who was becoming dictator in one country after another.

MOST OF THE PRESS approved of what the army had done. Secretary Hurley said, "Mac did a great job. He is the man of the hour." But these sentiments were not shared at the governor's mansion in Albany, the capital of the state of New York.

When Eleanor Roosevelt read the newspaper accounts of these events, she was overcome, she said, by "a feeling of horror." Her husband, the governor, asked, "Why didn't Hoover offer the men coffee and sandwiches, instead of turning Pat Hurley and Doug MacArthur loose?"

All eyes were turned to Albany that summer, for Governor Roosevelt was running for the presidency in the autumn. He provided one alternative to Republican President Hoover, who was standing for reelection. Another was the Christian Socialist Norman Thomas, riding a wave, unique to that year, of widespread disenchantment with the American system of free enterprise.

It was a time—again, in that sense, unique—when many questioned whether the United States would continue to choose its leaders by popular election. The charismatic demagogue Huey Long, who had established one-man rule in his home state of Louisiana, was ambitious to play a role on the national scene; it was not implausible to see in him a future dictator. The other most dangerous man in the country, Roosevelt told one of his political intimates, was MacArthur.

The general saw things the other way around; in his view, he had saved constitutional government in his attack on the bonus army. To prove his point, he filed a lawsuit against the authors of *More Merry-Go-Round*, who turned out to be the columnists Drew Pearson and Robert S. Allen. Among other things, he alleged that they had portrayed him as "dictatorial" and that they had falsely claimed he had disobeyed orders from his civilian superiors.

But an attorney for Pearson and Allen indicated that he was going to call for testimony from Isabel Rosario Cooper, MacArthur's Eurasian mistress. The general sent Eisenhower to look for her, but Ike reported back that he could not find her. The columnists, having bought MacArthur's love letters from her, kept her in hiding.

So MacArthur withdrew his lawsuit, leaving the popular impression that he could not challenge the columnists' portrayal of his conduct in the bonus march affair as "unwarranted, unnecessary . . . brutal"—and dictatorial. The general paid the columnists $15,000 (which they turned over to the girl) to keep his affair with her a secret. MacArthur and Isabel Cooper were both unmarried; thus it might have been thought that he had no reason to hush things up—especially at such a high cost, not only in cash but in the impression he gave the public that he could not defend his conduct against accusations that he was a would-be dictator. However, to those who knew him well, the explanation, though odd, was obvious. As a military colleague remarked years later in amazement, it was because there was one person MacArthur could not allow to learn about the Eurasian girl: "his *mother* . . . !"


IN THE MARGINS OF A BOOK that described how troops suppressed mobs in the dying days of the Roman Republic, Patton noted after the bonus march that "the U.S. Army is too small for foreign wars but is very useful at home." He did not note that, in the end, the Roman armies brought down the Republic.

Army-backed dictatorships were taking control elsewhere, and an obvious question was: Can it happen here? But a less obvious question was raised by the first part of Patton's comment: at a time when predatory dictatorships bent on war and conquest were on the move, could an America whose army was "too small for foreign wars" continue to go it alone in world politics?

It could be done, but only by remaining isolated from the affairs and troubles of countries outside our hemisphere. Such was the view of publisher William Randolph Hearst, who sought a Democratic candidate for the presidency in 1932 who would champion his views.

# 37

# RUMORS OF WARS

*Ye shall hear of wars and rumors of wars. . . .*
*For nation shall rise against nation.*
                                        —Matthew 24:6–7

IN THE FALL OF 1931, as MacArthur paid his first visit to Europe
as chief of staff and heard talk of impending war, the multimillionaire press
lord William Randolph Hearst, too, visited Europe and heard the same talk.
Though he had not succeeded in becoming mayor, senator, governor, or
president, Hearst had come close in some cases; and he remained, as he
approached his seventieth birthday, an immensely powerful figure in the
United States, whose chain of newspapers and magazines swayed large segments of public opinion.

Hearst had firsthand knowledge of how the United States could be
enticed into a foreign conflict: years before he had done it himself. His and
other sensation-mongering newspapers had been partly responsible for starting the Spanish-American War of 1898. From the outset in 1914 he had
been keenly aware of how the United States was being pulled into the world
war—but had fought against it, for hatred of the British empire was a
constant feature of his otherwise inconsistent politics.

Over the radio in September 1931, Hearst warned Americans that they
should not repeat the mistake they had made in 1917; Europe was preparing
for war, and the United States should take care not to be dragged into it.

Hearst led his newspapers into an antiwar crusade. He created a "Mothers of America" movement to campaign against war. He had financial interests in the motion picture industry, and made use of the power that gave
him to propagate antiwar sentiment; for inclusion in films, he personally
wrote such dialogue as: "The next war will depopulate the earth."

WILLIAM BULLITT was another American in Europe who feared that
the United States once again might be pulled into the Continent's quarrels.
In Russia in 1914 he had imagined that he could play a personal role in
averting the catastrophe. But in the aftermath of the dizzying 1920s, it took
time for him to regain his equilibrium and sense of mission.

The jazz age of the 1920s—"the most expensive orgy in history," in F. Scott Fitzgerald's words—was over. But for those who had lived it to the fullest, even those like Bill Bullitt who had escaped financial ruin,* the crash brought about emotional and intellectual disorientations: crises of faith and of identity. It was tempting in retrospect to see the reckless living-for-the-moment of the twenties as vain and shallow, and to repent by turning back to serious matters: to works of the mind, or to public service. Such, at any rate, was Bullitt's inclination.

Bullitt no longer was disposed to live the life of a playboy artist. Though the author of a best-selling novel, he found himself blocked; he could write nothing else. Louise Bryant, his second wife, had given up her own flourishing career as a journalist to help him; now she had contracted an incurable illness called Dercum's disease and could not even help herself.

Always a heavy drinker, Louise began to drink before breakfast and went on drinking all day. She seems to have been taking drugs, and was going to pieces visibly. By the end of 1929 it was easy for Bullitt to show that she could no longer function effectively either as a wife or as a mother. In December 1929 Bullitt filed for a divorce, which he obtained in 1930, winning sole custody of their six-year-old daughter, Anne. Though he had committed adulteries of his own, notably with the newspaper heiress "Cissy" Patterson in an escapade on the French Riviera, Bullitt in his lawsuit accused his wife of having run away with a lesbian lover. During the decade-long party American writers had thrown in Paris in the 1920s, Louise Bryant's wildness had seemed attractive and fun, but in the bleak morning-after light of 1930, it did not.

In an effort to understand her psychological problems—or perhaps his own—Bullitt traveled to Vienna and consulted Dr. Sigmund Freud. An improbable friendship blossomed. It ripened into a literary partnership, as Bullitt and Freud discussed the outlines of a book they both wanted to write, but for which each had need of the other.

The book was to be a psychological portrait of Woodrow Wilson. Bullitt was to supply the personal and political data for the biography, from which Freud would construct a theory of why the President behaved as he did. They did go ahead to do the book, but decided not to publish it until it was politic to do so.†

Edward House, with whom Bullitt had kept in touch even during his artist-playboy years, had more pressing tasks in hand for him. For House once again had a candidate; two decades after finding a kindred soul in Governor Wilson of New Jersey, he had found another winner in Governor Roosevelt of New York—to whom Bullitt could be of use.

---

* His brother Orville had sold them out of the market at the top, before the collapse.
† It was published in 1967.

Picking up his 1914–19 life where it had left off, Bullitt traveled up and down Europe, talking to politicians and journalists of all sorts. Bullitt had a genius for friendship, and was on close terms with more European statesmen than any other American of his time. He resumed writing reports to House on current politics, much as he had during the Wilson administration. House helped Bullitt to put himself in a position to play a role again in American foreign policy if Roosevelt were to win the 1932 elections.

Of course, Wilsonian loyalists were in Roosevelt's entourage; and they might blackball Bullitt for his disloyalty to the President in 1919. In this regard House himself was traveling on a passport that—known only to himself—had long since been canceled. As Wilson's sometime closest friend and political partner, he still spoke as though he were the dead man's envoy among the living. He did not reveal that his authority had been revoked by Wilson five years before the paralyzed President died. House kept secret the news of their bitter break; indeed, an authoritative four-volume work on House's role by his collaborator Charles Seymour improved upon the past by claiming that the intimacy between Wilson and House had never been broken: it had merely lapsed because of Wilson's illness. House therefore seemed to be in a position, if anybody among the living was, to forgive Bullitt in Wilson's name.

In December 1931 House asked Bullitt's permission to show one of his political letters from Europe to Roosevelt. It evidently was what Bullitt had been angling for. Bullitt replied: "I should be glad to have you show Roosevelt my letter and I hope you will, as you suggest, let him know that I might not be altogether useless." Bullitt had known Roosevelt only slightly during the Wilson administration, and counted on House to bring him into the inner circle of the New Yorker who was the leading contender to win the 1932 Democratic nomination.


BULLITT'S OLD FRIEND Walter Lippmann had carved out a unique niche for himself with his phenomenally successful syndicated newspaper column, which appeared in the *Herald Tribune* and more than a hundred other papers throughout the country. In the serious press, which aimed at objectively presenting the facts, Lippmann instead provided opinion and analysis that made sense of the news by putting it in a personal perspective. He did not even try to look at events from a detached point of view; he deliberately looked at them from his own. He had become in some ways the equivalent of a Hindu *pandit*; and that is what (in its anglicized form) he was called—a pundit.

It had become clear by 1930, as a Republican administration led America into an abyss, that the 1932 Democratic presidential nomination would be well worth having. Lippmann was insistent that the nominee must *not* be the popular governor of New York, Franklin Roosevelt, whom he had known in Wilson's Washington and whose most remarked-upon gift—of which Lippmann took a dim view—was to seem all things to all men.

To a friend, Lippmann wrote in 1930, "I very much hope that you are right in thinking that he has destroyed his chances of a presidential nomination. He never was big enough for that." In 1931 he wrote, "I never felt so confident as I do now that the weakness of the man will become revealed to the general public well in advance of the conventions." Roosevelt, according to him, "just doesn't happen to have a very good mind. . . . [H]e never really comes to grips with a problem which has any large dimensions. . . . He has never thought much, or understood much, about the great subjects which must concern the next President. . . ." He was no more than a "kind of amiable boy scout."

In 1932 he wrote, "What a weaseling mind he has; how much he would like to have everybody vote for him!" In his column he charged that Roosevelt was "without a firm grasp of public affairs and without any strong convictions . . ." and was "a pleasant man who, without any important qualifications for the office, would very much like to be President."

Other keen observers of the political scene were in agreement, and Lippmann himself refused to retract; referring back to these remarks years later, he said: "That I will maintain to my dying day was true of the Franklin Roosevelt of 1932." Indeed, one of the great mysteries of American history is how the charming, superficial mama's boy with an undergraduate sense of humor, easily bored, and with no interest in hearing explanations became a national and a world leader. Those who knew him as President continued to find him an intellectual lightweight with an astonishingly short attention span.

The widespread theory is that FDR's bout with crippling infantile paralysis, which began in 1921 and lasted for the rest of his life, matured him. If so, it was poetically right that his closest companion in youthful debauches and follies, the philandering and hard-drinking Livingston Davis, should have committed suicide during the presidential primary season of 1932: it echoed the despair and death of Falstaff when young Prince Hal put aside the wild companions of his youth to assume greatness as Henry V.

But Shakespeare's Henry V had grown to be a different man from the carousing young wastrel he once had been, while there had been no such revolution in Roosevelt's character. The shallow young assistant secretary of the navy, who nonetheless had been the only American official with the genius to see in August 1914 what the European war would mean, remained an intellectually shallow man when as President he saved democracy, first in America and then in the world. "A second-class intellect. But a first-class temperament!" The description of FDR in 1933 attributed to Justice Oliver Wendell Holmes suggests the elusive but undeniable quality of the President's greatness.

Lippmann was right to think that Roosevelt had the mindlessness of a fraternity man, but it transpired that he was wrong to think the less of him for it. The genius in action of the frivolous Hudson Valley squire who would rather be amused than informed was a mystery to contemporaries and remains a mystery to historians. But so great a difference did he make that it is almost impossible to imagine what would have happened to the United States if his candidacy had gone down the drain after the first few ballots at the Democratic National Convention of 1932.


IN 1932 WILLIAM RANDOLPH HEARST, an opinion maker of rather a different sort than Lippmann, decided to back a Democratic candidate for the presidency, rather than to run for the nomination himself as he had in the past. Though Roosevelt, whose internationalism alienated Hearst, held an early lead, he had no lock on the nomination; and a number of other names were being brought forward (even, in the end, that of Walter Lippmann). Hearst's inclination was to support Congressman John Nance Garner of Texas, the Democratic Speaker of the House, with whom he had become friendly when they were both serving their first terms in Congress starting in 1903. But he took the precaution of first making sure that Garner stood with him on the issues that mattered most. A Hearst envoy, sent to question Garner, was able to reassure the publisher on that point: Garner was totally opposed to American involvement in the affairs and wars of Europe.

Garner had not been regarded as a major contender, but he became one in early January 1932 when Hearst took to the airwaves and proclaimed that "we should personally see to it that a man is elected to the Presidency this year whose guiding motto is 'America first.'" John Nance Garner, he told a surprised America, was that man.

Edward House immediately contacted Hearst, seeking his support for Roosevelt and assuring him that the New York governor was no internationalist. Hearst was skeptical. Roosevelt, he wrote House on January 21, "made his numerous declarations publicly when he said that he *was* an internationalist. He should make his declaration publicly that he has changed his mind and . . . that he is *now* in favor of not joining the League [of Nations] . . . . I must say frankly that if Mr. Roosevelt is not willing to make public declaration of his change of heart, and wants only to make his statement to me privately, I would not believe him. . . ."

On February 2, typically trying to have it both ways in a speech delivered in Albany to the New York Grange, Roosevelt said that he had no apology to make for having supported American entry into the League of Nations in 1920, and that if circumstances had not changed, "I would still favor America's entry into the League. But the League of Nations today is not the League of Nations conceived by Woodrow Wilson. It might have been had the United States joined . . . ," but we had not, and the League now dealt with "strictly European political national difficulties. In these the United States should have no part. . . . The League has not developed . . . along the course contemplated by its founder. . . ." The members of the League, instead of being guided by its ideals, had embarked on rearmament programs so that "American participation in the League would not serve the highest purpose of the prevention of war . . . in accordance with fundamental American ideals. . . . [T]herefore I do not favor American participation."

This somewhat tortured explanation of Roosevelt's position was not enough for Hearst, who threw money and resources behind his candidate with such effectiveness that in June 1932 Garner came into the Democratic National Convention in Chicago with the California and Texas delegations behind him.

Two-thirds of the delegates—770 votes—were needed to win. On the first roll call of the Chicago convention, Roosevelt received a shade more than 666 votes; Alfred E. Smith, who last time around, in 1928, had won the nomination but lost the election, had nearly 202; and Garner, a bit more than 90. There was little change on the second and third ballots, and Roosevelt's campaign manager worried that if the fourth ballot proved inconclusive, too, the convention would move to a compromise candidate such as former War Secretary Newton D. Baker, a political heir of Woodrow Wilson's.

From his hilltop castle of San Simeon in California, Hearst kept in constant telephone contact with his men on the floor of the convention. Garner had little chance of winning further support. Smith was better positioned, but he was Hearst's bitter enemy, to be stopped at all cost. Joseph Kennedy phoned Hearst to warn that if Roosevelt fell short on the next ballot, the candidate would be Baker, the most internationalist of all.

Hearst saw that for one ballot more his control of the Garner bloc enabled him to swing the nomination to Roosevelt; afterward his 90 votes might not be able to swing the nomination to anyone, so nobody would have to make a deal with him to obtain his support.

He phoned the Roosevelt people in Chicago to demand assurances that if their man won, there would be no internationalism, no involvement in Europe or its affairs; and "almost tearfully," according to an eyewitness account, FDR's managers agreed. The publisher then called his own people in Washington and Chicago. Hearst's man in Washington relayed the tycoon's message to Garner, who consented; the deal was struck.

The Garner delegations of Texas and California then announced their switch to Roosevelt. The convention nominated Franklin Delano Roosevelt for President, with 945 votes out of 1,154, and John Nance Garner for Vice President on a unanimous voice vote.

It was the custom for nominees to be notified of their selection several weeks later, and to accept then. But Roosevelt immediately flew from Albany to Chicago to deliver his acceptance speech to the convention. He said he was breaking with "absurd conventions." It was a foretaste of things to come: Roosevelt was not going to play by the rules—or at any rate, not by the old ones.

## 38

# THE EMERGENCE OF FDR

ROOSEVELT WAS NOT AN INTELLECTUAL. It was unlikely to have occurred to him that the role he was about to play on the stage of history had been foreshadowed in a literary classic, let alone one 3,000 years old. Yet it sheds some light on his performance to think of him in terms of Odysseus, the hero of Homer's epic poem of life and death in the long-ago Bronze Age.

When the *Odyssey* begins, its hero has spent many years fighting overseas in the Greek expedition against Troy. His side has won. The war is over now. He longs to return to house and family, and the *Odyssey* is the story of his adventures in trying to go home. He became, for all time, the model of the voyager in life.

He wants to go back to things as they were, but everywhere about him he finds people and things changing, often for the worse. Gods become humans; humans become animals. Mastering change is the art of survival in the world through which the voyager wanders.

Change was the central feature of the voyager's world—as it was of the world of Roosevelt's generation. Indeed, Roosevelt's contemporaries had lived through greater and faster change than any other generation in history. When they were young, they rode in carriages drawn by horses, as Trojans had done in the Bronze Age; now they flew in airplanes. They were born into a world of lamps and campfires, not unlike those of Greeks and Trojans, but now they lit up the night with electricity. The voices of their parents— back in the days when they had been young—could have been heard no farther than the distance of a shout, but now a person on one side of the Atlantic Ocean could carry on a normal conversation with someone on the other side.

After all the tremendous dislocations and changes caused by the Great War, in which for the first time a couple of million of young Americans were sent to a foreign continent, Americans wanted to go home to normalcy and the world they had left behind. They were not allowed to do so. Everything had changed.

The social shifts ignited by the war exploded in the 1920s. The role of women changed, and with it the norms of accepted behavior; relations between the sexes changed, along with the code of sexual behavior. Senators and soldiers and journalists who were attempting to grapple with bewildering political and economic dislocations were doing so, it should always be remembered, against the background of personal lives that had become at least equally problematical. Nobody had drawn the guidelines yet; it was all too new. As will be seen, faced with the question of how to deal with a wife who had become an alcoholic, or even whether to consult a psychologist about her, William Bullitt and James Forrestal, men who might well belong to the same club, took quite different approaches.

The worldwide rise of dictatorships after the war, the discrediting of the remaining democracies, and the collapse of the world's economies and financial institutions, coming on top of all the other confusing changes, seemed to leave nothing to hang on to. The Americans whose support Roosevelt solicited in 1932 were disoriented. They did not know what to believe. But FDR did.

In the faraway and largely imaginary world of the *Odyssey*, the voyager deals with the often magical transformations in shape and identity around him by quick changes into disguises of his own. Asked by a stranger who he is, he always invents a new identity for himself and tells an improvised story of how he happened to have been cast up upon this particular shore. Before he recognizes the affectionate goddess who watches over him, he lies even to her—to her vast amusement. He saves the truth only for members of his family—and even to them, only after he has told them invented tales designed to prepare them to hear the truth.

Roosevelt, too, was a teller of stories. It was his mode of persuasion. He employed speech not to reveal, but to convince. In the bureaucratic jargon of a later time, he told the truth only on a need-to-know basis.

Like Odysseus, too, he succeeded because, in a world in which others had forgotten who they were and had lost faith in the directional signs that tell which is north and which south, he knew who he was, where he was, and where he wanted to go. He had an instinct for which changes were real and which merely apparent. Undizzied by the world's revolutions, the astonishingly complex man who made himself appear so simple appeared to take his stand on firm ground as a Delano and a Roosevelt of the Hudson Valley.

AS ROOSEVELT WAS WINNING the Democratic nomination in Chicago with a promise of no more internationalism, William Bullitt, who allowed people to understand that he was Roosevelt's foreign policy representative, was visiting Moscow, the scene of his 1919 negotiations with Lenin: a mission that had led both to the triumph and to the tragedy of his earlier career. He led at least one American journalist in the Soviet capital, Eugene Lyons of the United Press, to believe that he was scouting out the land for the Democratic nominee. Lyons later quoted Bullitt as having said that "Franklin Roosevelt will be the next President, and American recognition of the Soviet government will be one of the first acts of his administration."

Before leaving Moscow, Bullitt insisted on placing a wreath on the grave of his friend John Reed. Times had changed; only with the greatest difficulty was the necessary permit obtained from the Soviet authorities. Bullitt still shared the romantic revolutionary outlook on Lenin's early communism expressed by the dead poet and journalist: a man he had so much admired, whose life he had wanted to live, and whose wife he had married. When Bullitt came away from the grave, "tears were rolling down his cheeks," wrote Lyons, "and his features were drawn with sorrow."

In July Bullitt returned to the United States to seek a role in the presidential campaign, but it proved unexpectedly difficult to be introduced to the candidate. Impatient with House, Bullitt turned to Louis Wehle, who had known Roosevelt since Harvard and who claimed to have been the first Democrat to promote Roosevelt for a spot on the 1920 national ticket.

Wehle wanted to be reassured about Bullitt's politics; and as Roosevelt had retreated from internationalism to win Hearst's support, so Bullitt now recanted his pro-Soviet views to gain a position with Roosevelt. Wehle later wrote that "we ironed out such difficulties as there were between us. Whatever Bullitt's original thoughts may have been about the possibilities of the Soviet system when it and Bullitt were both young, he had clearly become thoroughly disillusioned by the development of the U.S.S.R. under Stalin. He now condemned it and every part of it; and he now understood the extent of the Soviets' subversive activities in the United States during his long absences." (It is interesting to note that communist sympathizers, whom Bullitt now deprecated, had been organized throughout the United States in what were known, in honor of the friend Bullitt so admired, as John Reed Clubs.)

Wehle was unable to find a place for Bullitt on the Albany campaign staff—which was what Bullitt wanted—but did obtain a letter from Roosevelt formally accepting Bullitt's services as a foreign policy adviser. Bullitt then sent Roosevelt a letter of support, prudently attaching a donation ("Enclosed is my cheque for a thousand dollars. I wish I could send more, but I have no more to send"). The Democratic party was much in need of money, and the handful of rich men who supported it—among them, stock market manipulator Joseph Kennedy and Jesse Straus, the president of Macy's department store—were so few in number that they could feel sure of personal recognition if the ticket were to win.

Wehle finally succeeded in arranging a personal meeting between Bullitt and Roosevelt in Albany October 5. They charmed each other, and even though Roosevelt's friend William Phillips, an assistant secretary of state under Wilson and soon to be FDR's undersecretary, still blamed him for disloyalty in 1919, Roosevelt welcomed Bullitt back into the Democratic inner circle.

ROOSEVELT WON THE NOVEMBER 8, 1932, election with more than 57 percent of the popular vote and 88 percent of the electoral vote. But in those times a new inaugural did not take place until March; for the next four months, the government would mark time, waiting for Roosevelt's day to come.

At Wehle's suggestion, Roosevelt sent Bullitt on two private fact-finding trips to Europe after the elections. The focus of concern was repayment of the outstanding debts owed by the European countries to the United States. Bullitt was hopeful and wrong; he believed that Britain and France would pay. He also was optimistic about Germany: "Hitler is finished," he wrote, and "Hitler's influence is waning so fast that the Government is no longer afraid of the growth of the Nazi movement."

News of Bullitt's mission leaked to the press, and there was a furor: by law (the Logan Act) private citizens are forbidden to conduct American foreign policy on their own. Irate remarks were made in the Senate, with the mention of stiff penalties. When Bullitt returned to Washington, he was teased at a cocktail party by Senator Huey Long with "Damn near sent you to jail for twenty years, hey, boy?"

Nothing was to be done in policy making before March 4, 1933. Until then hope and the economy went down the drain, as the Hoover administration expired slowly.

IN JANUARY 1933 President-elect Roosevelt revealed to a Hearst emissary the two-step approach he would take in dealing with the deepening economic crisis. He would be an economic nationalist in the Hearst mould "for the present emergency." That meant doing whatever was necessary to raise price levels in the United States, no matter how unsettling that might be for foreign currencies. As he saw it, the United States had to be revived first; once that was done, it would be time to start working with others.

Roosevelt candidly told Hearst's envoy about step number two. When the emergency was over, he proposed to pursue a policy of tariff reduction and free trade, because in his view trade barriers hurt rather than helped. That had been Wilson's view as well, and it was the view of Cordell Hull, the longtime congressman and senator from Tennessee and Wilson loyalist whom he was going to appoint secretary of state.

These policies, explained in advance to Hearst, were those that Roosevelt outlined in his inaugural address on March 4. He explained that "I favor as a practical policy the putting of first things first." Though "I shall spare no effort to restore world trade," first the country would have to deal with the "emergency here at home" by "the establishment of a sound national economy." He was telling the country that he was an American nationalist who was taking a two-step approach to a Depression that he regarded as an emergency, like a flood or a hurricane. For the duration of the emergency, isolationism was the right policy. Once the emergency was over, the right thing would be to go back to economic internationalism.

AT THIS DISTANCE IN TIME it is difficult to convey the extraordinary effect of Roosevelt's inaugural address. It is true that he struck the right note: to a country that despaired of the do-nothing policies of Hoover and the long interregnum in which nobody was in charge, he pledged "action now," and warned that he might have to exercise the emergency powers usually granted to a President only in wartime. That was the main thing people wanted; they wanted the government to do something.

But the great effect was that of the new President's personality. He enjoyed life. He loved power. As it turned out, he would never give an appointee undivided authority; he wanted always to have the final word himself. And as would be seen even later, he adored being President so much that he could never bring himself to give it up.

He was serene and absolutely sure of himself. The sentence in his speech that put heart back into the country—"The only thing we have to fear is fear itself"—must have had so powerful an effect because it so well expressed his outlook: he was without fear. He radiated the sense that once he took charge, there would be nothing to worry about.

Never can one speech have made such a difference. It was a memorable occasion: a turning point because the country regained faith in itself and in its leadership. People who were at the 1933 inaugural never forgot it. A distinguished *New Yorker* journalist later remembered that as a boy of nineteen, he had been in Washington on that windy, misty winter Saturday. He had no ticket, and could not get close to the Capitol, where the ceremony would take place. So he found a tree without leaves and climbed it to see over the heads of the crowd. Other inhabitants of the tree were a woman in rags, an elderly man in patches, and a girl with red hair. The four of them sat on their branches and, along with tens of millions of other Americans whose clothes and lives were also in tatters, were reassured. As the four climbed down from their tree to go their ways, the redhead said: "I think we'll live."

WALTER LIPPMANN WROTE in May 1933 that "the nation, which had lost confidence in everything and everybody, has regained confidence. . . ." Hearst told FDR, "I guess at your next election we will make it unanimous." In the radio broadcasts that he made as "fireside chats," the President restored the country's faith in its institutions; and during the now-legendary first hundred days of the new administration, FDR saved the American banking, economic, and political systems.

In a diary entry Roosevelt's secretary of the interior, Harold Ickes, suggested the sense of breezy improvisation with which the most important question of world finance—whether to stay with the gold standard—was resolved. "One night Bullitt was at the White House and found the President in the long corridor on the second floor. . . . He asked Bullitt what ought to be done and Bullitt said that we ought to go off gold. Then Senator Key Pittman"—the new chairman of the Senate Foreign Relations Committee, from silver-producing Nevada—"came in and his opinion was asked. He said, 'Go off gold.' Raymond Moley"—a professor and a leading Roosevelt adviser—"was the third who came in and gave the same advice. There followed Secretary of the Treasury Woodin"—the cabinet officer within whose province the issue fell—"and the President waved cheerfully at him and said, 'Hello, Will, we have just gone off gold.' Woodin, taken aback, said: 'Have we?' "

Philadelphia banker Orville Bullitt was appalled to learn of the decision—and even more so that this question of high finance apparently had been decided on the basis of advice from such as his older brother, Bill, "whom I told that he had no right to an opinion as he had never even been able to balance his checkbook."


ROOSEVELT SOON MADE IT CLEAR that he meant what he said: in the first instance the United States would go it alone. A sixty-six-nation World Monetary and Economic Conference convened in London in June 1933. The official head of the American delegation was newly appointed Secretary of State Hull, but his authority was undercut by Roosevelt adviser Raymond Moley, who spoke as though he were the President's personal representative, and also by Bullitt (special assistant to the secretary of state and executive officer of the American delegation), who communicated directly with the White House.

In the end FDR undercut them all. The conference was jolted by a direct message from Roosevelt, apparently composed on the spur of the moment, saying that the United States was going to make decisions affecting its currency not in collaboration with the other countries, but on its own. He said flatly that the delegates were wasting time in seeking short-term stabilization of currencies when instead the governments should be curing "fundamental economic ills."

The conference lingered on for a short time afterward, but the Roosevelt message had aborted it. The foreign delegates were shocked by FDR's attitude. The American delegates were left to reflect on how their President had pulled out the rug from under them in public.

Of course, in appointing Hull to head the American delegation to London, Roosevelt had told him that except in minor matters he was not to depart from written instructions without asking Washington for permission and that "neither you nor any other member of the Delegation is to carry on, formally or informally, any discussion of either war debts or disarmament. These two problems will be handled by me in Washington." It ought to have been clear that FDR intended to be not only his own secretary of the Treasury but also his own secretary of state.

THE PRESIDENT SEEMINGLY HAD no legal power to pump up American price levels—which is what he intended to do. He became impatient with the administration lawyers who told him so. Henry Morgenthau, Jr., the Hudson Valley neighbor he had brought into politics, obtained a written legal opinion saying the President had the authority to do what he had it in mind to do. Many were shocked, and young attorney Dean Acheson, undersecretary of the Treasury, resigned from the government; but FDR soon promoted Morgenthau to Treasury secretary.

FDR reversed course on gold to some extent in 1934. He was an experimenter; he gave things a try, and then did what worked. A sailor since youth, he took pleasure in tacking with the wind. He took account of the tides in political affairs, and seized opportunities as they arose. To some his experiments in policy resembled the radical solutions being proposed by antidemocratic forces in Europe. Less than a year after FDR's inaugural, Hamilton Fish Armstrong, editor of the quarterly *Foreign Affairs*, had occasion to write him that "the Administration's social, economic and financial program (incidentally, I believe in it thoroughly) has unfortunately been interpreted in Europe as putting you in the ranks of the 'dictators.' I know that is not at all the case. . . . But the fact remains that in Europe it is commonly said that the American citadel of democracy has capitulated. . . . I suggest that you take an early opportunity to re-affirm publicly and emphatically, your belief in liberalism and democracy. . . . The peoples of Europe need to be reminded that the most powerful nation in the world has not yet decided that the only alternatives to choose between are communist dictatorship or fascist dictatorship."

But in a dangerous world (Bullitt had reported from London in the summer of 1933 that "the general opinion here is that war in Europe is inevitable"), the choices everywhere increasingly *were* between one dictator and another; therefore, in foreign policy an isolationist and disarmed United States had no effective strategy at hand except to play off one dictatorship against the other—a strategy of balance of power that Woodrow Wilson had denounced and Americans traditionally had abhorred as European and immoral. Here, too, FDR refused to be bound by the rules.

# 39

# A FOREIGN POLICY AT
# MINIMUM COST

IN A SENSE, any history of FDR's foreign policy from the time he took office in 1933 until the Munich Pact in late 1938 is misleading. It misleads because it is unbalanced: it focuses on the 1 percent and leaves out the 99 percent. It ignores the main part of what Roosevelt was doing, which was entirely in the domestic sphere. He was battling the Depression; trying to put the country back to work; attempting to make the workings of society more fair; and restoring faith in American democracy. No external threat to the security of the United States seemed to loom on the horizon. Americans still imagined that the outside world could not touch them. Foreign policy in those years still was a sideshow, to which the President could devote only his spare time—and not even very much of that.

Roosevelt believed that he could not afford the time or the resources to conduct a full-scale foreign policy until the economic emergency was over, but from the beginning he showed a sure understanding of the few foreign policy steps that it was absolutely essential to take and that could be taken at minimum cost.

His world outlook had been shaped when he was young. The theories of Admiral Alfred Thayer Mahan were a formative influence on his generation. However he did so, he assimilated Mahan's views. He looked at strategy in global terms. He was fascinated by geopolitics: the military and political consequences of geographical realities. With Mahan, he believed in the overriding importance of obtaining control of the seas; and later—long after Mahan's death—he became a convert to the view that control of the air matters greatly. He took his views from Theodore Roosevelt and from TR's intellectual and social set: Mahan, Cabot Lodge, and the Adamses. His first priority, like theirs, was clearing the Western Hemisphere of any threats to the United States; and his second, clearing the Atlantic and Pacific oceans of any such threats. But he departed from his mentors in his view of how to achieve the first goal.

In his presidential inaugural speech, he proclaimed that "in the field of world policy, I would dedicate this Nation to the policy of the good neighbor." The next month he told the governing board of the Pan-

American Union that he committed the United States to the independence and equality of the states of the hemisphere. It transpired that this was not mere rhetoric. At the Montevideo conference of the Pan-American Union (December 1933) and afterward, the Roosevelt administration renounced the right of the United States to unilaterally intervene in the affairs of its Caribbean and Latin American neighbors, as it had done so conspicuously in the past.

Roosevelt's new approach—his good-neighbor policy—was to try to win the friendship, or at any rate dampen the enmity, of the other states of the Western Hemisphere. The promise of the new policy was that it would avert danger to the United States from within the hemisphere at the least possible cost.

ROOSEVELT'S INTENTION was to see what could be accomplished in world affairs, without cost to the United States, by opening up communications with the Soviet Union. His problem was that the Department of State did not want to make the attempt. The East Europe desk head, Robert Kelley, was opposed to any such move. Moreover, it was under Kelley's guidance that the younger Soviet specialists in the State Department had been trained and intellectually formed.

So Roosevelt turned (as he was to do so often whenever the relevant executive department had to be gone around) to Henry Morgenthau, Jr.; then he asked Felix Frankfurter to use his contacts to find a Soviet official with whom Morgenthau could be in touch. But soon another possibility arose out of a conversation Roosevelt had with one of his campaign fundraisers.

Louis Wehle, pushing forward the claims of campaign contributor Bill Bullitt, asked FDR to appoint Bullitt ambassador to France. Roosevelt said the job already was spoken for; he had promised it to Jesse Straus, a much more major campaign contributor. Wehle then proposed Russia, citing Bullitt's special qualifications, his friendship with Lenin, and his acquaintance with the current Soviet leaders.

But the position of ambassador to the Soviet Union did not exist: the United States, alone among the world's major powers, did not have diplomatic relations with Moscow. This was more of an inconvenience to Americans than to Russians—who could do business in the open society of the United States, without going through official channels, more easily than could Americans in the closed society of the USSR.

Most Americans did not care whether the Soviet Union was recognized or not, but most of those who did care were in favor of recognition. A September 1933 poll of newspapers showed that 63 percent were in favor of recognition and only 27 percent were opposed to it. The Roman Catholic

Church was a focal point of opposition, but FDR overcame it: he held an hourlong meeting with Father Edmund A. Walsh of Georgetown University, the Catholic institution in Washington that functions as a training ground for the foreign service, after which Walsh stated in public that recognition of Russia was a decision that should be entrusted to the President in the exercise of his own good judgment. Thereupon, having escaped from his domestic political constraints, Roosevelt took the initiative in restoring relations with Russia.

Bullitt was not only a natural candidate for ambassadorship; he was also the natural choice to negotiate the diplomatic recognition as a result of which an American ambassador would be appointed. He had been in favor of establishing normal relations with Moscow since 1919; in 1933 he became, along with Morgenthau, FDR's agent in dealing with the Bolsheviks, as years before he had been the agent of House and Wilson.

The United States wanted Russia's promise to repay at least some of her wartime debt, and a pledge that communist subversion in America would be halted.* The USSR desired American backing against the threat of war with Japan. These were among the objectives aimed at in the 1933 negotiations, which ended successfully in American recognition of the Soviet Union on November 16–17 and the appointment of Bullitt as America's ambassador November 18.

It was an appointment much remarked upon. In Great Britain, Bullitt's behavior at the London economic conference had been thought shameful. Prime Minister Ramsay MacDonald, though a personal friend, had discovered his secretary was being taken to dinner and courted by Bullitt, who asked her to reveal confidential information. When Bullitt's appointment as ambassador was announced, a British Foreign Office official in London remarked that "I think Mr. Bullitt may do less harm in Moscow than in Washington, though he is the kind of man who does harm anywhere." The British ambassador in Washington commented that "he may be regarded as thoroughly untrustworthy, and completely unscrupulous."

It was bad enough that in London he had been caught out by MacDonald; in Washington Bullitt, whether or not he was aware of it, maneuvered himself into an even more awkward situation.

Unknown to most people at the time and to historians until relatively recently, the President and his wife remained married in name only. Historians, who seem to know everything, tell us that in 1933 it was almost two decades since the sexual relationship of the Roosevelts had come to an end. Now Franklin had at least one love of his own, and Eleanor had several.

---

* For domestic political reasons, these were pledges that Roosevelt had to obtain; but it is not clear whether he ever expected the Soviets to honor them. Bullitt, who harbored illusions that the President did not, fully expected the Russians to keep their word, and was furious when it became clear years later that they had no intention of doing so.

Since the tumultuous, youthful years when their marriage nearly broke up because of the Lucy Mercer affair, the two had learned to wish each other well in living separate personal lives; indeed, Roosevelt, who believed in making everybody happy, had arranged to build a house of their own for Eleanor and her lady friends on Roosevelt's grounds. At the same time Franklin and Eleanor, publicly very much a couple, developed a political partnership of value to them both, in which her humanity and idealism complemented his practice of the art of the possible.

Indeed, in the years to come Eleanor Roosevelt was to carve out for herself a role unique in American history. She was more than accessible to the public; constantly on the road, she went out to the country, seeing for herself and listening to what others had to say. Her reluctance to compromise principle, her goodness, her sympathy, and her almost palpable desire to help won her a position of independent moral authority. She had an activist character; when she saw or heard of something wrong, her reaction was to do something about it.

Of course, opponents of her politics made fun of her drabness and awkwardness. Even they, however, described her as a "do-gooder," though they did not intend that to be praise.

One of Eleanor's intimate friends in 1933, as for many years past, was Lorena Hickok, a top Associated Press journalist who had become an investigative field reporter for FDR's social services chief, Harry Hopkins. Franklin's close relationship was with his secretary, Marguerite ("Missy") LeHand, with whom Franklin had lived for years. Franklin and Missy were lovers in most senses and perhaps all.

Nonetheless, there were others in Missy's life: men who could offer her marriage. One such relation seems to have ended badly in late 1932. It was a few months later that Missy met handsome, charming, wealthy, womanizing Bill Bullitt.

Bullitt had a lifelong tendency, whether in the White House, the Kremlin, or any one of the seats of government in Europe, to blunder into situations of whose political currents, emotional eddies, and treacherous depths he was quite unaware. With his quickness in jumping to a conclusion, his sense of drama, and his firm conviction that he was the smartest person in any room, he was often mistaken in believing that he knew what game was being played.

Seemingly ignorant of the Roosevelts' marital arrangements and apparently under the impression that Missy was unattached, he seriously flirted with her, perhaps seduced her, and possibly gave her to understand that he was thinking of marrying her. FDR smiled on the relationship, as he had on the previous relationship that had ended badly. This called for explanation, but Bullitt seemed not to know that it did. For the decade to come, Bullitt, in his foreign policy career, was to rely entirely on FDR's friendship and support; it seems never to have occurred to him that he might have endangered that friendship by interfering with the President's relationship with what may have been his mistress.

Roosevelt's attitude was puzzling to his wife, even though she knew him to be broad-minded. But it seemed less puzzling after the announcement that Bullitt was to go away. Eleanor wrote Lorena Hickok on the day of the announcement that "Bullitt goes as Ambassador. I wonder if that is why F.D.R. has been so content to let Missy play with him! She'll have another embassy to visit next summer. . . ." Another explanation was that Roosevelt wanted Missy to discover how unreliable other men—men other than himself—were.

So the appointment of the first U.S. ambassador to the Soviet Union inspired emotions less tepid, and excited comments less conventional, than was usual with such official assignments. Attended, even within his own family, by mixed wishes for his success ("BULLITT'S UNCLE SAYS SOVIET DEAL DISGRACES UNITED STATES" was one newspaper headline), Bullitt embarked December 1, 1933, on his latest mission to Moscow.

Crossing the continent of Europe en route to his new post, Bullitt stopped for lunch with U.S. Ambassador William E. Dodd in Berlin. Dodd was a University of Chicago history professor whose appointment had been suggested by Colonel House. He had served as a German expert on the Inquiry team at the Paris Peace Conference of 1919, and had thought Bullitt's resignation letter at the time "bombastic and unreasonable." Like Undersecretary of State William Phillips, he believed that Bullitt's conduct in 1919 had been a betrayal of Wilson, Lansing, and the State Department, and that it remained unforgivable.

Bullitt went on his way to Russia, where he had to start from scratch in organizing an embassy. In retrospect it is clear that he was establishing the embryo of the foreign service that would wage the cold war. It was, in that sense, Bullitt rather than Dean Acheson who was present at the creation of post–Second World War American foreign policy. Bullitt understood that the embassy would need security arrangements that would not have been necessary in the pre-1914 world of polite diplomacy; he appointed as his security chief a young naval officer, Roscoe Hillenkoetter, who would later become head of the CIA.

It is said that their training under the regime of the State Department's Kelley led Bullitt's Moscow staff to take a hostile view of the Soviet Union. Certainly Loy Henderson, later a formidable figure in the State Department mandarinate, and future ambassadors to Russia George Kennan and Charles Bohlen were critical of the Stalin regime.

Born in Milwaukee and schooled at Princeton, Kennan, who was to become an architect of American foreign policy in the 1940s, was twenty-nine years old at the time. As a candidate for appointment to the newly established American Foreign Service, he had appeared before an oral examining panel (it "utterly terrified me," he later wrote) headed by the now formidable Joseph Grew. In 1928 he had been sent to Berlin and the Baltic republics to be trained as a Russian specialist.

Bohlen, the same age, trained in the Baltic states at about the same time that Kennan did. The grandson of a senator who became the first U.S. ambassador to France,* he had the easy charm that comes with birth into wealth and society. His fun-loving nature was a contrast to that of the serious Kennan, who became his lifelong best friend.

Kennan later described Bullitt, his new boss, as "a striking man: young, handsome, urbane, full of charm and enthusiasm, a product of Philadelphia society and Yale . . . and with a flamboyance of personality that is right out of F. Scott Fitzgerald."

"As the old American friend of new Russia," wrote Janet Flanner (the "Genet" who was the *New Yorker's* correspondent in Paris), Bullitt "was received with fantastic acclaim. When he rode in the streets he was cheered, at the Opera the Muscovites rose to shout his name. . . ." But it was Bullitt himself who told Flanner all this, in an interview that took place about five years later, and it gives some sense of the high drama in which he imagined himself to be playing a leading role.

Bullitt was won over by the compliments showered upon him. Writing to Roosevelt, he quoted Mikhail Kalinin (who occupied the ceremonial position of president of the Soviet Union) as saying "that he and everyone else in Russia considered you completely out of the class of the leaders of capitalist states; that it was clear to them all that you really cared about the welfare of the laboring men and the farmers. . . ." Meanwhile, the Communist party press claimed to have discovered previously unknown statements by Lenin praising Bullitt: "Apparently he really liked me," Bullitt marveled.

On December 20, 1933, Kliment Voroshilov, supreme Soviet military commander, invited Bullitt to dinner at the Kremlin to meet the Soviet leaders. Explaining why his own qualities made him such a success in Moscow, Bullitt told FDR, "The men at the head of the Soviet Government are really intelligent, sophisticated, vigorous human beings and they cannot be persuaded to waste their time with the ordinary conventional diplomatist." And they appreciated the intelligence of the aides he had chosen: "They were, for example, delighted by young Kennan who went in with me."

As Bullitt looked around the room, flatteringly filled in his honor with the important Soviet figures that other diplomats never got a chance to meet, Maksim Litvinov, the foreign minister, said: "This is the whole 'gang' that really runs things—the inside directorate."

---

* Previous envoys had held ministerial rather than ambassadorial rank.

After eating "every conceivable kind of caviar and crab and other Russian delicacy" with drinks, they sat down to an elaborate banquet punctuated by the frequent downing of vodka. The glasses of vodka had to be emptied—had to be drunk "bottoms up"—each time someone rose to offer a toast, Bullitt reported to Roosevelt, and "there were perhaps fifty toasts. . . . Everyone at the table got into the mood of a college fraternity banquet, and discretion was conspicuous by its absence. Litvinov whispered to me, 'You told me you wouldn't stay here if you were going to be treated as an outsider. Do you realize that everyone at this table has completely forgotten that anyone is here except the members of the inner gang?' "

After dinner, the party adjourned to a drawing room, and Stalin sat beside Bullitt for a long talk. "He said he hoped that I would feel myself completely at home in the Soviet Union," Bullitt told Roosevelt, "that he and all the members of the Government had felt that I was a friend for so long, that they had such admiration for yourself and the things you were trying to do in America that they felt we could cooperate with the greatest intimacy." Stalin "gave me the feeling that he was speaking honestly. . . . As I got up to leave, Stalin said to me, 'I want you to understand that if you want to see me at any time, day or night, you have only to let me know and I will see you at once.' "

As Bullitt noted, that was extraordinary, "as he has hitherto refused to see any Ambassador at any time." And then "Stalin took my head in his two hands and gave me a large kiss! I swallowed my astonishment, and, when he turned up his face for a return kiss, I delivered it."

During the course of the evening, the Soviet leaders told Bullitt that Japan was likely to attack Russia; Stalin spoke of it as a certainty. Stalin said that in this connection Russia needed 250,000 tons of steel rails at once to complete a railroad line to the Pacific port of Vladivostok, and wanted help—which Bullitt promised to him—in expediting their purchase in the United States.


THE FEAR of Japanese imperial expansion had hung over Asian and international politics for years. It was therefore to take his place in the front lines, as it were, in dealing with the leading threat to world peace that Joseph Grew embarked for Japan in March 1932 as America's new ambassador. Grew, whose career experience, aided by wealth and social position, had made him one of the leading mandarins of the Department of State, arrived in Japan to take up his post—only to find, within a matter of months, that his tenure as ambassador was in doubt.

For the election of a Democratic President had drawn into question the continuation in office of Republican-era appointees. Even though the creation in the 1920s of a professional U.S. foreign service had brought lower-level jobs into nonpartisan civil service status, ambassadorships remained political appointments.

Just as he had written Roosevelt to help save his job when Wilson was elected, Grew in 1932 contacted Roosevelt's friends Undersecretary of State William Phillips and Colonel House for their help in keeping him in his job now that Roosevelt was elected. Grew questioned whether his old college clubmate had the courage to resist "party hacks" who would want to reward the party faithful with ambassadorial posts, and doubted whether Roosevelt (whom he had accused of "gutter" politics in 1920) had "genuine honesty of purpose"; but he wrote "Dear Frank" a letter of congratulations on winning the election, saying that "Groton, Harvard, and the Fly are immensely proud and they have good right to be."

In fact, Grew's position never was in danger; and within a short time he began to appreciate the qualities of the new President. "Isn't it fine the way the President is supporting the career diplomats?" he wrote happily to one of his peers. He uttered "a most fervent prayer for Frank's success" when he read the inaugural address, and found the President's methods thereafter "intensely refreshing."

Whether or not Grew was the ideal ambassador, Alice Grew was by birth and upbringing the ideal ambassador's wife. She spoke Japanese, which her husband did not. The daughter of a Boston Cabot and a direct descendant of Benjamin Franklin, Alice also was a great-grandniece of Commodore Matthew Perry, who had forcibly opened up Japan to the modern world in 1853–54. The ambassador might well have reflected how different 1933 would have been had Alice's Uncle Matthew left Japan in self-imposed isolation, a feudal society cut off from the rest of mankind.

As it was, the Grews arrived in Tokyo at a time of great tension in relations between Japan and the outside world. Japan had just quit the League of Nations rather than accept interference with her program of conquest in Manchuria. Grew recognized, as Willard Straight had done decades before, that if the United States was not prepared to back up words with deeds, its words would not be heeded; and his counsel to an America that disapproved of Japanese actions but was not prepared to do anything about it was, in essence, to keep quiet.

In May 1933 Grew sent Secretary Hull a detailed appreciation of Japanese power. He wrote that "Japan probably has the most complete, well-balanced, coordinated and therefore powerful fighting machine in the world today. I do not refer to the army alone, but to the combination of sea, land and air forces, backed up as they are by enormous reserves of trained men, by industrial units coordinated with the fighting machine and by large reserves of supplies. . . . [T]aken as a whole the machine, I believe, is equal, if not superior, to that of any other nation. . . . Relative to the strength which could conceivably be brought against it, I consider Japan's fighting machine immeasurably stronger than any other. . . . More than . . . the strength of its fighting machine, however, the thing which makes the Japanese nation actually so powerful and potentially so menacing, is the national morale and esprit de corps . . . which perhaps has not been equalled since the days when the Mongol hordes followed Genghis Khan. . . ."

In September 1933 Grew reported to Washington that "eventual war between Japan and Soviet Russia is inevitable"—but not imminent. A question therefore arose as to what the United States ought to do in an effort to serve its own interests and those of world peace.

When Maksim Litvinov was in Washington, he had asked the State Department for a U.S.-USSR alliance against Japan, and had been curtly turned down by Phillips. Along with Stalin and the other Russian leaders, Litvinov imagined that Bullitt exercised great influence over Roosevelt, and broached the subject anew with the new ambassador in Moscow. Bullitt tried to explain that such an alliance was out of the question, and that the United States intended to keep on good terms with Japan, to which Litvinov responded: "Anything that could be done to make the Japanese believe that the United States was ready to cooperate with Russia, even though there might be no basis for the belief, would be valuable."

That is part of what Roosevelt accomplished simply by recognizing the Soviet Union. In the political circumstances of the time, it was all that he could do, but it was enough to raise the possibility—of which policy makers in Japan would have to take account—of joint action by the United States and the Soviet Union should an expansionist Japan go too far. Whether in part because of that, or entirely for such other reasons as the Soviet military buildup in the Far East, Japan seemingly moderated her policies in the years immediately following the restoration of U.S. ties with Russia. Grew himself believed, as he wrote Secretary Hull February 8, 1934, that "our recognition of the Soviet Union has injected a restraining influence, probably of greater effect than any other single integral."

In turn, as Bullitt reported to Roosevelt, the Soviet leaders, having abandoned hope of winning an American alliance and no longer fearing an imminent Japanese attack, felt no further need to court Bullitt or the United States. "The Japanese have let us down badly," Bullitt quoted a colleague as remarking wryly; and the "honeymoon atmosphere" in Moscow had "evaporated completely."

Although Bullitt thought it "almost impossible to imagine a situation which would cause us to have exceedingly bad relations with the Soviet Government for the simple reason that the two countries have no major conflicting interests," he recognized that the Russians no longer gave priority to their relationship with the United States, and that as a result he himself was in for a dull few years in bleak, gray, cold, friendless Moscow.

Bullitt was not a foreign service person by temperament; it was not in his nature to spend his life doing routine, day-to-day, nine-to-five chores. He was in his element only when reporting a scoop or scoring a coup. It was typical of his mode of operation that he strapped some of his earliest dispatches to the leg of the comedian Harpo Marx, who had been performing in the Soviet Union and was returning to the United States. " 'Just forget you're carrying it,' said the ambassador. 'Except,' he added, 'when you go in the shower.' " According to Marx's autobiography, published a quarter-century later, the comedian worried constantly during his voyage, ducked or hid whenever he felt people were looking at him or following him, developed a limp from self-consciousness, and finally kept to his room. The packet of unopened letters was duly collected by two men who identified themselves as government agents when Marx's ocean liner docked in New York. Marx never was told the nature of the secret papers he had carried.

Maybe it was a hoax. Marx may have invented the story. Or it could have been a joke that Bullitt played on him. But it says something about the ambassador that he just might have done it.

Bullitt was bored in Russia, and played truant. He traveled in Europe, in Asia, and sometimes back to America; he was away from the Moscow embassy literally half the time. He had gone to Russia with high ambitions but they had been frustrated.

It seems unlikely that his President ever shared either the high hopes or the disappointment. Roosevelt, by recognizing the Soviet Union, had made a move on the diplomatic chessboard that somewhat improved America's position in regard to Japan and perhaps even Germany. There is no reason to believe he expected anything more would come of it, and because of domestic political pressures and economic priorities, it was about all that he could do.

As in the good-neighbor policy, FDR was turning away from the approaches adopted by earlier administrations. Sending in the marines was the wrong thing to do when a Caribbean people chose a leader the President of the United States disliked. Refusing to recognize that a communist regime governed the Soviet Union was the wrong way to deal with a reality of which any participant in world politics would have to take account.

While taking a more constructive approach to international affairs, FDR at the same time was advancing America's national security interests. The good-neighbor policy helped make the Western Hemisphere more secure for the United States, and the recognition of Russia, with its implied warning to Japan, helped mitigate the threat to U.S. interests in the Pacific.

This indeed was a foreign policy pursued at minimum cost. It was all the foreign policy the President felt the United States could afford while he devoted full time and resources to pulling America out of the Depression. But in life, if not in theory, it often happens that dangers materialize before we are ready for them. So it was in 1933. FDR was not to be given the time to cure the Depression *before* dealing with mortal dangers from outside. He was going to be called upon to save the country at home and abroad— at the same time.

SECRETARY OF LABOR Frances Perkins, who had been a member of Roosevelt's cabinet since Albany days, asked the President in 1933 to propose American membership in the International Labor Organization. He authorized her to take the initiative, but told her to stress that the ILO was distinct from the League of Nations. He cautioned her to work with Hull and with those in the Congress who took an interest in foreign affairs, and to keep in mind that she must avoid Wilson's mistakes.

In October 1933 FDR sent for ILO director Harold Butler, whom he had met in 1919. "I'm going to join the I.L.O.," Roosevelt told him, but he could not say when. In politics timing is everything, he said. Throwing back his head and giving his roar of a laugh, the President said that "if you got your timing right you could do anything."

# 40

# UNPREPAREDNESS AS A
# NATIONAL POLICY

BERLIN. MIDDAY ON MONDAY, January 30, 1933. Eighty-four-year-old President Paul von Hindenburg appointed Adolf Hitler, leader of the National Socialist Workers ("Nazi") party, chancellor of Germany. On February 3 Hitler went to the apartments of the army's commander in chief to tell the assembled commanders of the German armed forces that, in disregard of the Treaty of Versailles, he would embark on a program of massive rearmament. He was going to claim in public that his aim in doing so was to solve the unemployment problem with which Germany, like other industrial industries, was plagued.* But in truth it was not in order to solve an economic problem that Hitler proposed to build a war machine; it was in order to wage war.

Like many and perhaps most of his countrymen, Hitler desired to annex those neighboring territories in which large German minority populations were now ruled by others. Like the kaiser's ministers during the First World War, he hoped to control Belgium and destroy the power of the French state. Like the younger Moltke, he pictured the politics of central and eastern Europe as a battle between Germans and Slavs.

But for him these goals were mere stepping-stones: preliminaries to the real struggle to achieve what he saw as Germany's destiny. For while his ranting and raving might sound incoherent, he brought with him, from the stagnant cesspools of race hatred in which he had been generated, an outlook different from that of the conservatives and reactionaries who were his political rivals on the Right. What was distinctive in Hitler's vision was indicated by the name of his party newspaper: *Volkischer Beobachter*—"The Racist Observer." Racism was not just his bias, but the core of his agenda; it was not a mere rhetoric, but a program of action. He proclaimed that Germans were not a nation, but a race—and not just a race, but the superior race. To realize itself, the German race would have to do three things: give

---

* Indeed, rearmament did solve the problem, and in 1936 the British economist John Maynard Keynes would publish a treatise that explained, among other things, why a program that created a massive demand for goods and services would have that effect.

total obedience to himself as its one leader ("fuehrer"); destroy the evil within it and purify its bloodstream by rooting out—by murdering, in the end—everyone of Jewish ancestry; and expand its living space by conquering eastern Europe and western Russia, killing or enslaving the Slavs who lived in those lands. Whether Hitler had formulated a further goal of world domination, for which he was to bid in 1941, is still debated, but it was at least implicit in his concept of the master race.

When Hitler was appointed chancellor, Franz von Papen, his vice chancellor, was not alone in believing that the Nazi leader could and would be tamed, used ("We have hired him," sneered von Papen), and then discarded. But like Lenin after the coup that brought him to power in Russia, Hitler moved immediately (through Hermann Goering, Prussian minister of the interior) to establish an overwhelming secret political police force to terrorize dissenters into submission. Within a year Hitler had destroyed Germany's federal, parliamentary, and constitutional structure and taken full power into his own hands as dictator.

The new German chancellor had been in office only several months, and the new American President only several weeks, when Roosevelt told the departing French ambassador to the U.S. that the situation in Germany was "alarming" and that "Hitler is a madman and his counsellors, some of whom I know personally, are even madder than he is." But uncertain of Hitler's ultimate intentions, the leaders of Germany's neighbors were not so sure. Dismissing what Hitler and his lieutenants said and wrote as mere blustering and posturing, from 1932 until 1939 they would see in his step-by-step overthrow of the Treaty of Versailles—and in his annexation of neighboring German-inhabited territories—no more than what any normal mainstream politician would have aimed at accomplishing. Moreover, in their hearts western Europeans agreed that it was right for Germany to win on these issues, for by the 1930s it was widely admitted that the arrangements arrived at in Versailles in 1919 were in every sense indefensible.

It was only in 1939, after Germany had taken all that could be viewed as hers by right, that the point was reached when a mainstream nationalist leader ought to have stopped—but that Hitler did not. It was only then that he proved by actions as well as words that he was not the man-you-can-do-business-with that Europeans had hoped he was; that instead he was the megalomaniac racist his writings and speeches proclaimed him to be. It was only then that there was hard proof that he was going to start a war to conquer Europe—but by then Germany had been rearming for six years, and it was plausible to argue, as defeatists did everywhere, that it was too late to stop him.

To be strong enough to have deterred Hitler, Germany's neighbors would have had to have begun rearming when Hitler did; to have stopped him thereafter, they would have had to have gone at least to the brink of war—and perhaps over it. But the democracies in the interwar years were unwilling to undertake such full-blooded policies. Everything they had learned in the trenches and on the slaughtering fields of the western front in 1914–18 disposed them not to do so.

They thought that their experience had shown them that wars solve nothing. They now saw the 1914–18 conflict as one of the most terrible and costly mistakes of all time. For even from the point of view of Great Britain and the United States, countries that had *won* the Great War, the world was worse off than it had been before 1914. They had entered the war to defend against what they had believed to be a German assault on Western civilization; they now believed that they had been wrong about that, and were determined not to make the same mistake twice.

In the words of the English historian A. J. P. Taylor, "Few educated people now believed that the war had been caused by a deliberate German aggression." Indeed, it was not until the 1960s that Fritz Fischer and his followers began publishing the evidence that some in the inner group of Germany's leaders consciously had opted for war. "In the general opinion wars started by mistake. . . . Or they were caused by great armaments. Or they were caused by 'grievances'; the clear moral here was that these, now predominantly German, should be redressed. Or finally they were caused by 'capitalism.' . . ."

These British beliefs were shared in the United States, especially (paradoxical though it may seem) in the anti-English regions of the Middle and Far West, where Britain's desire to disentangle itself from the Continent was paralleled by an American desire to disentangle itself from Britain.


IN BRITAIN it was only the party out of power—George Lansbury's socialist Labour party—that believed in disarming unilaterally. In America it had for many years been the policy of the government. The United States had disarmed itself on the ground and in the air, having reduced its army, in particular, to a skeleton force equipped only with antiquated weaponry. Traditionally Americans had believed that military expenditures impoverish a nation, so in the Great Depression, spending money on a military establishment seemed not just unnecessary but ruinous. Moreover, the notion that defense of the country's interests might require it at some future point to go to war was thought to be wrong morally as well as practically.

A poll of nearly 20,000 American Protestant clergymen published in 1931 showed 62 percent refusing to sanction or support any future war. Replying as army chief of staff, Douglas MacArthur protested that patriotism, which is shown by fighting and perhaps dying for your country, always had gone hand in hand with religion; but he failed to persuade.

Yet the experience of an international preparatory commission on disarmament that began work in Geneva in May 1926 provided some evidence that the pacifist goal was at best elusive. Members of the commission met and wrangled for five years before adjourning in January 1931 without having accomplished anything of note. Germany, meanwhile, secretly had been rearming the whole time.

In 1932 the League of Nations called a new Conference for the Reduction and Limitation of Armaments. As Roosevelt took office in 1933, it was about to collapse: Hitler had instructed his delegates to agree to nothing that would stand in the way of his planned rearmament program, while France sought an accord that would provide her with security—that is to say, a pact (which the Germans would never accept) to set arms limitations at levels guaranteeing France a substantial margin of superiority over Germany.

MacArthur offered Roosevelt a suggestion that American delegates to the conference might put forward in order to get the talks back on track: they might distinguish between defensive arms and offensive ones. If everybody would keep only the one kind and destroy the other, every country would be able to defend itself but no country would be able to attack another.

Though a flawed idea,* it was appealing, and FDR seized upon it. He had been advised that Hitler planned a major address for May 17, 1933, that, unless headed off, might bring down the curtain on the disarmament conference. Roosevelt decided to speak to the peoples of the world, as Wilson would have done. His longtime adviser, Felix Frankfurter, was "excited by your suggestion of appealing, through the heads of states, to the peoples of Europe to save the Disarmament Conference. There is every reason for hoping that the peoples of Europe will respond. [Your address] would touch the imagination and hopes of men everywhere."

So on May 12 Roosevelt launched an appeal to the heads of the nations then meeting at the Geneva disarmament conference and at the London economic conference. In it he asserted that there are only two reasons why countries arm themselves. One, felt by "only a small minority" of countries, is a "desire to enlarge their territories." For the overwhelming majority, however, "the fear of nations that they will be invaded" is the only reason to maintain armed forces. By agreeing to destroy all offensive weapons, the nations of the world could therefore achieve security. They would remain

---

* When a similar proposal was made a year earlier by British foreign secretary Sir John Simon, Winston Churchill demolished it in a House of Commons speech, citing specific examples of weapons that could be used for either offense or defense. It is not the weapon itself, Churchill showed, but the use to which it is put that makes it either offensive or defensive. This had been shown, too, in the course of the proceedings of the 1926–31 Disarmament Commission, which had bogged down in unresolvable disputes about which weapons were offensive.

fully able to defend themselves, while at the same time securing the peace by eliminating the weapons that alone make aggression possible.

Applause greeted the President's speech everywhere in the world, and he congratulated himself; he told his friend Henry Morgenthau that "I think I have averted a war." But if he really thought so, he deluded himself—and Morgenthau.

On reflection, he recognized that since Germany could not be trusted, France should not be expected to disarm; off the record he told reporters at a press conference on August 25 that "if I were a Frenchman and were certain in my own mind that Germany was not living up to treaties, I wouldn't scrap a thing and neither would any of us. . . . I would not disarm unless I had assurance that the other fellow is going to disarm."

In the autumn Roosevelt wrote to Ambassador Dodd in Berlin that "Walter Lippmann was here last week and made the interesting suggestion that about 8 per cent of the population of the entire world, i.e. Germany and Japan, is able, because of imperialistic attitude, to prevent peaceful guarantees and armament reductions on the part of the other 92 per cent of the world." This way of looking at it struck the President, who now had a ready explanation for why schemes of general disarmament seem never to work: there are always a few troublemakers who spoil things for all the rest.

In the autumn of 1933 Germany broke up the disarmament conference. In turn, that deprived FDR of the only excuse the U.S. public deemed valid for pursuing an active foreign policy in Europe.


ROOSEVELT HAD CAMPAIGNED for the presidency on a platform that called for balancing the federal budget; in office he continued to take the orthodox view that cutting government expenses would restore the economy. So it was a challenging assignment for MacArthur and his aide Ike Eisenhower to persuade the President and the Congress to continue army appropriations at their current levels, low though they were.

MacArthur and the army made themselves helpful in advancing one of FDR's most innovative and successful programs: raising and training a civilian corps of unemployed young people to do conservation work in national forests. It was called the Civilian Conservation Corps, known as the CCC. Colonel George Marshall, who established about a dozen and a half CCC camps in and around South Carolina,* proved particularly effective in these endeavors. The army was invaluable; in only two months, MacArthur signed up 275,000 recruits, trained them, and sent them to camps in almost every state of the union.

---

* The friendship Marshall developed in the course of this work with South Carolina Senator Byrnes later was to prove a pivotal relationship for him in his dealings with Congress.

In turn the CCC and such other New Deal programs as the Civil Works Administration and the Public Works Administration provided extra funding for the army, while other New Deal moneys for the unemployed went into naval construction to build up the fleet. Whether or not in pursuit of a deliberately deceptive plan, the President provided, under the heading of relief funds appropriated as such by Congress, the extra money needed to keep the armed forces in business.

Considering the immense egotism of a number of the personalities involved, MacArthur developed a good working relationship with the administration. He enjoyed the privileges of an insider: he was allowed to slip into the White House by the back door and was accorded direct access to the President. But he was not able to fathom FDR, nor was he able to read what was in Roosevelt's mind in regard to the issue that affected him personally: his future as chief of staff after 1934, when his term of duty was believed to run out.

Contrary to the general view, there was no fixed term to the position (although people assumed it to be a four-year job, to which nobody had ever been reappointed). In the spring of 1934 MacArthur suddenly feared that he had lost his chance to stay on. Along with the war secretary, he had met Roosevelt to protest the Budget Bureau's proposal to cut army appropriations for the next fiscal year; and carried away, in words repeated endlessly ever since by biographers and historians, he had abused and insulted the President.*

As he denounced his commander in chief to his face, the general was seized by the nervous cramps that often came upon him when with surface calm he displayed reckless courage. The result was the exchange of comments with the secretary of war that MacArthur later recorded. Though FDR had rebuked MacArthur, he had shown a willingness to compromise on the budget issue—and the secretary of war congratulated MacArthur:

SECRETARY: "You've saved the Army!"

MACARTHUR (*trembling and retching*): "But I just vomited on the steps of the White House."

As to MacArthur's tenure as chief of staff, Roosevelt handled the issue adroitly. He extended MacArthur's term without renewing it. The general would stay on, said the President, until a successor was chosen; yet no successor would be chosen until MacArthur had finished shepherding the army's legislative program through Congress.

---

* "When we lose the next war, and an American boy with an enemy bayonet through his belly and an enemy foot on his dying throat spits out his last curse, I want the name not to be MacArthur, but Roosevelt!"

Supporters of the controversial general were delighted that he was remaining, while opponents and enemies rejoiced that he was not nominated for a second term. Antimilitary congressmen may well have been more disposed to compromise on the substance of the army's ambitious program in order to speed the day when it was enacted and MacArthur sent away.

In the first half of 1935, the Congress was persuaded by MacArthur to increase military spending to levels unknown for more than a decade. The equipment of the armed forces would remain obsolete, but at least a start would be made on rebuilding manpower. "For the first time since 1922," MacArthur proclaimed jubilantly, there was a reasonable prospect that the army might become large and efficient enough to meet "the country's minimum needs." According to *The New York Times*, it was "the prevalent war talk" that got the appropriations through Congress; but the persuasive chief of staff deserved credit, too. Roosevelt had reaped the rewards—in more ways than one—of extending MacArthur's tour of duty.

It was only when the name of his replacement was announced that MacArthur realized he had been kept in office just long enough so that his handpicked successor became too close to retirement age to be appointed. The President chose Malin Craig instead, an officer supported by Pershing and the "Chaumont clique" of which George Marshall* was a luminary and which MacArthur considered to be a nest of his personal enemies. MacArthur exploded in rage when he heard the news.

Saying farewell, FDR awarded MacArthur another medal and told him, "Douglas, if war should suddenly come, don't wait for orders to come home. Grab the first transportation you can find. I want you to command my armies." Pershing sent him an autographed photo. The time had come for him to accept the gold watch, bid the company good-bye, and retire.

By prior arrangement, MacArthur, bringing along his aide Eisenhower (who did not want to go), went back in 1935 to the land with which he and his father were so closely associated: the Philippine Islands, a commonwealth scheduled to become independent in 1946. He went there as head of the American military mission. His mother followed him back to the Orient; she died and was interred there, later to be reburied at Arlington National Cemetery.

MacArthur lived a lordly life in the Eastern splendor of his retirement: he occupied the air-conditioned, six-room penthouse of the Manila Hotel.

---

* In 1933 a political lawyer who was commander of the Illinois National Guard asked MacArthur to send him an infantry colonel to serve as senior instructor. Strikes and riots were expected in Illinois, and the services of an outstanding professional military man were required. MacArthur personally chose Marshall ("Suggest Lieutenant Colonel George C. Marshall. He has no superior among Infantry Colonels"), pulling him off his CCC assignment in South Carolina. MacArthur denied Marshall's appeal to be left where he was, despite a personal telephoned plea from General Pershing in support of Marshall's request. Former Vice President Charles G. Dawes cried: "What! He can't do that. Hell, no! Not George Marshall. He's too big a man for this job. In fact he's the best goddamned officer in the U.S. Army."

In 1936 the Philippines made MacArthur a field marshal, and he designed a uniform for himself of black pants, white tunic, and gold braid to go with the title. At the end of 1937 he retired from the U.S. Army, but stayed on as the Philippines' military adviser. He married again and became a father. Though he sometimes spoke of returning to Milwaukee, Manila had become more his first than his second home.

He was back at the spot where he and his generation had come up against their first great foreign policy challenge—and had refused to face it. Annexing the Philippines (and Hawaii) in the 1890s had moved America's security frontier from the near side of the Pacific to the far, from the coast of California to that of Asia. It had brought the United States into a line with which an expansionist Japan would collide. So Washington should have thought through some policy for either averting or else dealing with the clash with Japan—but it had not.

Having chosen to draw the line where they had, Americans should have developed a strategy to defend it; instead they decided it was indefensible. Early in the century, the army had concluded that in the event of war U.S. forces in the Philippines would have to be abandoned to their fate in case of invasion. America's vulnerable garrison ought therefore to have been withdrawn as soon as possible, before any such invasion could materialize; but Washington, in its nationalist pride, was unwilling to consider that. The incoherent American military doctrine for the Philippines in case of war was "no improvements, no reinforcements, no withdrawal."

In his musical-comedy field marshal's uniform, with a make-believe military command, MacArthur was carrying out an assignment that made sense only in the let's-pretend world of Americans who believed that if their country was sufficiently defenseless, it (and its far outlying territories) would never be attacked.

So the foreign policy situation of Americans in the early and middle 1930s was this: They were living through exceptionally dangerous years. Abroad, aggressive dictators and militarists were on the march. Even at home democracy seemed, at least in the early thirties, to be at some risk, however small; and across the oceans democracy was visibly under siege. On the face of it the United States should have been mobilizing its armed strength to defend the American democracy against whatever perils lay ahead. But instead—paradoxically—Americans sought safety in showing the world that they had disarmed and in trusting the outside world to therefore leave them alone.

# PART SEVEN

# THE LAST, BEST HOPE

*If Italy, Germany and Japan at some critical moment move at the same time in their spheres, I cannot see any way to stop dictatorships. One of the Ministers here said to me today: "In that case I would commit suicide; your country alone can save civilization."*

—William E. Dodd, U.S. ambassador to Germany,
in a letter from Berlin, October 31, 1935

# 41

# CURBING THE PRESIDENT'S POWERS

IN THE EARLY 1930s Mussolini's Italy intrigued to create openings for conquest in the Balkans. It also staked out a claim to control Austria, and in 1935–36 invaded Ethiopia to carve out an African empire. Hitler's Germany, withdrawing from the League of Nations in October 1933, took back the Saar from France after a plebiscite in January 1935. In March 1935 it reintroduced conscription and renounced the disarmament clauses of the Treaty of Versailles, and the following year marched into and remilitarized the Rhineland.

Never had it seemed more evident to Americans that their proper role was to keep as much distance as possible between themselves and Europe, to provide an example to others, and to keep the flame of civilization alive on their side of the water.

With Europe moving ever closer to war, the tide of pacifism in the United States rose ever higher. Such powerful works as Erich Maria Remarque's novel *All Quiet on the Western Front*, the John Dos Passos trilogy *USA*, and Walter Millis's popular history *The Road to War* reinforced the widespread view that the world war had been wicked and pointless, that American entry into it had been a terrible mistake, and that either Woodrow Wilson had misled the country or his advisers had misled Wilson. The leaders of the Wilson administration were pictured as a cabal of guilty men by writers and journalists who argued that not only the suffering and deaths in combat, but also the economic misery of the Depression of the 1930s, flowed directly from the war—and a Gallup Poll showed that 71 percent of the public agreed.

THE TWO LEADERS who were putting millions of people back to work in the 1930s were Adolf Hitler and Harry Hopkins. Hitler was employing his people in the war industry. Hopkins was employing his people in public works—which somehow did not seem equally legitimate to the critics of the New Deal, who became increasingly vocal from 1934 onward: to them public payroll jobs were not real jobs.

In 1933 the whole of America seemed to support FDR. But once he had revived the country's financial institutions (by 1934 banks were sound and stock exchanges were liquid), many of those with jobs or wealth were angered that he did not stop. He did not surrender the extraordinary powers with which he endowed the presidency. Nor did he regard the emergency as having ended. He had solved the problems affecting people who had money, but not those of people who had none and had no jobs.

The President saw mass unemployment as a problem that government should deal with, and saw it as a part of the emergency that required emergency presidential powers. He also seemed to regard extreme poverty and social injustices as problems governments should solve. Starting in 1934 even within his own Democratic party, there was a conservative revolt against these views. People who did not object to FDR's cutting corners in 1933 called it illegal, unconstitutional, and dictatorial in 1934 and 1935. They objected strongly to his tax and other proposals that tended to redistribute wealth.

Harry Hopkins, with his eternally rumpled suits, became the personification of the Roosevelt New Deal, and was especially loathed by the President's critics. He had come from Iowa, where his father had owned a harness store. He was a professional social worker, and FDR had brought him along from the state government in Albany.

It was Hopkins who spearheaded the government's public works program. He was a superb administrator. By the middle of FDR's second term, he had overseen the public spending of almost $10 billion, and had made sure that the money was spent honestly.

It was a mark of the New Dealers that they worked hard and enjoyed their work. The President set the example. At 8:30 a.m., taking breakfast in bed, he already was busy reading the newspapers. After being wheeled into the Oval Office at 10 a.m., he would work all day, taking lunch at his desk, and stopping only after a 5 p.m. session with his staff. He met once a week with his cabinet and twice a week with the press.

In still photos one sees his face tilted upward, and his cigarette holder tilted upward, at an angle everyone calls jaunty. In newsreel photos he tosses his head from side to side, like a thoroughbred on show. His most characteristic gesture was to throw back his head and roar with laughter. He enjoyed living—and governing—hugely.

Those who feared that FDR was becoming a dictator at home overlapped with those who feared that presidents have too much power in foreign affairs. The Great War had been a tragic mistake; the United States had been brought into it by presidential leadership, so no future President should be allowed, like Wilson, to mislead or be misled—such was a common view. Legislation to restrict the powers of the President was pressed by a bewildering variety of groups. Roosevelt's objective was to hold the line against them.

Antimilitary movements were formed on university campuses across the country. A third of college students said they would not fight in a future war unless America was invaded; more than another third said they would not fight even then. A letter to President Roosevelt on May 15, 1934, from the presidents of nearly 200 colleges and universities asked him to support legislation that among other things would embargo all trade with or loans to belligerents in foreign wars, and would nationalize the armaments business.

The Hearst press kept to its isolationist theme, but FDR tried to hold the support of the eccentric magnate himself. When Hearst returned from a European trip in the autumn of 1934, Roosevelt sent him a friendly note: "Dear W.R.: I am delighted to hear from Joe"—Joseph P. Kennedy—"that you are coming down to see me on Monday. If you have not made other arrangements, I hope you will stay with us Monday night at the White House."

Kennedy, though bitterly disappointed that FDR had not yet rewarded him with high office, continued to function as the President's link not only with Hearst, but also with FDR's even more dangerous former supporter, Father Charles E. Coughlin.

Coughlin was a priest whose church was located in a suburb of Detroit, but who spoke to the whole country every week, at first over the CBS network and later over his own. He was a cleric who had discovered a vocation as a radio speaker; with his extraordinary voice, he had become the star of the new medium of mass communication. When the "radio priest" appealed for funds, he received more than a million envelopes in reply. "So great was his weekly harvest of currency," writes a historian of those years, "that he had become the country's principal speculator in silver"; and "his flock had become the largest in the history of Christianity." By 1934 he was receiving more mail than anybody else in the United States. Seven and a half million people signed up for membership in his National Union for Social Justice. By 1936 Coughlin's radio audience was estimated to be 46 million people, a shade more than the total number of voters in the presidential elections that year. His message was hatred and violence, especially of and against Jews.

Coughlin, like Hearst and Huey Long, was an important supporter of Roosevelt in 1932 who now joined with a strange assortment of allies to curb the President's power to involve the United States in international affairs. Within the Congress the chief leaders of the movement were former Progressive Republican supporters of TR or Robert La Follette, Sr., from the West, including Senator Gerald Nye of North Dakota. Among those who in 1932 had broken with the Republican party to form the National Progressive League for Franklin D. Roosevelt were Senators Hiram Johnson of California, Robert La Follette Jr. of Wisconsin, George Norris of Nebraska, and Burton Wheeler of Montana. Such isolationist allies of theirs as Senator William Borah of Idaho were prepared to support at least parts of FDR's domestic program.

These were supporters whom Roosevelt could not afford to alienate, even when they curbed his foreign policy powers, as they did by enacting Hiram Johnson's law (1934) forbidding American loans to countries that had not repaid loans from the world war (i.e., all borrower belligerent countries except Finland).


THE FELLOWSHIP OF CONCILIATION, the National Council for the Prevention of War, World Peaceways, and the Women's International League for Peace and Freedom were among the pacifist organizations that in 1932 and 1933 demanded that the U.S. Senate investigate the role of the armaments industry in fomenting international strife; but it was the executive secretary of the Women's International League, Dorothy Detzer, who actually pushed the Senate into action. It was she who arranged a crucial alliance between her chosen Senate leader, Gerald Nye, and Senator Arthur Vandenberg, the former TR enthusiast and newspaper editor from Michigan. With the support of the veterans' organization the American Legion, Vandenberg was trying to see that war profiteering was curbed in any future conflict. Detzer shaped the Nye-Vandenberg resolution steering the hearings away from the Foreign Relations Committee and into a more pliable special committee, and she engineered the selection of Nye as chairman. The publication of two widely read exposés of the arms trade and an article along similar lines in Henry Luce's new *Fortune* magazine, in addition to a massive nationwide lobbying campaign, made it difficult for Roosevelt to oppose the holding of Senate hearings, even though they seemed likely to spin out of the control of the administration and its Senate allies.

The Nye Committee (1934–36) uncovered nothing new, but it won headlines in sensationalizing existing information about the profits made by munitions firms, and in propagating conspiracy theories about the eastern banks and their ties to the Wilson administration. Nye and his colleagues tried to prove that arms firms foment wars in order to sell more product.

Roosevelt wrote to Colonel House (September 17, 1935) that "you may be interested to know that some of the Congressmen and Senators who are suggesting wild-eyed measures to keep us out of war are now declaring that you and Lansing and Page forced Wilson into the war! I . . . explained that I was in Washington myself the whole of that period, that none of them were there and that their historical analysis was wholly inaccurate. . . . The trouble is that they belong to the very large and perhaps increasing school of thought which holds that we can and should withdraw wholly within ourselves and cut off all but the most perfunctory relationships with other nations. They imagine that if the civilization of Europe is about to destroy itself through internal strife it might just as well go ahead and do it and that the United States can stand idly by."

But FDR was defeated in his maneuvers against the Nye Committee. His plan to supersede it by appointing an executive committee of his own, dominated by respected elder statesman Bernard Baruch, miscarried. Soon Baruch found himself under attack by Long and Coughlin, and was obliged to enlist his senatorial ally James F. Byrnes of South Carolina to defend his own record.

Isolationism was at floodtide, and starting in 1935 the Congress enacted Neutrality Acts that required the President to embargo arms traffic to all sides in the event of war. FDR maneuvered to obtain language that would allow him discretionary power, sufficient at least to allow him to embargo only one side—to aid the League of Nations, for example, if it really could bring itself to take a stand against Italy for invading Ethiopia.* It was precisely to keep the President from committing the United States to the side of the democracies against the dictators that the Congress curbed his powers.

FROM BERLIN Ambassador Dodd reported to Washington on November 5, 1934, that "there is great preparation for war. . . . [T]he object is to put France out of business. The result . . . will of course mean annexations and the predominance of the whole of Europe." To the President, he wondered (May 9, 1935), "What can anyone now do to change the fixed drift everywhere towards war?" He pointed out that in Germany "children at ages of eight to twelve are taught . . . to throw bombs; from twelve to eighteen they practice with rifles. . . ." He also noted that "Germany and Japan have some entente" and that "every leading diplomat here" believes that Hitler's "fixed purpose" is war. At the outset of 1936, Dodd sensed that "a dictatorial front" had been formed by Germany, Italy, and Japan: an alliance potentially so powerful as to threaten everyone else.

In January 1936 Wall Street lawyer John Foster Dulles came by the Berlin embassy. Dulles told Dodd: "My sister lives here. She is an enthusiastic Hitlerite." Miss Dulles had taken her brother to see a motion picture film that showed Germany's armed forces "defending" their country by

---

* Though the invasion of Ethiopia was not one requiring discretionary power. Italy was in a position to buy arms and oil while Ethiopia was not, so to impartially embargo all sides in reality embargoed only Italy.

devastating foreign cities. Dulles said that "such a display in the United States would be hissed off the screen." According to Dodd, "Dulles said he had served in the State Department with Secretary Lansing when Wilson was President and that he was indignant at the charges of the Senate Committee that Wilson entered the World War to make money for the United States."

On April 1 Dodd presciently wrote FDR that "Germany's dictatorship is now stronger than ever. If she keeps the pace three more years she can beat the whole of Europe in a war." Later (October 19, 1936) he reported to FDR that "Hitler and Mussolini intend to control all Europe."

But the President was receiving contrary analyses and predictions from his increasingly anti-Soviet ambassador to Moscow, the world traveler William Bullitt, who often seemed to be reporting from every European capital other than the one to which he was accredited. (Bullitt, wrote Dodd in 1936 after a morning spent with him, is "not one whose judgment can be relied on. He is ambitious for promotion to high position but does not seem to me to appraise situations too well.") Bullitt denounced Britain and France for trying to bring the Soviet Union into an alliance to deter Hitler from starting a war.

In 1936 Dodd looked into the future and foresaw that the Dutch ambassador to Germany was right in saying that "we shall probably never have another happy day in our lives." Bill Bullitt envisioned things differently: He reported from London that British politicians had played up the German threat in order to justify their excessive military budget. He also ridiculed the view he had heard expressed in London that "within three years"—which was to say, by 1939—"England will have to choose between making war on Germany or permitting Germany to dominate Czechoslovakia, Austria, Hungary, and Rumania preparatory to an attack on the Soviet Union": in other words, exactly what was going to happen. Bullitt wrote FDR that "strangely enough, all the old anti-Bolshevik fanatics like Winston Churchill are trumpeting this Bolshevik thesis . . . !"

Both Bullitt and Dodd seemed to believe that FDR agreed with them. Indeed, he encouraged them to think so.


IN THE WINTER OF 1935 Roosevelt wrote to his old friend and ambassador to Italy, Breckinridge Long, that "these are without doubt the most hair-trigger times the world has gone through in your lifetime and mine. I do not even exclude June and July 1914. . . ." To a skeptical friend, Ray Stannard Baker, FDR predicted that "in the near future" the public would see that foreign affairs questions had become even more vital than the nation's domestic ones. But until that time came, Roosevelt in public would continue to be the nationalist isolationist leader intent on fostering economic revival and reform at home.

As the 1936 elections approached, the President found an astonishing variety of opponents arrayed against him. Huey Long had been removed from the scene by assassination, but his lieutenant Gerald L. K. Smith joined with Father Coughlin in promoting a third-party ticket headed by Congressman William Lemke that grouped populist, race-hatred, and religious-hatred movements from all over the country. Familiar figures of the Democratic old guard, embittered by the New Deal's reforms, supported the Republicans, led by former presidential candidates Al Smith and John W. Davis—though such younger critics of FDR as Dean Acheson remained loyal to the Democratic ticket. Walter Lippmann, who had hesitated to vote for Arthur Vandenberg for President,* switched to the Republican side when the senator's candidacy faded and Governor Alfred Landon of Kansas won the nomination instead.

In the domestic sphere, Roosevelt had little difficulty in making his case; the voters knew that times were better and prosperity was returning. In foreign policy FDR aggressively seized the disarmament and isolationist issues as his own, claiming credit for having avoided the foreign entanglements into which the Congress in any event would never have let him enter, and allowing the public to understand that if reelected, he would launch a plan that might bring about world peace.

On November 3 FDR won reelection by the largest plurality in history, winning more than 60 percent of the popular vote and carrying all but two states. His victory in the electoral college (523 to 8) was the greatest since 1820, when President James Monroe ran without an opponent and won with 231 votes out of 235.

A FEW MONTHS before the 1936 American elections took place, a group of Spanish generals led a revolt against their country's elected government. The Spanish government asked France for aid; the rebels appealed to Italy. Taking the position that other countries should not interfere in the internal affairs of Spain, Roosevelt was able to present himself to the electorate as the man who was keeping the United States out of the war. Clearly the electorate approved.

* See pages 351–2.

## 42

# STAYING OUT OF IT

IN THE 1930s Americans knew that the principles of morality and political justice in which they believed were being systematically violated abroad, and that deeds of sickening and heartbreaking cruelty were being perpetrated by predatory powers in Europe, Africa, and Asia; but they felt strongly that it was none of their concern. They read in their newspapers that Mussolini's armies used poison gas and airplanes and a whole range of modern weaponry against native Ethiopians armed only with spears. They could have learned—had they inquired—that Germans committed terrible crimes daily against the half million among them of Jewish ancestry or belief.

It was not that Americans were ignorant of such things; it was that they chose to ignore them. Years earlier, Woodrow Wilson had persuaded his countrymen for a time that they could and should change the world, but his experience had taught them (or so they now believed) that it was a mistake even to try.

In its isolationism the United States of the 1930s was going back to the principles of its Founding Fathers, but not in its immigration policy. From the administration of George Washington to that of Woodrow Wilson, America always had welcomed whoever sought to enter. The interwar United States broke with that policy and therefore with its past. The country that once said, "Give me your tired, your poor/ Your huddled masses yearning to breathe free, . . . Send these, the homeless . . ." now no longer welcomed them. The Immigration Act of 1924 introduced a permanent quota; it was fixed in 1929 at 150,000 people a year. Those who most urgently pressed against the gates were the masses of European Jews. There was no hope for them if they could not find a haven; but between 1933 and 1941, only 8,500 of them were admitted. President Roosevelt has been criticized for having found it politically inexpedient to try to help: for having abandoned hundreds of thousands and later millions to their horrifying fate in Europe. But he seems to have correctly gauged the prevailing American mood. Americans wanted to have nothing to do with the emerging tragedies overseas.

According to a public opinion poll taken in 1937, only 26 percent of Americans thought the United States should have joined the League of Nations after the world war. Even the beleaguered League of Nations Association, a dwindling band of Wilson's disciples, now recognized that the League had failed. James Shotwell, one of the leaders of Wilson's Inquiry, headed the association with the help of Clark Eichelberger, a lecturer and editor; their argument was that if the United States had joined the League in 1919, the League *would* have been effective. America, Britain, and France would not have gone their separate ways; in the 1930s they would have allied against the aggressors. Shotwell and Eichelberger missed the point that joining the League did not change a country's foreign policy. For, when Roosevelt sent a delegation to the world economic conference in London in 1933, that did not pull him into collaboration with other world leaders; on the contrary, his delegation went to London to explain that FDR's America would go it alone. Similarly, if the United States had been a member of the League of Nations, the American ambassador to the League would have said in Geneva what American ambassadors said in Moscow and Paris and London: that the President and people of the United States refused to be drawn into the quarrels of countries outside the Western Hemisphere.

The American people had learned that righting international wrongs meant fighting, and they were determined not to do that. As they saw it, this was somebody else's fight, not theirs.


NOBODY CAUGHT THE POPULAR MOOD better than did Arthur Vandenberg, who initially had been appointed to the Senate in 1928 to fill the unexpired term of a sitting senator who had died in office.* Bulky, bushy-browed, and an old-fashioned orator, the middle western Republican was the popular caricature of a senator. A onetime TR fan who had been won over by Wilson to the cause of American entry into the world war, he made an initial effort to be fair to the Democratic Roosevelt. Unlike the old guard in his party whose entire program seemed to the public to consist in voting no, he supported the New Deal when he felt he could, and tried to propose constructive alternatives when he could not. This led the *Christian Science Monitor* in 1936 to comment that "Senator Vandenberg more than anyone is keeping alive the two-party system in the Senate," while Arthur Krock of *The New York Times* said that Vandenberg had become the

---

* Vandenberg had been so convinced that the governor who owed him the appointment to the Senate was going to betray him by naming someone else, that when an official letter from the governor arrived, he threw it in the wastepaper basket unopened. Only three days later, driven by insistent reports of his appointment, did he lead his newspaper staff into the basement to search through bales of bundled trash to find what did indeed turn out to be his appointment to the Senate.

de facto Republican leader in the Senate. In early press speculation about the 1936 and then the 1940 elections, his was the leading name mentioned for the Republican presidential nomination.

Vandenberg's greatest achievement during FDR's first administration was his enactment of Federal Deposit Insurance for bank accounts. It proved to be a major step in saving the American banking system. For unclear reasons, Roosevelt fought against the proposal all along the line. But once it was on the statute books and became an evident success, the President claimed credit for it. From that time on, Vandenberg, never the most temperate of men, felt a personal hostility toward FDR that time would not dim.

In foreign affairs Vandenberg, often inconsistent and sometimes incoherent, underwent a major change in beliefs during the 1930s. It was his membership in the Nye Committee that did it. The testimony that he heard convinced him that he had been wrong to support TR's preparedness program and wrong to support Wilson's call to arms in 1917. He became an isolationist; indeed, he was the leader of the isolationist bloc on Capitol Hill, assuming eventually the mantle of his older colleague Senator William Borah. Year after year Vandenberg stood alongside Nye in playing a major role in shaping the Neutrality Acts that, in overseas conflicts, deprived the President of the power to align the United States with either side.

ON AUGUST 25, 1936, FDR appointed William Bullitt U.S. ambassador to France. It made Bullitt happy on two counts: he was glad to leave the Soviet Union, which he had come to loathe for breaking its promises,* and he was delighted to be sent to France, his favorite foreign country. His tour of duty at the Paris embassy was to prove the zenith of his career.

Bullitt soon became in effect Roosevelt's ambassador to the whole of Europe. James Farley, FDR's campaign manager, wrote that "all diplomatic messages from the State Department to continental embassies and legations funneled through" Bullitt's embassy. "Bullitt dispatched couriers throughout Europe, as telephone and telegraph wires were known to be tapped. The Embassy had a direct wire to Washington through which Roosevelt and Bullitt maintained constant communication. From what I saw, Bullitt was closer than anyone in the diplomatic service to the President."

Bullitt allowed it to be understood that he and Roosevelt were old friends from the days of the Wilson administration, whose offices in those days had been only three doors away, and that he might well be FDR's

---

* The promises made in obtaining U.S. recognition in 1933: to repay wartime debts to America and to stop subversion within the United States. Bullitt, having helped to negotiate these terms at the time, seemed to take it personally that the Russians reneged on them.

handpicked successor as President of the United States. He seemed to know everyone in European politics, and to be confided in by all of them: "Bullitt practically sleeps with the French Cabinet," Interior Secretary Harold Ickes noted in his diary.

The American embassy off the Place de la Concorde, with its Louis XV facade, is a building of great beauty; and even the somewhat tasteless house at 2, avenue d'Iéna that then served as the ambassador's official residence commanded a spectacular view over the Trocadéro gardens and the river Seine to the Eiffel Tower. Bullitt also kept a small apartment of his own near the Rond-point des Champs-Élysées, with a tiny room for his Chinese manservant; an alcove off the living/dining room served as a bedroom for himself.

Bullitt added to these facilities the eighteenth-century Château Firmin, rented from the Institut de France, with which came the use of the celebrated park of Chantilly ("I am very proud that my Ambassador has rented the Park and the Great Chateau of Chantilly. May the ghost of the Great Conde haunt you . . . ," wrote Roosevelt in a teasing letter) and proximity to the racetrack: a sporting man in so many ways, Bullitt had a passion for horse races.

Bald on top, but with a pink, boyish face and expressive features, a fresh carnation always in the buttonhole, the headstrong but irresistibly charming American ambassador whose ancestors were French provided some of the most splendid entertainments in Paris. His chef was superb. The wine cellar he swiftly assembled was magnificent. At a ball for 600 guests, he served almost that number of bottles of champagne—vintage 1928, the greatest year since the Franco-Prussian war. At intimate dinner parties, he poured Château Mouton 1858, the first great year under Rothschild ownership, and the year with which Bordeaux's golden age began. He allowed the president of the Chamber of Deputies (the French equivalent of the Speaker of the House) to drink him out of the 1864s—another of Bordeaux's legendary vintages. To the *New Yorker*, he revealed that he spent $12,500 a year more than his income—at that time, a quite considerable sum.

Bullitt had brought his State Department secretary with him to take dictation in the middle of the night, to rise before dawn to do the marketing as fresh produce poured into Paris from the countryside, to read through and organize all incoming communications for the ambassador, to manage the households, and to oversee the work of the embassy. This rough-cut, street-smart young hustler from the Pennsylvania coalfields who looked something like a weasel was named Carmel Offie. Bullitt delighted in polishing Offie and then showing him off, as did Henry Higgins with Eliza Doolittle; and like Henry with Eliza, he fitted Offie to move in the highest society.

"You will be pleased to learn," Bullitt reported to Roosevelt in late

1936, "that last night Offie was the guest of honor at Maxim's at a dinner given by the Marquis and the Marquise de Polignac, who are the greatest snobs in France. Inasmuch as de Polignacs habitually ignore everyone from this Embassy, including the Ambassadors, I think you will agree with me that our child is already going fast and far. The Marquise herself drove him home at midnight!"

Ever faithful, Offie served as a foreign service officer, a fixer, a go-between, a valet, a companion, a secretary, an adviser, and a procurer of anything that Bullitt wanted procured for himself or his guests. The seamy side of the life he led in the shadows may well have been unknown to Bullitt; only later did his name appear in police dossiers and intelligence files—and only much later was the information used against him by his, and Bullitt's, enemies.

Meanwhile Offie's doings were reported in the lively chronicle of society scandal and political gossip with which Bullitt, as a sort of latter-day Madame de Sévigné, regaled his President in frequent and chatty letters. The desk-bound, wheelchair-bound chief executive was enabled through them to live vicariously the Paris high life he once had been able to enjoy himself. They provided a distraction at an opportune moment; for during his second term of office, Roosevelt was having a rotten time.


HIS AIDE LOUIS HOWE, the only person from whom he would accept criticism and correction, had died; and the extent of Roosevelt's personal triumph at the polls was so great as to go to anybody's head. Even his wife now confided that "I realize more and more that F.D.R. is a great man." Perhaps the 1936 election results had been too overwhelming a success, for on the morrow of them, Roosevelt lost his political balance. In 1937–38 he embarked on a program of financial conservatism, deflating the economy and aiming at a balanced budget at a time when in retrospect just the opposite—reflation and deficit spending—was called for. His policies brought down the stock market and the economy; both crashed. Millions were thrown out of work. Many of the gains of his first term were wiped out.

The President lost control of Congress. For a time he was unable to secure the enactment of any proposed legislation. His longtime political ally James F. Byrnes, de facto Democratic leader in the Senate, opposed him not merely on an antilynching bill to protect blacks against mob killings (enactment of which would be "betraying the trust of the Southern people," said one of Byrnes's fellow southern Democrats), but also on economic legislation. Byrnes "has jumped over the traces and gone conservative," noted Harold Ickes. And in the Senate, by and large, it was true that wherever Byrnes, a bellwether figure, went, the other senators went, too.

Much of FDR's first-term program had been invalidated by the Supreme Court in 1935, and when in his second term the President asked to enlarge the Court in order to pack it with his own supporters, the Congress turned him down. Now the chief executive found himself losing a war against both the legislature and the judiciary.

Strife between labor union organizers and the corporations that shut them out burst into violence in Roosevelt's second term. Employers used mobsters against union picketers while union men staged sit-in strikes to paralyze businesses. The public blamed the President for not putting an end to the riots and the sit-ins.

Roosevelt came to sense a gigantic plot against him, in which an array of business and allied interests were conspiring to bring down the government. As the 1938 midterm elections approached, he decided to try to purge his enemies within the Democratic party. In the elections he carried his case against disloyal senators and congressmen to the people—and mostly lost. Many of those whom he had attempted to purge were back in Washington with a mandate from the people to oppose him.

Riding the anti-Roosevelt wave, formidable new figures came to the Capitol to join the fray. A leading figure among them, whom FDR had seen in Paris in 1919, was Robert A. Taft. A fierce foe of government spending, Taft was elected to the Senate in 1938, and his name and outstanding intellect placed him immediately in the front ranks of Republican contenders for the presidency. On his second day in the Senate, Taft, who was deeply suspicious of foreigners and foreign entanglements, accused FDR of trying to involve the country in overseas conflicts in order to "take the minds of the people off their troubles at home."

Hounded by political enemies, Roosevelt must have felt immense relief in turning away from the apparently insoluble problems of the American economy and of American society, and taking the time to read the dispatches of his irrepressible ambassador to France.


BULLITT, AS HIS LETTERS to Roosevelt show, found himself in full sympathy with the foreign policy of the French government. The government was led by the country's first Socialist prime minister, Léon Blum, and it was sustained by a Popular Front in which a spectrum of parties of the Left were allied. Yet in the matter of the Spanish war, it would not support the elected leftist republican government in Madrid against a rightist military rebellion that began in the summer of 1936, just after Blum became premier and just before Bullitt arrived in Paris as ambassador. Within a week of the rebellion, Fascist Italy and Nazi Germany had agreed to dispatch war supplies to the Spanish Nationalists (as the rebels were called). Italian and German aviators and troops followed later; eventually

Italy was to supply 50,000. Stalin replied by sending Soviet arms to the Loyalist forces of the increasingly leftist government of the republic. As time went on, leftist volunteers from various countries found their way into the ranks of the Loyalist army, notably in the International Brigades that were dominated by communists and in which Stalinists waged an interior civil war against Trotskyites.

Blum's France followed the line of Stanley Baldwin's Britain: at all costs, the fighting in Spain must not be allowed to lead to a European war. In pursuance of that policy, Britain and France negotiated and signed an agreement with Italy, Germany, and Russia in which the signatory countries agreed not to intervene in the Spanish war: not to aid either side with troops or supplies. Britain and France mostly kept to their word, but Italy, Germany, and Russia cheated and continued to back their respective Spanish allies.

Bullitt's advice to his President was to stay out of harm's way. The "odor which pervades every conversation I have in Paris whether with Frenchmen, Englishmen, Belgians, or Czechs," he wrote on November 24, 1936, "is the emanation of a violent nervous desire to get us into the next war." He added that "it will be difficult for me to make you realize the extent to which French Cabinet Ministers and representatives of all the countries of Europe in Paris talk as if they had within them the same phonograph record—playing the theme, 'War is inevitable and Europe is doomed to destruction unless President Roosevelt intervenes.' " He found it impossible to get them to understand that there was nothing the President could do to help them.

Bullitt reported on December 1, 1936, that he had emphasized to Premier Blum "the absolute determination of the United States to stay out not only of any wars on the continent of Europe but out of any engagements or commitments which might possibly lead to our involvement in wars."

The following month he wrote that "the only policy for us is to stay as far out of the mess as possible." At the end of 1937 he commended to Roosevelt a book by the British philosopher Bertrand Russell that "holds out as the one hope of the world the possibility that the United States will stay out of the war . . . and will have, at the end of the holocaust, a civilization intact and of sufficient strength to pick up the pieces and put them together again."

Bullitt was openly anti-English, an attitude he claimed to derive from Revolutionary War ancestors. After a midnight conversation April 30, 1937, with Sir Eric Phipps—the British ambassador to Germany who became ambassador to France, and who "did not see the faintest possibility of coming to any agreement with Hitler" and believed in rearming as fast as possible—Bullitt reported to Secretary Hull that "the policy of Great Britain is still to keep the continent of Europe divided." Cynically, he misinterpreted what Phipps told him, assuming that the true motive of the British government was to foment discord between Germany and her neighbors in order to play one side off against the other.

Bullitt arrived at a program of his own for dealing with the simmering European crisis. His idea was to promote a reconciliation between France and Germany, who then could combine against the real threat to Europe: the Soviet Union.

As for the Far East, Bullitt saw no grave problem there. He wrote Roosevelt that "the far-off bugaboo of complete Japanese domination of Asia and an eventual attack on us seems to me no basis whatsoever for present-day policy."

IN AUGUST 1936 the Japanese cabinet adopted a far-reaching program of national policy that called for Japanese hegemony in China, Southeast Asia, and the western Pacific. To frighten off possible Soviet interference with the carrying out of the program, Japan signed an Anti-Comintern Pact with Germany later that year. Apparently the cabinet did not expect interference by the United States.

Earlier that year, the foreign news editor of the United Press wire service had written to and then met with President Roosevelt to propose a plan to improve relations between the United States and Japan. His idea was to establish a baseball world series between the two countries. Like everyone else who communicated with the President, he came away persuaded that Roosevelt agreed with him—had, indeed, "grasped the significance at once." In September 1936 the editor set out for Japan, bearing with him a letter of introduction from FDR to American ambassador Grew.

A minor and murky episode in July 1937 that led to an exchange of fire at midnight between Japanese and Chinese troops at the Marco Polo Bridge in Wanping, near Peking, provided an excuse for Japan to initiate the invasion contemplated by her newly adopted national program. Although war was not declared by either side, the Japanese army took the offensive against the Chinese, driving south and west, and capturing the Chinese capital city of Nanking in December. The Japanese victors subjected Nanking to horrors that were calculated to terrorize all China.

Governments around the world sent notes to Japan and China urging restraint, to no avail.

Roosevelt was moved to make an eloquent speech that autumn in which, using phrases suggested by Harold Ickes, he compared aggression to a contagious disease and urged "quarantining" the aggressors. Though his words were seized upon hopefully by advocates of collective security, it transpired that the President had no specific program of action to propose.

American passions had begun to run high about foreign events. In the continuing Far East crisis, Americans were sympathetic, as they always had been, to China. Looking in the other direction, across the Atlantic, Catholics in particular were aroused by Loyalist attacks on churches, priests, and nuns in Spain, while those on the Left increasingly were drawn to the cause of the Republic as against the military rebels and their Nazi and Fascist combat allies. Yet public opinion continued to be strongly isolationist; no matter who they were rooting for to win, Americans insisted they themselves would remain on the sidelines.

In later years it would become apparent that Stalin had taken advantage of the Spanish war to liquidate the followers of Trotsky and other rival communist leaders, and to take control of the European Left. But at the time, especially to the young, it seemed as though the Soviet Union was the only organized force actively opposing Nazism and Fascism in the world. Some of the brightest spirits in the younger generation turned to, or at least sympathized with, Russia and the Communist party apparatus she controlled.

Not untypical of the divide between the generations—in values and standards of behavior as well as in tastes and politics—was the situation in the American embassy in Berlin. Soon to be replaced by someone less openly critical of the Nazi regime,* Ambassador Dodd, who in 1936 predicted that by 1939 Germany would be able to "beat the whole of Europe in a war," simply despaired. A deeply conservative person who admired the traditions of aristocratic Germany, he was offended by the raucousness of the Nazi regime. He retreated from the modern world into his studies of Wilson, Jefferson, and the gallant ways of the Old South.

Meanwhile his daughter Martha, a socially and sexually active girl in her mid-twenties who in college had bedded her English literature professor, Robert Morss Lovett, and then perhaps Carl Sandburg, George Jean Nathan, and even Thornton Wilder when she worked as assistant literary editor of the Chicago *Tribune*, now took political activists as her lovers, too, in the delirium of Berlin. She was described by Thomas Wolfe, the author of *Look Homeward, Angel*, as "a little middle western flirt—with . . . a little 'sure that will be swell' sort of voice." The novelist, suddenly one of the most famous writers in the world, was on a trip to Germany, where he was greatly admired.† Intoxicated with fame, words, alcohol, sexual conquests, and acclaim, the giant of a man who did everything to excess was the greatest catch in town for a literary autograph hunter; and Wolfe told a friend that Martha was "like a butterfly hovering about my penis."

Reckless and indiscreet, Martha lurched with indiscriminate enthusi-

---

* Hugh R. Wilson, a career diplomat.
† New details of his brief fling with Martha Dodd soon are to be supplied by Shareen Brysac, chronicler of the Berlin set in which Martha moved.

asm from Nazism to communism, carried on with spies of various nationalities, and eventually fell in love with a Russian diplomat who appears to have been the resident station chief of the Soviet secret service.

Martha's father confided his secrets to her. She read the embassy mail and typed the most confidential outgoing documents herself. A convicted spy for the Soviet Union testified in his (and her) trial in 1957 that it was originally at the request of her Russian lover, Boris Vinogradov, that she began turning over the embassy's secrets and its files to the Soviet Union.

In 1937 Martha and Boris composed a joint letter to Stalin asking his permission to marry. They received no response; but not long afterward, Vinogradov was recalled home and executed.

Decades later Martha denied that it was for her lover's sake that she had done what she had done; it was, she said, because it was the only way open to fight Nazism and Fascism at a time when America refused to join in the fight.

THE ISOLATIONIST ASSUMPTION was that if the United States stayed out of things, it would be left alone. George S. Messersmith, a career diplomat who had served in Germany and Austria and who had just returned to Washington to serve as assistant secretary of state, challenged that view in a memo to Secretary Hull (October 11, 1937). He argued that "the United States are the ultimate object of attack of the powers grouped in this new system of force and lawlessness"—Germany, Italy, and Japan—so that it would be wiser for America to join the fray earlier rather than later. For otherwise, "when the time comes for them to deal with the United States . . . ," our "country will be practically alone for the rest will have been cleared out of the way."

# 43

## THE MARCH TOWARD WAR

BERLIN. THE REICH CHANCELLERY on the Wilhelmstrasse. November 5, 1937, 4:15 p.m. The fuehrer, attended by only one aide, addressed the German foreign minister and four uniformed chiefs of the armed forces to reveal his plans for the future. Hitler began by asserting that the remarks he was about to make were so important that, "in the event of his death, they should be regarded as his last will and testament."

Apart from air force commander Goering, the men to whom he spoke were conservative professionals with roots in the prewar elite. They knew that Germany lacked the resources to wage a long war, and though unwilling to oppose their leader, at least openly, they worried that Hitler's recklessness might embroil her in a war she might lose. Their nerves would have crumbled if Britain and France had stood firm when Hitler reoccupied the Rhineland or when he openly ordered full rearmament.

Now Hitler outlined an even more dangerous plan of action: a timetable of conquest calling for Germany to invade, occupy, and annex Austria and Czechoslovakia. Hitler's point was that the industry, agriculture, and manpower of those countries then could be exploited by Germany, so strengthening her that she could go on to further conquests.

The chiefs of the foreign office, the armed forces, the army, and the navy questioned whether Germany was ready for the major war that might ensue. Might this plan not lead Germany into another disaster of 1918–19 proportions?

The fuehrer swept away not only the questions but also the questioners: within three months all were dismissed from their jobs, replaced by those who harbored neither doubts nor fears as to where Hitler was leading them. The Nazi revolution in Germany, as the journalist and historian William L. Shirer later commented, now was complete.


THE NEW DEAL REVOLUTION in the United States was, if not complete, then at least far along. It had brought vast new powers to the federal government and therefore had attracted talented and ambitious people from all over the country to the nation's capital. It was appropriate that

Walter Lippmann should now be writing no longer from New York, but from Washington, D.C., as the sleepy and still provincial southern city verged on becoming an important center of world news.

But it was accident rather than design that moved him there. Lippmann's best friend had been Hamilton Fish Armstrong, editor of *Foreign Affairs*, the magisterial publication of the Council on Foreign Relations in New York. Armstrong and his wife, Helen, shared Lippmann's intellectual passions, interests, and concerns, so Lippmann had spent much time in their company, sometimes with his party-loving wife, Faye, but more often by himself.

In 1937 Lippmann and Helen Armstrong became lovers, and they planned a secret tryst in Europe for that summer. A rationalist all his life, detached and cool, Lippmann, suddenly in the grip of his emotions, was driven to indiscretion. He wrote passionate letters to Helen, one of which fell into her husband's hands. The violently bitter breakup of both marriages followed.

Not even New York, America's metropolis, was a big enough city to contain both luminaries of the American foreign policy establishment, who now no longer spoke to each other. Lippmann moved to Washington and, after both divorces became final, married Helen.

LIPPMANN'S OLD FRIEND BULLITT, though accredited only to France, was acting as an American observer of the entire European scene—just as he had in Wilson administration days. He reported to Washington his conversations with leading European political personalities, including German officials to whom he alone seemed to have access. At the end of 1937, America's roving ambassador to France spoke at length with the number two man in the Nazi regime, Hermann Goering, who purported to confide to him the full details of Hitler's plans. Goering explained that there no longer was any conflict between France and Germany, because Germany had given up all thought of regaining Alsace-Lorraine. Germany was France's friend and was ready to sign a full treaty of alliance with her. All that Germany wanted (Goering said, lying) was to unite with Austria and with the German-inhabited section of Czechoslovakia, the Sudetenland, for "Germany had no desire to have territory in Europe except territory inhabited by Germans." Once Hitler had rounded out Germany by uniting Austria and the Sudetenland with her, he would call a halt; there would be no further conquests.

Bullitt, who actively was promoting a Franco-German alliance, believed what he was told. So did the newly appointed undersecretary of state, Sumner Welles, who responded to him that "your conversation with Goering is one of the most important pieces of information which has reached

the Department in many a month. I wish to the good Lord that during the
past years we had been getting this type of information from Berlin." For,
like Bullitt, Welles considered Ambassador Dodd a failure for being so
openly critical of the Nazis that he was denied access to them and intimacy
with them. Welles had even taken steps to secure Dodd's recall.

Welles's star was in the ascendant in Washington. Tall and handsome,
he was a product of Groton and Harvard. His mother had been one of the
best friends of Eleanor Roosevelt's mother. Ten years younger than the President, Welles had been a page at his wedding and had been sponsored by
Roosevelt for a State Department career. He had been FDR's first ambassador to Cuba, and when his policy there led to disaster, he had been promoted (to assistant secretary of state) rather than dismissed. Though haughty
and disdainful with others (and therefore widely disliked), Welles was on
easy terms with FDR, with whom he shared an overweening pride of birth.
From the time of his appointment as undersecretary in 1937, Welles dealt
directly with the President instead of through his long-suffering nominal
chief, Secretary Hull, whom FDR found admirable but boring.

It was Welles, then, sharing Bullitt's view that the United States
needed an envoy in Berlin more acceptable to the Nazi regime, who took
steps to accomplish that end. But it was the Soviet Union, not Germany,
that FDR himself seemed intent on accommodating. It seems not to have
been Welles, or even Hull, but the President who took the much-resented
step of dissolving the Russian Division in the Department of State, apparently because of its anti-Soviet views; and in 1936, to fill Bullitt's place at
the Moscow embassy, he appointed Joseph Davies, a politician who found
no fault with the USSR.

Another FDR decision—this time, one that Bullitt approved—was to
send Joseph P. Kennedy as U.S. ambassador to Britain. The Boston Irish
speculator and wheeler-dealer (or swindler, some said), who had served as
first chairman of the Securities and Exchange Commission, had been the
President's liaison with Hearst, Coughlin, and other demagogues of the
Right, and had the confidence of isolationist leaders—Republican as well
as Democrat. Nursing a grudge that came from not having been rewarded
adequately by FDR until now,* Kennedy soon began to see himself as a
1940 presidential candidate; he lavished financial favors on *New York Times*
Washington bureau chief Arthur Krock and other newsmen to promote his
interests.

Kennedy admired the way the Paris embassy was run, and arranged
for his two oldest sons, Joe junior and Jack, to do brief stints there. As
always, Bullitt had discovered talent, bringing forward promising young
diplomats Robert Murphy and Douglas MacArthur II (the general's

---

* Some would have seen the SEC chairmanship as reward enough, but Kennedy did not.

nephew), and taking along with him from his Moscow embassy future CIA director Roscoe Hillenkoetter. But it was Carmel Offie whose services Kennedy most coveted; he offered to put him on his personal payroll.

Kennedy (from London) would consult Offie (in Paris) by telephone several times a day, and when his son Jack, the future president, did his monthlong stint at the Paris embassy in the spring of 1939, staying at Bullitt's otherwise deserted official residence on the avenue d'Iéna, it was Offie who entertained him and showed him around. Offie later recalled that Jack, who was then twenty-one years old, "did not learn much French but . . . had a good time" because Offie got him "invited to various parties in the diplomatic corps" where he "could meet young ladies. . . ." In a thankyou note young Kennedy sent Bullitt from Poland, as he continued his travels, he wrote: "That month ranks as just about the best I've ever put in." To a friend back home he wrote that "Bullitt has turned out to be a hell of a good guy. Live like a king . . . as Offie and I are the only ones there + about 30 lackies."

IN MARCH 1938 German troops invaded and occupied Austria, which Germany then annexed. Ambassador Kennedy believed these events did not "affect our country or my job." He deplored "the semi-hysterical attitude which the professional diplomats here adopt. . . ." He foresaw no further danger.

Later that month Konrad Henlein, the leader of the Nazi-subsidized German-speaking party in Czechoslovakia, was instructed by Hitler to ask concessions from the Czech government that could not be granted: "We must always demand so much we can never be satisfied," said Henlein in summarizing his instructions. On May 7 the British and French ministers in Prague urged the Czech government "to go to the utmost limit" in meeting Henlein's requirements.

The crisis in Europe was approaching its yearlong climax. Unlike Kennedy, Bullitt was aware of the imminence of crisis; but like the European politicians and officials with whom he dined, he believed that—at some price, however high—the German government could be appeased. His concern was that the Czech government would not pitch its offer high enough.

In his château at Chantilly, surrounded by woods and serenaded by nightingales, Bullitt wrote to Roosevelt on June 13 that he felt "like a participant in the last days of Pompeii." That, he told the President, was the mood of all Paris; "I know no informed Frenchman who does not feel that he is living in the last days of his civilization. . . ."

Bullitt reported to FDR the gist of his conversations with the French chief of staff and with the general who in wartime would be France's frontline commander. What they had to say was disheartening. In effect, the

French generals envisaged a replay of their strategy in the First World War. On the outbreak of the war, they planned to attack German fortifications and expected French manpower losses to be so horrendous in doing so that it would mean "the death of a race." But at that price they could deadlock the Germans until a British naval blockade starved the Germans into submission.

"There is beginning to be a general conviction throughout Europe that the United States will be drawn into war," Bullitt continued. "This conviction is helpful insofar as it may tend to diminish the readiness of Germany to go to war; but we shall find ourselves violently unpopular in both France and England when it becomes clear that we intend to maintain our neutrality."

Bullitt's proposed policy was on the one hand to persuade the French of the truth—which was that the United States would remain neutral—while on the other hand bluffing Germany by hinting at what was not true: that America might intervene on behalf of France and Britain. As to what the United States in fact should do, Bullitt wrote that "I remain as convinced as ever that we should not permit ourselves to be drawn in. I believe that if war starts, the destruction on the Continent of Europe will be so great that, unless we are able to remain strong and relatively untouched, there will be no nation on earth left to pick up the pieces. If we should stay out, we could at least help to keep alive whatever human beings may remain alive in Europe."

As always, Bullitt found time and place for gaiety even as he relayed his somber report. He told the President that Harold Ickes, a widower who had remarried the month before, had visited Paris with his bride on their honeymoon; Bullitt had taken the couple to dinner two nights before. He had also entertained them at his country estate, and then had put them up in a small hotel in Paris where reporters would not find them. "Mrs. Ickes is charming," Bullitt remarked. "How Ickes accomplished that is beyond me."

Then there was the wife of Joseph E. Davies, briefly ambassador to Russia and now the newly appointed ambassador to Belgium. Instead of remaining at her husband's post in Brussels, "she has taken a large house in Paris, ostensibly for one of her daughters, and is having it done over for her own occupancy." An informant had told Bullitt that "she had said to him that she knew she would be bored by Brussels, so she had decided to spend *all* her time in Paris!" Bullitt's comment was: "War will, at least, save me from that."

FDR, NOTING THAT BULLITT was predicting that war might be close at hand, gave little hint of his own thinking—or even of whether he was thinking very much about it at all. "Dear Bill," FDR wrote in reply. "May God in His infinite wisdom prove that you are wrong. I know you share this hope with me."

It was the summer of 1938, and the question was about to be put to the test. In July Walter Lippmann, who despite the move from New York to Washington kept to his regular schedule of travel abroad and discussion with foreign leaders, visited Czechoslovakia, the focal point at the time of Germany's unwanted attentions; afterward he discussed matters with Bullitt. Lippmann had come away from a long meeting with Czech president Edvard Beneš with the impression that Czechoslovakia would resist a German invasion and that Britain and France would come to her aid. If that became clear in advance, Lippmann reasoned, Hitler might not attack.

But Bullitt, like the leaders of Britain and France, was still thinking in terms not of scaring off Germany, but of buying her off. Like them, he believed that Germany would not attack if Czechoslovakia made concessions that were sufficiently enormous.

Bowing to pressure from his country's British and French allies, Beneš on September 5 asked the leaders of the German-speaking party to write down on paper all of their demands, and promised in advance to accept whatever they asked. But acting on Hitler's instructions, Henlein and his colleagues refused to accept even this blank check, and broke off negotiations.

British prime minister Neville Chamberlain flew to Germany to offer one concession after another, but Hitler kept raising his demands as negotiations continued throughout the month of September. But in the course of a shouting, screaming, hysterical speech to a mass audience in Berlin September 26, Hitler, who had made (and broken) similar promises before, denied that he wanted to rule Czechs and pledged that Sudeten Czechoslovakia was the last territorial claim that he would make in Europe.

The British and French governments were determined to take Hitler at his word. At 1 a.m. September 30, Hitler, Mussolini, Chamberlain, and French premier Édouard Daladier, meeting in Munich, signed the pact that permitted Germany to occupy and annex Sudeten Czechoslovakia, together with the entire formidable Czech fortification system. Hitler was disappointed by the capitulation of Chamberlain and Daladier; he had hoped to provoke a war. But his fearful generals—certain that the Allies, protected by the Czech fortifications, would have won the war—were amazed and ecstatic.

Ten days after signing the Munich Pact, Hitler gave orders to his forces to plan the takeover of the rest of Czechoslovakia.

WAVING IN THE AIR the piece of paper that was his agreement with Hitler, Chamberlain exulted to the cheering crowds that had come out in

London to welcome him home: "I've got it!" In Paris on October 1, the day after the Munich Pact was signed, Bullitt went by the home of French foreign minister Georges Bonnet, just back from the signing in Germany, to offer his own congratulations. Bullitt, in the words of his biographers, "appeared . . . with an armful of roses, tears in his eyes, and a 'fraternal and joyous salutation of America' on his lips."

But a couple of days later, on October 3, Bullitt lunched with his close friend Premier Daladier, who disagreed with Bonnet. Daladier told Bullitt that the Munich Pact was a disaster for France. Indeed, said the premier, he had expected that the crowd waiting to welcome his returning airplane had come to lynch him for having signed it. He would not have signed it, he said, if he had had three or four thousand warplanes to back him up. He said that Chamberlain had been duped; that Hitler, despite his promise not to do so, would make new territorial demands in six months; and that France would have to regain a national spirit within the year in order to oppose Germany. In material terms, he believed, what France needed was an effective air force.

Bullitt, who tended to take his views from France's leaders, instantly changed his mind about the European situation. No longer did he believe that Germany was, or could be, appeased: he recognized that new demands would be made on the democracies. He now felt that America should strengthen herself and strengthen France. Fear of Russia was overtaken in his mind by fear of Germany. His new view of the situation was reinforced by Hitler, who publicly proclaimed the need for Germany to rearm further.

Bullitt cabled FDR to alert him to the urgent need for America's rearmament. The President, who may have needed no prompting, proposed a politically astute response to the fears that had been raised by the foreign crisis—and one in line with his primary strategic concern for the security of the Western Hemisphere. He urged the Congress to authorize an additional $300 million for Western Hemisphere defense, a program appealing to isolationists and interventionists alike.

Briefed by French officials, including his old banker friend Jean Monnet, Bullitt caught the next ocean liner to the United States, the *Normandie*. On October 13 he was closeted with FDR at the White House until late into the night. FDR saw that the Munich Pact merely postponed the opening date of the coming war in Europe—and ensured that it would be fought on terms much more favorable to Germany. At a time when the air strength of the United States itself was centered on only nineteen modern bombers, Bullitt urged the President to build thousands of warplanes and somehow supply them to France. No notes were taken, but the meeting was decisive; by bedtime FDR, in a fit of enthusiasm, had decided to produce military aircraft in overwhelming numbers.

The next morning Roosevelt told reporters he would ask Congress to give the army an additional $500 million to be spent on warplanes. He told the War Department to plan a major expansion of the air force. America had the capacity to make only about 1,200 planes a year; but FDR decided the country would build 8,000, 10,000, 15,000, 20,000, or 24,000 a year.* He told the New York *Herald Tribune* that "neither we, nor any nation, will accept disarmament while neighbor nations arm to the teeth."

Bullitt's cable from France, followed by his meeting with FDR on October 13, had been crucial in turning around the American position on what to do about the threat of a new war in Europe. Until October 1938 the American reaction to the threat of war had been to preach and practice disarmament. Now FDR's new policy was rearmament.

Yet Bullitt and Roosevelt had thought nothing through. It is easier to imagine them in their all-night session as college fraternity brothers than as policy planners. For in deciding to ask Congress for money that would be spent entirely on planes, it had escaped their notice that they would also need money for hangars to house the planes, and for airstrips on which the planes could land, and for pilots to fly the planes, and for ground crews to service them, and for fuel to power them.

Such needs as these were drawn to the President's attention when he met with his military chiefs and some of his civilian advisers November 14 and again in late December. Roosevelt told them that the United States needed "a huge air force so that we do not need a huge army." Echoing Bullitt, who echoed Daladier, he asserted that "had we had this summer 5,000 planes and the capacity immediately to produce 10,000 a year . . . Hitler would not have dared to take the stand he did." Too late, the American President and the French premier had come around to the view that Germany would back down before a show of force—which might have been true two or three years earlier, but was not in the cards after Munich.

But Deputy Chief of Staff George Marshall persuaded FDR's intimate adviser Harry Hopkins, and then the reluctant President himself, that designing armed forces to carry out only one strategy—in this case, deterrence through air power—was imprudent. There had to be balance in the buildup of the American armed forces, Marshall argued, for the United States had to be prepared to meet the entire range of possibilities that might arise in future, and therefore unforeseeable, circumstances.

IN A JANUARY 1939 White House meeting with the navy, war, and Treasury secretaries and other administration officials, Bullitt sat next to Roosevelt while the President emphasized his desire to support France in the ongoing European political crisis. Bullitt then stressed the urgency of

---

* All of these were figures mentioned at one time or another by the President in the next year or two.

supplying the French with the Douglas bomber, which incorporated the most advanced American aviation technology. War Secretary Harry Woodring, an isolationist from Kansas and an opponent in any event of rearmament, objected that giving the Douglas to France would be transferring government military secrets to a foreign country.

It would indeed be politically risky to do that, especially as the American public apparently assumed that the large air fleet FDR proposed to assemble was entirely for the use of the United States. In fact, the substantial number of planes the President was talking about were intended by him in large part for France and Britain. Afraid that the army or the navy, if entrusted with administration of his program, would try to keep the aircraft for themselves, he turned the matter over to the reliable Henry Morgenthau. In making his end run around the State Department to recognize Russia in 1933, FDR had put the matter in the hands of Morgenthau and Bullitt; now, to bypass the War and Navy departments, he turned to them again. For Treasury, though, that meant running the risk of taking the blame if what was afoot became known to the Congress or the public.

So when FDR directed Morgenthau to order the release of Douglas aircraft to France, close friend though he was, he replied: "Mr. President, I want this in writing." When Treasury officials then sent letters containing the necessary orders to the White House for FDR's signature, they were returned—unsigned. Bullitt then took a hand in the matter, and secured Roosevelt's signatures: he pushed the reluctant President into taking the responsibility for his directive.

But on January 23 one of the new bombers crashed in California while on a test flight, and it became known that a passenger who died was from the French Ministry of Aviation. The secret therefore was out, and on January 27 the President, through a smoke screen of evasions, admitted that he had it in mind to supply aircraft to France. He then explained and defended his policy in secret to members of the Senate Military Affairs Committee.

But when the press reported that in the secret session the President had argued that "America's security frontier now lay on the river Rhine," FDR denied that he had said it. He had not, but it was a fair description of the views he had expressed. As many have remarked, it was always Roosevelt's practice to lead with somebody else's chin. Now he found himself out front and in an exposed position, and retreated rapidly.

FDR arranged a public press interview to restate simply (he said) the fundamentals of U.S. foreign policy as his administration conceived them to be: "We are against any entangling alliances, obviously"; we are for free trade, peace, and national independence; and "we are in complete sympathy with any and every effort to reduce or limit armaments." The public was reassured, but the President's statements were thoroughly and deliberately misleading. He might "sympathize" with reducing armaments, but was urging Congress to let him build tens of thousands of warplanes. He was not being candid with the American people about his real purposes.

Though historians are unlikely ever to agree as to what were FDR's intentions at any given time, what he had in mind in the autumn of 1938 and the winter of 1939 can be inferred from how he reacted to events. He was told by Bullitt of Daladier's view that Hitler would make new demands within months. The massive aviation production program he suddenly espoused after his all-night talk with Bullitt showed that he had been converted to the Daladier and Bullitt view that with a few thousand military aircraft to back them up, France and Britain could force Hitler to back down. His decision to produce far more planes than the United States could then use shows that FDR proposed to produce those aircraft for the Allies. He intended to supply them to France and perhaps Britain, not to keep them—at least not all of them, and maybe not even most of them—for the United States.

FDR was not thinking of bringing the United States into a war, or at least not into a land war, for he did not propose to strengthen America's skeleton army. Bullitt had infected him with enthusiasm for the notion that airplanes would keep war away from America's shores. It was George Marshall, not the President, who argued that the country should take steps to enable it to wage war if necessary.

So by the winter of 1939 FDR had come to believe that Hitler would make further demands on Germany's neighbors and had to be stopped; that France and Britain could stop him, short of war, if they had enough warplanes; that only the United States could supply them with the quantity of aircraft they needed; and—perhaps most important—that it was in America's interest to supply the European democracies with whatever they needed to take their stand and bring Nazi Germany's expansion to a halt.

# 44

# THE BELL TOLLS

IN ORDER FOR THE UNITED STATES to have been able to back them up, France and Britain would have had to take a stand. But in the winter of 1938–39, that was something they felt no need to do. Proud of his pact with Hitler, Neville Chamberlain sent out Christmas cards picturing the airplane in which he had flown to Munich. On March 9 he told an off-the-record press conference that relations with Germany and Italy were improving, that trade discussions with the German government were about to begin, and that he expected a disarmament conference to convene, perhaps before the end of the year.

Guided by the prime minister, a close political ally delivered a speech the following day—March 10—suggesting that a golden age of peace and prosperity was dawning for Britain and Europe. It may have been on March 10, too, that the political cartoonist of *Punch* finished his drawing for the next issue: it showed John Bull awakening from a nightmare labeled "WAR SCARE" (which is shown flying out the window) with the relieved words, "Thank goodness that's over!" The cartoon was entitled "The Ides of March" and appeared in print March 15, 1939.

As it happened, March 15 was the day that the German army, breaking the Munich Pact, invaded and occupied what remained of Czechoslovakia. Hitler slept in Prague that night, in the fortified castle on the crest of the hill that dominates the city. Once the residence of the ancient kings of Bohemia, it had served until that very night as the palace of the president of what had been the republic of Czechoslovakia.

As a pretext for the invasion, the German government had engineered the secession of Slovakia under pro-Nazi leaders. In turn the secession of Slovakia provided England with an excuse for standing aside. The prime minister admitted to the House of Commons on March 15 that Great Britain, as a party to the Munich Pact, and indeed its prime mover, had "a moral obligation" to come to Czechoslovakia's defense. But, he argued, the secession of Slovakia meant that Czechoslovakia was no longer a nation. Thus, Britain's guarantee of her security "has now ceased to exist" and "His

Majesty's Government cannot accordingly hold themselves any longer bound by this obligation."

IN THE WINTER OF 1939 Chamberlain proposed to send as his new ambassador to the United States Lord Lothian, who as Philip Kerr had headed Prime Minister Lloyd George's secretariat in the First World War. Kerr, who had sympathized with the stated foreign policy goals of Hitler's government all along, was one of the original supporters of the appeasement policy. He now was in the process of changing his mind. In conversations with President Roosevelt that winter, he seemingly took the position that Britain was unable to hold the line anymore against such dynamic expansionist powers as Hitler's Germany, and that Britain's burden of upholding the balance of power in Europe and Asia from now on would have to be taken over by the United States. Roosevelt would have none of it.

"I wish the British would stop this 'we who are about to die, salute thee' attitude," wrote the President afterward. "I got mad clear through and told him"—Lothian—"that just so long as he or Britishers like him took that attitude of complete despair, the British would not be worth saving anyway. What the British need today is a good stiff grog, inducing not only the desire to save civilization but the continued belief that they can do it."

IF THE COUNTRIES of Europe and Asia, one after another, were to let themselves fall into the grip of Germany and her allies without putting up a fight in their own defense, should the United States therefore, as Roosevelt's remarks implied, abandon them to their fate? Grappling with the question in the winter of 1939, Walter Lippmann's restless mind was led to new conclusions. He was always in the immediate intellectual advance guard of his peers, and his twists and turns of opinion were a reliable leading indicator of imminent shifts in the views of his generation in the course of its lifelong foreign policy education.

In 1914–15 Lippmann had believed that America had to stay out of the European war; in 1916–17 he had known that America had to enter it. After the war was over, he had concluded that America should never had gone into it. In 1916–18 he had crusaded for the League of Nations; in 1919 he had urged his fellow Americans to reject it. He had advised Franklin Roosevelt and written in support of him as President, but had voted against him both in 1932 and 1936. Now he turned his protean mind to foreign policy assumptions that he had shared with most other Americans in the 1930s—until the winter of 1939.

It was now Lippmann's view that staying out of foreign conflicts was not the safe and prudent policy he and others had thought it to be. Writing to Thomas Lamont of the Morgan bank, a friend and colleague from Wilson administration days, he warned that "the policy of neutrality and isolation involves the risk which nobody had foreseen until recently, that the victim of the aggression will not only be overcome, but in being overcome will be the ally of the aggressor . . ." so that "a power that had been on our side of the scale will be transferred to the other side."

Thus, in taking back Germany's industrial heartland, the Saar and the Rhineland, and later (in 1938–39) taking Czechoslovakia, with its Skoda armaments works that were among Europe's most important manufacturers of war matériel, Hitler added strength to strength; he had made the Germany of 1936, which could have been defeated by practically anybody in Europe, into the Germany of 1939, which could be defeated by practically nobody in Europe.

And what of Japan? asked Lippmann. By not only vanquishing China, but enlisting China's resources and her hundreds of millions of people into Japanese service, could it now dominate Asia?

And what if France and Britain were overcome by Germany and converted into Germany's vassals in a war against the United States? At the back of Lippmann's mind was the dreaded question of what would happen if Britain's Royal Navy, which ruled the world's oceans and for so long had shielded America from overseas threats, were turned over to German conquerors for use against the United States?

Suddenly it seemed the height of folly to have waited while Germany and Japan seized, devoured, and digested their neighbors one by one. When Germany attacked Czechoslovakia, had she not really attacked the security of Great Britain? If Germany now attacked Britain, would she not be threatening the national security of the United States?

THE WINTER OF 1939 was one of the coldest Europe and the United States had known. The state of international affairs, too, was bleak. Roosevelt, who now believed that he had been wrong, told his cabinet that he had acted in good faith in imposing an embargo on shipments of supplies to the Spanish republic. The fall of Barcelona in January 1939 doomed the Loyalist forces to defeat in the three-year war that had taken almost a million lives. Interior Secretary Ickes bitterly confided to his diary his regrets that the American embargo had helped keep the republic from winning the "fight for her life and the lives of some of the rest of us, as events will very likely prove."

For the conspicuous part played by the armed forces of Hitler's Germany and Mussolini's Italy in bringing about the victory of Francisco

Franco's Nationalist coalition suggested that Franco's regime would be manipulated by Rome and Berlin. Indeed, on March 27, 1939, the day before Franco's troops entered the starving capital city of Madrid and four days before the formal termination of the civil war, Spain adhered to the Anti-Comintern Pact uniting Germany, Italy, and Japan in a common policy. This seemed to confirm that the American, British, and French embargo on aid to the Loyalists had placed a potential enemy in the coming European war on France's vulnerable Pyrenean frontier. Too late, Roosevelt began to suspect that the Loyalist cause in Spain might have been America's cause, too. For that was what the broad spectrum of writers and intellectuals on the American Left were saying: people who voted for Roosevelt but whose views were articulated more often by his wife than by him.

Eleanor Roosevelt had made a career of being FDR's conscience, but in the Spanish affair he had not listened to her or it. A passionate partisan of the Loyalists, she was bitter that he had ignored her views and, typically, blamed herself. To a guest for dinner at the White House, she remarked: "We were morally right, but too weak. We should have pushed *him* harder"—nodding toward her silent, ignored, but unprotesting husband at the head of the table.

Only a few years back, Americans had believed that nothing that happened on the other side of the oceans was of concern to them. Now the writers and artists who often were the first in their midst to sense and express a shift in the intellectual winds were saying just the opposite: that nothing that happens to human beings anywhere can be of indifference to Americans. The view was perhaps most notably phrased in a book published the following year: Ernest Hemingway's novel of the Spanish civil war, *For Whom the Bell Tolls*. The title was from the lines in which John Donne, the seventeenth-century English poet and churchman, reflected on the tolling of bells to signal the death of he knew not whom, writing that "any man's death diminishes me, because I am involved in mankind; and therefore never send to know for whom the bell tolls; it tolls for thee."

IT WAS AS THOUGH a fog had started to lift. Gradually the leaders of the European democracies could see—indistinctly at first through the haze, and only later in clear outline—the hostile armies that were approaching for the attack.

Within a couple of days after the British prime minister had washed his hands of the guarantee to Czechoslovakia, he learned that even ardent Conservatives were appalled. The feeling in Parliament, according to that keen observer Harold Nicolson, "is that Chamberlain will either have to go or completely reverse his policy." Scheduled to speak in public on March 17, Chamberlain discarded his text and prepared another, defending his foreign policy record but finally posing the question of whether Germany and her allies might not be planning to conquer the world.

In the couple of weeks that followed, Chamberlain's ministers, stampeded by a false rumor that Germany was about to attack Romania, attempted to construct a military alliance that would deter Germany by threatening her with a two-front war. Both Poland and the Soviet Union were approached by the British to join the alliance, but as the former refused to ally with the latter, a choice had to be made; Britain chose Poland. Then another false report—this one, that an attack on Poland was imminent— moved Chamberlain to make a rash pledge. Hoping to gain time to put together the alliance that would deter Hitler, the British prime minister told a crowded and cheering House of Commons on March 31 that if, while his negotiations were taking place, Polish independence were threatened and the Poles resisted, Britain and France would come to their aid.

So the line was drawn; and Chamberlain had gambled his career, his government's existence, his country's future, and the peace of the world on his stubborn belief that Hitler would never dare to cross that line.


UNTIL 1939 HITLER'S VICTIMS had submitted unresistingly. Bill Bullitt predicted (on March 23, 1939) that now that would change; he wrote to FDR that "some day someone will have enough guts to pull a trigger and the affair will begin." He added that in France, "everyone believes that war is inevitable and that it will come quickly." War before May 15 was, he reported (on April 4), "possible" but not "certain."

As usual his reports to the President were filled with the anecdotes and gossip that Roosevelt so enjoyed. The French premier had asked for advice on how to increase the national birthrate; Bullitt told FDR, "I do not know quite what to suggest unless it is to have Joe Kennedy transferred to Paris!" And on that subject: "Joe Kennedy phones several times a week to say that he is about to resign. I don't believe for one minute that he will."

Bullitt's views mirrored those of the French politicians with whom he was on intimate terms. "The trouble with Bullitt," FDR complained, "is in the morning he will send me a telegram, 'Everything is lovely,' and then he will go out to have lunch with some French official, and I get a telegram that everything is going to hell."

Passionately committed to the French cause, Bullitt foresaw the need to build an American army that could be sent to Europe and suggested to Roosevelt on March 23, 1939, that "it might be worthwhile to bring back Douglas MacArthur . . . to direct our activities in France." Described by a Polish diplomat as "President Roosevelt's right-hand man in . . . foreign affairs," he acted as go-between in building the French alliance with Poland.

*Time* magazine (March 6, 1939) called him "President Roosevelt's most trusted adviser on foreign affairs."

Joseph Kennedy, his colleague in London, shared the views of the British prime minister almost as much as Bullitt did those of the French. An enthusiastic supporter of Chamberlain and appeasement, Kennedy still believed in 1939 what Bullitt had believed until 1938: that the United States could and should stay out of the coming European war, and that the great danger to Europe was posed not by Nazi Germany, but by Soviet Russia. In February 1939 he cheerfully wrote FDR that "England is on its way" and "that Germany will not attack." His hopeful belief was that Poland should agree to whatever demands Hitler made upon her, so as to allow an unimpeded Germany to invade Russia. But at times he despaired, believing that Britain might be headed for a war she was militarily unprepared to fight. He could not bring himself to follow instructions from Washington that he try to stiffen Chamberlain's resolve.

At a dinner June 14 Walter Lippmann, on a visit to England, mentioned that Kennedy was telling friends that when war came, Britain would be defeated and would make her peace with Germany. Seated next to Lippmann at dinner was Winston Churchill, the Conservative rebel who had lived in the political wilderness, out of office, out of power, and out of favor, throughout the decade of the 1930s.

"No, the Ambassador should not have spoken so, Mr. Lippmann," said Churchill. "He should not have said that dreadful word. Yet supposing (as I do not for one moment suppose) that Mr. Kennedy were correct in his tragic utterance, then I for one would willingly lay down my life in combat, rather than, in fear of defeat, surrender to the menaces of these most sinister men. It will then be for you, for the Americans, to preserve and to maintain the great heritage of the English-speaking peoples. . . ."


BEFORE, DURING, AND AFTER the Czech crisis of 1938, Roosevelt had launched appeals for peace. As German pressures mounted in the Polish crisis of 1939, Roosevelt had Undersecretary of State Welles and Assistant Secretary Adolph Berle draft an appeal, which the President sent to the German and Polish leaders in late August, suggesting that their differences be the subject of conciliation or arbitration, and reiterating the American view that political goals should not be achieved by armed force. Berle's view was that these messages "have all that quality of naivete which is the prerogative alone of the United States. Nevertheless they have to be sent." FDR was conscious of the debilitating confusion as to who was responsible for the outbreak of the First World War, and remarked: "This puts the bee on Germany, which nobody did in 1914."

An editorial in the New York *Herald Tribune* said it well: "Mere pleas, mere appeals to reason, count for nothing. . . . Yet such is the temper of the American people that they are glad the President made his appeals. They would have felt, had he not made them, that perhaps he had over-looked a chance to preserve peace."

The President predicted to Berle that war would break out in Europe September 10. Aware that the Soviet Union was considering which side to join, Roosevelt sent secret messages urging the Russian leaders to throw in their lot with France and Britain. But he was not taken entirely by surprise by the news that Moscow instead had come to an understanding with Berlin: that Nazi Germany and Soviet Russia had negotiated a nonaggression treaty that was signed and announced the night of August 23–24. Its secret clauses divided all of eastern Europe into Nazi and Soviet spheres. Even without knowing those clauses, the world was shocked by the cynicism of Nazis and communists in negotiating a partnership even though each had claimed the ideology of the other was the incarnation of evil.

Chamberlain and Daladier had refused to face the unpleasant truth that the western European democracies needed an alliance with Russia—however despicable her government might be—to stand a chance of defeating Ger-many. So the Soviet Union had gone over to the other side; and Britain and France were left holding a commitment to defend Poland that they could no longer redeem.

Chamberlain and Daladier saw the tragic irony of their position: they would have to go to war on Poland's behalf even though they now knew they could not save her. To Daladier, who seems to have understood that France had to fight Germany someday anyway, this was less embittering than it was to Chamberlain, who saw the coming conflict as pointless: as a war without a purpose. The British leader saw no way out—unless Poland should release the democracies from their commitment to defend her.

Acting on behalf of the Chamberlain government, Kennedy sent a proposal to Washington that the American government should pressure the Poles into surrendering to Germany's demands without a fight. FDR and Secretary of State Hull refused to do that. Acting on his own, Kennedy then persuaded the British government to try to force the Poles to let Cham-berlain and his foreign secretary negotiate with Germany on their behalf, as they had done for the Czechs the year before at Munich. The Poles purposely delayed their reply.

Meeting with the prime minister or the foreign secretary several times a day, Kennedy overflowed with ideas for new concessions that could be made to Germany. He was undeterred by a report from Berlin that Hitler said "it was useless for the British to bother about Poland since he and the Russians had agreed to cut it up." Kennedy's thought was that Hitler might be persuaded to forgo claims to Polish territory in return for one or two billion dollars.

Kennedy, Bullitt, and Roosevelt talked with one another over the telephone all through the August crisis. Historians lack written evidence of what they said to one another. One can guess that Bullitt continued, as he always had, to retail as his own the views of the French premier and France's military chiefs. At least these were views of some sophistication. Those of the brash businessman who served as ambassador in London showed little understanding of the foreign situation; they would serve as an argument against the American practice of filling ambassadorial posts with those whose only qualification for the job is the making of campaign contributions.

Over a game of golf years later, Kennedy gave James Forrestal his version of the Polish crisis. His view was that Britain and France ought simply to have walked away from their guarantee to Poland. Left to themselves, according to Kennedy, that is what they would have done.* Kennedy—much overestimating American influence—said that it was FDR who pushed Britain and France into making a stand, and that it was Bullitt who persuaded FDR to do so. If it had not been for the Americans, France and Britain would have done nothing; Germany, after taking Poland, would have gone on to invade the Soviet Union; and the rest of the world would have been left in peace because (Kennedy indicated, misunderstanding Nazi intentions) Hitler would not have attacked the west European democracies. So that in Kennedy's view, the one person most responsible for the outbreak of the Second World War was not Adolf Hitler but William Christian Bullitt.

TO THE AVERAGE AMERICAN the crisis in Europe still seemed far away. More than 25 million visitors to the New York World's Fair were captivated by the bright prospects of the world of the future. Millions of others, looking back nearly a century to the Civil War, awaited the opening, scheduled for the end of the year, of *Gone With the Wind*, touted as the greatest motion picture of all time. Shirley Temple beguiled the nation in *The Little Princess*.

Even those abroad were unaware of how swiftly the August crisis was racing toward its climax. While American tourists, Franklin Roosevelt's mother among them, continued their leisurely summer travels, German troops massed on the Polish frontier. Bullitt told FDR that "storm warnings

---

* Minutes of the August 23, 1939, meeting of the French cabinet and military chiefs show this to be untrue; the military leaders advised that there was no choice but to go to war over Poland.

are out in Europe," and on August 24 he cabled: "I told your mother . . .
I thought she should return to America today. . . . [S]he agreed and will
leave . . . this afternoon." A couple of days later young John F. Kennedy,
in Germany on a pleasure jaunt, having bought a new German movie camera
and projector, was asked by the Berlin embassy to leave for London with a
secret message for his father: war would commence in one week.

AT TEN MINUTES BEFORE THREE on the morning of Friday,
September 1, 1939, the telephone beside Roosevelt's bed in the White
House rang. He switched on the lights, looked at the time, then reached
over and answered the phone.

"This is Bill Bullitt, Mr. President," said the voice at the other end of
the line. He was calling to report that German troops had invaded Poland
and already had penetrated "deep" into the country.

Roosevelt immediately called the undersecretary and secretary of state,
the secretary of war, and the acting secretary of the navy with the news.
Then he went back to sleep. At 6:30 a.m. the telephone awakened him.
Again it was Bullitt from Paris. His news was that Daladier had told him
that France and Britain were going to war.

So the cease-fire of November 1918 had not brought an end to the
war between Germany and her neighbors; after an armistice of twenty-one
years, the battle to stop the Reich from achieving mastery in Europe—and
after Europe, the world—had resumed.

# PART EIGHT

# WILL AMERICA GET INTO IT AGAIN?

# 45

## REPLAY

*. . . history does in fact repeat.*
—Franklin Roosevelt

ROOSEVELT, MEETING WITH HIS CABINET two days later, told its members about Bullitt phoning him from Europe September 1 with the fateful news.

"An unknown and unknowable destiny yawned before mankind that morning," he said. "Yet, I was almost startled by a strange feeling of familiarity—a feeling that I had been through it all before. But after all it was not strange. During the long years of the World War"—the 1914 war that America had entered in 1917—"the telephone at my bedside with a direct wire to the Navy Department"—for Roosevelt then had been assistant secretary of the navy—"had time and again brought me other tragic messages in the night. . . ."

"I had in fact been through it all before," he concluded. "It was not strange to me but more like picking up again an interrupted routine." Looking into the future, he told the cabinet that what would be distinctive about the days that lay ahead was that they would be "crowded with the same problems, the same anxieties that filled to the brim those September days of 1914. For history does in fact repeat."

Americans of Roosevelt's generation, who throughout the 1920s and 1930s had regretted so deeply what they believed to have been their tragic mistakes in war and peace during the Wilson administration, were about to be granted what mortals rarely are given: they were being allowed to do it over again. They were being given another chance.

And because Americans usually walk away from the past and ignore history, what was unique in the years to come was the extent to which, unlike Americans of any other time, they kept looking over their shoulders. Time and again they looked back. They made decisions and took positions in the light of what they or their counterparts had said or done twenty or twenty-five years before.

SEPTEMBER 1. IN HIS ROOM at the Manila Hotel, Lieutenant Colonel Dwight Eisenhower heard the news of war. Suddenly everything came together for him. He had never wanted to go out to the Philippines with MacArthur, and his tour of duty there had been an unhappy one. His former hero worship of the general had turned to strong dislike—or to something even more than that.*

Eisenhower's great regret was that he had not been able to get overseas in the Great War. The news coming over the radio suggested that he might have a second shot at it; his four-year tour of duty in the Philippines was coming to an end, and he had long before decided that in 1939 he would return to a post in the United States.

Jumping into the elevator, he rode up to the penthouse of the Manila Hotel. "General," he told MacArthur, "in my opinion the United States cannot remain out of this war for long. I want to go home as soon as possible. I want to participate. . . ." MacArthur attempted to dissuade him, but in the end let him go.

So at the last possible moment as the vessels were leaving dock, Eisenhower jumped from MacArthur's ship to Marshall's. In a bit more than a year, Ike would be drafting Marshall's letters and orders to MacArthur.


ROOSEVELT ADDRESSED THE PEOPLE of the United States in a "fireside chat" over the radio on the evening of Sunday, September 3. His subject was American neutrality in the war that had just broken out in Europe. Conscious, as were his listeners, that twenty-five years before, Woodrow Wilson had appealed to Americans to be neutral not just in deed, but also in thought, Roosevelt said: "I cannot ask that every American remain neutral in thought. . . . Even a neutral cannot be asked to close his mind or conscience."

Indeed, the moral difference between the Allies and their enemies was clear in 1939. It had not been in 1914, when supporting the British and French meant also supporting despotic tsarist Russia. Now, in the aftermath of the Nazi-Soviet nonaggression pact of August 1939, despotic Stalinist Russia was on the German side. So the war declared by Daladier and Chamberlain was an unambiguous conflict between democracies and dictators.

Moreover, in 1914 the public was in genuine doubt as to who had caused the war. But there could be no doubt about who started the war of 1939. And in countless pleas, messages, speeches, and proposals of media-

---

* When the relevant portions of his diaries are opened to scholars, it will be interesting to read Ike's comments about his boss.

tions throughout the 1930s, and at the risk of seeming naive, simple, and uncomprehending, Roosevelt had urged conciliation, negotiation, arbitration, and peace. In his fireside chat, FDR reminded Americans that their government had left no stone unturned in its efforts to prevent the war. The government now aimed at true neutrality.

But Americans were also aware that although President Wilson had proclaimed neutrality at the beginning of the Great War, in the end he had sent an American Expeditionary Force overseas. Roosevelt made clear that he was not going to repeat that experiment: "Let no man or woman thoughtlessly or falsely talk of America sending its armies to European fields."

WHEN THE WAR NEWS hit the New York Stock Exchange, the industrial averages soared from 134 to 138, the percentage equivalent of going up more than 100 points today. The 1914 war had brought riches to the United States, and investors bet that the 1939 war would do the same.

It certainly would do so if the President could induce the Congress to revise the Neutrality Acts so as to allow Americans to sell supplies to the Allies on a cash-and-carry basis: the Allies to pay cash, then carry away the goods in their own merchant vessels so that all risk of being torpedoed by German U-boats was theirs.

The public was in favor of the President's proposals. A Gallup Poll taken in October 1939 showed that 62 percent of the population favored extending all aid to the Allies short of war. Selling goods to them was not even extending aid; it was doing good business at a profit.

There were persuasive isolationist as well as internationalist arguments for going along with the President's proposals. The best way "to keep Americans 3,000 miles from the war and keep the war 3,000 miles from Americans," according to Walter Lippmann, was to send war supplies to Britain and France to help them win on their own. For if they were to lose, he thought, America would be compelled to fight. Yet the country was in no position to do so: quarrels with Japan pinned down the American navy in the Pacific; and the United States "could not, would not, and should not send an army overseas."

Appealing to Arthur Vandenberg, the Republican foreign policy leader in the Senate and once a fellow journalist, Lippmann argued that America ran no risks by selling arms to the Allies for cash: that an embargo on financing the Allies and on shipping supplies to them provided the "one effective way of preventing our being drawn into the war." He reminded anybody who needed reminding that in 1917 it had been the attacks on American merchant vessels carrying goods to the Allies that had brought the country into the war. The danger could be averted this time around by ensuring that war supplies were carried by Allied rather than American merchantmen.

Vandenberg had been there himself; he had lived through the same years that Lippmann had. He had been, like Lippmann, a TR supporter who had gone over to Wilson—and in part because he had been convinced by Wilson then, he was not convinced by Roosevelt now. "The story of 1917–18 is already repeating itself," he said. "Pressure and propaganda are at work to drive us into the new World War." And he foresaw that "the same emotions which demand the repeal of the embargo will subsequently demand still more effective aid for Britain, France, and Poland. . . ."

Vandenberg's instincts told him that the United States should either be all the way in or all the way out; the policy of backing the Allies without joining them bothered him. For one thing, he felt they could not stop Germany on their own; if the Germans were to be defeated, the United States at some point would have to come in to do it. Nor was it right to let Britons, Frenchmen, and Poles do all the fighting, for if it really was America's cause they were upholding, Americans should be fighting by their side. But in Vandenberg's view, what was happening in Europe was not America's business; the responsibility of the United States was limited to defending the Western Hemisphere.

Vandenberg frequently took lunch with Robert Taft, who in his brief service in the Senate was already looked to as the intellectual leader of his party. The pedantic and uncompromising Taft, at the top of his class at Yale and Harvard Law, but colorless, passionless, and humorless, and the owl-faced, beetle-browed, and pompous Vandenberg, with his overblown rhetoric and the tendency to violent swings of opinion that made him seem like some vessel in rough seas rolling from starboard to port, were an odd couple of middle western politicians, but together they led the Republican minority in the Senate.

Taft was pro-Ally but antiwar. His wife, Martha, was if anything even more against entering the war than he was. He favored aiding the Allies so that they could win the war without America being drawn into it. He voted for even more rapid production of aircraft than the administration asked.

Taft was at one with Vandenberg in violently distrusting the President. The Republican leaders regarded Roosevelt as devious and opportunistic, and believed he exercised too much power. Imagining him as a war President, they must have been reminded of Wilson's autocratic and one-party government in war and peace in 1917–20.

Even before the outbreak of war, Taft had warned that "we have moved far toward totalitarian government already. The additional powers sought by the President in case of war . . . would create a Socialist dictatorship which it would be impossible to dissolve once the war is over." His strongly held view was that "we should be prepared to defend our own shores but we should not undertake to defend the ideals of democracies in foreign countries." Why try to straighten out the affairs of foreign countries? he asked. If America's New Dealers could not manage the United States, how could they run the world any better?

Several months after the outbreak of war, Taft said: "While I certainly do not consider myself an isolationist, I feel it would be a great mistake for us to participate in the European War. I do not believe that we could materially affect the outcome"—remembering the First World War, in which the United States was not ready to fight until too late in the day— "and I do not believe we have shown any ability to make a peace after the war is over"—for had he not been in Paris in 1919, and believed President Wilson to have made a shambles of the postwar settlement? "In the meantime," he concluded, by going to war "we would certainly destroy democracy in this country."

ROOSEVELT, TOO, remembered Wilson's mistakes, among them his unwillingness to work with Congress or with the other political party. A few days after Germany invaded Poland, the President placed a phone call to South Carolina to ask the help of James F. Byrnes, one of the many senators he had estranged in his efforts to purge "disloyal" Democrats— several of whom were Byrnes's friends—in the 1938 elections. Now Roosevelt moved to make peace.

The President "is preparing to compose his ancient quarrel with Congress," wrote the journalists Joseph Alsop and Robert Kintner, by asking "the Democratic moderate [Byrnes] . . . to share in the Senate management of the embargo repeal. . . ." Byrnes was invited by Roosevelt to a conference in Washington, to be held before a special session of Congress convened. So were other congressional leaders of both parties, and the 1936 Republican presidential and vice-presidential candidates. At the conference Roosevelt was, in Byrnes's words, "conciliatory and persuasive."

The Congress granted the President's request. The neutrality laws were changed. The United States now had a bipartisan strategy for dealing with the crisis in Europe. It was to ensure an Allied victory by selling Britain and France all the weapons they might need, and to do so at a profit and without running the risk that the United States might be drawn into the war.

GEORGE MARSHALL, acting chief of staff of the American army during July and August, became chief September 1, 1939, the day Poland was invaded. While waiting for Quarters Number One at Fort Myer to be ready for occupancy, he had been staying with Colonel George Patton, whose family was away (and who exulted in a letter to his wife: "I have just consummated a pretty snappy move! . . . [H]e and I are batching it. I think that once I can get my natural charm working I won't need any letters from John J. P[ershing] or any one else").

Though Marshall was Pershing's principal protégé, and the old general had campaigned long and hard to ensure that his former aide rose to the top, in the end it had been Harry Hopkins who persuaded Roosevelt to appoint Marshall to the job. But by the time Marshall was sworn in, Hopkins, ill and going through bouts of hospitalization, was not at hand to provide political guidance and to help him develop a close relationship with the President.

By an executive order issued July 5, FDR had positioned himself to take a more direct role in commanding the armed forces; on certain issues the service chiefs were now to report directly to him as commander in chief rather than to the secretary of war or the secretary of the navy. The new system made it all the more important for Marshall to develop an easy working relationship with the President; yet the general's own stern nature made that difficult for him to do.

Unsmiling and unbending, the tall, ramrod-straight general, formal in manner and manners, was disciplined and organized, and was offended aesthetically by his commander in chief, who was none of those things. Ignoring the prompting of Hopkins, Marshall kept his relationship with the President on a professional basis. He did not visit Roosevelt at his Hyde Park or Warm Springs homes; and he refused to laugh at the President's jokes. So he forfeited his chance of influencing FDR the way Hopkins and other favorites did. He left the President to his natural inclinations as a convert to airpower and a big-navy man. FDR had no intention of leading America into a land war, and therefore remained indifferent to the needs of the army.

The War Department, in a state of permanent civil war between Secretary Woodring and Assistant Secretary Louis Johnson—two ambitious politicians, one of them isolationist and the other not, each of whom spent his time seeking to get the other fired—was of no help to Marshall in trying to find political support in the executive department for his plans to develop an effective army.

So Marshall fell back on the help of Senator Byrnes of South Carolina, whom he had known years before in running the CCC program in that state. One of the triumphs that Byrnes made possible for Marshall was obtaining from Congress the power to weed out, or leapfrog, inefficient senior officers.

Marshall was ruthlessly impartial, sparing no friends. Consulting the little black book that he had filled with the names of promising young officers, he brought them forward and put them to the test of varied commands and duties: Dwight Eisenhower, Omar Bradley, Maxwell Taylor, Walter Bedell Smith, Matthew Ridgway, J. Lawton Collins, and others.

Under his guidance original training programs were developed that would make possible the rapid creation of a mass army should the need arise. In doing so he was thinking ahead to contingencies that the country's political chiefs were ignoring.

Similarly the army, planning ahead, looked at the choices that might have to be faced if the United States came into conflict with Japan and Germany at the same time. Army planners reached the conclusion that Germany was the more dangerous, so that priority should be given to the European war.*

America's political leaders in 1939 had grown to manhood in the era of the Spanish-American War, and had lived ever since with the question that the war of 1898 had opened up: whether the United States, in its world policy, should put Europe or Asia first. A few would continue to debate that issue in years to come. But for the most part they were going to allow it to be decided on military grounds—just as President Wilson had left the chief question of his presidency, whether or not to send an American army to fight a land war in Europe, to the discretion of General Pershing.

"Time—time more than anything else" was Marshall's driving obsession, for the great formative experience of his life had been the world war in which the United States had been too late: too late in producing war matériel to be able to supply even its own army, and too late to create an army that could launch a broad offensive of its own.

"We must be prepared the next time we are involved in war, to fight immediately, that is within a few weeks . . . ," the chief of staff wrote to one of his generals. The last time—a year and a half after the United States entered the war—the American commander, Pershing, still had not been ready to order the first American offensive. Marshall believed that Americans would not be given the luxury of waiting so long in the blitzkrieg age.

A naturally taciturn person not given to revealing his private thoughts, he apparently did not reflect, at least out loud, on the curious chain of circumstances that had led him to take up in 1939 what he had left off doing in 1918.

ON SEPTEMBER 3, the day Great Britain declared war on Germany, Winston Churchill was asked to Prime Minister Chamberlain's rooms at the

---

* The first draft of the army's plan was completed in January 1939.

House of Commons. There Chamberlain invited his sixty-four-year-old critic, a pariah in the House of Commons for most of a decade, and one who had been given up long since for politically dead, to join the cabinet in the position he had held at the start of the Great War: First Lord of the Admiralty. Churchill accepted and sent a message to the Admiralty that he would come by later that day.

After an afternoon war cabinet meeting at Downing Street, Churchill, following the route so familiar to him in the great days of his career, crossed Horse Guards Parade to Admiralty House. He made directly for the First Lord's room, which he had not entered since leaving it in disgrace—blamed, perhaps unfairly, for the disastrous Dardanelles expedition in 1915—a quarter of a century earlier. No sooner was he through the door than he rushed over to a cupboard in the paneling and, in the words of his private secretary, "he flung the door open with a dramatic gesture—there, behind the panelling was a large map showing the disposition of all German ships on the day he had left the Admiralty in 1915."

"Where is the octagonal table?" Churchill demanded; he told the naval assistant assigned to him that he wanted it back. The officer dashed off to consult urgently with housekeepers, and before long a remembered piece of furniture was restored to service.

"He also told me," the naval assistant later recalled, "that on the back of the sofa there should be a chart box. It was there with charts in it, which I showed him. He said, 'I thought so. These are the same charts that I used in this room in 1915.' "


A BIT MORE THAN A WEEK LATER, Churchill received a letter from the President of the United States. "It is because you and I occupied similar positions in the World War"—wrote the onetime assistant secretary of the navy, greatly exaggerating the importance of his own position in 1914 compared with Churchill's—"that I want you to know how glad I am that you are back again in the Admiralty." Roosevelt suggested that Churchill should "keep me in touch personally about anything you want me to know about." Churchill obtained permission from Chamberlain and the cabinet to meet FDR's request. Thus began the unprecedented private correspondence between the two public men that brought about, for a time, the first alliance into which the United States had ever entered.

When Ambassador Kennedy asked Roosevelt why he was corresponding with Churchill, the President replied: "I have always disliked him since the time I went to England in 1918. He acted like a stinker at a dinner, lording it all over us. . . . I'm giving him attention now because there is a strong possibility that he will become the prime minister and I want to get my hand in now."

"Your letter," Churchill wrote Roosevelt, "takes me back to 1914 and it is certainly a most unusual experience to occupy the same post fighting the same enemy 25 years later." Emphasizing the link between them, the British leader employed the code name "Naval Person" in his cables to FDR.

THE COURSE OF THE WAR, however, ran differently than it had in 1914, and in ways that at first were startling and then became merely puzzling.

The German attack on Poland was the shock. It was the world's first experience of blitzkrieg, and the Polish army was not equipped either mentally or materially to deal with it. The war pitted 2,000 German aircraft against 600 mostly out-of-date Polish planes that in any event were destroyed on the ground in the first days of the war. So Germany now controlled the skies over Poland, from which fighters and Stuka dive-bombers streaked down to strafe and bomb at will, cutting the lines of transportation and knocking out the communications of the defending forces.

Poland was proud of its horse cavalry, but it belonged to another era and proved no match in mobility for the German mechanized divisions that raced through and behind the lines of the defenders to encircle them. Within days of the invasion the German forces succeeded in shattering the Polish army into isolated pieces. But before Germany could complete her lightning victory, the Soviet Union invaded Poland from the other side and occupied the share of the country that Hitler had agreed (in the nonaggression pact the month before) should go to Russia.

The French high command had hoped the Poles would hold out for months while France mobilized. Poland was nonetheless swallowed up, and disappeared from the map of Europe in less than four weeks. Hitler wanted to turn immediately against France and her allies. He ordered his generals to fall upon the democracies of western Europe in order to render them incapable of resisting the "continued expansion of the German people." He scheduled the attack to begin November 12, 1939.

What puzzled the Western world in the autumn of 1939 was that no such German assault occurred. It is now known that the German army was not really ready for war in 1939 and that its generals were disturbed by Hitler's unrealistically speeded-up timetable. The Polish campaign left in its wake shortages of ammunition and vehicles that could not be supplied, and a breakdown of machinery that could not be repaired, for months to come. Twenty-nine times Hitler set the date for his armies to attack in the west, only to be forced to postpone because the army was not yet ready to roll forward.

Had they known that much of the German army was *hors de combat*, the Allied commanders might have realized that this was their opportunity to attack. Or perhaps they would not have, for it was a common view that the coming of the autumn rains had made military movement impractical. Then, too, as Bullitt reported to Roosevelt, "It is the opinion of the French General Staff that whichever army attacks first the lines of fortifications that now divide France and Germany will be defeated."

An eerie silence hung over Europe. The French called it a *drôle de guerre*—a funny kind of war; the British called it the "Great Bore War"; and old isolationist Senator Borah called it "the phony war." A British war correspondent touring the French front lines wrote: "Across the river a young German was standing in the sun, naked to the waist, washing himself. It annoyed me that it should be possible for him to go on washing calmly there with two machine-guns on the opposite bank. I asked the French sentry why he did not fire. . . . '*Ils ne sont pas méchants,*' he said—they're not bad chaps—'and if we fire, they will fire back.' "

It was difficult for the United States government to know what to make of the situation, especially after Bullitt phoned the State Department November 28 with the news that the Soviet Union was about to invade Finland. Would this be done by prearrangement with Germany? Did the news mean that Russia and Germany were working together? Or did it mean, on the contrary, that the two predators were about to come into conflict? And did the quiet on the western front mean that Germany was going to call off her war against France and Britain? In Washington nobody knew.

Perhaps a world settlement was at hand. In early December 1939 FDR told two of his intimates, Morgenthau and Berle, that he "proposed to make peace next spring on the basis of having everybody produce everything they could; take what was needed; and put the rest into a pool; and let the countries which needed the balance draw it as needed through the cartels."

His apparent assumption was that the war had come about because of economic scarcity, but if he really held that belief, he forgot it soon. A few days later the President was talking of the war as a crisis that was spiritual. It was in his mind to enter into diplomatic relations with the Vatican, a move that might well please Catholic voters in the 1940 elections. He did so in connection with a Christmas message to the pope (December 1939), in which he wrote in high-flown language of his faith in lofty moral values. He sent similar messages to the president of the Jewish Theological Seminary of America and to the president of the Federal Council of the Churches of Christ in America.

Delighted by the prophetic posture he had struck in dealing with the Catholic, Protestant, and Jewish faiths, Roosevelt was restrained only with difficulty by the State Department from communicating in the same elevated tone with the patriarch of the Greek Orthodox faith in Istanbul (the former Constantinople) and with Muslim dignitaries throughout Asia.

Despite the evident pleasure he took in portraying himself as a wise man who sees through the ephemera of wars and politics to the spiritual values that are timeless—and the no less evident political advantage to be gained by appearing so—Roosevelt was not a Wilsonian optimist: "I do not entertain the thought of some of the statesmen of 1918 that the world can make, or we can help the world to achieve lasting peace," he wrote to William Allen White in January 1940. He saw little hope of achieving even the small improvement in the international situation for which he would settle. Influenced perhaps by reports from Bullitt and Kennedy that France and Britain might lose the war, the President wondered whether it would not be worse if they patched together a peace agreement immediately that would fall apart in a few years.

Yet Europeans began to think it was just such a patched-up truce that FDR was seeking, for in March he allowed Sumner Welles to embark on a self-promoting, fact-finding trip to Europe to ask if there were a chance of making peace. The purpose of the Welles mission never was very clear, but it was not what the British government thought it was: an attempt to drive the Allies into coming to some arrangement with Hitler. Sir Robert Vansittart, chief diplomatic adviser to the British government, wrote in a memorandum that "the Prime Minister says . . . that President Roosevelt is ready to play a dirty trick on the world and risk the ultimate destruction of the Western Democracies in order to secure the re-election of a democratic candidate in the United States."

PERHAPS THE MOST IMPORTANT NEWS affecting the approaching American presidential elections was the least noticed at the time: it was the deterioration in the health of Harry Hopkins, the President's closest associate in the domestic management of the New Deal. Hopkins seemed to be the only person FDR could bear to think of succeeding him in the presidency; he had started to groom Hopkins as his candidate, and began in 1938 by appointing him to a cabinet position (as secretary of commerce) to give him political visibility. The President seemed to be sincere in pushing the Hopkins candidacy, though with FDR one never knew for sure.

But Hopkins fell ill with everything from flu and nutritional disorders to cancer, and by September 1939—when Roosevelt received the news of

Germany's invasion of Poland and saw the war crisis of 1914 repeating itself—Hopkins was given only about four weeks to live.

So as Roosevelt moved to try to lead America unharmed through the world crisis, he was left with only one candidate to back for the Democratic presidential nomination in 1940: himself. Of course, he did not admit that to anyone.

# 46

# FDR's New World Strategy

THE WORLD STRATEGY that Roosevelt had developed in 1939 and with which he entered 1940 rested on the assumption that given sufficient supplies, Britain and France eventually could win the war in Europe. It was a reasonable assumption and one that was held widely. If it held good, then FDR could pursue a foreign policy that allowed him to have it not merely both ways, but all ways, in a presidential election year.

The American public was pro-Ally but still antiwar, and the President's policy of equipping Britain and France to defeat Germany on their own was calculated to satisfy both of those not necessarily compatible feelings—while at the same time accomplishing long-standing domestic policy objectives in creating jobs and wealth. Indeed, as stock price movements on the New York Stock Exchange had anticipated, rearmament in the end would eliminate the problems in the American economy that the New Deal had never been able to solve.

IN THE WINTER OF 1940 Kennedy and Bullitt found themselves on vacation in the United States at the same time. Privately Kennedy had grown to have a low opinion of Bullitt ("He is . . . rattlebrained. . . . His judgment is pathetic and I am afraid of his influence on F.D.R. because they think alike . . ."), but had continued to maintain an outward show of cordiality.

Learning that Bullitt was giving an interview to Joseph Patterson, owner of the New York *Daily News*, and *News* writer Doris Fleeson, Kennedy came by. He was a friend of the two journalists, and interrupted their conversation with Bullitt to interject views of his own. Kennedy violently denounced Roosevelt, and when the journalists left, Bullitt told him he was being disloyal and should not speak that way in front of the press. Bullitt later informed Ickes that "Joe said he would say what he god-damned pleased before whom he god-damned pleased"—to which Bullitt had replied that Kennedy was "abysmally ignorant on foreign affairs" and should keep his mouth shut. Bullitt told Ickes that he would never speak to Kennedy again.

IN THE SPRING OF 1940, as Britain and France continued to quarrel about how to respond to the Soviet threat in Finland, the German war machine sprang to life. On April 9 Nazi forces invaded Norway and Denmark, overrunning both countries swiftly and providing a foretaste of wars of the future: the Oslo and Stavanger airfields were captured by the first paratroop attacks ever mounted.

In Washington on the night of April 10, after the United States had received the news from Europe that Denmark had surrendered, General Marshall attended a dinner to which Senator Byrnes had invited him and a handful of Senate leaders. The suggestion had come from South Carolina financier Bernard Baruch, who was closely associated with Byrnes. Baruch had told Marshall that "the Army has never gotten its real story over" and had suggested that Byrnes arrange the meeting.

Marshall was desperate. He could not obtain the money to build his army. Congress would not provide the sums needed, and the President, whose strategy did not envisage the need for an army, seemingly took no interest in the matter. All night and into the morning Marshall told the senators at the Byrnes dinner of the shortages the War Department could not fill. Marshall told them: "I feel culpable. My job as Chief of Staff is to convince you of our needs and I have utterly failed. I don't know what to do."

A Colorado senator, Alva Adams, a leader of the Democratic party in the Senate, made a decision for himself and the others: "You get every God damn thing you want," he said.

Several weeks later Marshall testified before a Senate subcommittee that "I am more of a pacifist than you think. I went through one war and I do not want to see another." Missouri senator Harry S Truman responded: "General, I think that all of us who were in it feel that way."

On May 10 German forces, overshadowed by a sky dark with their military aircraft, swept into and through the Low Countries of Holland and Belgium. France's vulnerable northern flank—from Montmédy, below the Ardennes forest, where the fortified Maginot Line ended, all the way across to the English Channel—lay exposed.

As news of the German victories was received at the War Department in Washington, Marshall told Treasury Secretary Morgenthau that it was terrifying how much it would cost to buy the military equipment the United States needed. "I don't scare easily," Morgenthau replied. The immediate requirement, said Marshall, was for twice the yearly appropriation the President had asked in January, adding that the very thought of the dollar figure "makes me dizzy." Morgenthau said: "It makes me dizzy if we don't get it."

On May 13 Morgenthau brought along Marshall to see the President. FDR now said that the United States would build not 10,000 or 25,000, but 50,000 airplanes a year. He turned down the request Morgenthau had made on the army's behalf and refused to hear Marshall, claiming, "I know exactly what he will say." Enraged, Marshall lectured the President point by point on the deficiencies in the primitive American defense program. Subdued and impressed, the President told Marshall to come back the next day to talk things over.

THE WAR BROUGHT LEADERSHIP CHANGES throughout the Western world. In France in March, Daladier was replaced as premier by Paul Reynaud, who for years had preached resistance to Nazi Germany. In England in May, Chamberlain was succeeded by Winston Churchill. In his correspondence with FDR, "Naval Person," having left the Admiralty to become prime minister, now styled himself "Former Naval Person."

In the United States a surge of feeling for the Allies upset earlier calculations as to the political terms on which the presidential campaign would be fought: it had looked like a contest between a Republican isolationist and a Democratic internationalist, but did not turn out that way.

In 1938 James Farley, the canny political professional who served as chairman of the Democratic National Committee, echoed the opinion of Washington insiders in predicting that the Republicans "will undoubtedly nominate Senator Vandenberg for the presidency in 1940." But after the 1938 elections Vandenberg had to divide the isolationist vote with others. A May 1939 Gallup Poll showed New York district attorney Thomas E. Dewey ahead; next came newly elected Senator Taft and Vandenberg in what was close to a tie. Still, in 1940 the columnist Drew Pearson quoted Joseph Kennedy as naming Vandenberg his "favorite Republican candidate" for the presidency; Kennedy said that he would "back Arthur against half the Democratic candidates."

But Republican voters were looking for new faces, and Arthur Vandenberg resembled too closely a caricature of an old-fashioned senator. Journalist Dorothy Thompson remarked that "Senator Vandenberg simply does not speak the language of anybody under the age of 40 in this country."

Dewey, an attractive thirty-eight-year-old prosecutor from New York who had earned a national reputation for his crusade against organized crime, held a large lead in the polls from the start. He doomed Vandenberg's candidacy by beating him in the Wisconsin and Nebraska primaries of April 1940. Dewey's campaign was well financed and organized, and he held on to a commanding lead over Taft. But in the shadow of the European war, Dewey, with no experience of political office or foreign affairs, suddenly looked much too young to be President; and his isolationist views increasingly alienated the internationalist-minded eastern seaboard bankers, law-yers, and businessmen whose candidate he had been.

The emergence of Wendell Willkie as the Republican candidate was one of the most astonishing stories in modern American political history. Willkie, forty-eight, a world war veteran, was an attorney from Indiana who had made a success as a Wall Street utility holding company executive. He had been a Democrat, was not a politician, and was imbued with a pure Wilsonian vision: his first quarrel with FDR's politics was with Roosevelt's abandonment of support for the League of Nations.

Willkie had outgrown the hometown girl he had married as a young man, and for years had kept company with actresses, models, and showgirls. That phase ended in late 1937 when he met Irita Van Doren, book editor of the New York *Herald Tribune.* She became the only woman in his life, and she edited him as though he were one of the book reviews submitted to her: polishing him, giving him style, cutting out flaws, sharpening him.

Willkie had won headlines through the years for his long battle (on behalf of the utility company he headed) against what he pictured as the antibusiness tendencies of the New Deal. Propelled into national promi-nence by an inspirational article he wrote for *Fortune* magazine and by an April 9, 1940, appearance on a radio quiz show, "Information Please," in which he captivated a mass audience, Willkie's cause caught fire. He worked something in the nature of religious conversions: people who met him sud-denly *believed.*

Taft was still tipped by the professionals to win on the third or fourth ballot. But on June 2, 1940, Taft attended a dinner party given by Ogden Reid, publisher of the New York *Herald Tribune,* a leading voice of Repub-licanism, where he was drawn into a shouting match with Dorothy Thomp-son and others on the subject of the European war. Thoughts that he might not be totally unacceptable as a nominee went out the window. Willkie, at the same dinner, worked his magic on the other guests.

Walter Lippmann, who in the past had admired Taft, revised his opin-ion in light of the European war. He wrote that Taft "has all the limitations of Neville Chamberlain, the same complacency, the same incapacity to fore-see, the same apathy in action. . . . [T]o nominate him now would be to invite for the nation a disaster . . . [and] for Mr. Taft a tragic ordeal."

Lippmann was no kinder to the front-runner, Dewey. As the Repub-licans were about to convene, he wrote: "For eighteen months the Repub-lican party has been walking in its sleep. At no one of the critical junctures of this period has the party understood the situation or proposed measures to deal with it or offered the country positive leadership. . . . One can, I think, search the speeches of Mr. Taft and Mr. Dewey, and search them in vain, for any evidence of foresight as to what has happened, for a single proposal which was sought, in advance of the Administration, to strengthen the national defense. The speeches of Messrs. Taft and Dewey during these critical months make Mr. Neville Chamberlain seem like a far-sighted and strong statesman."

Lippmann's friend Thomas Lamont, who had connections with businesses and banks all over the country, used his network on Willkie's behalf. Twenty-eight-year-old Wall Street lawyer Oren Root sent out a sort of chain letter (each asked the recipient to send out fifteen more) asking pledges of support for Willkie, and starting with mailings to Yale and Princeton alumni, wound up three weeks later with 200,000 pledges. Willkie clubs sprung up all over the country.

Willkie made a virtue of having no campaign organization. He had no floor manager at the Republican National Convention in Philadelphia at the end of June. But with thousands of spectators in the galleries shouting "We want Willkie!" and with Vandenberg unable to hold even his home state of Michigan for himself or for Taft, the nomination went to Willkie on the sixth ballot—the only spontaneous, grassroots candidacy that anyone could remember ever having succeeded.

The novelty of it distracted attention from something else that was remarkable: the profound shift in sentiment within the until-then isolationist Republican party. The party nominated an internationally minded figure from the Atlantic seaboard for the first time since 1916. The battle for the nomination had not been, as had been expected, between a middle westerner and an easterner, but between two easterners: New York lawyer Dewey, who led on the first three ballots, and New York lawyer Willkie, who took the nomination away from him by leading on the next three. The new majority in the Republican party was internationalist*; it had been willing to nominate Dewey only so long as foreign policy was not an issue, and when the European war came to the fore, it dumped Dewey and gave the nomination to Willkie instead.

After winning the nomination, Willkie was contacted by Dewey's foreign policy adviser John Foster Dulles, the New York lawyer who was one of the inner circle of four running the Dewey campaign. Dulles offered his services, and those of his brother Allen, in advising on foreign policy and in preparing a statement on American foreign policy.

Dulles was considered a fellow isolationist by Bob Taft, his friend since young manhood, but in fact he was closer to holding a pro-German position. His legal career in important part consisted in representing companies (Solvay, International Nickel, Consolidated Silesian Coal and Steel) that were partners of German companies in cartels. He blamed the outbreak of war on the refusal of Britain and France to let Germany make changes peacefully.

---

* And remained so. For the next two decades, delegates for whom the 1940 choice would have been between Dewey and Willkie beat those for whom it would have been between Taft and Vandenberg.

While acting as Dewey's foreign policy expert, he denied (March 1940) that the war "involved a great moral issue, with right wholly on one side of the Allies and wrong wholly on the side of Germany."

Willkie thanked Dulles for his offer of advice and said he would call him—but never did. He had taken the nomination away from people of Dulles's political persuasion. The shift within the Republican party, and the nomination of a candidate at least as pro-Ally as was FDR, was a foreign policy gift to Roosevelt; between June and November 1940 the President would be much freer politically to help Britain, if he chose to do so, than he would have been had Taft or Vandenberg been his opponent.


WHILE TAFT, Vandenberg, Dewey, and Willkie were battling for the nomination, the German armies that had swept through the Low Countries on May 10 were moving forward with terrifying speed. In the six weeks that followed, they changed the face of Europe.

Generals on both sides had estimated it would take nine days for the Germans to cross Belgium and reach the Meuse, but the tank commander General Heinz Guderian did it in two. Crossing the river on May 13— south of where the French had anticipated an attack—he took them by surprise, unnerved them, and broke through their lines. Surprising them again by turning west, and ignoring orders from superiors including Hitler himself to pause, Guderian's legions roared 135 miles across northern France to the Atlantic in a week, encircling the entire British, Belgian, and northern French armies, and separating them from their supply bases as well as from the main French armies to their south. The British Expeditionary Force was down to its last rations; in a few days the troops would begin to starve. Meanwhile, the Germans were poised to win the race to the English Channel ports and cut off the British from their island homeland by standing between them and the sea.

On May 25 a British officer attached to the French high command reported to London "that the French were very downhearted and did not mean to stay in the war." The next day Premier Reynaud told Churchill "that the war could not be won on land" and that Marshal Philippe Pétain, the elderly general who had joined the government, might insist on suing for an armistice. Then Belgium surrendered.

The British cabinet discussed whether Hitler might agree to make peace on terms that England could accept, with Churchill angrily telling Foreign Secretary Halifax that it would be a fatal mistake even to inquire. Churchill asked his military chiefs whether the British Isles could hold out alone. They said yes, even though his question was whether it could be done with only a navy and an air force, for he assumed that the army, trapped on the Continent, would be destroyed. It was an assumption shared by all. "London people cried openly in the buses, in the streets, for the English army which was lost," a young writer later remembered.

Churchill's government decided to save what it could of the British Expeditionary Force, which had retreated to Dunkerque, a French town on the North Sea coast. After the port of Dunkerque was destroyed by German bombers, Allied troops lined up on a beach ten miles long to be ferried out to sea. With German forces holding back to regroup, a motley armada of about 500 civilian-manned British vessels—sailboats, river ferries, trawlers, and fishing smacks—crossed the narrow seas from England to join about 250 vessels of the Royal Navy in saving nearly all 200,000 British soldiers, and some 140,000 French and Belgian, from the wreckage of Europe.

The tragedy of the evacuation was that 150,000 French troops were left behind. The long-term effect of the evacuation was to drive a wedge between France and Britain emotionally and politically, as each in years to come blamed the other for having abandoned the common cause. Its immediate effect was to separate the Allies physically so that the German high command could deal with them one at a time, and plan to finish with France by the end of spring and with Britain by the end of summer.

Salvation now could come only from the New World. Harold Laski, the left-wing British author and teacher, wrote from England on June 10, 1940, to his old friend Felix Frankfurter in Washington, urging Americans to organize in time. "Make them learn the lesson a million of us are going to die for, because Chamberlain would not learn it," he wrote; for "unless you learn the lesson, your fate will be no different from that which threatens us. . . . [I]f you do not get ready now, you will have your Dunkirk too; and were that to come, there would be no prospect for the sons of men. . . ." He ended on a distinct note of farewell: "My America has been a great America. I hope all of you who love it, will do all in your power to keep it a great America. Then, one day, the world's great age may indeed begin anew."

On June 10, too, there appeared a syndicated newspaper article by Walter Lippmann, a close friend and colleague of Frankfurter's from the days of the Great War, who realized suddenly that it was the failure to understand the earlier conflict that had blinded his contemporaries. He charged that the reason Americans had misunderstood the significance of what was happening in the 1939–40 European war was that they had not comprehended why the United States had entered the world war in 1917. They had been "duped by a falsification of history" and "miseducated by a swarm of innocent but ignorant historians." Reminding himself of what he had written in 1917, he explained that Britain's independence and Anglo-American control of the Atlantic Ocean were indispensable elements of

America's security. That was why the United States in 1917 could not have allowed German U-boats to cut off what Lippmann had termed "the Atlantic highway," and it was why the United States in 1940 could not allow the British Isles to fall into German hands.

Even as Lippmann's article was being read across America, Britain was coming closer by the day to becoming isolated. France and her army were disintegrating. Soon after Dunkerque, Reynaud's government declared Paris an open city and fled the capital for Tours and then Bordeaux, supposedly to make a stand, though the supposition proved unwarranted. Reynaud, as Churchill reported to Roosevelt, "has a young general de Gaulle who believes much can be done"; but most others no longer held any such belief.

With a courage bordering on rashness, the British prime minister continued flying to France to attend meetings with French officials. On June 12 he wrote Roosevelt that he had told the French government "we thought Hitler could not win the war or the mastery of the world until he had disposed of us which has not been found easy in the past and which perhaps will not be found easy now. I made it clear to the French that we had good hopes of victory and anyhow had no doubts whatever of what our duty was."

But on June 16 Reynaud resigned as premier, and his successor, Marshal Pétain, was determined to surrender. It was a stupefying end to the battle for France: Roosevelt had thought Germany might well lose, and not even Hitler had imagined that Germany would win in a mere six weeks. German superiority in numbers had not been great enough to account for what had happened; indeed, it is not clear that the Germans *had* superiority in numbers. Most of the world—which had thought the French army the most powerful in the world, and had expected another inch-by-inch war that would last four years until it ended in an Allied victory—could neither comprehend the speed and nature of the disaster nor understand how it had occurred.

The rout of the French army left Ambassador Bullitt with a personal mission: the protection of Paris. On June 8 he had ordered twelve submachine guns with ammunition to be installed in the American embassy; and the following day he announced that he would not leave Paris to go southward with the rest of the diplomatic corps and the government. He told Reynaud "that no American Ambassador in history had ever left Paris" and that he had no intention of being the first to do so. He decided to act, with the approval of the French government, as the "guardian of the civil authority" in arranging peaceful German entrance to the city and in attempting to save Paris from possible destruction.

The State Department's view was that Bullitt's job was to accompany the French government, and Secretary Hull wanted to order him to do so. But years before, Bullitt in conversation with FDR had imagined a situation in which German armies might enter Paris; he had asked the President not to let the State Department order him to leave the city, saying that he would be forced to disobey such an order.

The President kept his word. "You said you would see to it that I should not receive such an order and I am grateful to you for remembering," Bullitt cabled Roosevelt June 12. "My deepest personal reason for staying in Paris is that whatever I have as character, good or bad, is based on the fact that since the age of four I have never run away from anything however painful or dangerous when I thought it was my duty to take a stand. If I should leave Paris now I would be no longer myself."

The German army marched into Paris early the morning of June 14. The news sent a stab of pain through the many Americans, including hundreds of thousands of veterans of Pershing's army, to whom Paris meant their youth. In Washington, in a scene significant only in that it was occurring in so many other places, Librarian of Congress Archibald MacLeish (who in 1935 had written, "I should do everything in my power to prevent the United States going to war under *any* circumstances") was found at his desk in tears. The next day he lunched with Interior Secretary Ickes and urged that America declare war.

Bullitt stayed in Paris for only about two weeks after the Germans entered. Having helped to arrange an orderly transfer of authority to German military officials, there then was little left for him to do. He cabled Washington repeatedly to call attention to the plight of the refugees who clogged the paths and highways of Europe in hopeless attempted flight from the Nazis; he also reported that from Paris alone a million more had taken the road south, where nothing awaited but starvation. But Washington and the Red Cross did nothing, and Bullitt pleaded in vain with Hull: "There are now six million persons in southwestern France who will die unless American aid for them is organized immediately."

Bullitt did not realize that he had disappointed FDR. By failing to follow the French government southwest to Bordeaux, he had forfeited the last chance to exert America's full influence on the cabinet to keep France in the war. Just as Joe Kennedy had not followed FDR's orders to stiffen the Chamberlain government's resolve to fight, so had Bullitt—in Washington's view and in that of General de Gaulle—not gone the last mile to keep the Reynaud government in the war.

Moreover, FDR, whose first priority was the security of the Western Hemisphere, saw French West Africa in enemy hands as a dagger pointed at South America. His policy was to win the friendship of General Maxime Weygand, the French commander in chief in Africa, so as to keep French Africa from being used against the Americas. Robert Murphy, of Bullitt's embassy staff, worked at winning over Weygand; but it was a task that Roosevelt felt Ambassador Bullitt should be doing himself.

In mid-July Bullitt left Lisbon for the United States. He expected to be named secretary of war or secretary of the navy, the two positions that FDR had offered him. But by the time he reported to the President, the political situation had changed.

IN PART it may have had something to do with the President's health. A few months earlier—in February—Bullitt (on leave from Paris), Roosevelt, and Missy LeHand had an intimate dinner together in the White House in the course of which FDR reportedly collapsed. It was, of course, hushed up. But a physical attack—if that is what it was—often leaves an emotional legacy of mood changes, and Roosevelt became moody about Democratic politics.

His candidate for the presidency, Harry Hopkins, had been eliminated from the race by ill health, and Roosevelt really had no second choice. He had grown to dislike his party, with its backward-looking southern Bourbons, its corrupt big-city bosses, and its big-business interests—a coalition that had named the Democratic party's 1924 and 1928 nominees and that would name its 1940 nominee if he stood aside and let it happen.

As feudal barons had defied their kings during Europe's Middle Ages, so the powerful lords of the Senate—of both parties—defied the White House. Roosevelt's attempt to defeat Democratic senators who opposed him had failed in 1938, but in 1940 he made another ill-judged try: he seemed to back a candidate against Missouri's Senator Truman, who was seeking a second term. Truman had provided FDR with at least one important victory on a crucial vote in the Senate. Moreover, he was a champion of small business against the corporate giants that Roosevelt opposed. But he also (though personally honest) had been the candidate of a corrupt Kansas City political machine; perhaps for that reason, Roosevelt preferred Truman's opponent. Truman was popular with fellow senators, and Jimmy Byrnes had Bernard Baruch contribute $4,000 toward his election—which proved to be half of his entire campaign fund. It was a close race, but Truman won and Roosevelt cannot have been pleased.

But what mostly must have contributed to putting FDR into a strangely dark mood was that the props had been kicked out from under his strategy for staying out of the world crisis. His assumption that the Allies would fight on to victory was jolted by the fall of France. Abandoned by her ally, England continued to defy Germany, but one did not need to be as defeatist as Ambassador Kennedy to fear that she could not hold out for long. On June 27 Marshall and other army and naval planners advised Roosevelt to send no further military supplies to Britain since her survival was uncertain and whatever was sent her might fall into German hands once England was overrun. In July 1940 FDR sent a special envoy, William J.

Donovan, to Britain to report whether she could and would endure. Later he sent a team of military officers. He knew Kennedy's views, but wanted a second opinion—and then a third.

THE FALL OF FRANCE in 1940 either marked or made a revolution in world affairs. Global politics were turned upside down. All bets were off; all reckonings had to be figured again from scratch.

Since sometime in the seventeenth century, events had been dominated by the ambitions and actions, rivalries and alliances, wars and diplomatic combinations of France and Great Britain: the one supreme* on land; the other, at sea. Whether as friends or enemies, whether fighting alongside or against each other, they had set the course of history and politics. The United States was born out of the tension between the two great European powers; and the historical era of their predominance was the only international environment the country ever had known.

When Pétain surrendered to Hitler, this long-standing structure of world politics disintegrated. New powers linked to one another—Nazi Germany, Fascist Italy, imperial Japan, and communist Russia—stood poised to achieve mastery in the world unless somebody stopped them.

FDR had not intended to be a foreign policy President, let alone a war president, when he took office in 1933. He had not intended to involve his country in the conflicts of the outside world; his generation had explored that route in the First World War and had learned, to their cost, where it led.

The collapse of France changed Roosevelt's calculations. It was the decisive foreign policy event in his presidency, for before it occurred, he had seen no need to bring the United States into the war. After it happened, however, he saw no way to keep America out of it. The magnitude of the German triumph was such that it was inconceivable Britain could come back to win on her own. The best that could be hoped for was that she could stay in the fight until the president elected in November could somehow induce an unwilling American public to join in it, too.

FDR still believed (as did Churchill) that the war could be won solely by airpower—that is to say, by bombers. He did not believe that it would be necessary to send U.S. armies overseas. In campaigning for the presidency, he was not being entirely untruthful in saying he would not send American boys to die on foreign battlefields, for he did not intend to do so. But he did mean to fight Nazi Germany, and was convinced that to bring the

---

* Though France had lost the 1870–71 war to Prussian-led Germany, she reversed its results by winning the 1914–18 war against Germany.

country around to his views, he would need to make new appointments.

Taking a dim view of his party, his Congress, most of his cabinet colleagues, and all of the candidates who proposed to take his place, FDR, who already had decided to carry on himself, decided to do so with a new team.

# 47

## FDR's NEW TEAM
## AND NEW TERM

ON MAY 10, the day Germany invaded the Low Countries, Harry Hopkins dined with the President and his wife. He felt too ill to return home, and at the urging of the Roosevelts, spent the night at the White House. He stayed on. He left the White House only three and a half years later, and never recovered.

His health shattered, Hopkins no longer harbored personal ambitions. He devoted his remaining years and energies to FDR. He spent all his waking hours with the President or acting for him; he served as Roosevelt's other self, looking, listening, speaking, and (at terrible cost to his frail body) traveling for the even less mobile FDR.

Hopkins knew nothing of foreign policy or military affairs, but had a practical and inquiring mind and was briefed by Roosevelt. From the middle of 1940 on, in pursuing world war and world peace, the Roosevelt story became the story of Roosevelt and Hopkins.


EVER SINCE THE MUNICH PACT at the end of 1938, Roosevelt had been thinking of forming a coalition government to face the war threat. As a member of the last Democratic administration, he had seen for himself what disasters Woodrow Wilson had brought about by trying to direct and inspire a war effort—which, in order to succeed, necessarily had to be a *national* effort—while presiding over a one-party government that inevitably was perceived as partisan.

In December 1939 the post of secretary of the navy fell open, and FDR made his first move in the direction of coalition by offering it to Frank Knox, owner of the Chicago *Daily News* and Republican candidate for vice president in the last elections. Knox said that if the time ever came when he could accept such an offer, he would want a Republican named as secretary of war, too—preferably William J. Donovan, war hero, Wall Street lawyer, progressive New York Republican, and law school classmate of

Roosevelt's.* But Knox told the President that the time was not yet ripe for him to join the cabinet.

So Roosevelt appointed the acting navy secretary, Charles Edison, to the post. When Edison turned out to be inadequate, Roosevelt, who hated to fire anyone, arranged for him to be nominated governor of New Jersey to be rid of him. So the job was open, and FDR offered it to Bullitt, who accepted and expected to be sworn in after returning from France in the summer of 1940.

That left the War Department with its paralyzing feud between isolationist Secretary Harry Woodring and internationalist Assistant Secretary Louis Johnson, to whom FDR had promised the succession once Woodring somehow could be removed. Roosevelt also had offered the War Department job to Bullitt.

The situation, already complex, became more complicated still as a result of initiatives by private citizens. Moved by the war news from Europe, individual Americans who held no political office but had become impatient with the President's caution in responding to the overseas threat prepared to take matters in hand.

Wall Street lawyer Grenville Clark had been a class ahead of FDR at Harvard. They had started in law practice together in the first decade of the century: both had been employed as law clerks by the same Manhattan firm, and at the same time. Clark had achieved fame early by running the TR-inspired preparedness movement—the Plattsburg Movement—during the early years of the Great War, before the United States entered it. Now he took the lead in lobbying for military conscription: the draft.

To accomplish their program, Clark and the friends with whom he met at the Harvard Club decided to have their own proconscription candidate named secretary of war. Their candidate, perhaps the only person with the stature and leadership qualities to get such a program through Congress, was elder statesman Henry Stimson, former Republican secretary of war and secretary of state. Stimson was of an age (seventy-two) when he might require considerable assistance in administering his department, so Clark and his friends hit on the idea of pushing a two-man "ticket": Stimson for secretary and Judge Robert Patterson for assistant secretary: both ex-Plattsburg trainees who had served on the western front. Clark enlisted the help of Stimson's former protégé, Felix Frankfurter, now a Supreme Court justice but still one of FDR's political advisers. Frankfurter, who always had been devoted to Stimson, took the matter in hand. The President was persuaded, and on June 19 finally induced Woodring to resign.

But before contacting Stimson about War, FDR phoned Knox to renew

---

* Though a Republican, Donovan performed foreign fact-finding missions for FDR even before joining the government on a full-time basis.

his invitation for Navy. Knox had worked for Vandenberg's Michigan newspaper and had been associated with the Hearst press, but FDR liked him immensely and now offered him his choice of Navy or War. Knox picked Navy. So FDR did give War to Stimson and, eventually, Patterson.* The appointment of these outstanding national figures from the Republican party strengthened FDR with both the voters and the Congress.

Stimson and Knox recruited outstanding staffs. As his undersecretary, Knox chose Wall Street investment banker James Forrestal of the investment banking house Dillon Read, an ex-Plattsburg trainee who had failed to get an overseas assignment in 1918 and was eager to serve.

Forrestal was contacted on the issue of aircraft production by his close friend, Wall Street banker Robert Lovett of Brown Brothers Harriman, a navy flier in the Great War. Lovett said the government was submitting its orders to what in effect was a handcraft industry, and should instead have airplanes made by the automobile companies, who alone knew how to mass produce. Lovett went to work on the matter at War, eventually becoming a special assistant secretary. Another of Stimson's recruits was former Plattsburg man and Wall Street lawyer John McCloy, who had become an expert on the subject of First World War German intelligence in the course of a complex lawsuit. Then there was Harvey Bundy, a lawyer who had worked for Stimson at State in the waning days of the Hoover administration, and who in Wilson days had been, alongside Walter Lippmann and Felix Frankfurter, a lodger at the "House of Truth."† Another recruit was George Harrison, former president of the New York Federal Reserve.

Of the six men at the top of Stimson's department—Stimson himself, Patterson, Bundy, Harrison, Lovett, and McCloy—two had clerked for Justice Holmes, three were Plattsburg veterans, four were from the Yale secret society Skull and Bones, five were Harvard Law, and all six were Republicans from the financial districts of New York and Boston. War and Navy had become a congenial Republican government within a government, staffed by a body of capable men who had gone to the same schools, belonged to the same clubs, and had done business with one another all their adult lives.

CONSIDERING THE QUANTITY and quality of the people who left their businesses and banks and law firms in the summer of 1940 to temporarily work with or permanently join the Roosevelt administration, it seems all the more curious that the President gave no sign that his government would continue beyond the end of the year. FDR played with his

---

* In the summer of 1941 Donovan was named to create and head a new intelligence agency that proved to be a forerunner of the CIA. So of those whom FDR was going to appoint secretary of war, only Bullitt and Louis Johnson (fired as assistant secretary to make way for Patterson) were without jobs.
† See page 133.

stamp collection and spent much of his time planning what he and his friend Harry Hopkins would do in private life. The two of them would publish a small newspaper or found a college or run a fishing resort in the Florida Keys or open a hot-dog stand; such at least was the impression conveyed by the playwright Robert Sherwood, the biographer of the two men.

Nobody knows exactly when FDR decided to defy precedent and run for a third term, nor even when he admitted to himself that he had made up his mind. In early July 1940 Roosevelt and Hopkins held an intimate political dinner to discuss the matter with Senator Byrnes and Democratic political chiefs Edward Flynn of New York, Mayor Edward Kelly of Chicago, and Frank Walker, future chairman of the Democratic National Committee. FDR told the others that he was under great pressure to run for reelection, that he himself was loath to break with the tradition that a president should not serve for more than two terms, but that there was no other candidate the party could choose who could succeed. What should he do? he asked; and his guests of course said that he should run again.

What bothered Byrnes was that the President had held the identical conversation with him six months earlier, in January 1940, at which time they had agreed he would run again. Nor did one need to be as astute as Byrnes to guess that the President had held the same well-rehearsed conversation with many others throughout the year. Yet by pretending to be undecided about his plans, FDR kept rival candidacies from developing.

But the bewildered and frustrated rank-and-file delegates chosen to attend the Democratic National Convention had no clue as to what was going to happen. They convened in Chicago in the middle of July with no clear lead from the President. In deference to FDR, no candidate from his wing of the party had stepped forward. The only candidates were conservative members of his administration who opposed his policies: Vice President Garner and the Democratic National Committee chairman, Postmaster General James Farley.

Asked by party leaders what to do at the convention ("Suppose at some point we want to know your directions on strategy—whom do we ask?"), FDR replied: "In that event, if I were you, I'd consult Jimmy Byrnes." And Byrnes did indeed play a major role in such matters as drafting the platform. But then Harry Hopkins arrived in Chicago for the convention. From a bathroom phone, he had the only direct line to the White House, so he was the man to see and to talk to. He also seemed to have a sort of script; for what followed, under his direction, was in the nature of a drama plotted out in advance.

A message from the President was read to the delegates in which, without saying he would refuse the nomination if the convention insisted on offering it, he said he did not wish to run or serve again. This stunned the delegates, who sat in silence, not knowing what they were supposed to do.

Then loudspeakers blared: "We want Roosevelt! Everybody wants Roosevelt!" The booming voice was that of Chicago's superintendent of sewers, broadcasting from his quarters underneath the stadium. At his cry, other operatives of Mayor Kelly's Chicago political machine and their political allies led the delegates in demonstrating in the aisles for fifty-three minutes crying, "Roosevelt! Roosevelt!" The next day they voted to nominate FDR.

Responding over the radio, the President said: "Lying awake, as I have, on many nights, I have asked myself whether I have the right, as Commander in Chief of the Army and Navy, to call on men and women to serve their country . . . and, at the same time, decline to serve my country in my own personal capacity, if I am called upon to do so by the people of my country." There could be but one answer: he had no such right. He was obliged to accept the nomination.

To the dismay of the delegates, who believed that at least the choice of a Vice President would be left up to them, they then were instructed to vote for liberal Secretary of Agriculture Henry Wallace, a former Republican, as the President's running mate. This, too, was a decision that emerged from FDR's well-practiced conversations with party leaders behind closed doors.

At the White House political dinner described previously, attended in early July by FDR, Hopkins, Byrnes, Kelly, Flynn, and Walker, the President raised the question of the vice-presidential nomination. He said that Garner did not want to run for Vice President again (which presumably expressed less than Roosevelt's whole thought, for Garner was running for the presidential nomination).

FDR then said that his first choice for a replacement candidate was Byrnes. Shrewdly, Byrnes himself raised the obvious objection: he came from the Deep South. But Byrnes did not know that Flynn was a houseguest at the White House, that he had already discussed the vice presidency with FDR, and that Roosevelt had brought up the name of Byrnes knowing what Flynn was about to say in vetoing the nomination. Byrnes, said Flynn, was a Catholic who had turned Protestant, and as such would lose the ticket many votes.

Byrnes was not the only politician cast for a part in what they did not realize was a prescripted drama, designed to satisfy their egos but not their ambitions, that Roosevelt and his few intimates had rehearsed. All over Chicago there were men whom FDR had named as his first choice for President, Vice President, or the cabinet, but whom he was somehow prevented from pushing forward.

The logic of the Wallace choice never was clear to the convention, and only a personal appearance and plea by Eleanor Roosevelt persuaded the convention to accept it. It was as though FDR, in his moodiness, was taking pleasure in forcing the party to admit that it had to do whatever he said. He seemed to be choosing Wallace not because the agriculture secretary had a following, but because he did not: as Vice President he would pose no political threat.

The instincts of the disgruntled delegates were right; they were not nominating a ticket that if elected would provide a Democratic administration from 1941 to 1945. Nor would the new administration really prove to be a coalition of Democrats and Republicans, though many in later years would claim that it was. The incoming administration would be a coalition of Theodore Roosevelt's followers and Franklin Roosevelt's followers: it would be a TR-FDR coalition.

Harold Ickes, who would continue to be interior secretary, was a Bull Moose Republican from the 1912 campaign. Of the new appointees, a significant number—half of the six men who ran the new War Department— were veterans of the TR-inspired Plattsburg Movement in 1916. The secretaries of the armed forces were TR Republicans; indeed, the new navy secretary, Colonel Frank Knox, had been one of TR's Rough Riders, and a lifelong friend. The new Vice President was from TR's faction of the Republican party, the Progressives, as was William Donovan, who was about to head the forerunner of the CIA.

What loomed ahead, therefore, if FDR won the 1940 general elections, was that the Rough Riders would ride again.


THREE CONFLICTS BEGAN in the summer of 1940 that took place at about the same time and affected one another: (1) the presidential contest in the United States, (2) the efforts of private American citizens to pry loose from their government some reconditioned American destroyers the British desperately needed, and (3) across the Atlantic, the loneliest and most decisive struggle of the war: the Battle of Britain.

On July 2 Hitler ordered plans to be drawn up for the invasion of the British Isles. His army delivered the plans July 17. The German army's conception was that the air force would play the role of artillery, pounding the enemy with explosives before the attack, then softening up the defenders and opening up gaping holes in their lines. Then German troops would cross the English Channel as if it were a river and pour through the holes in British lines. Hitler scheduled the invasion for September 15; the Luftwaffe commenced the buildup toward its assigned task with a concentrated air campaign conducted from July 10 to August 12 against shipping in the Channel.

The air barrage against the British Isles themselves began August 13. Germany's object was to destroy England's airfields and airplane factories in order to win command of the skies. It was a close-run thing, with the outnumbered British for a time losing twice as many pilots as they were able to train for replacements.

The fate of the world was at stake, but it would be decided by only a couple of thousand men put up by the two sides. The rest of humanity could only watch as helpless bystanders as the pilots of RAF Fighter Command's 600 single-seat Hurricanes and Spitfires were pitted against the nearly 1,200 bombers and more than 800 fighters of Goering's Luftwaffe. It was pilot and ground crew against pilot and ground crew. By mid-September the Germans had lost. Hitler postponed the invasion of England to October, then until spring, then indefinitely.

But meanwhile the Germans began the "blitz": the nighttime bombing of London by armadas of as many as a thousand planes. It was aimed at civilians—at ordinary people and their houses, and at their places of business and entertainment—and it was much more unnerving than daytime bombing because it took place in the dark. This was an aspect of the war that was made vivid for millions on the other side of the Atlantic by the radio broadcasts of intrepid American reporters.

For it was the moment when radio replaced the press as the principal supplier of news to the masses: a step on the road that, a half-century later, led to the Gulf war being watched as it happened on television. Best remembered of the pioneer radio correspondents who brought something of the reality of London under aerial siege into American homes in 1940–41 is Edward R. Murrow of the CBS network, whose somber and understatedly dramatic opening words, "This . . . is London," are known even to millions too young to have heard him at the time. Murrow went to wherever the action was, and allowed his audience to listen to it. In the background Americans heard air raid sirens, shouts and screams, the shrieks and whines of incoming bombs, the roar of explosions. According to one account of his innovative techniques, "He sometimes broadcast air raids from roof tops, with as many as a dozen microphones scattered to pick up the sound." The crackling noise of static on the overseas line conveyed a sense of the fragility of America's tie to the last fighting outpost of the Western world: it said more effectively than words could have done that this was a line that at any minute could be cut.

The President, in response to pleas from Churchill, sent to Britain such guns and ammunition as America could spare. But Roosevelt, who remembered the British empire as it was in his youth—the greatest and wealthiest of the world's powers—seemed unable to grasp by how narrow a financial margin Churchill's England clung to survival. He saw no reason why the British should not pay cash for supplies.

On the other hand he feared that Britain, though able to fight on, might give in to Germany through moral weakness, as she had done throughout the 1930s. If so, whatever ships or planes America delivered to England might be delivered by England to Germany. This was one reason for his continued refusal to help England in the way most urgently needed: the loan of overage American destroyers recently reconditioned. One of the other and more important reasons was that Congress almost certainly would refuse to let him do it.

Churchill first raised this subject with him in May 1940, but Roosevelt said that "to his regret . . . the United States of America could not spare any." In June, with Italy entering the war and France disintegrating, Churchill told Roosevelt that "nothing is so important as for us to have the thirty or forty old destroyers you have already had reconditioned." At about the same time he made the same point to Bullitt in Paris. But from Washington the British ambassador reported to the prime minister "that the President is not convinced that our need for destroyers is serious."

Churchill's greatest immediate fear in regard to the war at sea was that the French battle fleet would be turned over to Germany by the Vichy government. He met the threat head-on by sending a British squadron to Algeria, where about a tenth of the French war fleet berthed, with an ultimatum to either sail to British ports or be attacked. The French resisted, so on July 3 the British blew one after another of their ally's warships out of the water.

Roosevelt approved of the decision, and may even have begun to believe that Britain had regained her fighting spirit. But if so, it had no effect on his continuing disinclination to lend Churchill the destroyers Great Britain so badly needed.

On July 31 Churchill cabled FDR that German control of the French coastline allowed the enemy to launch attacks at British shipping from many points along that coast. To counter such attacks while also defending against a cross-Channel invasion, holding the Straits of Gibraltar against attacks from the Mediterranean, and patrolling the northern seas against attacks from Scandinavia had stretched the Royal Navy to its limits. Churchill claimed that for lack of "50 of your oldest destroyers," all could be lost. "The whole fate of the war may be decided by this minor and easily remediable factor." He pleaded: "Mr. President, with great respect I must tell you that in the long history of the world, this is a thing to do now."

Private American citizens, meeting in New York City, were moved to action on the destroyer issue, as others had been in pushing through military conscription and in placing Stimson and Patterson in the War Department. The earlier group, assembled by Grenville Clark, had met at the Harvard Club; this one convened a block away, at the Century Association. The roughly twenty-seven members of the Century group included university presidents, clergymen, newspaper columnists, businessmen, retired admirals, and a Hollywood producer, among others. Henry Luce, founding owner and publisher of *Time*, *Life*, and *Fortune*, and Democratic lawyer Dean Acheson, closest friend of Roosevelt's advisers Frankfurter and MacLeish, were among the members able to reach into one presidential camp or the other.

The journalist Joseph Alsop, who had looked into the matter, told the others that Churchill desperately needed the destroyers and that America could spare them. Eighty-year-old General Pershing made a radio address, drafted by Walter Lippmann and Herbert Agar, saying that the immediate transfer of the destroyers might save America from another war. White House adviser-attorney Benjamin Cohen and Dean Acheson found a legal way for the President to transfer the destroyers without having to ask the approval of Congress (where a filibuster would have killed it); he could do it by executive decree.

Century group members worked to persuade Roosevelt and Willkie to let the destroyer transfer proceed without becoming a campaign issue. The cabinet urged the President to do it.

Churchill seems to have been the first to suggest that it might help if Britain leased some bases to the United States in return. Henry Luce seized on the point that America ought to be compensated. The British ambassador, Lord Lothian, mentioned the quid pro quo idea to Walter Lippmann, who later remembered it as an idea that he and Lothian had originated.

FDR then went forward with it, bargaining hard and obtaining from Britain the use of Caribbean bases far more valuable than the aging destroyers. Not merely in appearance, but in reality, he had given nothing away. He showed himself to the voters as a shrewd trader who had gotten the better of the British.

Of course, the isolationist press nonetheless attacked. Alsop had anticipated the onslaught by soliciting support from the other leading newspaper opinion writers, their views to be published the moment the news was announced that the President was transferring the destroyers by executive order. "I got firm commitments from all the major columnists save one," he later wrote. "Although Walter Lippmann supported the movement to the hilt early on . . . , in the end he became alarmed about the extreme use of executive prerogative and chose, as Walter sometimes did, to write on both sides of the issue."


AS THE POLITICAL CAMPAIGN MOVED toward its climax, both candidates were driven to appeal to the great majority of voters who feared that American troops were about to be sent to Europe's battlefields. Conscious that the slogan "He kept us out of war!" had won the 1916 elections for Woodrow Wilson, but that Wilson then had turned around and led the country into the conflict, Willkie charged that FDR, too, might pledge peace but if reelected would lead America into war.

Roosevelt worried that Joe Kennedy might turn against him and confirm Willkie's charges. The archisolationist and proappeaser, who spent his nights in the English countryside because he was afraid of the German bombs that fell on London, was still at his ambassadorial post in Britain but only with many recriminations on both sides. The Foreign Office file on him contained such comments as: "He thinks and hopes that we shall be defeated. . . . We consider that he is undoubtedly a coward. . . . Mr. Kennedy is a very foul specimen of double crosser and defeatist. He thinks of nothing but his own pocket."

At Byrnes's suggestion, FDR offered to name Kennedy chairman of the Democratic National Committee, but the ambassador refused. Taking a leave of absence from his post in London, Kennedy prepared to debark for a holiday in the United States. Roosevelt had Byrnes cable Kennedy asking him to say nothing on his return to America until the President had a chance to talk to him.

The arriving Kennedys were spirited to the White House for a dinner with the President and the Byrneses, at which Missy LeHand was hostess. As Byrnes described the man and the occasion, "Kennedy is not a bashful man. He is a forceful talker, and in his vocabulary are many words not found in dictionaries. He used some of them in his denunciation of the State Department and of the treatment accorded him."

To Byrnes's surprise, FDR did not defend State, but said that he "understood entirely . . . how Kennedy felt; as a matter of fact, he thought that Kennedy's views were charitable, and it was only because of the war that he, Roosevelt, had put up with similar treatment. He was determined that after the election there would be some real housecleaning, so that friends of his, like Joe, would never again be subjected to such outrageous treatment."

Roosevelt then asked his friend to make a radio speech advocating his reelection, and the moment Kennedy agreed, LeHand jumped up and phoned to book the radio time.

Later, in a major final campaign talk in Boston October 30, FDR drove to the stadium with members of the Kennedy family and went out of his way to praise Kennedy: "that Boston boy, beloved by all of Boston and a lot of other places, my Ambassador to the Court of St. James's, Joe Kennedy." In the course of FDR's speech, in a phrase often quoted later, the President pledged: "And while I am talking to you mothers and fathers, I give you one more assurance. I have said this before, but I shall say it again and again and again: Your boys are not going to be sent into any foreign wars." ("That hypocritical son of a bitch!" said Willkie on hearing those sentences. "This is going to beat me!")

Willkie was untroubled by the possibility that he might be defeated if his relationship with Irita Van Doren were revealed by the press. "Everybody knows about us—all the newspapers in New York," he said, and nobody would give them away in public. Roosevelt, whose marital arrangements were similarly unconventional, felt that Willkie displayed poor political judgment in allowing the press to know.

However, FDR was glad that Willkie's situation helped preclude the Republicans from publishing a cache of letters from Henry Wallace to the White Russian he addressed as "Dear Guru," in which his strange philosophical beliefs, couched in the language of mysticism, could easily have been quoted to make Wallace sound at best ridiculous and at worst a lunatic.

On the night of election day, Tuesday, November 4, FDR and his family and friends were gathered at his home in Hyde Park to hear the returns.

Roosevelt won the presidential elections against Willkie 55 to 45 percent. Churchill wired his congratulations on November 6: "I look forward to being able to interchange my thoughts with you," he wrote. Exciting times lay ahead, said Churchill: "Things are afoot which will be remembered as long as the English language is spoken in any quarter of the globe. . . ."

# 48

## MAKING CHURCHILL A PARTNER

WITH THE ELECTIONS OVER, Roosevelt and Hopkins left Washington December 2, 1940, for a couple of weeks of cruising in the Caribbean. They fished and relaxed in the sunshine by day, and played poker or watched Hollywood films by night.

U.S. Navy seaplanes flew every so often from Washington to wherever the President's party had anchored, bringing legislation to sign, messages, and mail. On December 9 Roosevelt received and read a 4,000-word letter telegram from Churchill that had been sent to the White House and forwarded to the Caribbean. It was an overall view of the war situation in the coming year. FDR, resting and relaxing aboard ship in the soothing tropics, was able to give it his full attention.

Churchill proposed that, as it had done when Roosevelt was assistant navy secretary in the Wilson administration, the United States should assert its doctrine of freedom of the seas: that American merchant vessels would be free to sail or trade, unmolested, anywhere in the world. In exercise of that right America should then send supplies to England in convoys guarded by the U.S. Navy, and thus break the effective blockade of the British Isles imposed by German U-boat warfare. Roosevelt did not respond to this request.

The prime minister then asked for a great increase in America's supply of war matériel to Britain, but stated bluntly that his government was running out of cash to pay for supplies. He wrote that it "would not be in the moral or economic interests of either of our countries" to leave a postwar Britain "stripped to the bone."

Ever since the fighting had begun in Europe, FDR had been told repeatedly that Britain would soon reach the point where she could no longer pay her way. He had refused to believe it. For whatever reason, he seemed to believe it now.

He thought about it for a while, and then came up with his plan for giving the British whatever they needed free of charge. He called it "lend-lease." Afterward scholars were able to track down the origins of the phrase: in May 1940 Bullitt had proposed that the U.S. "lease" warships to France, and in August Ickes argued that to transfer warships to England was to "lend" a fire extinguisher to a neighbor whose house was on fire. In December 1940 the idea emerged whole from the President's head, and once he had told newsmen that sending supplies to Britain was—in his and Ickes's immensely persuasive analogy—like lending a garden hose to a neighbor whose house was on fire, the campaign for public support was won.

Of course, it was a misnomer: the supplies sent to Britain pursuant to the new program were neither loaned nor leased; they were given. Senator Taft pointed that out, in a fight (in which he was joined by Vandenberg, Nye, and Wheeler in the Senate, and outside it by Herbert Hoover, Alfred Landon, and Thomas Dewey) to prevent enactment of lend-lease; but the Congress, urged on also by Wendell Willkie, passed the necessary legislation, which shrewdly had been numbered Bill 1776.


BOTH ROOSEVELT AND HOPKINS were intensely curious about Churchill, if somewhat skeptical. Roosevelt had been introduced to him once, but that was more than twenty years earlier, a fleeting and inconsequential encounter. In those days Roosevelt had been of so little importance in world affairs compared with Churchill that the famous Englishman had taken no notice of him and now was under the impression that they had never met. (This hurt Roosevelt's feelings, and upon realizing it, the prime minister decided that he remembered FDR well.)

As for Hopkins, he had little experience of foreigners or of foreign countries, and was suspicious of them. But as FDR wanted to get a personal sense of what Churchill really was like—as a human being and as a politician—and of what his beliefs and goals were, Hopkins, though he hated air travel, volunteered to fly to London to spend time with the prime minister and report back.

The trip to London took five days. On arrival he interviewed Edward R. Murrow, telling him off the record that "I've come here to try to be a catalytic agent between two prima donnas." He went to the Foreign Office and met the incoming foreign secretary, Anthony Eden, and then the outgoing one, Lord Halifax, who was being sent out to Washington as ambassador. He was put off by Eden's upper-class dandy manner and found Halifax "a hopeless Tory," which would not matter during the war, but (Hopkins wrote to Roosevelt) "I should not like to see him have much to say about a later peace—I should like to have Eden say less."

Hopkins then met Churchill, with whom he took lunch. "I told him," wrote Hopkins, "there was a feeling in some quarters that he, Churchill, did not like America, Americans, or Roosevelt. This set him off on a bitter tho fairly constrained attack on Ambassador Kennedy who he believes is responsible for this impression. He denied it vigorously. . . ."

Hopkins spent days and nights with Churchill as the prime minister went about directing the war, holding meetings, receiving reports, and dining with friends and colleagues. Hopkins met all sorts of other people, too, in and out of the government. He stayed at a hotel in Mayfair, still a center of London nightlife, though lit up now not by the limelight of floorshows, but by explosions and fires, and noisy not with revelry but with the drone of warplane engines, the wail of sirens, and the many sounds of aerial bombardment. He noted that German bombs spared nobody, that they had struck working-class neighborhoods but also Buckingham Palace and Downing Street. He observed that Churchill's sleeping quarters, across the street from the prime minister's official residence, did not provide the British leader with time out from the blitz—though a bomb shelter was in the process of being built that at last would allow him to sleep in peace.

Hopkins wrote out in longhand a letter to the President briefly summarizing his findings: "The people here are amazing from Churchill down and if courage alone can win—the result will be inevitable. But they need our help desperately and I am sure you will let nothing stand in the way. . . . *Churchill* is the gov't in every sense of the word—he controls the grand strategy and often the details—labor trusts him—the army, navy, air force are behind him to a man. The politicians and upper crust pretend to like him. . . ." These were meaningful words from a working-class American predisposed to dislike English aristocrats and their airs.

"I cannot believe that it is true that Churchill dislikes either you or America—it just doesn't make sense. . . ."

Hopkins ordinarily did not offer advice to Roosevelt. His role was to understand more perfectly than anyone else the workings of the President's mind: to grasp what it was that FDR wanted done, and then to do it. But now he came close to advocating a course of action. To the man to whom he was closest in the world, he wrote: "This island needs our help now Mr. President with everything we can give them."

"*. . .* AMERICA'S WORLD DUTY could be successfully performed only in partnership with Britain": these words, addressed by Hopkins to his British hosts in the course of an off-the-record speech given to newspaper owners and executives, forecast the relationship that was about to develop.

It was Churchill who made the relationship possible, not merely because he represented so clean and complete a break with Britain's appeasement past that Hopkins felt Roosevelt could trust him, but because he realized his world had changed—so much so that England now could survive only with American support. To obtain that support was one of his chief concerns.

Without knowing the President, Churchill somehow recognized that Roosevelt would tolerate no equals; so he made it clear that he deferred to FDR. He did not claim an entirely balanced partnership. On January 19, during the Hopkins visit, the prime minister called FDR on the telephone. He began: "Mr. President, it's me—Winston—speaking. . . ."

AT THE END OF HIS SIX-WEEK TRIP, Hopkins brought back to Washington a shopping list of supplies urgently needed by Britain. Waiting to meet Hopkins as his plane landed was his friend W. Averell Harriman, who pleaded for a job in the war effort and offered to do anything as an aide to Hopkins, including carry his bags. He had bungled his role in the Great War and now seized his second chance.

Hopkins talked to Roosevelt, who sent for Harriman and appointed him lend-lease "expediter" in London—the personal link between Britain's government and Hopkins, who would oversee the lend-lease program from the White House. As Hopkins's man in London, would Harriman report through the State Department or directly to the White House? "I don't know," Roosevelt told journalists who asked, "and I don't give a damn, you know."

WHILE HOPKINS was setting up the program under which the American economy was mobilizing behind the British war effort, the uniformed heads of America's armed forces were forging their own transatlantic alliance. The initiative came from an old friend of FDR's, Admiral Harold R. Stark, chief of naval operations, who submitted a memorandum to the President just after the November 1940 elections in which he argued that the continued existence of the British empire was vital to the defense of the Western Hemisphere. He asked Roosevelt to choose between the options that would confront the United States if the country were drawn into a two-ocean war against Germany and Japan, and he asked permission to engage in staff talks with Britain's military chiefs in order to formulate joint contingency plans.

Typically the President took no position with respect to the memorandum. He would not say which of the four strategic options he would choose: priority to the Atlantic, priority to the Pacific, split the fleet evenly between the two, or withdraw from both. But FDR, without approving, did not object to the staff talks Stark proposed.

Delegates from the British chiefs of staff secretly came to the United States at the end of January 1941. In the course of talks with American military leaders over the next two months, they arrived at a common strategy that they would propose to their two governments in the event that the United States were to enter the war against Germany.

Meanwhile, the President explained the current strategy to the American people in terms anyone could understand. "A nation can have peace with the Nazis only at the price of total surrender . . . ," he said; so Germany must be stopped. He explained the existing division of labor between the United States and Britain in a ringing phrase, suggested by Hopkins: "We must be the great arsenal of democracy." America would supply the wherewithal for England to defeat Germany.

Churchill said the same thing in his own way: "Give us the tools, and we will finish the job." He said that "in the last war the United States sent two million men across the Atlantic. But this is not a war of vast armies. . . . We do not need the gallant armies which are forming throughout the American Union. We do not need them this year, nor next year; nor any year that I can foresee."

Though many doubted at the time, and at least some doubt it still, Churchill seems to have been telling the truth about what he believed in early 1941. At the time, it was what FDR seems to have believed, too. Both leaders still held an exaggerated faith in what could be accomplished by air power alone. Neither of them foresaw the need to send an American Expeditionary Force to Europe.

One of the best clues to Roosevelt's thinking is provided by Robert Sherwood, who spent much time in the White House as one of Roosevelt's speechwriters. He wrote that as FDR worked on speeches, "he would look up at the portrait of Woodrow Wilson over the mantelpiece. The tragedy of Wilson was always somewhere within the rim of his consciousness. Roosevelt could never forget Wilson's mistakes . . . and there was no motivating force in all of Roosevelt's wartime political policy stronger than the determination to prevent repetition of the same mistakes."

One of Wilson's great mistakes, it was widely believed in 1941, had been to send the American army overseas. To the extent that FDR had thought things through in 1941—although his tendency mostly was to *not* think things through—he seems to have believed that even if the United States went to war, it would not wage it on the ground. He believed that if drawn into the fighting, the United States would continue to supply Britain's military needs while waging a purely naval and air force war.

Hopkins told Roosevelt that Churchill was of the same view: "He believes that this war will never see great forces massed against one another." Churchill believed that the war would be won by an overwhelming preponderance of air power.

The immediate question, as in the Great War, was how to protect the Atlantic sea-lanes against German U-boats. Pressed by Knox and Stimson, the President on April 10, 1941, moved the eastern boundary of the American "defense zone" in the Atlantic Ocean—an area forbidden to foreign warships—to the twenty-sixth meridian, to include the Azores; but he still would not authorize the escorting of convoys.

THROUGHOUT 1 9 4 0 AND 1 9 4 1 there was widespread public debate in the United States about staying out of the European war.

The Committee to Defend America by Aiding the Allies was formed in the spring of 1940 by William Allen White, editor of the Emporia (Kansas) *Gazette*, with assistance from Clark Eichelberger, national director of the League of Nations Association. As its name suggested, the White committee argued that supplying Britain and letting her do the fighting was the best way to keep the United States from being attacked.

The Century Association group, which played so great a role in pushing through the destroyers-for-bases arrangement, seceded from the White committee. Its members believed that Britain, even if well supplied, could not defeat Germany on her own. They felt the United States had to enter the war to win it.

The America First Committee, also formed in 1940, claimed a membership of 800,000 and was led by, among others, aviation pioneer Charles Lindbergh. Like his congressman father in the Great War, Lindbergh opposed American intervention against Germany. His committee drew support from people who were opposed to the administration's policy from a variety of points of view. There were true isolationists: people, in other words, who believed in defending only the Western Hemisphere. Then there were those who, though internationalists, believed the United States should act on its own rather than in alliance with foreign countries, or (though these tended to overlap) who gave priority to the Pacific and Asia rather than to the Atlantic and Europe. There were left-wingers, Progressives, and pacifists like Robert Maynard Hutchins of the University of Chicago, who still believed, as they had in the early 1930s, that wars were started by and served only the interests of imperialists and arms manufacturers. And there were right-wingers, pro-Nazis, pro-Germans, Anglophobes, and anti-Semites. Their cause was spearheaded by Colonel Robert McCormick's Chicago *Tribune*.

As in the years leading up to American entry into the Great War, though to a much lesser extent, arguments about policy and principle sometimes cloaked what really were regional or ethnic differences. Thus the anti-Roosevelt coalition of Republicans and old-guard southern Democrats that at times controlled the Senate disintegrated on the lend-lease issue when the South defected; for the old Confederacy was the most pro-British section of the country.

The President seemed, as he had all along, to be led by public opinion, which on the whole rejected the views of both America First and the Century and overwhelmingly favored a strategy of giving England all aid—but short of war.


THE GERMAN ARMY'S 1941 campaign season began March 1, when its troops crossed the Danube from Hungary to Romania on pontoon bridges. German forces were moving south, passing by permission through Balkan states of the Axis alliance, Hungary, Romania, and Bulgaria, toward Greece and the Mediterranean. On April 6, before dawn, German warplanes struck crippling blows at Greece and Yugoslavia; waves of Nazi invaders then flooded into both countries at sunrise.

The Yugoslav army surrendered April 17. The Greek army gave up on April 27. The last remnants of the British army in Greece were evacuated from the beaches by the end of April. Mainland Greece and all of the islands except Crete were in German or Italian hands by May 11. The British threw in additional forces to make a stand in Crete, but suffered disaster; German paratroops landed on the island May 20 and overcame the last pocket of resistance eleven days later.

The Germans seemed invincible. With summertime weather still ahead of them, the question was only where they would march next. Rumors and even some hard information pointed toward the Soviet Union; but an invasion of the British Isles seemed to make more sense.

The British empire in the Arab world seemed to be collapsing. A single German division under General Erwin Rommel, sent to rescue beleaguered Italians in Libya, drove Britain's Middle Eastern armies all the way back to the Egyptian frontier, threatening to cut the imperial lifeline: the Suez Canal. At the same time, pro-Nazi Arab nationalist officers seized power in Iraq; British troops and their local allies scrambled as quickly as they could to regain the upper hand, but for a while it looked as though the empire's land road to India, too, had been severed.

So FDR could not be sure in the spring of 1941 that Britain would survive. Though Stimson continued to push him to assign American warships to convoy duty, Roosevelt resisted; his first priority was to hold the Atlantic as a shield protecting the Western Hemisphere. Helping Britain took second place to that. Moreover, American war production was not yet at levels adequate to supply both Britain and the United States should a convoy system lead to war.


THE WALL STREET EXECUTIVES and lawyers that Stimson and Knox had brought into government to administer the American military buildup found in Washington a city and a life very different from what they had left. The capital city was backward, and suffered from being at once a small town and an overcrowded city. Its facilities for transportation, entertainment, and social life were limited both in quality and in quantity.

It went without saying that the social life of fine manners and elevated conversation presided over by Nannie Lodge and Elizabeth Cameron in the days of the Republican Roosevelt was as faded as the leaves of a nineteenth-century scrapbook. The Democratic Roosevelt and his wife set almost as unsocial an example as the Wilsons had; meals served by them at the White House were notoriously bad, and the cocktails the President took such pride in mixing were mediocre. One reason that Hopkins had been surprised to find Churchill enjoying the house-party company of witty, learned, and talented people on weekends, when he allowed himself to relax, was that it was so different from what he was used to back in Washington: Roosevelt disliked social life and preferred to go to sleep well before midnight.

Washington was a one-industry, one-company town, and it was not easy for the wives who arrived from Manhattan to adjust to a life that was so much less than metropolitan. They found themselves suddenly deprived of theater, opera, art galleries, fashion houses, nightclubs, and a galaxy of restaurants, and stranded in a town in which all conversation centered on their husbands' work.

Worst hit of all seemed to be Josephine Forrestal, wife of the hard-driving investment banker who now filled the position that Franklin Roosevelt had held in the 1917 war, with a higher title (undersecretary of the navy, rather than assistant secretary) but also much greater responsibilities. It was his job to help Frank Knox streamline the antiquated Navy Department and try to turn America's peacetime navy into the most powerful fighting fleet in the world in a hurry. A man who moved with the coiled tension of a jungle cat about to spring, Forrestal worked at his job sixteen hours a day.

Fear and anxiety caused by the war, and especially the terrifying news of the apparently unstoppable sweep of German armor across the face of Europe, is said by Forrestal's latest biographers to have been at the back of the breakdown Mrs. Forrestal suffered. There were more specific sources of strain as well, among them the need to hold her own in lunchtime and dinnertime conversations about politics, a subject in which she took no interest and did not feel at home.

Her unrestrained alcoholism, the terrible seizures that led to scenes and unforgivable insults, and her obscene language—"She was vulgar beyond belief," said a friend—soon became common knowledge and left her a social outcast. "Wives would literally flee," said another friend, if they heard she was coming.

Adele Lovett, Robert's wife, decided that Josephine had gone "plumb crazy"; and it turned out that she had. At the end of 1940, she suffered a nervous breakdown and entered a world of hallucinations: "the Reds" were out to destroy her and her family, she cried.

Adele Lovett persuaded the Forrestals to hospitalize Josephine for psychiatric help, but after two weeks she left the hospital, declined further treatment, and along with her husband, refused to admit that the breakdown had happened. Forrestal neither divorced her nor sent her to an institution, but instead tried with no success to hide a condition that neither he nor she would admit was an illness.

It meant that at a typical dinner party, "Jim spent the entire evening with his head in his hands" as one outrage followed another; that a butler had to be instructed to watch her constantly; and that Forrestal repeatedly was interrupted at work: once she kicked a little child in the street and her husband had to send a naval aide to pull her away before the police could arrest her. Forrestal acted as though the situation did not exist, except that he resumed the active womanizing for which he had been known earlier in life.

THE SPRING OF 1941 was a depressing one for FDR. He was given no relief from the war news, and the news was terrible. The Germans were victorious on every front. It was not easy even to imagine how they could be stopped. And the President himself was almost continuously unwell: colds, influenza, anemia, bleeding hemorrhoids. He took to his bed.

Misjudging the situation, Bill Bullitt, who wanted to see the President, decided that the White House staff was being overly protective of Roosevelt's health. Bullitt had grievances and wanted to air them.

Though he did not know it, Bullitt's troubles had begun on his return from France, when he had told reporters that the Vichy government was not fascist and that Marshal Pétain was a great patriot. "Billy was all wet about Pétain" and "Pétain was able to twist Bullitt around his finger," FDR told a friend of Bullitt's—though typically not Bullitt himself. He assured Bullitt that he remained ambassador to France and that after he had taken his holiday in the United States, he would be going back to France: to its new capital at Vichy. But at the same time, FDR set about finding himself a new ambassador, preferably a military figure who might be able to influence Pétain on a soldier-to-soldier basis. Even though Pétain had sold out to the Germans, thought the President, some use might be made of him.

FDR had offered the job first to Pershing (who refused) and then to Admiral William D. Leahy, the former chief of naval operations (who accepted). Newspapers quoted Bullitt as saying that he was staying on— indeed, he had a letter from FDR saying so—and yet they reported that Leahy was in fact replacing him. To Bullitt's bitter you-told-me-I-was-staying-on accusations, the President replied: "I know, Bill. But I forgot. . . . Just let it go." That was not good enough for Bullitt, who kept hammering away: ". . . what on earth am I going to do after you put me in that awful position? . . . What am I going to say to the press? This is shocking. . . . Well, this is certainly a funny one, if anything ever was funny. It certainly leaves me in a spot." On and on he went, despite FDR's repeated admonition to "let it go."

Kennedy had resigned himself to returning to private life, and had channeled his political ambitions into the career of his oldest son. But Bullitt would *not* let go. He was critical of the President's policy toward the European war. He muttered against Hopkins and his ignorance of foreign affairs—for Hopkins and Harriman now were the President's eyes and ears in Europe, while Hopkins had become FDR's chief foreign policy confidant. Believing that these were positions he once had filled, and knowing that he did not do so now, Bullitt was jealous.

But mostly Bullitt attacked Roosevelt's friend Sumner Welles, a contemporary and rival, whom he blamed for taking the undersecretary job at State that Bullitt had wanted for his family friend R. Walton ("Judge") Moore. Welles also stood in Bullitt's way if, as seems likely, the discarded ambassador to France now aimed at becoming undersecretary or secretary of state himself.

On April 23, 1941, Bullitt was admitted to see the ailing President. He said that Judge Moore, on his deathbed, had entrusted him with certain papers of utmost importance to be given to the President—which Bullitt now did. The papers showed that when drunk, aboard a train, Welles had made homosexual propositions to black sleeping-car porters. Bullitt said that "Moore had felt that the maintenance of Welles in public office was a menace to the country since he was subject to blackmail by foreign powers. . . ."

From the FBI, Roosevelt knew that Bullitt had collected the documents himself and therefore was inventing some or perhaps even all of what he was saying about Moore and the scene at his deathbed.

Bullitt claimed he already had discussed the matter with Hull, who had said that "he considered Welles was worse than a murderer." Roosevelt said the problem had been dealt with, for he had taken steps to ensure that Welles would never do it again, but Bullitt said that was not the point: "the question was not one of future acts but of past crimes. . . ."

The President said that he did not want to let Welles go because he was useful. But Bullitt returned to the charge: FDR, he said, "was thinking of asking Americans to die in a crusade for all that was decent in human life. He could not have among the leaders of a crusade a criminal like Welles."

Bullitt said that he personally would refuse to take any State Department job unless Welles was fired. He hinted that the information in his possession might give rise to a criminal prosecution that would besmirch the Roosevelt administration. He closed with what sounded like an ultimatum: he would expect to hear from Roosevelt by the end of the week.

The President rang for his military aide, General Edwin ("Pa") Watson. "Pa, I don't feel well," he said. "Please cancel all my appointments for the rest of the day." He wanted to be taken back to his room.

It was a kind of ugliness Roosevelt could not face—or at any rate, chose not to. He would do nothing about Bullitt or Welles. Bullitt was to continue his campaign against Welles, always on the edge of making his charges in public, for the next two years; and Roosevelt and his man in the State Department would live in the shadow of that.


THE LARGEST ATTACK in military history took the Soviet Union completely by surprise at three in the morning, Sunday, June 22, 1941. The United States and Great Britain had warned the Soviets of the impending German invasion, which they had learned of through their own intelligence sources, but Joseph Stalin refused to believe them.

Thousands of warplanes, thousands of tanks, hundreds of thousands of motor vehicles, and 3 million German troops burst into the Soviet domains. Stalin, suffering some sort of breakdown, retreated to his dacha and stayed incommunicado for a week as the panzers ripped through his empire.

The War Department and the army advised the President that the Soviet Union could hold out for no more than three months. But even that much respite, Stimson pointed out, would allow the United States Navy to begin escorting convoys across the Atlantic to England while German attention was directed elsewhere. And Roosevelt, looking forward hopefully to the autumn rains and winter snows that could hamper or stop the German invasion of Russia, cheerfully observed that if the Soviets could survive for three months, they could survive for nine—until spring.

Churchill's response to the German invasion had been an immediate offer of all possible aid. Roosevelt was less forthcoming, but after a few weeks he let his fact finder investigate. Hopkins flew to Moscow at the end of July to establish contact and to lay the groundwork for later extension of lend-lease to Russia. He planned then to join FDR and Churchill on the momentous occasion of their first conference.

From Russia, Hopkins, seemingly on the verge of death but able to recover after sleeping night and day, returned to Britain, where he boarded a British battleship, the *Prince of Wales*. Churchill, with a staff, joined him, and they embarked for Newfoundland in Canada, where by secret prearrangement they were met by an American heavy cruiser, the *Augusta*, carrying FDR, Welles, Harriman, and the American army, navy, and air force chiefs.

At the Atlantic Conference (August 9–12), the President and the prime minister, meeting in person for the first time since they were introduced two decades earlier, developed an easy personal relationship. FDR welcomed Churchill to dinner aboard the *Augusta* the first night. The following morning, August 10, Roosevelt and his party went to the *Prince of Wales* for Sunday services. The British and American crews joined in singing hymns chosen by Churchill: "O God Our Help in Ages Past," "Onward Christian Soldiers," and "Eternal Father Strong to Save."

On August 11 the work of the conference began on three levels. Diplomats held talks with their opposite numbers, as did military leaders; while the President and the prime minister held talks of their own. After listening to a report by Hopkins on his trip to Moscow, FDR followed Churchill's lead in proposing massive aid to the Soviet Union.

Little took place in the way of military planning. Members of the American delegation stressed that the United States had no intention of entering the war. The British military chiefs were disappointed to find the Americans "living in a different world," remote from the European conflict. The army seemed at least a year or two away from being able to think of anything but trying to equip itself. From Washington came the welcome news that the Congress, albeit by a margin of only one vote, had given General Marshall the extended conscription program for which he had pleaded; now it was possible to start to create an American army that at least could defend itself if attacked.

In Newfoundland FDR was able to address his fear that Britain, as in the earlier European war, might make secret territorial or other pledges to Russia's government or to other Allied governments about the postwar settlement. A high official of the British Foreign Office supplied the necessary assurances. Showing that he had avoided yet another of Wilson's mistakes, FDR demonstrated that he had pinned down Britain to an unselfish set of war goals while he still exercised enough leverage over British policy to do so. The goals proclaimed by the two leaders and known as the Atlantic Charter drew a line between them and their Axis enemies. The charter in effect said that the United States and Britain, unlike the Axis powers, did not intend to acquire any new territory at a peace settlement, and that they would fully respect the legitimate rights of all peoples and countries everywhere.

The final communiqué pledged the United States and Great Britain to "respect the right of all peoples to choose the form of government under which they will live; and they wish to see sovereign rights restored to those who have been forcibly deprived of them." Was this a promise to liberate countries ruled by the British empire? In the years that followed Churchill said no, that the language should be interpreted restrictively, while Roosevelt felt otherwise.

Thus the apparent unity achieved at the conference masked continuing fundamental differences between the two countries on world politics. Earlier in the year FDR already had staked out a position more visionary than Churchill's by setting out (in his State of the Union message to Congress) the four freedoms that he said everybody should enjoy: freedom of speech and expression; religious freedom; freedom from want; and freedom from fear, to be secured in part by universal disarmament.

But on the establishment of a new League of Nations in the postwar world, it was the prime minister, not the President, who took the more idealistic stance. In his draft of the charter, Churchill proposed pledging support for a postwar international organization; but FDR struck out that pledge, and instead inserted a demand that the aggressor states, once defeated, be disarmed. FDR said that raising the League issue would be bad politics in the United States, where it would excite "suspicions and opposition." Besides, he said, he did not believe a League would be effective. He said he preferred a postwar settlement in which the globe was policed by the United States and Great Britain* at least for the time being, for FDR said that "the time had come to be realistic."

For Churchill, a potential domestic political problem was caused by *not* raising the League issue. He felt obliged to cable London urgently to Clement Attlee, leader of the opposition Labour party and a member of the coalition cabinet, to secure his agreement to the President's proposed language. Labour, pacifist in the 1920s and 1930s, was of course very pro-League and could be expected to be disappointed that no mention of international organization was made in the Atlantic Charter.

On the American side, Welles was dismayed by Roosevelt's disparagement of the League. FDR told him that "nothing could be more futile than the reconstitution of a body such as . . . the League of Nations." Welles argued that at least there should be an assembly in which the small countries could, if nothing else, complain in public. He and Hopkins argued against the President, who in the end allowed Welles to insert vague language referring to a "wider and permanent system of general security." This final language showed that the continuing intellectual hold of Woodrow Wilson on his onetime followers in the Roosevelt administration was so strong that not even the President himself could overcome it completely.

A couple of months after the Atlantic Charter was proclaimed, the debate within the Roosevelt coalition between the followers of TR and those

---

* The Soviet Union, fighting at the time for sheer survival, did not enter into Roosevelt's calculations as a great power.

of Woodrow Wilson became public. In a speech to the American Bar Association, Navy secretary Knox proposed that after the war, the American and British navies should join together to police the world. He said that such a force could guarantee peace for at least a century. His was a vision inspired by TR and FDR.

Welles replied in a speech at Wilson's tomb. He appealed to the American people to "turn again for light and for inspiration to the ideals of that great seer, statesman, patriot, and lover of his fellow men—Woodrow Wilson. . . ."

THE ATLANTIC CONFERENCE disbanded in mid-August 1941 with much accomplished. As a partnership between Britain and the United States now had been established, a joint mission headed by Harriman and Lord Beaverbrook, Churchill's minister of aircraft production, was sent out to Russia to set up a supply operation on behalf of the two countries.

A second major outcome of the conference was an American commitment to the battle of the Atlantic. The U.S. Navy was ordered to escort convoys all across the western Atlantic to the maritime frontiers of Britain, a line drawn by the President on a map he tore out of a *National Geographic* magazine. This in turn freed the Royal Navy to guard convoys sent to Murmansk for Russia. The Americans were under public orders from their President to shoot German U-boats on sight. America had become some sort of a belligerent in the conflict without having fully joined in it.

On returning to England, Churchill told his war cabinet that FDR had said he would become more and more provocative to Germany in the Atlantic and that "everything was to be done to force an 'incident.'" If indeed Roosevelt said so, he was far in advance of the diplomatic and military members of his delegation, who gave their British counterparts quite a different impression. The meeting in Newfoundland had been, in Churchill's words, "something really big." He had made a giant step toward forging the special and personal relationship with FDR that would make it possible to win the war.

Two months after the conference, Roosevelt wrote a letter to Churchill in which for the first time he addressed him as "Dear Winston." A few days later he sent a longhand note, ending: "I wish I could see you again!"

# 49

## A SECOND SUMMONS
## TO GREATNESS

*There is a lot of talk around town to the effect that the Japanese, in case*
*of a break with the United States, are planning to go all out in a surprise*
*mass attack on Pearl Harbor. I rather guess that the boys in Hawaii*
*are not precisely asleep.*

> —Joseph Grew, U.S. ambassador to Japan,
> from Tokyo, January 27, 1941

IN EARLY AUGUST the German armies in Russia slowed. The re-
treating Soviet forces, though they had suffered staggering losses, had not
collapsed. The brutality of German occupation began to unite the diverse
nationalities of the Soviet Union against the invaders; and their determination to fight on meant that Hitler's goal of ending the war in September
could not be met.

But within weeks the Germans were back on the offensive. In the late
summer and early autumn of 1941 they scored two of the greatest victories
in military history: vast encirclements, one around Kiev, the other around
the river town of Vyazma on the road to Moscow, in which a million and
a half Russian prisoners were taken. In all, the Russians had lost 4 million
men, killed or captured; the Germans, only 560,000.

In early September Stalin wrote to Churchill that the Soviet Union
was being destroyed with impunity by the Nazis because they knew the
threat from the west was mere bluff. Their strategy always had been to pick
off countries one at a time, and now they were conquering Russia secure in
the knowledge that Britain would not come to her aid. Unless Britain
opened a second front by invading France or the Balkans, and sent vast
supplies to the Soviet Union immediately, Russia would be defeated. The
Soviet ambassador who delivered the letter hinted that unless Britain fulfilled Stalin's demands, the Soviet ruler might come to terms with Hitler:
he might sign a separate peace.

Churchill could not promise the second front, but pledged half the
tanks and planes Stalin demanded, saying the United States would supply

the other half. Apologizing later to his American partner for making guarantees in his name, Churchill told FDR that the "moment may be decisive."

THERE WAS NOT ENOUGH to go around: that was the challenge faced by Roosevelt in the autumn of 1941. There was not enough to supply both the United States and Britain, not enough to supply both Britain and Russia, not enough to supply both the army and the navy, and not enough to supply both the Pacific and Atlantic fleets.

Because of design changes, production of the B-17 "flying fortress" came to a halt during the summer; only one bomber was turned out in July. There were also design problems with naval vessels coming out of the docks. New-product development was not yet completed for many of the weapons systems; wrinkles had not yet been ironed out; smooth mass-production assembly lines were not in operation.

So the President had to choose who was to get the scarce supplies—and decided to restrict the expansion of the American army in order to be able to send its equipment to the Soviet Union. He was placing a very heavy bet on Russia's ability to survive—and giving high priority to keeping Japan from attacking her.

JAPAN WAS AN ALLY of Germany and Italy by the terms of an Axis Pact reached in the autumn of 1940, in which the two European dictatorships recognized Japan's right to dominate "Greater East Asia." When she was on the verge of invading the British homeland, Germany encouraged Japan to attack the British empire in Asia and the Pacific. Minimizing the risk that the United States might then come to Britain's aid, Hitler promised (April 4, 1941) that if America did intervene, Germany would declare war on her. But after invading Russia, Germany changed the order of her priorities. Hitler instead tried to persuade Japan to attack Russia, while FDR focused his attention on keeping Japan from doing so.

For most of the twentieth century, the United States and Japan had been at odds. At issue was the question of China, whose independence and territorial integrity America wished to see respected, and whose markets America wished to see open to all. The quarrel intensified in 1931 with Japan's invasion of northern China—Manchuria—and in 1937 with Japan's attack on China proper. It heightened in July 1941 when Japan occupied French Indochina. Washington responded by freezing Japanese assets and by imposing a complex payments scheme that in effect rationed raw materials and oil sold to Japan. It was in the nature of an embargo, but was intended to be less than total.

With no raw materials of her own, Japan was vulnerable to a cutoff of supplies, especially oil. The question was how she would react to it. Roosevelt told Ickes that "the Japs are having a real drag-down and knockout fight among themselves . . ." as to whether to attack north (i.e., Russia), south (i.e., Britain), or not at all. He said that "it is terribly important . . . for us to help to keep peace in the Pacific" because "I simply have not got enough Navy to go around. . . ." To have to send ships to the Pacific would weaken chances for America to win the battle of the Atlantic.

U.S. policy took high risks in hopes of high rewards. If Japan backed down, Roosevelt, at no cost, would liberate both the Soviet Union and the United States from the threat of a two-front war. The risk was that embargoing Japan would instead drive her to fight, in which case the two-front war would not merely occur but would occur at the very worst time.

Why not hold off from pressuring Japan? That was the strategy Walter Lippmann urged in 1940. He wrote that a conflict with Japan "must be avoided at all cost. . . . Japan cannot threaten the independence of any state in this hemisphere . . . whereas a victorious Germany can and will. For this reason it seems to me self-evident that we must find a basis of compromise with the Japanese. . . ."

Yet when Japan occupied Indochina in July 1941, he favored an embargo: "economic paralysis" might check Japanese imperialism, he wrote. Stimson, who had considered imposing sanctions even in the 1931 crisis, said that history showed that if America took a firm stand, Japan would back down. Chiang Kai-shek, China's leader, told FDR that sanctions would bring Japan to the peace table. A historian of the period has written that "Morgenthau, Ickes, Stanley K. Hornbeck, the State Department's most senior Far Eastern advisor, congressional leaders, and, according to an opinion poll, 75 percent of the American public agreed."

But Roosevelt's military chiefs feared that the embargo, far from bringing Japan to the peace table, risked igniting a war in the Pacific—which the United States could not afford for the time being. They seemed to be saying that in the spring of 1942 FDR could do whatever he liked in regard to Japan, but not now.

The intelligence and war plans division of the army sent a memorandum November 1, 1941, to Marshall stating that "a primary objective of our policy should be to avoid a two-front war. . . ." America should avoid the risk of war with Japan now, "which would lessen the main effort against Germany. With Germany defeated, the Far Eastern situation can be readily retrieved."

The navy, too, worried that the administration's policies might bring about a war against Japan prematurely. Admiral Stark initiated several meetings at which he and General Marshall warned the President and the State Department that America would not be ready to fight Japan until spring, and that war in the Pacific therefore had to be avoided at least until then. Stark and Marshall reiterated this point in a memorandum to the President November 5.

The chief of staff explained it to the press, too. Seven Washington correspondents were called by the War Department early the morning of November 15 to attend a secret conference with General Marshall at 10:15 a.m. The seven consisted of representatives of the three wire services, AP, UP, and INS; of two newspapers, *The New York Times* and the *Herald Tribune*; and of two weekly newsmagazines, *Time* and *Newsweek*. According to notes of the meeting: "The U.S. is on the brink of war with the Japanese," said the General. Our position is highly favorable in this respect: We have access to a leak in all the information they are receiving. . . ." As a result the United States was aware that Japan did not know how powerful the U.S. position in the Philippines had become.

By spring the United States would have so strong a bomber fleet in the Philippines that the American air force could destroy Japan. Marshall said that in the spring this information would be quietly leaked to the Japanese so that they could back down without losing face in public "and war might be averted. The last thing the U.S. wants is a war with Japanese which would divide our strength."

Marshall said that "if war with the Japanese does come, we'll fight mercilessly. Flying fortresses will be dispatched immediately to set the paper cities of Japan on fire." Marshall showed maps of Japanese bases throughout the Pacific, and explained that U.S. aircraft would destroy them all. "Our aim is to blanket the whole area with air power. Our own fleet, meanwhile, will remain out of range of Japanese air power, at Hawaii."

But this assumed that the American aircraft were in place. A problem would arise if the Japanese attacked before the Americans were ready, which is to say, before winter. "The danger period," Marshall warned, "is the first ten days of December."


DURING THE DANGER PERIOD before the United States was militarily prepared, America would continue to supply Japan with oil and other strategic supplies, but only in limited quantities: that was the compromise on which FDR settled. He would keep the Japanese under pressure so as to exert a restraining influence, without exerting so much pressure as to drive them into doing something rash.

In part because an oil shortage in the United States led to a domestic outcry that drove FDR to ban most exports, and in part because the newly appointed assistant secretary of state for economic affairs, Dean Acheson, zealously used bureaucratic obstructionism to prevent Japanese applications from being approved, the supply of oil to Japan was in fact cut off totally.

By the time FDR realized what Acheson had done, he seems to have felt that it was too late to back down: he had to stay with the policy of placing a total embargo on oil shipments to Japan, or else risk seeming to appease her.

Ambassador Grew had warned Roosevelt repeatedly that "if we once start sanctions against Japan we must see them through to the end, and the end may conceivably be war." There were those who said that Japan, knowing the United States to be so much more powerful than herself, never would start a war because it would be suicidal. But Grew, in a cable to the State Department on November 3, warned that Japanese culture and thinking were quite different from America's, and that the Japanese would make an "all-out, do-or-die" effort to break out of economic strangulation "even to the point of risking national hara-kiri rather than yield to pressure from abroad."

The United States had deciphered one of the Japanese diplomatic codes, and routinely intercepted and often could read Japanese cables (a source of information the American government called "MAGIC"). From these it seemed there was much activity by Japanese officials in 1941 focused on the unwillingness of the Roosevelt administration to permit Japanese expansion to continue unchecked.

But in the autumn of 1941, American military leaders believed the immediate future to be brighter than it was. Even Marshall had become infected with the excessive enthusiasm for the B-17 bomber that the others felt, and shared the belief that within months the Japanese military machine would be defenseless against it. Then, too, the recall of sixty-one-year-old Douglas MacArthur to active duty excited optimism. The lavishly paid field marshal of the Philippines, with his sense of theater and sense of destiny, was once again a working general in the United States Army, given three stars and command of the United States Army forces in the Far East. It was not yet evident what years of Oriental adulation, indolence, and luxury had done to him.

MacArthur being MacArthur, he insisted that long-standing plans to abandon the Philippines in the event of war be changed. He proposed (as had his former aide Eisenhower, now with the Third Army in San Antonio) to gamble everything on stopping invaders of the 7,100 islands on the beaches—and Marshall approved. MacArthur expected the Japanese to invade in April 1942 with a limited number of troops, and he counted on his new B-17s to sink the fleet ferrying them to the attack. Neither MacArthur nor his fellow generals then knew, among other things, what difficulty a B-17 would have in trying to bomb a moving vessel.

The important thing, FDR's military chiefs kept telling him, was to stall the Japanese—to arrive at some temporary understanding with them, or at any rate to keep alive their hopes that negotiations might succeed. They had to be kept from attacking in 1941.

IN 1941 three-quarters of Japan's foreign trade and nine-tenths of her oil supplies had been cut off by the United States, Britain, and the Dutch East Indies. Japanese military leaders advised that their country's economy would collapse by spring. The military machine would be paralyzed. For lack of fuel, ships would not be able to leave port, airplanes would not be able to fly, tanks would grind to a halt. The country's existence was at stake. A decision was reached by the government's ministers at an imperial conference November 5: Japan would go to war if the embargo were not lifted by November 25 or if diplomacy had not succeeded by December 1.

From MAGIC and other sources, FDR learned in November 1941 that Japan would move south (rather than north against Russia), that the move somehow would involve the United States, and that the Japanese were working according to a timetable that required the United States to lift its embargo by November 25.

Roosevelt was pulled by his military advisers to yield to Japan for the moment. But he was coaxed the other way by the need to reassure those who were fighting for the American cause. China was in dire straits. The battle of the Atlantic was being lost; the German U-boat fleet tripled in size in 1941, and as Stimson learned, the navy was "thoroughly scared about their inability to stamp out the sub menace." In Russia the Germans had made a supreme effort: Guderian's panzers were in the suburbs of Moscow and poised to encircle the capital city. FDR told Morgenthau November 26 that the situation in the Soviet Union was "awful" and that Moscow was "falling."

If America were seen to back down in the face of Japanese threats at that moment—with Allied fortunes, forces, and nerves all stretched to breaking point—might it not deprive the Allies of that last ounce of faith that kept them fighting? For FDR knew that a belief that the United States soon would come to the rescue sustained the leaders as well as the peoples who held out against the Axis powers; an act of appeasement might weaken that belief.

Whether for that reason or another, the President refused to make concessions to Japan, however temporary. He did not know that at dawn November 26, Tokyo time, a Japanese naval striking force had begun the long voyage that would lead it to the Hawaiian Islands, but he did know that time was running out. He was aware that his decision to stand firm meant that Japan would attack—somewhere, and soon.

He had been advised that the United States would have to enter the war against Germany sometime; "Stimson and Marshall feel that we can't win without getting into the war but they have no idea how that is going to be accomplished," Hopkins noted. FDR was understood by many to say that he could bring the country into the war only if Germany would attack. He then dared her to attack by sending his fleets to sink German U-boats, but the Germans did not rise to the provocation.

Of course, he realized that in a sense it was too soon to enter the war against Germany. Until American production was sufficient to supply his own forces as well as Russia's and Britain's, the common cause was better served by staying out of it. And it would be best to overcome Germany before engaging in conflict against Japan.

War with Japan in 1941 would be a war at the wrong time against the wrong country. But it was the only war the other side was willing to start; if Hitler honored his reiterated pledge to side with Japan, it could become the right war: the war FDR knew America was destined to fight.


IT WAS A NOVEMBER EVENING in Washington. The dinner party was at the home of wealthy socialite Cissy Patterson, owner of the Washington *Times Herald*. As so often happened that year, the evening turned into an argument about the war. Senator Burton Wheeler, a Montana Republican who had opposed American participation in the Great War and had stood for isolationism for decades, attacked his fellow guest Undersecretary of the Navy James Forrestal. Wheeler said that war would bring misery to the country, and that the electorate would punish Roosevelt's supporters if they brought America into it.

As the evening went on, each of the guests was called upon to take a stand. One of the youngest, twenty-four-year-old Ensign John F. Kennedy, said that he had been an isolationist, but that his opinion was changing. He did not have to explain that it might be awkward for a son of Joe Kennedy's to admit to such a shift, which in effect meant that he had gone over to the other side.

Forrestal made it easier for the young sailor; he said that he had been an isolationist, too. But he had come to the conclusion "that America must be the dominant power of the 20th century." Kennedy would record in his notes that Forrestal, speaking of Hitler, said: "We would have to fight him some day—it was best to take him on now, while we had allies."


THE WAR AND NAVY DEPARTMENTS put all American Pacific commands on alert November 24. Cordell Hull reported that negotiations with the Japanese in Washington had come to an impasse; the Pacific commands were warned that it was possible the Japanese might launch a surprise attack, perhaps on Guam or the Philippines.

On November 27, with news arriving of vast Japanese convoys on the move, Stimson cabled an additional alert to MacArthur, telling him, however, that in case of war "THE UNITED STATES DESIRED THAT JAPAN COMMIT THE FIRST OVERT ACT."

President Roosevelt met with Hull, Stimson, Knox, and his two service chiefs, General Marshall and Admiral Stark, on Sunday, November 30. FDR told them he believed that Japan might attack as soon as the next day (Monday, December 1), "for the Japanese are notorious for making an attack without warning. The question is how we should maneuver them into the position of firing the first shot without allowing too much danger to ourselves."

Yet December 1 came and went, with no Japanese attack. So did December 2.

Unseen, unheard, undetected, on December 3 the Japanese striking force en route to Hawaii crossed the international date line on an unfrequented course on which it could expect to remain unobserved and to encounter no traffic.

All attention was focused on Japanese armies and fleets visibly on the move in Southeast Asia and in the far western Pacific. Where were they headed? American and British observers could only guess: Thailand, perhaps, or Borneo or Malaya. Marshall was certain it was the Philippines.

ON DECEMBER 4, Robert McCormick's fervently isolationist Chicago *Tribune*, in an effort to prove the administration was planning to enter the European conflict, printed the complete secret mobilization plans prepared by the U.S. Army and Navy for use in event of war. It was curious: only a quarter of a century before, McCormick had published stories proving that America was shockingly *un*prepared for war on the basis of secret information leaked to him by his then friend Navy Assistant Secretary Franklin Roosevelt.

IN WASHINGTON, at 9:30 in the evening on Saturday, December 6, an assistant to the White House naval aide handed FDR a long cable, just decoded by MAGIC. It was a message from Tokyo to the Japanese ambassador to the United States. It instructed him to break off negotiations. The President was quick to grasp its implications: "This means war," he told Hopkins, who agreed. Hopkins said he wished the country did not have to wait for Japan to attack at a time and place of her own choosing; it was too bad the United States could not strike the first blow. "No, we can't do that," said Roosevelt. "We are a democracy and a peaceful people."

Where would the Japanese attack? Roosevelt and Hopkins both mentioned countries in the vicinity of Japanese military bases in Indochina. For some time past, the President had worried aloud to Hopkins that Japan might invade British and Dutch possessions but not American ones, so as to make it politically difficult for him to commit America to the common defense effort.

The following morning, Sunday, December 7, Roosevelt reread the Japanese message and discussed it with Hull, Knox, and Stimson, and took a less alarmist view of what it meant. Of course, it showed that negotiations were stalled. But it did not necessarily mean war—though Stimson noted that "Hull is very certain that the Japs are planning some deviltry and we are all wondering when the blow will strike."

At morning's end Eleanor Roosevelt had a party of thirty guests— friends, relatives, and people to whom she owed invitations—to lunch in the Blue Room of the White House. The President begged off, pleading a cold and a headache. Roosevelt and Hopkins took lunch at the President's desk.

After lunch—at 1:40 p.m.—the telephone rang. It was Navy Secretary Knox. He told the President that the navy had picked up an air raid alarm from its base at Pearl Harbor, outside Honolulu, on the island of Oahu in Hawaii, and that it was not a drill. "No!" said Roosevelt.

Hopkins said it must be a mistake; Japan would not attack in Hawaii. FDR disagreed; it was what Japan would do precisely because nobody expected it.

Hopkins and Roosevelt did nothing for the next twenty minutes or so, while the President thought things through. Then FDR phoned Hull, who was scheduled to receive Japan's envoys—at their request—to accept a message they said they wished to deliver. FDR told Hull to hear them out icily, but to volunteer no information of the attack.

As the navy had not told the army, FDR called Stimson, who thought the President was talking about a Japanese attack in the Gulf of Siam. "Oh, no," said the President, "I don't mean that. They are attacking Hawaii. They are now bombing Hawaii."

At 2:20 FDR received a phone call from Admiral Stark, who supplied the first details of the attack. At 2:30 Roosevelt called in his press secretary and dictated a news release. A half hour later he dictated a further press release.

At 3:00 the President met with Hull, Stimson, Knox, Stark, and Marshall. Even before the attack it had been their view that the United States had to get into the European war, and that the Japanese had supplied the opportunity. But they agreed that the war would be long and serious.

Phone calls kept coming in. FDR's friend Henry Morgenthau phoned from a New York City hotel. His chauffeur had just driven him and his family back from a two-hour Sunday lunch at Voisin, a luxurious French restaurant only a few blocks away. As Treasury secretary, he had an official Coast Guard twin-engine airplane at his disposal with which to return to the capital. Morgenthau put so much heroic self-dramatization into the tones with which he said "Sir, I have just heard the news. . . . I'll fly right back to Washington" that Roosevelt teased: "Be careful you don't get shot down, Henry."

In midafternoon, U.S. Ambassador John Winant in London phoned the White House and put Churchill on the line. "Mr. President, what's this I hear about Japan?" the prime minister asked. "It's quite true," said Roosevelt. "They have attacked us at Pearl Harbor. We are all in the same boat now."

Edward R. Murrow's wife, Janet, called to say that she assumed the White House dinner to which she and her husband were invited that night was to be canceled. No, said Eleanor Roosevelt, who took the call, "We still have to eat. We still want you to come."

Crowds gathered outside the White House to watch the famous figures arrive. When the Murrows arrived for dinner at eight, they had to make their way through throngs inside as well as out. In the family dining room Mrs. Roosevelt served them and a few friends and relatives scrambled eggs, milk, and pudding.

FDR ate in his study, where he received a stream of visitors. Beer and sandwiches were served to the politicians and officials who circulated through the corridors of the President's mansion. At 8:20 the first cabinet member arrived—Jesse Jones, the secretary of commerce—followed by Vice President Wallace, then the others, with Navy's Knox last of all.

The Murrows rose to leave after dinner, but although Mrs. Murrow returned to their hotel, he stayed on when Mrs. Roosevelt asked him to wait to see the President. Seated on a bench in the hallway, he watched the cabinet members go to their meeting with FDR and Hopkins in the Oval Office with "amazement and anger" on their faces.

Roosevelt asked Knox to brief the cabinet, some of whose members knew little about what had happened.* He then read out loud the draft of a message to Congress—which, except for a sentence suggested by Hopkins, he had written himself—asking for a declaration of war. Welles and Hull had a draft of their own, which was long and detailed; humoring them, FDR promised to consider it. Somebody suggested tying in Germany to his

---

* Some 190 Japanese carrier-based aircraft had attacked, followed by a second wave of 170; 2,403 Americans were killed and 1,178 were wounded. Eight battleships and ten other ships were destroyed or seriously damaged, and almost all American military aircraft on the island of Oahu—some 347 in all—were destroyed. Only the aircraft carriers, which happened to be at sea, escaped damage.

war message, but the President ruled that out: he did not have evidence of German collusion in the Japanese attack.

After the cabinet concluded, Roosevelt met with congressional leaders, with whom he agreed on a time for him to address a joint session of the House and the Senate the following day, December 8. They decided to schedule his speech for shortly after noon. He did not say what he was going to tell the two houses of Congress when he spoke to them, nor did he inform them that he was going to ask for a declaration of war.

About a half hour after midnight, the President sent everyone home to bed.


FEW MILITARY DEBACLES seem more difficult to understand or can have been so exhaustively studied as the American failure to anticipate an attack on Pearl Harbor. Roosevelt wanted Germany or, if that were not possible, Japan to attack somewhere in the world, but not to do significant damage: sinking an American merchant vessel on the high seas might have accomplished his goal. The last thing in the world that America's big-navy President wanted was to lose his battleship fleet at the outset of a war.

Warnings were ignored or misunderstood—but by everyone, not just the country's military and civilian leaders. If there was a plot to leave the country open to attack, all Americans were party to it. Claims that FDR— and therefore, necessarily, Stimson, Knox, Marshall, and Stark—deliberately allowed the assault to happen are ridiculous for many reasons, but not least because they fail to come to grips with the fact that an almost willful refusal to recognize that the Japanese *really* were attacking can be found at every level of the armed forces, down to the lowliest. At Pearl Harbor, the approaching Japanese armada was sighted by radar; but the sailor who reported it was told to forget it—that it must be American forces the radar was picking up. From one end of the Pacific to the other, the story was the same: either nobody was on duty, or the person on duty saw a blip on the screen, awakened a lieutenant to report it, and was told to disregard it by the lieutenant, who then rolled over and went back to sleep.

"Living in a different world": that, it will be remembered, was a British military appreciation of the American military at the Atlantic Conference. The Americans engaged in drills, exercises, and war games. Young American soldiers and sailors never had responded to a military alert that was real— which was why on December 7 their reaction was to turn off the alarm and go back to sleep. They were peacetime people with peacetime priorities. They arrived late, left early, and took off weekends.

A vivid illustration of the mentality that led to Pearl Harbor was provided in the Philippines the following day. Word of the Japanese attack had been received. MacArthur knew that the Japanese had destroyed the

American airplanes in Hawaii lined up in a row on the ground; orders had been received by MacArthur's air commander from the chief of the army air force in Washington to disperse all U.S. planes at Clark and other fields so that the same thing would not happen in the Philippines.

Yet nine hours after MacArthur learned of the Pearl Harbor attack, his airplanes—including the large fleet of B-17s that were supposed to win the Pacific war for America—were still lined up neatly at Clark and the other fields, as though intended for Japanese target practice. With no experience of warfare with modern weapons, MacArthur had not provided for enough fighter protection for his bombers, nor for antiaircraft defenses for his airfields, nor for adequate radar.

When a lone American radar operator at Iba Field, eighty-five miles from Manila, picked up the blip on the screen that was the Japanese armada of 200 warplanes en route to the Philippine airfields, warnings were sent to Clark by teletype, radio, and telephone. The teletype message did not get through because the teletypist at Clark was out to lunch. The radio went out of commission—perhaps jammed by the Japanese, perhaps in need of repair. The telephone call went through, however. The lieutenant at Clark who answered it took the message and promised to pass the word of the impending attack "at the earliest opportunity," but in the end did not tell anyone. Perhaps he had heard alarms before and nothing had happened. In the real world, *his* real world, airplanes did not rain down bombs that exploded. Nor did anyone fire live ammunition—at Americans. Those were things that happened only in the movies.

When Marshall heard the news that MacArthur had allowed his air fleet, too, to be destroyed on the ground, hours *after* having been told of Pearl Harbor—after having been warned, and after having been explicitly told by Washington to disperse the planes—he could hardly believe it. But when scholars after the war studied the story of the road to Pearl Harbor, they found it difficult to understand Marshall's behavior, either. How had he allowed himself to fall asleep at the wheel? Why had he not seen that the attack on Hawaii was coming? Why had he not put America's armed forces on a proper alert?

In part it was because Marshall and his top commanders believed that a Japanese attack on Pearl Harbor was impossible: that the American fortress on Oahu was invulnerable, and that the range of Japanese weapons capability did not extend that far. In part it may have been a racist belief that the Japanese could not pose a real threat to white people, that they were "natives" who could be defeated easily. Then, too, there was a cry-wolf aspect to the ominous signs Marshall detected that Japan would strike soon; the United States had received so many warnings of attacks on so many places in Asia and the Pacific for so long that it could not give credence to, or respond to, them all. A constraint on the Roosevelt administration was that it did not want to go on a military alert so sudden, conspicuous, or alarming that isolationist senators could charge that Roosevelt was provoking an enemy attack. Even without that constraint, it might not have been possible for Washington on a moment's notice to wake up America's dormant armed forces. A peacetime army rarely knows how to go on an effective alert; soldiers and their weapons usually have to undergo the test of combat to learn how to function properly and to correct the inevitable flaws in performance.

But above all, what seems to have been responsible for the mental blackout of Americans as the Japanese moved to attack was an enormous failure of the imagination. Americans could not believe that a country overseas ever would attack American territory. The Atlantic and the Pacific, policed by the Royal Navy, always had shielded the United States. Americans took the shield for granted; most were unaware why it was there, and therefore gave no thought to the possibility that it might be there no longer.

In 1853–54 American warships commanded by Mrs. Joseph Grew's great-granduncle Matthew Perry forced Japan to come out of its secure isolation to take part in the affairs of the rest of the world. Japanese warplanes performed the same service for the United States in 1941.

A FAIR INDICATION of the state of mind of civilian America on December 7 was provided, as many have remarked, at Griffith Stadium in Washington, D.C., where the local football team, the Redskins, played its final game of the season against the Philadelphia Eagles. Messages kept arriving for journalists, military personnel, and government officials telling them of the Japanese attack and calling them out of the stands and to their stations. But the sellout crowd refused to be distracted from the game.

The stadium management would not announce the Japanese attack over the public address system, a decision approved by the owner of the Redskins, who explained that Pearl Harbor was not sports news. The Washington bureau chief of INS sent an employee to the White House to cover the war story while he himself remained at the stadium to watch the end of the game. The Washington *Post* headline the following day was "WAR'S OUTBREAK IS DEEP SECRET TO 27,702 REDSKIN GAME FANS."

ON DECEMBER 8, Americans began to take precautions.

The news of Pearl Harbor brought the Archibald MacLeishes rushing back from the Dean Achesons' country home in Maryland, where the two couples had spent the weekend. As librarian of Congress, MacLeish had prepared a contingency plan that he began putting into effect. To the invulnerable vaults of Fort Knox, Kentucky, he shipped for safekeeping the icons of the American political faith: the Declaration of Independence, the Constitution, the Bill of Rights, the Gutenberg Bible, and the Magna Carta.

At the White House, it struck the Secret Service that the President now needed extra protection against assassination. He was scheduled to address Congress after noon; early in the morning Mike Reilly, the Secret Service chief, began looking for a bulletproof limousine in which to drive him there. Federal regulations prevented the government from buying any automobile that expensive, but Reilly got hold of an armored limousine the Treasury had seized from Chicago gangster chieftain Al Capone when convicting him. Reilly washed it, oiled it, filled it up with gas, and brought it around to the White House to transport the President.

"I hope Mr. Capone won't mind," said FDR. Woodrow Wilson had been the first President to ride to his inauguration in an automobile; now his successor was the first to ride in an armored car. America was moving rapidly into the twentieth century.

The President had asked Wilson's widow to accompany Mrs. Roosevelt to the joint session of Congress assembling to hear him that day. Shortly after noon Eleanor Roosevelt seated herself next to Edith Galt Wilson in the White House gallery in the chambers of the House of Representatives.

Roosevelt entered, was greeted by loud applause, and spoke—unlike Wilson in 1917, out of whose shadow he was walking—with calculated brevity and understatement. He branded December 7 a date that "will live in infamy" and asked for a declaration of war against Japan. He did not show his concern that Germany now might pull back from the brink—an unnecessary concern, as it turned out, for within days Hitler kept his word to Japan: Germany declared war on the United States. So did Italy.

The ancient Romans had a deity named Janus whom they depicted as having opposite heads, looking both backward and forward at the same time. Like him, the President looked back: in bringing the two First Ladies together in the gallery on that historic occasion, stressing unity and continuity, he evoked the spirits of Eleanor's uncle and of Edith's husband, the presiding geniuses under whom he and his generation had served their apprenticeships in world affairs. It was in making their way between the strongly contrasting views and instincts of those two powerful antagonists that he and his peers had achieved their intellectual formation and had tried to answer for themselves the question of what role the United States should play in the world outside the Western Hemisphere.

Like Janus, too, the President looked forward. Under his leadership, the country was plunging into a war to be fought against great odds and on an unprecedented scale. At stake was nothing less than all the future of the human race. As their first blunderings at Pearl Harbor and in the Philippines had shown, Americans were embarking in waters they had not yet fathomed. Children of TR but also of Woodrow Wilson; products of the

Great War, the roaring jazz age, and the Great Depression; they were now, however incomplete their education, called upon to leave schooling behind and to take the field.

Janus, who took his name from the entrance door, was the god of *beginnings*. As FDR's Americans set out upon their voyage into the unknown, the god must have given them his most especial blessing.

# A Brief Tour of the American Age

# 50

# THE MAGNIFICENT COUNTRY

THE INDUSTRIAL EXPRESSWAY was built in 1942. The road stretched from Detroit to the new bomber factory at Willow Run, Michigan, some thirty miles away. On it, workers, raw materials, and component parts were brought from the city to the industrial works. As a British commentator recently observed, "By 1943 (when Willow Run was turning out a B-24 bomber every hour) the expressway was an artery of what was then almost certainly the world's greatest centre of high-technology manufacturing. . . . Germany was being defeated by Detroit. The engines of the Red Army's tanks were made in Michigan."

The road became a symbol of America's awesome productive capacity. It was one element that went to make up the picture the world had of the United States in the 1940s. Another was the bountifulness of American agriculture. Above all, there was the country's apparently inexhaustible supplies of raw materials and money.

The abundance was allied to generosity. Fixed forever in the photo album of twentieth-century memories are the shots of American soldiers—GIs—giving candy bars and chewing gum to Europe's deprived children.

Compared especially with the emaciated children in the photos, the GIs were big. A healthy diet had made them tall, but they were big people, too, in other than the physical sense. They had a bigness of spirit. While Europeans focused on their own narrow interests and were splintered into classes and clans separated by blood feuds, Americans pictured themselves—and were pictured by others—as people who rose above differences and divisions and thought in terms not just of their own village or pasture or river valley, but of the globe itself.

Nobody better embodied their liberality and greatness than did their President. FDR infused wartime America with his own carefree and forward-looking spirit. When he announced production goals for aircraft or tanks that experts derided as absurdly high, he did so because he knew that Americans would rise to a daunting challenge—and would enjoy doing so. They liked to feel that nothing was beyond them.

Learning, as he did in so many respects, from Wilson's mistakes, Roosevelt did not campaign for the Democrats in the congressional elections of

1942. As the nation's wartime commander in chief, he had risen above party. He had become the President of all the people.

Photographs of FDR with his wartime colleagues, Churchill and Stalin, show the President as preeminent. His posture looks welcoming; he seems always to be the host. Relaxed, at his ease, he is posed to act as chairman and to set the agenda. His air of authority is that of one born to command.

He is the picture of what Aristotle famously described as "the magnificent man." He is the person who does things on a great scale, but suits the size of his gesture to that of the occasion. He will not stoop to pennypinching, "for there is something paltry about exact book-keeping"; but he will lavish his means only on undertakings worthy of him.

So, too, the wartime United States that expressed itself through FDR: to itself and to others it seemed to be "the magnificent country." It assumed the aspect of its great leader. The creation of that image of magnificence was a wonderful act of political imagination—more so, rather than less so, because it was somewhat at variance with the facts.


THE UNITED STATES was far behind other major countries militarily. In Roosevelt's war, as in Wilson's, time was what stood in the way. In December 1941 the country was not ready. For years George Marshall had been preaching the importance of factoring lead time into military planning: that between the day a weapons system is conceived and the day it is ready to be deployed in the field, one must allow for a period of years. But he had been preaching to the deaf.

Although, in accordance with plans formulated in advance, priority was given to the Atlantic, it was in the Pacific that America caught up first. The Japanese offensive pointing at Australia was blunted by American naval aircraft in the Coral Sea on May 6–7, 1942, the first sea battle in history in which the enemy fleets never caught sight of one another. Japan then was turned back early the following month in the battle of Midway Island, when the whole Japanese battle fleet was attacked by warplanes operating from a badly outnumbered U.S. naval task force. The navy fliers demolished the Japanese and sank all four of their aircraft carriers. It was a conclusive engagement; Japan was on the defensive for the rest of the war, could no longer win, and in that sense posed no further threat.

The battle of the Atlantic was a war against U-boats. It was the critical endeavor in the American struggle with Germany. Until it was won, the United States could not mount and continue to support and supply an invasion of western Europe. But it was not until sometime in 1943—a long time into the war—that the U-boats were vanquished, and by then the Germans already had suffered their decisive defeat on land: in Russia, at the Battle of Stalingrad.

While waiting, America's leaders were determined to engage the German armies somewhere, both to take pressure off Soviet Russia and to demonstrate that they were trying to do so: they aimed to keep Stalin from negotiating a separate peace. In November 1942 American and British troops under Eisenhower's command landed in, and subsequently liberated, French North Africa, linking up with British troops fresh from their victory over General Rommel's Afrika Korps at El Alamein in Egypt. Eisenhower's forces followed up their conquest of Morocco, Algeria, and Tunisia by invasions of Sicily and Italy in July and September 1943.

With the Atlantic and the Mediterranean under their control, the United States and Britain at last were ready to join issue with Nazi Germany on what had been the central battlefields of the earlier world war. On June 6, 1944, the Allied forces landed in France. Hitler's Germany was caught between Eisenhower's forces attacking from the west and Soviet troops advancing from the east. After nearly a year of savage fighting on both fronts, Germany surrendered in May 1945.

In the Pacific, America waged two campaigns. As commander in his own southern sphere, MacArthur led an army campaign that culminated in his return to the Philippines on October 20, 1944. Meanwhile, to his north, the navy and marines attacked and captured island after island.

On August 6, 1945, American airmen dropped a secret new weapon, the atomic bomb, on Japan. Two days later the Soviet Union declared war, and the following day Americans dropped a second A-bomb. In mid-August Japan surrendered.

In outline that was the story of the war, but it should be evident that no summary can encompass it adequately. Too much happened. It was too large. Tens of millions of civilians as well as soldiers were caught up in it personally over the course of years, each with his or her own individual story. In terms of scale, it was the biggest thing in history.


THE STRATEGIES eventually pursued in their respective campaigns by such different personalities as MacArthur and Eisenhower had as a point in common that they were available only to generals whose countries could command overwhelming superiority. It was only in the later stages of the war—when, in terms of war production, the United States was starting to become the magnificent country it had been taken to be from the start—that such strategies became feasible.

MacArthur got off to a shaky start in the war. It is commonly accepted that he was disastrously inadequate as a commander in 1941–42. But he recovered his grip the next year, and scored a decisive triumph in the Bismarck Sea in March 1943. Ahead of him lay Rabaul, capital and port of the island of New Britain, which 100,000 entrenched Japanese troops had converted into a seemingly impregnable fortress. It was the enemy strong point in the region, but MacArthur's decision, in line with that of the chiefs of staff, was to leave it alone and go around it. Thereby he left 100,000 Japanese soldiers stranded, cut off as if they had been besieged. They were surrounded not by troops, but by the impassable ocean. Their ships and planes having been destroyed by the Americans, they were marooned. Ignored, they were obliged to sit out the war in helpless rage and frustration.

Having done it once, MacArthur did it again, making it the trademark of his mature strategy. Repeatedly he would order his forces to sweep around the Japanese in vast encircling movements, saving time and the lives of his men, and consigning one enemy bastion after another to Rabaul-like irrelevance. It was a lordly strategy made possible only by a complete command of the seas and the skies that rendered the enemy earthbound and immobile.

Eisenhower's strategy was the reverse of dashing. He felt no need to match the brilliant generalship of his adversaries. His was the caution of a commander who knows that the crushing weight of the reinforcements eventually available to him makes victory certain unless he commits some terrible blunder. A superb coalition leader, as Fox Conner had trained him to be, he directed a chorus of prima donnas with soothing skill and focused on avoiding mistakes and limiting risks.

It did not matter that the enemy often was equipped with weapons of superior design. The Germans produced better tanks and guns; the Japanese flew better fighter planes. The wartime Senate Special Committee to Investigate the National Defense Program, chaired by Senator Truman, discovered that workmanship in American factories was shoddy and quality control was lacking. Defense contractors were supplying the armed forces with equipment that they knew was flawed: Curtiss-Wright was delivering faulty engines for combat aircraft; Glenn Martin testified that his company was building airplanes with wings that were not wide enough—and that he saw no reason to change, for he already had the contract. No matter. However qualitatively inferior American military goods might be, the country could produce them in such quantity as to overwhelm.

Then, too, there was the matter of organizing the economy for war. Conscious of Wilson's failings in this regard, and prodded by Bernard Baruch even before the United States entered the war, Roosevelt knew in some part of his mind that he ought to appoint somebody to be in overall charge. But he could never bear to part with the power. Industrialists Edward Stettinius Jr., Donald Nelson, and Charles E. Wilson, and banker Ferdinand Eberstadt were among those who tried bringing order out of the chaos. Most effective of all was James Byrnes, who resigned the Supreme Court seat with which FDR had rewarded him in order to try to run the civilian side of the war effort. From May 29, 1943, he served as "assistant President." Somehow miracles of mobilization already had occurred—even without the coordination and central direction that many felt were required.

MAGNIFICENCE SUGGESTS a polished style and culture, but these were not the traits that Europeans discerned in their liberators. The GIs were friendly, open, generous, and decent; but the peoples they freed, and who by and large had cut a poor figure in the war, salvaged some of their pride by looking down on the Americans for lack of manners, learning, and breeding.

This European sense of superiority was not easily supportable—even though it continued to be maintained—once the troops had seen the death camps. True, the immensity of the horror made it not at first comprehensible—not, at least, as a whole; that took time. And it was only over time, too, that the true story came out, that the Germans were not alone in the genocide; that French, Polish, and other enthusiastic assistants joined in consigning millions to the flames.

But to see the ovens into which humans were fed was enough to implicate the high culture of Europe; its value was drawn into question once it was suspected that such a culture had culminated in Dachau and Auschwitz. And by way of contrast, how could one look down on the typical GI who showered gifts on little children—without regard to whose little children they were?*

Observing the works of Nazi Germany and her willing aiders and abettors in German-occupied Europe had the effect of reminding the United States of what it stood for. Americans told themselves, and others, that theirs was a country in which every person was as good as everybody else—a land tolerant of differences but conscious that beneath surface differences all were children of one God.

Those who lived through the 1940s will remember the motion picture films then and afterward about the war and the names of the men in a typical army platoon—as the movies had it: Smith, O'Brien, Campbell, Kozlowski, Jones, Giannini, Suarez, Cohen. That was the way the country wanted to be seen: as a spacious, liberal-spirited New World that had risen above the hatreds that had destroyed the Old.

AND, OF COURSE, that was not really true.

It was evident even in those years, when FDR's was America's face to

---

\* Yet a generation of postwar European intellectuals grew up in the cafés of Saint-Germain-des-Prés and elsewhere defining their literary and artistic superiority by a deliberate anti-Americanism.

the world, that the picture of the United States as the magnificent country required significant qualification. Whatever the movies might say, the armed forces were racially segregated; there were wartime race riots in such cities as Detroit and Los Angeles; and the Ku Klux Klan still held a following. Anti-Semitism was deep and widespread, as was ethnic feuding.

Even the material aspect of American magnificence was not entirely what it seemed. The picture of the United States as endlessly and effortlessly wealthy, though in line with life as a privileged few that included FDR had lived it, bore no relation to the common experience of Americans or to the prewar decade of soup kitchens and apparently incurable mass unemployment. It was difficult to reconcile even with the personal experiences of Roosevelt's political contemporaries. Marshall, Eisenhower, and Vandenberg all had fathers who were wiped out financially in one or another of the depressions, panics, and crashes that were a recurring feature of the American landscape. Truman's father was ruined in the market. So was Roosevelt's grandfather Delano, who made a new fortune only by returning to China.

Those who were Roosevelt's age had witnessed the humiliating spectacle of their government losing control of finance and credit in the crashes of 1893 and 1907. In their childhood their country was the world's major debtor nation, and the debts were repaid only with moneys unexpectedly flowing in from the European war. As they entered their middle years, their generation rode the roller coaster that led to the 1929 crash. Along with the Great War, it was the Great Depression of the 1930s that had shaped them: terrible poverty, no jobs, no future, and no way out—until the war, not the New Deal, bailed them out.

Their experience of America therefore was not of a piece with the picture of the United States that FDR summoned up in the wartime years. That is why the creation of the image of magnificence was so great an achievement—and why the decision to try to live up to it was so morally admirable.

IN RETROSPECT what fascinates is that the magnificent country was not what America was, but what she started to become. Though the peacetime United States had suffered from mass unemployment and though Roosevelt and Vice President Wallace were mocked for looking ahead to full employment for Americans in the postwar world, it turned out under FDR's successors that a full-employment society *could* be achieved in America.

Racial segregation in the armed forces came to an end—though not until after the Korean War showed it caused battles to be lost that might otherwise be won. The need for everyone to stick together in order to wage the Second World War did much to ease ethnic tensions. Middle western cities that were rife with anti-Semitism in 1939 witnessed the flourishing of interfaith Christian-Jewish civic associations in the post-1945 world. The hatred people felt for persons of other religions or ethnic backgrounds did not disappear, but a crucial change had occurred during the war: Americans, even those who felt the hatreds, now recognized that such feelings were wrong. They tried to rid themselves of prejudice, and knew they should feel ashamed if they could not.

Socrates taught one of the central rules of classical Western ethics: if you want to *appear* beautiful or brave or wise, you ought to want all the more to actually *be* beautiful or brave or wise. Be what you wish to seem: the message of Socrates calls for an effort that the United States under FDR and his successors had the rare strength of character to be willing to undertake. America's magnificence in the last Roosevelt years lay not so much in what she was but in what she was going to try to become.

In this the country reflected its leader's approach to life and politics. He looked up; he looked ahead—and as a Roosevelt he knew that Americans perform best when rising to meet a seemingly impossible challenge.

# AMERICA AGAINST THE ALLIES

THE INNER HISTORY of an alliance is the story of its tensions, rivalries, and, sometimes, betrayals. Alongside these usual sources of discord, the United States brought to the broad coalition fighting the Second World War a unique one: the sense of separate purpose that had led Wilson in 1917 to term his country an associated power rather than an ally.

Two days before the attack on Pearl Harbor, William Bullitt sent a longhand note with unsolicited advice to Roosevelt: "Don't let Churchill get you into any more specific engagements than those in the Atlantic Charter. Try to keep him from engaging himself vis-a-vis Russia. The Treaties—if made—will be as difficult for you to handle as the secret Treaties were for Wilson."

It was natural for an American to suppose that whatever bargain Churchill and Stalin might make would be secret, cynical, selfish, and—if ever revealed to the public—shocking.

That was why FDR, in the Atlantic Conference of August 1941, had focused on obtaining from Churchill's government details of all commitments made to allies, along with a pledge not to enter into secret treaties in future. The principles of the United States in this regard were that all commitments and war goals should be made public, and that all military decisions should be arrived at with a view to winning the war rather than to achieving some hidden agenda of political or territorial objectives in the postwar world.

FRANCE WAS THE FIRST ALLY to find herself at odds with FDR—not least because he did not regard her as a genuine ally. As long as the regime presided over by Marshal Pétain in Vichy lasted, he recognized it as the legitimate government of France. As a student of Mahan, the President was sensitive to the geographical importance of French North and West Africa in regard to the south Atlantic highway to Latin America; he had instructed Robert Murphy of the Vichy embassy, one of Bullitt's protégés, to court the friendship of the French military authorities in Africa.*

A logical next step was for Murphy, as political adviser to Eisenhower, to negotiate with the local Vichy authorities in Algeria and Morocco to offer no opposition to Ike's invasion forces in 1942. The understandable objective Murphy pursued was to save the lives of American soldiers. In pursuit of the same goal, Eisenhower and Murphy arrived at an agreement with Vichy defense minister Admiral Jean-François Darlan in November 1942. In return for Darlan's help in persuading his forces not to oppose the Allies, the admiral was appointed civil administrator of the territory, and Vichy colonial officials were allowed to remain in place.

A storm of protest blew up in the United States and Britain. The Vichy government was in the nature of a fascist regime, yet the Anglo-American armies—as protesters pointed out—were propping it up rather than destroying it. Churchill and FDR considered disavowing the agreement. Eventually and reluctantly, however, the President was persuaded by Eisenhower to endorse the Darlan decision as a "temporary expedient justified solely by the stress of battle." The assassination of Darlan December 24, 1942, by a French royalist† was a stroke of luck for Roosevelt that did away with the problems Ike and the admiral had caused.

But the removal of Darlan did not bring FDR any closer to Brigadier General Charles de Gaulle, a solitary figure who claimed to speak for Frenchmen who had refused to accept Pétain's surrender to Germany. It was by no means clear in 1942 that de Gaulle represented anybody but himself. The President had a good debating point in his assertion that it was not for others to select a leader for France; after she had been liberated, elections would be held, and she then would choose a leader for herself. But it followed that France would have no spokesman in the councils of the Allies for the duration of the war, and indeed would not be a participant in the war.

That was the crux of FDR's position: he did not recognize France as an ally. In reality, she was not one. In 1942 there was no meaningful French resistance movement. Under German rule Paris wined, dined, and glittered as before. The Vichy regime did Hitler's bidding with enthusiasm. But Roosevelt seemed to be doing more than facing facts; he was taking advantage of them to demote France from the ranks of the great powers. His plan for Britain and the United States to police the postwar world, and disarm everybody else, relegated France to the position of Belgium, Holland, or Greece. In mid-1942 Roosevelt went further and classified France with Germany, Italy, and Japan, calling the French "associates of the aggressors."

* See page 401.
† He seems to have believed that de Gaulle held royalist sympathies and intended, if victorious, to place the Comte de Paris on the throne. But his true motives, his background, and the question of whether he was acting on the prompting of others remain subjects of debate.

The Vichy regime could be expected to accept an inferior status in the postwar world. In its dealings with the Germans, it already had agreed to a subordinate role for France in world affairs. Meanwhile, the Pétain government seemed much more open to American than to British influence; and—such was FDR's gamble—it would keep the Germans from using its territory in Europe and Africa in making war on the United States. So both during and after the war, Vichy would do all that Roosevelt now asked of France.

Moreover, in maintaining that Pétain, not de Gaulle, was the leader who commanded the loyalty of France (in 1942), FDR almost certainly was right. He was being realistic. But he was not being generous.*

FDR may have been affected by France's behavior in his own political lifetime. In Paris at the end of the First World War, she had blocked Wilson's plan for a liberal peace. In 1919 she had overruled the United States, and in the end had forced a treaty on Germany so onerous that it was predictable Germany would go to war someday to get it changed. Then, in the 1930s, she had lacked the nerve to defend the treaty—the treaty *she* had insisted on imposing—when Germany rebelled against it. She could have faced down Germany at the Rhineland in 1936, but did not. In 1939–40, when the war came that her Versailles treaty helped cause, she lacked the courage to fight on; despite what even might have been superiority in numbers of troops and war machines, she had surrendered.

Roosevelt despised people who give up. It could well have been his view of the ignoble role France had played between 1919 and 1940 that shaped his attitude toward de Gaulle, even though the general's own conduct had been heroic at all times.† It was only reluctantly, and under the influence of Eisenhower and the British, that the President moved toward some sort of official recognition of de Gaulle's standing. Even so, he foresaw political chaos once France was liberated. And he looked forward to disbanding the French colonial empire, taking over its naval bases in Africa and Indochina for America's use in policing the disarmed postwar world.

WHEN HE HEARD THE NEWS of the attack on Pearl Harbor, de Gaulle remarked that the war was over. From that it followed that the battle to shape the postwar world had begun. De Gaulle took that as a

---

* Churchill (a de Gaulle supporter at least at first) and the British Foreign Office *were* being generous in helping de Gaulle pretend that he incarnated France and therefore that France had not surrendered in 1940. It was a conscious act of mythmaking on their part. They wanted France to keep her pride so that she could become a great nation again. This (though France often had been a rival and even an enemy) was in Britain's enlightened self-interest; and American officials took a cynical view of the British government's motives in backing de Gaulle.

† Though, in Roosevelt's view, de Gaulle now spent his time making trouble for the Allies rather than making war against the Germans.

starting point in alliance politics: he left to Marshall, Eisenhower, and others
the task of winning the war, and devoted his attentions to elbowing Britain
and America aside to make room for France in the front ranks of the Allies.
That he added to the difficulties of fighting the war did not concern him.
One can easily come away from a reading of his war memoirs with a sense
that his—and France's—enemies were the United States and England rather
than Germany and Italy.

This ran exactly counter to the American sense of how a government
should wage war—without regard to politics, and with priority given to
winning—and explains why Britain's protégé, de Gaulle's Free France, was
so unpopular not merely with Roosevelt, but also with such other members
of his administration as Secretary of State Hull. For much the same reasons,
another ally unpopular with Americans—at any rate, those in the field—
was Chiang Kai-shek's government of China.

China was a protégé of the Americans, pictured by them as a great
power even though she was far from being that yet. But the high hopes
and idealism lavished on the sleeping giant tended not to survive any prolonged encounter with Chiang's regime. One American after another came
away disgusted by the financial corruption of Chinese officialdom and by
the web of political intrigue.

It became evident to Americans on the spot that Chiang was less concerned with fighting the war than with preserving his own power and the
wealth of his family and associates. To him the chief enemy was the communist enclave in the northwest. The communists, however, whatever their
true intentions may have been, in public took the patriotic line that the
war against Japan came first.

That posed a dilemma for the United States, unwilling because of
anticommunism to back the only force in China that could and would fight
effectively against the Japanese, yet loath to continue pouring resources into
the bottomless pit of Chinese Nationalist corruption. In terms of the American political outlook, there was no answer to the question of what to do
about China.


GREAT BRITAIN IN 1941 became the first real ally the United
States had ever had. FDR had made a start in his initial meeting with
Churchill at sea off the Newfoundland coast in August 1941. But it was
an uncertain beginning, for Marshall and others in the President's inner
circle remained suspicious of British intentions. When the Japanese struck
at Pearl Harbor and the prime minister offered to come over to America
immediately to discuss joint strategy—now that America was in the war—
Washington's first instinct was to ask him to wait. Unsent drafts of the
President's reply suggest that his military advisers were distrustful of their

new ally. They suspected that Churchill would propose a grand strategy aimed at using American troops to achieve British imperial gains in the postwar world. Wisely, FDR overcame these fears and settled on asking the prime minister to hold off his visit only for a week.

Churchill and his aides arrived in Washington December 22 for a conference that the prime minister code-named ARCADIA and that was to last three weeks. Insofar as relations between the two English-speaking democracies were concerned, it proved to be the most important conference of the war. Moved, despite themselves, by George Marshall's powerful persuasiveness, participants agreed on the principle of entrusting a single officer with overall command of each theater of operations—which meant not only that an Englishman could direct American armies, but that an air force officer could give orders to naval fleets.

Another visible manifestation of the real partnership of the two countries was the establishment in Washington of a combined Joint Chiefs of Staff—the heads of the American army, navy, and army air force, together with representatives of their opposite numbers in London—to hammer out agreement on the conduct of the war as a whole. From the point of view of waging war, it was about as close as an alliance could come to unity.

The U.S.-British partnership was at the center of the ARCADIA scheme. Orbiting around it were the countries associated with it in the war, which FDR had the happy notion of calling the "United Nations."* These included the Soviet Union, which had survived the initial German assault. Though not regarded at the time as a major power, Russia as of December 1941 had come to be thought of as a country that Hitler might not be able to occupy.

Close friendships developed quickly between the Americans and their British colleagues. Churchill, who stayed at the White House, pushed Roosevelt's wheelchair to the elevator each night as a gesture of respect. He wrote to his wife: "The Americans are magnificent in their breadth of view."

In 1942 British researchers into the military uses of atomic energy turned over their information to the United States; the following year FDR reciprocated by promising Churchill full sharing of data. Yet the good faith tended to be one-sided. Churchill discovered that British intelligence, having broken the U.S. cipher, had been spying on the Americans—and promptly informed Roosevelt; but FDR said nothing to the prime minister about similar American activities.

Neither Marshall nor Eisenhower had battlefield experience. The British commanders could not very well point that out, but they had seen their country nearly go down the drain in the First World War by mounting the direct attacks on entrenched enemy positions that the Americans now urged.

* The Declaration of the United Nations was signed in Washington on January 1, 1942.

Marshall wanted to launch an amphibious assault on German-held France immediately. Problems encountered later in the opening trial of arms against German troops in French North Africa confirmed the judgment that U.S. forces were far from ready: that such an assault might have been suicidal. British military leaders were proposing peripheral strategies in 1941–42, not necessarily or at least not entirely from imperialistic motives, but instead because their experience had taught them, wrongly or rightly, that it was the only way to win without suffering a bloodbath. The experience of D day showed that Churchill and FDR were right to postpone that event until 1944, and Marshall was wrong.* But American military leaders would not credit the sincerity of the motives of their English colleagues.

Suspicions of British imperialism persisted. It was in part FDR's idea, inspired by Mahan, to invade French North Africa, but Marshall, who was opposed, ascribed it to Churchill; he believed it was intended only to further British postwar interests, and reacted by proposing to shift priority from the European theater to the Pacific—in which he was overruled by the President. But Roosevelt, too, disapproved of European empires, and repeatedly criticized the prime minister on that score, urging him, among other things, to free India.

IN JANUARY 1943 Roosevelt and Churchill met in a suburb of Casablanca, on the Atlantic coast of Morocco, to discuss next steps in the war. Coming after the Newfoundland and Washington conferences of 1941, it was their third wartime meeting. The prime minister was an old hand at flying into war zones; but for the President, the airplane trip thousands of miles across the Atlantic was a novel and exhilarating experience.

Stalin, who had been invited, claimed that he was unable to join them. His presence, however, was felt. The leaders of the democracies were keenly aware that the communist dictator demanded the launching of an invasion of western Europe as a proof of their loyalty to their alliance with the Soviet Union.

Nazi Germany still was undefeated. German troops still held the line outside Stalingrad and battled British and American troops in Tunisia; German submarines still waged the Battle of the Atlantic and impeded the American effort to ship a mass army across the ocean to England in order to invade France. But the President and the prime minister clearly felt that their countries were on the road to victory.

Among their military decisions were agreements to give top priority

---

* But Marshall was right to worry that, as in the First World War, the American army might be ready to launch its attack too late.

to the battle of the Atlantic; to complete the North African campaign and then go on to invade Sicily; to increase strategic bombing of Germany and build up forces in Britain to invade France; and to launch various operations in Burma, China, and the Pacific.

The most controversial issue then and now was when to open up a "second front" by invading western Europe in force. Its implications were political as well as military. It had a direct bearing on the shape of the postwar world. It was debated at the Casablanca conference and continued to be argued passionately throughout 1943.

Marshall and America's other military leaders worried about the Pacific campaign against Japan because, despite aid from British Commonwealth and other forces, it was a war waged largely by the United States. America's strategy was to hold Japan at bay while defeating Germany first. But this gave the Japanese time to build up their defenses. The more time they were given, the greater American casualties eventually were likely to be. It followed that Marshall and his colleagues wanted not merely to defeat Germany, but to do so in the quickest possible way. They were prepared to take risks if necessary in order to save time. They wanted to try for a knockout blow immediately by sending their armies to liberate France and invade Germany.

General Albert C. Wedemeyer, one of Marshall's chief operations planners along with Eisenhower, spoke for the influential group of American army leaders who believed that British opposition to an immediate assault on the coast of France was inspired by political rather than military calculations. According to Wedemeyer, the British were paying mere lip service to the concept of a cross-Channel operation while they really were devoted to a war of attrition in which Germany and the Soviet Union would bleed each other white. Only when Germany disintegrated would they wish to invade Europe. This would allow them to dominate the Continent in the postwar world, playing off an enfeebled Germany against an enfeebled Soviet Union. Their preferred wartime strategy of focusing on the Mediterranean theater of operations would allow them also to hold on to the maritime road to the Middle East and their empire in Asia and the Pacific.

The Soviet wartime strategy of focusing all resources on defeating Germany in Europe was in accord with the thinking of America's generals. Marshall and his colleagues were not necessarily blind to the possibility that the strategy they favored might expose Europe to a Soviet threat in the postwar world. But Marshall believed that his advice as a military man should be strictly military and that he should leave political considerations to the civilian commander in chief. Like Roosevelt, Marshall also seems to have believed that any postwar Soviet threat to Europe was Britain's problem, not America's. Until 1943, at least, it was commonly believed that Britain was strong enough to deal with the problem by herself.

But FDR's views diverged from those of his military advisers. Despite their reluctance, he had ordered them to invade French North Africa, not merely because to his Mahan-influenced mind it was of strategic importance, but because he wanted to see American troops engaged in battle against Germans as soon as possible, committing the United States to his priority of defeating Germany first. Victory in North Africa would create a momentum of its own, leading on to the invasion of Sicily (as decided at Casablanca) and then of Italy. All of these—the assaults on North Africa, Sicily, and Italy—were urged by Churchill and agreed to by Roosevelt. FDR seemed to be siding with the British against his own generals.

Fears were in evidence on Capitol Hill that at Casablanca the President was subordinating his country's interests to those of British imperialism. Questions were asked by the chairman of the Senate Committee on Foreign Relations. Only reassurances by Marshall, who was trusted universally, sufficed to quiet these concerns.

At the close of the Casablanca conference on January 24, Roosevelt announced that the war goal pursued by the United States and Great Britain was the "unconditional surrender" of their enemies. FDR may have intended thereby to help overcome the doubts raised by the Darlan deal as to whether he sincerely intended to destroy fascism; and in a statement of clarification he explained that he intended to eradicate not the civilian populations, but the vicious political philosophies, of the enemy powers. He also may have intended the unconditional surrender formula to reassure the Soviet Union that the democracies would not negotiate a separate peace at Russia's expense. Then, too, FDR may have hoped to avoid the mistakes Wilson had made in 1918 in offering peace terms that misled the German people.

AT THE CLOSE of the Casablanca conference, Churchill took Roosevelt on a pleasure jaunt. It was a measure of how well things had gone in the previous year that they felt they could afford to relax. They headed for the Moroccan oasis of Marrakesh, a hundred miles from the ocean, and a refuge from both the Atlantic and the Sahara.

Marrakesh is a pink city, watered by streams and rivers, lined with orange trees and palms, and filled with gardens and cool hidden courtyards. Early one evening, Churchill had servants make a chair of their arms to carry FDR up to a villa rooftop to see the sun set over the distant snow-capped Atlas mountain range. Churchill had painted the scene years earlier, and did so again on his trip with Roosevelt; it was the only painting he did during the war. He told FDR that the sunset at Marrakesh was the most beautiful scene in the world.

After viewing the sunset, the two leaders went down to dinner. Over the meal they spoke to and of each other with great affection. Enchanted,

Roosevelt spoke of his political dreams. He said he wanted to see a global immunization program that would eradicate disease; compulsory education for everyone; and a birth control system.

It was a foretaste of what America would bring to the world of the twentieth century: the President of the United States addressed the concerns not of his own country alone, but of the planet.


ROOSEVELT CRUSADED, as had Wilson, for free trade in the post-war world. At times he saw Britain through the eyes of his grandfather Delano, as a commercial rival; he then urged the abolition of the tariff wall built around the commonwealth system.

The President was under domestic political pressure to treat England as a business competitor. That became clear in the autumn of 1943, when a bipartisan group of five traveling senators called the United States a "global sucker" for not making wartime aid contingent on the granting of commercial concessions. The five included powerful Senator Richard Russell, a Georgia Democrat, and young Senator Henry Cabot Lodge of Massachusetts, a leader of the internationalist wing of the Republican party and the grandson of the man who had defeated Wilson and the League of Nations in 1919–20.

England's imperialism remained unpopular with the American public. In a June 1942 poll, 56 percent of Americans called the British "oppressors" who had taken unfair advantage of the peoples they ruled. Those who did so might not have believed recent calculations that the empire provided Britain in the late 1930s with only about 1 percent of her income.

Roosevelt was voicing his country's sentiments when he told the press: "There never has been, there isn't now and there never will be, any race on earth fit to serve as masters of their fellow men. . . . We believe that any nationality, no matter how small, has the inherent right to its own nationhood."

Although Churchill stoutly argued that "British imperialism has spread and is spreading democracy more widely than any other system of government since the beginning of time," his views fell on deaf ears. A report from the United States to the British Foreign Office warned that "official opinion is tending towards the conclusion that as part of the post-war settlement the existing Colonial Empires ought to be liquidated. . . ."

Beginning perhaps in 1943, as Allied fortunes improved, the American government became more critical of Britain. As victory and a peace settlement drew nearer, the U.S. desire to dissolve European colonial empires came more to the fore. So did the question of which governments to restore in liberated Europe; Secretary Hull claimed the British "attitude is probably dictated by their desire to protect . . . monarchial institutions." They proposed to crown kings, he said, while the United States cast its vote for establishing republics.

"Winston and I will write the Peace Treaty," FDR had said; but as the United States increased its contribution to the war effort, American leaders began to ask why Britain should have an equal voice in deciding the fate of postwar Europe. "We are going to pay for it," said Treasury Secretary Morgenthau. "The English are going to be busted. . . . I think it had better be Franklin Roosevelt, without Winston, [who] writes the peace treaty. . . ."

FDR told his Joint Chiefs of Staff in 1943 that political motives lay behind a whole range of British proposals and initiatives, from elevating France to great-power status, to overall strategy in the Mediterranean and in the Southeast Asia campaign, to planning for the postwar Balkans. He warned against allowing England to get the United States "roped into accepting any European spheres of influence." For while Roosevelt did not want Churchill to take control of part of Europe by agreement with Stalin, neither did he want him to set up a bloc in Europe against Stalin—to oppose the USSR—which might lead to a new war.

WHEN GERMANY INVADED the Soviet Union and the Western democracies offered aid, Stalin's first demand was for recognition of his country's 1941 frontiers: the ones set by agreement with Hitler. Churchill came to believe he should consent, but Roosevelt was adamantly opposed. On the specific issues, he refused to concede that the Baltic republics or a large chunk of Poland should belong to Russia; in general, he was opposed to a redrawing of frontiers until the war was won. Sumner Welles told the British Foreign Office that its proposed appeasement of Stalin would be another Munich.

Churchill was afraid Russia might negotiate a separate peace if her demands were not met. Stalin linked his territorial claims to his insistence that America and Britain invade France to open up a second front in the European war against Germany: he insisted on having either one or the other.

In the spring of 1942 Roosevelt told Soviet foreign minister Molotov that he looked forward to establishing a new world order after the war, based on cooperation of the great powers. He said that he envisaged the Soviet Union as one of the policemen of the postwar world. Along with the United States and Britain—and perhaps China—they would be the only countries allowed to have arms. The others would be demilitarized. Moreover, the colonial empires of the European powers would be taken away and entrusted to the three or four great powers.

This did not satisfy Molotov, who wanted to occupy countries next door rather than in Africa or the Pacific, and who repeatedly asked for an assurance that a second front would be opened in 1942.

Roosevelt decided that if he could meet Stalin personally—and preferably alone—he could convince him to put aside his territorial demands for the duration of the war. He persuaded himself that it was not merely the State Department but also the British who stood in the way of reaching an agreement. "I know you will not mind my being brutally frank," he wrote Churchill in 1942, "when I tell you that I think I can personally handle Stalin better than your Foreign Office or my State Department. Stalin hates the guts of all your top people. He thinks he likes me better and I hope he will continue to do so."

A report from army intelligence claimed that Russians "do not understand our altruism" in sending lend-lease supplies and "fail completely to cooperate with us"—interestingly enough, because of British interference. The report warned of a possible new Nazi-Soviet deal arising from Russian distrust of the West caused by British behavior.

# 52

# THE ORIGINS OF THE
# COLD WAR

AS HE WAS SO OFTEN, Bullitt was the first: in this case, the first
within the government to focus on the Russian threat. Working out of the
Navy Department, where he was supplied with special projects from time
to time to keep him busy, he bombarded the President in the middle of
the war with long memorandums warning that this was the time for a
showdown with the Soviet Union. "You have your power now," he wrote,
but "you will lose it the day Germany collapses. Wilson could have written
his own ticket before the Armistice of 1918. You may be able to write
yours—now."

He was wrong on both counts. At no point after the United States
entered the First World War was Wilson able to obtain Allied agreement
to America's proposed war goals; the President proclaimed the Fourteen
Points unilaterally precisely because he knew Britain and France would not
accept them.

As for the Soviet Union: even in the first days of the German invasion,
when survival for more than a few weeks seemed unlikely, Moscow clung
to its claims on the Baltic republics and Poland. Stalin could not be coerced
into agreeing to FDR's postwar plans for these areas; if he had promised to
do so, it is a fair guess that once his armies were in control of the situation,
he would not have kept his word.

In a memo dated January 29, 1943, Bullitt ridiculed the prevailing
view that Stalin had changed his beliefs, and the Soviet government its
nature. Russia's expansionism, he wrote, was like that of an amoeba. "He
moves where opposition is weak. He stops where opposition is strong. He
puts out pseudopodia like an amoeba. . . . If the pseudopodia meet no
obstacle, the Soviet Union flows on."

Attacking what really was FDR's plan, but ascribing it to the British,
Bullitt argued that instead of disarming the continent of Europe after the
war, the United States should organize a united, integrated, and rearmed
Europe that would stand in the way of Soviet expansion.

It should be carrot and stick, wrote Bullitt. FDR should arrange a
face-to-face meeting with Stalin and offer him aid and credits in rebuilding

the devastated Soviet Union in return for cooperation. But what if Stalin said no?

For one lucid moment before darkness descended on Bullitt's mind, he saw all the way through to the core and essence of it: *the Red Army was going to keep whatever territory it won.* What that meant—though many Americans would not recognize or accept it, either at the time or later—was that the only way to prevent Soviet domination of central and eastern Europe was for the U.S. Army to liberate those areas from Nazi Germany before the Russians could get there.

So Bullitt proposed to change America's war strategy in order to get there first. He wrote that the United States could do it "if we make our attack on the Axis not by way of France and Italy but by way of Salonika and Constantinople." Of course, he knew that American doctrine required that strategy be adopted for military rather than political purposes. But he argued that his idea of attacking through Greece and Turkey was every bit as sound from a military point of view as that of attacking via Italy and France. "And if military considerations are equal, the strategic plan that promises political success is to be preferred to the strategic plan that promises political disaster."

There is no evidence that Bullitt's memorandums were considered seriously. Marshall never wavered in his belief that, to the extent possible, all forces should be concentrated on a cross-Channel invasion of France.

Bullitt coupled his strategic proposals with notions for cleaning out and streamlining the State Department. His purpose in suggesting changes at State was transparent: he was back to what was both his obsession and his undoing. He had the ever-faithful Carmel Offie distribute documents all over Capitol Hill describing Sumner Welles's homosexual escapades— to which he himself added details of what he claimed were indiscretions on the part of Mrs. Welles that compromised national security.

After a terminally bitter argument with Hull, Welles was fired in 1943, bringing his career in the government to an end—and Bullitt's. FDR would have nothing further to do with the ambassador who once had amused him.

Bullitt went around Washington pouring out to others his dark prophecies as to what the Soviet Union would do. Britain's ambassador in Washington and former foreign secretary, Lord Halifax, reported in 1943 that he had found Bullitt "very anti-Russian. He thinks we and his own Government are completely blind to the kind of thing he anticipates Stalin will want to do. As he sees it he will seek to dominate and control all Central and South-Eastern European Governments . . . and one of these days we shall all wake up to find Russia a great menace to our free democracies. I told him that this was not the impression gathered by those who had had to do with Stalin, but this naturally made no impression on him. He is a strange fellow, and I don't think judgment is his strongest quality."

IN THE AUTUMN OF 1943 Harriman was sent out to Moscow as U.S. ambassador. He had graduated with Bullitt in the Yale class of '13, was to serve in the post first held by Bullitt, and was assisted by the stars of Bullitt's original staff, first Charles Bohlen, and then George Kennan. Like Bullitt, Harriman urged dangling the prospect of postwar credits in front of Stalin to secure his cooperation. And like Bullitt, though for different reasons, Harriman was unable to get through directly to the President. In Harriman's case it was because his conduit, the ailing Harry Hopkins, had lost his place in the President's full confidence—for reasons as vague as those that led Wilson to break with House.

From 1943 on, the President was alone in shaping America's grand strategy for war and peace. In the past he had talked over these issues with Hopkins and Welles. Now he had nobody.

FDR became the solitary master of the White House map room, where developments on all fronts could be followed on detailed maps. The room served as intelligence headquarters at the highest level; on its military channels FDR communicated directly with Churchill, Stalin, and others and reached agreements. There and there alone were to be found the files of messages and transcriptions of telephone conversations that spelled out America's commitments to and from her allies.

So secret was the map room that even the secretary of state—Hull— knew nothing of it.

THERE WERE VAST QUANTITIES of new data about the Soviet Union that the President had to assimilate in adjusting his policies to a fast-moving and confusing situation.

One item: Stalin, who had a secret atomic bomb program of his own, had learned (as Roosevelt and Churchill found out) of the Anglo-American partnership in developing an atomic bomb.

Another: Churchill had new evidence, which he forwarded to Roosevelt in the summer of 1943, of Stalin's wickedness: it transpired that the 10,000 or 15,000 Polish officers killed at Katyn Wood in 1940 in order to destroy the nation's elite had been killed not by the Germans, but by the Russians.

FDR's request that the combined Joint Chiefs plan for U.S. and British troops to race to Berlin before the Russians shows that he believed that military operations might be conducted with political objectives in mind. But for whatever reason he continued to object to Churchill's attempts to bargain with Stalin, and he persistently deplored British proposals to campaign in the Balkans and the Mediterranean as politically motivated.

Roosevelt could not help but be impressed by the disproportionate contribution the Soviet Union was making to the war against Hitler. Some 80 percent of Germany's forces were engaged by Russia. The destruction wrought by the Nazi invaders was on a scale that challenged the imagination. Describing Soviet losses for the whole of the war, an American historian has written: "German invaders had destroyed over 1,700 cities and towns and more than 70,000 villages and hamlets. They demolished more than six million buildings and over 31,000 industrial enterprises. They wrecked 61 of the largest power stations, 1,100 coal pits, and more than 3,000 oil wells. They dismantled 40,000 miles of railroad track, blew up 56,000 miles of main road, and ruined 90,000 bridges. The Germans ransacked the countryside, destroying tens of thousands of collective farms and machine and tractor stations. They stole and slaughtered 17 million head of cattle, 20 million hogs, 27 million sheep and goats, 110 million poultry, and 7 million horses. More than 20 million Soviet lives were lost in the war. . . ." More recent estimates have put the number of Soviet dead at upwards of 25 million. This compares with 400,000 battle deaths suffered by the United States in the Second World War against Japan, Germany, and Italy.

More to the point as far as inter-Allied politics was concerned, at Stalingrad in 1943 the Red Army had won the victory that proved to be the turning point in the war. By mid-1944, when the United States and Britain now planned to invade France, the Russians were going to be poised to march into Poland. Never was the realism of Stalin made more clear. From the beginning he had said that America and Britain had to choose one or the other: either they landed in Normandy in 1942 or 1943, or else they accepted the Soviet frontiers he claimed in eastern Europe; for his armies would get to such countries as Poland and Romania first. (Of course, he may have been lying. He might have taken central and eastern Europe even if the Western powers *had* invaded France in 1942 or 1943.)

The situation confronting FDR as he planned a face-to-face meeting with Stalin and Churchill at Teheran at the end of 1943 was like that encountered by Wilson at Paris in 1919. Roosevelt had lived through that episode and knew it well. In the First World War the United States had been too late; France was in a position to claim that she had won the war, and therefore was able to impose her own peace terms. In the Second World War, the United States was too late again: D day should have been in 1942 or 1943 if America were to stand a chance of freeing central and eastern Europe. Yet that might not have been possible. A U.S. invasion of France in 1942 or 1943 might well have been defeated.

Now Stalin would take half of Europe and do as he chose with it.

Roosevelt, who had a kind of pride in power just as he had pride of birth, was drawn away from Churchill and toward Stalin by the disappointing performance of Britain's ground forces in various campaigns and the extraordinary accomplishments of Russia's.

Roosevelt nonetheless made an effort to persuade the Soviet dictator to modify his goals. At the end of 1943 FDR had his long-awaited chance to meet privately (at first) with Stalin at the Teheran conference. Differences were papered over, but Stalin would not budge; he would keep his 1941 frontiers, including the Baltic republics and a section of Poland. It was Roosevelt who backed down.

The President now treated Churchill as only a minor partner. Ickes recorded in his diary that "the Roosevelt-Stalin axis is gaining strength and the Roosevelt-Churchill axis is losing strength in about equal ratio." Apparently imagining that Stalin was opposed to empires, FDR spoke to him of dismantling Britain's—and may have been surprised by the communist leader's response: that "because of the British military contribution, the Soviet government considers that there should be no reduction in the British Empire, but on the contrary it should if necessary be increased by turning over to Great Britain on the basis of trusteeship certain bases and strongpoints throughout the world."

Or perhaps Roosevelt was not surprised, for there were times when he was ruthlessly realistic. On returning from Teheran in January 1944, FDR told Otto, heir to the Hapsburg throne, that he "had told the Russians they could take over and control completely as their sphere—so completely that the United States could from this moment on have no further policies with regard to them"—not only the Baltic countries and eastern Poland, but Finland, Romania, and Bulgaria.


A COINCIDENCE that had consequences was that Bullitt had been placed in the Navy Department. The position created for him was special assistant to the secretary. The undersecretary, James Forrestal, was repelled but also fascinated by communism, and was in search of some way to understand it. He fell (Forrestal's most recent biographers tell us) under Bullitt's influence.

Forrestal agreed entirely that the Soviet Union was expansionist and dangerous. From Bullitt he derived the key perception that communism was a kind of religion. It apparently was new to him—though John Maynard Keynes had made the point in a well-known essay in 1925—and it struck a responsive chord in one whose central inner conflict was the attempt to escape his religion.

Forrestal began to take a serious interest in the reports of Ambassador Harriman, whose views were similar to Bullitt's though not identical to them. Harriman seemed more inclined to believe the United States *could* do business with the Soviets—but only by being tough with them, not friendly and generous.

The picture painted by Bullitt was darker. He saw communism as relentlessly expansionist—and Forrestal was inclined to share that vision, too. In their emerging view, the Soviet Union had stopped being an ally and was about to become an enemy. Forrestal was to become a leader of the American crusade against world communism.

# 53

# WILSON'S WAY

NINETEEN FORTY-THREE proved to be the pivotal year in the European war. The Allies completed their conquest of North Africa, which, in turn, opened the Mediterranean to their shipping. They took Sicily. They obtained Italy's surrender; and, against stubborn German resistance, they invaded the southern tip of the Italian peninsula.

The most important military event of the year was the Soviet Union's defeat of Germany in mammoth clashes of arms on the eastern front. After the Red Army won the largest tank battle in history—the battle of Kursk—what began to emerge was that a fundamental shift in the balance of power was taking place: the Soviet Union, which had been considered a negligible military factor as late as 1941, was on its way to becoming the greatest land power in the world.

Roosevelt and Churchill held a half dozen conferences during the course of 1943, reaching strategic decisions and then modifying or abandoning them as circumstances quickly changed. The main question they had to resolve (but which they postponed repeatedly) was when American and British forces would launch their long-mooted invasion of France. By the autumn it became clear that the Allies had destroyed the German submarine menace, winning the battle of the Atlantic and making it possible for the United States to ship a mass army across the ocean to England to mount such an invasion.

The invasion date finally was set at the Teheran conference. This was the last of the 1943 meetings, though the first that was attended by Stalin. It took place in the capital of Iran, a country partially occupied by British-led and Russian-led forces in the Second World War as in the First.

Teheran was the most important of the 1943 conferences because at it the leaders of the Big Three—the United States, Great Britain, and the Soviet Union—reached agreement at last on their grand strategy in the war. Although the British still were inclined to postpone the cross-Channel invasion until 1945 or even 1946, FDR imposed the date of late spring 1944. Stalin and Churchill accepted that date; and the three leaders agreed that the United States and Great Britain also would launch an assault on France's Mediterranean coast at about the same time. In turn Stalin promised to order a major Soviet offensive on the eastern front timed to coincide with the two invasions of France. This was their perfected war plan, and they kept to it on schedule.

The three leaders also reached some broad agreements about the postwar world. It was common ground, especially as between Roosevelt and Stalin, that Germany should be dismembered and her power to make war destroyed. It was agreed, too, both that there should be an international organization and that the peace should be kept by a concert of the several great powers.

FDR sketched out on a sheet of paper how this might look. There would be an Assembly, consisting of the governments of the forty or so United Nations, to make nonbinding recommendations; and an Executive to deal, also in a nonbinding way, with all nonmilitary questions. Then there would be the "Four Policemen," the Big Three plus China, to enforce the peace. FDR had been expressing ideas along these lines at least since 1942. He claimed to be too realistic to expect his proposed international organization to keep the peace forever, but hoped that it might do so for a few decades.

Stalin was somewhat skeptical. He argued that the Germans were so powerful that even if dismembered, they would manage to reunite eventually. Against such a threat, FDR's international organization, he claimed, would prove inadequate. Instead the Allies should retain strategic points around the world with which to keep potential aggressors subdued. His posture was similar to that of Clemenceau at the Paris conference a quarter of a century before. Like Clemenceau, he doubted that Germans could be reformed.

Stalin was skeptical, too, about elevating China to the level of the Big Three and about deputizing her to play a role in European affairs. China, like Germany, historically posed a danger that Russians dreaded; and while Stalin did not point that out, he made clear that he felt she should be confined to her own sphere in Asia.

FDR did not disagree. His scheme, as he explained it, did not call for a Chinese presence in Europe or indeed anywhere outside of Asia. The United States would not be involved in policing postwar Europe either; Roosevelt made it clear that the American public would insist on withdrawing from the Continent. Control of Europe would be shared in the postwar world by Great Britain and the Soviet Union. That was a key element in FDR's plan; and Stalin gave the impression of being at least open to persuasion.

Churchill and Stalin seemed disposed to listen sympathetically to Roosevelt's plan for restructuring world politics, but FDR was unable to explain clearly what he had in mind. On the one hand, he did not intend for the three or four great powers to act jointly in peacekeeping operations all around the globe. In his plan each would act only within its own region: Europe was to be policed by Britain and Russia; the Western Hemisphere, by the United States. On the other hand, he opposed establishing spheres of influence. But he could not explain why his scheme would not do just that.*

The Woodrow Wilson part of FDR seemed to be genuinely opposed to exclusive spheres of influence on moral principle. Yet the Theodore Roosevelt part of him recognized that the establishment of spheres might be the only way to do political business in an imperfect world—while the FDR in him cautioned not to reveal that to the public.

Others in American public life, many of them with minds less complicated, were also considering how to remake the world. Their schemes, like Roosevelt's, failed to explain how goals were to be achieved with the specified means.

Looking ahead to the 1944 presidential elections, the chairman of the Republican National Committee, Harrison E. Spangler, convened a party conference at Mackinac Island, Michigan, in September 1943 to adopt an agreed plan for postwar policy. All factions in the party were represented at Mackinac except for Willkie's followers, regarded by the others as extreme internationalists. Vandenberg was principally responsible for the resulting Mackinac Declaration, which endorsed American membership in an international organization but stressed that the United States would not be bound by its decisions. This program was open to the objection that if its members were not bound by its decisions, the organization could not be effective.

Thomas E. Dewey was the leading candidate for the Republican nomination. His foreign policy adviser, John Foster Dulles, had become a lay religious leader with a special interest in plans for postwar world institutions. Dulles sponsored a plan for an international organization whose decisions could be imposed only through moral force. As moral force had not deterred Hitler or Mussolini, it was not clear why it would deter Stalin or others. Privately Dulles held more realistic views.

Walter Lippmann scored a popular success in 1943 with his book *U.S. Foreign Policy: Shield of the Republic*, in which he argued that world peace could best be secured by a continuing alliance of the United States, the Soviet Union, and Great Britain. The following year, as the differences between the three countries became more evident, he published *U.S. War Aims*, advocating the establishment of spheres of influence and the adoption of a policy of live and let live. The book proved to be a failure, eclipsed by

---

* Perhaps he was reaching for some sort of concept in which each great power would exercise merely a limited peacekeeping responsibility in its sphere while not interfering in other respects with the independence of the countries in its sphere, and without closing them off from outside influences or from relationships with other great powers.

Sumner Welles's *The Time for Decision*, a Wilsonian work calling for a new League of Nations. Of course, the old one had not worked.

In the spring of 1944 Cordell Hull, loyal Wilsonian that he was, assembled a bipartisan group of eight senators, including Vandenberg, to work with the State Department on its draft of a proposed United Nations Charter. Vandenberg approved of it, but felt the United States should not join the UN unless Britain and the Soviet Union agreed to peace terms America would deem just. There was no realistic possibility that this condition would be met; Russia was going to keep the neighboring lands that she occupied.

In late June 1944 the Republican National Convention assembled in Chicago and nominated Dewey for President on the first ballot. Taft was running for reelection to the Senate that year, and in his place Ohio governor John W. Bricker headed the forces of isolationism at the convention. Dewey chose Bricker to run with him for Vice President. The foreign policy platform, reflecting the views and language of Dulles and Vandenberg, cautiously favored U.S. participation in a postwar international peacekeeping organization.

The Democrats, too, met in Chicago, in July. Sensing a conservative swing in the electorate, FDR, in poor health but running for a fourth term as President, seemingly allowed party officials to designate the vice-presidential nominee. Under the surface of events, he moved deviously to select a candidate himself—someone who would not hurt the ticket in an election that he feared might be close.

The incumbent, Henry Wallace, was a liability who had to be disposed of because his fringe spiritualist beliefs and leftist politics threatened to disquiet the mainstream of the electorate. But dropping the Vice President would risk forfeiting the enthusiasm of FDR's core of supporters to whom Wallace's idealism, vision, and eloquence were of especial importance. If their hero were to be sacrificed, the rival clan would have to suffer a sacrifice in return.

Once again pushing forward and then pulling the rug out from under his oldest political associate, FDR launched a boom for James Byrnes as *his* candidate—and then allowed political boss Ed Flynn of the Bronx to veto the "assistant President" as a liability in courting Catholic and black voters, and organized labor to veto him as too conservative.

Having appeared to let the Right veto the candidate of the Left, and the Left veto the candidate of the Right, FDR allowed the real contest to go forward between the two names acceptable to everyone, and therefore to him: William O. Douglas and Harry S Truman. FDR somewhat preferred Douglas, but let the leaders of the party organization—many of whom seem to have secretly believed that Roosevelt might die in office—choose Truman instead, putting the middle-of-the-road Missouri senator in line for the White House.

The Democratic foreign policy platform strongly endorsed creation of an international organization "endowed with power to employ armed forces when necessary to prevent aggression and preserve peace," but did not provide details of how this would be done.

The Republicans were placing their emphasis on retaining full freedom of action for the United States, while the Democrats were putting theirs on giving up enough national decision-making power to the United Nations so that it could be effective. But both pledged themselves to institutionalized international cooperation—which probably was as much as the electorate cared to know.

With foreign policy effectively excluded from the campaign, FDR won the November election. But as Roosevelt had foreseen, though his aides had not, his margin of victory over his Republican challenger was smaller than in 1940: 7.5 percent instead of 9.88 percent.

As the 1944 presidential campaign was taking place, representatives of the various United Nations were meeting at Bretton Woods, New Hampshire (July 1–22), and in the Dumbarton Oaks mansion in Georgetown, a section of Washington (August 21–October 7), to draw partial blueprints for, respectively, international financial institutions and a postwar international organization to preserve the peace.

Both conferences were held in an attempt to realize the new and largely American vision of a unitary world whose affairs would be dealt with by international institutions. At Bretton Woods, the United States sat down with 44 wartime allies to devise a postwar monetary order. Holding to her traditional goal, America hoped to break down blocs and barriers and to establish a stable global financial order within which her citizens could trade, invest, and do business anywhere in the world. The United States and Great Britain were the only two real financial powers at Bretton Woods, and the story of the conference is that of the dialogue and negotiations between the two. They were the most ambitious economic talks in history, aimed, as they were, at designing a new system for the entire world.

FDR would have preferred Dumbarton Oaks, too, to be essentially a negotiation between the great powers, but American internationalist opinion in both the Democratic and Republican parties was too much under the influence of Woodrow Wilson for that to be practical politics. The plans for an international organization to keep the peace, carried forward by the Dumbarton Oaks meeting, necessarily represented a compromise between FDR's concepts, embodied in the Security Council, and Wilson's, embodied in the General Assembly.

The productive functioning of international institutions depended on continuing cooperation between the various governments, and especially those of the three allied great powers. But in 1944 there was even more reason than there had been in 1943 to question whether that cooperation could in fact be relied upon. Buoyed with success, the Russians might well harden their position on postwar boundaries and on the future of eastern Europe.

Roosevelt was hopeful but also realistic. During the presidential campaign, he told Hull: "In regard to the Soviet government, it is true that we have no idea as yet what they have in mind, but we have to remember that in their occupied territory they will do more or less as they wish. We cannot afford to get into a position of merely recording protests on our part unless there is some chance of some of the protests being heeded."

WESTERN LEADERS blinded themselves to the obvious: it was not just the United States that wanted to remake the world in its own image; so did the Soviet Union. Unlike a Woodrow Wilson—or a Leon Trotsky— Stalin was no believer in trying to change the whole world at once. He moved a step at a time. Victory in the Second World War would bring him control of neighboring countries. He would give priority in the years afterward to consolidating that control. In twenty years there might be another major war, in the chaotic aftermath of which he could annex an additional large portion of the globe. In the end his regime was destined to have it all; his version of Marxism told him that. So he could wait.

As communist leaders explained long afterward, the plan to buy Stalin's cooperation with postwar credits was a nonstarter. No amount of credits from the United States would induce him to abandon his goals.

Indeed U.S. aid was in some ways dangerous to him: subversive of his regime. Harriman was not the first American ambassador to notice that the Soviet government denied to its people that the streams of supplies from the United States came from abroad. To accept help meant to open up Soviet society to foreign influence, and Stalin's purposes were better served by keeping the lands he served closed off from the rest of the world.

To imagine that the men in the Kremlin would abjure their political religion in return for economic benefits was to underestimate the depth of their commitment to their faith. "Roosevelt believed in dollars," Foreign Minister Molotov recalled decades later. "Not that he didn't believe in anything else, but he considered his people to be so rich, and we so poor and so worn out, that we would come begging. . . . That's where they miscalculated. That's where they weren't Marxists and we were. They woke up only when half of Europe was taken from them."

Stalin's theories left him impervious to demonstrations of Western friendliness. Marxism, which pictures events as being driven by objective social forces, is one of those philosophies that leave no room for individual humans to make a difference. If Churchill and Roosevelt promised sincerely that Britain and America would live forever in peace and harmony with a communist Russia, it would only mean that Churchill and Roosevelt were mistaken.

The Soviet dictator seems to have assumed his allies would understand that he would take control of the countries the Red Army conquered. Stalin told a group of Yugoslav communists: "Whoever occupies a territory also imposes on it his own social system" as far "as his army can reach." Churchill therefore spoke a language the Kremlin understood, in offering, for example, to recognize Russia's hold on Romania if Stalin would recognize Britain's control of Greece. That was Moscow's way of doing business.

When FDR spoke of the Big Three working together, however, he spoke in terms whose meaning the Russians must have found elusive. If there were to be two halves to the world, the Soviets could have one for their closed communist system and the Anglo-Americans could have the other; and the two could coexist. But if the President, in suggesting a three-power world directorate, meant that there was to be only *one* world order, the issue would have to be joined as to whose kind of world it would be. To the extent that FDR was Rooseveltian—a realist willing to divide the world into spheres of exclusive control or influence—he could have a deal with Stalin. But to the extent that he was Wilsonian—an idealist determined to set the entire world free—he could only in the end have a war with Russia, whether hot or cold.

# 54

# HANDING OVER COMMAND

IN LATER YEARS Bullitt would allow it to be understood that he broke with FDR on the question of Soviet Russia. In fact, it was FDR who broke with him. Hull tried to obtain some sort of diplomatic appointment for Bullitt, but could not; the President never would forgive what he had done to Welles. Sardonically, FDR joked about sending him as minister to Saudi Arabia—having in mind, no doubt, a very large desert and a very small canteen of water.

As a boy, Bullitt must have read adventure stories in which the hero, ruined, runs away to join the foreign legion and wins glory. He did much the same thing. His career at an end, he asked Stimson to let him go on active duty with the army; Stimson refused. He then applied to join the forces of Free France. De Gaulle replied by hand: "There are some consolations. Your letter, for me, is one. It will be for all the French. Come now! Good and dear American friend. Our ranks are open to you. You will return with us into wounded Paris. . . ."

Commissioned a major in the infantry, he served from the summer of 1944 as aide to the commanding general of the French First Army, which invaded the Riviera coast and drove north along the Rhône and then on to Alsace and the Rhine. He was promoted to lieutenant colonel, awarded the Croix de Guerre, and admitted to the Legion of Honor. On Bastille Day 1945 Bullitt was among the French officers who drove up the Champs-Élysées leading the victory parade, taking the salute from de Gaulle in the reviewing stand.

IN RETROSPECT, 1945 was a time of things and people and jobs coming to an end. The expected face was not behind the desk in the familiar office. Hull, very ill, and tired of not being consulted or even informed about the President's foreign policy, resigned. He and Welles no longer headed the State Department. Stettinius, the former lend-lease chief, now was secretary of state, and Grew was undersecretary. Frank Knox had died in April 1944, and Forrestal had become secretary of the navy.

In the depths of winter the President unwillingly voyaged to and from Yalta in the Crimea for what was to prove the last of his wartime conferences with Stalin and Churchill. On doctor's orders he had lost weight—thirty-five pounds—and he looked frighteningly ill. But this was a meeting that he had to attend.

The concerns that drove the President to make his final journey were so much creatures of that fleeting moment that only a year or two later, political colleagues and military advisers would forget why he went and what he accomplished there.

Roosevelt journeyed to Yalta because General Marshall strongly urged him to get Stalin's confirmation that the Soviet Union would enter the war against Japan and would do so within ninety days after Germany surrendered.* The chief of staff told the President that getting such a commitment was absolutely essential. The United States expected to lose at least hundreds of thousands of troops in invading the Japanese islands. Japanese plans called for a defending force of 3 million to meet the invaders on the beaches. Marshall believed that a Soviet attack pinning down a million Japanese troops in Manchuria would be indispensable. A MacArthur spokesman told journalists that "we must not invade Japan proper unless the Russian army is previously committed to action"; the general used such strong language along the same lines in appealing to Washington that the Joint Chiefs finally urged Roosevelt in effect to give Stalin whatever he asked in return for coming into the Far Eastern war.

That the Russians would ask for something in return was taken for granted. "They simply cannot understand giving without taking," remarked Marshall's representative in Moscow, General John Deane. Harriman was able to give Roosevelt some idea in advance of what Stalin would ask.

FDR's triumph at the Yalta Conference (February 4–11, 1945) was that he won the very promise his generals told him they needed so much from Stalin: Russia would attack Japan—and in return for doing so, would have the Kuril Islands, the half of Sakhalin Island occupied by Japan, and concessions in northern China. Since the Soviet decision to declare war on Japan had to be kept a secret from the Japanese until it happened, the entire agreement had to remain secret.

From Wilson administration days, warning bells should have sounded in some part of Roosevelt's brain. He knew that the American public deplored secret deals, especially those promising territorial acquisitions to allies: it was the very point that he had made to Churchill in framing the Atlantic Charter in 1941. And he was aware of the uproar that would be

---

* Forrest C. Pogue, author of the classic biography of Marshall, dissents from the common view that Marshall brought pressure to bear on Roosevelt to obtain such a commitment.

caused when it became known that he had made pledges to Russia at China's expense. Wilson had been most vulnerable on the issue of concessions to Japan in China's Shantung province.

Yet what else could he do? If his generals were right, he was saving perhaps as many as a million American lives. Unfortunately for Roosevelt's reputation for statesmanship, Marshall, MacArthur, and his other generals were not right. They were as wrong as they had been when they estimated that Nazi Germany would defeat Soviet Russia in a few weeks, or as Marshall had been when he warned that Britain probably would fall in 1940 or when he told journalists in November 1941 that the American fleet had been sent to Pearl Harbor because then it would be safely "out of range of Japanese air power."* At Yalta, Roosevelt was misled not by Stalin or Molotov, but by Marshall, MacArthur, and the American Joint Chiefs.

Harriman was among the first to suspect—and then, only after the conference at Yalta had concluded—that the Soviet government actually *wanted* to enter the Far East war. The Japanese were on their last legs; they were nearing collapse. In attacking them Stalin rightly expected relatively easy pickings. For whatever reason, Marshall and his American military colleagues—MacArthur included—seem to have had no inkling of this. Even with the use of the A-bomb, they expected the rest of the Japanese war to be hard fought.

But their mistake did not matter all that much; in the end, the secret concessions made to the Soviet Union in Asia had no significant effect on world politics.


THERE WERE 700 MEMBERS of the Anglo-American delegations at Yalta. Many of them were interested in technical or detailed matters that were of little interest to the President. A question of great moment to them, and to the Congress and the American public, was the number of votes each country should have in the proposed United Nations Organization. FDR seems to have regarded the issue as unimportant; in his conception, all decisions would be made by unanimous agreement of the United States, Russia, and Britain (with France and China), so that the voting would be something of a charade. If seven countries were of one opinion, and forty-four were of the other opinion, the seven would win—if they included the Big Five. Therefore, the President cared little whether the Soviet Union was awarded one vote or, as Stalin asked, three. Yet the question excited the American electorate.

So the UN question was discussed, voting rights included; some further agreements were reached on the structure of a postwar peacekeeping orga-

* See page 433.

nization. But the drafting of the charter of the organization, and negotiation of the many details and questions that would have to be resolved, were postponed until a conference could convene dedicated solely to the creation of the United Nations. That conference was to take place in San Francisco in the spring of 1945.

The future of Germany also was discussed. Roosevelt always had taken the European view that the Reich was too powerful. Wilson's program had been to change Germany; FDR's, to break her into little pieces. Though generally known in American government circles as the "Morgenthau plan," it was at least as much Roosevelt's as Morgenthau's, and it had been the program of the Big Three throughout the war. It called for changing Germany from an industrial to a pastoral society. It also called for splitting her up into several disarmed units. Into how many segments to divide up the country—and along which lines—had been the subject of lively discussion at the Teheran conference.

Below the level of the President, however, the American government had never thought of Germany's future in such terms. Stimson blamed the Second World War on the harsh terms of the Versailles treaty, and proposed this time to be generous. His War Department and Hull's State Department always had been opposed to dismemberment. They had used delaying tactics with considerable success. In the autumn of 1944 details of the Morgenthau plan were leaked to the press, and the resulting furor led Roosevelt to back off from sponsoring it.

The future of Germany was the question the Big Three had to resolve if they were to make peace. At Yalta, Stalin pressed for a definite and detailed dismemberment decision, but Churchill argued for not deciding how to cut up Germany until expert studies had been made; at FDR's suggestion it was agreed to postpone the map-making for thirty days. Whatever his motive may have been at the time, Churchill told his private secretary a month later that "he hardly liked to consider dismembering Germany until his doubts about Russia's intentions had been cleared away." For, of course, if Russia had become an enemy, German power would be needed to counterbalance her; and if so, 1945 had stopped being postwar and had started to become what might well be prewar.


THOUGH IT WAS NOT HIS MAIN PURPOSE in undergoing the hardship of the voyage to Yalta,* politics drove FDR to try to bring his two wayward allies back into line. In liberated Europe, Great Britain seemed to be crusading for monarchy and Soviet Russia for communism, while the United States understood it to be a war for democracy.

---

* Getting Russia to go to war with Japan was.

American public opinion was deeply disturbed by the actions of the British army in Greece. English troops were installing a royalist regime by force in a battle against pro-Ally guerrilla forces. Churchill said the guerrillas were communist-inspired, but at the time Americans did not believe it.

Meanwhile, the Soviet takeover of Poland threatened FDR with the loss of the major Polish-American voting bloc, and he worried that the public as a whole would be so disgusted by the spectacle of rival British and Russian imperialisms that it would once again turn away from participation in international affairs.

Before leaving for Europe, FDR had told congressional leaders that "the Russians had the power in Eastern Europe, that it was obviously impossible to have a break with them and that, therefore, the only practicable course was to use what influence we had to ameliorate the situation." So he understood his chances were not very good, but also that he had to try his best.

Most of the time at the Yalta Conference was spent disagreeing about Poland. Underneath the words spoken by the participants, it really was a discussion of Soviet expansion into all the surrounding territories in Europe. Stalin made no secret of his determination to guide the futures of the neighboring countries that his armies had occupied or were about to occupy.

FDR knew that he could not prevent Soviet expansion. That could only be done by force of arms, and neither he nor the American people were in a mood to provoke a war with Russia. Moreover, as soon as Germany collapsed, the President would need to pull his armies out of Europe in order to send them to war against Japan.

All that could be done was to occupy as much of Europe as possible before the Red Army did, but Roosevelt, in the American tradition, left such decisions to his generals—to be made on military grounds. It was for Eisenhower to choose whether to try to race the Russians to Berlin—and rather than take tens of thousands of casualties and at least some risk of an armed clash with the Red Army, Ike cautiously opted not to make the attempt. Events justified his decision: the United States received her agreed sector of Berlin to administer, without losing the 100,000 lives it would have taken to fight through to the German capital to win it on her own.

Without wanting it, FDR was confronted with a spheres-of-influence peace settlement, for the Soviet armies were carving out a sphere of their own in neighboring Europe in which the Kremlin's word was law. At the same time, they were leaving western Europe, Italy, and Greece to Britain and America as their sphere, to do with as they chose. It was a de facto partition of Europe.

FDR did not merely not want the Soviet Union to have its own sphere (in Stalin's sense) in Europe; he did not want the United States to have one, either. For one thing it would mean garrisoning Europe with American troops, and Roosevelt knew the public wanted the boys brought home as soon as possible.

Then there were the endless involvements in foreign feuds and disputes to which a protectorate in Europe would lead. A year earlier, confronted with a British plan for an American zone of occupation in western Europe, FDR wrote Churchill: "I am absolutely unwilling to police France and possibly Italy and the Balkans as well. After all, France is your baby and will take a lot of nursing in order to bring it to the point of walking alone." He wrote him again saying, " 'Do please don't' ask me to keep any American forces in France. I just cannot do it! . . . I denounce and protest the paternity of Belgium, France and Italy. You really ought to bring up and discipline your own children. In view of the fact that they may be your bulwark in future days, you should at least pay for their schooling now."


THE TALKS WITH STALIN about a new government for Poland were an effort by Roosevelt and Churchill to work out some rules of conduct to which the Soviet government would pledge itself in administering the European countries that were about to come within its sphere. It was the most they could hope to accomplish in the circumstances.

It could be argued that such a statement of principles might conceivably have imposed some restraint on Russian behavior, and it certainly would help FDR win support from the Congress, the press, and the public. Stalin duly signed the document: a Declaration on Liberated Europe. It was an imprecise agreement, left open to diverse interpretations—and as Roosevelt had told Stalin he needed it for domestic political reasons, Stalin may have assumed that all members of the U.S. delegation recognized that the declaration was being issued only for cosmetic purposes. FDR apart, the others in fact took it more or less seriously, and in months and years to come Americans were to blame either Stalin for breaking his word or Roosevelt for taking it.

About at least this one thing critics of FDR at Yalta were wrong: he was not defrauded by the declaration. Even if it turned out to be a piece of paper worth not little, but nothing, the President had not been outbargained, for he had given nothing for it. And since he was getting it, so to speak, free of charge, why not take it?

George Kennan, then little known and not listened to, an officer of the American embassy in Moscow, believed the United States should be honest about the hard, unpleasant facts FDR was obliged to recognize at Yalta. He argued that the government should openly admit that the Soviet army had conquered half of Europe and was likely to hold on to it; that within its sphere, the Kremlin would do unilaterally whatever it chose; that there was nothing in the realm of practical politics that America could do about it; and that in consequence Europe had been partitioned into two spheres, one Soviet and one Western. Kennan was right; that *was* the truth about Yalta.

But it was not FDR's way to tell the public the truth if it was unpalatable.

ROOSEVELT HAD INSISTED that James Byrnes accompany him to Yalta. Byrnes managed all domestic policy for the President and argued that he should not leave Washington. Perhaps he was flattered by the invitation, or maybe he felt obliged to obey orders. For whatever reason, he went along with FDR.

Twice in a row, in 1940 and 1944, Byrnes's old friend Roosevelt had manipulated him, putting him up for Vice President and then arranging for someone to knock him down. It could be argued that by making such a point of the need for his presence on the world stage at Yalta, FDR was trying to make things up to him. Byrnes himself professed to be mystified. Thirteen years later he wrote: "Why the President insisted on my going I still do not know." But by then he really did know the reason: FDR was setting him up to be used once again.

The President managed the Yalta schedule in such a way that Byrnes attended only those sessions in which events occurred that FDR wanted the Congress and the public to know about, such as Stalin's promises of democracy in eastern Europe. Everybody knew of Byrnes's pride in his shorthand; he took notes and returned to Washington early, with the authoritative record on paper (of which he was also very proud) of what had happened.

As the first one back, and the custodian of a written record, Byrnes provided the initial authoritative account of the Yalta Conference to political Washington. FDR was known to be slippery, but Byrnes was trusted; his glowing account of what had been accomplished helped gain enthusiastic acceptance of the accords.

The President himself returned from the Crimea only slowly—and painfully. Bullitt's man Carmel Offie saw Roosevelt aboard ship on the return voyage and remembered later that "he looked ghastly, sort of dead and dug up." The President's personal aide, Pa Watson, was under an oxygen tent and died on the way home. Harry Hopkins was carried off in a stretcher, to be nursed back to sufficient strength so that he could be flown back to the Mayo Clinic. A friend of Roosevelt's from college days was shocked by what he saw when he came aboard: "This is a ship of death," he said.

Roosevelt returned to the United States and told the Congress and the public the opposite of the truth about the Crimean conference—which is what they wanted to hear. The Yalta settlement, he reported, "ought to spell the end of the system of unilateral action, the exclusive alliances, the spheres of influence, the balances of power, and all the other expedients that have been tried for centuries—and have always failed." In fact it *was* a spheres-of-influence agreement. The President may have believed that if he did not call it that, the public might learn to live with it.

But the President in the end could not hold things together, and his last few weeks after returning from Yalta were a time of disintegration. At a preliminary San Francisco conference to plan the United Nations, news came out of Stalin's claim to have extra votes. "This will *raise hell*," wrote Senator Vandenberg, one of the delegates, in his diary on March 23. "We began to get some of the inside 'bad news' from Yalta today. It is typical of the baffling secrecy which leaves one eternally uncertain of what deals have been made."

On April 3 Vandenberg wrote: "There is a general disposition to *stop this Stalin* appeasement. It *has* to stop *sometime.*" The President himself allowed it to be understood that he was troubled by Soviet behavior. Stettinius, who reflected his views, had told the War and Navy secretaries on March 13: "A most successful meeting at Yalta, particularly . . . as regards Russian-American relationship. Every evidence . . . of the Russian desire to cooperate along all lines with U.S. . . . ." But on April 2 he told Forrestal and Stimson "of serious deterioration in our relations with Russia."

Forrestal copied page after page of Harriman's cables into his diary. (From Moscow: "I cannot list the almost daily affronts and total disregard which the Soviets evince in matters of interest to us.") Harriman suggested that Stalin and Molotov might believe they had been given the green light to do as they wished in Poland because of FDR's willingness to accept the loose language of the declaration issued at Yalta. It was only by being tough, Harriman reiterated, that the United States could do business with the Stalin regime.

One of Harriman's cables was handed to Roosevelt on his last day in Washington* before leaving for Warm Springs for a rest. He read it, and banged his fist on the arms of his wheelchair. "Averell is right; we can't do business with Stalin," he said. "He has broken every one of the promises he made at Yalta."

Yet he continued to believe that problems should not be confronted. On April 11, 1945, the last full day of his life, he sent a short cable to Churchill in which he said: "I would minimize the general Soviet problem

* March 24, 1945.

as much as possible because these problems, in one form or another, seem to arise every day and most of them straighten out. . . ." But he added: "We must be firm, however. . . ."


FDR BELIEVED that if he smiled on the goddess who presided over his destiny, she would smile upon him. He also believed that if he ignored disagreeable facts and situations, eventually they would go away. Given time, he could reconcile the apparently irreconcilable. The main thing was never to lose faith.

He would never accept the end of his youthful love affair with Lucy Mercer. The secret leaked out: she had been with him on the day of his death. It later transpired that she had been with him often; that after the death of her husband, she had come back to him.

In Warm Springs, Georgia, in the early afternoon of April 12, the President was sitting for a portrait. He said something amusing. Lucy smiled. He was looking at her. Then he tried to put his hands to his head; he whispered, "I have a terrible headache," and a bit more than two hours later was dead of a massive stroke. An elderly house servant who was in the room when Roosevelt was stricken said: "The last I remember he was looking into the smiling face of a beautiful woman."


LESS THAN FOUR HOURS after FDR's death, following a hasty search of the White House bookcases for a Bible on which to take an oath, Harry S Truman was sworn in as President by Chief Justice Harlan F. Stone. Secretary of State Stettinius, whom Truman soon replaced with Byrnes, asked whether the next San Francisco conference, scheduled to convene in less than two weeks, should be postponed. The conference, following on the earlier San Francisco meeting, was to be devoted to drafting the final charter of the United Nations. Truman replied that the conference "should be held as directed by the President"—still meaning, by that, Franklin Roosevelt.

A memorial appearing in *Yank*, the soldiers' magazine, said that FDR "was the Commander in Chief, not only of our armed forces, but of our generation."

After the funeral service for FDR, Harry Hopkins told Robert Sherwood that "he was going to turn in his resignation at once and he thought the whole Cabinet should do likewise and get out. . . . [H]e said, 'Truman has got to have his own people around him, not Roosevelt's. If we were around, we'd always be looking at him and he'd know we were thinking, "The *President* wouldn't do it that way." ' "

# 55

## ONE WORLD—OR TWO?

AMERICA HAD BEEN HERE BEFORE. It was uncanny how the experience of the First World War seemed to be repeating itself. Once again American troops had arrived in France at least a year too late; the ally with the most powerful army was chiefly responsible for winning the war on the ground, and was imposing its own peace terms, of which the United States disapproved; in the hour of victory over Germany, the menace of Russian communism suddenly loomed up, threatening all Europe; and the President of the United States was stricken while attempting to patch up a lasting peace.

All that was missing was the final scene: the withdrawal of the United States from international politics. Political leaders of both parties were keenly aware of this, and Republican foreign policy strategists led by Vandenberg and Dulles were as determined as the Democrats not to let it happen again. The foreign policy thinking of the Truman years has to be understood against the background of the overriding fear of America's leaders that U.S. voters might once again want to turn their backs on the world.

A quarter of a century earlier, the American political establishment had not followed Woodrow Wilson. Regretting it, they did so now.


IN AN OFTEN QUOTED OBSERVATION, F. Scott Fitzgerald remarked that "the test of a first-rate intelligence is the ability to hold two opposed ideas in the mind at the same time, and still retain the ability to function." By that he meant, he explained, "for example, [to] be able to see that things are hopeless and yet be determined to make them otherwise."

Much of that quality was on display in the United States in the months immediately following FDR's death. Leaders of both parties, joining together, went about creating the sort of new institutions to deal with world problems that Wilson had advocated—international institutions that could function only on the basis of voluntary cooperation between countries—even though they were on notice that the element essential to making such institutions work would be missing. Soviet Russia, with the world's strongest army, would not cooperate in building a unitary new world order.

It was curious timing. For the first time, the United States was prepared to participate in an international alliance. Only Taft and Herbert Hoover remained isolationist; even Vandenberg, in a famous Senate speech in January 1945, admitted that he had been wrong and now was a convert to internationalism. The willingness of right-wing middle western Republican leaders to ally with a Russia that was communist had been a long time in coming, but when it came, it turned out that the leaders in the Kremlin would not enter into a permanent alliance with open societies.

PEPPERY HARRY TRUMAN, a short, combative, folksy blend of simplicity and shrewdness, had barely known FDR. In his three months as Vice President he had not been briefed on what the country's military and civilian leaders were doing. He had little time in which to learn a lot.

Two days after becoming President, he had lunch at his desk with Harry Hopkins, the single person best qualified to tell him the inside story of everything. In his diary Truman recorded: "Discussed the whole history of the Roosevelt administration 1933 to date—particular emphasis on the foreign visits. . . . We discussed Stalin, Churchill, de Gaulle, Cairo, Casablanca, Tehran, and Yalta." To that meeting, his diary indicates with a humor that may have been conscious, Truman devoted a half hour.

He quickly formed opinions about the other major world leaders. He explained to Mrs. Roosevelt that "the difficulties with Churchill are very nearly as exasperating as they are with the Russians." He claimed that "Russians distribute lies about us. . . . Our papers lie about . . . the Russians—and the British out lie . . . us both."

Truman received a variety of advice from his senior advisers as to what to do about the Soviet Union. Harriman warned that unless America were to adopt a firm attitude, the Russians might continue to turn neighboring states into communist vassals; and he told Forrestal that the United States "might well have to face"—from Soviet communism—"an ideological warfare just as vigorous and dangerous as Fascism or Nazism."

At a White House meeting April 23, Stettinius, who knew no better, said that the Kremlin had broken its Yalta pledge to allow Poland a freely elected democratic government. Notes of the meeting show that Admiral Leahy replied "that he had left Yalta with the impression that the Soviet government had no intention of permitting free government to operate in Poland, and that he would have been surprised had the Soviet government behaved any differently than it did." Stimson, pointing out that the Russians had kept their word in military matters, urged going slowly in breaking with them, and said that they might interpret their political pledges differently: according to their own lights, they might be fulfilling their promises.

Marshall cautioned against acting in such a way that Russia would delay entering the Far East war, as her help was greatly needed.

According to one set of notes of the meeting, "The President said . . . that he felt our agreements with the Soviet Union so far had been a one-way street and that he could not continue; it was now or never. He intended to go on with the plans for San Francisco"—the conference to create the postwar United Nations peacekeeping organization—"and if the Russians did not wish to join us they could go to hell. . . ." Shortly afterward Truman met with Molotov and gave the Soviet minister a tough and pointed lecture, telling him that if Russian leaders did not want to be talked to like that in future, all they had to do was keep their promises.

Harriman, on the suggestion of his aide Chip Bohlen, proposed that Truman send the ailing Harry Hopkins on a mission to Moscow to meet with Stalin and resolve matters. The President did so, but feeling that he had serious problems with Great Britain, too, he sent another envoy to London. He asked another invalid veteran of the Roosevelt years, former ambassador to Russia Joseph Davies, to undertake the trip. Truman held Davies in high regard, though it is not easy to understand why. In London Davies told the prime minister that his (Churchill's) warnings about the Soviet threat were like those the world had heard from Hitler and Goebbels. He counseled the British leader to give more credence to the Kremlin's professions of good faith. Davies reported to Truman that Churchill "was basically more concerned over preserving England's position in Europe than in preserving peace." FDR's chief of staff, Leahy, endorsing Davies's report, commented to the new President that "this is consistent with our staff estimate of Churchill's attitude throughout the war."

In the same vein, before leaving for Moscow, Hopkins told Forrestal, Harriman, and Bohlen "that he was skeptical about Churchill, at least in the . . . Anglo-American-Russian relationship; that he thought it was of vital importance that we not be maneuvered into a position where Great Britain had us lined up with them as a bloc against Russia to implement England's European policy."

Sending Hopkins off on his mission, Truman noted in his diary that he had told his special envoy to "make it clear to Uncle Joe Stalin that I knew what I wanted—and that I intended to get it—peace for the world for at least 90 years. That Poland, Rumania, Bulgaria, Czeckoslovakia [*sic*], Austria, Yugo-Slavia, Latvia, Lithuania, Estonia et al. made no difference to U.S. interests. . . . That Poland should have 'free elections,' at least as free as Hague, Tom Pendergast . . ." or any other crooked machine politician would allow. "Uncle Joe should make some sort of gesture—whether he means or not to keep it. . . . Any smart political boss will do that."

Truman indicated that "to have a reasonably lasting peace the three great powers must be able to trust one another and they must themselves honestly want it. They must also have the confidence of the *smaller* nations. Russia hasn't the confidence of the small nations, nor has Britain. We have. I want peace and I'm willing to fight for it. It is my opinion we'll get it."

Truman's envoy Hopkins received a warm reception when he arrived in Russia, obtained agreement from Stalin on the issues necessary to let the San Francisco conference go forward to create the United Nations Charter, and received reassurances as well on the date of Russian entry into the war against Japan.

THE TRANSITIONAL YEARS following Roosevelt's death were marked in the administration by the coexistence of inconsistent points of view, by rapid and often complete changes of opinion, and by frequent misunderstandings of foreign politics—while the mercurial President seemed impulsive in his judgments and erratic in his behavior.

Truman told his diary (June 7, 1945): "I'm not afraid of Russia. They've always been our friends and I can't see any reason why they shouldn't always be." Naively, he compared the average Soviet citizen, who had no voice in his government, to "a stock holder in the Standard Oil of New Jersey"—presumably someone who owned only one share.

He continued to misunderstand both Stalin and his one-man dictatorship. Truman wrote (July 17, 1945): "I can deal with Stalin. He is honest—but smart as hell." As late as 1948 Truman said in public that "I like Old Joe," describing the Soviet leader as "a decent fellow [who] is a prisoner of the Politburo . . . ," adding that Stalin "can't do what he wants to do. He makes agreements, and if he could, he would keep them; but the people who run the government are very specific in saying that he can't keep them."

Truman shocked both Britain and the USSR by terminating the lend-lease program on which the two of them had come to depend. For England, the cutoff was a disaster. But a Gallup Poll showed 60 percent of Americans opposed to any aid to Britain at all.

Then, at Potsdam, the last of the Big Three conferences—and the one during which Churchill learned that he had been voted out of office—Truman shifted the U.S. position on Germany. Though at the time that country was divided "temporarily" into zones of military occupation by the Allied forces, she would not, it was decided, eventually be dismembered. This created a dangerous new source of tensions between Russia and the West: a prize so dangerous in enemy hands that each would have to try to win it.

The goal of the United Nations alliance had been to destroy Nazi Germany. It was an ambiguous objective because it used two words to describe the enemy instead of one. Nazis were the enemy to Stimson, Hull, Churchill, and Truman; Germans were, to Roosevelt and Stalin. From Stalin's perspective, Truman's walking away from FDR's commitment to dismember Germany might well have looked like America's unilateral renunciation of her alliance with Russia. Truman did not see it that way, and evidently had no inkling, either, that Stalin might see it that way.

From the Moscow embassy, Harriman continued to urge getting tough with the Russians. Truman wavered uneasily between doing so and not. The Russian dictator kept his promise to declare war on Japan, but after the dropping of the two atom bombs, Emperor Hirohito surrendered, rendering Soviet help unnecessary. At that point American leaders would have preferred Stalin to break his word. Japan surrendered two days after Russia entered the war. Harriman, without even consulting Washington, refused the Soviet request to participate in the ceremony of accepting Japan's capitulation; and Byrnes repeated to Molotov that there would be no Russian forces in the army of occupation.

Still, there were the promises made to Stalin at Yalta—matters such as the Kuril Islands—and now Americans began to be aware of these. It proved a great embarrassment to Truman, and even more so to Byrnes. In FDR's last years, Byrnes had handled domestic affairs while the President did foreign affairs; when Truman took office, he intended to do just the reverse, letting Byrnes manage foreign policy while he concentrated on matters at home. Byrnes was a senior statesman, but his only claim to expertise in foreign policy was that he had been at Yalta. Before Truman had been President for two weeks, Byrnes presented him with a red leather-bound copy of the shorthand notes he had taken at the conference, which, given his skill as a professional court reporter, could be argued were the authentic record of the proceedings. He was staking out a claim to be the specialist in the Yalta accords.

But month after month new details surfaced of secret agreements, made when Byrnes was not present, that contradicted the assertions made by the administration about U.S.-Soviet commitments. By the summer of 1945, the President knew that he had been wrong about the Polish accord between Stalin and FDR—and he still could not find the only American copy of the Far East pact between the two men. Yalta, supposedly his strength, was blowing up in Byrnes's face—and in Truman's. Truman was not to blame, Byrnes told him, for the "duplicity and hypocrisy which had been practiced by the President"—i.e., Roosevelt—but the American public might not agree.

Byrnes made a game effort to deal with the situation in such a way as to protect Truman, himself, FDR's reputation, and the Democratic administration. He used stick and carrot. Backed by the implicit threat of the

U.S. atom bomb, but offering the prospect of an opportunity for Russia to share in the atomic energy monopoly, he threw himself into making the best deal he could with the Soviet Union.

At the London meeting of foreign ministers in September 1945, Byrnes tried to work things out. The American public position was that at Yalta, Stalin had promised democracy in eastern Europe. Byrnes now knew that was not so, but could not admit it because he was the one who had been maneuvered into telling everyone that in the first place. He therefore tried to obtain concessions from Russia, however small or cosmetic, so that he could go back to Washington saying that the Soviet Union was now keeping its word.

He tried to wrap it all up: "We have pushed these babies as far as they will go," he told John Foster Dulles, a Republican member of his team, "and I think we better start thinking about compromise." But Dulles would not go along with that. He threatened to break with the administration and attack publicly if Byrnes did not stand firm on making the Russians live up to their alleged commitments.

So Byrnes moved away from compromise and no longer could reach an agreement with the other side. A Soviet staff member complained to Charles Bohlen that although he had been told the secretary was "practical," he was not showing himself so. "When is he going to start trading?" asked the Russian.

Byrnes found himself out on a limb. He knew the Soviet Union would not introduce democracy into eastern Europe; could not be forced to do so, short of going to war; and did not believe it had pledged to do so. But he also realized that the people of the United States could not be told any of those things without courting disaster for his administration and his party in the next elections. American public opinion was moving in an anti-Soviet direction. Byrnes had been left behind by the mainstream. Leahy accused him of appeasement. Truman started to distance himself from the secretary.

The idea of sharing atomic energy secrets with the USSR—and doing so without first consulting the Senate—aroused the wrath of Vandenberg and other leading members of the Foreign Relations Committee. They blamed Byrnes; Truman, they felt, simply did not understand.

Byrnes became aware of these currents of opinion, and moved to take a harder line against Russia. He shored up his position, but in doing so gave up his chance—if he ever had one—of bridging the gulf between the reality of Yalta and the misleading presentation of it he had made at the time.

In the spring of 1946 Undersecretary of State Dean Acheson handed his letter of resignation to Byrnes. "You're smarter than I thought," Byrnes said, preempting his aide by writing out a similar letter of his own. "You didn't have a copyright on that idea, you know," Byrnes told Acheson. But for the time being the President kept Byrnes in office, and Byrnes kept Acheson in office.

FEW PERIODS can have been more closely scrutinized by historians than that of the first Truman administration, the years in which the duel between the wartime allies began to take shape. Until and unless new revelations emerge from the Soviet archives, the most illuminating explanation of what happened from Moscow's point of view may well be that provided in 1946 by Maksim Litvinov, the out-of-favor former Soviet foreign minister who had given up hope for himself and the world and who spoke freely to the U.S. ambassador (and later to a CBS correspondent, newly arrived in Moscow). What he said was reported to Washington by cable, and the quotes that follow are from the cable.

The root cause of the quarrel between the Soviet Union and the West was, according to Litvinov, the "ideological conception prevailing here of inevitability of conflict between Communist and capitalist worlds." Only a few months earlier, on February 9, Stalin, in his first major postwar address, announced that heavy industry (which Western observers took to mean rearmament) would be his government's chief priority; fulfillment of consumer needs would have to be postponed. Reminding his listeners that dangers might arise in the future, he said that "no peaceful international order is possible" between the communist bloc and the camp of capitalism and imperialism. At the time, George Kennan had cabled the State Department from Moscow: "As Department is aware, there has been pronounced reemphasis upon Marxist-Leninist doctrine here during and since final stage of war in Europe."

Litvinov did not blame the Soviet regime for not wanting to cooperate in the work of the United Nations and other international institutions, for, he said, it was "not unreasonable for USSR to be suspicious of any forum in which she would constantly be outvoted." But he was critical of his country's return to an "outmoded" concept of "geographical security."

He rightly saw that "each side wants unified Germany under its control," and he called the German issue the greatest single problem in the world.

Could America reach a friendly settlement with Moscow by recognizing Russia's right to govern the countries she had taken over in the war as she saw fit? Would the Soviet Union then be satisfied with what it had? It was on this point that Litvinov was especially interesting. Asked what would happen if the West gave in to *all* of the Soviet demands, "he said it would lead to West being faced after period of time with next series of demands." So the inevitable conflict was a self-fulfilling prophecy; animated by a belief in it, the Soviet Union would refuse to be reconciled on any basis, and would stalk the Western countries until an opportune time and place for a showdown appeared.

Litvinov's view was bleak: "I now feel," he said, "that the best that can be hoped for is a prolonged armed truce."


RUSSIA ALWAYS HAD BEEN EXPANSIONIST. It has been calculated that at the time of the Russian revolutions, the tsars had been conquering and occupying neighboring territories at the rate of fifty square miles a day for 400 years. It was a cautious and continuing expansion, and it was special in that it seemed to be motivated not by ambition, but by fear. Russians never could feel secure; they were driven to protect themselves by seizing whatever lay on the other side of their frontiers.

Historians have noted that whereas imperial Britain employed a strategy of propping up buffer states to keep harm at bay, the Russians always preferred partitions: as lands entered into their political orbit, they felt comfortable only in taking physical possession of them.

Theirs had always been an authoritarian government and a closed society. Russia was a domain of secrets and conspiracies, of plots and assassinations, whose people were distrustful of one another and deeply mistrustful of foreigners.

So at the end of the Second World War, Stalin was acting as a tsar would have acted. But Marxism, which is open to many interpretations, was able to provide him with a more flattering explanation of what he was doing. In consolidating Russia's hold on eastern Europe, in maintaining a closed economy and society cut off from the West, and in remaining implacably hostile to Western efforts to bring the Soviet Union into partnership with Britain and America, he could believe he was pursuing a fated conflict between the representatives of the working classes and their enemies that only a superficial thinker—a non-Marxist like Truman—would imagine could be worked out peacefully: compromised or patched up.

In 1946 leaders of the American government decided that the Soviet Union was irreconcilably hostile, and also that it would expand if it were unopposed. The amoeba was not mentioned, but in the inner circles of the Truman administration in 1946, the interpretation of Soviet thinking and behavior was similar to Bullitt's in 1943. It was no coincidence. The driving force in creating an American doctrine regarding Soviet relations was James Forrestal, the navy secretary who had come under Bullitt's influence three years before.

Forrestal had been searching for an authoritative statement of the sources of Soviet behavior—in simple American slang, of what made them tick. Unexpectedly, George Kennan supplied it to him. For years Kennan had been frustrated by his inability to get Washington to listen to his views.

Kennan was in acting charge of the Moscow embassy while Harriman was in America; and when a routine inquiry arrived from the Treasury asking about difficulties with the Soviet Union, Kennan seized the opportunity to reply—at length.

So wordy was this cable of February 22, 1946, that it has been known ever since as the "Long Telegram." Harriman, struck by it, showed it to Forrestal. It was exactly what the secretary wanted, and appeared at the very moment he wanted it.

Forrestal circulated the Long Telegram within the Truman administration and ordered several thousand top-ranking military officers to read it. He became Kennan's political patron, and brought him back to Washington.

Like Bullitt, his former chief, Kennan claimed that it was in the nature of Soviet Russia to push against her frontiers. If the door she pushed against was closed, she would stop pushing for the time being; but if it were open, she would go on through it. The role of America and her allies was to counter Russia's push to expand. Confined to her own frontiers for a long period of time, the USSR might collapse from internal tensions, or might evolve in ways that the United States would welcome. That, in rough and brief terms, was the doctrine that the Truman administration eventually adopted under the patronage of Forrestal and under the name of "containment," although as it transpired, different people were to interpret containment in vastly different ways.

The month after the Long Telegram arrived, Winston Churchill, encouraged by Truman to speak at an educational institution in Truman's home state, went to Missouri. American hospitality failed to rise to the occasion: once arrived in Fulton, where Westminster College was located, the thirsty British leader discovered that the town was "dry," and only after a wide-ranging search by Truman's personal aide was an essential pint of whiskey located. The President himself introduced the former prime minister, who delivered a typically eloquent address. Speaking of the Soviet Union in terms of friendship and admiration, Churchill said that facts nonetheless had to be faced: that the Kremlin had rung down an "iron curtain" across Europe, behind which they had imposed a brutal and totalitarian rule. Churchill argued that the Anglo-American democracies should unite and build up their strength to deter the evils that might lie ahead.

Across America the response was hostile. Churchill was attacked on many counts, and Truman, who may have agreed with him, was moved by politics to disassociate himself from what his guest had said at Fulton. The President claimed not to have known the contents of Churchill's speech in advance.

In a zigzag typical of his foreign policy at the time, Truman nonetheless stood firm in the spring and summer when faced with what he viewed as attempts by the Kremlin to disrupt Iran and intimidate Turkey. Angry at the Soviet regime, Truman showed the side of him that was to become a cold war crusader.

In order to win over Henry Wallace and others friendly to Russia, Truman asked his special counsel, Clark Clifford, to provide him with a report that detailed Soviet treaty-breaking. To the President, who was on weak ground here, the basic issue was that the Russian leaders did not keep their word. The report proved to be a long and detailed document, drafted for Clifford by George Elsey, the naval officer in charge of the map room at the White House. Expressing essentially the same views as those outlined in Kennan's Long Telegram, but in a much more alarming way, the Clifford-Elsey report was a top secret summary of the outlook of selected American officials: Forrestal, Leahy, Patterson, Kennan, Bohlen, Acheson, and others.

"Powerful stuff," said Truman when he read it. He ordered Clifford to bring all twenty copies of it to him immediately. He then hid them, saying, "If it leaked, it would blow the roof off the White House."

WHAT WAS CONFUSING about the emerging conflict between the United States and the USSR was that it was about more than one thing.

First, it was about America's refusal to accept continued Russian rule of the countries the Red Army had occupied during the war. On the one hand, the United States, which promptly demobilized and disarmed in 1945, gave no thought to the question of how America could force Russia to retreat; on the other hand, Americans refused to make peace with the existing situation.

Next there was the issue of Soviet expansionism: the Russian tendency to push against the frontier. It would have been entirely coherent for American leaders to argue in 1946 (though none did) that it was legitimate for the Soviets to hold the frontier line with which they emerged from the war—but not to go beyond it. Presumably that is the position Great Britain would have taken had Churchill returned to office and had he continued the policies he advocated during the war. The point to note here is that the quarrel with Russia for expanding to her 1945 boundaries was separate and distinct from the quarrel with her for attempting to go beyond them.

A third quarrel was about potential subversion of governments outside the Soviet sphere. In France and Italy, for example, there were large parties of the revolutionary Left. They were born before the Soviet state, and would have existed even if the Soviet Union did not. But they had come under Russia's control, taking money and orders from Moscow. And they were in a position to threaten to pull down some of the European governments that the United States was attempting to prop up.

The Clifford-Elsey report discussed the danger posed by this disciplined worldwide party apparatus. It was the doctrine behind it—communism—that most disturbed and indeed obsessed Forrestal. Whichever way America's leaders looked at it in 1946 and succeeding years, this threat to the stability of countries within the Western sphere of influence in Europe (the sphere FDR intended for Britain, but which was on the verge of becoming American) was yet a third cause of the conflict with the Soviet Union.

The dark prospect from Washington was that just as the first half of the century had been spent waging war about where the German frontier ought to be, so the second half would be spent waging war about where communist Russia's frontier should be.

PARALLEL TO THE CONFLICTS about the existing and perhaps moving frontier of the Soviet sphere was the even greater quarrel about the nature of that sphere. In seeking to establish a new and stable world order that would provide a framework for a long-lasting peace between the great powers, Americans naturally thought in terms of one world. Stalin's determination to cut off his sphere from the rest of the globe was something they could not understand at first. It took time for them to realize how dangerous foreign contacts, ideas, and even goods were to the police-state Soviet empire. Only then could they see that the Russians objected not only to the specific one-world design of an FDR, but to the very notion of one world—unless it were ruled from Moscow. Until then, two worlds were all they would accept. Wilson's way was not for them.

# 56

# TR's WAY

IN EUROPE IN THE IMMEDIATE postwar years, communism and Russia were not the chief concerns. The overriding issues were the breakdown of civil society and of the economy. "The human problem the war will leave behind it has not yet been imagined, much less faced by anybody. There has never been such destruction, such disintegration of the structure of life," wrote Anne O'Hare McCormick in *The New York Times* on March 14, 1945. The extent of the devastation and of the collapse of civilized life was beyond comprehension—or at least beyond that of the American public at the end of the war. Americans expected that their forces in Europe could pack up and leave, that the financial support they had provided to countries abroad could now be stopped, and that their responsibilities were at an end.

But tens of millions of Europeans had no light, no heat, no home, and no food; and across the Continent, economic activity had ground to a halt. There was little power: Germany and Britain, the chief prewar suppliers of coal, no longer could export. Transport was paralyzed: even if 4,000 kilometers of France's railroad tracks and five-sixths of her locomotives had not been destroyed, her trains could not have moved for lack of fuel. The same was true of Holland, 60 percent of whose transport had been demolished, and of other countries as well.

Factories had been reduced to rubble, and in central Europe two-thirds of the industry had been carted off to Russia by the Red Army. There were shortages of everything. In Vienna there were no nails to hold down the lids of coffins, and many Austrians dressed in recycled rags. There were no clothes to be had in Norway, Holland, and Greece; shops were closed.

Streaming across the face of the Continent were 20 million homeless refugees, displaced from wherever they once had lived by the settlement terms of the war—some headed one way, some another.

In the summer of 1946 the United Nations Economic and Social Council was told that 100 million Europeans were starving—eating less than the body needed to function—and that an additional 40 million were just on the line.

The connection between country and city had been cut. Urban areas no longer produced industrial wares with which to bargain, and currencies were losing value in an inflationary, black-market world of shortages and profiteers; farmers therefore kept what they had. Factory workers without jobs or food turned in troubling numbers to strikes, to demonstrations, and to the communist parties of their countries.

THE FIFTEEN WEEKS in which postwar American foreign policy was created began on a cold, gray, and rainy Friday afternoon. It was February 21, 1947, and movers and packers already had taken many of the files from the old State, War and Navy Departments Building* to the new State Department quarters at Twenty-first Street and Virginia Avenue.

A last-minute phone call from the British ambassador saying that he had notes of such importance that they had to be delivered to the secretary himself came too late: George Marshall, recently appointed to the job,† normally would have been available but had left for Princeton, where he was scheduled to deliver a speech the following day. Undersecretary Dean Acheson suggested that the ambassador might honor the spirit of his instructions by having a member of his staff deliver the documents to Old State, to be handed to Marshall first thing Monday morning.

For whatever reason, Acheson himself was unavailable. So was the assistant secretary for European affairs. So H. M. Sichel, first secretary of the British embassy, found himself delivering his government's communications to the assistant secretary for the Near East, Loy Henderson.

Henderson quickly saw the importance of the notes from London. Typically understated in style, they announced in effect that Great Britain had decided to stop being a world power. Under a Labour government, she already was in the process of withdrawing from India, Burma, Egypt, and Palestine. The specific message to Marshall was that England no longer could afford to shore up the opposition to threatened Soviet expansion in Greece and Turkey. British aid to Greece would terminate March 31. If America wanted to take over the British position, she therefore should do so effective April 1.

Henderson, along with Assistant Secretary for Europe John D. Hickerson and Acheson, immediately initiated a decision-making process that led on March 12 to the proposal by the President of a Greek-Turkish aid

---

* Six years earlier, the War Department had moved out of the building and into the largest office complex in the world, the Pentagon.

† Marshall had replaced James Byrnes, his former political sponsor and, to some extent, Truman's. Truman claimed that Byrnes had tried to conduct foreign policy without consulting the President, but the evidence suggests that Truman was exaggerating, and he probably fired Byrnes for other reasons.

bill; subsequently enacted by Congress in the context of the Truman Doctrine, it was a sweeping and arguably much too far-reaching pledge of U.S. support for the independence of free peoples everywhere.

Several things were especially striking about this rapid American decision. One was the unusual unity with which the State Department, the Congress, both political parties, and the office of the President worked together to shape the program. Another was that the only obstacle to be overcome was that senators worried they might be "pulling Britain's chestnuts out of the fire." A third point was the shared recognition that the newly created United Nations Organization already had become irrelevant to the world of the 1940s: it would be quite useless in dealing with precisely the sort of problem that the public expected the UN to solve—a threat to the independence and territorial integrity of the member states. The fourth was that at a meeting of congressional leaders with the President, Marshall, and Acheson, it was accepted that the American people would not support the policy if candidly and openly presented in the way Marshall thought about it: as a program of aid to two countries of strategic importance to the United States in maintaining the existing balance of power. Acheson instead described it to the senators, in an extemporaneous speech, as a program to stop communism from infecting first one country and then another; and Vandenberg told the administration (which agreed with him) that he could get the necessary support for it only if the policy were proposed to the country on Acheson's terms. So the Truman Doctrine was born: the U.S. taking England's place in upholding the European balance of power in the eastern Mediterranean, but pretending instead to be mounting a worldwide ideological crusade against communism.

ALL THAT FOLLOWED was implicit in the decision to support Greece and Turkey. It was logical to ask, as Acheson did March 5 after meetings with Forrestal and Robert Patterson, what other countries might need similar aid—and to ask a committee to study the question and report. After the President addressed Congress a week later to propose supporting the two countries, the press raised the same issue. The Washington *Post* and *The New York Times* told their readers that helping Greece and Turkey was just a "starter." Columnists James Reston, Marquis Childs, and Joseph Alsop all foresaw the need for massive financial programs to reconstruct Europe.

Walter Lippmann addressed on March 13 the essential issue: that priorities would have to be established. "Never was it so necessary to define our commitments by a unified strategical conception as to where our available power, prestige, money, and expertness, which are not unlimited, can be invested with the best prospect of achieving the best that is judged to be possible."

On April 5 he told his readers: "The truth is that political and economic measures on a scale which no responsible statesman has yet ventured to hint at will be needed in the next year or so. To prevent the crisis which will otherwise engulf Europe and spread chaos throughout the world, the measures will have to be very large—in Europe, no less than an economic union, and over here no less than the equivalent to a revival of Lend-Lease."

Some of the best foreign policy minds in the United States were seizing on the same point at the same time: as Lippmann wrote May 1, "if we allocate our contributions to each European government separately," that would "merely put them all on the dole." For the United States to finance the successful reconstruction of Europe, the Continent would have to make itself into a viable economic proposition. Instead of remaining fragmented into many small national markets, it would have to reduce trade barriers and aim at creating a Europe-wide market.

The logic of their international situation led American leaders in 1947 to arrive at the same position Woodrow Wilson had taken for theoretical reasons in 1917: the world would become safe for America only when Europe was converted into something somewhat like another United States.

GEORGE KENNAN, appointed to head the new Policy Planning Staff in the State Department, told Marshall that the reconstruction of the European economy required the recovery of Germany. In a public speech some months earlier, Republican spokesman John Foster Dulles came to the same conclusion from the opposite direction. The logic that compelled him to support German reunification drove him to advocate European unity. William Fulbright in the Senate and Hale Boggs in the House were Democratic sponsors of a congressional resolution calling for creation of a United States of Europe.

In April Marshall attended a foreign ministers conference in Moscow, and Dulles came along as an adviser. Failure to reach a settlement with the Soviet Union at the meeting, and the news of the terrible conditions prevailing on the Continent, led the bipartisan American delegation to conclude that a new sort of lend-lease program (for FDR had taught the country to think in such terms) indeed had to be initiated. On his return to Washington, Marshall directed Kennan to put his Policy Planning Staff together and propose details of such a program in two weeks. Kennan took three. He made good use of the work done by the committee Acheson had put into motion in March, and of the resources of Undersecretary of State for Economic Affairs Will Clayton.

On June 5 Marshall outlined the plan that carries his name in a commencement speech at Harvard University. He invited the countries of Europe to take the initiative in drawing up a program for their own recovery that the United States could support. His speech, which was drafted by Bohlen, had none of the anticommunist rhetoric that had been so striking in the Greece-Turkey message to Congress that Acheson had drafted for Truman. Marshall said: "Our policy is directed not against any country or doctrine, but against hunger, poverty, desperation and chaos. Its purpose should be the revival of a working economy in the world so as to permit the emergence of political and social conditions in which free institutions can exist."

The Marshall Plan therefore was an offer addressed to all of Europe, including the Soviet Union and its newly acquired satellite countries in central and eastern Europe. Czechoslovakia was pulled back from accepting by Moscow; the Soviet Union kept the countries in its sphere from joining the plan. Their refusal of it marked the economic division of Europe into West and East, in which international organizations dealing with investment, trade, currency, and similar issues—the World Bank, the International Monetary Fund, the various European recovery agencies, the General Agreement on Tariffs and Trade (GATT), and the like—functioned for the non-Soviet world, while the Russian-dominated part of the world kept to itself.

The plan went hand in hand with American support for the drawing together and possible unification of western Europe and—most intensely feared by the Kremlin—of western Germany. Indeed, the Truman administration was advancing along a road that would lead two years later to the merger of American, British, and French zones into a new German state, the Federal Republic. Seeing the direction in which the Americans were moving, Stalin reacted violently. In 1945 and 1946 he had kept to the agreement he had made partitioning Europe; within the British sphere, he had abandoned the communists of Greece to Churchill's armies, and he had ordered the Communist party of France to help de Gaulle and his successors restore that country's infrastructure and economy. In 1947, retaliating against Washington's policy for Germany, Stalin had a chief aide instruct the leaders of western Europe's communist parties to change course. In a secret meeting to which they were summoned in Poland in September 1947, they were ordered to subvert the governments and sabotage the economies of their respective countries.

So as the United States went to work to restore the prosperity of Europe, west of the Russian sphere, Soviet leaders ordered their followers to disrupt it.

THE BIRTH OF THE MARSHALL PLAN in 1947 gave rise to an economic alliance between the United States and western Europe. At that time, the U.S. government had no intention of also entering into a military alliance.

The strategy the United States should adopt in response to the Soviet threat was the subject of the famous debate in print that year between George Kennan, writing under the nom de plume "X" in the pages of *Foreign Affairs*, and Walter Lippmann. Kennan's identity soon became known, and he emerged as a public figure. Viewing Soviet Russia as Bullitt had done in his amoeba memorandum,* he argued that she would flow forward (perhaps like a river that has overflowed its banks?) at every point that it was not checked; what therefore was called for was containment—a sort of wall or dike around the Soviet bloc.

Lippmann replied in a series of articles, reprinted in book form, that gave currency to "the cold war" as a description of the strange U.S.-Soviet duel that was to take center stage in world politics for decades to come. He argued that the United States should react to Soviet moves only at points and on battlefields and with weapons of America's own choosing.

To garrison the whole length of the Soviet frontier was beyond America's resources; it would require the United States to acquire dozens of puppet, client, and allied countries all around the globe to fight America's fights. But as such satellites as were available to the United States in Asia and the Middle East were too flimsy to hold back the Soviet Union, America would find itself not defended by a ring of client states, but defending them.

Instead of recruiting new allies in the vastnesses of Eurasia, the United States, Lippmann argued, should limit itself to perfecting its natural alliances with countries of the Western Hemisphere—and with those of western Europe, which when restored to health would be able to contribute significantly to the common defense.

The two men were more in agreement than was supposed at the time, for Kennan regretted not having limited and qualified a number of his statements. But the "X" article was enduringly valuable in making the point that rather than fight a war against Soviet Russia, the United States should hold the line against its expansionism and await its collapse from within.

LIKE HITLER, Stalin gained control of Czechoslovakia in two stages. The second of them—the total takeover—was dramatized by the fate of Czech foreign minister Jan Masaryk, son of the republic's founder, a much-loved man of liberal ideals and the only noncommunist remaining in the cabinet. Nobody could have tried harder to work in partnership with the Soviet Union and the Communist party. But at the end he knew that even

* See page 465.

he was a marked man. He sent the woman he loved, Marcia Davenport, an American novelist, to the safety of London, promising to escape and join her within days. On March 10, 1948, he was pushed from the fourth-floor window of the foreign ministry to his death in what was made to look like a suicide.* For many, his murder removed the last lingering illusions about Soviet intentions.

The next day Norway told the United States and Britain that she had been informed the Soviet Union was about to attempt to intimidate her into a treaty making far-reaching concessions. Finland already had been bullied into signing such a treaty, but the Norwegian government had decided to refuse.

Britain was in the process of negotiating the first stages of a European consortium to become America's partner in the Marshall Plan. Norway asked Britain "what help Norway might expect to receive if attacked." Within days the British and other European negotiators turned the proposed Western European Union into a defensive military alliance. Truman told Congress that the United States should help. From its spies, the USSR knew that Kennan and Bohlen were among the high American officials opposed to going any further than supplying Europe with arms, and that many in Congress opposed entering into any military alliance with western Europe.

Nonetheless, the Soviet Union escalated the conflict and on April 1 cut off western rail access to Berlin as the start of a full-scale blockade. The local American military commander, General Lucius Clay, proposed to send a convoy through to run the blockade. His British counterpart, General Sir Brian Robertson, told him it could not be done: the Russians had only to blow up the bridge over the Elbe and the convoy would be stranded in the Soviet zone. Robertson suggested instead supplying Berlin by air.

To recommendations that he abandon the city, Truman said: "We are going to stay. Period." He added: "The Russians have no right to get us out." He ordered the airlift that saved the city.

Truman had referred to Vandenberg, chairman of the Foreign Relations Committee, the politically explosive issue of how America should respond to the western European defensive alliance that British foreign secretary Ernest Bevin was whipping into shape. Spurred on by the Soviet blockade, Vandenberg decided that the United States should enter into an alliance with the Europeans and (with an eye to the 1948 elections) that the Republican Senate rather than the Democratic President should take the initiative in doing it. "Why should Truman get all the credit?" he asked.

Thus the North Atlantic Treaty Organization (NATO) was born. It was the sort of alliance Theodore Roosevelt had espoused: like-minded nations pursuing a common goal. The NATO treaty pledged each country

---

* Some still believe the official story that it was a suicide.

that signed it to regard an attack on another—in Europe or North America—as an attack on itself. Once the airlift had beaten the Berlin blockade, Truman therefore felt free to cut the defense budget. Backed by the atomic bomb, the public warning that the United States would go to war would, he felt, deter the Soviet Union from attacking western Europe.

THE AMERICANS WANT an integrated Europe looking like the United States of America." Such was the assessment of a British civil servant, and it may not have been wide of the mark. But it was not what they got, and what they got was not entirely of their doing.

Initially the United States invested $12.5 billion—somewhat more than $70 billion in today's dollars—in the Marshall Plan.* It provided the short-term liquidity, and restored the business confidence, that enabled Europe to finance her own reconstruction. The first tranche of $6.8 billion amounted to 18 percent of the 1949 U.S. budget. Yet in the plan's first two years, some 80 to 90 percent of capital formation came from Europe herself.

Truman intended to appoint Dean Acheson or Will Clayton to oversee the plan. Either man might have done so with a broad strategic conception in mind. But Vandenberg vetoed them, fearing that Marshall Plan funds somehow might flow into Democratic party coffers, and insisting that the administrator should be a businessman, not a politician. He selected the nominee: Paul Hoffman, an automobile company executive. Under Hoffman, an array of American business, community, and labor leaders offered advice and guidance, but it was the Europeans themselves (as Marshall had intended) who shaped their own economic recovery.

It was curiously and uniquely American to appoint a businessman to oversee the creation of a new Europe and to imagine that to be a nonpolitical function. Nor was there a parallel for an American automobile company executive, on orders from Washington, helping Italians and Frenchmen and Germans to put together car companies that could compete against U.S. motorcar manufacturers.

Of course, in designing the new Europe the United States did not have it entirely its own way. Britain stood in the way of the integrated economic system—the free trade—that the United States advocated, and France blocked the integrated European army that America proposed in order to allow German rearmament to take place under controlled conditions. American economic and political goals were best realized by the Schuman Plan

---

* Writing in *The New York Times* (March 7, 1990), Zbigniew Brzezinski estimated that between 1946 and 1955, the United States contributed to western European recovery in all (including the Marshall Plan) a sum equal in 1989 dollars to $170 billion.

for a united coal and steel community, but it was a Frenchman (Jean Monnet) who was the chief architect of it.

Still, the chief objective of the Marshall Plan was to restore the vitality of the countries of western Europe so that they could function, if they chose, as America's allies; and that objective was achieved.

BETWEEN THE END of the Second World War and the outbreak of the Korean War, the United States, which until then never had joined alliances outside of the Western Hemisphere, constructed and entered not one but two parallel—and in a way, alternative—international alliance systems intended to prevent the outbreak of a major war.

One centered around the United Nations, a creation Wilsonian in conception, but modified in light of FDR's insight that the world could be run only by the great powers acting in concert, and that if the great powers are divided—as they were in the late 1940s—the world cannot be run at all. Like a sort of Sleeping Beauty, the United Nations system of administering the affairs of one world was left in repose until international politics should change in such a way as to bring it to life and allow it to function.

The other alliance system, nominally operating as a self-defense organization pursuant to the UN Charter, was a Theodore Roosevelt sort of conception. The Atlantic alliance, in its several forms, was a grouping of countries brought together by a shared interest in protecting the existing balance of power against Soviet attempts to overthrow it. Having experimented with both, Truman, Marshall, Acheson, Kennan, and their colleagues found that it was the second alliance system that was the more useful in answering America's needs in their time.

# 57

# BREAKING WITH THE PAST—
# AND PAYING THE PRICE FOR IT

WE MUST NEVER FIGHT ANOTHER WAR the way we fought
the last two," Truman told his aide Clark Clifford. "I have the feeling that
if the Army and the Navy had fought our enemies as hard as they fought
each other, the war would have ended much earlier." In his view the United
States was "damn lucky" to have won the Second World War. Soon after
he became President, Truman decided to unify the armed services and to
organize a national security structure suited to the twentieth century. In
recognizing that the United States would be fighting wars in the future,
the President was departing from tradition.

TRUMAN'S GOOD QUALITIES, including his willingness to face
facts, were not appreciated in his first years as President. His party lost the
1946 congressional elections the year after he took office. It was so complete
a political disaster that Arkansas Democratic senator J. William Fulbright,
an admirer of the British parliamentary system of government, called on
Truman to resign in favor of the Senate leader, Vandenberg, a Republican.
And despite the Truman administration's inspiring foreign policy leadership
in 1947, it was generally not so much predicted as assumed that Truman
would lose a four-way 1948 presidential race to the Republican candidate,
New York governor Dewey.

Dewey, an isolationist before the war, had moved with the times. With
his authorization, his foreign policy adviser and intended secretary of state,
John Foster Dulles, had played a key role in shaping the administration's
bipartisan foreign policy. Unity was to be the Republican theme; foreign
policy was not at issue in the campaign once Dewey had crushed Taft at
the Republican convention in Philadelphia.

After Dewey won the nomination, he assembled a group of about
twenty advisers and party leaders at the Bellevue-Stratford Hotel to discuss
the choice of his vice-presidential nominee. Taft, who was invited but did
not appear, sent word urging the selection of Bricker, who had run with
Dewey in 1944. But Vandenberg spoke for an emerging consensus in ad-

vising *"not* to build a *hybrid* ticket—not to choose a V.P. who was not in full harmony with the platform and with . . . support of international cooperation." He said that "we could not go to the country with a ticket which did no more than personify the *split* on this issue among Republicans in Congress." So compromise with isolationism, as in the balanced Dewey-Bricker nominations of 1944, was rejected. In the end, California governor Earl Warren and former Minnesota governor Harold Stassen, internationalists both, were the only candidates given serious consideration for the nomination, and Warren was chosen.

Dewey's selection of Warren as a running mate also signaled a continuing change in the Republican party that in turn reflected demographic shifts within the country. In 1944 the New Yorker had followed a pattern as old as the Republican party in uniting with an Ohio man; but in 1948 he looked to California. Starting in that year, the Republicans were to nominate a Californian on their national ticket in six out of seven elections.

The move from an Ohio–New York axis to a California–New York combination represented a shift to a more outward-looking attitude, as both seaboards were open to foreign contacts, goods, and ideas, while the interior of the country—the Middle West—by definition was insular.

But the evolution of the Republican party was set back temporarily by the 1948 election results. With the Democratic party split in three (Truman, left-wing Progressive candidate Henry Wallace, and states'-rights southerner Strom Thurmond, all running for President), and with a powerful ticket of their own, the Republicans looked unbeatable. When they did lose, they felt cheated—and were driven to desperate tactics.

It is entirely possible that America would have been spared some of the more ugly by-products of the cold war had the Dewey-Warren slate prevailed. The isolationist bloc (which flourished only within the Republican party) would have surrendered four years earlier than in fact it did, for it would have been subject to its own party's discipline; it would have been forced to support an internationalist administration that was Republican.

Much of the anticommunist hysteria whipped up by the frustrated Republican losers of the 1948 elections in an effort to discredit the Truman administration—and, on the other hand, indulged in defensively by the administration to prove itself more anti-Red than its critics—might have been avoided had the Republicans won. The height of the Red-baiting era in the middle of the century corresponds almost exactly with the presidential term that Truman took away from Dewey: 1949–53.

THE CALL FOR an anticommunist crusade issued by Truman and Acheson at Vandenberg's suggestion did succeed in rallying support for their anti-Russian programs, but unexpectedly, it supplied ammunition to the opposition as well. For anticommunism proved to be a two-edged sword. Congressmen who opposed the high taxes needed to sustain a large foreign policy and military budget could claim the two were not necessary. They were able to argue that the real danger was not that posed by the Red Army: the genuine threat was from within. Firing alleged subversives, blacklisting performers, and banning books from library shelves provided an alternative to voting funds for foreign aid—or even to expanding and strengthening the armed forces.

Senator Joseph McCarthy, the demagogue who gave his name to witch-hunting at midcentury, represented Wisconsin voters, many of them German-American, who had been opposed to American entry into the two world wars. In the prevailing hysteria they took revenge on the liberal internationalists of the eastern seaboard, whom they held responsible for leading the country into wars against Germany.

The communist victory in the Chinese civil war in 1949 was confusing and troubling to Americans, and it was exploited by the McCarthy wing of the Republican party. Had Dewey been President, perhaps such partisan bitterness could have been avoided. It should have been evident that no matter which party held the White House, the United States could have done nothing to prevent Mao Tse-tung's victory.

It should have been clear, too, that whatever else might be said against him, Mao was not really Stalin's man but an indigenous leader with an agenda of his own. The Kremlin in fact had supported Chiang Kai-shek, and Mao had won leadership of the Communist party only by defeating the Moscow-anointed faction. Observers with a long view of history foresaw that China was potentially Russia's most dangerous adversary.

Yet the Democrats were blamed—successfully—for having let Nationalist China be driven from the mainland. Even in the absence of evidence (and there seems to be none), it is hard to believe that this did not affect Truman and Acheson in their decision the following year to take a stand in Korea.

We do not know what decision a President Dewey would have made the first week in June 1950 after North Korean tanks smashed across the thirty-eighth parallel on their way to destroy South Korea in a blitzkrieg. But the initial reaction of political significance happened to be that of Dulles, then in Japan, who was Secretary Acheson's adviser and would have been Dewey's secretary. If South Korea could not hold the line, Dulles cabled to Washington, "U.S. force should be used even though this risks Russian countermoves. To sit by while Korea is overrun by unprovoked armed attack would start disastrous chain of events leading most probably to world war." This was advice that would have been politically easier for a Dewey to ignore than for a Truman, who allegedly had lost China.

How to react was one of the most complex questions an American president has been called upon to decide. Endorsing a recommendation of the Joint Chiefs of Staff, Truman in April 1948 had approved this policy statement: "The United States should not become so irrevocably involved in the Korean situation that an action taken by . . . any other power in Korea could be considered a *casus belli* for the United States." U.S. troops had been withdrawn from South Korea* in 1949 because the military establishment thought it served no purpose for them to be there. For different reasons, the relevant military and political leaders of the Truman administration had all concluded that U.S. forces ought not to be left in vulnerable enclaves on the mainland of Asia but instead should hold a line of islands off the Asian coast, shielded by the fleet.

Holding South Korea was not a vital interest. Its loss in theory might threaten Japan, but in practice not, for the U.S. Navy ruled the waters that flowed between them. Allies elsewhere would not lose confidence in the value of America's guarantee, as South Korea did not have an American guarantee. South Korea was in a different category than they were: by the NATO treaty, America was pledged to defend such countries as Belgium and Holland, but there was no American commitment to protect South Korea. Then, too, the attack was not by the Soviet Union, but by a client state not inconceivably pursuing its own interests.

Yet it was a brazen aggression by what seemed at the time to be a monolithic, Russian-directed international communist bloc,† and it trampled upon a UN-sponsored line of division between the two Koreas. Truman's first instinct was to regard it as a test of his and America's manhood—and to meet it. Later he talked about how the UN would be destroyed if North Korea were allowed to get away with the invasion;‡ it was a common belief at the time that the League of Nations had collapsed because of its failure to stop the Japanese invasion of Manchuria and the Italian invasion of Ethiopia. The challenge to the Truman Doctrine bothered him, too; he may not have remembered that his promise to protect free

---

* Except for a Military Advisory Group of 500 officers and men.

† In retrospect, it seems to have been North Korea, rather than Russia, that initiated the proposal to attack. According to Georgi Arbatov, director of the Institute of U.S. and Canada Studies in Moscow (1990), it was Kim Il Sung, North Korea's dictator, who proposed the attack to Stalin, who rejected the proposal. Kim then brought the idea to China's leader, and Mao said yes. Kim then came back to Moscow, where Stalin said yes rather than look less courageous than Mao. More recent evidence to be discussed in a forthcoming book by Professor John Lewis Gaddis will offer a different interpretation, showing Stalin to have played a more positive role, but will confirm that the initiating force was Kim.

‡ At a meeting with congressional leaders in the Cabinet Room of the White House at 11:30 a.m., June 27, 1950, Acheson briefed those assembled on the Korean situation. When he had finished, Truman thanked him, "but pointed out that the Secretary had overlooked a most important element in the situation"—that the UN Security Council had passed a resolution pursuant to which the U.S. was acting. According to official notes of the meeting, "the Secretary of State was quite obviously embarrassed at his failure in mentioning the United Nations." The UN loomed much larger in Truman's thinking than in Acheson's.

peoples everywhere against communist aggression was supposed to be mere rhetoric for domestic political consumption.

In the map room of the White House, its commanding officer, George Elsey, made a memo of what Truman said to him June 26. "But what he was worried about, the President said, was the Middle East. He put his finger on Iran and said: 'Here is where they will start trouble if we aren't careful.'

" 'Korea,' he said, 'is the Greece of the Far East. If we are tough enough now, if we stand up to them like we did in Greece three years ago, they won't take any next steps. But if we just stand by, they'll move into Iran and they'll take over the whole Middle East.' "

All of the civilian and military administration figures with whom Truman met believed as he did that U.S. forces should act to throw the invaders back. No one seemed to question that. Yet it was an extremely odd decision that marked another great break with the American past.

Americans never before had gone to war unless they believed the other side had attacked the United States.* It was axiomatic as late as 1941 that the United States would not go to war unless the other side struck first— at America. The gravest threat posed by Nazi Germany to American vital interests—and the virtual certainty that if Hitler conquered Britain and Russia, he would employ all the resources of Eurasia to build up his war machine to attack an isolated Western Hemisphere—was insufficient to move the United States to join in the fight. It was a country that waited for others to attack it first. In the spring of 1917 Wilson had known it was likely that German U-boats would sink American vessels, but realized he could do nothing (and did not want to do anything) until their torpedoes sank ships. FDR was aware the Japanese would attack in late 1941 or early 1942—but by the rules of American politics he had to wait until they did.

Yet suddenly, based on the lessons drawn from their experience of Germany's creeping aggressions in the 1930s (which they wrongly likened to the Korean situation), Truman's generation was prepared to go to war at the other extreme: the United States or an ally not attacked; the attack not mounted by Russia or by a country even potentially dangerous to the United States; the territory at stake of no value to America or Russia; the regime attacked, a dictatorship; the conflict located on the far side of the world, in a place few Americans had heard of; and the battlefield, chosen by the other side, one on which the odds were stacked against the United States.

John Foster Dulles had a theory of his own as to why South Korea had to be kept out of the communist bloc—and why Vietnam had to be kept out of it, too. He believed that if South Korea and Vietnam were taken

---

* Or its ships, which are American territory.

over by the Russian-Chinese combine, their markets would be closed to Japan. Dulles imagined that these were the export markets on which Japanese industry would depend in the years to come; to deprive Japan of them would be to strangle its nascent economy—and drive the country to the communist side.

Dulles was peering into one of the more clouded of crystal balls. The notion that the Japanese would not be able to compete in the world's export markets—other than Korea and Vietnam—proved to be one of the more wide-of-the-mark predictions of modern times. In any event, Truman, who made the decision to go into Korea, quite clearly was not thinking in terms of export markets. His thinking, and that of most of his aides, came out of their past as witnesses to history, and however inaccurately, they saw themselves as taking the stand that Chamberlain failed to take at Munich.

It is still not entirely clear why Truman did not ask Congress for a declaration of war. True, presidents had sent armed forces into action—on raids and expeditions and Caribbean invasions—somewhere between 100 and 200 times without asking for such a declaration; but Korea was the first real war that a President started on his own. That, too, represented a great break with the American past.

THE FIRST COUPLE OF YEARS of the presidential term to which Truman was elected on his own proved to be a testing time for his leadership. The detonation of the first Russian atomic bomb in 1949, the communist victory in the Chinese civil war, and the North Korean invasion of the south led the President to adopt a response to the Soviet threat that was more military and more militant than had been the case before. The new approach was embodied in the National Security Council policy paper known as NSC 68, which argued that the Soviet Union aimed at domination of the whole world, and that the United States should give priority to massive rearmament. The paper was drafted by the council before the Korean attack, but was not approved or signed by Truman until after it.

In part the shift in emphasis evidenced by NSC 68 may have been the result of a turnover within the State Department: Paul Nitze, who drafted the document, replaced George Kennan as head of the Policy Planning Staff, while Dean Acheson succeeded Marshall as secretary. At the time, Acheson and Nitze tended to employ a hard anticommunist rhetoric that Marshall and Kennan tended to avoid; this may have indicated policy differences on matters of substance as well as style. But the NSC 68 recommendation of rearmament, even if it came about because of a change in the government's men, was inspired at least as much by a change in the country's circumstances. The paper was a response to the communist takeover of China and to the invalidation of America's world strategy as a result of the explosion by Russia of the A-bomb. Until then, the demobilized and disarmed United States had indulged in believing that its atomic monopoly was a threat sufficient to counter the Red Army. Now, clearly, it was not; so if war came, America would have to go up against Russia—and now China, too—man for man and tank for tank. What Acheson and Nitze had seen, the public saw too once the Korean War began.

Ever since taking office Truman had tried to evade it, but now the bill came due for payment. Breaking with a tradition going back to the Founding Fathers, he would have to create a standing army. Building a modern defense establishment meant departing from the principles of small government and low taxes that had always been central to the Republic's values. It meant becoming like the European nations Americans always had denounced: like a Prussia with a permanent war economy. That was the cost of becoming and remaining involved in world politics. It was only because of the North Korean attack that the country allowed Truman to follow this path.

One surge in the size of the American government had taken place under FDR in fighting the Depression. Now Truman initiated another to fight the cold war—and to be prepared to fight any other kind of war. He gave his approval to NSC 68. The national security government was to continue growing through the second half of the twentieth century.

Truman, Acheson, Marshall, and Eisenhower would have been shocked—as young men in 1901—to learn where it would all end (though, of course, it never ends). Theodore Roosevelt, their newly inducted President, had a White House staff of thirty-five; Ronald Reagan was to have one of 3,366—plus an additional 3,000 on a part-time basis. And in 1992, for the first time, more Americans worked in government than in manufacturing.

IN THE DARK DAYS of the Korean War, Truman called FDR's generals back to the colors. He phoned Marshall, who was trout fishing in Michigan in retirement, and appointed him secretary of defense. He contacted Eisenhower, who had entered a new civilian career as president of Columbia University, and sent him to Europe as head of NATO forces.

He placed MacArthur in command of United States and United Nations forces in Korea, and the old soldier achieved an astounding and almost miraculous victory by his landing at Inchon September 15. He seemed to have won the war. After hard fighting in the South Korean capital of Seoul, the northern invaders fled back home. MacArthur pursued them.

But the Chinese, hitherto on the sidelines, then announced that the war was going to be fought by their own rules. China declared that if MacArthur's troops entered North Korea, the Chinese would enter the war.

A billion Chinese with the Soviet Union behind them: that was rather too much for the Truman administration to handle. Yet stopping MacArthur's advance at the frontier line seemed to solve nothing; the North Koreans could simply wait until they had rebuilt their forces and then, if they chose, reinvade.

If the Chinese stood behind their threat, MacArthur's forces had only two choices, neither of them acceptable: to stay where they were, standing guard forever against the next invasion; or to invade the north and become involved in an endless war against China's unlimited manpower.

MacArthur chose to believe the Chinese were bluffing. With the approval of Truman—whose initial view after North Korea's attack had been that the invaders should be thrown back only to their own frontier—he ordered the U.S.–UN armies in early October to cross the thirty-eighth parallel and keep on heading north. He led his forces to disaster, dividing them—as Korea's topography requires, for the mountains run north–south—and storming all the way up to the Yalu River frontier with China. He charged, in a line that was thin and discontinuous, setting up his troops for a counterpunch as waves of Chinese "volunteers" crossed the river in late October and smashed into and through them, sending the American armies reeling back to face annihilation with backs against the sea.

From the heights of success at Inchon to the lower depths of the Yalu retreat, no general can have seen his fortunes plunge so far in so short a time. In despair that his troops would not be able to hold the line—any line—MacArthur demanded that the war be widened. With the limited forces at his disposal, he told Washington, he could not cope with the enemy. Full-scale war against China and Russia suddenly loomed ahead as possibilities, as did the use of atomic bombs.

On November 28, 1950, Truman met with his advisers and made the crucial decision not to widen the conflict: which is to say, to not risk starting the Third World War—even though refusing to widen the war, according to MacArthur, meant losing it. Even for Truman, whose strength was facing facts, these were hard ones to look in the face. Losing a war, for the first time in American history. Watching the complete destruction of the American and United Nations forces in Korea—and accepting that and making no reply. Bearing responsibility for having sent in the troops in the first place. Becoming the greatest failure as a war leader in the history of the American presidency.

Two days before Christmas, MacArthur's field commander was killed. On Christmas day Matthew Ridgway, perhaps America's most competent general, arrived to replace him. MacArthur gave him full authority.

Within weeks, Ridgway had stopped what Truman's latest biographer has called "the longest retreat in American military history." Then he turned the troops around. A month after he arrived, Ridgway started the U.S.-UN forces moving forward again. He had shown that MacArthur was wrong; it could be done without starting a wider war—though perhaps nobody but Ridgway could have done it.

Washington could breathe easy. But the narrowness of the escape retrospectively threw doubt on the wisdom of having intervened in the Korean conflict. So did the limitations on what Ridgway could accomplish: liberation of South Korea, with a standstill near the prewar frontier, but no victory over North Korea. As Acheson pointed out: "We can't defeat the Chinese in Korea" because "they can put in more than we can." But the American people would not sustain for long a war of attrition with no hope of winning in sight. Truman fired MacArthur for insubordination in April 1951, but it was the general's view that there is no substitute for victory that rang true to the public.

Nor was the public necessarily wrong. When the administration thought it had the chance to take the whole of Korea, it had reached for it. Only when that goal proved to be beyond its grasp did the American government let it be known that the stalemate arrived at near the thirty-eighth parallel was its objective. It was a freak stroke of luck that the United States had held on to even that—or indeed any portion of the Korean peninsula. Before Ridgway took up his command, all that Secretary of Defense Marshall asked was to "get out with honor."

When they defended the rightness of their decisions, Truman and Acheson could be understood to suggest that when similar challenges were posed in the future, they would once again allow America to be drawn into limited wars: where it was heads, the United States does not win; tails, the United States loses.

The administration took the view that in the atomic era, to risk war against other great powers would be suicidal. The Truman government also had decided and said that it made no strategic sense to try to defend South Korea. Yet inflamed by an act of communist aggression, Truman and his advisers forgot their prudence and their strategy. Maddened by the waving Red flag, they charged blindly past the wrong place: a spot chosen by the matador. It was the price of the frenzy they themselves had aroused, in which American public figures now felt obliged to prove their patriotism by showing they were not soft on communism.

JAMES FORRESTAL'S MANY FRIENDS and allies tried to minimize the significance of the form his mental breakdown took, not wanting it to color appreciation of his views while he was still in control of himself. He always had been tense and moody, and his lifelong conflicts about his religious and family origins apparently were severe. Whenever he invited political or business colleagues to the house, he had to worry about what drunken scene or crazed conduct to expect from his wife. Enemies among newspaper columnists printed what he claimed were lies about him. At one cabinet meeting, Clark Clifford, seated behind him, watched in fascinated horror as Forrestal, with his fingernail, scratched a spot at the back of his head—first until it was raw, and then until it bled.

Forrestal suffered from severe nervous exhaustion, and as his service as secretary of defense—America's first head of the unified armed services—came to an end in 1949, he was a physical wreck and virtually unable to speak. That his wife had paranoid delusions that Reds were plotting against her may have been related in some way to his own similar fears. He claimed that Russians were about to invade the United States, or perhaps already had. Visiting his friend Robert Lovett in Florida, Forrestal confided, as he had to his old Wall Street colleague Ferdinand Eberstadt: "The Russians are after me, the FBI is watching me, the Zionists are after me." He searched the closets at Lovett's house and looked under the beds.

It was his wife, whom he had refused to send to a mental institution because it would ruin her reputation, who decided not to send him to one because it would ruin his. He was sent instead to a hospital, while columnist Drew Pearson charged in print and over the air that the American atom bomb arsenal had been in the hands of a madman.

That same year, Forrestal jumped to his death from a window of Bethesda Naval Hospital outside Washington. A new biography suggests that his suicide may have been triggered by the poem he was copying out at the time. What had stopped his copying, and seemingly had plunged him into gloom, was the word "nightingale." It was a code word for a secret operation he had authorized, the organization of an underground army in Soviet Russia. The army was to be composed of Ukrainians who, in Hitler's service during the war, had carried out mass murders of Jews and fellow Ukrainians. It would have made a great scoop for Drew Pearson: "FORRESTAL HIRES NAZI DEATH SQUADS TO WORK FOR U.S."

DURING BOTH WORLD WARS it had been America's intention to remake the enemy powers when the fighting was over. Wilson hoped to turn Germany into a civilian democracy—that was what the war was all about, he had told Congress in 1917—but in the end he never had the chance. In 1945 Truman, MacArthur, and their aides meant to rebuild Germany and Japan in America's liberal democratic image. But barely had they made a start of it when the cold war forced them to make compromises. To fight the Russians in Europe, they sometimes had to recruit the very forces against which they had been crusading under FDR.

As Acheson wrote, summarizing his views as of 1949: "To me, one conclusion seemed plain beyond doubt. Western Europe and the U.S. could not contain the Soviet Union and suppress Germany and Japan at the same time." Nor, in that endeavor, could they do without the aid of the rocket scientists, industrialists, intelligence officers, and others who had been the willing servants of Nazi Germany and Tojo's Japan, many of whom the Allies had earlier planned to punish for war crimes.

The balancing act performed by American occupation officials in building democracy in Japan and western Germany, while at the same time employing people deeply implicated in the shameful past, was a challenging one.

A MONTH AFTER BECOMING PRESIDENT, Truman wrote in his diary: "We want no Gestapo or Secret Police. F.B.I. is tending in that direction. They are dabbling in sex life scandals and plain blackmail when they should be catching criminals. . . . *This must stop.*"

Truman also disliked the idea of having an espionage service, yet some sort of centralized foreign intelligence and/or operations directorate was an essential element of the national security government Truman and Clifford were creating; and between 1946 and 1950 they thrashed out the question of what it should be.

After false starts by three predecessors, General Walter Bedell Smith, a Marshall protégé who had headed Eisenhower's staff in the European war and later served as ambassador to the Soviet Union, took charge in 1950 and created the modern CIA—which among other things mounted clandestine operations. But the public never felt comfortable with such covert activities; they were not in the American tradition. Having to stoop to such practices was one of the costs of the cold war.

To ENJOY THE PRIVILEGE of operating beyond the law, licensed by a government to commit what otherwise would be crimes, is a heady experience, a constant temptation, and a power that can corrupt. But it was not the grant of the power, but its grant to an entity beyond his control, that aroused the jealousy of J. Edgar Hoover, director of the Federal Bureau of Investigation—the FBI. He was frustrated by the independence of the emerging CIA, and it became evident that he coveted the entire world of American secret agents for his own domain.

It was typical that by the summer of 1950 Hoover had authorized a surveillance of the CIA's Carmel Offie, the former Bullitt aide who had been forced to resign from the State Department; and it was to last more than twenty years. Offie had mysteriously become wealthy a decade before. By

1942 he had a house in Georgetown where Bullitt used to stay, and Vice President Wallace wrote in his diary that "Bill said that Offie had sponged off him for many years and now he was sponging off Offie."

When brought into the CIA by its head of covert operations, Frank G. Wisner, Offie began to recruit all sorts of people, and Wisner's widow later said that "before long he was starting to bring in people Frank didn't know, friends of Bill Bullitt's." He rebuilt ties with people who had worked for the Nazis and now could be used against Russia, and with the many exiled eastern Europeans of shady past with whom he had contacts. This was the dark side of the crusade against communism. Offie represented something that would be attacked by critics who believed the United States was selling its soul in order to beat the Russians.

Hoover, now generally believed to have been homosexual, also was a homophobe and was enraged that a "degenerate" such as Offie could hold office. It was Offie, of course, a homosexual himself, who had been in charge of Bullitt's campaign to smear Sumner Welles for his homosexuality.

Hoover joined forces with Senator Joseph McCarthy, whose attacks on Offie as a high official who "spent his time hanging around the men's room in Lafayette Park" brought about his instant resignation from the CIA. But Offie found immediate employment with the American Federation of Labor, in a program he had set up for the CIA to counter communist influence.

The FBI could not get at him because he was not employed by the government. Hoover was furious: "Offie is dangerous to the security of the country," he wrote, and "it is outrageous for such a character to escape prosecution on such a technicality."

The FBI file expanded as more and more unsubstantiated charges went into it: gunrunning, white slavery, election fraud, bribery, and while on trips to Rome, "chicken-hawking behind the Vatican in recognizable embassy cars."


IN A SENSE Bullitt, along with Offie, had been a forerunner of the witch-hunters by hounding Welles out of government as an alleged security risk. Now, joining the McCarthyite throng who won headlines by denouncing others—often falsely—he turned his back on friends and colleagues of a lifetime and charged that communist sympathizers were in the top ranks of the government, having come in with the New Deal: "the State Department and the Foreign Service are still rancid with these men." Bullitt, Offie, and Offie's enemy, Hoover, had all descended into the same sewer. And it could be argued that this was a result—though perhaps not a necessary one—of the decision to fight the unscrupulous communist empire with its own weapons, which brought with it a certain moral corruption that proved contagious.

In the pages of *Life* magazine, Bullitt outlined his thesis that because FDR had not listened to him, the Soviet Union had been allowed to expand. As an insider who supposedly knew all the secrets, Bullitt wove a story of a feeble, incompetent, dying President tricked by Stalin at Teheran and Yalta into giving Russia central and eastern Europe. George Elsey, keeper of the map room at the White House and the man who *really* knew all the secrets, was furious. In comments to Chip Bohlen, FDR's interpreter at Yalta who had been with the President at all meetings with Russians, Elsey wrote on White House stationery (April 3, 1948): "real slander" and "lying in his teeth." But it was Bullitt's version that survived in popular mythology.

Louis Wehle, who had introduced Bullitt to FDR in 1932, had become a Republican, and in 1948 promised Bullitt that he would be named undersecretary of state—the long-sought-for Sumner Welles job—if the Dewey-Warren ticket won. But by 1953, when a Republican President finally was inaugurated, Bullitt's political credit was exhausted, and his friends long since were estranged.

## 58

# FORGING A CONSENSUS

EVER SINCE 1898, the fundamental question about American foreign relations had been whether the United States would choose to play a continuing role in world affairs. The showdown on that issue was scheduled to occur on the floor of the Republican National Convention in Chicago in July 1952.

Only in the Republican party did isolationists still command a mass following. Yet they had lost every nomination since 1936, and even they must have sensed that 1952 was their last opportunity. Their candidate was Senator Robert A. Taft—"Mr. Republican"—the hero of the conservative wing of a party in which liberals were in the minority. A liberal-minded internationalist New York lawyer had taken the Republican nomination from an Ohio conservative isolationist—and then had gone on to lose the general elections—three times in a row: in 1940, 1944, and 1948. In 1952 there was a widespread feeling that it was only fair to give Taft his chance.

The emergence of Dwight Eisenhower as a candidate meant that Taft would have to fight for it. Now NATO commander, Ike was a national hero. A seeming nonpartisan, he for years had hidden his ambition to be President and had given no indication of party preference. Democrats had longed to nominate him in 1948, but for various reasons the timing was not right: it was the wrong year for him* as well as the wrong party.

In a year in which any Republican nominee looked to be the likely winner, Ike had framed the issue masterfully. Disclaiming personal ambition, he had offered to support Taft if the senator would pledge himself to international alliance in the cause of collective security. Of course, the Ohioan would not renounce the views of a lifetime, so Eisenhower—as he told visitors to NATO headquarters—felt it his *duty* to seek the nomination in order to lead the party and therefore the country away from isolationism.

Dewey placed his organization, which had proven twice that it was the best in the business of winning Republican conventions, at Eisenhower's

---

* Among clouds hanging over his candidacy in 1948 were rumors of his wartime love affair with Kay Summersby, his driver and secretary. Her popular book about working for Eisenhower defused that issue before the 1952 elections.

disposal, under the leadership of its manager, New York lawyer Herbert Brownell. Although Taft believed he was coming into Chicago with enough pledges to win, Brownell outmaneuvered the Ohioan on a series of procedural issues affecting the seating of delegates. On the first ballot, Ike, with 595 votes, was nine short of victory, and Taft had 500. Then Minnesota switched the nineteen votes it was casting for favorite son Harold Stassen to Eisenhower.

Minnesota's shift finished isolationism as a political force in American life. After Eisenhower won the general election over Adlai Stevenson and was sworn in as President, Taft became his loyal Senate majority leader. When Taft died shortly afterward, the "fortress America" strategy was buried with him.

In Taft's last months it became evident that what was required was a revolution in the thinking of his colleagues. They were used to blaming big government and large budgets on the Democrats. On April 3, 1953, Eisenhower's press secretary received a telephoned report from the Senate Appropriations Committee that "Senator Taft blew up and said the overall budget was the same as the Truman budget; he did not think he could publicly defend it nor could other Republicans in Congress and we would lose the Congress."

Again Taft and his colleagues wanted to renounce the accords reached with the Soviet Union at Yalta, while the Eisenhower administration was willing only to denounce Russia for having "perverted" those agreements. For the administration knew that the commitments made at Yalta were those America favored: introduction of democracy in eastern Europe, for example. The Taft wing of the party remained a prisoner of its own propaganda: when both Taft and Dulles charged that FDR had given the countries of eastern Europe into capitivity, the difference between them was that Taft believed what he was saying while Dulles was consciously lying.

ISOLATIONISM HAVING BEEN DEALT WITH, other foreign policy approaches were available to be examined. For in the long years of government by Roosevelt and Truman, the Republican party had become the refuge of critics of administration foreign policy from almost every angle. In the Eisenhower years all the right-wing alternatives to the hitherto bipartisan foreign policy of the United States came up for review, to be rejected or to be tested but in any event to be resolved.

Yet the story of how all of them were discarded is unclear: the record of the Eisenhower administration, though extremely well documented, and though the subject of penetrating studies, is more murky than that of others. In part, this has to do with Ike himself, a military politician who was an expert in the arts of deception. Privately he had a short and violent temper;

in public he wore a relaxed grin. Throughout his career, he had been known for the clarity of his style, but at presidential press conferences he so scrambled his sentences that he seemed to be talking nonsense; it was difficult to pin him down and he always could retract what anybody thought he might have said. As President, he gave the impression of spending full time on the golf links and leaving decisions to Dulles and others; it now transpires that he was in total command but had placed his officials in a position where they, and not he, were the ones blamed for whatever went wrong.

Brownell and Lucius Clay cleared the cabinet appointments, and for secretary of state gave no serious consideration to anyone other than John Foster Dulles. Later rumors that John McCloy's name was in contention seem, on the available evidence, not to have been true. British foreign secretary Eden, on his behalf and Churchill's, recommended against the choice of Dulles, but were told that their arguments were useless. Dulles's facial tic, a reminder of his youthful endeavors to surmount British imperial trade barriers in the tropics, boded ill for the Churchill and Eden governments.

In his own way Dulles was as deceiving as Eisenhower, and with the recent opening of his archives, historians are changing a good many judgments about him. An earlier view, associated with his lay religious activities, was that he was rigid and doctrinaire. Taft, who knew him when they were both students, was closer to the mark in worrying that he was a waverer. They had been isolationists together in the 1930s and early 1940s, but when the political winds shifted, Taft looked around and saw that Dulles had become a leader of the Republican internationalists. Taft was concerned that Dulles was "likely to let himself be pushed around by those who are with him," but was resigned to accepting him as "probably the best appointment that could be made."

Dulles wrote the foreign policy plank in the 1952 Republican platform. It attacked the Democrats for appeasing communism, losing China, shielding traitors, aiming at national socialism, making unspecified blunders at Teheran, Yalta, and Potsdam, and much more to the same effect—after which nobody could have guessed that for years Dulles had been part of the bipartisan team that was formulating that policy. "We charge that they have plunged us into war in Korea without the consent of our citizens . . ." seems especially hard coming from the first person in June 1950 to cable Washington from Asia to send in the armed forces.

Dulles criticized the policy of containment as "negative, futile and immoral." He promised that Eisenhower instead would pursue a policy of "liberation": that Soviet rule in Europe would be rolled back.

Encouraged by the rhetoric of the Eisenhower administration, East Germans in 1953 and Hungarians in 1956 revolted against Soviet rule and called on the United States for help. America made no effort to rescue them, and the revolts were crushed by the Russians. Dulles's pledges of liberation rang hollow.

Had Dulles consciously been lying when he claimed he knew an alternative to the containment policy? Had he known (but how could he *not* have known?) that the only way to liberate Eastern Europe in the 1950s was to go to war with Russia, and that neither he nor Eisenhower—nor the people of the United States—were prepared to do that?

So it was to be with one issue after another in the Eisenhower administration. Dulles claimed to have found the solution to the problem of how to reduce the ruinously expensive military budget required to deter Soviet aggression. "Massive retaliation" was his answer: give up buying costly conventional weapons, and in case of conflict threaten to unleash a nuclear war. But once the Russians had nuclear weapons of their own, that was not a strategy but the road to suicide. How could Dulles not have known that?

EISENHOWER EXUDED CONFIDENCE that if elected, he would know what to do about Korea. It was a trap that Truman had not known how to escape. The basic problem was one of geography and population: Korea was next to communist China, which had a billion people. If the United States sent a million troops, China could send two million; if ten million, then twenty. There was no way to top China's bid.

The full story of how and why North Korea agreed to a cease-fire still has not emerged. Stalin's death must have played a big role: in the communist world a period of quiet to sort things out might have been a strongly felt need. But mostly it seems to have been the result of China's economic and military exhaustion.*

It seems to have been the Korean War experience that led MacArthur to modify his worldview in an important way. Before he had been relieved of his command by Truman, the only ways he could think of to break out of the trap involved taking huge risks. The trap, of course, was caused by China's "privileged sanctuary" position: officially not at war, she remained immune to attack, while free to slip a few hundred thousand more "volunteers" across the border anytime the North Koreans seemed to need help. MacArthur proposed attacking China, which might have brought her fully into the war and might have brought in her ally the Soviet Union as well. Soon after leaving the army, he developed a plan that he hoped Eisenhower and Dulles would adopt: the communist leaders would be offered a comprehensive world settlement, with the threat that if they refused it, the

---

* The claim that it was because Dulles threatened to use nuclear weapons has not been substantiated, at least as yet.

United States would drop atom bombs on North Korea and would bomb China to the point where she could no longer wage modern war.

In the past it was only after MacArthur had run terrible risks and come away from them that he would start to tremble and become ill. Perhaps it was some similar effect that resulted in his change of mind, years after he had retired to civilian life and a business career. MacArthur had been in the trap of Korea; he had seen that he would have to risk a nuclear world war to fight his way out of it; and by the end of the Eisenhower administration, he had drawn the conclusion that American generals should not be ordered into China or the countries that neighbor her.

His advice in the 1960s to President Kennedy and then, from his deathbed, to President Johnson was to never again send U.S. troops to fight on the mainland of Asia. All of his life he had been urging America to commit the bulk of its armed forces to Asia first and to Europe only second. In the end he seems to have changed his mind.


AMERICANS BORN IN THE 1880s and early 1890s had been living with these questions all their lives, and now, in the last half of the 1950s, had resolved them. By the time of the second Eisenhower administration, it had become common ground for that generation that the United States should play an abiding role in international affairs; that it should do so in alliance with other nations, and in institutionalized cooperation with them; that it should police the world's oceans; that it has vital interests outside of the Western Hemisphere and should defend them; that the United States should defend Germany and Japan so that those nations need not remilitarize in order to defend themselves; that preserving the independence of Great Britain and of the countries of Western Europe is among America's vital interests; that America's most intimate political and military association should be with Europe; and that if needed, American armies should be sent to war on the continent of Europe but not that of Asia.

# 59

# AMERICA'S TRIUMPH

THE UNITED STATES had come to England's aid in her darkest hour, yet in other respects she had been less than a friend. "[I]f only America were not so unsympathetic & indeed unhelpful to us—over Egypt, India . . . ," and the rest of the remaining and former empire, lamented Clementine Churchill (February 13, 1954) to her husband, prime minister again since the autumn of 1951. She was echoing a familiar British complaint. A couple of months before, Eisenhower had proposed in a speech to the UN to refer to the "obsolete Colonial mold," and had been persuaded to delete that "obnoxious phrase" only by Churchill's personal intervention.

In the summer of 1954 Eisenhower sent Churchill a long letter critical of Britain's overseas imperialism. The prime minister replied August 8 that "I read with great interest all that you have written me about what is called Colonialism, namely: bringing forward backward races and opening up the jungles. I was brought up to feel proud of much that we had done. Certainly in India, with all its history . . . of despotic rule, Britain has a story to tell which will look quite well against the background of the coming hundred years"—that is, in comparison with what the first century of Indian independence, 1947–2047, was likely to bring.

It was a debate that had gone on since the time of Washington, Jefferson, and Adams. British leaders found it hard to believe that in the twentieth century—for was not the war of 1776 finished yet?—Americans would still harbor such sentiments and indeed take anticolonialism seriously. But they were wrong to underestimate the tenacity with which such views were held. Antifascism and anticommunism might come and go, but anticolonialism was the principal political plank in the enduring foreign policy of the United States. The fact that in exercising hegemony within the Western Hemisphere, or in occupying territories abroad in pursuit of military or commercial advantage, the United States itself practiced what looked to others like imperialism was something that Americans at mid-century usually chose not to notice.

It was not just a high-minded academic like Wilson or a crusty old isolationist like Senator Borah; even Franklin Roosevelt, an urbane man of the world who had traveled on the Continent, felt uneasy in both world wars in having Britain and France for allies, because the Europeans still clung to colonial empires.

Indeed, one of the troubling limitations of NATO since its inception had been the American intention to defend Britain, France, and the others only within their own continent. The United States was determined not to be drawn into preserving Europe's possessions overseas. The curious result was that America, though an ally of the NATO countries in Europe, was their critic, sometimes their rival, potentially their adversary, and conceivably even their enemy in other quarters of the globe.

THE AMERICAN DILEMMA in the colonialist world was that Washington wanted to overthrow the existing European imperial regimes without allowing the indigenous rebels, who almost always seemed to the United States to be communists, to take power.

An immediate problem when Eisenhower took office was the revolt in French Indochina led by the communist but nationalist Ho Chi Minh. Despite French pleas, the President did not supply the important assistance that Paris asked; rather, he discussed the possibility of doing so, and instead of saying no, posed conditions that were not met: that Congress should support such American intervention; that Britain and other allies should participate, too; and that all of the Joint Chiefs should recommend taking such action (which General Ridgway, the army chief of staff, refused to do).

Eisenhower and Dulles were contemptuous of the French for losing the Indochina War, yet tried to persuade them not to negotiate an end to it. When the French nonetheless made peace in Geneva in 1954, the U.S. government launched a clandestine campaign of subversion in North Vietnam and a political program aimed at replacing France as the sponsor of the noncommunist regime in South Vietnam.

Having succeeded in assuming responsibility for supporting the fragile new government of South Vietnam, the United States sought to make of it a nationalist regime: a local force both anti-imperialist and anticommunist, offering honest and effective leadership, that could command a mass popular following and that possessed the strength to win either an election or a civil war—but that also would accept guidance from the United States. Such a government was never found for South Vietnam.

Dulles and Eisenhower did not face the stark question of what they would do if the only choice were between a European colonial regime and a native government not unfriendly to communism. It was a question they were going to be forced to answer in the Egyptian crisis that exploded two years later.

THE ROAD TO SUEZ, the highway of empire and the crossroads of history, began, as it was to end, with a recognition by the British cabinet that the country was living beyond its means. As Churchill returned to office, Anthony Eden at the Foreign Office addressed the question of how to pay for maintaining Britain as a world power. His answer was to draw the United States, through NATO, into playing a greater role in Europe; and then to secure American help in garrisoning the Middle East, the second most important theater. "The more gradually and inconspicuously we can transfer the real burdens from our own to American shoulders, the less damage we shall do to our position and influence in the world," Eden wrote.

The United States, to which the Churchill government continued handing over responsibilities in the Middle East, had embarked on a new course under Eisenhower. Like his best friend in the cabinet, the powerful Treasury secretary and big-business executive George Humphrey, Ike believed that America's strength lay in the health of her economy; the way to preserve that health was to shrink government, reduce or eliminate budget deficits, and lower taxes. Loath to order an ever more costly military buildup, the President turned to the CIA to deal with the Middle East and other Third World situations by covert operations that, in comparison with regular warfare by modern armies, would be extremely inexpensive.

By coincidence the instrument was ready at hand just when needed. After all the organizational battles about what it should be and who should be in charge of what, the CIA came into its own as an entity only in the 1950s, under General Walter Bedell Smith (October 1950–February 1953) and his deputy Allen Dulles, who succeeded to the directorship when Smith moved to the State Department and Eisenhower became President.

Within the clandestine operations division, there was a continuing tension between its two branches. The older of the two, the Office of Special Operations (OSO) was a sort of continuation of the wartime OSS and dealt with espionage and counterespionage: spying on the Soviet bloc and uncovering Soviet spies in the West. It functioned behind the iron curtain. To the extent that it functioned in the Third World, it did so only to obtain additional information about the Russian empire and its clandestine operations. The OSO did not take much interest in the Third World as such.

The Office of Policy Coordination (OPC) was created by order of President Truman to engage in covert operations. It originally was under the direction of George Kennan at the State Department and was headed at first by Frank Wisner and Carmel Offie. It took the OPC a few years to learn what was, for Americans, a new business. It undertook to secretly manipulate the politics of other countries, particularly Third World countries emerging from colonialist rule.

The more colorful operatives of the OPC were in the Theodore Roosevelt mold—and some were even his relatives. Like TR, they spoke many languages and prided themselves on being tough. Like TR's political partner Henry Cabot Lodge, they were American nationalists—very much like the English and intensely competitive with them.

Apparently the first OPC field operation was in 1949, and its first completely successful one was in 1952. With Eisenhower's inauguration in 1953, it was ready to go to work.

Its services were required in Iran, whose nationalist and republican prime minister, Dr. Muhammad Mussadegh, had nationalized all foreign oil assets in May 1951. These were chiefly those of the British-owned Anglo-Persian Oil Company, with its important refinery at Abadan. For two years Britain and Iran had argued about the payment due to the owners, while Britain organized a boycott of Iran. Mussadegh drew on deep reserves of antiforeign feeling in whipping up mass domestic support for his program. The shah fled, first to his castle on the Caspian Sea, then to Rome. This was the crisis that Churchill's cabinet blamed on the previous Labour government, and in which London asked Washington for help.

At Britain's call for help, Wisner's operatives were sent in to straighten out Iran. They arranged the overthrow of Mussadegh and the return of the shah. Having done so, they took for the United States 40 percent of what had been Britain's monopoly of Iranian oil.

Then there was Egypt. Moving into a political vacuum left by Britain, the CIA set out to back a potential new leader for the country. Allen Dulles for a time preferred Gamal Abdel Nasser, the most charismatic of the young officers who successfully plotted the overthrow of King Farouk I.

The CIA in Washington acted (until 1956) as Nasser's friend at court, while in Egypt it taught his secret police how to foil a coup d'état. An agency team set up an anti-American propaganda program for his use in case he had to out-demagogue opponents. But whether the CIA contributed to Nasser's success is hard to say, for he was an immensely shrewd and popular politician with a mass following throughout the Middle East.

European governments fighting to hold on to their positions in the region blamed their desperate situation on him. Successive French cabinets, losing a war in Algeria that in intensity approached a civil war, claimed that it was only Nasser's support and inspiration that sustained the rebel forces. Eden, who followed Churchill as prime minister, became hysterical when it looked as though the kingdom of Jordan, the Colonial Office's own creation, with its Sandhurst-trained monarch and its British-officered army, was being seduced by the Egyptian leader. Of Nasser, Eden said: "I want him murdered."

While Allen Dulles still was trying to build Nasser up,* his older brother began trying to tear him down. The secretary of state saw in the Egyptian someone who could not be counted on to resist the Soviet Union. John Foster Dulles therefore backed another candidate for leadership of the Arab world; he turned to the Iraqi dictator, Nuri Said.

Nasser met this challenge by one of his own; breaking the rules set for him by the Western powers, he ordered massive quantities of arms from the Soviet bloc. Secretary Dulles escalated the conflict; he punished the Arab leader publicly by pulling out the financing from Egypt's cherished project of building a new dam at Aswan, and in blunt terms meant to humiliate. Nasser reescalated in a speech July 26, 1956, by announcing the transfer to Egypt's ownership of all shares in the Compagnie Universelle du Canal Maritime de Suez, the company that leased and operated the Suez Canal concession. He proposed to pay for the Aswan Dam with the profits from Suez. The owners of the shares he was taking were almost entirely European; his promise to pay them the closing market price for their stock holdings was either disregarded or not believed in Europe.

In both the CIA's pro-Nasser activities and the State Department's active anti-Nasser policies, the ones getting hurt were Britain and France, the two bystanders. Eisenhower and John Foster Dulles hoped to see Nasser eliminated someday, but felt no urgency about it; their preference was to do nothing for the moment, and perhaps remove the Egyptian dictator from the scene at some later point when nobody was looking.

France (because of Algeria) and Britain (because of Jordan) had decided to overthrow Nasser even before the nationalization of the canal company, which they took as their excuse. But the nationalization alerted the world to the possibility of an Anglo-French riposte. Eisenhower strongly cautioned Paris and, above all, London not to use force.

Misunderstanding was mutual. Ike and Dulles told each other, and Eden, that if Britain and France attacked, the United States would not assist them—but never so much as hinted that America might actually *oppose* them. Deputy Undersecretary of State Robert Murphy, a special envoy from Eisenhower, cabled Washington from London that Eden and Chancellor of the Exchequer Harold Macmillan "said British government has decided to drive Nasser out of Egypt. The decision they declared is firm. They expressed simple conviction military action is necessary and inevitable." Murphy went on to quote the British leaders as saying they hoped the United States would support them, but would understand if it chose not to do so. For whatever reason, the Eisenhower administration seems to have believed this was merely a proposed course of action and that London and Paris would not actually launch a military operation without first advising Washington.

---

* Eventually Allen Dulles became disillusioned with Nasser.

But then—as the U.S. government continued to bombard Downing Street with advice to avoid the use of force—on social occasions Europeans stopped talking when Americans entered the room. It became evident they were planning something but not saying what. They put the scheme into operation in late autumn (U.S. intelligence figured it out only just beforehand), and it turned out to be a plan too complicated to work, covered by a story too transparently false to be believed.

Israel, which had suffered border attacks from Egypt for years, was secretly invited by France to invade Sinai and drive to the Suez Canal. By prearrangement, France and England then announced that they were sending their armies to the canal zone to separate the two antagonists and protect the maritime passageway. The Israelis advanced too quickly, and the Europeans too slowly; then the Soviet government issued threats suggesting that it would bomb England and France unless they withdrew.

Eisenhower and Dulles were enraged—not by the Russians, but by the British, French, and Israelis. Recently released records suggest that they were animated even more by a personal sense of betrayal than by policy considerations. Reasonably or otherwise, they felt they had been lied to by people they had regarded as trusted friends. At a guess—and it is no more than that—Eisenhower, who as Allied and NATO generalissimo had been accustomed to issuing orders to Britain and France for fifteen years, was angry that his counsel to them in this case had not been taken as more in the nature of a command.

Eisenhower and Dulles took the position that the United States must be seen by the Third World not to stand aside—which was something they had suggested beforehand—but to actively oppose the European invasion. They wanted the peoples of Africa, Asia, and Latin America to be shown that America was against imperialism. But they employed the wrong tactics to realize such a strategy: instead of seeming to take sides against Britain and France, while in reality not harming them, the Eisenhower administration did it the other way around. There should have been speeches and gestures: appearances, not realities. Instead, the United States acted invisibly but with paralyzing effectiveness to halt their allies by financial maneuverings of which the public was unaware.

Treasury Secretary Humphrey cut off the financial support that alone enabled Britain to prop up the value of her currency. The British Treasury suddenly was faced with the prospect of financial disaster: a run on the pound, the collapse of sterling, a plunge into chaos. Yet only a handful of people understood that such was the case. Until Macmillan, the British equivalent of secretary of the Treasury, told them, even his colleagues in the British cabinet did not know it. Macmillan had favored the Suez expedition, but now effectively stopped it. The United States had defeated the Europeans—but in secret.

The short-term consequences for the United States were disastrous. The Third World public to which the administration suddenly attached such importance believed it had seen the last desperate venture of imperial Europe defeated—not by the United States, but by the Soviet Union. Russian influence in the Middle East grew. America's principal allies were weakened. France, shocked into a realization that U.S. backing could not be relied upon, began work on building her own nuclear arsenal.

But although neither Eisenhower nor Dulles had reason to believe it would happen, the long-term results were those the United States had wanted to bring about for two centuries: persuaded, finally, that America would not support them in playing an imperial role, the powers of Europe, unable to pay for their empires on their own, set out to divest themselves of their colonies. Macmillan, taking Eden's place as prime minister, set the program in motion in London. De Gaulle, when he returned to power at the end of the 1950s, did the same in Paris. Belgium, Spain, and others followed suit, as Portugal did later for reasons of her own. Perhaps it would have happened in any event, even had there been no prodding by the United States, but it seems unlikely it would have happened so quickly.

The American Revolution of 1776 had come to fruition. Its goals had been fully achieved at last. The era of European world domination had come to an end. It was perhaps the most important happening of the twentieth century. In the year Eisenhower was born, nearly half the land surface of the earth was ruled by either the British queen or the Russian tsar. Now the countries of the world were given back to the peoples who inhabited them. An international law periodical published in 1982 reported that "since 1945, Britain has relinquished 5,200,000 square miles of colonial possessions with some 800 million inhabitants." And that was Britain alone; it took no account of what France, Belgium, and others had surrendered.

THE UNITED STATES HAD OTHER, but less focused, ideas of the changes Europe should make in herself. Many of these involved the formation of some sort of pan-European union. By eliminating tariff and other customs barriers, the countries of Europe could create a market large enough to support industries that could play in the same league that American businesses did. By establishing one army, Europe, with a population larger than that of the Soviet Union, would be able to defend herself. By transcending nationalisms, the peoples of Britain and the Continent could solve the problem of Germany being too powerful for her neighbors.

Yet Europeans would not always travel in the directions the United

States pointed out to them. France blocked American-backed initiatives such as the European army. In the Eisenhower years, it looked very much as though de Gaulle's vision of a "Europe of fatherlands" would prevail. Then, and for years afterward, it seemed that American reasoning had been superficial; it had taken no account of history. André Malraux, man of letters and politics, remarked that Europe "does not exist and never has. It is the last of the great myths." In the Middle Ages, he said, it was decided "that there was a Europe because there was Christianity. Christianity was serious. Europe is a dream—for Europeans but also for others. I would like to know how serious the American dream of Europe was. Did the leaders of America really ever believe in it?"

The Americans did believe in it; and in the end de Gaulle, who had summoned up French nationalism to block it, said it was *his* conception that was the dream. After leaving office, he told Malraux: "I held up the corpse of France in my arms and I made the world believe France was living. And I, General de Gaulle, I knew she was dead."

As of this writing, European unity is far from achieved. But the links, however loose, are there, including the various institutions of the European Community, and what has come into being is at least somewhat like what the United States proposed decades ago. As with so many American objectives, it has taken far more time than Truman's and Marshall's and Eisenhower's generation expected. But in the end, the Continent has moved in the direction pioneered by the United States.

THE GIS WHO LIBERATED EUROPE held an unthinking belief that teaching people to play baseball and drink cola and eat hamburgers helped to spread Americanism. Somehow they were right. Again, it took decades. But the coming of the consumer society and the communications revolution to Europe and the rest of the world did accomplish what Wilson's political children set out to do: make the rest of the world more like the United States. Now in all corners of the globe people dress, eat, drink, and dance like Americans; they listen to American-style popular music, see Hollywood movies, get their news from Cable News Network, and hire Washington political-media firms to manage their election campaigns.

The rest of the world took its issue-oriented politics—and its issues as well—from the United States.* The environment ("conservation," as it was called when Theodore Roosevelt invented it as a political program), antitrust regulation, securities and stock exchange laws, the women's movement: all were invented in America. Once they were the politics of the New World; now they are the new politics of the entire world.

* Which, to be fair, learned from England.

The American theory was that defeated enemies, Germany and Japan, should not be destroyed but reoriented: restored, but taught to channel their resources into achieving economic rather than military or political hegemony. It was a road that Walter Rathenau and other German civilian leaders had pointed out to their countrymen in the early days of the century, but that they had not taken, either then or in the 1930s. Yet the American victors in the Second World War had given Germany a third chance.

Events so far suggest that the bet placed by the Truman administration was the right one: that rebuilding Germany and Japan, and trusting the willingness and ability of their peoples to change their militarist outlook to a civilian one,* was the course to take—rather than sentencing them to a Carthaginian destruction, as FDR would have done at least with Germany.

But history is never over. Truman's bet continues to ride—and the fate of much of the world continues to ride with it.


E I S E N H O W E R  A N D  D U L L E S continued the containment policy outlined by George Kennan and amended by Paul Nitze during the Truman administration, but only grudgingly, and in default of having any workable alternative. They were impatient with containment because they wanted quick results—which seemed not to be forthcoming.

Like Acheson, Dulles believed that the Soviet system, though inferior to America's in many ways, held certain advantages in the long run. In early 1959 he told congressmen that because of the regimented nature of their societies, communist countries had "possibilities for economic growth which we do not possess in a free society." The contrary view ascribed to Bernard Baruch and Joseph Kennedy—that Americans should *encourage* Russia and all other rival countries to be communist because communism is such an inefficient system that the United States could keep on beating them—was regarded as a joke rather than a serious theory.

Dulles did see Kennan's point that Soviet Russia might collapse someday as a result of internal contradictions; and he saw, too, that should a split between Russia and China occur, their rivalry could neutralize the danger either of them posed to the United States. But Dulles, who in 1955 said that such a split might be a year or even "some years away," in 1956 remarked gloomily that "[t]hese natural rivalries might take 100 years to assert themselves."

---

* Lessons have been learned. Paradoxically, Japan, which started its wars in the first half of the century in order to capture natural resources, was enabled to become an economic winner in the second half by not having any of her own: she was free to buy raw materials at the cheapest price available in any market, and thus become a low-cost manufacturer.

IN FACT, the rivalry between the two great communist powers began to evidence itself in the 1950s, during Dulles's lifetime, and the internal collapse of the Soviet Union took less than half a century.

The cold war was a disagreement about the settlement of the Second World War, which ended in 1945.* In 1989 the Soviet Union began the process of surrendering the sphere in central and eastern Europe that FDR, Truman, and their successors had been unwilling for Russia to have. That was what the argument initially had been about, and the Kremlin gave it up. Then came the almost incredible headlines: Russia dissolved the Soviet Union and gave up communism.

It was one of the most astonishing things in history, both in itself and in that it completed the accomplishment of the seemingly impossible American program of remaking the world. When Woodrow Wilson proclaimed his goals in 1917, he had given no practical thought to how they could be achieved. And since, in the circumstances of the time (and indeed in any circumstances then foreseeable), they would have been impossible of realization, a foreign policy realist in 1917 would have had to believe either that the President was indulging in meaningless rhetoric or that he was out of his mind. But in the 1990s what Wilson proposed had come to pass— partly because the world had changed greatly and in ways he could not have foreseen, but also as a partial result of purposeful actions by the generation that he had educated and brought into politics.

What seemed so far-fetched as to border on craziness was Wilson's further belief that somehow America's victorious allies, too, could be changed by the United States: forced to give up their empires and their frontiers, and to move toward some sort of federation. Wilson could not explain (because he did not know) how victor countries could be forced to do anything against their will. Yet without intending to, Eisenhower and Dulles at Suez managed the accomplishment of defeating America's allies after first defeating most of her enemies.


THE FINAL CONTEST to be resolved was America's continuing battle with Russia—part one thing, and part the other: the country that in both world wars had started as an ally and ended as an enemy. What was re-markable was that in the conflict with the Soviet Union, the United States pursued a rational strategy that worked. History is the story of ironies: of moves meant to achieve one purpose that instead achieve another. Here was

---

* But in a sense it did not end until August 31, 1994, when the last Soviet troops left Germany and the Baltic republics.

the extraordinary exception. Kennan's theory, adopted by the American government, was that if the United States held the line long enough, the Soviet Union would collapse from within—and that is what actually happened.

In the First World War, Wilson had inspired people Franklin Roosevelt's and Harry Truman's and Dwight Eisenhower's age to go out and change the politics of the rest of the planet. It took nearly a century; it was by no means entirely of their doing, and for the most part they did not realize where the forces would lead that they were putting in motion—but, in the end, they did it.

# EPILOGUE

## TALES OF THE AMERICAN AGE

IT WAS A FAST AND UNEXPECTED FINISH. Coming only a
half-century after the United States seemingly solved the problems of
German and Japanese expansionism, and less than forty years after America
helped to push the countries of Western Europe into releasing their overseas
colonies, the sudden and dramatic collapse of the last remaining empire—
that of the Soviet Union—was so tidy and satisfying as an ending that it
is tempting to think that it *was* one: that history is a novel, and this its
last page. For someone trying to make sense of what happened, the challenge
is to tell what the plots and subplots were: what the stories were, in other
words, that led to the end of empires and the emergence, for the time being,
of the United States as the sole global power.

AFTERWARD, people tend to see a certain inevitability in events. In
the era of Roman triumph, Virgil in the *Aeneid* pictured the evolution of a
small and rustic republic into the imperial mistress of the Mediterranean
world as foreordained. Now there is a fast-expanding literature on the rise
of the United States suggesting that it, too, was no accident.

America's rise to world power can be told as the story of a small but
ambitious rural eighteenth-century republic restlessly expanding its territories, its markets, and its power until, at the end of the twentieth century,
it dominated the planet.

There is even some truth in that account. The early Republic was
expansionist, and aimed to take possession of as much as possible of North
America—preferably all of it. To the post–Civil War United States, Central
America and the Caribbean islands proved tempting as well. But that was
the end of it. The generation with which this book has been concerned was
content with the country's existing frontiers. The fever of imperialism that
raged at the time of the Spanish-American War died down quickly. And
the quantum leap—the great expansion of the United States in the twentieth century from merely hemispheric to global power—was neither
planned nor intended. It was not even desired.

Isolationism—the insistence on remaining within the Western Hemisphere and avoiding engagements in or with Europe—was so completely the dominant mood of the American people and leaders alike during most of the political lifetime of the FDR generation, that it is the key to understanding that generation's history. That FDR and his contemporaries were burdened with this obsolete tradition—an anachronistic way of thinking and feeling—was the challenge they had to confront; that they overcame isolationism is the thing that they did.

This is one reason why the ascent of the Americans to supremacy is not—like the rise of Alexander's Greeks or Genghis Khan's Mongols or Süleyman the Magnificent's Turks—a tale of empire wanted and achieved. Empire (in the usual sense) had never been the Americans' dream; even in their expansionist phase, they had wanted only to possess more land, not rule more people. Nor was it empire that they were given, or that they were willing to accept: the most they would take was the leadership of countries whose independence the United States not only respected but shored up.

Unlike other countries that achieved mastery in their own times and places, the United States sought to avoid the involvement in wars and politics abroad that empire brings. Americans of all political parties fiercely resisted the idea of sending armies overseas. They consented to do so only when the United States was attacked, and even then insisted on bringing their soldiers home as soon as possible. FDR's bitterest wartime argument with Churchill was over Britain's plan to have the United States stay to take control of France, Belgium, Italy, and the Balkans; the American President refused. For thousands of years armed hordes had fought for the possession of these beautiful lands, but the United States regarded them as an unacceptable burden; let Britain deal with them, said Roosevelt.

So while Rome's growth from a small republic to a world empire was a tale of triumph, America's was not: becoming a global superpower was a kind of defeat, for it was not what the country wanted. The United States asked to be left alone in the Western Hemisphere. Its goal was to not be bothered by the problems of the rest of the world. But by 1950 it had lost in that endeavor. Lost, too, was the freedom from government that isolation made possible and that settlers had come to the New World to find. Presidents Roosevelt, Truman, and Eisenhower all sought to demobilize the troops and slash military spending; their hopes were dashed by the militarization of the cold war.

Uniquely, America's was the story of a world power in large part reluctant to be one. It could be told as a tale of innocence lost, but also as one of maturity gained.


THE GENERATION with which this book has been concerned, and which in the end made the critical decision to turn its back on isolationism, was formed intellectually, in its youth, by the dialogue between Theodore Roosevelt and Woodrow Wilson—and while retaining some of Roosevelt's realism, was won over by the moral vision of Wilson. It was Wilson who made it possible for idealistic young Americans to abandon their innate isolationism: who showed them how they could retain their fundamental belief in the unique historical mission of the United States even while advocating participation by America in the sordidness of world politics.

Wilson's doctrine was that America could engage in international relations and still remain true to herself if she crossed the oceans only for the purpose of purifying what she found on the far side of them. Under Wilson the United States went to war to end war, and entered politics to abolish politics. America would become part of the world only to change it: to remake it in her image.

Anyone who fails to recognize their belief that they were in world politics only to achieve a moral purpose misunderstands Truman, Eisenhower, Acheson, Dulles, and their contemporaries. At times they may have been deluding themselves about the purity of their motives, for self-awareness was not one of their strengths, but so far as we know, in their own minds their object was to put things right: to change the world into a civilized and law-abiding community of constitutional democracies. It may be true that in justifying the means by the ends, they ignored the moral ambiguities inherent in stooping to fight the enemy on his own low level; but they clung to Jay Gatsby's American faith that the dream can remain uncorrupted even if the dreamer does not.

At Bretton Woods and afterward, American officials went about trying to construct a postwar economic system that would be as open and global as possible. They believed this would benefit the United States and all other countries as well. In the interwar years they had seen the crippling effect of trade barriers, autocratic policies, and beggar-thy-neighbor practices; learning from that experience, they crusaded for an open world economy.

In tones ranging from gentle teasing to ungentle derision, critics have pointed out that the United States fostered policies that greatly benefited American economic interests and led to their worldwide growth. On two counts this is odd criticism. In the first place, surely it is no bad thing for a government to pursue policies that benefit its country; one ought rather to criticize it for doing the reverse. In the second, the spectacular growth in the worldwide economic activity of Japan, Germany, and others proves the Americans of 1944–45 to have been right in arguing that an open world system would reward other countries as well as the United States. The achievement of a global economy, paralleled by an explosion in technology and a revolution in communications, and sparked by an unleashing of creative capitalist energies in the Pacific Rim and elsewhere around the world, has vindicated the vision of FDR's lieutenants.

Some historians have argued that it is useful to think of the world economy the United States created as a sort of informal empire. The father of this school of thought is said to have been William Appleman Williams, a powerfully suggestive and original scholar whose challenges to conventional interpretations of American history and policy inspired generations of talented younger academics to strike out on new paths of their own. It does not derogate from the value of the stimulating views that he expressed to point out that events have not always borne them out.

Turning today, for example, to his famous work *The Tragedy of American Diplomacy*, one sees that he was right to say that the idea that the Soviet Union eventually "will collapse" was "at the base of our containment policy"; but that he was wrong to dismiss that idea, as he did in quoting approvingly the words of an expert on Russian affairs that to believe the Soviet Union might collapse "seems unrealistic."

In a later work, *The Roots of the Modern American Empire*, Williams developed his theory that American leaders aimed at creating an informal economic world empire. Rightly, he pointed out that important groups and individuals in the United States in the nineteenth and early twentieth centuries believed in capturing markets abroad for America's surplus production, first of agricultural products (according to Williams) and later of manufactured goods. But then he went on to argue that American leaders in the post–Second World War era also intentionally were creating a world in which the other countries subject to American influence were made into mere captive markets and thus were integrated in the economy of the United States, rather than being allowed to have independent economies of their own.

Had Williams been right, presumably the Japanese domestic market, for example, now would be flooded with American products while the United States would be a market closed to Japanese goods; and an outstanding financial problem would be the enormous balance of payments surplus piled up year after year by the United States in its trade with its onetime Pacific enemy. Readers of the financial press need not be reminded that this is not what happened.

In the clarity of retrospect it seems that Williams, at least in this respect, got both the intentions of American policy makers and the consequences of their actions wrong. The United States has no empire, not even an economic one. Is not today's world economy at least as much Japan's or Germany's "empire" as America's? And surely Harry Truman, for example, whose thought processes can be gleaned from his diaries and conversation, was not planning to create what he thought of as an empire.

Of course, the economic planning a half-century ago was not done by the half-dozen or so people at the top who formulated America's grand strategy. Presidents Roosevelt, Truman, and Eisenhower, and the few with whom they shared the power of making foreign policy, were mostly ignorant of economics and tended to ignore economic factors. John Foster Dulles was perhaps the only one of them who consciously formulated American policy with a view to controlling markets and advancing business interests—and as has been seen, got it wrong, imagining as he did that Japanese goods could not compete in the world market.

Nor were they, to any great extent, thinking in realpolitik terms. In the course of the twentieth century, in addition to helping to free Europe's colonies, FDR, Truman, Eisenhower, and their contemporaries turned back three attempts to overthrow the European balance of power: two by Germany, and one by Russia. But that is not what they said they were doing and may not even have been what they thought they were doing. They claimed that democracy was defeating fascism and communism. Their analyses of foreign politics often were wrong, and of international relations at times close to childish; for some of them did not fully recognize the essential role of power politics in world affairs,* and cherished their Wilsonian faith that world opinion would force other governments to walk a straight line. But the point is: that *is* the way they talked—and thought. Surprisingly, perhaps, they seem to have meant what they said. They did not do what they did for the same reasons an international relations professor, let alone one in the 1990s, would have done it or explained it. They did it for reasons of their own. And it is *their* reasons that have to be investigated if an essentially biographical narrative such as this is to be a true one: if history, in other words, is to be given back to those who lived it.

W H E N  T H E  I D E A of writing this book was proposed, a question asked by potential publishers was how it would relate to *The Wise Men* by Walter Isaacson and Evan Thomas, a group biography of Acheson, Bohlen, Harriman, Kennan, Lovett, and McCloy that sets out to show that they were a sort of band of brothers: close friends—mostly of the same social background, schools, and clubs—who shared values and outlook, and as a team helped make and/or administer American policy during and after the Second World War. It is a useful and suggestive work that performs a valuable service in drawing attention to the essential clubbishness of particular subgroups within the government. The Army and Navy departments under Stimson and Knox were an especially strong example of that. Isaacson and Thomas illuminated an important truth about a significant inner group.

The truth is just the reverse about the generation of leaders with which

---

* The teaching of international relations, giving due appreciation to power realities, began in the United States in the last half of the 1940s. Those most influenced by it were students who would not themselves become policy makers until a later date.

the preceding pages have been concerned. With its complementary thesis, this book sets out to be the mirror opposite of *The Wise Men*. Looking not at an inner group of friends but at members of the generation as a whole, and at its representative leaders of government and opinion, what it shows is not how much alike they were, but how startlingly diverse they were: FDR, privately tutored, touring Europe as a child, while at the age of five MacArthur was marching through hostile Apache territory; the young Eisenhower working in the creamery of a German religious order in small-town Kansas while Felix Frankfurter was escaping the attentions of Irish street fighters in the immigrant ghettos of New York City. Unlike the tale of the Wise Men, theirs was a story of people starting from vastly different backgrounds and schooling and opinions, changing their minds many times in the course of their lifetime about what America's role ought to be in world affairs, and only at the end arriving at a more or less common point of view. During most of their lifetime, all they had in common was that they were being shaped by the same political experiences.

As a generation, their big moment—big either because it was the one they had, or because it was the one they spent the rest of their lives regretting that they had missed—came during the First World War and the Paris negotiations that followed it. It was not only for themselves; for the world, too, they saw the war and peace of that time as the most important things that had happened in history.

Their encounter with Woodrow Wilson left a decisive impression on them. Much of what FDR did or did not do was the result of his effort to avoid Wilson's mistakes, while others like Byrnes, Truman, and Dulles were trying to live up to the principles of the President who had inspired and taught them when they were young.

Wilson's failure hit them especially hard. *The Education of Henry Adams*, the autobiography that Eleanor Roosevelt gave to Franklin as a gift, reminded readers when it was published in 1918 that a life is an education; but it was disorienting to discover that education, too, can mislead.

They had been brought up as isolationists. Nonetheless, they had come over to Wilson's faith in idealistic internationalism, and then they had seen themselves proven wrong about that—and indeed mocked, by the cynicism with which the Allied leaders exploited the 1918 victory for selfish and imperialist purposes. So that it was a sort of double distilled isolationism they felt in the interwar years. It was a belief to which they were born and bred, and to which they had returned after having strayed and been taught a hard lesson. Overwhelmingly, Americans in 1937 did not want to be involved in a new European war; but what is more significant is that 71 percent of them thought it a mistake to have participated in the last one.

That is what made it high drama when, after the fall of France, America's leaders recognized that the war to save civilization was their fight, too.

It was late in the day; only a dwindling band of English aviators stood between the Hitler-Stalin-Mussolini-Tojo combine and mastery of the world. FDR, whose habit in politics was to put things off, had let it go until about one second before midnight.

SOME OF THESE MEN gave the others a bad press. William Bullitt, one of the first of his generation to rush into print, made himself the hero of stories in which former patrons and allies came off badly. In almost constant pain from lymphatic leukemia, back injuries, and leg injuries resulting from a wartime traffic accident, and embittered by being left out in the cold in American politics,* he began publishing his inside account of American foreign policy. His articles started to appear in the mid-1940s in such popular magazines as *Life* and *Look*. Taking his revenge on FDR, he told tales of a younger Roosevelt sometimes smart enough to take his cue from Bullitt, and an old, sick, foolish Roosevelt duped by Stalin during the war. Later he impugned the loyalty of State Department officers, turned on Marshall for the "loss" of China, scolded President Eisenhower by accusing him of following an appeasement policy, and told President de Gaulle that he was a *salaud*—a piece of filth.

Bullitt reserved his greatest hatred for the President he believed had betrayed him when he was young: Wilson had left his mark on all that generation, but on Bullitt he left a wound that would never heal. For decades Bullitt nurtured his plan for revenge. Among his papers, in manuscript form, was the poisonous biography of Wilson that Sigmund Freud in some fashion had collaborated with him in producing. After Mrs. Wilson died in 1961, Bullitt felt free to publish it. It was printed and distributed in December 1966 with a publication date of 1967 on its title page.

In January and February 1967 Bullitt lay on his deathbed. His book was widely reviewed and universally condemned. The Harvard psychiatrist Robert Coles called it "a mischievous and preposterous joke, a sort of caricature . . . or else an awful and unrelenting slander." The English historian A. J. P. Taylor wrote: "The book is a disgrace . . . and . . . contributes nothing to historical understanding."

But of all of this, Bullitt remained unaware. At his bedside his brother and sister-in-law, his cousin, his daughter, and the ever-loyal Carmel Offie†

---

* James Byrnes was another close associate of FDR's embittered by the treatment he had received from the late President. He returned home to South Carolina and was elected governor (1951–55). Acclimatizing politically, he became a racist whose parochialism seemed incomprehensible in a former national statesman. Like Bullitt, he wrote about Yalta; unlike Bullitt, he gave a fair account of what he knew of it. Byrnes died in 1972.

† Five years later Offie was killed in an airplane crash. His nemesis, J. Edgar Hoover, died in office two months later.

stood guard, shielding him from knowledge of the reviews. He died February 15. He may well have passed away believing happily that finally he had taken his revenge on Wilson.

BULLITT'S CRITICISM OF FDR and other contemporaries was unjustified; they had recognized the danger posed by Stalin, as they did the threat posed by Hitler, slowly but still in time. By exhausting all possibilities of legitimate accommodation with such regimes, they demonstrated that the blame for America's quarrel lay with the other side: an achievement of some value to a democratic government that wishes to mobilize the enthusiastic support of its own population as well as to appeal to public opinion abroad.

They *were* wrong about one major foreign power, but Bullitt was, too. That was England. Their persistent mistake was to overestimate Great Britain: what they regarded as her wealth, her power, her cunning, her bad faith, her imperial acquisitiveness, and her animus against liberal democracy.

In the early 1920s they were alarmed about Britain's rearmament when they should have been worrying about Germany's—and about British *dis*armament. They missed all the signs of Britain's industrial and imperial decline. In 1939 they assumed that the Allies, on their own, would defeat Germany. They thought of Churchill as an aristocrat and a reactionary. In 1940 FDR refused to believe that Britain's survival hung by a thread: he spoke as though Britons were malingering. He never really understood that Britain had run out of money and could not afford to pay for the war. He thought that after the war she would dominate all those parts of Europe that Russia did not. He and Hull believed that she planned to suppress democracies in Europe and restore monarchies. The American government pictured the British empire as an entity that would expand everywhere unless stopped—a description more suited to the Soviet Union. Churchill knew that he needed America on his side to balance the weight of Russia in the post-1945 world, but both FDR and Truman believed otherwise, picturing Britain and Russia as even in strength, and America's role as playing umpire between them.

FDR, Truman, and Eisenhower all tended to trust the Soviet Union as a function of distrusting imperial Britain. They were confused because Churchill spoke in favor of imperialism, and Stalin against it, even though at the time Britain was liberating neighboring countries and Russia was enslaving them. Though the Truman Doctrine called upon the United States to defend Greece and Turkey against communist aggression and subversion, even the most right-wing of senators initially reacted against it because they feared it might serve the interests of the British empire.

By 1961 the survivors of the FDR-Truman-Eisenhower generation had come to agree, however reluctantly, on what the main lines of U.S. world policy ought to be. However, they still did not see—not even then—that once Britain had shed the remains of her empire, her interests—as well as her political and cultural values—had become so close to being identical to America's that some sort of global partnership, such as Churchill advocated, had become feasible. It remains an attractive possibility today, for all the obstacles that remain as well.

WHETHER IN JUDGING FDR, Truman, Eisenhower, and their contemporaries, or merely in seeking to understand them, the most important thing to note is that they were coping with change on an unprecedented scale: with more and greater change than had been experienced by any generation in history. It was true in all aspects of life. In warfare, for example, MacArthur, brought up in bow-and-arrow country during the Geronimo wars, became a general who considered using nuclear weapons. He and his contemporaries were born when Europe was dividing up Africa, as young men were indignant when Europe carved up the Middle East; and then only twenty-five years later, in one of the greatest of all reversals of fortune, they saw Europe herself partitioned.

The private lives of these public men has been touched upon in these pages only in order to give a sense of the challenging experience of a generation that was trying to deal with revolutionary changes in politics, economics, science, technology, and warfare while at the same time having to deal with profound changes in sexual mores and family life.

It is amazing that they were able to retain a degree of balance and perspective—enough to allow them, as world conquerors in 1945, to behave well, certainly as compared with the heads of other victorious great powers.

THE EARLIEST EMPIRES, those born in the river valleys of the Middle East, subjugated their neighbors in order to exact tribute, to tax, to loot, or to enslave them. Later conquerors—even those, like sixteenth-century Spain, claiming to be doing the Church's work by converting the heathen—in fact followed the same pattern.

The American notion, brought by Wilson's speeches to Paris in 1919, was that those who had won the world should serve the interests of all of its peoples, everywhere; but the Allies were prepared to incorporate such ideas only in their propaganda, not in their policy. Clemenceau's France and Lloyd George's Britain sought peace terms that would benefit only their own countries and empires—which is what countries always had done, and was, at least in part, what the United States did, too, whatever Wilson might say.

What was so startling about the conduct of the leaders of the American government after the Second World War was that to a considerable extent they practiced what Wilson had preached. In 1949 Churchill wrote: "Many nations have arrived at the summit of the world but none, before the United States, on this occasion, has chosen that moment of triumph, not for aggrandizement but for further self-sacrifice."

After the fact, and at this remove, it is taken for granted; but it should not be. It was one of the most unusual acts in the history of international warfare. Prior to twentieth-century America, the rule had been: losers pay. Now one of the victors chose to pay. A country that had been so isolationist that it regarded nothing that happened abroad as of vital concern took upon itself responsibility for the whole of the European continent: so far had it traveled in so short a time.

It was particularly remarkable in contrast with the behavior of America's rival, the Soviet Union. Russia looted the countries she occupied, seeking compensation for what she had lost in the war; while the United States, neither asking nor taking reparations, poured money into wartime allies and enemies alike in order to revive them, and offered to do the same for Russia and her client states.

Demanding a sphere of influence in Europe, the Soviet Union took something more—what might be called a sphere of control—but the United States took something less. America chose to restore the countries of Western Europe to independence. The United States in clandestine operations channeled funds to European political movements of both the Left and the Right, so as to promote pluralism; Moscow gave its moneys to Communist parties to push one line from which deviation was not permitted.

American officials were consciously pursuing their country's self-interest in fostering Europe's recovery, for they wanted Europe to be prosperous enough to buy American goods in large quantity. The merit of their policy was that it reflected an enlightened view of self-interest. And they carried out their policy generously. In the Marshall Plan, American businessmen made it possible for Western European companies to compete effectively—even against the American automobile industry and other key U.S. businesses. It is inconceivable that any other country would have put such a plan into operation. Certainly Russia, within its bloc of peoples and countries, did not do so.

During the cold war years, it was not uncommon to think of the twentieth century as a competition between the two great powers and their rival systems. On his deathbed in 1959, that is what John Foster Dulles told his brother Allen: that their lives had been coextensive with the contest that had opened up when Lenin and Wilson emerged at the same moment in history to challenge Old Europe from two different sides. It was a rivalry like that of Athens and Sparta, or Rome and Carthage.

It was a subject of lively debate within the generation to which the Dulles brothers belonged as to whether the Soviet Union was to be thought of in national or rather in ideological terms: whether it was merely tsarist Russia in disguise or the militant church of an atheist political religion. Certainly it was to some degree a mixture of the two; but whatever the Soviet leaders themselves might have thought, in practice they far more closely resembled the tsar than they did Karl Marx. And though they claimed that within their part of the world they were building a new social system, different from that of the West, they were not.

That was what was discovered when the iron curtain was lifted: behind it was an old world, not a new one. It had been supposed that Russia and the West were competing to build the social system of the future, but it turned out that there was no contest; the Soviet side did not have a modern society that they could enter in the competition. Their system of government, their farms, and their factories were all things out of the past.

The armed forces and the secret police functioned effectively, but that was all—and it was not enough. The system was intellectually bankrupt. It disintegrated when its leaders and managers lost faith in the official ideology. They had justified the workings of a brutal empire by a belief in its underlying mission. When they lost that belief, they saw their society as its subjects saw it: as just another despotism; another empire except for its totalitarianism, and nothing that would have surprised the last kaiser, the last sultan, or the last tsar.

IF THE SOVIET THREAT was narrower than the Dulleses had believed—more military and less philosophical—so was the American achievement broader. It was not just the empire of the Soviets that the United States had outlasted; it had outlasted them all. The United States had led the other countries into a world without empires. Americans of the 1990s could say that, with relatively few exceptions, no people in their time lived unwillingly under the rule of another—and that the FDR generation had played a significant role in causing that to be true.

FDR's policy at Teheran and Yalta had been to voice his disagreement with Russia—but not to go to war against her to get America's way. That was the essence, too, of the various Truman, Marshall, Acheson, and Kennan policies after the war: to hold the line against Soviet expansionism in the vital geopolitical regions, and wait for the communist bloc to collapse from within. Dulles and Eisenhower were dissatisfied with that approach, but could think of none other that was viable.

Their juniors claimed that they could do better. *New York Times* journalist James Reston remembers what John F. Kennedy told him in 1961, just after Kennedy became President. "It was now essential to demonstrate our firmness" to the Soviet leader Nikita Khrushchev, "and the place to do it, he remarked to my astonishment, was Vietnam! . . . I was speechless. . . . [T]he reference to Vietnam baffled me."

Kennedy, in drawing the line between his generation and Eisenhower's and Truman's, focused strategic attention on the areas outside of Europe and on the possibility of actually engaging the enemy in armed combat in such places. Presidents of his generation, from his day on, led the country on a long detour through the jungles, deserts, and urban slums of the Third World in search of victory over communism. It may be that in their wanderings through Southeast Asia, the Middle East, and Central America, they struck some mortal blow at the Soviet Union*; but as of now there is no compelling evidence that they did so. Instead, the victory seems to have been won in Europe, by the long-term strategy set in motion by the first Truman administration. To the extent that Kennedy and his successors, through Presidents Reagan and Bush, contributed to that result, it was by continuing the strategy of focusing American resources on the conflict with the Soviet Union, especially in Europe, rather than by dissipating resources in pursuing their own strategy of waging campaigns against client states on the periphery.

WHEN THE SOVIET EMPIRE DISSOLVED, the clock in many senses was put back to 1945. As the Second World War came to an end, the FDR and Truman administrations offered to help in the reconstruction of Russia and the countries that she was occupying. The Marshall Plan, the World Bank, and the International Monetary Fund all were open to participation by the Soviet bloc.† Roosevelt, Hopkins, and Harriman offered generous credits directly to the Soviet Union, but all of these opportunities and offers were rejected at the time by Stalin.

In the 1990s Russia and the other countries Stalin once ruled found themselves free to change their minds—and did so. They were eager to have done for them what the United States had done for Western Europe. But America, though she wished she could, no longer felt able to do it.

The curious thing was that the economy of the America of the 1990s that no longer could afford to finance Eastern Europe was—in absolute terms, though not in relation to other countries—much richer, bigger, and more powerful than the America of 1945 that offered to reconstruct both Eastern and Western Europe at the same time. The U.S. economy of the

---

* The only lethal blow struck at Russia in the Third World was the one she struck herself: her invasion of Afghanistan. The significant point is that the United States did not commit American forces to the campaign against Russia in Afghanistan.

† The Truman administration expected the Soviet Union to say no. But the administration did make the offer.

1990s dwarfed that of 1945; gross national product was more than twenty-five times greater.*

It was a generational difference. The United States that was personified by Roosevelt thrived on challenges, and had learned from the President to try to do what others said was impossible. Had FDR been told over dinner by ambassadors from former Soviet bloc countries that they were unable to find the American financing needed to reconstruct themselves as constitutional democracies, he would have thrown back his head and roared with laughter. "Come by my office tomorrow morning," he would have said, "and we'll take care of it."

---

* Yes, in the 1990s the United States has problems it did not have in 1945, including budget and trade deficits. But these, too, in the author's view, are essentially political problems. That is: what is difficult is not solving them but having the political will to do what is necessary to solve them. That also is the message in the text above.

# POSTSCRIPT

JUNE 1970. The palm-fringed Caribbean island, once a colony of the British empire, was independent now. Visiting for the first time, and touring inland by taxi, I caught sight of ruins through the underbrush. They looked to be the shattered remains of an American military airstrip, one of those bases England gave the United States in 1940 in return for destroyers. Nearby—in 1940, too—Roosevelt and Hopkins would have cruised while the President made up his mind to throw isolationism overboard and to set about saving the world.

That had been a turning point in the story of the American century. But it struck me that if my friends, instead of remaining on the beach to sunbathe, had joined me on the taxi tour, they would have been unlikely to hit on that particular association. At the time—in 1970—most of my friends were in their twenties or thirties. What little they knew of the early 1940s probably came from the movies: from *Casablanca* above all, the darling of campus cinemas and art theaters.

Seeing history through Hollywood's eyes is rarely to be recommended, but it occurred to me that in this one case it might be no bad thing. *Casablanca* taught the few lessons you most needed to know about what happened then. You would hear Humphrey Bogart's Rick Blaine say, "They're asleep all over America"—and in those distant days, they were indeed unaware that the threatened Nazi conquest of all Europe also jeopardized them. You would see in Rick the embodiment of all types and persuasions of Americans decades ago whose ideals had been betrayed once too often, and who now refused to be suckered again. As Rick says, "I'm the only cause I'm interested in."

But in the end you would witness Rick's dramatic discovery that what happens to people on the other side of the ocean is his concern, too. Of course, somewhere inside, he had known that all along. So it was with FDR's generation: after the 1940 election, they were caught up by some of the same ideals they had held in 1917. The blindfold came off their eyes; it now looked to them as though Woodrow Wilson had been right all along. They recognized again, as they had when they were young, that the United States was called upon to have a foreign policy. Many if not most of them also went back to Wilson's view that the goal of a foreign policy should be to do right.

The United States was to win wealth and power in the wars against the dictators, but it was not for that reason (though some historians believe otherwise) that it enlisted in the cause. Like Rick, who stopped putting himself first, FDR and his associates and immediate successors turned the country away from its exclusive concern with self: the historic isolationism that was its preferred course. They did that, and committed the United States instead to play an active role in world affairs, because they thought it was the right thing to do.

In the spring of 1970, on my windswept island, I stood before modest but visible remains of the first steps they took along the road. I wondered how the pieces I could see on the ground once had fitted together, and what the American air base had been like. But the taxi driver waved away my questions. He seemed to know only one thing about it: it was a relic of an era in which people were built on a more heroic scale. As though recalling some age in which gods and giants walked the earth, he said: "It's from the time of the Americans."

# Notes

## Prologue

PAGE

3 Washington, D.C., Friday, January 20, 1961: The factual details that follow are taken from *The New York Times,* Saturday, January 21, 1961; *Time,* January 27, 1961; Ambrose 1983–84; Wofford 1980; Eisenhower 1974; Schlesinger 1965; and Sorensen 1965.
"it's like being in the death cell": Ambrose 1983–84, 2:616.
"The President kept saying": Ibid., 2:604.

4 "the atmosphere in the West Wing": Eisenhower 1974, 287.

5 "grouped behind Kennedy": Sorensen 1965, 244–5.

6 "he was sixty-two": Schlesinger 1965, 140.
"seemed to be very much": Wofford 1980, 81.
"nothing vital": *Time,* January 27, 1961, 13.

## 1   *The Middle of the Journey*

11 "The buildings are low": Howells 1901, 343.
"Expositions are the timekeepers": Morgan 1963, 517.

13 Henry Adams . . . was inspired to believe: Adams 1918, 488–98.
Tulsa . . . consisted of only one street: Sullivan 1926–35, 1:21.

14 almost 40 *percent* of the country's white population: Sullivan 1926–35, 1:35.
"marshalled, herded": James 1907, 84.
"ingurgitation": Ibid.
a "spaciously organized cage": Ibid., 134.
"170,000 M. of railway": Baedeker 1893, xxvii.

15 "The collapse of the old order": James 1907, 386.
Asking how, in a great . . . society: Ibid., 418.

16 He traveled 18,000 miles: Werner 1929, 95.

17 "not a rich man": Chernow 1990, 159.

18 "local jealousies": Adams 1889, 107.
"government . . . politics": FitzGerald 1979, 48–9.

## 2   *Europe and Us*

19 "elsewhere" means Europe: James 1907, 327.
"The American stood in the world": Adams 1889, 109.
"Believing that in the long run": Ibid.

21 In the words of John Quincy Adams: LaFeber 1989, 80.
"true friends of mankind": Flexner 1965–72, 4:37.
*Daisy Miller* was inspired by a story: James 1934, 267.

22 relief in both countries when they did not go to war: Campbell 1976, 212.
in 1892 . . . raised their legations: Widenor 1980, 101n.

23 fond of Spring-Rice, "hated his country": Spring-Rice 1929, 1:54.
the circle of Henry Adams: O'Toole 1990; Samuels 1989.
six for breakfast: Spring-Rice 1929, 1:53.
"almost appalling": Dos Passos 1962, 2.
"The same important news": Ibid.
"God and man": Ibid.
"Isolation is no longer possible": Ibid.

24 "Don't . . . hurt him": Morgan 1963, 521.

## 3 *The Energies of TR*

25 One of the best-remembered theories of Henry Adams: Adams 1918, 379–90; Samuels 1989, 341–3.
in 1898 the world generated: Tuchman 1962b, 234.
The relative invention rate: Ibid., 235.

26 "wanted to put an end to all the evil": Dos Passos 1962, 7.
In 1900 the country produced: Sullivan 1926–35, 1:31.
From then to 1910: Cooper 1990, 82.
Telephones rose 600 percent: Ibid., 136.
the number of motor vehicles: Ibid., 82, 133.
some 40 percent of the country's industrial output: Ibid., 11.
J. P. Morgan . . . half as much annual revenue: Chernow 1990, 67.

27 "the enlargement of the scope . . . National Government": Cooper 1990, 61.
"ultimately every European power should be driven out": Widenor 1980, 109–10.

28 Henry James privately considered: Edel 1972, 265, 267.
Henry Adams . . . remarked: Samuels 1989, 351.
Hay told TR: O'Toole 1990, 362.

29 Taft . . . horse and buggy: Cooper 1990, 133.
TR . . . first . . . President to fly: Ibid., 135.

31 One day in January 1902: Hodgson 1990, 7–8.

## 4 *American Lives*

32 "Mrs. Roosevelt . . . had a connection": Ward 1985, 37.
"everyone is talking about . . . Theodore": Ibid.
"a Delano, not a Roosevelt": Ibid., 66.

33 "the key to his own . . . reticences": Schlesinger 1957–, 2:578.

thought that Roosevelt was "superficial" . . . "self-conscious" . . . "without convictions": Ward 1985, 315.

TR's family called him "Miss Nancy": Ibid.

had called him "the feather duster": Ibid., 251.

"a good little mother's boy": Ibid.

"The joke was on us": Ibid.

35    "could not imagine doing anything just for fun": Isaacson/Thomas 1986, 42.

"the idea of service": Ibid., 55.

"if . . . Groton boys do not enter political life": Ward 1985, 194.

36    his early life: The text paragraphs that follow are based on James 1970 and Manchester 1978.

The . . . Santa Fe Trail: *National Geographic*, March 1991, 98–123.

Historians doubt that he "trudged": James 1970, 52, and Manchester 1978, 54.

38    "the most promising student": James 1970, 60.

"believe in yourself": James 1970, 65.

Asian tour "was without doubt": Manchester 1978, 79.

39    his weight could go up to 320: LaFeber 1989, 241.

retired to his Pullman car and cried: Patterson 1972, 46.

Robert Alphonso Taft: The text follows Patterson 1972.

"What does your father do?": Ibid., 54.

40    Dulles: The text follows Pruessen 1982.

41    contributing $60,000: Lisagor/Lipsius 1988, 41.

at $12.50 a week: Ibid.

"the major benefit I got from Princeton": Pruessen 1982, 10.

George Catlett Marshall, Jr.: The text follows Cray 1990.

42    "I was an ardent Teddy fan": Tompkins 1970, 4.

Eisenhower: The text follows Ambrose 1983–84 and Lyon 1974.

"his heritage was ordinary": Ambrose 1983–84, 1:13.

43    "I have found out in later years": Ibid., 19.

44    Truman: The text follows Miller 1973 and McCullough 1992.

45    Byrnes: The text follows Byrnes 1958.

Joseph Patrick Kennedy: The text follows Whalen 1964 and Beschloss 1980.

"128 times": Beschloss 1980, 39.

"How can we make some money?": Ibid., 40.

46    "Every Groton fellow I know": Brownell/Billings 1987, 20.

"I'm going to be a lawyer": Ibid., 19.

47    Harriman . . . was listed: Isaacson/Thomas 1986, 82.

48    had danced with . . . MacLeish: Gentile, 24.

Saltonstall . . . a mentor: Ibid., 29.

49    "my heart shrivelled": Croly 1924, 91.

50    "the biggest game in the East": Ibid., 199.

51    "we had a kind of receivership": Lash 1975, 7.

52    "Walter Lippmann was brought up": Steel 1980, 3.

52   "the image of a great leader": Ibid., 4.
TR "was the first President": Ibid., 64.
Lippmann was . . . the "most brilliant young man": Ibid., xiii.

### 5   *Franklin Roosevelt Comes to Town*

57   "How would you like to come to Washington": Freidel 1952, 155.
Wilson . . . turned down someone: Ibid.
"Go, Frank, go": Ward 1989, 200.
TR wrote a . . . note: Daniels 1954, 66.
"His distinguished cousin TR": Ward 1989, 200.
"He's following in Teddy's footsteps": Ibid.
"I am truly glad of your appointment": Freidel 1952, 158.
58   [Roosevelt] reminded reporters: Ibid.
"I suppose that I . . . must follow": Ibid.
"on a summer sea": James Bryce, quoted in Widenor 1980, 123.
"not . . . too small": Roosevelt 1947–50, 2:200.
"somewhat at sea!": Ibid., 199.
59   "It is only once in a generation": Freidel 1952, 168.
Daniels's opinions: Ward 1989, 205.
"the funniest looking hillbilly": Daniels 1954, 54.
Lodge . . . communicated directly: Freidel 1952, 167.
60   Roosevelt corresponded with Grew: Ibid., 169.
their alcohol ration: Ibid., 159–60.
61   "to obtain . . . information": James 1970, 117.
"MacArthur was not a member of my command": Ibid., 123.
62   "might encourage any . . . staff officer": Ibid., 125.
"the greatest war": Ward 1989, 244.
"nobody seemed the least bit excited": Ibid.

### 6   *The Outbreak of the Great War*

63   stream that . . . ran red: West 1941, 297.
64   as an English historian suggested: Taylor 1964, 67.
"What are you doing?": West 1941, 349.
"It is nothing": Taylor 1964, 73.
65   publication . . . of . . . German documents: By Fritz Fischer, John Rohl,
and their colleagues.
66   "the militant war spirit": House 1926–28, 1:260–1.
67   as historians now have shown: Notably, Fritz Fischer.
Moltke . . . committed Germany: Craig 1978, 323.
68   "launch an immediate attack": Rohl 1973, 29.
the "military superiority of our enemies": Ibid., 31–2.
69   Moltke assured Conrad: Tuchman 1962a, 522 n192.

"some damned foolish thing": Tuchman 1962a, 91.

Some evidence uncovered relatively recently: Rohl 1973, 125.

"reproach him . . . with indecision": Fischer 1967, 55.

"I haven't chickened out": Morton 1989, 279.

70 "eliminates any reason for war": Fischer 1967, 71.

"How did all this happen?": Morton 1989, 313.

"The military keep on urging": Evans/von Strandman 1988, 121.

"neither London, nor Paris": Ibid., 102.

"a probability of 90 percent": Ibid., 115.

"Beaming faces": Ibid., 120.

"the mood is brilliant": Rohl 1973, 28.


### 7 ". . . I Was Going to Stop the War"

72 "I was young and . . . I hated war": Brownell/Billings 1987, 39.

"raging mad for war": Sullivan 1926–35, 5:4.

" 'War! War!' ": Ibid., 5.

in Munich students were chanting: Ibid.

73 "half the population of the city": Ibid., 3–4.

"a howling mob": Ibid., 5.

"a tomahawk . . . You've got to go in!": Lash 1975, 17.

"feeling chiefly very sad": Ward 1989, 244.

"I started in alone": Ibid.

no "conception of what a general European war means": Ibid.

"complete smash up": Ibid., 245.

74 "we had been thrown off our balance": Sullivan 1926–35, 5:46.

"prayer and supplication": Ibid., 44.

"to repair . . . to their places of worship": Ibid.

"if this Republic can live in peace": Ibid., 45.

"The European ideal bears its full fruit": Cooper 1990, 221.

"Aren't the nations of Europe . . . queer": Patterson 1972, 68.

"we never appreciated so keenly": Sullivan 1926–35, 5:32.

75 "out of the trenches by Christmas": Ibid., 169–70.

"10,000 howling men and women": Brownell/Billings 1987, 42.


### 8 America Quarrels with Both Sides

77 "it is a singular thing": Spring-Rice 1929, 2:218.

A poll of 400 newspaper editors: Cooper 1990, 230.

78 the . . . financial district "has simply broken into chaos": Churchill 1969, 3:1993.

"THE CREDIT OF ALL EUROPE": Chernow 1990, 185.

79 "read a page . . . 'Madison and I' ": Dos Passos 1962, 114.

Willard Straight . . . claimed: Chernow 1990, 187.

80 "Stettinius . . . the single most important": Ibid., 188–9.

"working . . . for the Allies, but also for money": Samuels 1989, 448.

80  "industrial depression, idle capital": Chernow 1990, 198.
81  Lindbergh . . . denounced the "money interests": Ibid., 192.
    "four boys and a dog": Ibid., 184.
    owing about $3.7 billion . . . owed about $3.8 billion: LaFeber 1989, 273.
82  6 percent in a poll: Cooper 1990, 234.
    A journalist . . . reported that Lippmann: Smith 1985, 467.
    Lippmann wrote to *The New Republic* correspondent: Blum 1985, 28.
    Taft . . . wrote him to say: Heckscher 1991, 364–5.
    "You people are not neutral": Dos Passos 1962, 128.
83  Lodge . . . later claimed: Widenor 1980, 212.
    Germany's ambassador wrote in his memoirs: Ibid., 216.
    Bryan had told the Austro-Hungarian ambassador: Dos Passos 1962, 127.

### 9  America Prepares—But for What?

85  League officials addressed 120,000: Rappaport 1962, 61.
86  Daniels . . . "ship for ship": Davis 1971, 392.
    "trust to the judgment of the real experts": Ward 1989, 303.
    "We have it in mind to be prepared": Smith 1985, 478.
    if TR had been President: Ward 1989, 303.
    "preparedness does not cause war": Tompkins 1970, 18.
87  the French . . . would "throw in every last man": Horne 1963, 36.
89  "That's why . . . discouraged about Wilson": Steel 1980, 94.
    "Who builds a world": Reed 1919, xiii.
    "a clash of traders": Ibid., xxvi.
    England . . . "grips the Red Sea": Ibid., xxvii.
90  "Russian ideals are the most exhilarating": Ibid., xxviii.
    "I do not suppose . . . any . . . fairness": Blum 1985, 38–9.
91  "I have come around . . . to Wilson": Smith 185, 496.
    TR accused the West . . . White replied: Ibid., 497.
92  House . . . told the Allied ambassadors . . . the German chancellor's promise: Lowe/Dockrill 1972, 2:238.
93  "God, God, where's the rest": Wilson 1986, 323.
95  the President learned that the Allies . . . had met secretly: LaFeber 1989, 275.
    "Let us build a navy bigger": Ibid., 276.
    House proposal "was not worth five minutes' thought": Lowe/Dockrill 1972, 3:560.
    Spring-Rice . . . warned London: Ibid., 558.

### 10  Berlin Decides

97  having loaned . . . so much: Brownell/Billings 1987, 54.
    "We were broad-minded": Bullitt 1917, 3.

"hated America": Ibid., 4.

"Harvard secretaries": Ibid., 13.

"scarcely any butter": Ibid.

98 "given up . . . starving": Ibid.

"the high price of caviar": Ibid.

no other people . . . had it "in" them: Ibid., 29.

"their confidence": Ibid., 139.

"Hoover . . . the greatest American": Ibid., 128.

"I wish I knew": Ibid., 30–1.

"I did not have a hand": Brownell/Billings 1987, 59.

"the most absurd": Bullitt 1917, 111.

"It would make us the most hated": Ibid.

"an even chance": Ibid.

99 "I can only pray": Gentile 1992, 45.

100 "with absolute certainty": Brownell/Billings 1987, 61.

"at the present moment": Ibid.

"a struggle whose outcome": Ibid.

the October 28 . . . issue of *The New Republic:* Ibid., 63.

101 "our Government should therefore be fully prepared": House 1926–28, 2:387.

102 "the American executive": Fromkin 1989, 253.

103 "my worst fears": House 1926–28, 2:412–13.

"for peace at almost any price": Ibid., 413.

104 the senator had looked "stunned": Ibid., 424.

"His Majesty doesn't understand": Tuchman 1958, 134.

"What's troubling him now?": Ibid.

"had vision but lacked nerve": Hough 1983, 302.

105 "if the military authorities consider the U-boat war essential": Tuchman 1958, 136–7.

"I guarantee on my word": Ibid., 137.

"We can take care of America": Ibid.

"I order . . . unrestricted submarine warfare": Ibid.

"If success beckons, . . . we must follow": Ibid., 136–7.

107 "the quintessence of a prig": LaFeber 1989, 278.

"fetid, ignominious": Ibid.

"brave and timely appeal": Cooper 1990, 259.

11 *America Finds a Foreign Policy*

110 "I know that it is very serious": Smith 1985, 511.

"I am finished": Ibid.

"could not get his balance": Heckscher 1991, 427.

"had begun to go from west to east": Ibid.

" 'white civilization' and its domination": LaFeber 1989, 278.

"to keep the white race strong": Tuchman 1958, 146.

111 "greater justice would be done": LaFeber 1989, 278.
"actual overt acts": Heckscher 1991, 429.
"We are the sincere friends": Ibid.
"a very timid man": Ward 1989, 338.
"something to boast of": Steel 1980, 110.
"The safety of the Atlantic highway": Ibid., 111.
an "Atlantic community": Ibid.
"vital highways": Ibid.
"the administration . . . expected": Blum 1985, 61–2.
112 "the war is not a first page story": Johnson 1947, 220.
113 "pitch me into the ash heap": Miller 1986, 94.
"I buried him today": Brownell/Billings 1987, 65.
114 "loathed in advance": Samuels 1989, 442.
a "protectorate against the will": Tompkins 1970, 17.
four-fifths of the . . . regular army: Tuchman 1958, 101.
116 "I want history to show . . . clean hands": Ward 1989, 338.
"the satisfaction of seeing you Secretary": Ibid., 337.
The Navy League's leader was ready: Ibid., 339.
117 "Lodge was a creature": Adams 1918, 419.
"no doubt . . . what your advice is": Heckscher 1991, 437.
"apathy of the Middle West": Fromkin 1989, 255.
118 the British ambassador had reported to London: Spring-Rice 1929, 2:254.
"it should be . . . between us and them": Fromkin 1989, 255.
"did not wish to be disturbed": Heckscher 1991, 438.
119 in an antechamber . . . he paused to prepare: Ferrell 1985, 1.

## 12   *A Missed Rendezvous*

125 "Wilson was my President": Tompkins 1970, 19.
"I do like the Kaiser": Cook 1983, 99.
"I have tried to say a little of what I feel": Blum 1985, 63–4.
127 "My failure to enter the army": Letter from Taft to Herbert Hoover, October 18, 1918. Taft papers, container 19.
128 "the greatest revival": Tompkins 1970, 20.
"an idealistic crusade": Pruessen 1982, 24.
"I see that you're another one of those goddamn leaders": Rogow 1963, 67.
129 "didn't appreciate . . . not going into the war": Whalen 1964, 59.
"Kennedy confessed": Ibid.
as he wrote to his brother: Letter from A. Harriman to R. Harriman, April 6, 1918. Harriman papers, container 2.
He was able to launch only one: History Card, August 3, 1918. Harriman papers, container 673.
"an awfully bad record": Letter from Chas. Schwab to Harriman, August 23, 1918. Harriman papers, container 674.

Harriman wrote (but did not send): Letter from Harriman to Schwab, August 29, 1918. Harriman papers, container 674.

"in no other way could I contribute": Isaacson/Thomas 1986, 85.

"he had long regretted": Harriman/Abel 1975, 6.

"That tended to square the balance": Ibid., 7.

Porter was the most shameless: Schwartz 1977, 46 et seq.

130 As . . . Churchill later told the story: Moran 1966, 184.

"You *must* resign": Ward 1989, 346.

TR "was *always* urging": Ibid.

131 "You didn't see me": Lash 1971, 226.

"deserved a good time": Ibid.

## 13   *Focusing on the Peace*

132 "unhappy results . . . appendicitis": Brownell/Billings 1987, 67.

The State Department . . . requested that he not be inducted: Bullitt 1972, xi.

133 "What I want to do": Steel 1980, 116.

134 Lippmann's memorandum: Blum 1985, 69–70.

"Lippmann is not only thoughtful": Steel 1980, 127.

135 Frankfurter . . . reported: Walworth 1977, 75 n5.

Wilson . . . read it "with . . . interest": Ibid.

"the aims and desires": Grew 1952, 1:330.

"my share": Ibid.

"the first American": Council on Foreign Relations 1972, 403.

136 "the work outlined": Steel 1980, 127.

"The job goes well": Ibid., 129.

137 "I hate this war!": Walworth 1986, 2.

## 14   *A War of Our Own*

141 "Don't let the British": Coffman 1977, 73.

"he questioned the desirability": Notes of W. H. Taft regarding interview with Wilson, December 12, 1917. Taft papers, container 19.

He made that clear to Arthur Balfour: Heckscher 1991, 448; Fowler 1969, 28.

142 "Good Lord! . . . You're not going to send soldiers": Kennedy 1980, 144.

"I will give you only two orders": Smith 1985, 582.

"a separate and distinct component": Dos Passos 1962, 245.

143 "there is no intention": Kennedy 1980, 159.

"even the naval part isn't organized": Pogue 1963–87, 1:144.

144 "here and there": Kennedy 1980, 173.

"our position will be stronger": Ibid.

Felix Frankfurter . . . reported: Heckscher 1991, 447.

145 "Our troops are the best": Cray 1990, 63.

## 15   *The AEF Is Too Late*

146   $81.75 a head: Ferrell 1985, 119.

147   only 500 were made in the USA: Kennedy 1980, 194 n5.
entire expense . . . $24 billion: Ferrell 1985, 84.
perhaps $22 billion: War Department (U.S.) *n.d.,* 147.
1970 dollars . . . $112 billion: Kennedy 1980, 139.

148   "I don't trust the Americans": Riddell 1986, 210.
"The chief danger . . . is . . . American trade": Kennedy 1980, 173.

149   friendship of Edward House . . . Wiseman: Fowler 1969.

## 16   *The Battle of Ideas*

150   TR argued . . . that the United States "did not go to war": Mayer 1959, 344–5.

153   "because of the Bolshevik peace proposals": House 1926–28, 3:279.
House agreed with . . . Briand: Ibid., 280.
"Our people and Congress will not fight": Ibid., 282.

154   House . . . cabled Wilson: Ibid., 286.
"impossible to omit foreign affairs": Wilson 1966–91, 45:187.
"an important decision the President and I made": House diary, December 18, 1917. House papers.
House "intimated": House 1926–28, 3:320.

155   "I could see . . . signs of weariness": Ibid., December 30, 1917.
Sisson . . . wired . . . "Re-state anti-imperialistic war aims": Kennan 1956–58, 1:251.

156   Wilson told Spring-Rice: Wilson 1966–91, 45:454–8.
Spring-Rice cabled the foreign secretary: Ibid.

157   "the selfishness which seems to lurk": House diary. House papers, vol. XIII (January 3, 1918).

158   "put words into the mouth of the President": Blum 1985, 86n.

158n. taped interviews: OH.
"shook the morale": OH, 11.
"You're going to have to disentangle": Ibid., 107.

159n. "We spent three weeks": Ibid., 12.
"Isaiah Bowman": Ibid., 109.
he and Admiral Grayson: Ibid., 120.
"it was we . . . in points": Ibid., 108.
"It was all keyed": Ibid., 109.
"I've never seen an adequate discussion": Ibid., 12.
Lippmann papers at Yale . . . memo . . . misidentified: Blum 1985, 84–5.

## 17 *Wilson Versus Lenin*

161 "the common people of the world desire": Wilson 1966–91, 46:167.
"They trust him": Ibid., 183.
"the air of Berlin and Vienna": Ibid., 184.

162 "Germany to-day is more unified": Ibid., 567–9.
"we had better fight": Ibid.
"Wilson was profoundly . . . disappointed": Heckscher 1991, 473.

163 "From this time on": Ibid.

164 "What the hell difference does it make?": Reed 1919, xxxii.
"I wouldn't ask Walter L for anything": Steel 1980, 138.
Reed . . . had "served for a time": Wilson 1966–91, 48:144–5.

165 "the world's greatest adventure": Heckscher 1991, 466.
"we have fallen down": Allen Dulles to John Foster Dulles, letter of April
29, 1918. J. F. Dulles papers, box 2.

166 "I am very jealous": Steel 1980, 147.
"I am very much puzzled": Ibid., 146.
"I have found his judgment most unsound": Ibid.


## 18 *How to Fight the War*

167 Wilson's idea: Coffman 1968, 97.
Roosevelt championed: Ibid., 99.
Lovett . . . way to go after the U-boats: Isaacson/Thomas 1986, 91–2.

168 "The only interest and romance": Coffman 1968, 187.
Biographers have blamed it: Blumenson 1985, 16–17.

169 "a fire-eater": Ibid., 95.
"darned sick of my job": Ibid., 96.
"I believe that . . . I have again fallen on my feet": Blumenson 1972, 432.
"What do you think of me": Ibid., 434.

170 "the Tanks . . . a great opportunity": Ibid., 463.
"feeling very low": Ibid., 476.
"unless I get some Tanks soon": Ibid., 477.

171 "stretch . . . like a rainbow": James 1970, 135.
"our methods are to be . . . our own": Ibid., 151–2.
"savage and merciless": Ibid., 157.
"MacArthur is one of the ablest": Ibid.

172 "Raids became . . . popular": Ibid., 165.
Duffy . . . said that "some older heads": Ibid.
"in earlier wars": Taylor 1963, 115.
"a blamed good thing for the army": James 1970, 165.
"greatest fighting" . . . officer: Manchester 1978, 103.
"the show-off": Ibid., 104.

173 "the most brilliant young officer in the army": Ibid., 172.
"the bloodiest fighting man": Ibid., 181.

173　　"The bravest of the brave": Ibid., 187–8.

　　　　"Have personally assumed command": Ibid., 190.


## 19　*The AEF Makes Its Move*

174　　Donovan . . . worried . . . 65 percent . . . 75 percent: Coffman 1968, 279.

　　　　"Sir, I am teaching them": Manchester 1978, 114.

175　　according to the War Department: War Department *n.d.,* 130.

　　　　"Get forward, then!": Coffman 1968, 279.

　　　　"I think each one wanted to leave": Blumenson 1972, 585.

　　　　"Don't worry, Major": Manchester 1978, 115.

176　　"Let's go!" cried Patton: Blumenson 1985, 113.

177　　"officers fell": James 1970, 222–3.


## 20　*An Army of Tourists*

178　　"afraid of a gun": Miller 1986, 103.

　　　　"I went to war": Ibid., 108.

　　　　had been "ready to get married": Ibid., 112.

　　　　New York . . . "a vast disappointment": Ibid., 113.

　　　　"Wall Street is an alley": Ibid., 114.

　　　　"a real Chateau": Ibid., 115.

179　　"You boys stick with me": Ibid., 119.

　　　　"His knees were knocking together": Ibid.

　　　　later army investigations would show: Ibid., 132.

　　　　"right tonight I'm where I want to be": Ibid., 133.

180　　Folies-Bergères "disgusting": Ibid., 146.

　　　　"gave all of us common people": Ibid.

　　　　"thousands of men who had never before recorded": Kennedy 1980, 205.

　　　　"a tired people": Ibid., 207.

181　　"anxious that Woodie cease his gallivantin' ": Miller 1986, 147.

　　　　"what effect the war": Turnbull 1962, 79.

182　　"probably going inside of two months": Fitzgerald 1963, 373.

　　　　"his throat straining": Fitzgerald 1933, book 1, xiii.

　　　　" 'This land here cost' ": Ibid.

　　　　"interesting . . . to list the authors": Cowley 1951, 38.

183　　"ambulance service had a lesson of its own": Ibid.

　　　　The war became "a spectacle": Ibid., 39.

　　　　"this spectatorial attitude": Ibid., 43.

　　　　"This ain't a war": Ibid., 44.

184　　"Archie . . . looking horribly badly": Ward 1989, 397.

　　　　"We boys . . . thought it was up to us": Ibid., 346.

　　　　"how am I going to break it to her?": Ibid., 389.

　　　　"if I had not myself gone to war": Ibid.

185　　"having joy ride": Ibid., 404.

"drank like undergraduates": Ibid., 407.
"The bottom dropped out": Ibid., 412.
"I can forgive": Ibid., 415.
"we'll spend the rest of our lives": Ambrose 1983–84, 1:65.

## 21  *Disillusion Before Versailles*

189 Dulles . . . formally requested: Letter of July 23, 1918, J. F. Dulles to
War Trade Board. J. F. Dulles papers, box 2.
Taft wrote to Herbert Hoover: Letter of October 18, 1918, Taft to Hoover.
Taft papers, container 19.

190 "the British and French . . . may demand": Croly 1924, 525–6.
"what do I take to you?": Ibid., 534.
"I was closer to Willard": Ibid., 544.

191 "to guard the military stores": Kennan 1956–58, 2:484.
"to make it safe for Russian forces": Ibid.

192 "on sentimental grounds": Ibid., 396.
"inability of the United States to furnish": Ibid.
"Why are you shaking your head": Ibid., 397.
"the Russian people in their endeavor": Ibid., 484.
"the hope and purpose of the Government": Ibid., 484–5.

193 "sick at heart": Brownell/Billings 1987, 69.
"One year ago today": Ibid.
Wilson "should be judged by what he was": Kennan 1956–58, 2:405.

## 22  *A Stab in the Back*

196 "The country . . . was afraid": Grew 1952, 1:333.
197 "A great piece of good fortune": Ibid., 331.
"army of officials": Ibid., 331–2.
"actual standard of power": Stevenson 1988, 227.

199 and Mrs. Wilson was sure of it: Walworth 1977, 44.
"too much success . . . of the Allies": Link 1957, 107–8.
"it was . . . agreed . . . not the case": Lowe/Dockrill 1972, 2:274.
"I must write you": Steel 1980, 150.

200 "the most colossal news fake": Kennedy 1980, 232.
"to fire on the German people": Watt 1968, 110.
"on the stroke of the eleventh hour": House/Seymour 1921, 14.

201 "the greatest day I have seen": Grew 1952, 1:357.
"the best and . . . the only practical one": Ibid., 356.

202 "government . . . by the German people": Mayer 1967, 63.

## 23  *The* George Washington *Goes to Europe*

207 "I told Howard": House diary, September 29, 1917. House papers.
"desired to be a peace commissioner": Ibid., October 13, 1917.
a statute enacted in 1913: Walworth 1977, 114.
"I assume . . . I shall . . . preside": Ibid., 116.
cabled [Wilson] November 14: Ibid., 118.

208 No point of dignity . . . "must prevent": Ibid., 119.
"it is universally expected": Ibid.
"I think he . . . wants to come": Ibid., 118 n33.

209 intended to "run it all": Ibid., 121.
"you carry overseas with you": Smith 1964, 35.
"greatest success . . . supremest tragedy": Walworth 1977, 136.
"everybody . . . skeptical and cynical": Wilson 1966–91, 53:350.

210 "at Château Thierry": Ibid., 352.
"Tell me what's right": Walworth 1977, 133.

211 "Bohemia will be a part": Brownell/Billings 1987, 77.
"Why should war be the only cause": Gilbert 1975, 171–2.

212 Churchill reminded . . . that the world remained dangerous: Ibid.; Gilbert
1978, 427 n1.
"planning to take what they can get": Walworth 1977, 134.

214 "We've lived in suspense": Ward 1989, 417–18.

215 "What do you think of your old husband": Gentile 1992, 69.
"watching us closely": Ibid., 71.
"royal battle": Ibid.
"terrible danger": Ibid.
"it looks as though it would be rotten": Ibid.

## 25  *Paris in the Plague Year*

220 "not a Conference . . . a very serious illness": Nicolson 1933, 84.
the virus was born . . . from the intermixture of . . . armies: McNeill
1976, 255.

221 "When President Wilson left Washington": Keynes 1920, 38.
"there waited the largest throng": Smith 1964, 37.
"I do not think there has been anything like it": Ibid., 39.
"no one ever had such cheers": Ibid.

222 Hughes . . . demanded to know: Heckscher 1991, 509.
Lord Curzon . . . suggested: Ibid., 510.
"old system" . . . good enough: Ibid.

## 26  *A Who's Who of Americans in Paris*

223 Lansing asked: Walworth 1977, 256.
White wondered: Ibid., 255.

224 Bullitt seems to have pressured House: Ibid., 261 n53.
At least one . . . suspected: Ibid.
Inquiry scholars . . . complained: Walworth 1986, 10 n15.

225 "You have made yourself indispensable": Walworth 1977, 250.
Baruch later implied: Baruch 1960, 96.
putting doubts into the President's mind: Walworth 1977, 262 n57.

226 "I never saw anything like Paris": Ward 1989, 423.

227 "women barely tore themselves away": Vansittart 1958, 202.
"The cheer": Cook 1992, 234.
"the scandals": Ibid.
"you wonder if there are any ladies": Ward 1989, 428.
"very little real beauty": Ibid., 429.

27   *A Clash by Night*

228 more than 1,000 Americans: Walworth 1986, 22.
perhaps . . . 1,300: Walworth 1977, 257 n35.
[everyone] . . . "keeping diaries": Mee 1980, 93.
"the best book": Frankfurter 1960, 161.
"a study of fog": Nicolson 1933, 6.

229 "Let it have our brand": Walworth 1977, 213.
"This government . . . will not agree": Ibid., 216.
"Do nothing else": Ibid., 217.
British ambassador . . . the hand that fed Europe: Ibid., 221.

230 Taft . . . sublet a furnished apartment: Documents from Europe 1917–19.
Sublease from Lt. F. R. Wulsin. Taft papers, container 19.
Lewis Strauss . . . reported: Mayer 1967, 368.
whichever had "a progressive program": Walworth 1977, 227.

231 "the President of the bourgeois U.S.": Mayer 1967, 396.
"an almost pathetic confidence": Walworth 1977, 34.

233 "On this day, forty-eight years ago": Mee 1980, 48.
"the fortunes of all peoples": Ibid.
"The greater the . . . catastrophes": Ibid., 49.
"the whole of it, and forever": Fromkin 1989, 439.

235 "What you have said today": Walworth 1986, 44.
the secretaries omitted to report: Ibid.
"a practical scheme to carry out His aims": Mee 1980, 63.
"the nucleus of world organization": Lippmann 1919, 51.
"Europe is being liquidated": Ibid., 33.

236 "The United States must go in": Ward 1989, 431.
Roosevelt . . . spoke . . . to . . . Sheffield Cowles: Ibid., 432.

## 28 *War or Peace with Communism?*

237 the United States lacked . . . data: Walworth 1986, 137.
Bullitt . . . suggested . . . missions . . . "to examine conditions": Ibid., 139.
to "cure him of Bolshevism": Ibid., 138.
"for the benefit of the American commissioners": Ibid.
Philip Kerr . . . supported the project: Ibid.
238 Cachin said the French Left: Ibid., 139.
Bolshevism as a "poison": Brownell/Billings 1987, 76.
"to prevent a contagious epidemic": Bullitt 1919, 26.
239 "Lenin was sent into Russia": Gilbert 1975, 355.
"prostitutes have disappeared": Brownell/Billings 1987, 86.
240 "we have seen the future": Ibid.
Lenin informed Bullitt . . . the West asked his government: Walworth 1986, 235.
"The Allies . . . well out of it": Kennan 1960, 132.
"existence . . . with the imperialist states . . . unthinkable": Walworth 1986, 234.
241 "how can you expect me to be sensible": Kennan 1960, 133.
"proposed recognition . . . caused consternation": Walworth 1986, 238.
"this murderous tyranny": Mayer 1967, 477.
242 Churchill urged . . . Wilson "not be allowed to weaken": Gilbert 1975, 276.
"of course . . . men of all nationalities": Brownell/Billings 1987, 93.
"There was some suggestion": Kennan 1960, 133.
"peoples of Europe . . . seeking": Mayer 1967, 570.
243 "constructive and kind . . . peaceful and constructive": Ibid.
"in self defense, to terror and massacres": Ibid.

## 29 *Wilson Collapses*

244 "You Americans are broken reeds": Harrod 1951, 253.
"The honeymoon . . . is over": Grew 1952, 1:372.
245 "the French press is complaining": Ibid., 373.
"The Americans . . . have angered the French": Ibid., 374.
"He and his conscience": Nicolson 1933, 198.
"the suspicion that America was asking": Ibid., 195.
246 "Woodrow . . . seemed to have aged": Watt 1968, 87.
246n. "was hysterical": Interview with Bullitt, April 2, 1951, by Arthur Walworth. Walworth papers.
247 "when House got to the point": Truman 1989, 355.
248 "Wilson very impatient": Mayer 1967, 571.
Baker wrote that House "now begins": Ibid.
Baker . . . "talked with the President": Ibid.

"I found the President . . . discouraged": Ibid., 572.

"a new premier . . . no better": Ibid.

249 "Nice people . . . views are identical": Nicolson 1933, 223.

250 the Japanese "will go home": Heckscher 1991, 567.

### 30   *Blood Money*

252 "if Germany were left . . . prostrate": Baruch 1960, 107.

one German mark . . . became one trillion: Craig 1978, 450.

Wilson wrote to Lloyd George: Harrod 1951, 247.

253 "paid less than five billion": Baruch 1960, 108.

"Great Britain . . . on the make": Walworth 1986, 522.

### 31   *Closing Up Shop at the Peace Talks*

255 "We lived many lives": Lawrence 1939, 142–3.

"Great dissatisfaction . . . slow": Riddell 1986, 261.

"Later saw . . . Kerr": Ibid.

"I thought it advisable": Ibid.

prime minister "is very angry": Ibid., 262.

256 "Do not disband your army": Fromkin 1989, 386.

"Commission . . . knows very little": Grew 1952, 1:384.

257 "Snoop around": Watt 1968, 103.

a "hopeless mess": Mee 1980, 210.

"without reading them ourselves": Ibid.

258 "flashed into our minds": Watt 1968, 407.

"never been so miserable": Harrod 1951, 249.

"disappointment . . . regret . . . depression": Watt 1968, 407.

"a terrible document": Ibid.

"If I were a German": Ibid.

259 "a lovely day": Nicolson 1933, 327.

"a smile on the face of the Tiger": Riddell 1986, 273.

260 "no statement of ideals": Berle 1973, 11.

"Yesterday Bullitt called me in": Ibid., 12.

"the greatest . . . since Jesus": Robert E. Lynch, Bullitt's secretary in 1919, in an interview with Arthur Walworth, March 22, 197? [date illegible]. Walworth papers.

"This isn't . . . peace": Brownell/Billings 1987, 94.

261 as some remembered it: Berle 1973, 13.

about thirty . . . as Bullitt . . . recalled: Interview with Arthur Walworth, April 2, 1951. Walworth papers.

John Storck: FRUS, Paris Peace Conference 1919, 11:569.

Joseph V. Fuller: Ibid., 571.

George B. Noble: Ibid., 572.

Adolf Berle: Ibid., 570.

261    Samuel Eliot Morison: Ibid., 571.
       "SENSATION": Berle 1973, 12.

262    White . . . lectured Bullitt: Walworth 1986, 395.
       "I was one of the millions": FRUS, Paris Peace Conference 1919, 11:573–4.
       "How about Bullitt?": Walworth 1986, 395 n56.

263    "bamboozled": Ibid., 240 n33.
       "I expect a compromise": Blum 1985, 114.
       "I can't see peace": Ibid.
       "IS IT PEACE?": Steel 1980, 158–9.
       "I can find no excuses": Blum 1985, 119.
       renouncing "the Imperial program": Steel 1980, 160–1.

264    "I can understand these things": Blum 1985, 122.
       "curious irresponsibility in . . . language": Steel 1980, 160.
       "unjust and unprincipled": Walworth 1986, 394.

265    "For 3 hours after dinner": Gilbert 1978, 670.
       commissioners wrote: FRUS, Paris Peace Conference 1919, 11:587.
       House wrote to Wilson: Ibid., 588.
       "The time to consider": Watt 1968, 450.
       "My months at the . . . Peace Conference": Fromkin 1989, 399.

266    "Paris . . . like . . . Congress": Frankfurter 1960, 162.
       secretariat "has had a very unhappy time": FRUS, Paris Peace Conference 1919, 11:598.

267    "sign their own death warrants": Ibid., 600.
       "I wish . . . the other road": House 1926–28, 4:489.
       "To bed": Nicolson 1933, 371.
       "What a wretched mess": Watt 1968, 11.
       "all a great pity": Ibid.

## 32   *The Idols Fall*

271    "no money, no offices": Moynihan 1960, 310.
       "Well, we have to do something": Ibid., 311.
       "as if he had known me all his life": Ibid., 312.

272    "apostles of Lenin in our own midst": LaFeber 1989, 310.

273    "I consider . . . the league . . . useless": Bullitt 1919, 102–3.

274    "the personal instrument of God": Frankfurter 1960, 167.
       "by the hand of God": Smith 1964, 167.

276    "You can go to it": Ward 1989, 470.
       "the only chance the Democrats have": Ibid., 471.
       "a lot of political bosses": Ibid.
       "a bewildered state of mind": Blum 1985, 134.

## 33   *The United States Signs Its Separate Peace*

279   "a darned fine sail": Ward 1989, 557.
"They'll vote for you": Ibid., 556.
"Frank Roosevelt . . . in the gutter": Heinrichs 1966, 48–9.

280   "The war has used up words": Reynolds 1976, 60–1.
"I was always embarrassed": Ibid., 61.

281   "through rough . . . technique": *The New York Times,* August 26, 1921, 2.
English newspaperman . . . remarked . . . lounge suits: Ibid.
"cut-and-dried": Ibid., 1.

## 34   *The Education of the Roosevelt Generation: First Lessons*

283   "disband their armies": Nye 1993, 49.

## 35   *Going on the Biggest Spree in History*

286   "watch the world go to hell": Brownell/Billings 1987, 96.

288   "we were tired of Great Causes": Fitzgerald 1931.
"we were the most powerful nation": Ibid.
"young liquor . . . young blood": Ibid.
"The people over thirty . . . had joined the dance": Ibid.
"the Jazz Age now raced along": Ibid.
"the attraction is purely physical": Manchester 1978, 142.

289   "I don't care what it costs": Ibid., 147.

290   "I see Bill Bullitt, in retrospect": Bullitt 1972, xv.

## 36   *The Age of the Dictators*

295   "during the second half of the twenties": Keylor 1992, 133.
"fascinating figure": James 1970, 345.

296   "If only your father": Manchester 1978, 158.
"takes . . . care of his mother": Pearson/Allen 1932, 209.
"he uses a . . . fan": Ibid.
"virtual dictator": Ibid.

297   "a matutinal rite": Allen 1939, 44.
wrong ". . . to consider . . . coercion": Steel 1980, 329.
"I don't see": Blum 1985, 279.

299   "troubled and confused": James 1970, 371.

300   "not going to take an upturn": Ambrose 1983–84, 1:88–9.
"nomads of the Depression": Manchester 1973, 20.

301   "I distinctly remember": Overheard by the author.
"I have bad news": Schlesinger 1957–, 1:267.

302   "I might as well starve": *Time,* August 8, 1932, 5.

303 "he said he was too busy": James 1970, 401.
    "the whole encampment . . . began burning": Ibid., 402.
    "a bad-looking mob": Ibid., 403–4.
    "this meeting led to the . . . impression": Ibid., 404–5.
    "Mac did a great job": *Time,* August 8, 1932, 7.
    "a feeling of horror": Manchester 1973, 18.
    "offer the men coffee": Ibid.
304 (Pearson and Allen) had portrayed him as "dictatorial": Manchester 1978,
    169.
    "unwarranted, unnecessary . . . brutal": Ibid.
    "his *mother* . . . !": Ibid., 170.
    "U.S. Army is too small": Nye 1993, 98.

## 37   Rumors of Wars

306 "The next war will depopulate": Swanberg 1961, 511.
307 "the most expensive orgy": Fitzgerald 1931.
308 "glad to have you show Roosevelt": Bullitt 1972, 17.
309 "I very much hope . . . you are right": Blum 1985, 268.
    "I never felt so confident": Ibid., 277.
    "doesn't . . . have a very good mind": Ibid., 280–1.
    "amiable boy scout": Ibid.
    "a weaseling mind": Ibid., 294.
    "without a firm grasp": Steel 1980, 291–2.
    "to my dying day": Ibid., 292.
310 "we should personally see to it": Swanberg 1961, 515.
    "made his . . . declarations publicly": Ibid., 516.
311 "I would still favor . . . entry": Nixon 1969, 1:23–4.
    "almost tearfully": Swanberg 1961, 518.

## 38   The Emergence of FDR

313 the *Odyssey:* I have drawn this reading of the work from the critic
    R. W. B. Lewis, whose "Homer and Virgil: The Double Themes," from
    an old issue of *Furioso* magazine, I have followed in the text.
315 "Roosevelt . . . next President": Brownell/Billings 1987, 126.
    "tears were rolling": Bullitt 1972, 18.
    "we ironed out": Wehle 1953, 113–14.
    "Enclosed is my cheque": Bullitt 1972, 20.
316 "Hitler is finished": Ibid., 23.
    "sent you to jail": Brownell/Billings 1987, 130.
    "the present emergency": Schlesinger 1957–, 2:192.
317 "I think we'll live": Philip Hamburger, *New Yorker,* February 8, 1993, 76.
318 "nation . . . lost confidence": Schlesinger 1957–, 2:13.
    "make it unanimous": Ibid.

"Bullitt was at the White House": Bullitt 1972, 32–3.

"no right to an opinion": Ibid., 33.

319    "fundamental economic ills": Schlesinger 1957–, 2:222.

"neither you nor any other member of the Delegation": Nixon 1969, 1:187–8.

"the Administration's . . . program": Ibid., 641–2.

320    "war in Europe is inevitable": Ibid., 291.

## 39    *A Foreign Policy at Minimum Cost*

322    A September 1933 poll: Davis 1986, 339.

323    "Bullitt may do less harm": Bullitt 1972, 58.

"thoroughly untrustworthy": Ibid.

325    "to let Missy play": Davis 1986, 340.

"BULLITT'S UNCLE": Bullitt 1972, 58.

"bombastic and unreasonable": Brownell/Billings 1987, 96.

It is said that their training under . . . Kelley: LaFeber 1989, 362.

326    "utterly terrified me": Kennan 1967, 18.

"a striking man": LaFeber 1989, 363.

"the old American friend": Brownell/Billings 1987, 142.

"he and everyone else": Bullitt 1972, 63.

"he really liked me": Ibid., 64.

"men at the head of the Soviet Government": Ibid., 65.

"delighted by young Kennan": Ibid.

"the whole 'gang' ": Ibid., 66–9.

328    "party hacks": Heinrichs 1966, 188.

"gutter" politics: Ibid., 189.

"Dear Frank": Ibid.

"Isn't it fine": Ibid., 190.

"most fervent prayer": Ibid.

"Japan . . . has the most . . . powerful": Nixon 1969, 1:179–80.

329    "war . . . inevitable": FRUS 1933, 3:412.

"Anything that could be done": Brownell/Billings 1987, 145.

"a restraining influence": FRUS 1934, 2:35.

"Japanese have let us down": Bullitt 1972, 83.

"honeymoon atmosphere": Ibid.

"impossible to imagine": Ibid., 97.

330    "forget you're carrying it": Marx 1961, 328.

331    "I'm going to join the I.L.O.": Moynihan 1960, 539.

## 40    *Unpreparedness as a National Policy*

333    "We have hired him": Craig 1978, 570.

"alarming . . . Hitler is a madman": Davis 1986, 125.

334    "Few educated people": Taylor 1965, 361–2.

334 A poll . . . 20,000 . . . clergymen: Manchester 1978, 163.
335 "excited by your suggestion": Freedman 1967, 130–1.
    a "desire to enlarge": Nixon 1969, 1:126–8.
335n. Churchill demolished it: Churchill 1948–53, 1:71–2.
336 "I . . . averted a war": Davis 1986, 127.
    "if I were a Frenchman": Nixon 1969, 1:374–5.
    "Walter Lippmann was here": Ibid., 485.
337 "You've saved the Army!": Ibid.
337n. "When we lose the next war": Manchester 1978, 169.
338 "the first time since 1922": James 1970, 450.
    "war talk": Ibid., 449.
    "Douglas, if war": Manchester 1978, 174.
338n. "Suggest . . . Marshall": Marshall 1981–86, 1:399 n3.
    "Hell, no!": James 1970, 436.
339 "no improvements": Ibid., 476.
341 "If Italy, Germany and Japan": Nixon 1969, 3:44.

41   *Curbing the President's Powers*

343 71 percent of the public agreed: Manchester 1973, 126.
345 A third . . . would not fight: Ibid.
    the presidents of . . . 200 colleges: Nixon 1969, 2:104–6.
    "Dear W.R.": Swanberg 1961, 529.
    "principal speculator in silver": Manchester 1973, 109.
346 Roosevelt wrote to . . . House: Roosevelt 1947–50, 3:506–7.
347 "preparation for war": Nixon 1969, 2:275–6.
    "fixed purpose": Ibid., 499.
    "a dictatorial front": Dodd 1941, 302.
    Dulles told Dodd: Ibid., 304.
348 "three more years": Nixon 1969, 3:278.
    Bullitt, wrote Dodd: Dodd 1941, 309.
    "another happy day": Ibid., 349.
    "fanatics like Winston Churchill": Nixon 1969, 3:205.
    "the most hair-trigger times": Ibid., 2:437.
    To . . . Baker . . . FDR predicted: Ibid., 3:50.

42   *Staying Out of It*

350 only 8,500 of them: LaFeber 1989, 368.
351 only 26 percent of Americans: Divine 1967, 28.
    "keeping alive the two-party system": Tompkins 1970, 130.
352 de facto Republican leader: Ibid.
    "all diplomatic messages": Bullitt 1972, 167.
353 "Bullitt practically sleeps": Ibid., 169.

"I am very proud": Ibid., xxxv.

354    "Offie was the guest of honor": Ibid., 172.

"F.D.R. is a great man": Davis 1993, 5n.

"betraying the trust": Freidel 1952, 247.

"has . . . gone conservative": Ibid., 222.

355    "take the minds . . . off their troubles": Patterson 1972, 196.

356    "odor which pervades": Bullitt 1972, 184.

"absolute determination . . . to stay out": Ibid., 197.

"the only policy . . . out of the mess": Ibid., 206.

Russell . . . "holds out": Ibid., 228.

"did not see the . . . possibility": FRUS 1937, 1:85.

357    "the far-off bugaboo": Bullitt 1972, 244.

1936 the Japanese cabinet adopted: Keylor 1992, 245.

"grasped the significance": Nixon 1969, 3:411.

358    "beat the whole of Europe": Ibid., 278.

"a . . . flirt": Donald 1987, 323.

"like a butterfly": Brysac, chapter 8.

359    A convicted spy: Ibid., chapter 7.

joint letter to Stalin: Ibid., chapter 9.

"the United States are the ultimate object": FRUS 1937, 1:141.

## 43   *The March Toward War*

360    "event of his death": Shirer 1960, 418.

Shirer later commented: Ibid., 437.

361    "Germany had no desire": FRUS 1937, 1:172.

"your conversation with Goering": Bullitt 1972, 240.

363    Jack . . . "had a good time": Ibid., 273.

"That month . . . best": Ibid.

"Live like a king": Hamilton 1992, 260.

did not "affect our country": Ibid., 223.

"we can never be satisfied": Shirer 1960, 488.

"go to the utmost limit": Ibid., 489.

"last days of Pompeii": Bullitt 1972, 267.

364    "the death of a race": Ibid., 268.

"a general conviction": Ibid., 269.

"I remain . . . convinced . . . not permit ourselves to be drawn in": Ibid., 270.

"Mrs. Ickes is charming": Ibid., 271.

"War will . . . save me": Ibid.

365    "Dear Bill . . . May God . . . prove": Ibid., 272.

366    "an armful of roses": Brownell/Billings 1987, 223.

367    "neither we, nor any nation": *Time*, November 7, 1938, 7.

"had we . . . 5,000 planes": Dallek 1979, 173.

368 "I want this in writing": Bullitt 1972, 303.
"against . . . entangling alliances": Langer/Gleason 1952, 1:49.

## 44 *The Bell Tolls*

370 "WAR SCARE": Watt 1989, 162.
"a moral obligation": Namier 1948, 69–70.
371 "I wish the British would stop": Davis 1993, 403.
372 "neutrality and isolation . . . a power . . . on our side": Blum 1985, 375.
"fight for her life": Davis 1993, 398.
373 "We were morally right": Ibid., 399.
"Chamberlain will either have to go": Watt 1989, 167.
374 "enough guts": Bullitt 1972, 332.
"possible" but not "certain": Brownell/Billings 1987, 232.
"have Joe Kennedy transferred": Bullitt 1972, 350.
"Kennedy phones . . . to resign": Ibid., 356.
"The trouble with Bullitt": Brownell/Billings 1987, 235.
"bring back Douglas MacArthur": Bullitt 1972, 334.
"Roosevelt's right-hand man": Brownell/Billings 1987, 234.
375 *Time* . . . called him: Ibid., 235.
"England is on its way": Whalen 1964, 257.
"No, the Ambassador should not": Gilbert 1977, 1074.
"that quality of naivete": Langer/Gleason 1952, 1:189.
"This puts the bee": Ibid., 190.
376 "Mere pleas": Ibid.
"it was useless for the British": Hamilton 1992, 276.
377 Kennedy gave . . . Forrestal his version: Whalen 1964, 258.
"storm warnings": Brownell/Billings 1987, 237.
378 "I told your mother": Ibid.
"This is Bill Bullitt": Davis 1993, 461.

## 45 *Replay*

381 "An unknown . . . destiny": Bullitt 1972, 366.
382 "General," he told MacArthur: Manchester 1978, 201.
"neutral in thought": Langer/Gleason 1952, 1:204.
383 "America sending its armies": Ibid.
Gallup Poll: Ibid., 288.
"Americans 3,000 miles from the war": Steel 1980, 379.
"could not, would not, and should not": Ibid., 380.
"one effective way of preventing our being drawn into": Ibid., 379.
384 "The story of 1917–18": Ketchum 1989, 226.
"far toward totalitarian government": Patterson 1972, 200.
385 "defend our own shores": Ibid., 198.
"not . . . an isolationist": Ibid., 215.

Joseph Alsop and Robert Kintner: Byrnes 1958, 111.

"conciliatory and persuasive": Ibid.

386   "a pretty snappy move!": Marshall 1981–86, 2:21.

387   "Time . . . more than anything": Cray 1990, 147.

"prepared . . . to fight immediately": Ibid., 151.

388   "flung the door open": Gilbert 1977, 1113.

"octagonal table": Gilbert 1983, 4.

"He also told me . . . chart box": Ibid.

"you and I occupied similar positions": Gilbert 1993, 76.

"have always disliked him": Beschloss 1980, 200.

389   "Your letter . . . takes me back": Gilbert 1993, 211.

2,000 German aircraft: Parker 1990, 22.

"continued expansion of the German people": Craig 1978, 716.

German army was not really ready: Ibid., 619, 717.

390   "whichever army attacks first": Bullitt 1972, 383.

"phony war": Horne 1969, 92.

"Across the river": Ibid., 94.

"peace next spring": Langer/Gleason 1952, 1:344.

391   "I do not entertain the thought": Ibid., 346.

"the Prime Minister says": Bullitt 1972, 404.

### 46   *FDR's New World Strategy*

393   "rattlebrained": Beschloss 1980, 203.

"Joe . . . would say what he god-damned pleased": Ibid.

394   "Army . . . real story": Cray 1990, 152.

"I feel culpable": Ibid.

"You get every . . . damn thing": Ibid.

"I am . . . a pacifist": Ibid.

"all . . . feel that way": Ibid., 153.

"I don't scare": Ibid., 154.

"makes me dizzy": Ibid.

395   "I know . . . what he will say": Ibid., 155.

"Vandenberg for the presidency": Tompkins 1970, 167.

Gallup Poll: Ibid., 170–1.

"favorite Republican": Ibid., 179.

"anybody under . . . 40": Ibid., 182.

396   "the limitations of . . . Chamberlain": Patterson 1972, 224.

"Republican . . . walking in its sleep": Sherwood 1948, 174.

398   "involved a great moral issue": Pruessen 1982, 188.

"French . . . downhearted": Gilbert 1983, 399.

"war could not be won": Ibid., 402–3.

399   "London people cried": Mitford 1945, chapter 19.

"Chamberlain would not learn": Freedman 1967, 536–7.

"duped by . . . history": Steel 1980, 382.

400     "young . . . de Gaulle": Kimball 1984, 1:44.

"Hitler could not win": Ibid.

"no American Ambassador . . . had ever left": Bullitt 1972, 456–7.

401     "You said you would see to it": Ibid., 466.

"everything in my power": Donaldson 1992, 333.

"six million . . . who will die": Bullitt 1972, 463.

## 47   *FDR's New Team and New Term*

408     The two of them would publish a small newspaper . . . Sherwood: Davis 1993, 584.

What bothered Byrnes . . . identical conversation: Byrnes 1958, 117–18.

"Suppose at some point we want to know": Sherwood 1948, 176.

411     "He sometimes broadcast . . . from roof tops": Gregory 1989, 3.

412     "America could not spare any": Gilbert 1983, 463.

"nothing . . . so important": Ibid., 493.

"the President is not convinced": Ibid.

"50 . . . destroyers . . . fate of the war": Kimball 1984, 1:57.

413     "I got firm commitments": Alsop/Platt 1992, 146–7.

414     "thinks . . . we shall be defeated": Bullitt 1972, 436–7.

"Kennedy is not a bashful man": Byrnes 1958, 126.

FDR . . . "understood entirely": Ibid.

"that Boston boy": Beschloss 1980, 221.

"son of a bitch!": Ibid.

415     "I look forward . . . Things are afoot": Kimball 1984, 1:81.

## 48   *Making Churchill a Partner*

416     "not be in the moral or economic": Kimball 1984, 1:108.

Bullitt . . . "lease": Kimball 1969, 68.

417     Ickes . . . "lend": Ibid., 77.

"two prima donnas": Sherwood 1948, 236.

"hopeless Tory": Ibid., 237.

"Churchill, did not like America": Ibid., 238.

418     "The people here are amazing": Ibid., 243.

"America's world duty": Ibid., 249.

419     "it's me—Winston": Kimball 1984, 1:128.

"I don't give a damn": Abramson 1992, 277.

420     "peace with the Nazis": Sherwood 1948, 226.

"arsenal of democracy": Ibid.

"Give us the tools": Gilbert 1983, 1010.

"the United States sent two million": Sherwood 1948, 262.

"he would look up at . . . Wilson": Ibid., 227.

"this war will never see great forces": Ibid., 239.

423     "vulgar beyond belief": Hoopes/Brinkley 1992, 133.

"Wives would . . . flee": Ibid.
"plumb crazy": Ibid.
424 "the Reds": Ibid., 132.
"head in his hands": Ibid., 134.
"Billy was all wet": Brownell/Billings 1987, 267.
425 "I know, Bill. . . . Just let it go": Bullitt 1972, 505.
All quotes re April Bullitt-FDR meeting on pages 425 and 426: Ibid., 512–14.
427 Americans "living in a different world": Gilbert 1983, 1161.
428 "suspicions and opposition": Divine 1967, 44.
"time . . . to be realistic": Ibid.
"nothing could be more futile": Welles 1946, 5.
429 Knox proposed: Divine 1967, 45.
"turn again for light . . . to . . . Wilson": Ibid.
"force an 'incident' ": Thorne 1978, 73.
"something really big": Heinrichs 1988, 151.
"Dear Winston": Kimball 1984, 1:249.
"see you again!": Ibid., 250.

## 49    *A Second Summons to Greatness*

430 "There is a lot of talk": Grew 1952, 2:1233.
431 "moment may be decisive": Gilbert 1983, 1183.
432 "Japs . . . drag-down and knock-out fight": Cray 1990, 227.
"avoided at all cost": Blum 1985, 392.
"economic paralysis": Steel 1980, 391.
"Morgenthau, Ickes": Dallek 1979, 236–7.
"a primary objective": Marshall 1981–86, 2:658.
433 Stark and Marshall . . . memorandum: Ibid., 660.
"on the brink of war": Ibid., 680.
"The danger period": Ibid.
434 "if we . . . start sanctions": Grew 1952, 2:1211.
"do-or-die": Ibid., 1287.
435 navy . . . "thoroughly scared": Heinrichs 1988, 205.
"awful" . . . Moscow was "falling": Ibid., 213.
436 "Stimson and Marshall feel": Sherwood 1948, 397.
"America must be . . . dominant": Hamilton 1992, 415.
437 "FIRST OVERT ACT": Manchester 1978, 223.
"Japanese are notorious": Cray 1990, 241.
"This means war": Sherwood 1948, 426.
438 "No, we can't do that": Ibid., 427.
"planning some deviltry": Ketchum 1989, 735.
"No!": Manchester 1973, 257.
"Oh, no . . . bombing Hawaii": Hodgson 1990, 242–3.
439 "I'll fly right back": Morgenthau 1991, 297.
"Mr. President . . . all in the same boat": Kimball 1984, 1:281.

439  "We still have to eat": Weintraub 1991, 328.
"amazement and anger": Ibid., 461.
441  "at the earliest opportunity": Manchester 1978, 237.
442  the owner of the Redskins . . . explained: Weintraub 1991, 306.
"WAR'S OUTBREAK IS DEEP SECRET": Ibid.
443  "I hope Mr. Capone": Brinkley 1988, 89.

## 50   The Magnificent Country

447  The Industrial Expressway: "The Old Country," A Survey of America,
*Economist,* October 26, 1991.
"By 1943 . . . greatest centre of high-technology": Michael Elliott,
Ibid., 3.
448  "the magnificent man": *Nicomachean Ethics,* book 4, chapter 2.
"something paltry": Ibid.
449  MacArthur . . . Rabaul: Manchester 1978, 5, 6.
450  Curtiss-Wright . . . Glenn Martin: McCullough 1992, 271–2.
453  Socrates taught: *Greater Hippias* 294:b.

## 51   America Against the Allies

454  "Don't let Churchill": Bullitt 1972, 531.
455  a "temporary expedient": Eisenhower 1986, 6.
"associates of the aggressors": Edmonds 1991, 343.
457  Unsent drafts . . . distrustful: Kimball 1984, 1:284.
458  "The Americans are magnificent": Gilbert 1986, 23.
British researchers . . . atomic energy: Ibid., 514.
spying on the Americans: Kimball 1984, 1:371.
459  intended . . . British postwar interests: Ibid., 577.
462  "global sucker": Ibid., 2:527.
June 1942 poll, 56 percent: Thorne 1978, 209.
only . . . 1 percent of her income: Ibid., 100n.
"any race . . . fit to serve as masters": Ibid., 103.
"British imperialism . . . is spreading democracy": Shawcross 1988, 61.
"official opinion . . . Empires ought to be liquidated": Thorne 1978, 220.
Hull . . . "monarchial institutions": Kimball 1984, 2:587.
463  "Winston and I": Blum 1970, 491.
"We are going to pay": Thorne 1978, 138.
FDR told his Joint Chiefs . . . political motives: Ibid., 274.
Roosevelt told . . . Molotov . . . new world order: Kimball 1984, 2:502.
464  "I know you will not mind . . . I can . . . handle Stalin": Gardner 1993,
130.
A report from army intelligence . . . that Russians "do not understand":
Ibid.

## 52   *The Origins of the Cold War*

465   "You have your power now": Bullitt 1972, 588.
"amoeba . . . pseudopodia": Ibid., 579.
466   "Salonika and Constantinople": Ibid., 588.
"if military considerations are equal": Ibid.
Offie . . . Mrs. Welles: Hersh 1992, 150–1.
Bullitt "very anti-Russian": Bullitt 1972, 595.
468   "German invaders had destroyed over 1,700 cities": Leffler 1992, 5.
469   "the Roosevelt-Stalin axis": Thorne 1978, 276.
"because of the British . . . contribution": Ibid., 361.
"the Russians . . . could take over": Bullitt 1972, 601.
fell . . . under Bullitt's influence: Hoopes/Brinkley 1992, 261.
John Maynard Keynes: Keynes 1932, 297.

## 53   *Wilson's Way*

476   "In regard to the Soviet government": Messer 1982, 42.
"Roosevelt believed in dollars": Gardner 1993, 181.
477   "Whoever occupies a territory": Ibid., 10.

## 54   *Handing Over Command*

478   "There are some consolations": Bullitt 1972, 604.
479   Japanese plans . . . 3 million: Cray 1990, 498.
MacArthur spokesman . . . "we must not invade": Manchester 1978, 499.
"giving without taking": Cray 1990, 498.
481   Churchill . . . "dismembering Germany": Gilbert 1986, 1265.
482   "the Russians had the power": Messer 1982, 42.
483   "France is your baby": Memorandum for Admiral Brown, "Zones of Occupation in Europe," August 31, 1944, 9–10. Elsey papers, box 3.
Kennan . . . United States should be honest: Abramson 1992, 391.
484   "Why the President insisted": Byrnes 1958, 253.
"looked ghastly": Bullitt 1972, 611.
"ship of death": Ibid.
485   Yalta . . . "ought to spell the end": Halle 1967, 27.
"This will *raise hell*": Vandenberg 1952, 159.
"*stop this Stalin*": Ibid., 141.
"successful meeting at Yalta": Forrestal 1951, 35.
"serious deterioration": Ibid., 38.
"almost daily affronts": Ibid., 40.
"Averell is right": Harriman 1971, 38 n3.
"minimize the . . . Soviet problem": Kimball 1984, 3:630.
486   "a terrible headache": Manchester 1973, 349.
"the smiling face of a beautiful woman": Ibid.

486 "as directed by the President": Ferrell 1980, 16.
*Yank* . . . "Commander in Chief": Sherwood 1948, 882.
"he was going to turn in his resignation": Ibid.

## 55 *One World—Or Two?*

487 Scott Fitzgerald: *The Crack-Up*, second paragraph.
488 "Discussed the whole history of the Roosevelt administration": Ferrell 1980, 18–19.
"difficulties with Churchill": Ibid., 21–2.
"Russians distribute lies": Ibid., 45.
Harriman warned . . . "ideological warfare": Forrestal 1951, 47.
Leahy . . . "left Yalta with the impression": Ibid., 51.
Stimson . . . Russians had kept their word: Ibid., 49.
489 Marshall cautioned . . . her help was greatly needed: Ibid., 51.
"The President said . . . Russians . . . could go to hell": Ibid., 50.
Davies reported: Cook 1989, 17.
Leahy, endorsing: Ibid.
Hopkins "skeptical about Churchill": Forrestal 1951, 58.
"make it clear. . . . Any smart political boss": Messer 1982, 82.
"a reasonably lasting peace": Ferrell 1980, 35.
490 "I'm not afraid of Russia": Ibid., 44.
"I can deal with Stalin": Ibid., 53.
"I like Old Joe": Clifford 1991, 200–1.
60 percent of Americans: Ibid., 20.
491 "duplicity and hypocrisy": Messer 1982, 29.
492 "We have pushed these babies as far": Ibid., 132.
"When . . . start trading?": Ibid., 133.
"You're smarter than I thought": Ibid., 179–80.
493 For all Litvinov quotes on pages 493 and 494: FRUS 1946, 6:763 et seq.
"no . . . order is possible": Cook 1989, 49.
"As Department is aware": Kennan cable to Secretary of State, February 19, 1946. Elsey papers, box 63.
494 fifty square miles a day: Fromkin 1989, 475.
496 "Powerful stuff": Clifford 1991, 123.

## 56 *TR's Way*

498 "The human problem the war will leave": Ellwood 1992, 29.
4,000 kilometers . . . railroad tracks: Ibid., 37.
In Vienna . . . no nails: Ibid., 31.
100 million . . . were starving: Ibid., 34.
499 The fifteen weeks: Jones 1955.
500 just a "starter": Ibid., 227.
"Never was it so necessary": Ibid.

501 "economic measures on a scale": Ibid., 229.
"if we allocate . . . on the dole": Ibid., 231.
Kennan . . . told Marshall . . . recovery of Germany: Cook 1989, 81.
Dulles . . . same conclusion: Jones 1955, 220.
502 "not against any country or doctrine": Cook 1989, 84.
504 "what help Norway might expect": Ibid., 123.
"We are going to stay": Ibid., 153.
"Why should Truman": Ibid., 161.
505 "Americans want an integrated Europe": Hogan 1987, 427.
80 to 90 percent: Ibid., 431.

## 57   Breaking with the Past—And Paying the Price for It

507 "never fight another war": Clifford 1991, 146.
508 "*not* to build a *hybrid* ticket": Vandenberg 1952, 440.
509 "U.S. force should be used": Harry S Truman Library. Student Research File, box 31: The Korean War.
510 "The United States should not become . . . involved": Ridgway 1967, 7.
510n. Georgi Arbatov: Stephen E. Ambrose, "Secrets of the Cold War," *New York Times,* December 27, 1990, A19.
"the Secretary had overlooked": Harry S Truman Library. Student Research File, box 31: The Korean War. Memorandum of presidential briefing June 27, 1950.
511 "But what he was worried about . . . 'Korea . . . the Greece' ": Harry S Truman Library. Student Research File, box 31: The Korean War. Elsey memorandum of June 26, 1950.
513 White House staff sizes: "Hide and Seek," *Wall Street Journal,* January 20, 1989, R20.
more Americans worked in government: *Economist,* August 8, 1992, 16.
514 "the longest retreat": McCullough 1992, 834.
515 "We can't defeat the Chinese": Ibid., 817.
"get out with honor": Ibid.
516 Clifford . . . watched in . . . horror: Clifford 1991, 172.
"The Russians . . . the FBI . . . the Zionists": Ibid., 174.
"nightingale": Hoopes/Brinkley 1992, 465.
517 "conclusion seemed plain": Acheson 1969, 338.
"We want no Gestapo": Ferrell 1980, 22.
surveillance of . . . Offie: Hersh 1992, 443.
518 "Offie had sponged": Ibid., 445.
"before long . . . people Frank didn't know": Ibid., 442.
"degenerate": Ibid., 443.
"men's room in LaFayette Park": Ibid., 442.
"Offie is dangerous": Ibid., 444.
"chicken-hawking behind the Vatican": Ibid., 448.

518  "State Department . . . still rancid with these men": Taft 1989, 150.

519  "real slander": Elsey papers, box 3: Yalta. September 3, 1948.

## 58  *Forging a Consensus*

521  "Senator Taft blew up": State Department to White House (Hagerty). April 3, 1953. Dulles/Eisenhower Library: telephone conversations. J. F. Dulles papers, box 10.

522  "likely to let himself be pushed around": Patterson 1972, 583.
"negative, futile": Immerman 1990, 4.

## 59  *America's Triumph*

525  "America . . . so unsympathetic": Gilbert 1988, 951.
"obsolete Colonial": Ibid., 929.
"what is called Colonialism": Ibid., 1295.

527  The road to Suez: See David Fromkin, "Eyeless in Suez," *The New Republic*, July 29, 1991, 39–42, and sources cited there.
"gradually . . . inconspicuously": *Economist*, June 2, 1990, 19.
the instrument was ready: For the organizational history of the CIA through 1953, see Darling 1990 and Montague 1992.

528  first . . . operation . . . in 1949: Copeland 1969, 50 et seq.; Copeland 1974, 203.
first . . . successful one . . . in 1952: Copeland 1974, 206.
40 percent of . . . Britain's . . . oil: Ibid.
Allen Dulles . . . preferred . . . Nasser: Kyle 1991, chapter 3.
The CIA . . . as Nasser's friend: Louis/Owen 1989, 95–8; Copeland 1969.
anti-American propaganda: Kyle 1991, chapter 3.
"I want him murdered": Ibid., 99. In another version, "destroyed." Horne 1989, 1:396.

529  "British government has decided": FRUS, 1955–57, vol. XVI, *Suez Crises*, document 33, 61.

531  "5,200,000 square miles": *American Journal of International Law*, January 1983, 109.

532  Europe "does not exist": *Time*, April 8, 1974, 34.
"the corpse of France": *International Herald Tribune*, August 7, 1972, 1.

533  "possibilities for . . . growth": Immerman 1990, 73.
"some years . . . 100 years": Ibid., 63.

## *Epilogue: Tales of the American Age*

540  "will collapse . . . seems unrealistic": Williams 1959, 206.
a later work: Williams 1969.

543  "preposterous": Brownell/Billings 1987, 329.
"a disgrace": Ibid., 330.

546  "further self-sacrifice": *Finest Hour* (International Churchill Societies), no. 72, Third Quarter 1991, back page. Speech notes for dinner given by Henry Luce, New York City, March 25, 1949.

On his deathbed in 1959: Memoirs (1962), 3. May 1959 entry. Allen Dulles papers, box 208.

547  "essential to demonstrate our firmness . . . Vietnam": Reston 1991, 291.

# BIBLIOGRAPHY

This is a list of the books from which I quoted, or from which I considered quoting, in one draft or another of the text. It does not include all the reference and other books that I consulted. It does not list books or archival papers that I read for background only; nor does it include the titles of books, many of them famous or said on good authority to be of great importance, that ought to be listed in any proper bibliography but that I have not read.

Therefore, it is not a bibliography in any comprehensive sense. Essentially it is a list of sources.

## Abbreviations

I have followed the usual practice in abbreviating the Foreign Relations of the United States series published by the Department of State as FRUS.

The Reminiscences of Walter Lippmann in the Columbia University Oral History Collection, a transcript of which is available for purchase from the University, is cited herein as OH.

Papers in various collections are abbreviated as follows:

| Papers | Abbreviation |
|---|---|
| Allen Dulles<br>Seeley G. Mudd Manuscript Library<br>Princeton University | Allen Dulles papers |
| John Foster Dulles<br>Seeley G. Mudd Manuscript Library<br>Princeton University | J. F. Dulles papers |
| George M. Elsey<br>Harry S Truman Library<br>Independence, Missouri | Elsey papers |
| W. Averell Harriman<br>Library of Congress | Harriman papers |
| Edward M. House<br>Manuscripts and Archives<br>Yale University Library<br>New Haven, Connecticut | House papers |

Robert A. Taft                                    Taft papers
Library of Congress

Arthur Walworth                                   Walworth papers
Yale University

## List of Sources

Abramson, Rudy. 1992. *Spanning the Century: The Life of W. Averell Harriman, 1891–1986.* New York: Morrow.

Acheson, Dean. 1961. *Sketches from Life of Men I Have Known.* New York: Harper.

———. 1965. *Morning and Noon.* Boston: Houghton Mifflin.

———. 1969. *Present at the Creation: My Years in the State Department.* New York: Norton.

Adams, Henry. 1889. Reprint edition 1986. *History of the United States of America During the Administrations of Thomas Jefferson.* New York: Library of America.

———. 1918. *The Education of Henry Adams: An Autobiography.* Boston: Houghton Mifflin.

Adams, Henry H. 1977. *Harry Hopkins.* New York: Putnam's.

Agar, Herbert. 1942. *A Time for Greatness.* Boston: Little, Brown.

Allen, Frederick Lewis. 1939. Reprint edition 1972. *Since Yesterday: The 1930s in America—September 3, 1929–September 3, 1939.* New York: Perennial Library.

Alsop, Joseph W., with Adam Platt. 1992. *"I've Seen the Best of It."* New York: Norton.

Ambrose, Stephen E. 1983–84. *Eisenhower.* 2 vols. New York: Simon & Schuster.

Baedeker, Karl (ed.). 1893. Reprint edition 1971. *The United States: With an Excursion into Mexico. A Handbook for Travellers.* New York: Da Capo Press.

Baker, Ray Stannard. 1923. *Woodrow Wilson and World Settlement.* 3 vols. Garden City, N.Y.: Doubleday, Page.

Baruch, Bernard M. 1960. *Baruch: The Public Years.* New York: Holt, Rinehart & Winston.

Berle, Adolf A. 1973. *Navigating the Rapids 1918–1971.* Edited by Beatrice Bishop Berle and Travis Beal Jacobs. New York: Harcourt Brace Jovanovich.

Beschloss, Michael R. 1980. *Kennedy and Roosevelt: The Uneasy Alliance.* New York: Norton.

Bird, Kai. 1992. *John J. McCloy: The Making of the American Establishment.* New York: Simon & Schuster.

Blum, John Morton. 1959–67. *From the Morgenthau Diaries.* 3 vols. Boston: Houghton Mifflin.

———. 1970. *Roosevelt and Morgenthau.* Boston: Houghton Mifflin.

———. 1976. *V Was for Victory: Politics and American Culture During World War II.* New York: Harcourt Brace Jovanovich.

——— (ed.). 1985. *Public Philosopher: Selected Letters of Walter Lippmann.* New York: Ticknor & Fields.

Blumenson, Martin. 1972. *The Patton Papers: 1885–1940.* Boston: Houghton Mifflin.

————. 1985. *Patton: The Man Behind the Legend 1885–1945.* New York: Morrow.

Brandon, Henry. 1988. *Special Relationships: A Foreign Correspondent's Memoirs from Roosevelt to Reagan.* New York: Atheneum.

Brands, H. W. 1993. *The Devil We Knew.* New York and Oxford: Oxford University Press.

Brinkley, David. 1988. *Washington Goes to War.* New York: Knopf.

Brownell, Herbert, with John P. Burke. 1993. *Advising Ike: The Memoirs of Attorney General Herbert Brownell.* Lawrence: University Press of Kansas.

Brownell, Will, and Richard N. Billings. 1987. *So Close to Greatness: A Biography of William C. Bullitt.* New York: Macmillan.

Brysac, Shareen. Biography in progress of Mildred Harnack-Fish.

Bullitt, Ernesta Drinker. 1917. *An Uncensored Diary: From the Central Empires.* Garden City, N.Y.: Doubleday, Page.

Bullitt, Orville H. (ed.). 1972. *For the President: Personal and Secret.* Boston: Houghton Mifflin.

Bullitt, William C. 1919. *The Bullitt Mission to Russia.* New York: Huebsch.

————. 1946. *The Great Globe Itself.* New York: Scribners.

Bundy, McGeorge. 1988. *Danger and Survival: Choices About the Bomb in the First Fifty Years.* New York: Random House.

Byrnes, James F. 1947. *Speaking Frankly.* New York: Harper.

————. 1958. *All in One Lifetime.* New York: Harper & Brothers.

Campbell, Charles S. 1976. *The Transformation of American Foreign Relations 1865–1900.* New York: Harper & Row.

Chace, James, and Caleb Carr. 1988. *America Invulnerable: The Quest for Absolute Security from 1812 to Star Wars.* New York: Summit.

Chernow, Ron. 1990. *The House of Morgan: An American Banking Dynasty and the Rise of Modern Finance.* New York: Atlantic Monthly Press.

Churchill, Randolph S. 1969. *Winston S. Churchill: Companion Volume II.* 3 vols. Boston: Houghton Mifflin.

Churchill, Winston S. 1948–53. *The Second World War.* 6 vols. Boston: Houghton Mifflin.

Clifford, Clark, with Richard Holbrooke. 1991. *Counsel to the President.* New York: Random House.

Coffman, Edward M. 1968. Reprint edition 1986. *The War to End All Wars: The American Military Experience in World War I.* Madison: University of Wisconsin Press.

————. 1977. "The American Military and Strategic Policy in World War I" in *War Aims and Strategic Policy in the Great War 1914–1918.* Edited by Barry Hunt and Adrian Preston. London: Croom Helm.

Cook, Beverly Blair. 1983. "Sentencing the Unpatriotic: Federal Trial Judges in Wisconsin During Four Wars" in *The Quest for Social Justice: The Morris Fromkin Memorial Lectures 1970–1980.* Edited by Ralph M. Aderman. Madison: University of Wisconsin Press.

Cook, Blanche Wiesen. 1992. *Eleanor Roosevelt.* New York: Viking.

Cook, Don. 1989. *Forging the Alliance: NATO, 1945–1950.* New York: Arbor House/Morrow.

Cooper, Jr., John Milton. 1990. *Pivotal Decades: The United States 1900–1920.* New York: Norton.

Copeland, Miles. 1969. *The Game of Nations: The Amorality of Power Politics.* New York: Simon & Schuster.

———. 1974. *Without Cloak or Dagger: The Truth About the New Espionage.* New York: Simon & Schuster.

Council on Foreign Relations. 1972. *The Foreign Affairs 50-Year Bibliography: New Evaluations of Significant Books on International Relations 1920–1970.* Edited by Byron Dexter. New York: Bowker.

Cowley, Malcolm. 1951. *Exile's Return: A Literary Odyssey of the 1920s.* New York: Viking.

Craig, Gordon A. 1978. *Germany 1866–1945.* New York: Oxford University Press.

Cray, Ed. 1990. *General of the Army: George C. Marshall—Soldier and Statesman.* New York: Norton.

Croly, Herbert. 1924. *Willard Straight.* New York: Macmillan.

Curry, George. 1965. *James F. Byrnes.* New York: Cooper Square.

Dallek, Robert. 1979. *Franklin D. Roosevelt and American Foreign Policy, 1932–1945.* New York: Oxford University Press.

Daniels, Jonathan. 1954. *The End of Innocence.* Philadelphia: Lippincott.

Darling, Arthur B. 1990. *The Central Intelligence Agency: An Instrument of Government, to 1950.* University Park: Pennsylvania State University Press.

Davis, Kenneth S. 1971. *FDR: The Beckoning of Destiny 1882–1928.* New York: Putnam's.

———. 1986. *FDR: The New Deal Years 1933–1937.* New York: Random House.

———. 1993. *FDR: Into the Storm 1937–1940, A History.* New York: Random House.

Diggins, John Patrick. 1988. *The Proud Decades: America in War and in Peace, 1941–1960.* New York: Norton.

Divine, Robert A. 1967. *Second Chance: The Triumph of Internationalism in America During World War II.* New York: Atheneum.

———. 1969. *Roosevelt and World War II.* Baltimore: Johns Hopkins.

Dodd, Martha. 1939. *Through Embassy Eyes.* New York: Harcourt, Brace.

Dodd, William E. 1941. *Ambassador Dodd's Diary: 1933–1938.* Edited by William E. Dodd, Jr., and Martha Dodd. New York: Harcourt, Brace.

Donald, David Herbert. 1987. *Look Homeward: A Life of Thomas Wolfe.* London: Bloomsbury.

Donaldson, Scott. 1992. *Archibald MacLeish: An American Life.* Boston: Houghton Mifflin.

Dorwart, Jeffery M. 1991. *Eberstadt and Forrestal: A National Security Partnership, 1909–1949.* College Station: Texas A&M University Press.

Dos Passos, John. 1962. Reprint edition 1963. *Mr. Wilson's War.* London: Hamish Hamilton.

Dulles, Foster Rhea. 1954. *America's Rise to World Power: 1898–1954.* New York: Harper & Row.

Edel, Leon. 1972. *Henry James: 1901–1916, The Master.* Philadelphia: Lippincott.

———. 1985. *Henry James: A Life.* New York: Harper & Row.

Edmonds, Robin. 1991. Reprint edition 1992. *The Big Three: Churchill, Roosevelt and Stalin in Peace and War.* London: Penguin.

Eisenhower, David. 1986. *Eisenhower: At War 1943–1945.* New York: Random House.

Eisenhower, John S. D. 1974. *Strictly Personal.* Garden City, N.Y.: Doubleday.

Ellwood, David W. 1992. *Rebuilding Europe: Western Europe, America and Postwar Reconstruction.* London: Longman.

Evans, R. J. W., and Hartmut Pogge von Strandman (eds.). 1988. Reprint edition 1991. *The Coming of the First World War.* Oxford: Clarendon Press.

Feis, Herbert. 1957. *Churchill Roosevelt Stalin: The War They Waged and the Peace They Sought.* Princeton: Princeton University Press.

———. 1960. *Between War and Peace: The Potsdam Conference.* Princeton: Princeton University Press.

Ferrell, Robert H. 1966. *George C. Marshall.* New York: Cooper Square.

———. 1985. *Woodrow Wilson and World War I: 1917–1921.* New York: Harper & Row.

——— (ed.). 1980. *Off the Record: The Private Papers of Harry S. Truman.* New York: Harper & Row.

Fischer, David Hackett. 1989. *Albion's Seed: Four British Folkways in America.* New York: Oxford University Press.

Fischer, Fritz. 1967. *Germany's Aims in the First World War.* New York: Norton.

———. 1974. *World Power or Decline: The Controversy over Germany's Aims in the First World War.* Translated by Lancelot L. Farrar, Robert Kimber, and Rita Kimber. New York: Norton.

———. 1975. *War of Illusions: German Policies from 1911 to 1914.* Translated by Marian Jackson. London: Chatto & Windus.

———. 1977. "German War Aims 1914–1918 and German Policy Before the War" in *War Aims and Strategic Policy in the Great War 1914–1918.* Edited by Barry Hunt and Adrian Preston. London: Croom Helm.

Fitzgerald, F. Scott. 1931. Reprint edition 1956. "Echoes of the Jazz Age," reprinted in *The Crack-Up.* New York: New Directions.

———. 1933. *Tender Is the Night.* New York: Scribners.

———. 1963. *The Letters of F. Scott Fitzgerald.* Edited by Andrew Turnbull. New York: Scribners.

FitzGerald, Frances. 1979. *America Revised: History Schoolbooks in the Twentieth Century.* Boston and Toronto: Little, Brown.

Flexner, James Thomas. 1965–72. *George Washington.* 4 vols. Boston and Toronto: Little, Brown.

Forrestal, James. 1951. *The Forrestal Diaries.* Edited by Walter Millis with the collaboration of E. S. Duffield. New York: Viking.

Fowler, W. B. 1969. *British-American Relations 1917–1918: The Role of Sir William Wiseman.* Princeton: Princeton University Press.

Frankfurter, Felix. 1960. *Felix Frankfurter Reminisces.* Recorded in talks with Dr. Harlan B. Phillips. New York: Reynal.

Freedman, Max (ed.). 1967. *Roosevelt and Frankfurter: Their Correspondence 1928–1945.* Boston and Toronto: Little, Brown.

Freidel, Frank. 1952. *Franklin D. Roosevelt: The Apprenticeship.* Boston: Little, Brown.

Freud, Sigmund, and William C. Bullitt. 1967. *Thomas Woodrow Wilson: A Psychological Study.* Boston: Houghton Mifflin.

Fromkin, David. 1989. *A Peace to End All Peace: Creating the Modern Middle East 1914–1922.* New York: Holt. London: Andre Deutsch.

Gaddis, John Lewis. 1987. *The Long Peace: Inquiries into the History of the Cold War.* New York: Oxford University Press.

Gardner, Lloyd C. 1970. *Architects of Illusion: Men and Ideas in American Foreign Policy 1941–1949.* Chicago: Quadrangle.

———. 1993. *Spheres of Influence: The Great Powers Partition Europe, from Munich to Yalta.* Chicago: Ivan R. Dee.

Gentile, Rick. 1992. Unpublished thesis in progress on the career of Secretary of State Christian A. Herter.

Gilbert, Martin. 1975. *Winston S. Churchill: The Stricken World: 1916–1922.* Boston: Houghton Mifflin.

———. 1977. *Winston S. Churchill: The Prophet of Truth: 1922–1939.* Boston: Houghton Mifflin.

———. 1978. *Winston S. Churchill: Companion,* Volume IV, Part 1, January 1917 to June 1919. Boston: Houghton Mifflin.

———. 1983. *Winston S. Churchill: Finest Hour: 1939–1941.* Boston: Houghton Mifflin.

———. 1986. *Winston S. Churchill: Road to Victory: 1941–45.* Boston: Houghton Mifflin.

———. 1988. *Winston S. Churchill: Never Despair: 1945–1965.* Boston: Houghton Mifflin.

———. 1993. *The Churchill War Papers: At the Admiralty, September 1939 to May 1940.* New York: Norton.

Gregory, Ross. 1989. *America 1941: A Nation at the Crossroads.* New York: Free Press.

Grew, Joseph Clark. 1944. *Ten Years in Japan.* New York: Simon & Schuster.

———. 1952. *Turbulent Era: A Diplomatic Record of Forty Years, 1904–1945.* 2 vols. Boston: Houghton Mifflin.

Halle, Louis J. 1967. Reprint edition 1991. *The Cold War as History.* New York: Harper Perennial.

Hamilton, Nigel. 1992. *J.F.K.: Reckless Youth.* New York: Random House.

Harriman, W. Averell. 1971. *America and Russia in a Changing World: A Half Century of Personal Observations.* Garden City, N.Y.: Doubleday.

Harriman, W. Averell, and Elie Abel. 1975. *Special Envoy to Churchill and Stalin 1941–1946.* New York: Random House.

Harrod, R. F. 1951. *The Life of John Maynard Keynes.* New York: Harcourt, Brace.

Heckscher, August. 1991. *Woodrow Wilson.* New York: Scribners.

Heinrichs, Jr., Waldo H. 1966. *American Ambassador: Joseph C. Grew and the Development of the United States Diplomatic Tradition.* Boston: Little, Brown.

————. 1988. *Threshold of War: Franklin D. Roosevelt and American Entry into World War II.* New York: Oxford University Press.

Hersh, Burton. 1992. *The Old Boys: The American Elite and the Origins of the CIA.* New York: Scribners.

Hodgson, Godfrey. 1990. *The Colonel: The Life and Wars of Henry Stimson 1867–1950.* New York: Knopf.

Hogan, Michael J. 1987. *The Marshall Plan: America, Britain, and the Reconstruction of Western Europe, 1947–1952.* Cambridge: Cambridge University Press.

Holborn, Hajo. 1970. Reprint edition 1971. *Germany and Europe: Historical Essays.* Garden City, N.Y.: Anchor.

Hoopes, Townsend, and Douglas Brinkley. 1992. *Driven Patriot: The Life and Times of James Forrestal.* New York: Knopf.

Horne, Alistair. 1963. *The Price of Glory: Verdun 1916.* New York: St. Martin's Press.

————. 1969. *To Lose a Battle: France 1940.* Boston: Little, Brown.

————. 1989. *Harold Macmillan.* 2 vols. New York: Viking.

Hough, Richard. 1983. *The Great War at Sea: 1914–1918.* Oxford: Oxford University Press.

House, Edward Mandell. 1926–28. *The Intimate Papers of Colonel House.* Edited by Charles Seymour. 4 vols. Boston: Houghton Mifflin.

House, Edward Mandell, and Charles Seymour (eds.). 1921. *What Really Happened at Paris: The Story of the Peace Conference, 1918–1919.* New York: Scribners.

Howells, W. D., Mark Twain, Nathaniel S. Shaler, and others. 1901. *The Niagara Book.* New York: Doubleday, Page.

Immerman, Richard H. (ed.). 1990. *John Foster Dulles and the Diplomacy of the Cold War.* Princeton: Princeton University Press.

Isaacson, Walter, and Evan Thomas. 1986. Reprint edition 1988. *The Wise Men: Six Friends and the World They Made.* New York: Touchstone.

James, D. Clayton. 1970. *The Years of MacArthur, Vol. I, 1880–1941.* Boston: Houghton Mifflin.

James, Henry. 1907. Reprint edition 1968. *The American Scene.* Bloomington: Indiana University Press.

————. 1934. *The Art of the Novel: Critical Prefaces.* New York: Scribners.

————. 1987. *Selected Letters.* Edited by Leon Edel. Cambridge, Mass., and London: Harvard University Press.

Janeway, Eliot. 1951. *The Struggle for Survival.* New York: Weybright & Telley.

Johnson, Walter. 1947. *William Allen White's America.* New York: Holt.

Jones, Joseph M. 1955. *The Fifteen Weeks (February 21 to June 5, 1947).* New York: Viking.

Kennan, George F. 1951. *American Diplomacy 1900–1950.* Chicago: University of Chicago Press.

————. 1956–58. *Soviet-American Relations, 1917–1920.* 2 vols. Princeton: Princeton University Press.

————. 1960. *Russia and the West Under Lenin and Stalin.* Boston: Little, Brown.

————. 1967. *Memoirs: 1925–1950.* Boston: Little, Brown.

————. 1972. *Memoirs: 1950–1963.* Boston: Little, Brown.

Kennedy, David M. 1980. *Over Here: The First World War and American Society.* New York: Oxford University Press.

Ketchum, Richard M. 1989. *The Borrowed Years 1938–1941: America on the Way to War.* New York: Random House.

Keylor, William R. 1992. *The Twentieth-Century World: An International History.* Second edition. New York: Oxford University Press.

Keynes, John Maynard. 1920. *The Economic Consequences of the Peace.* New York: Harcourt, Brace.

————. 1932. *Essays in Persuasion.* New York: Harcourt, Brace.

Kimball, Warren F. 1969. *The Most Unsordid Act: Lend-Lease, 1939–1941.* Baltimore: Johns Hopkins.

————. 1984. *Churchill and Roosevelt: The Complete Correspondence.* 3 vols. Princeton: Princeton University Press.

Krieger, Leonard, and Fritz Stern (eds.). 1968. Reprint edition 1969. *The Responsibility of Power: Historical Essays in Honor of Hajo Holborn.* Garden City, N.Y.: Anchor.

Krock, Arthur. 1968. *Memoirs: Sixty Years on the Firing Line.* New York: Funk & Wagnalls.

Kyle, Keith. 1991. *Suez.* New York: St. Martin's Press.

LaFeber, Walter. 1989. *The American Age: United States Foreign Policy at Home and Abroad Since 1750.* New York: Norton.

Langer, William L., and S. Everett Gleason. 1952. Reprint edition 1964. *The Challenge to Isolation, 1937–1940.* 2 vols. New York: Harper Torchback.

Larrabee, Eric. 1987. *Commander in Chief: Franklin Delano Roosevelt, His Lieutenants, and Their War.* New York: Harper & Row.

Lash, Joseph P. 1971. *Eleanor and Franklin: The Story of Their Relationship, Based on Eleanor Roosevelt's Private Papers.* New York: Norton.

———— (ed.). 1975. *From the Diaries of Felix Frankfurter.* New York: Norton.

Lawrence, T. E. 1939. *Oriental Assembly.* London: Williams & Norgate.

Leffler, Melvyn P. 1992. *A Preponderance of Power: National Security, the Truman Administration, and the Cold War.* Stanford: Stanford University Press.

Leuchtenburg, William E. (ed.). 1967. *Franklin D. Roosevelt: A Profile.* New York: Hill & Wang.

Levin, Jr., N. Gordon. 1968. Reprint edition 1973. *Woodrow Wilson and World Politics: America's Response to War and Revolution.* New York: Oxford University Press.

Link, Arthur S. 1957. *Wilson the Diplomatist: A Look at His Major Foreign Policies.* Baltimore: Johns Hopkins.

Lippmann, Walter. 1919. *The Political Scene: An Essay on the Victory of 1918.* New York: Holt.

————. 1922. *Public Opinion.* New York: Harcourt, Brace.

————. 1943. *U.S. Foreign Policy: Shield of the Republic.* Boston: Little, Brown.

————. 1944. *U.S. War Aims.* Boston: Little, Brown.

————. 1947. *The Cold War.* Boston: Little, Brown.

Lisagor, Nancy, and Frank Lipsius. 1988. *A Law unto Itself: The Untold Story of the Law Firm Sullivan & Cromwell.* New York: Morrow.

Louis, William Roger, and Roger Owen. 1989. *Suez 1956: The Crisis and Its Consequences.* Oxford: Clarendon Press.

Lowe, C. J., and M. L. Dockrill. 1972. *The Mirage of Power.* 3 vols. London: Routledge & Kegan Paul.

Lukacs, John. 1976. *The Last European War: September 1939/December 1941.* London: Routledge & Kegan Paul.

Lyon, Peter. 1974. *Eisenhower: Portrait of the Hero.* Boston: Little, Brown.

McCullough, David. 1992. *Truman.* New York: Simon & Schuster.

McLellan, David S. 1976. *Dean Acheson: The State Department Years.* New York: Dodd, Mead.

McNeill, William H. 1976. Reprint edition 1976. *Plagues and Peoples.* Garden City, N.Y.: Anchor.

Maier, Charles S. 1988. *The Unmasterable Past: History, Holocaust, and German National Identity.* Cambridge, Mass.: Harvard University Press.

Manchester, William. 1973. *The Story and the Dream: A Narrative History of America 1932–1972.* Boston: Little, Brown.

———. 1978. Reprint edition 1983. *American Caesar: Douglas MacArthur 1880–1964.* New York: Dell.

Marshall, George Catlett. 1981–86. *The Papers of George Catlett Marshall.* Edited by Larry Bland. 2 vols. Baltimore: Johns Hopkins.

Marx, Harpo. 1961. *Harpo Speaks!* New York: Bernard Geis.

Mayer, Arno, J. 1959. Reprint edition 1964. *Wilson vs. Lenin: Political Origins of the New Diplomacy, 1917–1918.* Cleveland: Meridian.

———. 1967. *Politics and Diplomacy of Peacemaking: Containment and Counterrevolution at Versailles, 1918–1919.* New York: Knopf.

Mee, Jr., Charles L. 1980. *The End of Order: Versailles 1919.* New York: Dutton.

Messer, Robert L. 1982. *The End of an Alliance: James F. Byrnes, Roosevelt, Truman, and the Origins of the Cold War.* Chapel Hill: University of North Carolina Press.

Miller, Merle. 1973. *Plain Speaking: An Oral Biography of Harry S Truman.* New York: Putnam's.

Miller, Richard Lawrence. 1986. *Truman: The Rise to Power.* New York: McGraw-Hill.

Mitford, Nancy. 1945. *The Pursuit of Love.* London: Hamish Hamilton.

Montague, Ludwell Lee. 1992. *General Walter Bedell Smith as Director of Central Intelligence.* University Park: Pennsylvania State University Press.

Moran, Lord. 1966. *Winston Churchill: The Struggle for Survival 1940–1965.* London: Constable.

Morgan, H. Wayne. 1963. *William McKinley and His America.* Syracuse, N.Y.: Syracuse University Press.

Morgenthau III, Henry. 1991. *Mostly Morgenthaus: A Family History.* New York: Ticknor & Fields.

Morton, Frederic. 1989. *Thunder at Twilight: Vienna 1913/1914.* New York: Scribners.

Moynihan, Daniel P. 1960. *The United States and the International Labor Organization: 1889–1934.* (Thesis) Fletcher School of Law and Diplomacy.

Namier, L. B. 1948. *Diplomatic Prelude: 1938–1939.* London: Macmillan.

Neal, Steve. 1984. *Dark Horse: A Biography of Wendell Willkie.* Garden City, N.Y.: Doubleday.

Nicolson, Harold. 1933. Reprint edition 1965. *Peacemaking 1919.* New York: Grosset & Dunlap.

Nixon, Edgar B. 1969. *Franklin D. Roosevelt and Foreign Affairs.* 3 vols. Cambridge, Mass.: Harvard University Press.

Nye, Roger H. 1993. *The Patton Mind: The Professional Development of an Extraordinary Leader.* Garden City Park, N.Y.: Avery.

O'Toole, Patricia. 1990. *The Five of Hearts: An Intimate Portrait of Henry Adams and His Friends.* New York: Clarkson Potter.

Parker, R. A. C. 1990. *Struggle for Survival: The History of the Second World War.* Oxford: Oxford University Press.

Patterson, James T. 1972. *Mr. Republican: A Biography of Robert A. Taft.* Boston: Houghton Mifflin.

Pearson, Drew, and Robert S. Allen. 1932. *More Merry-Go-Round.* New York: Liveright.

Perkins, Frances. 1946. *The Roosevelt I Knew.* New York: Viking.

Pogue, Forrest C. 1963–87. *George C. Marshall.* 4 vols. New York: Viking.

Pruessen, Ronald W. 1982. *John Foster Dulles: The Road to Power.* New York: Free Press.

Rappaport, Armin. 1962. *The Navy League of the United States.* Detroit: Wayne State University Press.

Reed, John. 1919. Reprint edition 1960. *Ten Days That Shook the World.* New York: Vintage.

Reston, James. 1991. *Deadline: A Memoir.* New York: Random House.

Reynolds, Michael. 1976. Reprint edition 1987. *Hemingway's First War: The Making of "A Farewell to Arms."* Oxford: Basil Blackwell.

Riddell, George Allardice. 1986. *The Riddell Diaries: 1908–1923.* Edited by J. M. McEwen. London: Athlone Press.

Ridgway, Matthew B. 1967. *The Korean War.* Garden City, N.Y.: Doubleday.

Rogow, Arnold A. 1963. *James Forrestal: A Study of Personality, Politics, and Policy.* New York: Macmillan.

Rohl, John (ed.). 1973. *1914: Delusion or Design: The Testimony of Two German Diplomats.* New York: St. Martin's Press.

Roosevelt, Elliot (ed.). 1947–50. *FDR: His Personal Letters.* 4 vols. New York: Duell, Sloan & Pearce.

Samuels, Ernest. 1989. *Henry Adams.* Cambridge, Mass.: Harvard University Press.

Schaffer, Ronald. 1991. *America in the Great War: The Rise of the War Welfare State.* New York: Oxford University Press.

Schaller, Michael. 1989. *Douglas MacArthur: The Far Eastern General.* New York: Oxford University Press.

Schlesinger, Jr., Arthur M. 1957–. *The Age of Roosevelt.* 3 vols. London: Heinemann.

———. 1965. *A Thousand Days: John F. Kennedy in the White House.* Boston: Houghton Mifflin.

Schwartz, Charles. 1977. *Cole Porter: A Biography.* New York: Dial Press.

Schwartz, Thomas Alan. 1991. *America's Germany: John J. McCloy and the Federal Republic of Germany.* Cambridge, Mass.: Harvard University Press.

Shawcross, William. 1988. *The Shah's Last Ride: The Fate of an Ally.* New York: Simon & Schuster.

Sherwood, Robert E. 1948. *Roosevelt and Hopkins: An Intimate History.* New York: Harper.

Shirer, William L. 1960. Reprint edition 1962. *The Rise and Fall of the Third Reich: A History of Nazi Germany.* Greenwich, Conn.: Crest.

Smith, Gaddis. 1972. *Dean Acheson.* New York: Cooper Square.

Smith, Gene. 1964. *When the Cheering Stopped: The Last Years of Woodrow Wilson.* New York: Morrow.

Smith, Page. 1985. *America Enters the World: A People's History of the Progressive Era and World War I.* New York: McGraw-Hill.

Sorensen, Theodore C. 1965. *Kennedy.* New York: Harper & Row.

Spring-Rice, Sir Cecil. 1929. *The Letters and Friendships of Sir Cecil Spring-Rice: A Record.* Edited by Stephen Swynn. 2 vols. Boston: Houghton Mifflin.

Steel, Ronald. 1980. *Walter Lippmann and the American Century.* Boston: Little, Brown.

Stern, Fritz. 1987. *Dreams and Delusions: The Drama of German History.* New York: Knopf.

Stevenson, David. 1988. Reprint edition 1991. *The First World War and International Politics.* Oxford: Oxford University Press.

Sullivan, Mark. 1926–35. *Our Times: The United States 1900–1925.* 6 vols. New York: Scribners.

Swanberg, W. A. 1961. Reprint edition 1986. *Citizen Hearst: A Biography of William Randolph Hearst.* New York: Collier Macmillan.

Taft, John. 1989. *American Power: The Rise and Decline of U.S. Globalism 1918–1988.* New York: Harper.

Taylor, A. J. P. 1954. *The Struggle for Mastery in Europe 1848–1918.* Oxford: Clarendon Press.

———. 1963. *The First World War: An Illustrated History.* London: Hamish Hamilton.

———. 1964. *Politics in Wartime, and Other Essays.* London: Hamish Hamilton.

———. 1965. *English History: 1914–1945.* Oxford: Clarendon Press.

Thorne, Christopher. 1978. Reprint edition 1979. *Allies of a Kind: The United States, Britain and the War Against Japan, 1941–1945.* Oxford: Oxford University Press.

Tompkins, C. David. 1970. *Senator Arthur H. Vandenberg: The Evolution of a Modern Republican, 1884–1945.* Lansing: Michigan State University Press.

Truman, Harry S. 1989. *Where the Buck Stops: The Personal and Private Writings of Harry S Truman.* Edited by Margaret Truman. New York: Warner.

Tuchman, Barbara. 1958. Reprint edition 1971. *The Zimmerman Telegram.* New York: Bantam.

———. 1962a. Reprint edition 1963. *The Guns of August.* New York: Dell.

———. 1962b. Reprint edition 1980. *The Proud Tower: A Portrait of the World Before the War 1890–1914.* London: Papermac.

Turnbull, Andrew. 1962. *Scott Fitzgerald.* New York: Scribners.

Tuttle, Dwight William. 1983. *Harry L. Hopkins and Anglo-Soviet Relations, 1941–1945.* New York: Garland.

Vandenberg, Arthur H. 1952. *The Private Papers of Senator Vandenberg.* Edited by Arthur H. Vandenberg, Jr., with the collaboration of Joe Alex Morris. Boston: Houghton Mifflin.

Vansittart, Lord. 1958. *The Mist Procession.* London: Hutchinson.

Walker, Richard L. 1965. *E. R. Stettinius, Jr.* New York: Cooper Square.

Walworth, Arthur. 1977. *America's Moment: 1918—American Diplomacy at the End of World War I.* New York: Norton.

———. 1986. *Wilson and His Peacemakers: American Diplomacy at the Paris Peace Conference, 1919.* New York: Norton.

War Department (U.S.). No date. *The Official Record of the United States' Part in the Great War.*

Ward, Geoffrey C. 1985. *Before the Trumpet: Young Franklin Roosevelt 1882–1905.* New York: Harper & Row.

———. 1989. *A First-Class Temperament: The Emergence of Franklin Roosevelt.* New York: Harper & Row.

Watt, Donald Cameron. 1989. *How War Came: The Immediate Origins of the Second World War, 1938–1939.* New York: Pantheon.

Watt, Richard M. 1968. *The Kings Depart—The Tragedy of Germany: Versailles and the German Revolution.* New York: Simon & Schuster.

Wehle, Louis B. 1953. *Hidden Threads of History: Wilson Through Roosevelt.* New York: Macmillan.

Weinstein, Edwin A. 1981. *Woodrow Wilson: A Medical and Psychological Biography.* Princeton: Princeton University Press.

Weintraub, Stanley. 1991. *Long Day's Journey into War.* New York: Dutton.

Welles, Sumner. 1944. *The Time for Decision.* New York: Harper.

———. 1946. *Where Are We Heading?* New York: Harper.

Werner, M. R. 1929. Reprint edition 1983. *Bryan.* New York: Chelsea House.

West, Rebecca. 1941. Reprint edition 1943. *Black Lamb and Grey Falcon: A Journey Through Yugoslavia.* New York: Viking.

Whalen, Richard J. 1964. Reprint edition 1966. *The Founding Father: The Story of Joseph P. Kennedy.* New York: Signet.

Widenor, William C. 1980. Reprint edition 1983. *Henry Cabot Lodge and the Search for an American Foreign Policy.* Berkeley: University of California Press.

Williams, William Appleman. 1959. *The Tragedy of American Diplomacy.* Cleveland: World.

———. 1969. *The Roots of the Modern American Empire: A Study of the Growth and Shaping of Social Consciousness in a Marketplace Society.* New York: Random House.

Wilson, Trevor. 1986. *The Myriad Faces of War: Britain and the Great War, 1914–1918*. Cambridge: Polity.

Wilson, Woodrow. 1966–91. *The Papers of Woodrow Wilson.* 65 vols. to date. Edited by Arthur S. Link. Princeton: Princeton University Press.

Wofford, Harris. 1980. *Of Kennedys and Kings: Making Sense of the Sixties.* New York: Farrar Straus Giroux.

Wohlstetter, Roberta. 1962. *Pearl Harbor: Warning and Decision.* Stanford: Stanford University Press.

# ACKNOWLEDGMENTS

For editing my writings and steering them to periodicals and publishers over the years, I owe more than words can say to James Chace, my campaign manager, chief strategist, and literary adviser ever since the days, decades ago, when we were comrades in arms in an unlikely outpost of the U.S. Army in the muddy wastelands of northeastern France. In a sense all of my books are dedicated to him.

Suzanne Gluck became my agent when my last book was caught in a publishing situation that everybody else said was hopeless. She did the seemingly impossible and rescued me and my book from a black hole. What she asked in return was that I write a book for her; so here it is.

I was the beneficiary of great generosity in the course of doing my research. John Taft loaned me the large collection of William Bullitt papers that he had assembled at great effort for his important book *American Power.* Shareen Brysac let me read and quote from sections of her biography in progress of Mildred Harnack-Fish. Rick Gentile allowed me to read and quote from chapters of his biography in progress of Secretary of State Christian Herter. Caleb Carr let me see his paper on Henry Cabot Lodge. Senator Daniel Patrick Moynihan sent me his enormously impressive Ph.D. thesis on the ILO.

Donald Oresman, keenest of bibliophiles, sent me essential but long-out-of-print books that nobody else could find. And Stanley Mallach, a scholarly resource, led me to a collection of secondhand books containing basic works that the New York Public Library no longer possessed but I could not do without. Professor Christian Herter kindly took me to lunch in Washington and answered questions about his father.

Professor Robert W. Tucker generously invited me to lunch at his home in Washington and saved me much time by steering me to books that would best answer my needs in writing about Wilson and his team at the Paris Peace Conference.

Dr. Nicholas Rizopoulos was, as always, an invaluable guide to archives, archivists, scholars, and scholarship. Professor Charles Kupchan showed me around the Princeton libraries.

Ashbel Green at Alfred A. Knopf is the editor, and the kind of editor, that writers dream of having but that few have the luck to encounter. He and his always helpful assistants Jennie McPhee and Jennifer Bernstein have cheered up my life; they do it so well, and they make it all so easy.

Marge Danser takes my longhand, which looks less legible than that of a Dead Sea scribe, and through the miracle of word processing turns it into what looks like a printed book. Roger Kimball did me yet another favor (he has done many) by finding Marge for me.

No task is more a true act of generosity than the critical reading of a manuscript. In addition to my editor and my agent, and to James Chace, those who went over the manuscript were Professors John Morton Blum, John Lewis Gaddis, and Alain Silvera, and Mr. Fareed Zakaria. As in places I have stubbornly insisted on doing things my way in the face of forcible objections, it seems especially appropriate to emphasize that none of these readers are responsible in any way for shortcomings in the book or for views expressed in it.

My deepest thanks to them all.


I also want to thank the libraries that have helped in my research, particularly: the Franklin D. Roosevelt, Harry S Truman, and Dwight D. Eisenhower presidential libraries and their staffs; the Harvey S. Firestone and Seeley G. Mudd libraries at Princeton University and their staffs; Judith Schiff, Chief Research Archivist at the Yale University Library; and Judy Simonsen and the Milwaukee County Historical Association.

# INDEX

## A NOTE ABOUT THE AUTHOR

David Fromkin is Professor of International Relations, History, and Law at Boston University, where he also serves as chairman of the International Relations Department and director of the Center for International Relations. His *A Peace to End All Peace*, a best-seller in paperback, was selected by *The New York Times Book Review* as one of the thirteen best books of 1989.

## A NOTE ON THE TYPE

The text of this book was set in Garamond No. 3. It is not a true copy of any of the designs of Claude Garamond (ca. 1480–1561), but an adaptation of his types, which set the European standard for two centuries. It probably owes as much to the designs of Jean Jannon, a Protestant printer working in Sedan in the early seventeenth century, who had worked with Garamond's romans earlier, in Paris, but who was denied their use because of Catholic censorship. Jannon's matrices came into the possession of the Imprimerie Nationale, where they were thought to be by Garamond himself, and were so described when the Imprimerie revived the type in 1900. This particular version is based on an adaptation by Morris Fuller Benton.

Composed by PennSet, Inc., Bloomsburg, Pennsylvania
Printed and bound by Quebecor Printing Fairfield, Fairfield, Pennsylvania
Designed by Robert C. Olsson